✠ Daily Office ✠

Readings for the

from the Early Church

✠ J. Robert Wright ✠

Church Publishing Incorporated, New York

Church Publishing Incorporated
445 Fifth Avenue
New York, NY 10016

10 9 8 7 6 5

Table of Contents

Publisher's Acknowledgements

The English translation of the non-biblical readings from *The Liturgy of the Hours* © 1974, International Committee on English in the Liturgy, Inc. All rights reserved. Alterations made with approval.

The text of the readings included in this publication taken from *Christian Readings* is used by permission of CATHOLIC BOOK PUBLISHING CORP. Copyright © 1972, 1973 by CATHOLIC BOOK PUBLISHING CORP. Alterations made with permission.

Other selections within this volume have been edited, have been altered by the publisher in some cases, and are used here, with permission of the following copyright holders who are listed below in alphabetical order.

CATHOLIC UNIVERSITY OF AMERICA PRESS, Baltimore, Md. From *St. Peter Chrysologus: Selected Sermons; St. Valerian: Homilies,* transl. George E. Ganss (Fathers of the Church, vol. 17), copyright © 1953.

CATHOLIC UNIVERSITY OF AMERICA PRESS, Baltimore, Md. From *St. Augustine: Letters, Volume 4,* transl. Wilfrid Parsons (Fathers of the Church, vol. 30), copyright © 1955.

FORWARD MOVEMENT PUBLICATIONS, Cincinnati, Ohio. From *Handbook of American Orthodoxy,* ed. J. Robert Wright, copyright © 1972.

WILLIAM B. EERDMANS PUBLISHING COMPANY, Grand Rapids, Mich. From *A Select Library of Nicene and Post-Nicene Fathers of the Christian Church,* Second Series, edited by Philip Schaff and Henry Wace, Volumes VIII, IX, and XIV, published 1889–1900.

PAULIST/NEWMAN PRESS, Mahwah, N.J. From *St. Gregory of Nyssa: The Lord's Prayer, The Beatitudes,* transl. Hilda C. Graef (Ancient Christian Writers, no. 18), copyright © 1954. Permission requested.

PAULIST/NEWMAN PRESS, Mahwah, N.J. From *Rufinus: A Commentary on the Apostles' Creed,* transl. J.N.D. Kelly (Ancient Christian Writers, no. 20), copyright © 1955. Permission requested.

PAULIST/NEWMAN PRESS, Mahwah, N.J. From *Origen: The Song of Songs: Commentary and Homilies,* ed. R.P. Lawson (Ancient Christian Writers, no. 26), published 1957. Permission requested.

PAULIST/NEWMAN PRESS, Mahwah, N.J. From J. M. Perrin, *Catherine of Siena,* copyright © 1965. Permission requested.

PAULIST/NEWMAN PRESS, Mahwah, N.J. From *Egeria: Diary of a Pilgrimage,* ed. George E. Gingras (Ancient Christian Writers, no. 38), copyright © 1970. Permission requested.

PENGUIN BOOKS, Baltimore, Md. From *Saint Augustine: Confessions,* ed. R.S. Pine-Coffin, copyright © 1961. Permission requested.

PENGUIN BOOKS, Baltimore, Md. From *Eusebius: The History of the Church from Christ to Constantine,* ed. G.A. Williamson, copyright 1965. Permission requested.

PENGUIN BOOKS, Baltimore, Md. From *Julian of Norwich: Revelations of Divine Love,* ed. Clifton Wolters, copyright © 1966. Permission requested.

PENGUIN BOOKS, Baltimore, Md. From *Augustine: Concerning the City of God against the Pagans,* transl. Henry Bettenson, copyright © 1972. Permission requested.

PENGUIN BOOKS, Baltimore, Md. From *The Prayers and Meditations of St. Anselm,* ed. Sister Benedicta Ward, copyright © 1973. Permission requested.

ST. PAUL PUBLICATIONS, Slough, England. From *The Awe-Inspiring Rites of Initiation,* ed. Edward Yarnold, first edition copyright © 1971.

ST. VLADIMIR'S SEMINARY PRESS, Crestwood, N.Y. From *St. John of Damascus: On the Divine Images,* ed. David Anderson, copyright 1980. Permission requested.

SPCK, London, England. From *Some Authentic Acts of the Early Martyrs,* ed. E.C.E. Owen, published 1927, 1933.

SPCK, London, England. From *St. Cyril of Jerusalem's Lectures on the Christian Sacraments,* ed. Frank Leslie Cross, copyright © 1951.

SPCK, London, England. From *Saint John Chrysostom: Six Books on the Priesthood,* ed. Graham Neville, copyright © 1964.

UNIVERSITY PRESS OF AMERICA, INC. From *A Lost Tradition: Women Writers of the Early Church,* ed. Patricia Wilson-Kastner et al., copyright 1981.

WESTMINSTER/JOHN KNOX PRESS, Atlanta, Georgia. From *Alexandrian Christianity,* ed. J.E.L. Oulton and Henry Chadwick (Volume 2: The Library of Christian Classics), published 1954.

WESTMINSTER/JOHN KNOX PRESS, Atlanta, Georgia. From *Early Latin Theology,* ed. S. L. Greenslade (Volume 5: The Library of Christian Classics), published 1956.

WESTMINSTER/JOHN KNOX PRESS, Atlanta, Georgia. From *Western Asceticism,* ed. Owen Chadwick (Volume 12: The Library of Christian Classics), published 1958.

Introduction

The ancient tradition of supplementing the scriptural lessons for the Daily Office with a reading taken from the writers of the period of the early church has been made permissible in the 1979 American *Book of Common Prayer*: "On occasion, at the discretion of the Minister, a reading from non-biblical Christian literature may follow the biblical Readings," (p.142). Such authorization could, of course, be construed as extending to cover all sorts of materials written even up to the present time. However, pride of place has traditionally been given to the writings dated prior to the divisions of the sixteenth-century reformation that are held in common by all Christians, and especially to those works that come from the patristic period of the early church.

It is the purpose of the present volume to make such readings from the early church available on a structured and rational basis that complements the liturgical calendar and scriptural lectionary of the 1979 *Book of Common Prayer* of the Episcopal Church. This lectionary is substantially the same as that for the Daily Office in the 1985 *Book of Alternative Services* of the Anglican Church of Canada as well as that in the 1978 *Lutheran Book of Worship*.

In the public or private recitation of the Daily Office, the use of these readings can appropriately follow right after the lesson or lessons read from Holy Scripture, or the reading can take the place of the hymn or anthem after the Collects, or it can come at the end of the Office in the morning or evening. Apart from the Daily Office, these readings can serve as the basis for a homily at the Eucharist, or for daily private meditation, or (by using the indexes at the end) as an introductory course in the theology of the early church. From a varied and frequent use of *Readings for the Daily Office from the Early Church,* therefore, one can be led to the core of the church's doctrinal tradition and to a deeper understanding of its basis in Holy Scripture as well as to a fuller appreciation of the various liturgical feasts and seasons.

These readings have been selected from some sixty-four early Christian writers to accompany each of the 453 liturgical days in the Daily Office Lectionary of *The Book of Common Prayer* (pp. 933–1001). The editor's goal has been to provide one selection for each day that can be used with

Morning Prayer or Evening Prayer in either Year One or Year Two.

As much as possible, use has been made of readings from *The Liturgy of the Hours* in the translations prepared in the early 1970s by the International Committee on English in the Liturgy, Inc. This is the updated series of post-biblical readings officially used in the Roman Catholic church since the revision of its Divine Office mandated by the Second Vatican Ecumenical Council, which can also be found excerpted in a volume called *The Office of Readings* (1983).

Approximately sixty-one percent of the readings in the present volume have been taken from the Roman Catholic Office and adapted to the calendar and lectionary of the Episcopal Church, either by matching them to one of the several scriptural readings assigned on each day, or by matching them to approximately the same season or place in the Episcopal Church's liturgical year. Thus, to a large extent, the common ecumenical tradition may be shared. Assistance has also been drawn from the volume edited by Brother Kenneth, C.G.A., *From the Fathers to the Churches* (Collins, London 1983), which is largely an adaptation of the office readings in the Roman Catholic Church to the new lectionary of the *Alternative Service Book 1980* of the Church of England. Other readings have been taken from a wide variety of additional sources encountered and/or translated by the editor in over twenty years of teaching patristic and medieval church history and theology.

Selections have been assigned by applying one or the other of the principles defined above. However, where these principles are more difficult to follow—especially for the propers of the season after Pentecost—many readings have been assigned more generally on the basis of edification or of spiritual nourishment. In addition, a deliberate attempt has been made to be more inclusive of writings by and about women from the early church than is the case with the readings that were chosen earlier for the Roman Catholic Office.

The assigned intention for the present volume has been to select readings from the major post-biblical authors, especially of the patristic period of the early church, that are held in common by all Christians prior to the divisions of the sixteenth-century reformation. A future publication now under way, chronologically more inclusive, will be a separate and smaller paperback volume for the "Lesser Feasts and Fasts" containing readings by or about all the persons commemorated in the Episcopal Church's lesser calendar right down to the present century.

With regard to the publication of *Readings for the Daily Office from the Early Church,* note should also be taken of several technical matters. Appreciation is hereby expressed to the various copyright holders listed in the section of "Publisher's Acknowledgements" for their gracious permission to use (in many cases) the English translations that are already available and that have been reprinted here. In other cases, emendations, alterations or fresh translations have been made. Brackets or occasionally parentheses usually indicate words supplied by the editor for the sake of clarity. In order to facilitate the reading of the text with fewer distractions, the style of the International Commission on English in the Liturgy has been followed in *not* using ellipsis points to indicate omissions. When possible, the publisher has made human gender language more inclusive, except in those instances where the context seemed to dictate the retention of traditional terminology.

A source reference is given at the bottom of each reading for easy location of the text in a scholarly edition, although it is not necessarily the immediate source of the translation used or adapted. The psalm numbering in these references is usually based on the divisions of the Vulgate psalter and not on the numbering schema followed in the 1979 American *Book of Common Prayer.* Passages from scripture, even though they may be paraphrases or otherwise inexact quotations, have been translated as they appear in the works of the authors themselves, except when edited, for example, for inclusive language. The dates in brackets at the end of the lines introducing each reading are those of each author's death, as in the official Calendar of the Episcopal Church, and are not the years when particular selections were written. At the end of this volume there are indexes of all the authors and of selected topics and theological themes.

A special word of thanks is due my editorial assistants, the Rev. Joseph Britton and the Rev. John Conners, as well as my consultants on inclusive language, Professors Richard Corney and Deirdre Good and the Rev. Ellen Barrett. Their conscientious and painstaking help has greatly facilitated the preparation of this volume.

Finally, I take pleasure in dedicating this book to the honor of the REV. CANON H. BOONE PORTER. His liturgical piety, historical scholarship, and independent critical acumen have long served as a remarkable stimulus and model for many of us who are attempting to synthesize the Church's classical tradition with its contemporary worship, mission, and ministry.

J. Robert Wright, D. Phil. (Oxon.), D.D., F.R. Hist.S.,
St. Mark's Professor of Ecclesiastical History
The General Theological Seminary
New York City

Abbreviations

Commonly Used for Source References

ACW = Ancient Christian Writers

CCL = Corpus Christianorum, Series Latina

CSEL = Corpus Scriptorum Ecclesiasticorum Latinorum

FC = Fathers of the Church

GCS = Griechischen Christlichen Schriftsteller

PG = Patrologia Graeco-Latina, ed. J.P. Migne

PL = Patrologia Latina, ed. J.P. Migne

SC = Sources Chrétiennes

1 Advent
To Last Epiphany

A reading from the Catechetical Instructions of Cyril, Bishop of Jerusalem [386]

We do not preach only one coming of Christ, but a second as well, much more glorious than the first. The first coming was marked by patience; the second will bring the crown of a divine kingdom.

In general, what relates to our Lord Jesus Christ has two aspects. There is a birth from God before the ages, and a birth from a virgin at the fullness of time. There is a hidden coming, like that of rain on fleece, and a coming before all eyes, still in the future.

At the first coming he was wrapped in swaddling clothes in a manger. At his second coming he will be clothed in light as in a garment. In the first coming he endured the cross, despising the shame; in the second coming he will be in glory, escorted by an army of angels. We look then beyond the first coming and await the second. At the first coming we said: "Blessed is he who comes in the name of the Lord." At the second we shall say it again; we shall go out with the angels to meet the Lord and cry out in adoration: "Blessed is he who comes in the name of the Lord."

The Savior will not come to be judged again, but to judge those by whom he was judged. At his own judgment he was silent; then he will address those who committed the outrages against him when they crucified him and will remind them: "You did these things, and I was silent."

His first coming was to fulfill his plan of love, to teach us by gentle persuasion. This time, whether we like it or not, we will be subjects of his kingdom by necessity. Malachi the prophet speaks of the two comings. "And the Lord whom you seek will come suddenly to his temple": that is one coming.

Again he says of another coming: "Look, the Lord almighty will come, and who will endure the day of his entry, or who will stand in his sight?

Because he comes like a refiner's fire, a fuller's herb, and he will sit refining and cleansing."

These two comings are also referred to by Paul in writing to Titus: "The grace of God the Savior has appeared to all humanity, instructing us to put aside impiety and worldly desires and live temperately, uprightly, and religiously in this present age, waiting for the joyful hope, the appearance of the glory of our great God and Savior, Jesus Christ." Notice how he speaks of a first coming for which he gives thanks, and a second, the one we still await.

That is why the faith we profess has been handed on to you in these words: "He ascended into heaven, and is seated at the right hand of the Father, and he will come again in glory to judge the living and the dead, and his kingdom will have no end."

Our Lord Jesus Christ will therefore come from heaven. He will come at the end of the world, in glory, at the last day. For there will be an end to this world, and the created world will be made new.

Catechesis 15, 1–3: PG 33, 870–874

Week of 1 Advent ✠ Monday

A reading from a scriptural commentary of Ephrem of Edessa, Deacon [373]

To prevent his disciples from asking the time of his coming, Christ said: "About that hour no one knows, neither the angels nor the Son. It is not for you to know times or moments." He has kept those things hidden so that we may keep watch, each of us thinking that he will come in our own day. If he had revealed the time of his coming, his coming would have lost its savor: it would no longer be an object of yearning for the nations and the age in which it will be revealed. He promised that he would come but did not say when he would come, and so all generations and ages await him eagerly.

Though the Lord has established the signs of his coming, the time of their fulfillment has not been plainly revealed. These signs have come and gone with a multiplicity of change; more than that, they are still present. His final coming is like his first. As holy persons and prophets waited for him, thinking that he would reveal himself in their own day, so today each of the faithful longs to welcome him in our own day, because Christ has not made plain the day of his coming.

He has not made it plain for this reason especially, that no one may think that he whose power and dominion rule all numbers and times is ruled by fate and time. He described the signs of his coming; how could what he has himself decided be hidden from him? Therefore, he used these words to increase respect for the signs of his coming, so that from that day forward all generations and ages might think that he would come again in their own day.

Keep watch; when the body is asleep nature takes control of us, and what is done is not done by our will but by force, by the impulse of nature. When deep listlessness takes possession of the soul, for example, faintheartedness or melancholy, the enemy overpowers it and makes it do what it does not will. The force of nature, the enemy of the soul, is in control.

When the Lord commanded us to be vigilant, he meant vigilance in both parts of ourselves: in the body, against the tendency to sleep; in the soul, against lethargy and timidity. As Scripture says: "Wake up, you just, and I have risen, and am still with you;" and again: "Do not lose heart. Therefore, having this ministry, we do not lose heart."

Commentary on the Diatessaron 18, 15–17: SC 121, 325–328

Week of 1 Advent ✠ Tuesday

A reading from a sermon of Gregory of Nazianzus, Bishop of Constantinople [389]

Although there are divers choices of life on this earth and God has many mansions reserved for and divided among us in accord with our merits, there is only one road to salvation for all. Everyone must practice the different virtues, or all of them, if possible. And all must move forward on their journey toward what awaits them. On foot they must follow him who gloriously leads the way and keeps us in step, who guides us along the narrow road, through the narrow gate to the wide expanse of celestial blessedness.

In obedience to Paul and Christ himself, we must look upon charity as the first and greatest commandment, the sum of the law and the teaching of the prophets. And the chief traits of charity are love for the poor and compassion for our kin. God is worshiped more by mercy than by any single act, for nothing is so appropriate as mercy in his regard, since mercy and truth go before him. We must offer him mercy for others rather than our judgment upon them. Furthermore, this kind of deed is repaid by nothing so much as kindliness, when one makes just recompense and places pity on the scales and in the balance.

We must open the heart of our compassion to all the poor and to those afflicted with misfortune no matter what the cause, in obedience to the exhortation to rejoice with the joyful and weep with the sorrowful. Since we ourselves are human beings, we must set before others the meal of kindness no matter why they need it—whether because they are widows, orphans, or exiles; or because they are brutalized by masters, crushed by rulers, dehumanized by tax-collectors, bloodied by robbers, or victimized by the insatiate greed of thieves, be it through confiscation of property or ship-wreck. All such people are equally deserving of mercy, and they look to us for their needs just as we look to God for ours.

Among these unfortunate people, those who are made to suffer unjustly deserve more pity than those who lead wretched lives. We should especially feel compassion for those who are afflicted with physical suffering and betrayed by this troublesome, wretched, and deceitful body of ours.

For we are spirit but we are flesh as well. God wants us to realize that we are at the same time most lordly and most lowly, earth dwellers and heavenward bent, transient yet immortal, heirs to the light and the fire but of the darkness as well—according to what we ourselves decide.

We are made up of this compound and I think the reason for it is that when we are exalted by our likeness to God we may also be humbled by the earth from which we are made.

As I lament the weakness of my flesh in considering the sufferings of others, I conclude that we must tend the bodies which share kinship and slavery with us. Though I condemn the body as an enemy because of its passions, I nevertheless embrace it as a friend because of him who bound me to it. We should tend the bodies of our neighbors as we tend our own—both those that are healthy and those afflicted with the sickness that consumes our own. For we are all one in Christ, whether we be rich or poor, slave or free, healthy or sick.

Oration 14, On the Love of the Poor 5–8: PG 35, 864–868

Week of 1 Advent ✠ Wednesday

A reading from the treatise On the Value of Patience by
Cyprian, Bishop and Martyr of Carthage [258]

Patience is a precept for salvation given us by our Lord, our teacher: "Whoever endures to the end will be saved." And again: "If you persevere in my word, you will truly be my disciples; you will know the truth, and the truth will set you free."

We must endure and persevere if we are to attain the truth and freedom we have been allowed to hope for; faith and hope are the very meaning of our being Christians, but if faith and hope are to bear their fruit, patience is necessary.

We do not seek glory now, in the present, but we look for future glory, as Saint Paul instructs us when he says: "By hope we were saved. Now hope which is seen is not hope; how can we hope for what is seen? But if we hope for what we do not see, we wait for it in patience." Patient waiting is necessary if we are to be perfected in what we have begun to be, and if we are to receive from God what we hope for and believe.

In another place the same Apostle instructs and teaches the just, and those active in good works, and those who store up for themselves treasures in heaven through the reward God gives them. They are to be patient also, for he says: "Therefore while we have time, let us do good to all, but especially to those who are of the household of the faith. But let us not grow weary in doing good, for we shall reap our reward in due season."

Paul warns us not to grow weary in good works through impatience, not to be distracted or overcome by temptations and so give up in the midst of our pilgrimage of praise and glory, and allow our past good deeds to count for nothing because what was begun falls short of completion.

Finally the Apostle, speaking of charity, unites it with endurance and patience. "Charity," he says, "is always patient and kind; it is not jealous, is not boastful, is not given to anger, does not think evil, loves all things, believes all things, hopes all things, endures all things." He shows that charity can be steadfast and persevering because it has learned how to endure all things.

And in another place he says: "Bear with one another lovingly, striving to keep the unity of the Spirit in the bond of peace." He shows that neither unity nor peace can be maintained unless we cherish each other with mutual forbearance and preserve the bond of harmony by means of patience.

On the Value of Patience 13, 15: CSEL 3, 406–408

Week of 1 Advent ✠ Thursday

A reading from a sermon of Gregory of Nazianzus, Bishop of Constantinople [389]

The very Son of God, older than the ages, the invisible, the incomprehensible, the incorporeal, the beginning of beginning, the light of light, the fountain of life and immortality, the image of the archetype, the immovable seal, the perfect likeness, the definition and word of the Father: he it is who comes to his own image and takes our nature for the good of our nature, and unites himself to an intelligent soul for the good of my soul, to purify like by like. He takes to himself all that is human, except for sin. He was conceived by the Virgin Mary, who had been first prepared in soul and body by the Spirit; his coming to birth had to be treated with honor, virginity had to receive new honor. He comes forth as God, in the human nature he has taken, one being, made of two contrary elements, flesh and spirit. Spirit gave divinity, flesh received it.

He who makes rich is made poor; he takes on the poverty of my flesh, that I may gain the riches of his divinity. He who is full is made empty; he is emptied for a brief space of his glory, that I may share in his fullness. What is this wealth of goodness? What is this mystery that surrounds me? I received the likeness of God, but failed to keep it. He takes on my flesh, to bring salvation to the image, immortality to the flesh. He enters into a second union with us, a union far more wonderful than the first.

Holiness had to be brought to us by the humanity assumed by one who was God, so that God might overcome the tyrant by force and so deliver us and lead us back to himself through the mediation of his Son. The Son arranged this for the honor of the Father, to whom the Son is clearly obedient in all things.

The Good Shepherd, who lays down his life for the sheep, came in search of the straying sheep to the mountains and hills on which you used to offer sacrifice. When he found it, he took it on the shoulders that bore the wood of the cross, and led it back to the life of heaven.

Christ, the light of all lights, follows John, the lamp that goes before him. The Word of God follows the voice in the wilderness; the bridegroom follows the bridegroom's friend, who prepares a worthy people for the Lord by cleansing them by water in preparation for the Spirit.

We need God to take our flesh and die, that we might live. We have died with him, that we may be purified. We have risen again with him, because we have died with him. We have been glorified with him, because we have risen again with him.

Oration 45, 9, 22, 26, 28: PG 36, 634–635, 654, 658–659, 662

Week of 1 Advent ✠ Friday

A reading from the Proslogion of Anselm, Archbishop of Canterbury [1109]

Insignificant one, escape from your everyday business for a short while, hide for a moment from your restless thoughts. Break off from your cares and troubles and be less concerned about your tasks and labors. Make a little time for God and rest a while in him.

Enter into your mind's inner chamber. Shut out everything but God and whatever helps you to seek him; and when you have shut the door, look for him. Speak now to God and say with your whole heart: "I seek your face; your face, Lord, I desire."

Lord, my God, teach my heart where and how to seek you, where and how to find you. Lord, if you are not here, where shall I look for you in your absence? Yet if you are everywhere, why do I not see you when you are present? But surely you dwell in "light inaccessible." And where is light inaccessible? How shall I approach light inaccessible? Or who will lead me and bring me into it that I may see you there? And then, by what signs and under what forms shall I seek you? I have never seen you, Lord my God; I do not know your face.

Lord most high, what shall this exile do, so far from you? What shall your servant do, tormented by love of you and cast so far from your face? I yearn to see you, and your face is too far from me. I desire to approach you, and your dwelling is unapproachable. I long to find you, and do not know your dwelling place. I strive to look for you, and do not know your face.

Lord, you are my God and you are my Lord, and I have never seen you. You have made me and remade me, and you have given me all the good things I possess, and still I do not know you. I was made in order to see you, and I have not yet done that for which I was made.

Lord, how long will it be? How long, Lord, will you forget us? How long will you turn your face away from us? When will you look upon us and hear us? When will you enlighten our eyes and show us your face? When will you give yourself back to us?

Look upon us, Lord, hear us and enlighten us, show us your very self. Restore yourself to us that it may go well with us whose life is so evil without you. Take pity on our efforts and our striving toward you, for we have no strength apart from you.

Teach me to seek you, and when I seek you show yourself to me, for I cannot seek you unless you teach me, nor can I find you unless you show yourself to me. Let me seek you in desiring you and desire you in seeking you, find you in loving you and love you in finding you.

Proslogion 1: Opera Omnia, ed. Schmitt, 1, 97–100

Week of 1 Advent ✠ Saturday

A reading from a sermon of Leo the Great, Bishop of Rome [461]

The practice of Christian wisdom does not consist in an abundance of words, or in acuteness of reasonings, or in the appetite for praise and glory. It consists in the true and voluntary humility which our Lord Jesus Christ, from his mother's bosom until the torture of the cross, chose and taught as being the fullness of strength.

One day when the disciples were asking among themselves as to who was of greatest importance in the kingdom of heaven, the evangelist recounts that Jesus "called a little child over and stood the child in their midst and said: 'I assure you, unless you change and become like little children, you will not enter the kingdom of God. Whoever strives to be lowly, becoming like this child, is of greatest importance in that heavenly reign.' "

Christ loves the childhood which he first assumed in his soul and body. Christ loves childhood: toward it he steers the conduct of adults and toward it he leads the aged; after its example he fashions those whom he raises to the eternal kingdom.

In order that we may be able to understand how it is possible to achieve such an admirable conversion, and through what transformation we must return to an attitude of children, let the words of St. Paul instruct us: "Do not be childish in your outlook. Be like children as far as evil is concerned." Hence, it is not a question of returning to the games of childhood nor to the blunderings of our beginnings, but of taking therefrom something which is suitable for the years of maturity. This is the rapid relaxing of inner tensions, the prompt return to calm, the total forgetfulness of offenses, the complete indifference to honors, sociability, and the feeling of natural equality.

It is this form of humility which the Lord teaches us when as a child he is worshiped by the astrologers. To show what glory he was preparing for those who followed him he consecrated the martyrdom of children born at the same time as himself; born in Bethlehem like Christ, they became associated with him by their age and their suffering.

Therefore, believers should love humility and refrain from all pride;

each should prefer our neighbor to ourselves and "no one should seek selfish interest but rather that of our neighbor." Thus, when all shall be filled with sentiments of benevolence, the poison of envy will disappear completely, "for everyone who seeks to be exalted shall be humbled and the one who becomes humble shall be exalted." This is attested by our Lord Jesus Christ himself, who with the Father and the Holy Spirit lives and reigns forever.

Sermon 7 for Epiphany 3–4: PL 54, 258–259

Week of 2 Advent ✠ Sunday

A reading from a commentary on Isaiah by Eusebius, Bishop of Caesarea [c. 340]

"The voice of one crying in the wilderness: Prepare the way of the Lord, make straight the paths of our God." The prophecy makes clear that it is to be fulfilled, not in Jerusalem but in the wilderness: it is there that the glory of the Lord is to appear, and God's salvation is to be made known to all humanity.

It was in the wilderness that God's saving presence was proclaimed by John the Baptist, and there that God's salvation was seen. The words of this prophecy were fulfilled when Christ and his glory were made manifest to all: after his baptism the heavens opened, and the Holy Spirit in the form of a dove rested on him, and the Father's voice was heard, bearing witness to the Son: "This is my beloved Son, listen to him."

The prophecy meant that God was to come to a deserted place, inaccessible from the beginning. None of the pagans had any knowledge of God, since his holy servants and prophets were kept from approaching them. The voice commands that a way be prepared for the Word of God: the rough and trackless ground is to be made level, so that our God may find a highway when he comes. "Prepare the way of the Lord": the way is the preaching of the Gospel, the new message of consolation, ready to bring to all humanity the knowledge of God's saving power.

"Climb on a high mountain, bearer of good news to Zion. Lift up your voice in strength, bearer of good news to Jerusalem." These words harmonize very well with the meaning of what has gone before. They refer opportunely to the evangelists and proclaim the coming of God to us, after speaking of the voice crying in the wilderness. Mention of the evangelists suitably follows the prophecy on John the Baptist.

What does Zion mean if not the city previously called Jerusalem? This is the mountain referred to in that passage from Scripture: "Here is mount Zion, where you dwelt." The Apostle says: "You have come to mount Zion." Does not this refer to the company of the apostles, chosen from the former people of the circumcision?

This is the Zion, the Jerusalem, that received God's salvation. It stands aloft on the mountain of God, that is, it is raised high on the only-begotten Word of God. It is commanded to climb the high mountain and announce the word of salvation. Who is the bearer of the good news but the company of the evangelists? What does it mean to bear the good news but to preach to all nations, but first of all to the cities of Judah, the coming of Christ on earth?

Commentary on Isaiah 40: PG 24, 366–367

Week of 2 Advent ✠ Monday

A reading from a sermon of Bernard, Abbot of Clairvaux [1153]

We know that there are three comings of the Lord. The third lies between the other two. It is invisible, while the other two are visible. In the first coming he was seen on earth, dwelling among the people; he himself testified that they saw him and hated him. In the final coming "all flesh will see the salvation of our God," and "they will look on him whom they have pierced." The intermediate coming is a hidden one. In his first coming our Lord came in our flesh and in our weakness; in this middle coming he comes in spirit and in power; in the final coming he will be seen in glory and majesty.

Because this coming lies between the other two, it is like a road on which we travel from the first coming to the last. In the first, Christ was our redemption; in the last, he will appear as our life; in this middle coming, he is our rest and consolation.

In case someone should think that what we say about this middle coming is sheer invention, listen to what our Lord himself says: "If anyone loves me, they will keep my word, and my Father will love them, and we will come to them." There is another passage of Scripture which reads: "Those who fear God will do good," but something further has been said about those who love, that is, that they will keep God's word. Where is God's word to be kept? Obviously in the heart, as the prophet says: "I have hidden your words in my heart, so that I may not sin against you."

Keep God's word in this way. Let it enter into your very being, let it take possession of your desires and your whole way of life. Feed on goodness, and your soul will delight in its richness. Remember to eat your bread, or your heart will wither away. Fill your soul with richness and strength.

If you keep the word of God in this way, it will also keep you. The Son with the Father will come to you. The great Prophet who will build the new Jerusalem will come, the one who makes all things new. This coming will fulfill what is written: "As we have borne the likeness of the earthly, we shall also bear the likeness of the heavenly."

Sermon 5 for Advent 1–3: ed. Cist. 4 (1966), 188–190

Week of 2 Advent ✠ Tuesday

A reading from the treatise Against Heresies by Irenaeus, Bishop of Lyons [c. 202]

The Lord, coming into his own creation in visible form, was sustained by his own creation which he himself sustains in being. His obedience on the tree of the cross reversed the disobedience at the tree in Eden; the good news of the truth announced by an angel to Mary, a virgin subject to a husband, undid the evil lie that seduced Eve, a virgin espoused to a husband.

As Eve was seduced by the word of an angel and so fled from God after disobeying his word, Mary in her turn was given the good news by the word of an angel, and bore God in obedience to his word. As Eve was seduced into disobedience to God, so Mary was persuaded into obedience to God; thus the Virgin Mary became the advocate of the virgin Eve.

Christ gathered all things into one, by gathering them into himself. He declared war against our enemy, crushed and trampled on the head of the one who at the beginning had taken us captive in Adam, in accordance with God's words to the serpent in Genesis: "I will put enmity between you and the woman, and between your seed and her seed."

The one lying in wait for the serpent's head is the one who was born in the likeness of Adam from the Virgin. This is the seed spoken of by Paul in the letter to the Galatians: "The law of works was in force until the seed should come to whom the promise was made." He shows this even more clearly in the same letter when he says: "When the fullness of time had come, God sent his Son, born of a woman." The enemy would not have been defeated fairly if the vanquisher had not been born of a woman, because it was through a woman that the enemy had gained mastery over humanity in the beginning, and set himself up as the adversary.

That is why the Lord proclaims himself the Son of Man, the one who renews in himself that first person from whom the human race was formed; as by one person's defeat our race fell into the bondage of death, so by another's victory we were to rise again to life.

Against Heresies 5, 19, 1; 20, 2; 21, 1: SC 153, 248–250, 260–264

Week of 2 Advent ✠ Wednesday

A reading from a commentary on the psalms by Augustine, Bishop of Hippo [430]

God established a time for his promises and a time for their fulfillment.

The time for promises was in the time of the prophets, until John the Baptist; from John until the end is the time of fulfillment.

God, who is faithful, put himself in our debt, not by receiving anything but by promising so much. A promise was not sufficient for him; he chose to commit himself in writing as well, as it were making a contract of his promises. He wanted us to be able to see the way in which his promises were redeemed when he began to discharge them. And so the time of the prophets was, as we have often said, the foretelling of the promises.

He promised eternal salvation, everlasting happiness with the angels, an immortal inheritance, endless glory, the joyful vision of his face, his holy dwelling in heaven, and after resurrection from the dead no further fear of dying. This is as it were his final promise, the goal of all our striving. When we reach it, we shall ask for nothing more. But as to the way in which we are to arrive at our final goal, he has revealed this also, by promise and prophecy.

He has promised humans divinity, mortals immortality, sinners justification, the poor a rising to glory.

But because God's promises seemed impossible to human beings—equality with the angels in exchange for mortality, corruption, poverty, weakness, dust and ashes—God not only made a written contract with them to win their belief but also established a mediator of his good faith, not a prince or angel or archangel, but his only Son. He wanted, through his Son, to show us and give us the way he would lead us to the goal he has promised.

It was not enough for God to make his Son our guide to the way; he made him the way itself, that you might travel with him as leader, and by him as the way.

Therefore, the only Son of God was to come among us, to take our human nature, and in this nature to be born as a man. He was to die, to rise again, to ascend into heaven, to sit at the right hand of the Father, and to fulfill his promises among the nations, and after that to come again, to exact now what he had asked for before, to separate those deserving his anger from those deserving his mercy, to execute his threats against the wicked, and to reward the just as he had promised.

All this had therefore to be prophesied, foretold, and impressed on us as an event in the future, in order that we might wait for it in faith, not find it a sudden and dreadful reality.

Commentary on Psalm 109, 1–3: CCL 40, 1601–1603

Week of 2 Advent ✠ Thursday

A reading from a commentary on the psalms by Augustine,
Bishop of Hippo [430]

"My soul pines for your salvation," that is, it languishes in its expectation. This is a happy weakness, for though it points up the desire for a good that is not yet obtained it also shows the eagerness with which it is sought. From whom do these words proceed—from the origins of humanity until the end of the world—if not from the chosen race, the royal priesthood, the purchased people, every one who, on this earth and in their time, has lived, lives, or will live in the desire for Christ?

The witness of this longing is the saintly and aged Simeon, who in receiving Christ in his arms exclaims: "Now, Master, you can dismiss your servant in peace; you have fulfilled your word. For my eyes have witnessed your saving deed." For "it was revealed to him by the Holy Spirit that he would not experience death until he had seen the Anointed of the Lord."

The desire of this old man is, according to our faith, the desire of all the saints of the previous ages. Thus, the Lord himself said to his disciples: "I assure you, many a prophet and many a saint longed to see what you see but did not see it, to hear what you hear but did not hear it." Hence, they also must be numbered among those who chant: "My soul pines for your salvation."

This desire of the saints was not fulfilled in the past and it will not be fulfilled in the future until the consummation of the ages, when "the Desired of all the nations" will come, as promised by the Prophet. Thus Paul can write: "From now on a merited crown awaits me; on that Day the Lord, just judge that he is, will award it to me—and not only to me, but to all who have looked for his appearing with eager longing."

The desire of which we are speaking arises from the love of Christ's appearance, and it is about this that Paul further states: "When Christ our life appears, then you shall appear with him in glory."

In the first ages, before the child-bearing of the Virgin, the Church counted saints who desired the coming of Christ in the flesh. In the post-Ascension ages in which we live, the same Church numbers other saints who desire the appearance of Christ to judge the living and the dead. Never, from the beginning till the end of times, has this desire of the Church known the slightest diminishment, except during the period when the Lord lived on earth in the company of his disciples.

Thus, it is the entire Body of Christ, groaning in this life, whom we must fittingly understand as chanting in this psalm: "My soul pines for your salvation; I hope in your word." His word is the promise; and hope enables us to wait with patience for that which is not seen by those who believe.

Commentary on Psalm 119, 20, 1: CCL 40, 1730–1731

Week of 2 Advent ✠ Friday

A reading from the homilies of John Chrysostom, Bishop of Constantinople [407]

When we despise the poor, we despise Christ; thus our blame is very great. Paul himself persecuted Christ in persecuting those who are his; that is why Christ is heard to say: "Why do you persecute me?" Hence, whenever we give, let us have the same dispositions as if we were giving to Christ, for his words are more sure than our vision. Therefore, when you see a poor person, remember these words in which Christ reveals to you that it is he himself whom you can nourish. For even if that which appears be not Christ, yet in this person's form it is Christ himself who receives and begs.

But are you ashamed to hear that Christ begs? Rather be ashamed when you do not give to him when he begs. Herein lies the shame, as well as the pain and the punishment. His begging stems from his goodness, and calls for our rejoicing; but your failure to give stems from your inhumanity. But if you do not believe now that in passing one who is poor you are really passing by Christ, you will believe it when he will bring you in the midst of his followers and say: "As often as you neglected to do it to one of these least ones, you neglected to do it to me."

What is the good of adorning Christ's table with golden vases if he himself is left to perish in hunger? First fill him when he is hungry, and then you can adorn his table with what remains. Tell me. Suppose you see someone without the necessary food, and neglect to appease that person's hunger, while you first overlay the table with silver; will the hungry one thank you, and not rather be indignant? Or again, suppose you see someone wrapped in rags and stiff with cold, and neglect giving them a garment while you build golden columns claiming thereby to honor them, will that person not say that you are mocking and regard it as a most extreme insult?

Tell yourself that you act exactly in this way toward Christ when he is going about as a wanderer and a stranger in need of lodging and you neglect to receive him but you deck out a pavement, and walls, and capitals of columns. You hang up silver lamps by means of chains but you will not even look upon him who is enchained in prison. And I say these things not to forbid munificence in these matters but to admonish you to do those other works together with these or rather even before these.

Someone might say: If it were granted me to entertain Paul as a guest, I would readily do so. Behold, it is in your power to entertain Paul's Master as your guest, and you will not do so, for "Whoever welcomes one such child for my sake welcomes me," says Christ. By how much more the brother or sister may be least, so much the more does Christ come to you through that person. Whoever receives the great, often does it out of vainglory also; but whoever receives the lowly, does it purely for the sake of Christ.

Homily 88 on Matthew: PG 58, 778-779; Homily 50 on Matthew: PG 58, 509; Homily 45 on Acts: PG 60, 318

Week of 2 Advent ✠ Saturday

A reading from a commentary on the Song of Songs by
Origen, Priest and Theologian [c. 254]

"I am dark and beautiful, O daughters of Jerusalem, as the tents of Cedar, as the curtains of Solomon." In some copies we read: I am "black" and beautiful.

The person of the Bride is introduced as speaking, but she speaks now not to those maidens who are wont to run with her, but to the daughters of Jerusalem. To these, since they have spoken slightingly about her as being ugly, she now makes answer, saying: "I am indeed dark—or black—as far as my complexion goes, O daughters of Jerusalem; but, should a person scrutinize the features of my inward parts, then I am beautiful. For the tents of Cedar, which is a great nation," she says, "also are black, and their very name of Cedar means blackness or darkness. The curtains of Solomon likewise are black; but that blackness of his curtains is not considered unbecoming for so great a king in all his glory. Do not reproach me for my color, then, O daughters of Jerusalem, seeing that my body lacks neither natural beauty, nor that which is acquired by practice."

This much is comprehended in the tale enacted, and is the superficial meaning of the story here set forth. But let us return to the mystical exposition. This Bride who speaks represents the Church gathered from among the Gentiles; but the daughters of Jerusalem to whom she addresses herself are the souls who are described as being "most dear because of the election of their ancestors, but enemies because of the Gospel." Those are, therefore, the daughters of this earthly Jerusalem who, seeing the Church of the Gentiles, despise and vilify her for her ignoble birth; for she is baseborn in their eyes, because she cannot count as hers the noble blood of Abraham and Isaac and Jacob, for all that she forgets her own people and her own family and comes to Christ.

The Bride knows that the daughters of the former people impute this to her, and that because of it they call her black, as one who has not been enlightened by the patriarchs' teaching. She answers their objections thus: "I am indeed black, O daughters of Jerusalem, in that I cannot claim descent from the famous, neither have I received the enlightenment of Moses' Law. But I have my own beauty, all the same. For in me too there is that primal thing, the Image of God wherein I was created; and, coming now to the Word of God, I have received my beauty. Because of my dark colouring you may compare me to the tents of Cedar and the curtains of Solomon; but even Cedar was descended from Ismael, being born his second son, and Ismael was not without a share in the divine blessing. You liken me even to the curtains of Solomon, which are none other than the curtains of the tabernacle of God—indeed I am surprised, O daughters of Jerusalem, that you should want to reproach me with the blackness of my hue. How have you come to forget what is written in your Law, as to what Mary suffered who spoke against Moses because he had taken a black Ethiopian to wife? How is it that you do not recognize the true fulfillment of that type in me? I am that Ethiopian. I am black indeed by reason of my lowly origin; but I am beautiful through penitence and faith. For I have taken to myself the Son of God, I have received 'the Word made flesh;' I have come to Him 'who is the Image of God, the Firstborn of every creature' and who is 'the brightness of the glory and the express Image of the substance of God,' and I have been made fair. What are you doing, then, reproaching one who turns away from sin, which reproach the Law entirely forbids? How do you come to glory in the Law, and yet to violate it?"

Commentary on the Song of Songs 2, 1: GCS 33, 113–114

Week of 3 Advent ✠ Sunday

A reading from the Letter to Diognetus [c. 124]

With goodness and kindness, like a king who sends his son, who is also a king, God sent God, the Word, among us. He sent him to save us through persuasion rather than violence, for there is no violence in God. He sent him to call us rather than to accuse us; he sent him to love rather than to judge.

No one has either seen him or made him known; it is he himself who has revealed himself. And he has manifested himself through faith, to which alone it is given to behold God. For God, the Lord and Creator of the universe, who made all things and arranged them in orderly fashion, has shown himself to be not only filled with love for us but also long-suffering in his dealings with us. Yes, he has always been, is, and will remain the same: kind, good, free from wrath, true, and the only one who is good; and he formed in his mind a great and ineffable plan which he communicated to his Son alone.

As long as he held and preserved his own wise counsel in concealment, he appeared to neglect us and to have no concern for us. But after he revealed through his beloved Son and manifested what things he had prepared from the beginning, he conferred every blessing all at once upon us, so that we should both share in his benefits and see and be active in his service. Who of us would ever have expected these things?

God had thus disposed everything on his part with his Son, but until these last times he has permitted us to be borne along by unruly impulses, drawn away by the desire of pleasure and various lusts. This does not mean that he took the slightest delight in our sins but that he simply endured them; nor that he approved this time of working iniquity, but rather that he in no way consented to it. He prepared for the present time of righteousness so that, convinced of our unworthiness to obtain life during that time on account of our faults, we might now become worthy of it through the effect of the divine goodness; and so that, after we had been shown incapable of entering into the kingdom of God by our own efforts, we might become capable to do so by the divine power.

He took on himself the burden of our iniquities, and he gave his own Son as a ransom for us, the holy one for transgressors, the blameless one for the wicked, the just one for the unjust, the incorruptible one for the corruptible, the immortal one for the mortal. Where except in his justice could we find that with which to cover our sins! By whom could we be justified—we who are wicked and ungodly—except by the only Son of

God! What a wondrous exchange, unsearchable operation, and unexpected benefits! The crime of a large number is covered over by the justice of a single just one.

In the past, he first convinced our nature of its inability to obtain life. Now he has shown us the Savior capable of saving even what was impossible to save. In these two ways, he willed to lead us to trust in his goodness, to esteem him as our nourisher, Father, teacher, counsellor, healer, and our wisdom, light, honor, glory, power, and life.

Chapters 7–9: Funk 1, 403–409

Week of 3 Advent ✠ Monday

A reading from a sermon of Bernard, Abbot of Clairvaux [1153]

"See," says the Prophet, "the name of the Lord coming from afar." Who could doubt it? Something tremendous was needed in the beginning if the majesty of God was to deign to come down from such a distance, for a sojourn so unworthy of it.

There was, indeed, something tremendous about it; great mercy, immense compassion, abundant charity. For what purpose do we believe Christ came? We shall find it without difficulty, since his words and his acts clearly reveal to us the reason for his coming.

It is to search for the hundredth lost sheep that he came down in all haste from the mountains. He came because of us, so that the mercies of the Lord might be revealed with greater clarity, and his wonderful works for humankind. What amazing condescension on the part of God, who searches for us, and what great dignity bestowed on the one thus sought!

If we want to glory in it, we can quite reasonably do so, not because we can be anything in ourselves, but because he who created us has made us of such great worth. Indeed, all the riches and glory of this world, and all that one could wish for in it, is a very small thing and even nothing, in comparison with this glory. "What are we that you make much of us, or pay us any heed?"

But then again, I should like to know why he determined to come among us himself and why it was not, rather, we who went to him. For it is our benefit which is concerned. And, what is more, it is not the custom of the rich to go to the poor, even if it is their intention to do something for them.

It was, therefore, really our responsibility to go to Jesus: but a double obstacle prevented it. For our eyes were blind, and he dwells in inaccessible light. We were lying paralyzed on our pallet, incapable of reaching the greatness of God.

That is why, in his immense goodness, our Savior, the doctor of our souls, came down from his great height and tempered for our sick eyes the dazzling brightness of his glory. He clothed himself, as it were, with a lantern, with that luminous body, I mean, free from every stain, which he put on.

There we see that swift and brilliant cloud on which, the Prophet had foretold, he would ride to come down to Egypt.

Sermon 1 for Advent 7–8: ed. Cist. 4 (1966), 166–167

Week of 3 Advent ✠ Tuesday

A reading from a letter by Catherine of Siena, Dominican Sister and Mystic [1380]

I have told you that we should not act, and I do not wish you to act, like so many foolhardy worldly people who break the commandments of Holy Church. "I am not worthy," they say. And so they spend long days in mortal sin, refusing the food of their souls. Oh, what absurd humility! Who does not see that you are not worthy? You say you are waiting for the time when you will be worthy. When will that be? Do not wait, because you will not be any more worthy on the last day than you were on the first. Even if all our actions are good, we shall never be worthy. But God is the one who is worthy and who, with His own great worth, makes us worthy. And His worth cannot decrease. But as for us, what should we do? We should prepare ourselves to keep the sweet commandment because, if we do not do so and neglect Communion, then, thinking that we shall avoid sin, we shall fall into it.

Therefore, to conclude, I do not want to see such folly in you but rather that you dispose yourself, as a faithful Christian, to receive Holy Communion in the manner I have just described.

Letter 246: ed. Perrin 1965, 178-179

Week of 3 Advent ✠ Wednesday

A reading from a sermon of Leo the Great, Bishop of Rome [461]

On all days and at all times, the birth of our Lord and Savior from the Virgin-mother occurs to the thoughts of the faithful who meditate on divine things; so much so that the mind is inspired to the acknowledgment of its Creator and—whether it be occupied with the groans of supplication, or with the shouts of praise, or with the offering of sacrifice—focuses its spiritual insight on nothing more frequently and more trustingly than on the fact that God, the Son of God, begotten of the eternal Father, was also born of a human birth. But this nativity which is to be adored in heaven and on earth is suggested to us by no day more than today.

The state of infancy which the Son of God did not find unworthy of his majesty gave way to the state of manhood with the passing of time and, once the triumph of his passion and resurrection had been accomplished, all the actions of humility undertaken for us came to an end. Nevertheless, in adoring the birth of our Savior, we find that we are celebrating the commencement of our own life. For the birth of Christ is the source of life for the Christian people, and the birthday of the Head is the birthday of the body.

Although every individual who is called has a turn, and all the children of the Church are separated from one another by intervals of time, yet as the entire body of the faithful being born in the font of baptism is crucified with Christ in his passion, raised again in his resurrection, and placed at the Father's right hand in his ascension, so with him are they born in this nativity. Every believer, in any part of the world, who is reborn in Christ quits the old paths of our original nature and passes into a new person by being re-born. Henceforth, we are no longer reckoned of our earthly parents' lineage but among the seed of the Savior, who became the Son of Man in order that we might have the power to be the children of God. For unless he came down to us in this humiliation, no one would reach his presence by any merits of our own.

Therefore, they who "were begotten not by blood, nor by carnal desire, nor by human will, but by God" must offer to the Father the unanimity of peace-loving children, and all the members of adoption must meet in the First-begotten of the new creation, who came to do not his own will but his who sent him. For the grace of the Father has adopted as heirs not those who are discordant nor those who are unlike him, but those who are one in sentiments and affection.

Those who are remodeled after the same image must have the same spirit as the model. The birthday of the Lord is the birthday of peace. Indeed, the Apostle says: "It is he who is our peace, who made the two of us one"; since whether we be Jew or Gentile, "through him we both have access in one Spirit to the Father."

Sermon 6 for Christmas 1, 2, 5: PL 54, 212–213, 215

Week of 3 Advent ✠ Thursday

A reading from the First Letter to the Corinthians by Clement, Bishop of Rome [c. 100]

In prayer and supplication we will ask that God who regulates all things may preserve intact throughout the world the precise number of his elect, through his beloved Son Jesus Christ. Through him he has called us out of darkness into the light, out of ignorance into the knowledge of his glory, so that we might hope, Lord, in your name, for it is the foundation of all creation.

You have opened the eyes of our hearts, that they might know you. You alone are Most High in the highest heavens; you are the Holy One who resides among the saints. You cast down the insolence of the proud and overturn the plots of the nations; you lift up the humble and put down the haughty. You enrich and impoverish; you kill and save and bestow life.

You are the unique Benefactor of spirits and the God of all flesh; you pierce the abyss with your gaze and scrutinize the works of humankind. You are the helper of those in danger, the savior of those in despair, the creator and guardian of every spirit! You multiply the nations over the earth, and from among them you choose those who will bring their love to you, through Jesus Christ your beloved Son; in him you instruct, sanctify, and honor us.

We beg you, Master, be our help and strength. Save those among us who are oppressed, have pity on the lowly, and lift up the fallen. Heal the sick, bring back the straying, and feed the hungry. Release those in prison, lift up those who falter, and strengthen the fainthearted. Let all nations come to know you the one God, with your Son Jesus Christ, and us your people and the sheep of your pasture.

Through your works, you have manifested the eternal ordering of the world, Lord, Creator of the universe. You remain the same throughout all generations: just in your judgments, admirable in power and magnifi-

cence, full of wisdom in creating, and prudent in strengthening everything in existence. You manifest your goodness toward all visible things,
and your fidelity toward those who trust in you, for you are merciful and
compassionate.

Forgive our transgressions, our errors, our lapses, and our weaknesses. Do not keep count of the sins of your servants but purify us
through the bath of your truth, and direct our steps. Help us to walk in
holiness of heart, and to do what is good and pleasing to your eyes and
in the eyes of our rulers.

Master, let your face shine on us to grant us every good in peace, to
protect us by your powerful hand, to deliver us from every evil by the
might of your arm, and to save us from the unjust hatred of our enemies.
Grant to us and to all who dwell on this earth, Lord, peace and harmony,
as you once did to our ancestors, when they devoutly invoked you, in
all confidence and uprightness of heart.

First Letter to the Corinthians 59–60: Funk 1, 175–179

Week of 3 Advent ✠ Friday

*A reading from The Imitation of Christ by Thomas a Kempis,
Priest [1471]*

Do not care much who is with you and who is against you; but make it
your greatest care that God is with you in everything you do.

Have a good conscience, and God will defend you securely; no one can
hurt you if God wishes to help you.

If you know how to suffer in silence, you will surely receive God's help.
Since he knows best the time and the way to set you free, resign yourself
to him, for God helps you and frees you from all confusion.

It is often good for us, and helps us to remain humble, if others know
our weaknesses and confront us with them.

When we humble ourselves for our faults, we more easily please others
and mollify those we have angered.

God protects and frees a humble person; he loves and consoles a
humble person; he favors a humble person; he showers the humble with
graces; then, after suffering, God raises the humble up to glory.

God reveals his secrets to a humble person and in his kindness invit-
ingly draws that person to himself. When humble people are brought to
confusion, they experience peace, because they stand firm in God and
not in this world. Do not think that you have made any progress unless
you feel that you are the lowest of all people.

Above all things, keep peace within yourself, then you will be able to create peace among others. It is better to be peaceful than learned.

The passionate person often thinks evil of a good person and easily believes the worst; a good and peaceful person turns all things to good.

One who lives at peace suspects no one. But one who is tense and agitated by evil is troubled with all kinds of suspicions; such a person is never at peace within, nor does such a one permit others to be at peace.

Such a person often speaks when one should be silent, and fails to say what would be truly useful. Such people are well aware of the obligations of others but neglect their own.

So be zealous first of all with yourself, and then you will be more justified in expressing zeal for your neighbor.

You are good at excusing and justifying your own deeds, and yet you will not listen to the excuses of others. It would be more just to accuse yourself and to excuse your neighbor.

If you wish others to put up with you, first put up with them.

The Imitation of Christ 2, 2-3

Week of 3 Advent ✠ Saturday

A reading from a commentary on Luke by Bede, the Venerable, Priest, and Monk of Jarrow [735]

Mary said: "My soul proclaims the greatness of the Lord, my spirit rejoices in God my Savior."

The Lord has exalted me by a gift so great, so unheard of, that language is useless to describe it; and the depths of love in my heart can scarcely grasp it. I offer then all the powers of my soul in praise and thanksgiving. As I contemplate his greatness, which knows no limits, I joyfully surrender my whole life, my senses, my judgment, for my spirit rejoices in the eternal Godhead of that Jesus, that Savior, whom I have conceived in this world of time.

"The Almighty has done great things for me, and holy is his name."

Mary looks back to the beginning of her song, where she said: "My soul proclaims the greatness of the Lord." Only that soul for whom the Lord in his love does great things can proclaim his greatness with fitting praise and encourage those who share her desire and purpose, saying: "Join with me in proclaiming the greatness of the Lord; let us extol his name together."

Those who know the Lord, yet refuse to proclaim his greatness and sanctify his name to the limit of their power, "will be called least in the kingdom of heaven." His name is called holy because in the sublimity of his unique power he surpasses every creature and is far removed from all that he has made.

"He has come to the help of his servant Israel for he has remembered his promise of mercy."

In a beautiful phrase Mary calls Israel the servant of the Lord. The Lord came to his aid to save him. Israel is an obedient and humble servant, in the words of Hosea: "Israel was a servant, and I loved him."

Those who refuse to be humble cannot be saved. They cannot say with the prophet: "See, God comes to my aid; the Lord is the helper of my soul." But "anyone who makes himself humble like a little child is greater in the kingdom of heaven."

"The promise he made to our ancestors, to Abraham and his children for ever."

This does not refer to the physical descendants of Abraham, but to his spiritual children. These are his descendants, sprung not from the flesh only, but who, whether circumcised or not, have followed him in faith. Circumcised as he was, Abraham believed, and this was credited to him as an act of righteousness.

The coming of the Savior was promised to Abraham and to his descendants for ever. These are the children of promise, to whom it is said: "If you belong to Christ, then you are descendants of Abraham, heirs in accordance with the promise."

Commentary on Luke 1, 46–55: CCL 120, 37–39

Week of 4 Advent ✠ Sunday

*A reading from the treatise Against Heresies by Irenaeus,
Bishop of Lyons [c. 202]*

God is the glory of humanity. Humankind is the vessel which receives God's action and all his wisdom and power.

Just as a doctor is judged in his care for the sick, so God is revealed in his conduct with us. That is Paul's reason for saying: "God has made the whole world prisoner of unbelief that he may have mercy on all." He was speaking of human beings, who were disobedient to God, and cast off from immortality, and then found mercy, receiving through the Son of God the adoption he brings.

If we, without being puffed up or boastful, have a right belief regarding created things and their divine Creator, who, having given them being, holds them all in his power, and if we persevere in God's love, and in obedience and gratitude to him, we will receive greater glory from him. It will be a glory which will grow ever brighter until we take on the likeness of the one who died for us.

He it was who took on the likeness of sinful flesh, to condemn sin and rid the flesh of sin, as now condemned. He wanted to invite us to take on his likeness, appointing us imitators of God, establishing us in a way of life in obedience to the Father that would lead to the vision of God, and endowing us with power to receive the Father. He is the Word of God who dwelt with us and became the Son of Man to open the way for us to receive God, for God to dwell with us, according to the will of the Father.

For this reason the Lord himself gave as the sign of our salvation, the one who was born of the Virgin, Emmanuel. It was "the Lord himself who saved them," for of themselves they had no power to be saved. For this reason Paul speaks of the weakness of human nature, and says: I know that no good dwells in my flesh. He means that the blessing of our salvation comes not from us but from God. Again, he says: "I am a wretched man; who will free me from this body doomed to die?" Then he speaks of a liberator, thanks to Jesus Christ our Lord.

Isaiah says the same: "Hands that are feeble, grow strong! Knees that are weak, take courage! Hearts that are faint, grow strong! Fear not—see, our God is judgment and he will repay. He himself will come and save us." He means that we could not be saved of ourselves but only with God's help.

Against Heresies 3, 20, 2–3: SC 34, 388–395

Week of 4 Advent ✠ Monday

A reading from the Letter to the Smyrnaeans by Ignatius, Bishop of Antioch, and Martyr [c. 115]

Ignatius, who is also called Theophorus, to the Church of God the Father and of the beloved Jesus Christ which is at Smyrna in Asia. Your Church has through mercy obtained every kind of gift, is filled with faith and love, and is lacking in no gift; it is most worthy of God and adorned with holiness. I wish you every happiness through the unblemished Spirit and the word of God.

I glorify God, Jesus Christ himself, who has given you such wisdom. I have noted that you have been made perfect in an unshakable faith, like people nailed to the cross of our Lord Jesus Christ both in the flesh and in the spirit, and confirmed in love through the blood of Christ. With respect to our Lord, you are fully convinced that he was truly of the race of David according to the flesh, and the Son of God according to the will and power of God.

You are certain that he was truly born of a virgin and baptized by John so that all righteousness might be fulfilled by him; and that in his body he was truly nailed to the cross for us under Pontius Pilate and Herod the tetrarch. And we are the fruit of this divinely blessed passion, so that, through his resurrection he might set up a standard in the one body of his Church throughout the ages for his holy and faithful followers, whether among Jews or Gentiles.

For he suffered all these things for our sakes, that we might be saved. And he suffered truly, and equally truly raised himself from the dead. He did not merely seem to suffer, as some unbelievers claim—the way they themselves seem to be Christians. And their lot will be in accordance with their belief, when they will be divested of their bodies and be mere evil spirits.

For my part, I know that even after his resurrection he was still in the body, and I believe that this is so now. When, for instance, he came to those who were with Peter, he said to them: "Take hold of me and handle me, and see that I am not a disembodied spirit." And as soon as they touched him, they believed, convinced by his flesh and spirit.

This is the reason why they despised death and triumphed over it. And after his resurrection he ate and drank with them like a man with a body, although in his spirit he was united with the Father.

To the Smyrnaeans, greeting, 1–3: PG 5, 707–710

Week of 4 Advent ✠ Tuesday

A reading from a commentary on the psalms by Augustine, Bishop of Hippo [430]

"All the trees of the forest will exult before the face of the Lord, for he has come, he has come to judge the earth." He has come the first time, and he will come again. At his first coming, his own voice declared in the gospel: "Hereafter you shall see the Son of Man coming upon the clouds." What does he mean by "hereafter?" Does he not mean that the Lord will come at a future time when all the nations of the earth will be striking their breasts in grief? Previously he came through his preachers, and he filled the whole world. Let us not resist his first coming, so that we may not dread the second.

What then should Christians do? We ought to use the world, not become its slaves. And what does this mean? It means having, as though not having. So says the Apostle: "Beloved, the appointed time is short: from now on let those who have wives live as though they had none; and those who mourn as though they were not mourning; and those who rejoice as though they were not rejoicing; and those who buy as though they had no goods; and those who deal with this world as though they had no dealings with it. For the form of this world is passing away. But I wish you to be without anxiety." The one who is without anxiety waits without fear until the Lord comes. For what sort of love of Christ is it to fear his coming? Do we not have to blush for shame? We love him, yet we fear his coming. Are we really certain that we love him? Or do we love our sins more? Therefore let us hate our sins and love him who will exact punishment for them. He will come whether we wish it or not. Do not think that because he is not coming just now, he will not come at all. He will come, you know not when; and provided he finds you prepared, your ignorance of the time of his coming will not be held against you.

"All the trees of the forest will exult." He has come the first time, and he will come again to judge the earth; he will find those rejoicing who believed in his first coming, "for he has come. He will judge the world with equity and the peoples in his truth." What are equity and truth? He will gather together with him for the judgment his chosen ones, but the others he will set apart; for he will place some on his right, others on his left. What is more equitable, what more true than that they should not themselves expect mercy from the judge, who themselves were unwilling to show mercy before the judge's coming. Those, however, who were willing to show mercy will be judged with mercy. For it will be said to those placed on his right: "Come, blessed of my Father, take possession of the kingdom which has been prepared for you from the beginning of the world." And he reckons to their account their works of mercy: "For I was hungry and you gave me to eat; I was thirsty and you gave me to drink."

What is imputed to those placed on his left side? That they refused to show mercy. And where will they go? "Depart into the everlasting fire." The hearing of this condemnation will cause much wailing. But what has another psalm said? "The just will be held in everlasting remembrance and will not fear the evil report." What is the evil report? "Depart into the everlasting fire, which was prepared for the devil and the devil's angels." Whoever rejoices to hear the good report will not fear the bad. This is equity, this is truth.

Or do you, because you are unjust, expect the judge not to be just? Or because you are a liar, will the truthful one not be true? Rather, if you wish to receive mercy, be merciful before he comes; forgive whatever has been done against you; give of your abundance. Of whose possessions do you give, if not from his? If you were to give of your own, it would be largess; but since you give of his, it is restitution. "For what have you that you have not received?" These are the sacrifices most pleasing to God: mercy, humility, praise, peace, charity. Such as these, then, let us bring and, free from fear, we shall await the coming of the judge "who will judge the world in equity and the peoples in his truth."

Commentary on Psalm 95, 14, 15: CCL 39, 1351–1353

Week of 4 Advent ✠ Wednesday

A reading from the treatise On the Incarnation by
Athanasius, Bishop of Alexandria [373]

The Word of God did not abandon the human race, his creatures, who are hurtling to their own ruin. By the offering of his body, the Word of God destroyed death which had united itself to them; by his teaching, he corrected their negligences; and by his power, he restored the human race.

Why was it necessary for the Word of God to become incarnate and not some other? Scripture indicates the reason by these words: "It was fitting that when bringing many heirs to glory, God, for whom and through whom all things exist, should make their leader in the work of salvation perfect through suffering." This signifies that the work of raising human beings from the ruin into which they had fallen pertained to none other than the Word of God, who had made them in the beginning.

By the sacrifice of his body, he put an end to the law which weighed upon them, and he renewed in us the principle of life by giving us the hope of the resurrection. For if it is through ourselves that death attained dominance over us, conversely, it is through the incarnation of the Word of God that death has been destroyed and that life has been resurrected, as indicated by the Apostle filled with Christ: "Death came through one person; hence the resurrection of the dead comes through another person also. Just as in Adam all die, so in Christ all will come to life again."

It is no longer as condemned that we die. Rather, we die with the hope of rising again from the dead, awaiting the universal resurrection which God will manifest to us in his own time, since he is both the author of it and gives us the grace for it.

When the figure of someone has been painted on wood, then effaced by external elements, we need the presence of the one whose portrait it was if we wish to restore that person's image on the same material. And if this material is not discarded, it is because of the image painted on it which we wish to restore. In like manner, the most holy Son of the Father, being the image of the Father, has come into our land to renew us who had been made similar to him and to seek us out when we had been lost, pardoning our sins, as Scripture states: "I have come to search out and save what was lost."

Thus, when he says: "Unless you be born again," he does not allude to birth from a woman, but to the rebirth and re-creation of humankind in his image.

On the Incarnation 10, 14: PG 25, 111–114, 119

Week of 4 Advent ✠ Thursday

A reading from a sermon of Augustine, Bishop of Hippo [430]

John is the voice, but the Lord "is the Word who was in the beginning." John is the voice that lasts for a time; from the beginning Christ is the Word who lives for ever.

Take away the word, the meaning, and what is the voice? Where there is no understanding, there is only a meaningless sound. The voice without the word strikes the ear but does not build up the heart.

However, let us observe what happens when we first seek to build up our hearts. When I think about what I am going to say, the word or message is already in my heart. When I want to speak to you, I look for a way to share with your heart what is already in mine.

In my search for a way to let this message reach you, so that the word already in my heart may find place also in yours, I use my voice to speak to you. The sound of my voice brings the meaning of the word to you and then passes away. The word which the sound has brought to you is now in your heart, and yet it is still also in mine.

When the word has been conveyed to you, does not the sound seem to say: "The word ought to grow, and I should diminish?" The sound of the voice has made itself heard in the service of the word, and has gone away, as though it were saying: "My joy is complete." Let us hold on to the word; we must not lose the word conceived inwardly in our hearts.

Do you need proof that the voice passes away but the divine Word remains? Where is John's baptism today? It served its purpose, and it went away. Now it is Christ's baptism that we celebrate. It is in Christ that we all believe; we hope for salvation in him. This is the message the voice cried out.

Because it is hard to distinguish word from voice, even John himself was thought to be the Christ. The voice was thought to be the word. But the voice acknowledged what it was, anxious not to give offense to the word. "I am not the Christ," he said, "nor Elijah, nor the prophet." And the question came: "Who are you, then?" He replied: "I am the voice of one crying in the wilderness: Prepare the way for the Lord."

"The voice of one crying in the wilderness" is the voice of one breaking the silence. "Prepare the way for the Lord," the voice says, as though it were saying: "I speak out in order to lead him into your hearts, but he does not choose to come where I lead him unless you prepare the way for him."

"To prepare the way" means to pray well; it means thinking humbly of oneself. We should take our lesson from John the Baptist. He is thought to be the Christ; he declares he is not what they think. He does not take advantage of their mistake to further his own glory.

If he had said, "I am the Christ," you can imagine how readily he would have been believed, since they believed he was the Christ even before he spoke. But he did not say it; he acknowledged what he was. He pointed out clearly who he was; he humbled himself.

He saw where his salvation lay. He understood that he was a lamp, and his fear was that it might be blown out by the wind of pride.

Sermon 293, 3: PL 38, 1328–1329

Week of 4 Advent ✠ Friday

A reading from a homily of Origen, Priest and Theologian
[c. 254]

We read these words in the prophet Isaiah: "A voice cries out: In the desert prepare the way of the Lord! Make straight in the wasteland a highway for our God." The Lord wishes to find a way by which he might enter your hearts and walk therein. Prepare this way for him of whom it is said: "Make straight in the wasteland a highway for our God." The voice cries out in the desert: "Prepare the way." This voice first reaches our ears, and then following it, or rather with it, the Word penetrates our understanding. It is in this sense that Christ was announced by John.

Let us see, therefore, what the voice announces concerning the Word. "Prepare," says the voice, "the way of Lord." What way are we to prepare for the Lord? Is it a material way? But can the Word of God take such a way? Ought we not rather to prepare an inner way for the Lord by making the paths of our heart straight and smooth? Indeed, this is the way by which the Word of God enters in order to take up his abode in the human heart made ready to receive him.

How great is the human heart! What width and capacity it possesses, provided it is pure! Do you wish to know its greatness and width? Look at the extent of the divine knowledge that it embraces. It tells us itself: "God gave me sound knowledge of existing things, that I might know the organization of the universe and the force of its elements, the beginning and the end and the mid-point of times, the changes in the sun's course and the variations of the seasons. Cycles of years, positions of the stars, natures of animals, tempers of beasts, powers of the winds and thoughts of people, uses of plants and virtues of roots."

Thus, you see that the human heart knows so many things and is of no small compass. And notice that its greatness is not one of size but of the power of thought by which it is capable of knowing so many truths.

In order to make everyone realize how great the human heart is, let us look at a few examples taken from everyday life. We still retain in our minds all the towns which we have ever visited. Their features, the location of their squares, walls, and buildings remain in our hearts. We keep the road which we have traveled painted and engraved in our memories; and the sea over which we have sailed is harbored in our silent thought. As I have just said, the human heart knows so many things and is of no small compass.

Now, if it is not small, and if it can grasp so much, we can prepare the way of the Lord there and make straight the way where the Word, the Wisdom of God, will walk. Let each of you prepare the way of the Lord by a good conscience; make straight the way so that the Word of God may walk within you without stumbling and may give you knowledge of his mysteries and of his coming.

Homily 21 on Luke: PG 13, 1855–1856

Week of 4 Advent ✠ December 24

A reading from a sermon of Augustine, Bishop of Hippo [430]

Awake! For your sake God has become human. "Awake, you who sleep, rise up from the dead, and Christ will give you light." I tell you again: for your sake, God became human.

You would have suffered eternal death, had he not been born in time. Never would you have been freed from sinful flesh, had he not taken on himself the likeness of sinful flesh. You would have suffered everlasting unhappiness, had it not been for this mercy. You would never have returned to life, had he not shared your death. You would have been lost if he had not hastened to your aid. You would have perished, had he not come.

Let us then joyfully celebrate the coming of our salvation and redemption. Let us celebrate the festive day on which he who is the great and eternal day came from the great and endless day of eternity into our own short day of time.

"He has become our righteousness, our sanctification, our redemption, so that, as it is written: Let you who glory glory in the Lord."

"Truth, then, has arisen from the earth:" Christ who said, "I am the Truth," was born of a virgin. "And righteousness looked down from heaven": because believing in this new-born child, we are justified not by ourselves but by God.

"Truth has arisen from the earth": because "the Word was made flesh. And righteousness looked down from heaven": because "every good gift and every perfect gift is from above."

"Truth has arisen from the earth": flesh from Mary. "And righteousness looked down from heaven": for "you can receive nothing unless it has been given you from heaven."

"Justified by faith, let us be at peace with God": for "righteousness and peace have embraced one another. Through our Lord Jesus Christ": for "Truth has arisen from the earth. Through whom we have access to that grace in which we stand, and our boast is in our hope of God's glory." He does not say: "of our glory," but "of God's glory": for "righteousness" has not proceeded from us but has "looked down from heaven." Therefore let those who glory, glory not in themselves, but "in the Lord."

For this reason, when our Lord was born of the Virgin, the message of the angelic voices was: "Glory to God in the highest, and peace to his people on earth."

For how could there be peace on earth unless "Truth has arisen from the earth," that is, unless Christ were born of our flesh? And "he is our peace who made the two into one:" that we might be people of good will, sweetly linked by the bond of unity.

Let us then rejoice in this grace, so that our glorying may bear witness to our good conscience by which we glory, not in ourselves, but in the Lord. That is why Scripture says: "He is my glory, the one who lifts up my head." For what greater grace could God have made to dawn on us than to make his only Son become the Son of Man, so that human beings might in their turn become children and heirs of God?

Ask if this were merited; ask for its reason, for its justification, and see whether you will find any other answer but sheer grace.

Sermon 185: PL 38, 997–999

Week of 4 Advent ✠ Christmas Eve

A reading from a sermon of Leo the Great, Bishop of Rome [461]

Dearly beloved, today our Savior is born; let us rejoice. Sadness should have no place on the birthday of life. The fear of death has been swallowed up; life brings us joy with the promise of eternal happiness.

No one is shut out from this joy; all share the same reason for rejoicing. Our Lord, victor over sin and death, finding no one free from sin, came to free us all. Let the saint rejoice seeing the palm of victory at hand. Let the sinner be glad receiving the offer of forgiveness. Let the pagan take courage on being summoned to life.

In the fullness of time, chosen in the unfathomable depths of God's wisdom, the Son of God took for himself our common humanity in order to reconcile it with its creator. He came to overthrow the devil, the origin of death, in that very nature by which the devil had overthrown humankind.

And so at the birth of our Lord the angels sing in joy: "Glory to God in the highest," and they proclaim "peace to his people on earth" as they see the heavenly Jerusalem being built from all the nations of the world. When the angels on high are so exultant at this marvelous work of God's goodness, what joy should it not bring to our lowly hearts?

Beloved, let us give thanks to God the Father, through his Son, in the Holy Spirit, because in his great love for us he took pity on us, "and when we were dead in our sins he brought us to life with Christ," so that in him we might be a new creation. Let us throw off our old nature and all its ways and, as we have come to birth in Christ, let us renounce the works of the flesh.

Christian, remember your dignity, and now that you share in God's own nature, do not return by sin to your former base condition. Bear in mind who is your head and of whose body you are a member. Do not forget that you have been rescued from the power of darkness and brought into the light of God's kingdom.

Through the sacrament of baptism you have become a temple of the Holy Spirit. Do not drive away so great a guest by evil conduct and become again a slave to the devil, for your liberty was bought by the blood of Christ.

Sermon 1 for the Nativity 1–3: PL 54, 190–193

Christmas Day and Following ✠ Christmas Day

A reading from a sermon of Gregory of Nazianzus, Bishop of Constantinople [389]

Christ is born: glorify him. Christ comes from heaven: go out to meet him. Christ descends to earth: let us be raised on high. Let all the world sing to the Lord; let the heavens rejoice and let the earth be glad, for his sake who was first in heaven and then on earth. Christ is here in the flesh: let us exult with fear and joy—with fear, because of our sins; with joy, because of the hope that he brings us.

Once more the darkness is dispersed; once more the light is created. Let the people that sat in the darkness of ignorance now look upon the light of knowledge. The things of old have passed away; behold, all things are made new. He who has no mother in heaven is now born without father on earth. The laws of nature are overthrown, for the upper world must be filled with citizens. He who is without flesh becomes incarnate; the Word puts on a body; the Invisible is seen; he whom no hand can touch is handled; the Timeless has a beginning; the Son of God becomes Son of Man—Jesus Christ, the same yesterday, today and for ever.

Light from light, the Word of the Father comes to his own image, in the human race. For the sake of my flesh he takes flesh; for the sake of my soul he is united to a rational soul, purifying like by like. In every way he becomes human, except for sin. O strange conjunction! The Self-existent comes into being; the Uncreated is created. He shares in the poverty of my flesh, that I may share in the riches of his Godhead.

Oration 38: PG 36, 311–314

Christmas Day and Following ✠ First Sunday after Christmas

A reading from a sermon of Bernard, Abbot of Clairvaux [1153]

"The goodness and humanity of God our Savior have appeared in our midst." We thank God for the many consolations he has given us during this sad exile of our pilgrimage here on earth. Before the Son of God became human his goodness was hidden, for God's mercy is eternal, but how could such goodness be recognized? It was promised, but it was not experienced, and as a result few believed in it. "Often and in many ways the Lord used to speak through the prophets." Among other things, God said: "I think thoughts of peace and not of affliction." But what did humans respond, thinking thoughts of affliction and knowing nothing of peace? They said: "Peace, peace, there is no peace." This response made the "angels of peace weep bitterly," saying: "Lord, who has believed our message?" But now they believe because they see with their own eyes, and because "God's testimony has now become even more credible." He has gone so far as to "pitch his tent in the sun" so even the dimmest eyes see him.

Notice that peace is not promised but sent to us; it is no longer deferred, it is given; peace is not prophesied but achieved. It is as if God the Father sent upon the earth a purse full of his mercy. This purse was burst open during the Lord's passion to pour forth its hidden contents—the price of our redemption. It was only a small purse, but it was very full. As the Scriptures tell us: "A little child has been given to us, but in him dwells all the fullness of the divine nature." The fullness of time brought with it the fullness of divinity. God's Son came in the flesh so that mortals could see and recognize God's kindness. When God reveals his humanity, his goodness cannot possibly remain hidden. To show his kindness what more could he do beyond taking my human form? My humanity, I say, not Adam's—that is, not such as he had before his fall.

How could he have shown his mercy more clearly than by taking on himself our condition? For our sake the Word of God became as grass. What better proof could he have given of his love? Scripture says: "Lord, what are we that you are mindful of us; why does your heart go out to us?" The incarnation teaches us how much God cares for us and what he thinks and feels about us. We should stop thinking of our own sufferings and remember what he has suffered. Let us think of all the Lord has done for us, and then we shall realize how his goodness appears through his humanity. The lesser he became through his human nature, the greater was his goodness; the more he lowered himself for me, the dearer he is to me. "The goodness and humanity of God our Savior have appeared," says the Apostle.

Truly great and manifest are the goodness and humanity of God. He has given us a most wonderful proof of his goodness by adding humanity to his own divine nature.

Sermon 1 for Epiphany 1–2: PL 133, 141–143

Christmas Day and Following ✠ December 29

A reading from a sermon of Gregory the Great, Bishop of Rome [604]

Why was it that at the time when the Lord was to be born the entire world was enrolled, unless that it might be openly demonstrated that the one had appeared in flesh who would enrol his elect in eternity? Against such it is said by the prophet concerning the wicked: "Let them be deleted from the book of the living and not be enrolled among the righteous."

Also, appropriately, he was born in Bethlehem, for Bethlehem, being interpreted, means "house of bread," and it is he who says "I am the living bread, which came down from heaven." And so the place in which the Lord would be born was already called "house of bread," because it was to be there that in the future the one would appear, in substance of our flesh, who would fill the hearts of the faithful with abundance.

And he was born, not in the house of his parents but upon a journey, so that he might truly show that, because of the humanity he had assumed, he was born as it were in a foreign land. Foreign, that is, not according to power but according to nature. For it is written concerning his power, "He came unto his own." But in his nature he was born before all time, although in our nature he came to us within time. Since, therefore, he appeared in time while remaining eternal, the place where he descended had to be foreign.

And because it is said by the prophet, "All flesh is grass," he, becoming human, turned our grass into grain, as he says of himself, "Unless a grain of wheat falls into the earth and dies, it remains alone." Wherefore when he was born he was laid in a manger, so that he might nourish all the faithful, even the holy animals, with the grain of his flesh.

The angel announces that a king is born, and the choirs of angels join their voices, and rejoicing together they cry, "Glory to God in the highest, and on earth peace to those of good will." Before our redeemer was born in the flesh there was a discord between us and the angels, from whose brightness and purity we stood afar, not only as the result of original sin but also because of our daily offenses. Because through sin we had become strangers to God, the angels as God's subjects had cut us off from their fellowship. But because we have now acknowledged our king, the angels have received us as fellow citizens.

Homily 8 for the Nativity: PL 76, 1103–1104

A reading from a treatise by Hippolytus, Priest or Bishop of Rome [c. 236]

Our faith is not founded upon empty words; nor are we carried away by mere caprice or beguiled by specious arguments. On the contrary, we put our faith in words spoken by the power of God, spoken by the Word himself at God's command. God wished to win us back from disobedience, not by using force to reduce us to slavery but by addressing to our free will a call to liberty.

The Word spoke first of all through the prophets, but because the message was couched in such obscure language that it could be only dimly apprehended, in the last days the Father sent the Word in person, commanding him to show himself openly so that the world could see him and be saved.

We know that by taking a body from the Virgin he refashioned our fallen nature. We know that his humanity was of the same clay as our own; if this were not so, he would hardly have been a teacher who could expect to be imitated. If he were of a different substance from me, he would surely not have ordered me to do as he did, when by my very nature I am so weak. Such a demand could not be reconciled with his goodness and justice.

No. He wanted us to consider him as no different from ourselves, and so he worked, he was hungry and thirsty, he slept. Without protest he endured his passion, he submitted to death and revealed his resurrection. In all these ways he offered his own humanity as the firstfruits of our race to keep us from losing heart when suffering comes our way, and to make us look forward to receiving the same reward as he did, since we know that we possess the same humanity.

When we have come to know the true God, both our bodies and our souls will be immortal and incorruptible. We shall enter the kingdom of heaven, because while we lived on earth we acknowledged heaven's King. Friends of God and co-heirs with Christ, we shall be subject to no evil desires or inclinations, or to any affliction of body or soul, for we shall have become divine. It was because of our human condition that God allowed us to endure these things, but when we have been deified and made immortal, God has promised us a share in his own attributes.

The saying "Know yourself" means therefore that we should recognize and acknowledge in ourselves the God who made us in his own image, for if we do this, we in turn will be recognized and acknowledged by our

Maker. So let us not be at enmity with ourselves, but change our way of life without delay. "For Christ who is God, exalted above all creation," has taken away our sin and has refashioned our fallen nature. In the beginning God made us in his image and so gave proof of his love for us. If we obey his holy commands and learn to imitate his goodness, we shall be like him and he will honor us. God is not beggarly, and for the sake of his own glory he has given us a share in his divinity.

On the Refutation of All Heresies 10, 33–34: PG 16, 3452–3453

Christmas Day and Following ✠ December 31

A reading from a treatise by Gregory of Nazianzus, Bishop of Constantinople [389]

God created humankind. He "formed us out of the clay of the ground" which he had made and breathed in us with his own breath, what Scripture calls a thinking soul and an image of God. He placed us on earth to watch over visible creation, to be initiated into the spiritual mystery, to have dominion over the things of the earth, and to be submissive to the Reign from on high. But we neglected to be obedient and, on that account, because of our sin, we were separated from the tree of life, from paradise and from God. Our condition required the most powerful remedy and this was granted us.

The very Word of God, more ancient than the ages, the invisible, the incomprehensible, the incorporeal, the principle issuing from the principle, the light born of light, the source of life and of immortality, the imprint of the divine model, the immutable seal, the perfect image, and the definitive word of the Father proceeds toward his own image, clothes himself with flesh to save the flesh, unites a thinking soul to himself for the sake of my soul so as to purify the like by the like, and assumes all that is human with the exception of sin. Conceived of the Virgin who had been purified by the Spirit in her body and soul, it is truly God who assumes humanity so that there is formed one only being issued from two opposites, the flesh and the spirit, one divinizing, the other divinized.

Marvelous union and paradoxical exchange! He who is becomes. The uncreated lets himself be created. He whom nothing can contain is contained in the womb of a thinking soul who stands midway between divinity and the heavy and brittle flesh. He who is the giver of riches becomes a beggar. He begs for my flesh to enrich me with his divinity. He who is fullness empties himself. He empties himself at the moment of his glory to enable me to share his fullness.

What is this abundance of goodness? What is this mystery that has relation to me? I had received the image and I have failed to preserve it. He received my flesh to save that image and make my flesh immortal. And he offers a second share that is much more astonishing than the first. He then came to share that which was highest. Now he comes to have a share in that which is weakest. This last gesture is even more divine than the first. And it is even more sublime for those who understand it.

Discourse 45, 7–9: PG 36, 631–635

Christmas Day and Following ✠ Eve of Holy Name

A reading from a sermon of Leo the Great, Bishop of Rome [461]

Although the state of infancy, which the majesty of the Son of God did not disdain to assume, developed with the passage of time into the maturity of humanity, and although after the triumph of the passion and the resurrection all his lowly acts undertaken on our behalf belong to the past, nevertheless today's feast renews for us the sacred beginning of Jesus' life, his birth from the Virgin Mary. In the very act in which we are reverencing the birth of our Savior, we are also celebrating our own new birth. For the birth of Christ is the origin of the Christian people; and the birthday of the head is also the birthday of the body.

Though each and every individual occupies a definite place in this body to which he has been called, and though all the progeny of the Church is differentiated and marked with the passage of time, nevertheless, as the whole community of the faithful, once begotten in the baptismal font, was crucified with Christ in the passion, raised up with him in the resurrection and at the ascension placed at the right hand of the Father, so too it is born with him in this Nativity.

For all believers regenerated in Christ, no matter in what part of the whole world they may be, break with that ancient way of life that derives from original sin, and by rebirth are transformed into new persons. Henceforth they are reckoned to be of the stock, not of their earthly father, but of Christ, who became Son of Man precisely so that they could become children of God; for unless in humility he had come down to us, none of us by our own merits could ever go up to him.

Therefore the greatness of the gift which he has bestowed on us demands an appreciation proportioned to its excellence; for blessed Paul the Apostle truly teaches: "We have received not the spirit of this world, but the Spirit which is from God, that we might understand the gifts bestowed on us by God." The only way that he can be worthily honored by us is by the presentation to him of that which he has already given to us.

But what can we find in the treasure of the Lord's bounty more in keeping with the glory of this feast than that peace which was first announced by the angelic choir on the day of his birth? For that peace, from which the children of God spring, sustains love and mothers unity; it refreshes the blessed and shelters eternity; its characteristic function and special blessing is to join to God those whom it separates from this world.

Therefore, may those "who were born, not of blood nor of the will of the flesh nor of the will of humankind, but of God," offer to the Father their harmony as children united in peace; and may all those whom he has adopted as his members meet in the firstborn of the new creation who came not to do his own will but the will of the one who sent him; for the grace of the Father has adopted as heirs neither the contentious nor the dissident, but those who are one in thought and love. The hearts and minds of those who have been reformed according to one and the same image should be in harmony with one another.

Sermon 6 for the Nativity 2–3, 5: PL 54, 213–216

Christmas Day and Following ✠ Holy Name

A reading from a letter by Athanasius, Bishop of Alexandria [373]

This explains the fact of Mary's presence: she is to provide the Word with a body of his own, to be offered for our sake. Scripture records her giving birth, and says: "She wrapped him in swaddling clothes." Her breasts, which fed him, were called blessed. Sacrifice was offered because the child was her firstborn. Gabriel used careful and prudent language when he announced his birth. He did not speak of "what will be born in you" to avoid the impression that a body would be introduced into her womb from outside; he spoke of "what will be born from you," so that we might know by faith that her child originated within her and from her.

By taking our nature and offering it in sacrifice, the Word was to destroy it completely and then invest it with his own nature, and so prompt the Apostle to say: "This corruptible body must put on incorruption; this mortal body must put on immortality."

This was not done in outward show only, as some have imagined. This is not so. Our Savior truly became human, and from this has followed the salvation of humanity as a whole. Our salvation is in no way fictitious, nor does it apply only to the body. The salvation of the whole person, that is, of soul and body, has really been achieved in the Word himself.

What was born of Mary was therefore human by nature, in accordance with the inspired Scriptures, and the body of the Lord was a true body: It was a true body because it was the same as ours. Mary, you see, is our sister, for we are all born from Adam.

The words of Saint John: "The Word was made flesh," bear the same meaning, as we may see from a similar turn of phrase in Saint Paul: "Christ was made a curse for our sake." Our body has acquired something great through its communion and union with the Word. From being mortal it has been made immortal; though it was a living body it has become a spiritual one; though it was made from the earth it has passed through the gates of heaven.

To Epictetus 5–9: PG 26, 1058, 1062–1066

Christmas Day and Following ✠ Second Sunday after Christmas

A reading from a sermon of Augustine, Bishop of Hippo [430]

Beloved, our Lord Jesus Christ, the eternal creator of all things, today became our Savior by being born of a mother. Of his own will he was born for us today, in time, so that he could lead us to his Father's eternity. God became human like us so that we might become God. The Lord of the angels became one of us today so that we could eat the bread of angels.

Today, the prophecy is fulfilled that said: "Pour down, heavens, from above, and let the clouds rain down righteousness: let the earth be opened and bring forth a savior." The Lord who had created all things is himself now created, so that he who was lost would be found. Thus humanity, in the words of the psalmist, confesses: "Before I was humbled, I sinned." We sinned and became guilty; God is born as one of us to free us from our guilt. We fell, but God descended; we fell miserably, but God descended mercifully; we fell through pride, God descended with his grace.

What miracles! What prodigies! The laws of nature are changed in the case of humankind. God is born. A virgin becomes pregnant. The Word of God marries the woman who knows no man. She is now at the same time both mother and virgin. She becomes a mother, yet she remains a virgin. The virgin bears a son, yet she does not know man; she remains untouched, yet she is not barren.

Sermon 13 on the Time: PL 39, 1097–1098

Christmas Day and Following ✠ January 2

A reading from a homily of Basil the Great, Bishop of Caesarea [379]

God on earth, God among us! No longer the God who gives his law amid flashes of lightning, to the sound of the trumpet on the smoking mountain, within the darkness of a terrifying storm, but the God who speaks gently and with kindness in a human body to his kindred. God in the flesh! It is no longer the God who acts only at particular instants, as in the prophets, but one who completely assumes our human nature and through his flesh, which is that of our race, lifts all humanity up to him.

How, then, you will say, did the light come everywhere, through one sole person? In what manner is the Godhead in the flesh? Like fire in iron: not by moving about, but by spreading itself. The fire, indeed, does not thrust itself toward the iron, but, remaining where it is, it distributes its own strength to it. In doing so, the fire is in no way diminished, but it completely fills the iron to which it spreads. In the same manner, God the Word who "dwelt among us" did not go outside himself; the Word which was "made flesh" underwent no change; heaven was not deprived of him who controlled it and the earth received within itself him who is in heaven.

Look deeply into this mystery. God comes in the flesh in order to destroy the death concealed in flesh. In the same way as remedies and medications triumph over the factors of corruption when they are assimilated into the body, and in the same way as the darkness which reigns in a house is dispelled by the entry of light, so death, which held human nature in its power, was annihilated by the coming of the Godhead. In the same way as ice, when in water, prevails over the liquid element as long as it is night, and darkness covers everything, but is dissolved when the sun comes up, under the warmth of its rays: so death reigned till the coming of Christ; but when the saving grace of God appeared and the sun of justice rose, death was swallowed up in this victory, being unable to endure the sojourn of the true Life among us. O, the depth of the goodness of God and of his love for all of us!

Let us give glory to God with the shepherds, let us dance in choir with the angels, for "this day a Savior has been born to us, the Messiah and Lord." He is the Lord who has appeared to us, not in his divine form, in order not to terrify us in our weakness, but in the form of a servant, that he might set free what had been reduced to servitude. Who could be so faint-hearted and so ungrateful as not to rejoice and exult in gladness for what is taking place? It is a festival that is common to all creation.

Let us too shout our joy; let us give to our festival the name of Theophany. Let us celebrate the salvation of the world, the day when humanity was born. Today Adam's condemnation has been lifted. We shall no longer say: "You are dust, and to dust you shall return," but, "United to him who is in heaven, you shall be lifted up to heaven."

Homily for the Birth of Christ 2, 6: PG 31, 1459–1462, 1471–1474

Christmas Day and Following ✠ January 3

A reading from a commentary on John by Augustine, Bishop of Hippo [430]

The Lord, the teacher of love, full of love, came in person "with summary judgment on the world," as had been foretold of him, and showed that the law and the prophets are summed up in two commandments of love.

Call to mind what these two commandments are. They ought to be very familiar to you; they should not only spring to mind when I mention them, but ought never to be absent from your hearts. Keep always in mind that we must love God and our neighbor: "Love God with your whole heart, your whole soul, and your whole mind, and your neighbor as yourself."

These two commandments must be always in your thoughts and in your hearts, treasured, acted on, fulfilled. Love of God is the first to be commanded, but love of neighbor is the first to be put into practice. In giving two commandments of love Christ would not commend to you first your neighbor and then God, but first God and then your neighbor.

Since you do not yet see God, you merit the vision of God by loving your neighbor. By loving your neighbor you prepare your eye to see God: Saint John says clearly: "If you do not love your neighbor whom you see, how will you love God whom you do not see!"

Consider what is said to you: Love God. If you say to me: Show me whom I am to love, what shall I say if not what Saint John says: "No one has ever seen God!" But in case you should think that you are completely cut off from the sight of God, he says: "God is love, and you who remain in love remain in God." Love your neighbor, then, and see within your-self the power by which you love your neighbor; there you will see God, as far as you are able.

Begin, then, to love your neighbor. "Break your bread to feed the hungry, and bring into your home the homeless poor; if you see some-one naked, clothe them, and do not look down on your own flesh and blood."

What will you gain by doing this? "Your light will then burst forth like the dawn." Your light is your God; God is your "dawn," for he will come to you when the night of time is over. God does not rise or set but remains for ever.

In loving your neighbor and caring for others, you are on a journey. Where are you traveling if not to the Lord God, to him whom we should love with our whole heart, our whole soul, our whole mind? We have not yet reached his presence, but we have our neighbor at our side. Support, then, this companion of your pilgrimage if you want to come into the presence of the one with whom you desire to remain for ever.

Treatise 17 on John 7–9: CCL 36, 174–175

Christmas Day and Following ✠ January 4

A reading from the treatise On the Holy Spirit by Basil the Great, Bishop of Caesarea [379]

A spiritual person is one who no longer lives by the flesh but is led by the Spirit of God, one called a child of God, remade in the likeness of God's Son. As the power of sight is active in a healthy eye, so the Holy Spirit is active in a purified soul.

We may form a word either as a thought in the heart or as a sound on the lips. So the Holy Spirit, bearing witness to our spirit, cries out in our hearts, saying: "Abba, Father," or speaks in our place, as Scripture says: "It is not you who speak; it is the Spirit of the Father who speaks in you."

In the distributing of the gifts we can see the Spirit as a whole in relation to the parts. We are all members of one another, but with different gifts according to the grace God gives us. So "the eye cannot say to the hand, I do not need you, nor can the head say to the feet, I have no need of you." All the members together make up the body of Christ in the unity of the Spirit, and render each other a necessary service through their gifts. God has arranged the various parts of the body according to his own will, but there exists among them all a spiritual fellowship which makes it natural for them to share one another's feelings and to be concerned for one another. "If one member suffers, all suffer with it; if one member is honored, all rejoice together." Moreover, as parts are present in a single whole, so each of us is in the Spirit since all who make up the one body have been baptized into the one Spirit.

As the Father is seen in the Son, so the Son is seen in the Spirit. To worship in the Spirit, then, is to have our minds open to the light, as we may learn from our Lord's words to the Samaritan woman. Misled by the tradition of her country, she imagined that it was necessary to worship in a certain place, but our Lord gave her a different teaching. He told her that one must worship in Spirit and in truth, and clearly by the truth he meant himself.

As we speak of worship in the Son because the Son is the image of God the Father, so we speak of worship in the Spirit because the Spirit is the manifestation of the divinity of the Lord. Through the light of the Spirit we behold the Son, the splendor of God's glory, and through the Son, the very stamp of the Father, we are led to him who is the source both of his stamp, who is the Son, and of its seal, who is the Holy Spirit.

On the Holy Spirit 26, 61, 64: PG 32, 179–182, 186

Christmas Day and Following ✠ January 5

A reading from the Five Hundred Chapters by Maximus the Confessor, Abbot [662]

The Word of God, born once in the flesh (such is his kindness and his goodness), is always willing to be born spiritually in those who desire him. In them he is born as an infant, as he fashions himself in them by means of their virtues. He reveals himself to the extent that he knows someone is capable of receiving him. He diminishes the revelation of his glory not out of selfishness but because he recognizes the capacity and resources of those who desire to see him. Yet, in the transcendence of mystery, he always remains invisible to all.

For this reason the apostle Paul, reflecting on the power of the mystery, said: "Jesus Christ, yesterday and today: he remains the same for ever." For he understands the mystery as ever new, never growing old through our understanding of it.

Christ is God, for he has given all things their being out of nothing. Yet he is born as one of us by taking to himself our nature, flesh endowed with intelligent spirit. A star glitters by day in the East and leads the wise men to the place where the incarnate Word lies, to show that the Word, contained in the Law and the Prophets, surpasses in a mystical way knowledge derived from the senses, and to lead the Gentiles to the full light of knowledge.

For surely the word of the Law and the Prophets when it is understood with faith is like a star which leads those who are called by the power of grace in accordance with his decree to recognize the Word incarnate.

Here is the reason why God became a perfect human, changing nothing of human nature, except to take away sin (which was never natural anyway). His flesh was set before that voracious, gaping dragon as bait to provoke him: flesh that would be deadly for the dragon, for it would utterly destroy him by the power of the Godhead hidden within it. For human nature, however, his flesh was to be a remedy since the power of the Godhead in it would restore human nature to its original grace.

The great mystery of the divine incarnation remains a mystery for ever. How can the Word made flesh be essentially the same person that is wholly with the Father? How can he who is by nature God become by nature entirely human without lacking either nature, neither the divine by which he is God nor the human by which he became one of us?

Faith alone grasps these mysteries. Faith alone is truly the substance and foundation of all that exceeds knowledge and understanding.

Five Hundred Chapters 1, 8–13: PG 90, 1182–1186

Christmas Day and Following ✠ Eve of Epiphany

A reading from a sermon of Leo the Great, Bishop of Rome [461]

The loving providence of God determined that in the last days he would aid the world, set on its course to destruction. He decreed that all nations should be saved in Christ.

A promise had been made to the holy patriarch Abraham in regard to these nations. He was to have a countless progeny, born not from his body but from the seed of faith. His descendants are therefore compared with the array of the stars. The father of all nations was to hope not in an earthly progeny but in a progeny from above.

Let the full number of the nations now take their place in the family of the patriarchs. Let the children of the promise now receive the blessing in the seed of Abraham. In the persons of the Magi let all people adore the Creator of the universe; let God be known, not in Judea only, but in the whole world, so that "his name may be great in all Israel."

Dear friends, now that we have received instruction in this revelation of God's grace, let us celebrate with spiritual joy the day of our first harvesting, of the first calling of the Gentiles. Let us give thanks to the merciful God, "who has made us worthy," in the words of the Apostle, "to share the position of the saints in light; who has rescued us from the power of darkness, and brought us into the kingdom of his beloved Son." As Isaiah prophesied: "The people of the Gentiles, who sat in darkness, have seen a great light, and for those who dwelt in the region of the shadow of death a light has dawned." He spoke of them to the Lord: "The Gentiles, who do not know you, will invoke you, and the peoples, who knew you not, will take refuge in you."

This is "the day that Abraham saw, and rejoiced to see," when he knew that the children born of his faith would be blessed in his seed, that is, in Christ. Believing that he would be the father of the nations, he looked into the future, "giving glory to God, in full awareness that God is able to do what he has promised."

This is the day that David prophesied in the psalms, when he said: "All the nations that you have brought into being will come and fall down in adoration in your presence, Lord, and glorify your name." Again, "the Lord has made known his salvation; in the sight of the nations he has revealed his justice."

This came to be fulfilled, as we know, from the time when the star beckoned the three wise men out of their distant country and led them to recognize and adore the King of heaven and earth. The obedience of the star calls us to imitate its humble service: to be servants, as best we can, of the grace that invites all of us to find Christ.

Dear friends, you must have the same zeal to be of help to one another; then, in the kingdom of God, to which faith and good works are the way, you will shine as children of the light: through our Lord Jesus Christ, who lives and reigns with God the Father and the Holy Spirit for ever and ever.

Sermon 3 for Epiphany 1–3, 5: PL 54, 240–244

The Epiphany and Following ✠ Epiphany

A reading from a sermon of Gregory of Nazianzus, Bishop of Constantinople [389]

Christ is bathed in light; let us also be bathed in light. Christ is baptized; let us also go down with him, and rise with him.

John is baptizing when Jesus draws near. Perhaps he comes to sanctify his baptizer; certainly he comes to bury sinful humanity in the waters. He comes to sanctify the Jordan for our sake and in readiness for us; he who is spirit and flesh comes to begin a new creation through the Spirit and water.

The Baptist protests; Jesus insists. Then John says: "I ought to be baptized by you." He is the lamp in the presence of the sun, the voice in the presence of the Word, the friend in the presence of the Bridegroom, the greatest of all born of woman in the presence of the firstborn of all creation, the one who leapt in his mother's womb in the presence of him who was adored in the womb, the forerunner and future forerunner in the presence of him who has already come and is to come again. "I ought to be baptized by you;" we should also add: "and for you," for John is to be baptized in blood, washed clean like Peter, not only by the washing of his feet.

Jesus rises from the waters; the world rises with him. The heavens like Paradise with its flaming sword, closed by Adam for himself and his descendants, are rent open. The Spirit comes to him as to an equal, bearing witness to his Godhead. A voice bears witness to him from heaven, his place of origin. The Spirit descends in bodily form like the dove that so long ago announced the ending of the flood and so gives honor to the body that is one with God.

Today let us do honor to Christ's baptism and celebrate this feast in holiness. Be cleansed entirely and continue to be cleansed. Nothing gives such pleasure to God as the conversion and salvation of human beings, for whom his every word and every revelation exist. He wants you to become a living force for all humanity, lights shining in the world. You are to be radiant lights as you stand beside Christ, the great light, bathed in the glory of him who is the light of heaven. You are to enjoy more and more the pure and dazzling light of the Trinity, as now you have received—though not in its fullness—a ray of its splendor, proceeding from the one God, in Christ Jesus our Lord, to whom be glory and power for ever and ever.

Oration 39, 14-16, 20: PG 36, 350-351, 354, 358-359

The Epiphany and Following ✠ January 7

A reading from a sermon of Peter Chrysologus, Bishop of Ravenna [450]

In the mystery of our Lord's incarnation there were clear indications of his eternal Godhead. Yet the great events we celebrate today disclose and reveal in different ways the fact that God himself took a human body. Mortals, enshrouded always in darkness, must not be left in ignorance, and so be deprived of what they can understand and retain only by grace.

In choosing to be born for us, God chose to be known by us. He therefore reveals himself in this way, in order that this great sacrament of his love may not be an occasion for us of great misunderstanding.

Today the Magi find, crying in a manger, the one they have followed as he shone in the sky. Today the Magi see clearly, in swaddling clothes, the one they have long awaited as he lay hidden among the stars.

Today the Magi gaze in deep wonder at what they see: heaven on earth, earth in heaven, humankind in God, God in human flesh, one whom the whole universe cannot contain now enclosed in a tiny body. As they look, they believe and do not question, as their symbolic gifts bear witness: incense for God, gold for a king, myrrh for one who is to die.

So the Gentiles, who were the last, become the first: the faith of the Magi is the first fruits of the belief of the Gentiles.

Today Christ enters the Jordan to wash away the sin of the world. John himself testifies that this is why he has come: "Behold the Lamb of God, behold him who takes away the sins of the world." Today a servant lays his hand on the Lord, a man lays his hand on God, John lays his hand on Christ, not to forgive but to receive forgiveness.

Today, as the psalmist prophesied: "The voice of the Lord is heard above the waters." What does the voice say? "This is my beloved son, in whom I am well pleased."

Today the Holy Spirit hovers over the waters in the likeness of a dove. A dove announced to Noah that the flood had disappeared from the earth; so now a dove is to reveal that the world's shipwreck is at an end for ever. The sign is no longer an olive-shoot of the old stock: instead, the Spirit pours out on Christ's head the full richness of a new anointing by the Father, to fulfill what the psalmist had prophesied: "Therefore God, your God, has anointed you with the oil of gladness above your fellows."

Today Christ works the first of his signs from heaven by turning water into wine. But water [mixed with wine] has still to be changed into the sacrament of his blood, so that Christ may offer spiritual drink from the chalice of his body, to fulfill the psalmist's prophecy: "How excellent is my chalice, warming my spirit."

Sermon 160: PL 52, 620–622

The Epiphany and Following ✠ January 8

A reading from the Ecclesiastical History of Eusebius, Bishop of Caesarea [c. 340]

Glory to God the almighty, the King of the universe, for all his gifts, and gratitude to Jesus Christ, the Savior and Redeemer of our souls, through whom we pray that this peace may be preserved for us stable and unshaken for ever: a peace that will keep us safe from troubles outside as well as from all anxieties and disturbances of soul. When this bright and radiant day, darkened by no cloud, shone with heavenly light on the churches of Christ throughout the world, even those outside our community, though they had not the same cause for rejoicing, shared at least some of the blessings that God had bestowed on us. For us above all, who had placed our hopes in Christ, there was inexpressible joy and a heavenly happiness shone on every face. Every place that a short time before had been laid waste by the tyrants' wickedness we now saw restored to life, recovering, as it seemed, from a long and deadly disease. Churches were once again rising from the ground high into the air, far surpassing in splendor and magnificence the ones that had previously been stormed and destroyed.

Then came the spectacle that we had prayed and hoped for: dedication festivals throughout the cities, and the consecration of the newly erected houses of worship. For this there were convocations of bishops, gatherings of pilgrims from far distant lands, warm and loving contact between the different communities, as the members of Christ's body united in complete harmony. The mysterious prophecy: "There came together bone to bone and joint to joint" was thus fulfilled, as were all the other prophecies which had been unerringly proclaimed by type and symbol. All the members were filled with the grace of the one divine Spirit, all were of one mind, with the same enthusiasm for the faith, and on the lips of all there was one hymn of praise.

Yes, and our bishops performed religious rites with full ceremonial, priests officiated at the liturgy, the solemn ritual of the Church, chanting psalms, proclaiming the other parts of our God-given Scriptures, and celebrating the divine mysteries. Baptism was also administered, the sacred symbol of our Savior's passion. Without the slightest distraction, men and women of all ages united in prayer and thanksgiving, their minds and hearts full of joy as they gave glory to God the giver of all good gifts.

Ecclesiastical History 10, 1–3: PG 20, 842–847

The Epiphany and Following ✠ January 9

A reading from the treatise On Baptism by Gregory, Bishop of Nyssa [c. 394]

Too long have your rolled in the mire; hasten—not at the voice of John, but of Christ—to Jerusalem. For indeed the river of grace flows everywhere.

Jerusalem does not rise in Palestine to disappear in some nearby sea. It spreads over the whole earth and flows into paradise, flowing in the opposite direction to those four rivers which come from paradise and bringing in things far more precious than those which come forth.

Those rivers carry perfumes, the fruit of the culture and germination of the earth. This river brings in men and women, begotten of the Holy Spirit.

Wherever you draw water, there also does this river flow; it is diverted throughout the whole earth, and it does not consume its water in those places into which it is divided. For it has a rich source, Christ, and flowing out from him it inundates the entire world.

This river is delightful and drinkable, attracting nothing that is salty and unpleasant. It is rendered sweet by the Spirit's coming, like the fount of Marah by the touch of the wood.

It can easily be crossed by those who are devout, but is too deep for those who are worldly-minded and cannot even be approached by them.

Imitate Jesus, Bear the gospel, as he bore the ark. Leave behind the desert, that is, sin. Cross the Jordan, and hasten to life according to the commands of Christ.

Hurry to that land which brings forth fruits of joy; where—as promised—there flow milk and honey.

Overturn Jericho, your former way of life; and do not let it be built up again.

All these things constitute types for us; and they all prefigure truths which have now been revealed.

Treatise on Baptism: PG 46, 419–422

The Epiphany and Following ✠ January 10

A reading from the treatise Against Heresies by Irenaeus,
Bishop of Lyons [c. 202]

No one can know the Father apart from God's Word, that is, unless the Son reveals him, and no one can know the Son unless the Father so wills. Now the Son fulfills the Father's good pleasure: the Father sends, the Son is sent, and he comes. The Father is beyond our sight and comprehension; but he is known by his Word, who tells us of him who surpasses all telling. In turn, the Father alone has knowledge of his Word. And the Lord has revealed both truths. Therefore, the Son reveals the knowledge of the Father by his revelation of himself. Knowledge of the Father consists in the self-revelation of the Son, for all is revealed through the Word.

The Father's purpose in revealing the Son was to make himself known to us all and so to welcome into eternal rest those who believe in him, establishing them in justice, preserving them from death. To believe in him means to do his will.

Through creation itself the Word reveals God the Creator. Through the world he reveals the Lord who made the world. Through all that is fashioned he reveals the artist who crafted it all. Through the Son the Word reveals the Father who begot him as Son. All speak of these things in the same language, but they do not believe them in the same way. Through the law and the prophets the Word revealed himself and his Father in the same way, and though all the people equally heard the message not all equally believed it. Through the Word, made visible and palpable, the Father was revealed, though not all equally believed in him. But all saw the Father in the Son, for the Father of the Son cannot be seen, but the Son of the Father can be seen.

The Son performs everything as a ministry to the Father, from beginning to end, and without the Son no one can know God. The way to know the Father is the Son. Knowledge of the Son is in the Father, and is revealed through the Son. For this reason the Lord said: "No one knows the Son except the Father; and no one knows the Father except the Son, and those to whom the Son has revealed him." The word "revealed" refers not only to the future—as though the Word began to reveal the Father only when he was born of Mary; it refers equally to all time. From the beginning the Son is present to creation, reveals the Father to all, to those the Father chooses, when the Father chooses, and as the Father chooses. So, there is in all and through all one God the

Father, one Word and Son, and one Spirit, and one salvation for all who believe in him.

Against Heresies 4, 6, 3–7: SC 100, 442, 446, 448–454

The Epiphany and Following ✠ January 11

A reading from The Educator by Clement of Alexandria, Priest [c. 210]

Our Educator is the holy God Jesus, the Word, who is the guide of all humanity. God himself, who loves us, is our Educator. Somewhere in a canticle the Holy Spirit says about him: "He provided sufficiently for the people in the wilderness. He led them about in the thirst of summer heat in a dry land, and instructed them, and guarded them as the apple of his eye, as an eagle protects her nest, and shows her fond solicitude for her young, spreads her wings, takes them, and bears them on her back. The Lord alone was their leader, no strange god was with them!"

In my opinion, Scripture is obviously offering a picture of the Educator of children and describing the guidance he imparts.

When he speaks in his own person, he also confesses himself to be the Educator: "I, the Lord, am your God, who brought you out of the land of Egypt." But who has the power to lead in or out? Is it not the Educator?

He is the one who appeared to Abraham and said to him: "I am your God; be pleasing before me," and formed him by a gradual process into a faithful child, truly as an educator would, saying: "Be blameless; and I will make my covenant between me and you, and your descendants." Here is a share in the Educator's friendship. Who, then, would train us more lovingly than he? Formerly, the older people had an old covenant; the law disciplined the people with fear, and the word was an angel. But the new and young people have received a new and young covenant, the Word has become flesh, fear has been turned to love, and the mystic angel has been born, Jesus.

Formerly, this same Educator said: "Fear the Lord your God." But to us he says: "Love the Lord your God." Hence, he tells us: "Cease from your own works, from your old sins"; "Learn to do good"; "You have loved justice and hated iniquity." This is my new covenant written in the old letter.

Hence, the newness of the word must not be made ground for reproach. For the Lord says through Jeremiah: "Say not, 'I am too young.' Before I formed you in the womb I knew you, before you were born I dedicated you." Perhaps this prophetic word refers to us: before the foundation of the world we were known by God as destined for the faith, but we are still only little children, because the will of God has only recently been fulfilled; we are only newlyborn in the scheme of our calling and salvation.

The Educator 1, 7: PG 8, 315–318

The Epiphany and Following ✠ January 12

A reading from The Educator by Clement of Alexandria, Priest [c. 210]

Jesus our Educator has laid out for us the true life and has effected the education of the one who abides in Christ. The cast and character of the life he enjoins is not very formidable, nor is it made altogether easy by reason of his benignity. He imposes commands, but at the same time gives them such a character that they can be carried out.

The view I take is that he himself formed us out of dust, regenerated us by water, enabled us to grow through the Spirit, educated us by the word, and directed us by sacred precepts toward our adoption as heirs and our salvation. And he did so in order that he might transform an earth-born human being into a holy and heavenly being by his coming and fulfill to the utmost that divine utterance: "Let us make humankind in our image, after our likeness." It is Christ, in fact, who became the perfect realization of what God spoke; the rest of humanity is conceived as being created merely in his image.

Hence, let us who are children of the good Father and nurslings of the good Educator fulfill the Father's will, pay heed to the Word, and be truly fashioned by the saving life of the Savior. Then, inasmuch as we shall already be leading a heavenly life which makes us divine, let us anoint ourselves with the perennially youthful oil of gladness, that incorruptible oil of sweet fragrance. This we do by regarding the Lord's life as a shining example of incorruptibility and by following in the footsteps of God.

His main concern is to consider the way and the means in which our life might be rendered better. In order to give us a life that is simple and unencumbered by cares, he sets before us the life of a wayfarer, one that is easy to lead and easy to leave on our journey toward the attainment of an eternal happiness. He teaches us that each one of us must be his own storehouse. "Enough, then, of worrying about tomorrow," that is, we who have devoted ourselves to Christ ought to be self-sufficient and our own servants, living life from day to day.

It is not for war that we are educated, but for peace. War requires great preparation, and self-indulgence craves profusion; but peace and love, simple and quiet sisters, require neither arms nor excessive preparation. The Word is their sustenance.

This Word has received the charge to show the way and to educate; from him we learn frugality and humility, and all that pertains to love of truth, love of humanity, and love of excellence. In short, through him we become like God by a participation in moral excellence. Hence, we must not retrogress into carelessness and sloth but labor unwearyingly. You will then become what we neither dare hope, nor can imagine.

The Educator 1, 12: PG 8, 367–370

The Epiphany and Following ✠ Eve of 1 Epiphany

A reading from the Revelations of Divine Love by Dame Julian of Norwich [c. 1417]

The purpose of this revelation was to teach our soul the wisdom of cleaving to the goodness of God. And so our customary practice of prayer was brought to mind: how through our ignorance and inexperience in the ways of love we spend so much time on petition. I saw that it is indeed more worthy of God and more truly pleasing to him that through his goodness we should pray with full confidence, and by grace cling to him with real understanding and unshakeable love, than that we should go on making as many petitions as our souls are capable of. For however numerous our petitions they still come short of being wholly worthy of him. For in his goodness is included all one can want, without exception.

To know the goodness of God is the highest prayer of all, and it is a prayer that accommodates itself to our most lowly needs. It quickens our soul, and vitalizes it, developing it in grace and virtue. Here is the grace most appropriate to our need, and most ready to help. Here is the grace which our soul is seeking now, and which it will ever seek until that day when we know for a fact that he has wholly united us to himself. He does not despise the work of his hands, nor does he disdain to serve us, however lowly our natural need may be. He loves the soul he has made in his own likeness.

Revelation 1, chapter 6: Colledge and Walsh 2, 304–306

Week of 1 Epiphany ✠ Sunday

A reading from the First Apology in Defense of Divine Images by John of Damascus, Priest [c. 760]

In former times God, who is without form or body, could never be depicted. But now when God is seen in the flesh conversing with humankind, I make an image of the God whom I see. I do not worship matter; I worship the Creator of matter who became matter for my sake, who willed to take his abode in matter; who worked out my salvation through matter. Never will I cease honoring the matter which wrought my salvation! I honor it, but not as God. How could God be born out of things which have no existence in themselves? God's body is God because it is joined to his person by a union which shall never pass away. The divine nature remains the same; the flesh created in time is quickened by a reason-endowed soul. Because of this I salute all remaining matter with reverence, because God has filled it with his grace and power. Through it my salvation has come to me. Was not the thrice-happy and thrice-blessed wood of the cross matter? Was not the holy and exalted mountain of Calvary matter? What of the life-bearing rock, the holy and life-giving tomb, the fountain of our resurrection, was it not matter? Is not the ink in the most holy Gospel-book matter? Is not the life-giving altar made of matter? From it we receive the bread of life! Are not gold and silver matter? From them we make crosses, patens, chalices! And over and above all these things, is not the Body and Blood of our Lord matter? Either do away with the honor and veneration these things deserve, or accept the tradition of the Church and the veneration of images.

Reverence God and his friends; follow the inspiration of the Holy Spirit. Do not despise matter, for it is not despicable. God has made nothing despicable. To think such things is Manichaeism. Only that which does not have its source in God is despicable—that which is our own invention, our willful choice to disregard the law of God—namely, sin.

Apology 1, 16: PG 94, 1245

Week of 1 Epiphany ✠ Monday

A reading from an instruction by Columbanus, Celtic Abbot [615]

Moses wrote in the law: "God made humankind in his image and likeness." Consider, I ask you, the dignity of these words. God is all-powerful. We cannot see or understand him, describe or assess him. Yet he fashioned us from clay and endowed us with the nobility of his own image. What have we in common with God? Or earth with spirit?—for "God is a spirit." It is a glorious privilege that God should grant us his eternal image and the likeness of his character. Our likeness to God, if we preserve it, imparts high dignity.

If we apply the virtues planted in our souls to the right purpose, we will be like God. God's commands have taught us to give him back the virtues he sowed in us in our first innocence. The first command is "to love our Lord with our whole heart because he loved us first" from the beginning, before our existence. Loving God renews his image in us. Anyone who loves God keeps his commandments, for he said: "If you love me, keep my commandments." His command is that we love each other. In his own words: "This is my command, that you love each other as I also have loved you."

True love is shown not merely "in word, but in deed and in truth." So we must turn back our image undefiled and holy to our God and Father, for he is holy; in the words of Scripture: "Be holy, for I am holy." We must restore his image with love, for he is love; in John's words: "God is love." We must restore it with loyalty and truth, for he is loyal and truthful. The image we depict must not be that of one who is unlike God; for one who is harsh and irascible and proud would display the image of a despot.

Let us not imprint on ourselves the image of a despot, but let Christ paint his image in us with his words: "My peace I give you, my peace I leave with you." But the knowledge that peace is good is of no benefit to us if we do not practice it. The most valuable objects are usually the most fragile; costly things require the most careful handling. Particularly fragile is that which is lost by wanton talk and destroyed with the slightest injury of a brother or sister. People like nothing better than discussing and minding the business of others, passing superfluous comments at random and criticizing people behind their backs. So those who cannot say: "The Lord has given me a discerning tongue, that I may with a word support those who are weary" should keep silent, or if they do say anything it should promote peace.

Instruction 11, 1–2: Opera, Dublin 1957, 106–107

Week of 1 Epiphany ✠ Tuesday

A reading from the Exposition of the Orthodox Faith by John of Damascus, Priest [c. 760]

Let them remember that in the beginning God created us after His own image. On what grounds, then, do we show reverence to each other unless because we are made after God's image? For as Basil, that much-versed expounder of divine things, says, the honor given to the image passes over to the prototype. Now a prototype is that which is imaged, from which the derivative is obtained.

In the Old Testament the use of images was not common. But after God in his heart of pity became in truth human for our salvation, not as he was seen by Abraham in the semblance of a person, nor as he was seen by the prophets, but in being truly human, and after he lived upon the earth and dwelt among the people, worked miracles, suffered, was crucified, rose again and was taken back to Heaven, since all these things actually took place and were seen by men and women, they were written for the remembrance and instruction of us who were not alive at that time in order that though we saw not, we may still, hearing and believing, obtain the blessing of the Lord. But seeing that not every one has a knowledge of letters nor time for reading, the Fathers gave their sanction to depicting these events on images as being acts of great heroism, in order that they should form a concise memorial of them. Often, doubtless, when we have not the Lord's passion in mind and see the image of Christ's crucifixion, his saving passion is brought back to remembrance, and we fall down and worship not the material but that which is imaged: just as we do not worship the material of which the Gospels are made, nor the material of the Cross, but that which these typify. For wherein does the cross, that typifies the Lord, differ from a cross that does not do so? It is just the same also in the case of the Mother of the Lord. For the honor which we give to her is referred to him who was made of her incarnate. And similarly also the brave acts of holy men and women stir us up to be brave and to emulate and imitate their valor and to glorify God.

The Fount of Knowledge 3, On the Orthodox Faith 4, 16: PG 94, 1169–1173

Week of 1 Epiphany ✠ Wednesday

A reading from the Decree of the Seventh Ecumenical Council, of Nicaea [787]

We keep unchanged all the ecclesiastical traditions handed down to us, whether in writing or verbally, one of which is the making of pictorial representations, agreeable to the history of the preaching of the Gospel, a tradition useful in many respects, but especially in this, that so the incarnation of the Word of God is shown forth as real and not merely fantastic, for these have mutual indications and without doubt have also mutual significations.

We, therefore, following the royal pathway and the divinely inspired authority of our Holy Fathers and the traditions of the Catholic Church (for, as we all know, the Holy Spirit indwells her), define with all certitude and accuracy that just as the figure of the precious and life-giving Cross, so also the venerable and holy images, as well in painting and mosaic as of other fit materials, should be set forth in the holy churches of God, and on the sacred vessels and on the vestments and on hangings and in pictures both in houses and by the wayside, to wit, the figure of our Lord God and Savior Jesus Christ, of our spotless Lady, the Mother of God, of the honorable Angels, of all saints and of all pious people. For by so much more frequently as they are seen in artistic representation, by so much more readily are people lifted up to the memory of their prototypes, and to a longing after them; and to these should be given due salutation and honorable reverence, not indeed that true worship of faith which pertains alone to the divine nature; but to these, as to the figure of the precious and life-giving Cross and to the Book of the Gospels and to the other holy objects, incense and lights may be offered according to ancient pious custom. For the honor which is paid to the image passes on to that which the image represents, and whoever reveres the image reveres in it the subject represented.

Alberigo, 135–136: Denzinger 600–603

Week of 1 Epiphany ✠ Thursday

*A reading from the treatise Against the Pagans by
Athanasius, Bishop of Alexandria [373]*

By his own wisdom and Word, who is our Lord and Savior Christ, the
all-holy Father (whose excellence far exceeds that of any creature) like
a skillful pilot guides to safety all creation, regulating and keeping it in
being, as he judges right. It is proper that creation should exist as he has
made it and as we see it happening, because this is his will, which no
one would deny. For if the movement of the universe were irrational, and
the world rolled on in random fashion, one would be justified in disbelieving what we say. But if the world is founded on reason, wisdom
and science, and is filled with orderly beauty, then it must owe its origin
and order to none other than the Word of God.

He is God, the living and creative God of the universe, the Word of the
good God, who is God in his own right. The Word is different from all
created things: he is the unique Word belonging only to the good Father.
This is the Word that created this whole world and enlightens it by his
loving wisdom. He who is the good Word of the good Father produced
the order in all creation, joining opposites together, and forming from
them one harmonious sound. He is God, one and only-begotten, who
proceeds in goodness from the Father as from the fountain of goodness,
and gives order, direction and unity to creation.

By his eternal Word the Father created all things and implanted a
nature in his creatures. He did not want to see them tossed about at the
mercy of their own natures, and so be reduced to nothingness. But in
his goodness he governs and sustains the whole of nature by his Word
(who is himself also God), so that under the guidance, providence and
ordering of that Word, the whole of nature might remain stable and
coherent in his light. Nature was to share in the Father's Word, whose
reality is true, and be helped by him to exist, for without him it would
cease to be. For unless the Word, who is the very "image of the invisible
God, the firstborn of all creation," kept it in existence it could not exist.
For whatever exists, whether visible or invisible, remains in existence
through him and in him, and he is also the head of the Church, as we
are taught by the ministers of truth in their sacred writings.

The almighty and most holy Word of the Father pervades the whole
of reality, everywhere unfolding his power and shining on all things
visible and invisible. He sustains it all and binds it together in himself.

He leaves nothing devoid of his power but gives life and keeps it in being throughout all of creation and in each individual creature.

Against the Pagans 40–42; PG 25, 79–83

Week of 1 Epiphany ✠ Friday

A reading from the treatise Against the Pagans by Athanasius, Bishop of Alexandria [373]

"In the beginning was the Word, and the Word was with God, and the Word was God. All things were made through him, and without him nothing was made." In these words John the theologian teaches that nothing exists or remains in being except in and through the Word.

Think of a musician tuning a lyre. By skill the musician adjusts high notes to low and intermediate notes to the rest, and produces a series of harmonies. So too the wisdom of God holds the world like a lyre and joins things in the air to those on earth, and things in heaven to those in the air, and brings each part into harmony with the whole. By his decree and will he regulates them all to produce the beauty and harmony of a single, well-ordered universe. While remaining unchanged with his Father, he moves all creation by his unchanging nature, according to the Father's will. To everything he gives existence and life in accordance with its nature, and so creates a wonderful and truly divine harmony.

To illustrate this profound mystery, let us take the example of a choir of many singers. A choir is composed of a variety of men, women and children, of both old and young. Under the direction of one conductor, each sings in the way that is natural: men with men's voices, boys with boys' voices, old people with old voices, young people with young voices. Yet all of them produce a single harmony. Or consider the example of our soul. It moves our senses according to their several functions so that in the presence of a single object they all act simultaneously: the eye sees, the ear hears, the hand touches, the nose smells, the tongue tastes, and often the other parts of the body act as well as, for example, the feet may walk.

Although this is only a poor comparison, it gives some idea of how the whole universe is governed. The Word of God has but to give a gesture of command and everything falls into place; each creature performs its own proper function, and all together constitute one single harmonious order.

Against the Pagans 42–43; PG 25, 83–87

Week of 1 Epiphany ✠ Saturday

A reading from the First Letter to the Corinthians by Clement, Bishop of Rome [c. 100]

God's blessing must be our objective, and the way to win it our study. Search the records of ancient times. Why was our father Abraham blessed? Was it not because his upright and straightforward conduct was inspired by faith? As for Isaac's faith, it was so strong that, assured of the outcome, he willingly allowed himself to be offered in sacrifice. Jacob had the humility to leave his native land on account of his brother, and go and serve Laban. He was given the twelve tribes of Israel.

Honest reflection upon each of these examples will make us realize the magnitude of God's gifts. All the priests and levites who served the altar of God were descended from Jacob. The humanity of the Lord Jesus derived from him. Through the tribe of Judah, kings, princes and rulers sprang from him. Nor are his other tribes without their honor, for God promised Abraham: "Your descendants shall be as the stars of heaven."

It is obvious, therefore, that none of these owed their honor and exaltation to themselves, or to their own labors, or to their deeds of virtue. No; they owed everything to God's will. So likewise with us, who by his will are called in Christ Jesus. We are not justified by our wisdom, intelligence, piety, or by any action of ours, however holy, but by faith, the one means by which God has justified us from the beginning. To him be glory for ever and ever.

What must we do then? Give up good works? Stop practicing Christian love? God forbid! We must be ready and eager for every opportunity to do good, and put our whole heart into it. Even the Creator and Lord of the universe rejoices in his works. By his supreme power he set the heavens in their place; by his infinite wisdom he gave them their order. He separated the land from the waters surrounding it and made his own will its firm foundation. By his command he brought to life the beasts that roam the earth. He created the sea and all its living creatures, and then by his power set bounds to it. Finally, with his own holy and undefiled hands, he formed humankind, the highest and most intelligent of his creatures, the copy of his own image. "Let us make humans," God said, "in our image and likeness. And God made human beings, male and female he made them." Then, when he had finished making all his creatures, God gave them his approval and blessing: "Increase and multiply," he charged them.

We must recognize, therefore, that all the upright have been graced by good works, and that even the Lord himself took delight in the glory his works gave him. This should inspire us with a resolute determination to do his will and make us put our whole strength into the work of living a Christian life.

First Letter to the Corinthians 31–33: Funk 1, 99–103

Week of 2 Epiphany ✠ Sunday

A reading from the treatise Against Heresies by Irenaeus, Bishop of Lyons [c. 202]

The oblation of the Church, which the Lord taught was to be offered throughout the whole world, has been regarded by God as a pure sacrifice, and is acceptable to him. Not that he needs sacrifice from us, but the one who makes the offering receives glory in that offering, provided that the gift is accepted. Through a gift both honor and love are shown to a king.

The Lord wants us to make our offering in all sincerity and freedom from sin. He declared this when he said: "When, therefore, you offer your gift at the altar and remember that your brother [or sister] holds something against you, leave your gift before the altar, and first go and be reconciled with your brother [or sister]; and then come back and offer your gift."

We must offer God the firstfruits of his creation, as Moses said: "You will not come empty-handed into the presence of the Lord your God." In showing gratitude to God for his gifts we are to be accounted pleasing to God, and so receive the honor that comes from God.

It is not oblations as such that have met with disapproval. There were oblations of old; there are oblations now. There were sacrifices among the people of Israel; there are sacrifices in the Church. Only the kind of oblation has been changed: now it is offered by free people, not by slaves. There is one and the same Lord, but the character of an oblation made by slaves is distinctive, so too that of an oblation made by the free: their oblations bear the mark of freedom.

With God there is nothing without purpose, nothing without its meaning and reason. Thus the people of Israel used to dedicate tithes of their possessions. But those who have been given freedom devote what they possess to the Lord's use. They give it all to the Lord, not simply what is of lesser value, cheerfully and freely because they hope for greater things, like the poor widow who put into God's treasury her whole livelihood.

We must make oblation to God, and in all things be found pleasing to God the Creator, in sound teaching, in sincere faith, in firm hope, in ardent love, as we offer the firstfruits of the creatures that are his. The Church alone offers this pure oblation to the Creator when it makes its offering to him from his creation, with thanksgiving.

We offer him what is his, and so we proclaim communion and unity and profess our belief in the resurrection of flesh and spirit. Just as bread from the earth, when it receives the invocation of God, is no longer common bread but the eucharist, made up of two elements, one earthly and one heavenly, so also our bodies, in receiving the eucharist, are no longer corruptible, for they have the hope of resurrection.

Against Heresies 4, 18, 1–2, 4, 5: SC 100, 596–598, 606, 610–612

Week of 2 Epiphany ✠ Monday

A reading from a sermon of Bede, the Venerable, Priest, and Monk of Jarrow [735]

The Holy Spirit will give to those who love God the perfect peace of eternity. But even now the Spirit gives them great peace when kindling in their hearts the celestial fire of love. In fact, the Apostle says: "This hope will not leave us disappointed, because the love of God has been poured out in our hearts through the Holy Spirit who has been given to us."

The true, indeed, the only peace for souls in this world consists in being filled with divine love and animated with heavenly hope to the point of setting no store on the successes and failures of this world, of stripping ourselves wholly of earthly desires, of renouncing all worldly covetousness and rejoicing in injuries and persecutions suffered for Christ's sake, so that we can say with the Apostle: "We boast of our hope for the glory of God. But not only that—we even boast of our afflictions!" The person who expects to find peace in riches and in the enjoyment of this world's goods is only self-deceived. The frequent troubles of life here below and the fact that this world will end should convince such people that they are building their foundations on sand.

On the other hand, all those who, touched by the breath of the Holy Spirit, have taken upon themselves the excellent yoke of God's love and who, following Christ's example, have learned to be gentle and lowly in heart—these do already rejoice in a peace which even now is the image of eternal rest. In the depths of their souls they are separated from the commotion of humanity, they have the joy of remembering the presence of their Creator wherever they may be, and they thirst for the attainment of perfect contemplation, saying with St. John the Apostle: "We know that when it comes to light we shall be like him, for we shall see him as he is."

If we want to be rewarded with this vision, we shall need to bear the gospel in mind unceasingly and to show ourselves heedless of all worldly attractions; then we shall be found worthy to receive the grace of the Holy Spirit which the world cannot receive. Let us love Christ and persevere in observing his commandments which we have begun to follow.

The more we love him, the more we shall merit to be loved by his Father, and then he himself will grant us the grace of his great love in eternity. In this life he gives us faith and hope; in the life to come we shall see him face to face and he will show himself to us in the glory which he had with his Father before the world was made.

Homily 12 for the Vigil of Pentecost: PL 94, 196–197

Week of 2 Epiphany ✠ Tuesday

A reading from the treatise On Noah and the Ark by Ambrose, Bishop of Milan [397]

Let us now attentively consider what it was the Lord God meant when, communing with himself, he said: "Never again will I curse the earth because of the deeds of humankind, since their hearts are resolutely bent upon evil from their youth." Never again, therefore, as long as the earth endures, shall God strike all flesh, as he had done. Although he had punished the whole human race, he nevertheless knew that, while punishment for the violation of law may engender fear and bring them to a knowledge of the truth, it will not change their nature. This can be corrected in some but cannot be changed in all.

The Lord then punished in order that we might fear him, but he refrained from punishing in order that we might be saved. He punished on that one occasion that it might serve as an example to move us to fear him. He spared humankind that same fate forever thereafter, lest the bitter poison of sin exercise a universal and never-ending tyranny of death and destruction. One who would wish to punish people too frequently for their sins would only show that it is vengeance rather than a desire to correct that is the motive.

It was for these reasons, therefore, that God said: "Never again will I curse the earth because of the deeds of humankind." By these words God wished to declare his love for the universality of humanity, without at the same time contributing to the negligence of individuals by giving them a false sense of security. For this reason God still continues to visit his punishments upon some, while sparing others.

God's words also show that he is inclined to lessen rather than increase the afflictions that weigh upon us, knowing, as he does, that we cannot be made to desist completely from committing sin. To attempt to remove evil from our hearts is as futile as the proverbial attempt to draw up water in a thinly woven net. "Never again," God says, "will I curse the earth because of the sins of humankind, since their hearts are resolutely bent upon sin from their youth."

Note how eagerly we sin, according to the testimony of God himself. For he says that it is our hearts that are resolutely bent upon evil. These words seem to state that this proneness of our hearts to sin is something that we positively desire, an attraction for evil that proceeds from the noblest of our faculties, our free will, and, what is even worse, that we seek to satisfy with no lack of eagerness or restraint.

The resolve and desire to commit sin begin at the period of youth so that, whereas a child sins because of weakness, a youthful person does so out of malice, deliberately desiring to commit sins and even proudly boasting of those crimes. Many of them look upon innocence as cowardice, while they regard wrong-doing as something worthy of praise. Shamelessly priding themselves on their sins of impurity, self-indulgence, and adultery, they become more and more habituated to these excesses, so that their guilt becomes ever greater as they pass from one period of their lives to the next.

However justly, therefore, he might do so, God nevertheless declares that the entire human race shall not be exterminated. "Never again," he says, "will I strike all flesh," though punishment will still be meted out but restricted to parts only of the human race.

Treatise on Noah and the Ark, chs. 22–23, nos. 80–82: CSEL 32, 1, 470–472

Week of 2 Epiphany ✠ Wednesday

A reading from a commentary on the psalms by Hilary,
Bishop of Poitiers [367]

"Behold, how good and pleasant it is for brothers [and sisters] to dwell in unity!" It is good and pleasant for brothers [and sisters] to dwell in unity, because when they do so their association creates the assembly of the Church. The term "brothers" [and "sisters"] describes the bond of affection arising from their singleness of purpose.

We read that when the apostles first preached, the chief instruction they gave lay in this saying: "The hearts and minds of all believers were one." So it is fitting for the people of God to be brothers [and sisters] under one Father, to be united under one Spirit, to live in harmony under one roof, to be limbs of one body.

It is pleasant and good for believers to dwell in unity. The prophet suggested a comparison for this good and pleasant activity when he said: "It is like the ointment on the head which ran down over the beard of Aaron, down upon the collar of his garment." Aaron's oil was made of the perfumes used to anoint a priest. It was God's decision that his priest should have this consecration first, and that our Lord too should be anointed, but not visibly, "by those who are joined with him." Aaron's anointing did not belong to this world; it was not done with the horn used for kings, but "with the oil of gladness." So afterward Aaron was called the anointed one as the Law prescribed.

When this oil is poured out upon those of unclean heart, it snuffs out their lives, but when it is received as an anointing of love, it exudes the sweet odor of harmony with God. As Paul says, "we are the goodly fragrance of Christ." So just as it was pleasing to God when Aaron was anointed priest with this oil, so it is good and pleasant for believers to dwell in unity.

Now the oil ran down from his head to his beard. A beard adorns a man of mature years. We must not be children before Christ except in the restricted scriptural sense of being children in wickedness but not in our way of thinking. Now Paul calls all who lack faith, children, because they are too weak to take solid food and still need milk. As he says: "I fed you with milk rather than the solid food for which you were not yet ready; and you are still not ready."

Commentary on Psalm 132: PLS 1, 244–245

Week of 2 Epiphany ✠ Thursday

A reading from the Letter to the Ephesians by Ignatius, Bishop of Antioch, and Martyr [c. 115]

It is right for you to give glory in every way to Jesus Christ who has given glory to you; you must be made holy in all things by being united in perfect obedience, in submission to the bishop and the presbyters.

I am not giving you orders as if I were a person of importance. Even if I am a prisoner for the name of Christ, I am not yet made perfect in Jesus Christ. I am now beginning to be a disciple and I am speaking to you as my fellow-disciples. It is you who should be strengthening me by your faith, your encouragement, your patience, your serenity. But since love will not allow me to be silent about you, I am taking the opportunity to urge you to be united in conformity with the mind of God. For Jesus Christ, our life, without whom we cannot live, is the mind of the Father, just as the bishops, appointed over the whole earth, are in conformity with the mind of Jesus Christ.

It is fitting, therefore, that you should be in agreement with the mind of the bishop as in fact you are. Your excellent presbyters, who are a credit to God, are as suited to the bishop as strings to a harp. So in your harmony of mind and heart the song you sing is Jesus Christ. Every one of you should form a choir, so that, in harmony of sound through harmony of hearts, and in unity taking the note from God, you may sing with one voice through Jesus Christ to the Father. If you do this, he will listen to you and see from your good works that you are members of his Son. It is then an advantage to you to live in perfect unity, so that at all times you may share in God.

If in a short space of time I have become so close a friend of your bishop—in a friendship not based on nature but on spiritual grounds—how much more blessed do I judge you to be, for you are as united with him as the Church is to Jesus Christ, and Jesus Christ to the Father, so that all things are in harmony through unity.

To the Ephesians 2, 2-5, 2: Funk 1, 175-177

Week of 2 Epiphany ✠ Friday

A reading from a homily of John Chrysostom, Bishop of Constantinople [407]

This one just person can teach all of us to trust in an eternal reward (knowing as we do the generosity of our merciful Lord), to face up readily to the tests of virtue, and to undertake, in the glad hope of recompense, all the seeming hardships and difficult tasks of life. Abraham—I urge you to note this carefully—made good use of his native talent and the knowledge that is inborn in our nature. Consequently, though he had no exterior teacher and was raised by pagan parents, God sought him out and appeared to him.

In his early years he did not adopt his parents' erroneous ways but lived piously before God and thus merited the divine visitation while he was still in Mesopotamia. St. Stephen stresses this point when he says: "The God of glory appeared to our father Abraham while he was still in Mesopotamia and before he settled in Haran."

Did you notice how the vision caused him to move to a new place? It is likely that even as he was deeply pious toward God he also revered his parents and that his love won his father to him and caused the latter, out of love for his son in return, to leave his native land and dwell in a foreign place.

When they reached Haran, they pitched their tents there. After Terah, Abraham's father, had died, God again commanded Abraham to depart: "Go forth from the land of your kinsfolk and from your father's house to a land that I will show you." Since they had come to Haran with all their kinsfolk and household, God could say in his command to Abraham: "from your land" and "from your kinsfolk," thus indicating that he should journey alone, without his brother Nahor, or anyone else. "From your land," because they had lived there quite some time and regarded the country as their native soil.

Though still mourning his parents and though the difficulties of the journey were great, Abraham was quick to obey the Lord, despite the fact that he did not know where the journey would end. "Go forth," the Lord said, not to this or that country but "to a land that I will show you." Yet, though the order was indefinite, Abraham inquired no further but carried it out.

Abraham thus showed his religious spirit in every way, even to the point of undertaking this journey. Consequently, once he had reached Palestine and entered Canaan, God appeared to him, intending to deepen Abraham's enthusiasm and to extend aid. God said to him: "To your descendants I will give this land."

God also straight-way promised Abraham what he most intensely desired, heirs of his own, and thus rewarded him for the great toils he had endured. Inasmuch as nature had deprived him of children and his advanced years forbade him to expect them now, God's promise stirred his eager servant to new heights and gave him the eagerness of youth as he faced new struggles.

Homily 36 on Genesis 1–2: PG 53, 333–334

Week of 2 Epiphany ✠ Saturday

A reading from the Letter to the Ephesians by Ignatius, Bishop of Antioch, and Martyr [c. 115]

I do not issue orders to you, as if I were some great person. For, though I am bound for the name [of Christ], I am not yet perfect in Jesus Christ. Indeed, I am now being initiated into discipleship, and I address you as my fellow disciples. Yes, I ought to be anointed by you with faith, encouragement, patience, and steadfastness. But inasmuch as love does not permit me to be silent when you are concerned, I have it taken upon myself first to exhort you to live in harmony with the mind of God. Surely, Jesus Christ, our inseparable life, for his part is the mind of the Father, just as the bishops, scattered throughout the world, represent for their part the mind of Jesus Christ.

Hence, it is proper for you to live in accordance with the mind of the bishop—which you are doing. For your justly renowned presbytery, worthy of God, harmonizes with the bishop as completely as the strings with a harp. This is why in your concord and harmonious love Jesus Christ is sung. But you, the rank and file, should also form a choir, so that, joining the symphony by your concord and taking up the song of God in unison, you may with one voice sing to the Father through Jesus Christ. Thus he will both hear you and perceive by your works that you are indeed the members of his Son. It is profitable, therefore, for you to live in blameless unity, that you may at all times enjoy communion with God.

Some there are, you know, accustomed to carrying about the name [of Jesus Christ] in wicked guile, while they practice what is at variance with it and an insult to God. You must flee from them as you would from wild beasts. For they are ravening dogs who bite secretly, and you must be on guard against them for they are hard to cure. There is only one Physician who is possessed both of flesh and spirit, born and unborn, God become human, true life in death; sprung both from Mary and from God, first subject to suffering and then incapable of it—Jesus Christ our Lord.

And pray without ceasing for others. For they offer ground for hoping that they may be converted and attain to God. See, then, that they may be instructed by your works, if in no other way. Be meek in response to their wrath, humble in opposition to their boasting, counter their blasphemies with your prayers, remain steadfast in contrast to their error, and manifest your meekness in the face of their cruelty.

While we take care not to imitate their conduct, let us be found their brothers and sisters in all true kindness. Let us strive to follow the Lord's example and see who can suffer greater wrong, who more deprivation, who more contempt. Thus no weed of the devil may be found in you; but you may remain in perfect chastity and sobriety through Jesus Christ, in body and soul.

Apart from him, let nothing fascinate you. In union with him I bear about these bonds, these spiritual jewels, of mine. May I be privileged through your prayers—in which I hope always to have a share—to wear them when I rise from the dead! Thus I may be found in the lot of the

Christians of Ephesus, who have ever been of the same mind with the apostles through the power of Jesus Christ.

To the Ephesians 3, 4, 7, 10–11: Funk 1, 217–223

Week of 3 Epiphany ✠ Sunday

A reading from a homily of John Chrysostom, Bishop of Constantinople [407]

"You are the salt of the earth." It is not for your own sake, he says, but for the world's sake that the word is entrusted to you. I am not sending you into two cities only or ten or twenty, not to a single nation, as I sent the prophets of old, but across land and sea, to the whole world. And that world is in a miserable state. For when he says: "You are the salt of the earth," he is indicating that all humanity had lost its savor and had been corrupted by sin. Therefore, he requires of these people those virtues which are especially useful and even necessary if they are to bear the burdens of the human race. For those who are kindly, modest, merciful and just will not keep their good works to themselves but will see to it that these admirable fountains send out their streams for the good of others. Again, those who are clean of heart, peacemakers and ardent for truth, will order their lives so as to contribute to the common good.

Do not think, he says, that you are destined for easy struggles or unimportant tasks. "You are the salt of the earth." What do these words imply? Did the disciples restore what had already turned rotten? Not at all. Salt cannot help what is already corrupted. That is not what they did. But what had first been renewed and freed from corruption and then turned over to them, they salted and preserved in the newness the Lord had bestowed. It took the power of Christ to free humanity from the corruption caused by sin; it was the task of the apostles through strenuous labor to keep that corruption from returning.

Have you noticed how, bit by bit, Christ shows them to be superior to the prophets? He says they are to be teachers not simply for Palestine but for the whole world. Do not be surprised, then, he says, that I address you apart from the others and involve you in such a dangerous enterprise. Consider the numerous and extensive cities, peoples and nations I will be sending you to govern. For this reason I would have you make others prudent, as well as being prudent yourselves. For unless you can do that, you will not be able to sustain even yourselves.

If others lose their savor, then your ministry will help them regain it.

But if you yourselves suffer that loss, you will drag others down with you. Therefore, the greater the undertakings put into your hands, the more zealous you must be. For this reason he says: "But if the salt becomes tasteless, how can its flavor be restored? It is good for nothing now, but to be thrown out and trampled under foot."

When they hear the words: "When they curse you and persecute you and accuse you of every evil," they may be afraid to come forward. Therefore he says: "Unless you are prepared for that sort of thing, it is in vain that I have chosen you. Curses shall necessarily be your lot but they shall not harm you and will simply be a testimony to your constancy. If through fear, however, you fail to show the forcefulness your mission demands, your lot will be much worse, for all will speak evil of you and despise you. That is what being trampled under foot means."

Then he passes on to a more exalted comparison: "You are the light of the world." Once again, "of the world": not of one nation or twenty cities, but of the whole world. The light he means is an intelligible light, far superior to the rays of the sun we see, just as the salt is a spiritual salt. First salt, then light, so that you may learn how profitable sharp words may be and how useful serious doctrine. Such teaching holds in check and prevents dissipation; it leads to virtue and sharpens the mind's eye. "A city set on a hill cannot be hidden; nor do you light a lamp and put it under a basket." Here again he is urging them to a careful manner of life and teaching them to be watchful, for they live under the eyes of all and have the whole world for the arena of their struggles.

Homily 15 on Matthew 6, 7: PG 57, 231–232

Week of 3 Epiphany ✠ Monday

A reading from a commentary on Galatians by Augustine, Bishop of Hippo [430]

Paul writes to the Galatians to make them understand that by God's grace they are no longer under the law. When the Gospel was preached to them, there were some among them of Jewish origin known as circumcisers—though they called themselves Christians—who did not grasp the gift they had received. They still wanted to be under the burden of the law. Now God had imposed that burden on those who were slaves to sin and not on servants of justice. That is to say, God had given a just law to the unjust in order to show them their sin, not to take it away. For sin is taken away only by the gift of faith that works through love. The Galatians had already received this gift, but the circumcisers claimed that the Gospel would not save them unless they underwent circumcision and were willing to observe also the other traditional Jewish rites.

The Galatians, therefore, began to question Paul's preaching of the Gospel because he did not require Gentiles to follow Jewish observances as other apostles had done. Even Peter had yielded to the scandalized protests of the circumcisers. He pretended to believe that the Gospel would not save the Gentiles unless they fulfilled the burden of the law. But Paul recalled him from such dissimulation, as is shown in this very same letter. A similar issue arises in Paul's letter to the Romans, but with an evident difference. Through his letter to them Paul was able to resolve the strife and controversy that had developed between the Jewish and Gentile converts.

In the present letter Paul is writing to persons who were profoundly influenced and disturbed by the circumcisers. The Galatians had begun to believe them and to think that Paul had not preached rightly, since he had not ordered them to be circumcised. And so the Apostle begins by saying: "I am amazed that you are so quickly deserting him who called you to the glory of Christ, and turning to another gospel."

After this there comes a brief introduction to the point at issue. But remember in the very opening of the letter Paul had said that he was an apostle "sent neither by human commission nor from human authorities," a statement that does not appear in any other letter of his. He is making it quite clear that the circumcisers, for their part, are not from God but from human beings, and that his authority in preaching the Gospel must be considered equal to that of the other apostles. For he was called to be an apostle "neither by human commission nor from human authorities," but through God the Father and his Son, Jesus Christ.

Explanation of Paul's Letter to the Galatians, preface: PL 35, 2105–2107

Week of 3 Epiphany ✠ Tuesday

A reading from the treatise On Abraham by Ambrose, Bishop of Milan [397]

Since Abraham did not look for a reward from people, he received it from God, as we read: "After these events, this word of the Lord came to Abraham in a vision: 'Fear not, Abraham! I am your shield; I will make your reward very great.'"

God is not slow to reward; he is quick to promise and magnanimous in giving, lest any delay cause weak souls to experience regret at having renounced present things. He compensates, so to speak, liberally and with interest, so that he might give more abundantly to those who have not fallen captive to the world's goods that have been offered them.

Therefore, let us consider what reward Abraham asks of the Lord. It is not riches that he requests, like a miser; it is not longevity, as if he feared death; and it is not power. It is rather a fitting recompense for his labor. "What will you give me?" he asks. "See, you have given me no offspring." And he adds: "Because you have given me no offspring, one of my servants will be my heir."

If the manner in which Abraham expresses himself is inadequate for the correction of morals, pay attention to the oracle of the Lord condemning the heritage to which Abraham makes allusion: "It is not a slave," it is written, "who will be your heir, but the one who will issue from your loins will be your heir." Who is this other heir of whom he speaks? True, Hagar will bear a son, Ishmael, but he is not the one in question; it is Isaac whom he has in mind. Thus he adds: "Who will issue from your loins." For the one who truly issues from Abraham is the one who was conceived in a legitimate marriage.

Furthermore, in Isaac, the legitimate heir, we can see the true legitimate heir who is the Lord Jesus. In the beginning of the gospel according to St. Matthew we hear him called the "son of Abraham." He gave himself as his legitimate heir, making illustrious the succession of its author, and through whom Abraham could regard heaven and have knowledge of a splendid posterity no less radiant than the brightness of the stars. For, just as one star differs from another in brightness, says the Apostle, "so is it with the resurrection of the dead."

The reason for this is to signify that by enabling them to share in his resurrection the Lord has made participants of the celestial kingdom out of those whom death was accustomed to keep buried underground.

But how did the race of Abraham expand if not through the heritage of faith, thanks to which we are established in heaven, rendered similar to angels, and equal to the stars? Therefore, he said: "Just so shall your descendants be. Abraham put his faith in God," adds the text. What did he believe? That Christ, taking a body, would become his heir. In order to make us realize that it is really this which Abraham believed, the Lord tells us: "Abraham saw my day and was glad." Thus "it was credited to him as an act of righteousness" in the sense that he did not seek to reason but believed without hesitation.

It is good that faith comes before reason so that we do not appear to demand our proofs from human beings, but rather from the Lord our God. How unfitting it is for us to believe human testimony concerning others and not to believe God's oracles concerning himself! Therefore, let us imitate Abraham so that we may be heirs of the land through the justice of faith, through which he was made an heir of the world.

Treatise on Abraham 1, ch. 3, nos. 18–21: CSEL 32, 1, 515–517

Week of 3 Epiphany ✠ Wednesday

A reading from the treatise On Abraham by Ambrose, Bishop of Milan [397]

Someone might say: "How can you propose Abraham as an example for us when he had a child by his servant?" or again: "How did it come about that one whose actions we so admire fell into this error?" Hence, to avoid giving the appearance of dodging this point in the manner of navigators—a point which many considered to be a highly slippery spot—we have decided to explain it. I am in no way absolving Abraham from having had a son by his servant—this shows that he possessed neither another nature nor another essence but shared in the universal and human fraility.

Some will register surprise that even while he spoke to the Lord Abraham had already enjoyed commerce with his servant, as it is written: "Sarah said to Abraham: 'The Lord has kept me from bearing children. Have intercourse, then, with my maid; perhaps I shall have sons through her.'" And so it was done.

However, let us consider first of all that Abraham lived before the law of Moses and before the gospel, and adultery did not yet appear to be forbidden. The penalty for this crime dates from the time of the law which repressed it. Before the law, it was not the object of any sanction; it only became such once the law was promulgated. Hence, Abraham did not commit any fault against the law; rather he preceded the law.

In paradise, God praised marriage but did not condemn adultery. For he does not will the death of the sinner; he promises what carries a reward but does not speak of what carries a punishment. He loves more to inspire through kindness than to frighten through cruelty. If while still a pagan, you sinned, you had an excuse; but once you have entered the Church, you have heard the law say to you: "You shall not commit adultery." Thus, you no longer have any excuse for your sin.

Secondly, it was neither out of obedience to the desire for some vague pleasure nor out of capitulation to the charms of a wanton beauty that Abraham preferred the company of a servant to the conjugal bed. Rather, it was out of the desire to seek a posterity and to ensure the propagation of his race—for the human race was still very sparse after the flood. It was thus an act of religion, so that each might render to nature its due. Similarly, it was to ensure that the human race would not become extinct that the daughters of the saintly Lot sought a posterity a bit later, and they excused their private fault by claiming to be rendering a public service.

Treatise on Abraham 1, ch. 4, nos. 22–24: CSEL 32, 1, 517–519

Week of 3 Epiphany ✠ Thursday

A reading from a homily of Origen, Priest and Theologian [c. 254]

"Abraham took wood for the burnt offering and placed it upon Isaac his son, and he took fire and a sword in his hands, and together they went off." Isaac himself carries the wood for his own holocaust: this is a figure of Christ. For he bore the burden of the cross, and yet to carry the wood for the holocaust is really the duty of the priest. He is then both victim and priest. This is the meaning of the expression: "together they went off." For when Abraham, who was to perform the sacrifice, carried the fire and the knife, Isaac did not walk behind him, but with him. In this way he showed that he exercised the priesthood equally with Abraham.

What happens after this? Isaac said to Abraham his father: "Father." This plea from the son was at that instant the voice of temptation. For do you not think the voice of the child who was about to be sacrificed struck a responsive chord in the heart of the father? Although Abraham did not waver because of his faith, he responded with a voice full of affection and asked: "What is it, my son?" Isaac answered him: "Here are the fire and the wood, but where is the sheep for the holocaust?" And Abraham replied: "God will provide for himself a sheep for the holocaust, my son."

The careful yet loving response of Abraham moves me greatly. I do not know what he saw in spirit, because he did not speak of the present but of the future: "God will provide for himself a sheep." His reply concerns the future, yet his son inquires about the present. Indeed, the Lord himself provided a sheep for himself in Christ.

Abraham extended his hand to take the sword and slay his son, and the angel of the Lord called to him from heaven and said: "Abraham, Abraham." And he responded: "Here I am." And the angel said: "Do not put your hand upon the boy or do anything to him, for now I know that you fear God." Compare these words to those of the Apostle when he speaks of God: "He did not spare his own Son but gave him up for us all." God emulates humanity with magnificent generosity. Abraham offered to God his mortal son who did not die, and God gave up his immortal Son who died for all of us.

"And Abraham, looking about him, saw a ram caught by the horns in a bush." We said before that Isaac is a type of Christ. Yet this also seems true of the ram. To understand how both are figures of Christ—Isaac who was not slain and the ram who was—is well worth our inquiry.

Christ is the Word of God, but "the Word became flesh." Christ therefore suffered and died, but in the flesh. In this respect, the ram is the type, just as John said: "Behold the lamb of God, behold him who takes away the sins of the world." The Word, however, remained incorruptible. This is Christ according to the spirit, and Isaac is the type. Therefore, Christ himself is both victim and priest according to the spirit. For he offers the victim to the Father according to the flesh, and he is himself offered on the altar of the cross.

Homily 8 on Genesis 6, 8, 9: PG 12, 206–209

Week of 3 Epiphany ✠ Friday

A reading from a letter by Ambrose, Bishop of Milan [397]

The person who puts to death by the Spirit the deeds of our sinful nature will live, says the Apostle. This is not surprising since one who has the Spirit of God becomes a child of God. So true is it that such a one is a child of God that this person receives not a spirit that enslaves but the Spirit that makes us heirs. So much so that the Holy Spirit bears witness to our spirit that we are children of God. This is the witness of the Holy Spirit who cries out in our hearts: "Abba, Father," as we read in the letter to the Galatians.

There is also that other great testimony to the fact that we are children of God: "we are heirs of God, co-heirs with Christ." A co-heir of Christ is one who is glorified along with Christ. The one who is glorified along with him is one who, by suffering for him, suffers along with him.

To encourage us in suffering, Paul adds that all our sufferings are small in comparison with the wonderful reward that will be revealed in us; our labors do not deserve the blessings that are to come. We shall be restored to the likeness of God, and counted worthy of seeing him face to face.

Paul enhances the greatness of the revelation that is to come by adding that creation also looks forward to this revealing of the children of God. Creation, he says, is at present condemned to frustration, not of its own choice, but it lives in hope. Its hope is in Christ, as it awaits the grace of his ministry; or it hopes that it will share in the glorious freedom of the children of God and be freed from its bondage to corruption, so that there will be one freedom, shared by creation and by the children of God when their glory will be revealed.

At present, however, while this revealing is delayed, all creation groans as it looks forward to the glory of adoption and redemption; it is already in labor with that spirit of salvation, and is anxious to be freed from its subjection to frustration.

The meaning is clear: those who have the firstfruits of the Spirit are groaning in expectation of the adoption of children. This adoption is that of the whole body of creation, when it will be as it were a child of God and see the divine, eternal goodness face to face. The adoption is present in the Church of the Lord when the Spirit cries out: "Abba, Father," as you read in the letter to the Galatians. But it will be perfect when all who are worthy of seeing the face of God rise in incorruption, in honor and in glory. Then our humanity will know that it has been truly redeemed. So Paul glories in saying: "We are saved by hope." Hope saves, just as faith does, for of faith it is said: "Your faith has saved you."

Letter 35, 4–6, 13: PL 16, 1078–1079, 1081

Week of 3 Epiphany ✠ Saturday

A reading from the Revelations of Divine Love by Dame Julian of Norwich [c. 1417]

And he showed me more, a little thing, the size of a hazelnut, on the palm of my hand, round like a ball. I looked at it thoughtfully and wondered: "What is this?" And the answer came: "It is all that is made." I marvelled that it continued to exist and did not suddenly disintegrate; it was so small. And again my mind supplied the answer: "It exists, both now and for ever, because God loves it." In short, everything owes its existence to the love of God.

This is his meaning, as if to say: "See, I have done all this long before your prayers; and now you exist, and pray to me." He means that we ought to know that the greatest deeds are already done, as Holy Church teaches.

From the time these things were first revealed I had often wanted to know what was our Lord's meaning. It was more than fifteen years after that I was answered in my spirit's understanding. "You would know our Lord's meaning in this thing? Know it well. Love was his meaning."

So it was that I learned that love was our Lord's meaning. And I saw for certain, both here and elsewhere, that before ever he made us, God loved us.

Revelations, chapters 5, 42, 86: Colledge and Walsh 2, 299–300, 471, 732–733

Week of 4 Epiphany ✠ Sunday

A reading from a sermon of Gregory of Nazianzus, Bishop of Constantinople [389]

We must open our hearts to all the poor and to all sufferers. But those who have a particular right to our compassion are the sick who are affected by leprosy and whose flesh and bones are being eaten away.

Under our eyes there is spread out a horrible and pitiful spectacle, and one that is incredible for those who happen not to know it: people who are living corpses, mutilated in several parts of their bodies, so that some are now unrecognizable. To make themselves known they mention the name of their father, of their mother, of their brother, the place where they lived formerly. They tell us: "I am the child of that man; that one is my mother; this is my name; once upon a time you were my friend and intimate with me."

Such is their language, for they can no longer make themselves recognizable by their features, by what was formerly characteristic of their face. Gnawed by the disease, they have lost their fortune, their parents, even their bodies. They are the only ones who have both pity and aversion toward themselves. They do not know whether they should weep over what their body has lost or over what it still has, over the disease that has devoured them or over what will become the prey of the disease in its future developments. Part of them has departed before their burial; the other part will not have anyone to give them a burial.

The very best and most charitable people are wholly indifferent in their regard. It is only in connection with them that we forget that we are flesh and that we are surrounded by a wretched body. So far are we from taking care of those who belong to our race, that running away from them seems to give security to our own bodies. Several of us come near a corpse from time to time, even when it emits a bad smell; many bear the smell of the corpse of an animal, or are willing to be stuck in the mud. But we run away from those people with all our powers. What insensibility! And we are almost indignant because we breathe the same air!

Who is more generous than a father? Who is more compassionate than a mother? Well, even nature shuts the door to the lepers. The father, while bemoaning the condition of the child he had begotten, whom he had raised, in whom he had thought to have what was like an eye for his whole life, and for whom he had addressed many prayers to God, now has expelled the child from his house both freely and against his wish. The mother recalls the sufferings she has undergone for her child and with a broken heart weeps over the one who though still alive is virtually dead. The poor woman would like to embrace her child, but she dreads the flesh of that child as she dreads an enemy.

The lepers are forbidden to go into the cities, into houses, into public places, on our roads, to our feasts, to our banquets, and, what a calamity! even in the water.

What then shall we do, we who have received a share in a great name, who have received a new name, the name which comes to us from Christ, we who are disciples of Christ, gentle and kind, of Christ who has borne our ills? What will our thoughts and our attitude be toward those sick human beings?

Oration 14, On the Love of the Poor, 6, 10–12, 15: PG 35, 864, 869–872, 876

Week of 4 Epiphany ✠ Monday

A reading from the Letter to the Smyrnaeans by Ignatius, Bishop of Antioch, and Martyr [c. 115]

From Ignatius, known as Theophorus, to the church of God the Father and of Jesus Christ, his beloved, at Smyrna in Asia, wishing you all joy in an immaculate spirit and the Word of God. By his mercy you have won every gift and lack none, filled as you are with faith and love, beloved of God and fruitful in sanctity.

I celebrate the glory of Jesus Christ as God, because he is responsible for your wisdom, well aware as I am of the perfection of your unshakable faith. You are like people who have been nailed body and soul to the cross of Jesus Christ, confirmed in love by his blood.

In regard to the Lord, you firmly believe that he was "of the race of David according to the flesh," but God's son by the will and power of God; truly born of the Virgin and baptized by John, "that all justice might be fulfilled;" truly nailed to a cross in the flesh for our sake under Pontius Pilate and the Tetrarch Herod, and of his most blessed passion we are the fruit. And thus, by his resurrection he raised up a standard over his saints and faithful ones for all time (both Jews and Gentiles alike) in the one body of his Church. For he endured all this for us, for our salvation; and he really suffered, and just as truly rose from the dead.

As for myself, I am convinced that he was united with his body even after the resurrection. When he visited Peter and his companions, he said to them: "Take hold of me, touch me and see that I am not a spirit without a body." Immediately they touched him and believed, clutching at his body and his very spirit. And for this reason they despised death and conquered it. In addition, after his resurrection, the Lord ate and drank with them like a real human being, even though in spirit he was united with his Father.

And so I am giving you serious instruction on these things, dearly beloved, even though I am aware that you believe them to be so.

To the Smyrnaeans 1–4: Funk 1, 235–237

Week of 4 Epiphany ✠ Tuesday

A reading from a commentary on John by Theodore, Bishop of Mopsuestia [428]

Adam is the origin of our present state; but that of the life to come will be Christ, our Lord. For just as Adam was the first human to die, and all humanity became mortal because of him, so Christ is the first to arise from the dead, and he has given the seed of resurrection to all who come after him. We enter this visible life by bodily birth, and that is why we are all corruptible. However, in the life to come we shall be transformed by the power of the Spirit, and that is why we shall rise incorruptible.

Although this will only happen in the future life, Christ our Lord has been pleased to take us there even now in a symbolic way by giving us baptism and a new birth in himself. This spiritual birth is the present figure of the resurrection and of that regeneration which will be fully actualized in us when we leave this present life. That is why baptism is also called regeneration.

The Apostle has expressed this better than anyone else in telling us: "We who were baptized into Christ Jesus were baptized into his death. Through baptism into his death we were buried with him, so that, just as Christ was raised from the dead by the glory of the Father, we too might live a new life. If we have been united with him through likeness to his death, so shall we be through a like resurrection."

Thus, St. Paul shows us plainly that birth in baptism is the figure of resurrection after death. This resurrection is wrought in us through the power of the Spirit, according to the saying: "What is sown in the earth is subject to decay, what rises is incorruptible. What is sown is ignoble, what rises is glorious. Weakness is sown, strength rises up. A natural body is put down and a spiritual body comes up."

In other words, just as here below our body, so long as the soul is present, rejoices in visible life, even so afterward it will receive eternal incorruptible life through the power of the Spirit.

It is the same with the birth that is given us at baptism and which is a figure of our resurrection: in this birth we receive grace through the same Spirit, but in measure and in the form of a token. We will receive it in plenitude when we do actually arise, and then incorruption will in fact be communicated to us.

That is why the Apostle, in speaking of the life to come, reassures his listeners with the words: "Not only that, but we ourselves, although we have the Spirit as firstfruits, groan inwardly while we await the redemption of our bodies." For if in this present life we have received the firstfruits of grace, we look forward to receiving it fully when the happiness of the resurrection will be given us.

Commentaries on John 2: CSCO 116, 55–56

Week of 4 Epiphany ✠ Wednesday

A reading from a treatise by Clement of Alexandria, Priest [c. 210]

Prayer, to speak somewhat boldly, is converse with God. Even if we address him in a whisper, without opening our lips or uttering a sound, still we cry to him in our heart. For God never ceases to listen to the inward converse of the heart. For this reason also we raise our head and lift the hands toward heaven, and stand on tiptoe as we join in the closing outburst of prayer, following the eager flight of the spirit into the intelligible world. And while we thus endeavor to detach the body from the earth by lifting it upwards along with the uttered words, we spurn the fetters of the flesh and constrain the soul, winged with desire of better things, to ascend into the holy place.

And since the east symbolizes the day of birth, and it is from thence that the light spreads after it has first "shone forth out of darkness," indeed, and from thence that the day of the knowledge of the truth dawned like the sun upon those who were lying in ignorance, therefore our prayers are directed towards the rise of dawn. It was for this reason that the most ancient temples looked toward the west in order that they who stood facing the images might be taught to turn eastwards. "Let my prayer ascend up as incense before thee, the lifting up of my hands be an evening sacrifice" is the language of the Psalms.

Stromata 7, 7, 39–40, 43: PG 9, 456, 461, 464

Week of 4 Epiphany ✠ Thursday

A reading from a sermon of Leo the Great, Bishop of Rome [461]

Our Lord Jesus Christ, born truly human without ever ceasing to be true God, began in his person a new creation and by the manner of his birth gave humanity a spiritual origin. What mind can grasp this mystery, what tongue can fittingly recount this gift of love? Guilt becomes innocence, old becomes new, strangers are adopted and outsiders are made heirs. Rouse yourself, and recognize the dignity of your nature. Remember that you were made in God's image; though corrupted in Adam, that image has been restored in Christ.

Use creatures as they should be used: the earth, the sea, the sky, the air, the springs and the rivers. Give praise and glory to their Creator for all that you find beautiful and wonderful in them. See with your bodily eyes the light that shines on earth, but embrace with your whole soul and all your affections "the true light which enlightens everyone who comes into this world." Speaking of this light the prophet said: "Draw close to him and let his light shine upon you and your face will not blush with shame." If we are indeed the temple of God and if the Spirit of God lives in us, then what every believer has within is greater than what the believer admires in the skies.

Our words and exhortations are not intended to make you disdain God's works or think there is anything contrary to your faith in creation, for the good God has himself made all things good. What we do ask is that you use reasonably and with moderation all the marvelous creatures which adorn this world; as the Apostle says: "The things that are seen are transient but the things that are unseen are eternal."

For we are born in the present only to be reborn in the future. Our attachment, therefore, should not be to the transitory; instead, we must be intent upon the eternal. Let us think of how divine grace has transformed our earthly natures so that we may contemplate more closely our heavenly hope. We hear the Apostle say: "You are dead and your life is hidden with Christ in God. But when Christ your life appears, then you will also appear in glory with him," who lives and reigns with the Father and the Holy Spirit for ever and ever.

Sermon for the Nativity 7, 2, 6; PL 54, 217–218, 220–221

A reading from The Educator by Clement of Alexandria, Priest [c. 210]

Our Lord once revealed very clearly to us what is to be understood by the name "little child." When a dispute arose among the apostles as to which of them was the greater, Jesus stood a little child in their midst and said: "Whoever would be lowly, becoming like this little child, is of greatest importance in the kingdom of heaven." Hence, he does not mean by "little child" one who has not yet reached the use of reason because of immaturity, as some have thought.

Similarly, when he says: "Unless you become like little children you shall not enter the kingdom of God," his words must not be mistaken to mean "without learning." We are not little ones in the sense that we roll on the ground or creep on the earth like serpents as we once did, crawling with our whole body about senseless lusts. On the contrary, we are little children in the sense that we stretch upward with our minds and are set loose from the world and our sins; we touch the earth only on the tip of our toes to appear to be in the world but we pursue holy wisdom, although this seems folly to those whose soul is excited by evil.

Hence, children are really those who know God alone as their Father, who are simple, little ones, without guile. To these, surely, who have made progress in the word he has proclaimed this utterance, bidding them to dismiss anxiety about the things of this world and exhorting them to devote themselves to the Father alone in imitation of children. That is why he goes on to tell them: "Enough, then, of worrying about tomorrow. Today has troubles enough of its own."

He thus enjoins them to lay aside the cares of this life and depend on the Father alone. Whoever fulfills this command is in reality a child and an heir both to God and to the world—to the world, in the sense of one who has lost his wits; to God, in the sense of one dearly beloved.

Indeed, if the detractors of spiritual childhood call us foolish, see that they are really speaking evil of the Lord. They imply that those who seek the protection of God are lacking in intelligence. But if they themselves understand the designation children in its true and mandatory sense of innocent ones, we glory in that name. Children are indeed the new spirits who were infantile in the old folly but have newly become wise and have sprung into being according to the new covenant. Only recently, in fact, has God become known by the coming of Christ: "No one knows the Father but the Son—and anyone to whom the Son wishes to reveal him."

Therefore, in contradistinction to the older people, the newer people are called young, for they have learned the new blessings. And we possess the exuberance of life's morning prime in this youth which knows no age; indeed, we are ever growing to maturity in intelligence, ever young, ever mild, ever new. For those who have become partakers of the Word must necessarily be new themselves. And whatever partakes of eternity assumes, by that very fact, the qualities of the incorruptible; hence, the name childhood designates for us a life-long springtime; since the truth which is in us as well as our habits saturated with the truth cannot be touched by old age. Surely, wisdom is ever-blooming, ever fixed on the same truth, and never changing.

The Educator 1, 5: PG 8, 267–270, 274

Week of 4 Epiphany ✠ Saturday

A reading from a commentary on the psalms by Augustine,
Bishop of Hippo [430]

God established a time for making his promises and a time for their fulfillment. The time for making his promises extended from the prophets to John the Baptist; and the time for fulfilling his promises, from John the Baptist to the end of the ages. God, who is faithful, has made himself our debtor, not by receiving anything but by promising such great things.

It was a very small thing to make promises, so he even wished to bind himself in writing, as it were giving us a contract of his promises; in order that when he should begin to carry out his promises we would be able to discern in the Scriptures the order for the fulfillment of the promises. Hence, the time of prophecy was the time for the foretelling of the promises, as we have mentioned more than once.

He promised eternal salvation, everlasting happiness with the angels, an unfading inheritance, endless glory, the joyful vision of his face, his holy dwelling in heaven, and after our resurrection from the dead the assurance of no further fear of death. This is (so to speak) his final promise toward which all our intentions should be focused; for when we have reached it, we shall require nothing more nor demand anything further.

Furthermore, our Lord also manifested in his promises and prophecies the way in which we would arrive at our final goal. He promised humans divinity, mortals immortality, sinners justification, the poor a rising to glory. Whatever he promised, he promised to those who were unworthy, so that it was not a case of a reward being promised to workers but of grace being given as a gift as its name indicates.

Hence, even those who live justly, insofar as humans can live justly, do so not through human merits but through divine help. No one lives justly unless that person has been justified, that is, been made just; and one is made just by him who can never be unjust. As a lamp is not lighted by itself, so the human soul does not give light to itself but calls out to God: "You indeed, O Lord, give light to my lamp."

But, my beloved, because God's promises seemed impossible to us—equality with the angels in exchange for mortality, corruption, poverty, weakness, dust and ashes—God not only made a written contract with us to win our belief, but also established a mediator of his good faith: not a prince or angel or archangel, but his only Son. He wanted, through his Son, to show and give us the way he would lead us to the goal he has promised.

It was not enough for God to make his Son our guide to the way; he made him the way itself, that you might travel with him as leader, and by him as the way.

Therefore, the only Son of God was to come to us, to become human, and in this nature to be born as one of us, to die, to rise again, to ascend to heaven, to sit at the right hand of the Father and to fulfill his promises among the nations; and after that to come again, to exact now what he had asked for before, to separate those deserving his anger from those deserving his mercy, to execute his threats against the wicked, and to reward the just as he had promised.

All this had to be prophesied, foretold, and promised as an event in the future so that it would not inspire fear by coming suddenly but would be believed in and expected.

Commentary on Psalm 109 (110), 1–3: CCL 40, 1601–1603

Week of 5 Epiphany ✠ Sunday

A reading from the treatise On Prayer *by Origen, Priest and Theologian [c. 254]*

"The kingdom of God," in the words of our Lord and Savior, "does not come for all to see; nor shall they say: Behold, here it is, or behold, there it is; but the kingdom of God is within us, for the word of God is very near, in our mouth and in our heart." Thus it is clear that one who prays for the coming of God's kingdom prays rightly to have it within, that there it may grow and bear fruit and become perfect. For God reigns in each of his holy ones. Anyone who is holy obeys the spiritual laws of God, who dwells in that person as in a well-ordered city. The Father is present in the perfect soul, and with the perfect soul Christ reigns, according to the words: "We shall come to that soul and make our home therein."

Thus the kingdom of God within us, as we continue to make progress, will reach its highest point when the Apostle's words are fulfilled, and Christ, having subjected all his enemies to himself, will hand over his "kingdom to God the Father, that God may be all in all." Therefore, let us pray unceasingly with that disposition of soul which the Word may make divine, saying to our Father who is in heaven: "Hallowed be your name; your kingdom come."

Note this too about the kingdom of God. It is not a "sharing of justice with iniquity," nor a "society of light with darkness," nor a "meeting of Christ with Belial." The kingdom of God cannot exist alongside the reign of sin.

Therefore, if we wish God to reign in us, in no way "should sin reign in our mortal body"; rather we should "mortify our members which are upon the earth" and bear fruit in the Spirit. There should be in us a kind of spiritual paradise where God may walk and be our sole ruler with his Christ. In us the Lord will sit at the right hand of that spiritual power which we wish to receive. And he will sit there until all his enemies who are within us become "his footstool," and every principality, power and virtue in us is cast out.

All this can happen in each one of us, and the last enemy, death, can be destroyed; then Christ will say in us: "O death, where is your sting? O hell, where is your victory?" And so, what is "corruptible" in us must be clothed with holiness and "incorruptibility;" and what is "mortal" must be clothed, now that death has been conquered, in the Father's "immortality." Then God will reign in us, and we shall enjoy even now the blessings of rebirth and resurrection.

Treatise on Prayer 25: PG 11, 495–499

Week of 5 Epiphany ✠ Monday

A reading from the treatise On Prayer by Origen, Priest and Theologian [c. 254]

So it is necessary not only to pray, but also to pray "as we ought," and to pray for what we ought. For it is not enough that we should be able to pray for what we ought, unless in addition we possess the "as we ought." And what does the "as we ought" profit us, if we do not know how to pray for what we ought?

Now, of these two things the one, that is to say, "what we ought," is concerned with the words of prayer; the other, "as we ought," with the condition of whoever who is praying. Examples of "what we ought" are: "Ask for the great things, and the little things shall be added unto you"; and "Ask for the heavenly things and the earthly things shall be added unto you"; and "Pray for them that despitefully use you"; and "Pray therefore the Lord of the harvest, that he send forth laborers into his harvest"; and "Pray that you enter not into temptation"; and "Pray that your flight be not in the winter, neither on a sabbath" and "And in praying use not vain repetitions"; and any other sayings like these. An example of "as we ought" is: "I desire therefore that the faithful pray in every place, lifting up holy hands, without wrath and disputing. Instruction on "as we ought" is also to be found in the passage: "If therefore you are offering your gift at the altar, and there remember that your brother [or sister] has anything against you, leave there your gift before the altar, and go your way, first be reconciled to your brother [or sister], and then come and offer your gift." For what greater gift can a reasonable creature present to God than a sweet-savoured word of prayer, offered by one whose conscience is void of the foul savour that comes from sin?

Treatise on Prayer 2, 1–2: PG 11, 417

Week of 5 Epiphany ✠ Tuesday

A reading from the Sayings of Syncletica, Mother of the Egyptian Desert [late fourth century]

Saint Syncletica said: If you live in a monastic community, do not wander from place to place: if you do, it will harm you. If a hen stops sitting on the eggs she will hatch no chickens, and the monk or nun who moves from place to place grows cold and dead in faith.

When the devil does not use the goads of poverty to tempt us, then wealth is used for the purpose. Unable to win by scorn and mockery, the adversary tries praise and flattery. Unable to win by providing health, Satan tries illness. Unable to win by comfort, Satan tries to ruin the soul by vexations which lead a person to act against the monastic vow. Satan inflicts severe sickness on people in order to tempt them, and so makes them weak, and thereby shakes the charity which they feel towards God.

Iron is cleaned of rust by fire. If you are righteous and suffer, you grow to a yet higher sanctity. Gold is tested by fire.

Sailors beginning a voyage set the sails and look for a favorable wind, and later they meet a contrary wind. Just because the wind has turned, they do not throw the cargo overboard or abandon ship. They wait a little and battle against the storm until they can again set a direct course. And when we run into headwinds, let us put up the cross for our sail, and we shall voyage through the world in safety.

An open treasury is quickly spent. And any virtue will be annihilated if it is published abroad and becomes famous. If you put wax in front of a fire it melts, and if you pour vain praises on the soul, it goes soft and weak in seeking goodness.

Verba Seniorum, ed. Rosweyde, 7, 15–16, 18; 8, 19: Western Asceticism, ed. Chadwick, 85–87, 101

Week of 5 Epiphany ✠ Wednesday

A reading from the treatise Against Heresies by Irenaeus, Bishop of Lyons [c. 202]

The history of Isaac is not devoid of a symbolic character. For in the Epistle to the Romans, the Apostle declares: "When Rebekah had conceived by one man, our father Isaac," she received answer from the Word "in order that God's decree might stand fast not by works but by the favor of him who calls." It was said to her: "Two nations are in your womb, two peoples are quarreling while still within you; but one shall surpass the other, and the older shall serve the younger."

It is evident from this that not only were there prophecies of the patriarchs but also that the children brought forth by Rebekah were a prediction of the two nations. Furthermore, the one would indeed be the greater and the other the less; the one also should be in bondage but the other free. But both should be of one and the same Father. Our God, one and the same, is also their God, who knows hidden things and all things before they happen; hence, he has said: "I have loved Jacob and hated Esau."

Moreover, if anyone will look into Jacob's actions, he will find them not lacking in meaning but full of import with respect to the dispensations. Thus, first of all, at his birth, because he took hold of his brother's heel, he was called Jacob, that is, "the supplanter"—one who holds but is not held, binds the feet but is not bound, strives and conquers, grasping in his hand his adversary's heel, that is, victory. For to this end was the Lord born, the type of whose birth was set forth beforehand, of whom John also says in the book of Revelation: "He rode forth victorious, to conquer yet again."

Secondly, Jacob received the rights of the firstborn when his brother regarded them with contempt; this paralleled the way in which the younger nation received Christ, the firstborn, when the elder nation rejected him with the words: "We have no king but Caesar." But in Christ every blessing is summed up, and therefore the latter people have snatched away the blessings of the former from the Father, just as Jacob took away the blessing from Esau.

For it is truly one and the same God who directed the patriarchs toward his dispensations, and "justifies the circumcised and the uncircumcised on the basis of faith." Just as we are prefigured in the first, so on the other hand are they represented in us, that is, in the Church, and receive the reward for those things which they accomplished.

Against Heresies 4, 21–22: SC 100, 2, 678–691

Week of 5 Epiphany ✠ Thursday

A reading from a homily of Origen, Priest and Theologian [c. 254]

God said to Jacob: "Do not be afraid to go down to Egypt." Jacob has no reason to fear because, as God at once promises him: "For there I will make you a great nation and I shall go down to Egypt with you and I shall bring you back here again." Though these words were spoken by God to Jacob, there is, I cannot help but suspect, a greater mystery hidden within them, that does not apply strictly to Jacob.

Let us examine, therefore, the possibility that Jacob is to be viewed here perhaps as a figure of someone else—either a figure of the Lord, who was sent by the Father to come down to the Egypt of this world, who here in the Church became a great nation, and who, when his mission was completed, returned to the Father—or a figure of our first parents who, when they were banished from Paradise and its delights, were sent into the Egypt of this world to labor and to suffer and above all to engage in that deadly conflict "against the principalities and powers and the rulers of this world of darkness" of which Egypt is a type and figure, a conflict which was foretold by God when he said to the serpent: "He (the seed of the woman) will strike at your head while you strike at his heel" and "I will put enmity between you and the woman and between your offspring and hers."

Yet, in this struggle God did not abandon those engaged in it but was always with them. He was pleased with Abel and reproached Cain. When Enoch invoked his name, he came to him. He saved Noah from the deluge, bidding him to build the ark of salvation. He was Abraham's guide, after he set out from his father's house and from his kindred. He blessed Isaac and Jacob and led the children of Israel out of Egypt. Through Moses he wrote down and gave the law to his people, and what still remained to be written he gave to them through the prophets.

Thus, through all these merciful interventions he fulfilled his promise to be with them in Egypt. As for the words: "I will bring you back at the end," these, I think, were fulfilled when in the fullness of time the only-begotten Son of God descended into hell and called Adam, our first parent, out of there to bring him back to God. While he hung on the cross, Christ said to the thief: "This day you will be with me in paradise." These words, however, are to be understood as addressed, not merely to the thief, but to all the saints for whom he descended into hell. Understood in this way rather than as spoken to Jacob alone, the words: "I will bring you back at the end" are seen to be more truly fulfilled.

But for each one of us also it is decreed that we go down into Egypt and meet its labors and sufferings and trials. And if we merit the presence of God with us and his assistance, God will make of us a great nation, that is, our virtues shall be many and our holiness great, since this is the way that the saints are said to multiply and grow. The words: "I will bring you back at the end" will also be fulfilled in us, when namely we, having accomplished all that was required of us, have attained to perfection in virtue.

Homily 15 on Genesis 5–6: PG 12, 244–245

Week of 5 Epiphany ✠ Friday

A reading from the treatise On Prayer by Origen, Priest and Theologian [c. 254]

That person "prays without ceasing" (virtuous deeds or commandments fulfilled being included as part of prayer) who combines with the prayer the needful deeds and the prayer with the fitting actions. For thus alone can we accept "pray without ceasing" as a practicable saying, if we speak of the whole life of the saint as one great unbroken prayer: of which prayer that which is commonly called prayer is a part. This ought to be engaged in not less than three times every day, as is clear from the case of Daniel, who when great danger hung over him "prayed three times a day." Peter also, going up to the housetop about the sixth hour to pray, when also he saw the vessel let down from heaven, let down by four corners, is evidence for the middle one of the three prayers, while the one before it is spoken of by David, "In the morning shalt thou hear my" prayer, "in the morning will I order [my prayer] unto thee and will look up"; and the final one is indicated in the words "the lifting up of my hands as the evening sacrifice." Indeed we shall not fittingly pass even the night time without this prayer: for David says, "At midnight did I rise to give thanks unto thee for the judgments of thy righteousness"; and Paul, as is stated in the Acts of the Apostles, about midnight in company with Silas, at Philippi, was praying and singing hymns unto God, so that even the prisoners listened to them.

Now if Jesus prays, and does not pray in vain, obtaining through prayer what he asks for (and perhaps he would not have received it without prayer), which of us may neglect prayer?

Treatise on Prayer 12, 2–13, 1: PG 11, 452–453

Week of 5 Epiphany ✠ Saturday

A reading from a homily of John Chrysostom, Bishop of Constantinople [407]

From the outset of his letter St. Paul reminds the Corinthians of the prophecy which says: "I will confound the wisdom of the wise"; he shows that the wisdom of God has destroyed, by what looked like foolishness, the wisdom of the world, and that the foolishness of God is wiser than we are; he shows also that not only did he teach by unlearned people, but he chose unlearned persons for his followers.

St. Paul then shows that even the matter of his own teaching and his way of preaching, which would ordinarily have troubled people, did not do so. Not only, he says, were the disciples ignorant, but I myself also, who preached to you: "So it was that when I came to you and preached Christ's message to you, I did so without any high pretensions to eloquence, or to philosophy. I had no thought of bringing you any other knowledge than that of Jesus Christ, and of him as crucified."

That is why, in a former passage, showing that it was Christ who had done everything and who had willed that the word should be preached by the unlearned, St. Paul had said: "Christ did not send me to baptize; he sent me to preach the gospel; not with an orator's cleverness." It was not, then, the will of Paul, but that of Christ, which is far greater, infinitely greater.

"So it is not to make a display of eloquence, nor am I armed with secular learning, that I am come to preach the mystery of Christ." Notice that he does not say: the word, but the mystery; and there again, there was something to turn away his hearers, for this mystery which he preached everywhere was the death of Christ. He said himself: "I had no thought of bringing you any other knowledge than that of Jesus Christ, and of him as crucified," as much as to say that he was altogether destitute of the wisdom of the world, and that he had come to them without high pretensions.

It is evident, however, that he might have possessed them, for if his garments raised the dead, his shadow expelled diseases, much more was his soul capable of the gift of eloquence. For this is an art which can be learned; but the other transcends all art; capable of accomplishing prodigies to which art cannot attain, it would have been easy for him to accomplish lesser things. But Christ did not wish it, for it was not expedient. St. Paul then had reason to say: "I had no thought of bringing you any other knowledge," for I will only what Christ wills.

It seems to me that Paul speaks here to the Corinthians more humbly than to any other Church, and it is in order to kill their pride. These words: "I had no thought of bringing you any other knowledge" allude directly to the wisdom of the world. Truth, then, is not diminished by being preached without the help of human wisdom; on the contrary, it is its best ornament. It is, indeed, that which shows best the divine character and heavenly origins of it. Therefore the Apostle adds: "God's power, not human wisdom, was to be the foundation of your faith."

Homily 6 on 1 Corinthians 1–5: PG 61, 47–50

Week of 6 Epiphany ✠ Sunday

A reading from a sermon of Caesarius, Bishop of Arles [543]

If anyone is in conflict with another, end the quarrel lest you yourself end badly. Do not consider this unimportant, my beloved. Let us call to mind that our life here is mortal and frail, that it is endangered by many and great temptations, and this makes us pray that we may not be overcome.

And so, we realize that a just person is not without some sins. But there is one remedy which enables us to keep alive. For God, our Master, told us to say in our prayers: "Forgive us the wrong we have done as we forgive those who wrong us." We have made a contract with God and taken a resolution, adding for safety's sake the condition that the wrong must be forgiven. This makes us ask with complete confidence to be forgiven provided we too forgive.

If, on the contrary, we do not forgive, how can we in good conscience hope that our sins will be forgiven? Let no one deceive themselves: God deceived no one. It is human to be angry, but I wish it were impossible. It is human to become angry but let us not water the small plant born of anger with various suspicions. Let us not permit it to develop into a tree of hatred. It happens also frequently that a parent is angry with a child, but the parent does not hate the child. The parent is angry because of wishing to correct the child. If this is the purpose, the anger is animated by love.

We read in Scripture: "Why look at the speck in another's eye when you miss the plank in your own?" You find fault with another person for being angry, and you keep hatred in yourself. Anger in comparison with hatred is only a speck, but if the speck is fostered, it becomes a plank. If, on the contrary, you pluck out the speck and cast it away, it will amount to nothing.

He says in another place: "Anyone who hates another is a murderer." One who hates another, walks around, goes out, comes in, marches on, is not burdened by any chains and is not shut up in any prison, but is bound by guilt. Do not think of such a one as not being imprisoned. The heart is that person's prison. When you hear: "One who hates another is in darkness all the while," lest you might despise that darkness, the evangelist adds: "Anyone who hates another is a murderer."

You have hated others and walk safely around and refuse to be reconciled with them, and God has given you time and opportunity. Yet you are a murderer and are still alive. If you felt God's wrath you would be suddenly snatched away with your hatred toward others. God spares you; spare others likewise; make up and seek reconciliation with them.

But suppose you want reconciliation and the other person does not want it. That is enough for you; you have something to grieve for, you have freed yourself. If you want agreement and that person refuses, say confidently: "Forgive us the wrong we have done as we forgive those who wrong us."

Sermon on Fraternal Harmony 1–2: PLS 4, 446–447

Week of 6 Epiphany ✠ Monday

A reading from the treatise On Isaac or the Soul by Ambrose, Bishop of Milan [397]

The Apostle declares: "You are my children, and you put me back in labor pains until Christ is formed in you." For she is in labor who receives the spirit of salvation in her womb and pours it out upon others. Hence, since Christ was already formed in her, the bride says: "Set me as a seal on your heart, as a seal on your arm." Christ is the seal on the forehead, the seal on the heart: on the forehead, that we may ever confess him: on the heart, that we always love him; a seal on the arm, that we may carry out his tasks.

Therefore, let his image radiate in our confession, let it radiate in our love, let it radiate in our works and deeds, so that all his beauty may be expressed in us if it is possible. Let him be our head, because "the head of everyone is Christ." Let him be our eye, that through him we may see the Father. Let him be our voice, that through him we may speak to the Father. Let him be our right hand, that through him we may bring our sacrifice to God the Father. He is also our seal, which is the sign of perfection and love, because the Father loved the Son and set his seal on him, as we read: "It is on him that God the Father has set his seal."

Therefore, Christ is our love. Love is good, when it has offered itself to death for transgressions; love is good, when it has remitted sins. Hence, let our soul put on love, a kind of love which is as "strong as death." For just as death is the end of sins, so is love as well, since the person who loves the Lord ceases to commit sin. For "love thinks no evil and does not rejoice in what is wrong, but endures all things." For if you do not seek your own goods, how will you seek those of others? Strong too is that death through the bath through which every sin is buried and every transgression pardoned.

Such was the love brought forward by that woman in the gospel, about whom the Lord says: "Her many sins are forgiven—because of her great love." Strong, too, is the death of the holy martyrs, which abolishes previous transgression, and hence—since it entails a love not less than theirs—death that is equal to the suffering of the martyrs is equally strong in order to take away the punishment of sins.

The Lord Jesus sent this fire on the earth, and faith shone forth, devotion was kindled, love was illuminated, and justice was resplendent. With this fire he inflamed the heart of his apostles, as Cleopas bears witness, saying: "Were not our hearts burning inside us as he explained the Scriptures?"

Therefore, the wings of fire are the flames of the divine Scriptures. Finally, he explained the Scriptures, and the fire went forth and penetrated into the hearts of his hearers.

Treatise on Isaac or the Soul 8, 74–77: CSEL 32.1, 693–695

Week of 6 Epiphany ✠ Tuesday

A reading from the treatise On Prayer by Origen, Priest and Theologian [c. 254]

When "the Father" of the saints is said to be "in heaven," we are not to suppose that he is circumscribed in bodily fashion and dwells "in heaven"; otherwise, if the heaven contained him, God would be found less than, because contained by, the heaven: but we must believe that by the ineffable power of his Godhead all things are contained and held together by him. And, speaking generally, sayings which taken literally are supposed by simple folk to assert that God is in a place, must instead be understood in a manner that befits grand and spiritual conceptions of God. Such are the following in the [Gospel] according to John: "Now before the feast of the passover, Jesus knowing that his hour was come that he should depart out of this world unto the Father, having loved his own which were in the world, he loved them unto the end"; and, a little further on: "knowing that the Father had given all things into his hands, and that he came forth from God, and goeth unto God"; and later on: "Ye heard how I said to you, I go away, and I come unto you. If ye loved me, ye would have rejoiced, because I go unto the Father"; and again, later on: "But now I go unto him that sent me; and none of you asketh me, whither goest thou?" If these words are to be taken in a local sense, it is obvious that we must do the same with: "Jesus answered and said unto them, If you love me, you will keep my word: and my Father will love you, and we will come unto you, and make our abode with you."

These sayings do not conceive of a local departure of the Father and the Son to one who loves the word of Jesus, nor are they to be taken in a local sense. But the Word of God, condescending for our sakes and being "humbled," as concerning his own dignity, when he is among us, is said to "depart out of this world to the Father," in order that we also may behold him there in his perfection, returning again to his own "fulness," after the emptiness wherewith he "emptied himself" when he was with us: where also we, using him as our guide, being "made full," shall be delivered from all emptiness. Let the Word of God, therefore, depart to "him that sent him," quitting the world, and let him "go unto the Father." And as for that passage at the end of the Gospel according to John, "Touch me not; for I am not yet ascended unto the Father," let us seek to conceive of it in a mystical sense: the ascent of the Son "unto the Father," when conceived of by us with holy insight in a manner befitting Deity, is an ascent of the mind rather than of the body.

I think it necessary to consider carefully these sayings in connection with the words "Our Father which art in heaven," in order to remove a mean conception of God held by those who consider that he is locally "in heaven," and to prevent anyone from saying that God is in a place after the manner of a body (from which it follows that he is a body)—a tenet which leads to most impious opinions, namely, to suppose that he is divisible, material, corruptible.

Treatise on Prayer 23, 1–3: PG 11, 485–492

Week of 6 Epiphany ✠ Wednesday

A reading from a commentary on John by Cyril, Bishop of Alexandria [444]

In a plan of surpassing beauty the Creator of the universe decreed the renewal of all things in Christ. In his design for restoring human nature to its original condition, he gave a promise that he would pour out on it the Holy Spirit along with his other gifts, for otherwise our nature could not enter once more into the peaceful and secure possession of those gifts.

He therefore appointed a time for the Holy Spirit to come upon us: this was the time of Christ's coming. He gave this promise when he said: "In those days," that is, the days of the Savior, "I will pour out a share of my Spirit on all humanity."

When the time came for this great act of unforced generosity, which revealed in our midst the only-begotten Son, clothed with flesh on this earth, born of woman, in accordance with Holy Scripture, God the Father gave the Spirit once again. Christ, as the firstfruits of our restored nature, was the first to receive the Spirit. John the Baptist bore witness to this when he said: "I saw the Spirit coming down from heaven, and it rested on him."

Christ "received the Spirit" insofar as he was human, and insofar as a human being could receive the Spirit. He did so in such a way that, though he is the Son of God the Father, begotten of his substance, even before the incarnation, indeed before all ages, yet he was not offended at hearing the Father say to him after he had become human: "You are my Son; today I have begotten you."

The Father says of Christ, who was God, begotten of him before the ages, that he has been "begotten today," for the Father is to accept us in Christ as his adopted children. The whole of our nature is present in

Christ, insofar as he is human. So the Father can be said to give the Spirit again to the Son, though the Son possesses the Spirit as his own, in order that we may receive the Spirit in Christ. The Son therefore took to himself the seed of Abraham, as Scripture says, and became like us in all things.

The only-begotten Son receives the Spirit, but not for his own advantage, for the Spirit is his, and is given in him and through him, as we have already said. He receives it to renew our nature in its entirety and to make it whole again, for in becoming human he took our entire nature to himself. If we reason correctly, and use also the testimony of Scripture, we can see that Christ did not receive the Spirit for himself, but rather for us in him; for it is also through Christ that all gifts come down to us.

Commentary on John 5, 2: PG 73, 751–754

Week of 6 Epiphany ✠ Thursday

A reading from the Confessions of Augustine, Bishop of Hippo [430]

I hear the voice of my God commanding me: "Let not your hearts be overburdened with self-indulgence and drunkenness." Drunkenness is far, far from me; your mercy will keep it from ever coming near me. But over-eating sometimes steals upon your servants; your mercy will remove it far from me. For "no one can be continent unless you give it." You grant many things to our prayers: and what good we received before we prayed, from you we received it. And that we should afterward know and acknowledge our receiving these things from you is also your gift.

I never was a drunkard, but I have known drunkards who have been made sober by you. Therefore, it was your work that they should not be so who never were such; and your work that they should not always be so who for some time had been such; from you also it was, that both should know that this was your work.

I have also heard another voice of yours: "Go not after your lusts, but turn away from your own will." By your gift I have heard also that sentence which I have loved much: "Neither shall we suffer any loss if we do not eat, nor if we do eat shall we suffer any advantage." That is to say, neither shall the one make me happy nor the other miserable.

Again, I have heard: "For I have learned to be self-suffering in whatever circumstance I am. I know how to live humbly and I know how to live in abundance. I can do all things in him who strengthens me." Behold, here a soldier of the heavenly camp, and not the dust which we are. But remember, O Lord, that we are dust, and out of dust you made us, and we were lost and are found. Nor could Paul do it of himself, because he was of the same dust, whom I so loved to hear saying through the breath of your inspiration: "I can do all things," says he, "in him who strengthens me."

Strengthen me that I also may be able. Grant what you command, and command what you will. Paul confesses that he has received this, and "what he glories of, he glories of in the Lord." I have heard another praying in order also to receive: "Take from me," says he, "the greediness of the belly." From this it is clear, my holy God, that you give when that is done, which you command to be done.

Being, therefore, placed, as I am, in the midst of these temptations, I fight every day against the concupiscence of eating and drinking, for it is no such thing as I can resolve to cut off once for all and touch no more, as I could do with regard to concubinage. Therefore, the bridle of the throat is to be held with a tempered hand, so as neither to be too loose nor too tight. And who is it, O Lord, who is not carried sometimes a little out of the bounds of necessity? Whoever it is, such a person is great; let such a one magnify your name.

But I am not such, for I am sinful. And yet I also magnify your name. And Christ intercedes to you for my sins who has overcome the world numbering me among the weaker members of his body, because that which is imperfect in me, your eyes have seen, and in your book all shall be written.

Confessions 10, 31: CSEL 33, 259–262

Week of 6 Epiphany ✠ Friday

A reading from a sermon of Gregory the Great, Bishop of Rome [604]

Some people advance to the point where they are able to distribute in the proper way the earthly goods they have received; they exert themselves in works of mercy and give aid to the oppressed. Such people "go," inasmuch as they devote themselves to their neighbors' good. The "wheels" which Ezekiel saw in his vision go with them; that is, the sacred Scriptures guide them as they move about their work.

There are others who hold so courageously to the faith they have received that they can put up with any adversity; they are not in the slightest degree drawn into the disobedience of disbelief, but on the contrary attack those who preach such disobedience and draw them back to the right path. With these who "stand" firm, the wheels too stand, for the words of sacred Scripture strengthen these people in their right ways. They hear it said: "Stand firm, and hold fast to the traditions you received"; and again: "Your adversary, the devil, goes about like a roaring lion seeking whom he may devour. Resist, strong in your faith."

There are still others who take no stock in earthly goods and will not stoop to possess the passing things of time; they fix their hearts on God in contemplation. When they are thus raised up the wheels too are raised up, for, in the measure that one advances toward the heights, the Scriptures speak of heights more lofty still. The "living creatures," in short, go to the aid of their neighbor, stand to guard themselves, and are raised up to the contemplation of God.

The wheels, however, also go and stand and are raised up because seekers find in the sacred Scriptures what suits their own nature. If you have advanced to the active life, the Scriptures go with you. If you have achieved an unshakable constancy of spirit, they stand with you. If by God's grace you have reached the contemplative life, they soar aloft with you.

The precepts contained in sacred Scripture bring us back to life when we are lying dead in sin. This is why we address the Lord almighty with the Psalmist: "Never will I forget your justifications, for through them you give me life."

In the darkness of our present life the Scripture is a light for our journey. That is why Peter can say: "You do well to fix your gaze upon it as upon a lamp burning in a dark place." It is also why the Psalmist says: "Your word, Lord, is a lamp to my feet and a light to my paths."

We know, however, that even this lamp of ours is darkened for us, unless the truth makes that light shine in our hearts. For this reason the Psalmist says: "You give light to my lamp, O Lord my God; you give light to my darkness." For what good is a lit lamp unless it casts light? But no created light illumines us unless it be illumined in turn by the uncreated light. Almighty God, therefore, has, for our salvation, spoken the words of the holy Testaments and opened their meaning to us.

Homily 7 on Ezekiel 15–17: PL 76, 847–848

Week of 6 Epiphany ✠ Saturday

A reading from the treatise On Prayer *by Origen, Priest and Theologian [c. 254]*

It seems to me that those who are about to come to prayer, if they withdraw and prepare themselves for a little while, will be more earnest and attentive in regard to their prayer as a whole. They should put aside every kind of distraction and disturbance of mind, and recollect as far as possible the greatness of God to whom they come, and that it is a sacrilege to approach God lightly and carelessly and with a kind of disdain; and they should cast off all alien thoughts. Thus ought they to come to prayer, as it were stretching out the soul before the hands, and directing the mind to God before the eyes, and raising up from the ground the reason and making it to stand towards the Lord of all. All malice towards anyone who appears to have wronged them they should cast aside insofar as they wish God to bear no malice towards themselves, since they have injured and sinned against many a neighbour, or else are conscious of deeds of various kinds that they have committed contrary to right reason. Neither ought they to doubt that, as there are countless attitudes of the body, that attitude in which the hands are stretched out and eyes lifted up is to be preferred to all others, since the body brings to prayer the image, as it were, of the qualities suitable to the soul. We mean, however, that these attitudes should be given preference unless an obstacle opposes. For where there is an obstacle it is permissible on an occasion to pray suitably in a sitting position, on account of a disease of the feet that may not be disregarded, or even lying down, through fever or some such sickness. And also, on account of circumstances, if we are sailing, let us say, or if our business does not allow us to withdraw and offer the prayer that is due, it is permitted to pray without even seeming to do so.

And as for kneeling, that it is necessary when one is about to accuse oneself of one's sins before God, supplicating him for healing therefrom and for forgiveness thereof, it ought to be known that it is a symbol of one who is abject and submissive. Paul says: "For this cause I bow my knees unto the Father, from whom every family in heaven and on earth is named." Spiritual kneeling, so named because every creature falls down before God "in the name of Jesus" and humbles itself before him, appears to me to be indicated in the words: "That in the name of Jesus every knee should bow, of things in heaven and things on earth and things under the earth."

Treatise on Prayer 31, 2–3: PG 11, 549–552

Week of 7 Epiphany ✠ Sunday

A reading from a scriptural commentary of Ephrem of Edessa, Deacon [373]

Lord, who can comprehend even one of your words? We lose more of it than we grasp, like those who drink from a living spring. For God's word offers different facets according to the capacity of the listener, and the Lord has portrayed his message in many colors, so that whoever gazes upon it can see in it what suits. Within it he has buried manifold treasures, so that each of us might grow rich in seeking them out.

The word of God is a tree of life that offers us blessed fruit from each of its branches. It is like that rock which was struck open in the wilderness, from which all were offered spiritual drink. As the Apostle says: "They ate spiritual food and they drank spiritual drink."

And so whenever you discover some part of the treasure, you should not think that you have exhausted God's word. Instead you should feel that this is all that you were able to find of the wealth contained in it. Nor should you say that the word is weak and sterile or look down on it simply because this portion was all that you happened to find. But precisely because you could not capture it all you should give thanks for its riches.

Be glad then that you are overwhelmed, and do not be saddened because the word of God has overcome you. A thirsty person is happy when drinking, and is not depressed because of being unable to exhaust the spring. So let this spring quench your thirst, and not your thirst the spring. For if you can satisfy your thirst without exhausting the spring, then when you thirst again you can drink from it once more; but if when your thirst is sated the spring is also dried up, then your victory would turn to your own harm.

Be thankful then for what you have received, and do not be saddened at all that such an abundance still remains. What you have received and attained is your present share, while what is left will be your heritage. For what you could not take at one time because of your weakness, you will be able to grasp at another if you only persevere. So do not foolishly try to drain in one draught what cannot be consumed all at once, and do not cease out of faintheartedness from what you will be able to absorb as time goes on.

Commentary on the Diatessaron 1, 18–19: SC 121, 52–53

Week of 7 Epiphany ✠ Monday

A reading from a sermon of Gregory, Bishop of Nyssa [c. 394]

"Blessed are the pure in heart, for they shall see God." I do not think that if the eye of one's soul has been purified, one is promised a direct vision of God; but perhaps this marvellous saying may suggest what the Word expresses more clearly when he says to others: "The kingdom of God is within you." By this we should learn that if one's heart has been purified from every creature and all unruly affections, one will see the Image of the Divine Nature in one's own beauty.

I think that in this short saying the Word expresses some such counsel as this: There is in you, human beings, a desire to contemplate the true good. But when you hear that the Divine Majesty is exalted above the heavens, that its glory is inexpressible, its beauty ineffable, and its nature inaccessible, do not despair of ever beholding what you desire. It is indeed within your reach; you have within yourselves the standard by which to apprehend the Divine. For he who made you did at the same time endow your nature with this wonderful quality. For God imprinted on it the likeness of the glories of his own nature, as if molding the form of a carving into wax.

But the evil that has been poured all around the nature bearing the Divine Image has rendered useless to you this wonderful thing, that lies hidden under vile coverings. If, therefore, you wash off by a good life the filth that has been stuck on your heart like plaster, the Divine Beauty will again shine forth in you.

To give an example. Though people who see the sun in a mirror do not gaze at the sky itself, yet they see the sun in the reflection of the mirror no less than those who look at its very orb. So, he says, it is also with you. Even though you are too weak to perceive the Light Itself, yet if you but return to the grace of the Image with which you were informed from the beginning, you will have all you seek in yourselves. For the Godhead is purity, freedom from passion, and separation from all evil. If therefore these things be in you, God is indeed in you.

Hence, if your thought is without any alloy of evil, free from passion, and alien from all stain, you are blessed because you are clear of sight.

You are able to perceive what is invisible to those who are not purified, because you have been cleansed; the darkness caused by material entanglements has been removed from the eyes of your soul, and so you see the blessed vision radiant in the pure heaven of your heart. But what is this vision? It is purity, sanctity, simplicity, and other such luminous reflections of the Divine Nature, in which God is contemplated.

Oration 6, on the Beatitudes: PG 44, 1269–1272

Week of 7 Epiphany ✠ Tuesday

A reading from a homily of Gregory, Bishop of Nyssa [c. 394]

We shall be blessed with clear vision if we keep our eyes fixed on Christ, for he, as Paul teaches, is our head, and there is in him no shadow of evil. Saint Paul himself and all who have reached the same heights of sanctity had their eyes fixed on Christ, and so have all who live and move and have their being in him.

As no darkness can be seen by anyone surrounded by light, so no trivialities can capture the attention of anyone who has eyes on Christ. The one who keeps his eyes upon the head and origin of the whole universe has them on virtue in all its perfection; on truth, on justice, on immortality and on everything else that is good, for Christ is goodness itself.

"The wise then, turn their eyes toward the One who is their head, but fools grope in darkness." No one who puts a lamp under a bed instead of on a lampstand will receive any light from it. People are often considered blind and useless when they make the supreme Good their aim and give themselves up to the contemplation of God, but Paul made a boast of this and proclaimed himself a fool for Christ's sake. The reason he said, "We are fools for Christ's sake" was that his mind was free from all earthly preoccupations. It was as though he said, "We are blind to the life here below because our eyes are raised toward the One who is our head."

And so, without board or lodging, he traveled from place to place, destitute, naked, exhausted by hunger and thirst. When people saw him in captivity, flogged, shipwrecked, led about in chains, they could scarcely help thinking him a pitiable sight. Nevertheless, even while he suffered all this at the hands of others, he always looked toward the One who is his head and he asked: "What can separate us from the love of Christ, which is in Jesus? Can affliction or distress? Can persecution, hunger, nakedness, danger or death?" In other words: "What can force me to take my eyes from him who is my head and to turn them toward things that are contemptible?"

He bids us follow his example: "Seek the things that are above," he says, which is only another way of saying: "Keep your eyes on Christ."

Homily on Ecclesiastes 5: PG 44, 683–686

Week of 7 Epiphany ✠ Wednesday

A reading from a homily of Gregory, Bishop of Nyssa [c. 394]

"There is a time to be born and a time to die." The fact that there is a natural link between birth and death is expressed very clearly in this text of Scripture. Death invariably follows birth, and everyone who is born comes at last to the grave.

"There is a time to be born and a time to die." God grant that mine may be a timely birth and a timely death! Of course no one imagines that the Speaker regards as acts of virtue our natural birth and death, in neither of which our own will plays any part. A woman does not give birth because she chooses to do so; neither does anyone die as a result of one's own decision. Obviously, there is neither virtue nor vice in anything that lies beyond our control. So we must consider what is meant by a timely birth and a timely death.

It seems to me that the birth referred to here is our salvation, as is suggested by the prophet Isaiah. This reaches its full term and is not stillborn when, having been conceived by the fear of God, the soul's own birth pangs bring it to the light of day. We are in a sense our own parents, and we give birth to ourselves by our own free choice of what is good. Such a choice becomes possible for us when we have received God into ourselves and have become children of God, children of the Most High. On the other hand, if what the Apostle calls "the form of Christ" has not been produced in us, we abort ourselves. The child of God must reach maturity.

Now if the meaning of a timely birth is clear, so also is the meaning of a timely death. For Saint Paul every moment was a time to die, as he proclaims in his letters: "I swear by the pride I take in you that I face death every day." Elsewhere he says, "For your sake we are put to death daily" and "we felt like those condemned to death." How Paul died daily is perfectly obvious. He never gave himself up to a sinful life but kept his body under constant control. He carried death with him, Christ's death, wherever he went. He was always being crucified with Christ. It was not his own life he lived; it was Christ who lived in him. This surely was a timely death—a death whose end was true life.

"I put to death and I shall give life," God says, teaching us that death to sin and life in the Spirit is his gift, and promising that whatever he puts to death he will restore to life again.

Homily on Ecclesiastes 6: PG 44, 702–703

Week of 7 Epiphany ✠ Thursday

A reading from a commentary on Ecclesiastes by Jerome, Priest, and Monk of Bethlehem [420]

All to whom God has given wealth and possessions and power to enjoy them, and to accept their lot, and to take pleasure in their labor—they have received a gift from God. For they will not notice the days of their lives as they pass because God has filled their hearts with joy. Compare them with the people who are anxious about their wealth and are full of vexation as they hoard up possessions that perish. Our text says that it is better to take delight in what you have. The first at least have some pleasure in what they have, while the second suffer from excessive anxiety. And the reason is that the ability to enjoy riches is a gift from God; "they do not count the days of their lives," for God allows them to enjoy life; without sadness or anxiety, they are filled with the delight of the moment. However, it is better to understand the text with the Apostle as referring to God's gift of spiritual food and drink; we are to contemplate goodness in his works, for it takes great work and study for us to contemplate true good. And this is our lot: to rejoice in study and work. This is a good goal, but not completely good "until Christ is revealed in our lives."

All our work is to satisfy our mouths, yet our spirits will be hungry. For what has the wise more than a fool, except the knowledge of how to live? All that we work for in this world is consumed by our mouths, chewed up by our teeth, and passed into the stomach for digestion. And even when something delights the taste, the pleasure lasts only as long as we can taste it.

But after all this, the minds of the eaters get no satisfaction, for we will want to eat again, and neither wise person nor fool can live without food, and even the poor seek nothing more than to keep their bodies alive and not die of starvation. Or again, it may be because the spirit gains nothing useful from feeding the body. Food is common to the wise and the foolish alike, and for the poor food is wealth.

However, it is better to understand the text as referring to the person in Ecclesiastes, who is learned in the sacred Scripture, and knows that neither mouth nor spirit is satisfied so long as that person still desires learning. In this the wise has the advantage over the fool. For if one knows oneself to be poor (and the poor are called blessed in the Gospel), one strives to understand the important things in life, and walks "the straight and narrow way which leads to life." The wise is poor in wickedness, and knows where Christ, who is our life, is to be found.

Commentary on Ecclesiastes 5–6, 432–434: PL 23, 1057–1059

Week of 7 Epiphany ✠ Friday

A reading from the Moral Reflections on Job by Gregory the Great, Bishop of Rome [604]

When Paul perceived within himself the riches of internal wisdom, yet saw the corruptibility of his own body, he was led to say: "We have this treasure in earthen vessels." Now in the blessed Job the earthen vessel felt the gaping sores without, while this treasure of wisdom remained whole and intact within. For outwardly his body was in agony, but inwardly from the treasure of wisdom came forth holy thoughts: "If we have received good from the hand of the Lord, why should we not endure evil?" The "good" here refers either to the temporal or to the eternal gifts of God, and the "evil" to the scourges of the present time, about which the Lord says through the prophet: "I am the Lord and there is no other. I form the light and create the darkness. I make peace and create evil."

"I form the light and create the darkness," for though outwardly these scourges create the darkness of anguish, inwardly knowledge enkindles the light in the mind. "I make peace and create evil," for peace with God is restored to us when those things which were rightly created for us, but are not ordinarily desired, are turned into scourges and become evil for us. It is through sin that we become opposed to God; therefore, it is fitting that we should return to his peace by way of scourges. In this manner, when everything created for good is turned into a source of pain for us, the mind of the chastened may be humbly renewed and restored to peace with the Creator.

We ought particularly to observe in Job's words how skillfully he meets his wife's persuading: "If we have received good from the hand of the Lord, why should we not endure evil?" It is a great comfort in tribulation if, in times of adversity, we recall the gifts our Creator has given us. Nor will overwhelming sorrow break us, if we quickly call to mind the gifts which have sustained us. For it is written: "On the day of prosperity do not forget affliction, and on the day of affliction do not forget prosperity." For if we receive God's gifts, but forget our affliction, we can fall through our own excessive joy. On the other hand, when we are bruised by the scourges, but are not at all consoled by the thought of the blessings we have been fortunate to receive, we are completely cast down.

Thus both attitudes must be united so that one may be supported by the other: the memory of the gift can temper the pain of the affliction, and the foreboding and fear of the affliction can modify the joy of the gift. And so the holy Job, to soothe his soul's depression in the midst of his wound, weighs the delightful gifts he has received even while he suffers from the scourges, saying: "If we have received good from the hand of the Lord, why should we not endure evil?"

Moral Reflections on Job 3, 15–16: PL 75, 606–608

Week of 7 Epiphany ✠ Saturday

A reading from a commentary on John by Cyril, Bishop of Alexandria [444]

In order, then, that we ourselves also may join together, and be blended into unity with God and with one another—although through the actual difference which exists in each of us we have a distinct individuality of soul and body—the Only-begotten has contrived means which his own due wisdom and counsel have sought out. For by one body, that is, his own, blessing through the mystery of the Eucharist those who believe in him, he makes us of the same body with himself and with one another.

Who could sunder or divide from their natural union with one another those who are knit together through his holy body, which is one in union with Christ? For if "we all partake of the one bread" we are all made one body; for Christ cannot suffer severance. Therefore, the Church has also become Christ's body, and we are also individually his members, according to the wisdom of Paul. Since all of us are united with Christ inasmuch as we have received him who is one and indivisible in our own bodies, we owe the service of our members to him rather than to ourselves.

The fact that those who partake of his holy flesh gain this actual physical unity with Christ is once more attested by Paul when he says, with reference to the mystery of godliness: "I am speaking of the mystery of Christ, unknown to people in former ages but now revealed by the Spirit to the holy apostles and prophets. It is no less than this: in Christ Jesus the Gentiles are now co-heirs with the Jews, members of the same body and sharers of the promise."

And if we are all of us of the same body with one another in Christ, and not only with one another but also with him who is in us through his flesh, are we not then all of us clearly one both with one another and with Christ? For Christ is the bond of union, since he is at once God and human.

With reference, then, to the unity that is by the Spirit (I mean the Holy Spirit), following in the same track of inquiry, we say once more that we all—receiving one and the same Spirit (I mean the Holy Spirit)—are somehow blended together with one another and with God. For although we are many, and Christ who is the Spirit of the Father and of his own Spirit dwells in each of us severally, the Spirit is still one and indivisible, binding together the dissevered spirits of the individualities of one and all of us.

We have a separate being in his own natural singleness into unity causing us all to be shown forth in him, through himself and as one. Just as the power of his holy flesh makes those in whom it exists to be of the same body, so also the indivisible Spirit of God who abides in all, being one, binds all together into spiritual unity.

Hence, the inspired Paul addresses us in this fashion: "Bear with one another lovingly. Make every effort to preserve the unity which has the Spirit as its origin and peace as its binding force. There is but one body and one Spirit, just as there is but one hope given all of you by your call. There is one Lord, one faith, one baptism; one God and Father of all, who is over all, and works through all, and is in all." For while the Spirit, who is one, abides in us, the one God and Father of all will be in us, binding together into unity with one another and with himself whatever partakes of the Spirit.

Commentary on John 11, 11: PG 74, 559–562

Week of 8 Epiphany ✠ Sunday

A reading from the Confessions of Augustine, Bishop of Hippo [430]

Lord, you know me. Let me know you. Let me come to know you even as I am known. You are the strength of my soul; enter it and make it a place suitable for your dwelling, a possession "without spot or blemish." This is my hope and the reason I speak. In this hope I rejoice, when I rejoice rightly. As for the other things of this life, the less they deserve tears, the more likely will they be lamented; and the more they deserve tears, the less likely will people sorrow for them. "For behold, you have loved the truth, because the one who does what is true enters into the light." I wish to do this truth before you alone by praising you, and before a multitude of witnesses by writing of you.

O Lord, the depths of my conscience lie exposed before your eyes. Could anything remain hidden in me, even though I did not want to confess it to you? In that case I would only be hiding you from myself, not myself from you. But now my sighs are sufficient evidence that I am displeased with myself; that you are my light and the source of my joy; that you are loved and desired. I am thoroughly ashamed of myself; I have renounced myself and chosen you, recognizing that I can please neither you nor myself unless you enable me to do so.

Whoever I may be, Lord, I lie exposed to your scrutiny. I have already told of the profit I gain when I confess to you. And I do not make my confession with bodily words, bodily speech, but with the words of my soul and the cry of my mind which you hear and understand. When I am wicked, my confession to you is an expression of displeasure with myself. But when I do good, it consists in not attributing this goodness to myself. "For you, O Lord, bless the just," but first "you justify the wicked." And so I make my confession before you in silence, and yet not in silence. My voice is silent, but my heart cries out.

You, O Lord, are my judge. "For though no one knows a person's innermost self except the spirit within," yet there is something within which even one's own spirit does not know. But you know all of a person, for you have made us all. As for me, I despise myself in your sight, knowing that I am but dust and ashes; yet I know something of you that I do not know of myself.

True, "we see now indistinctly as in a mirror, but not yet face to face." Therefore, so long as I am in exile from you, I am more present to myself than to you. Yet I do know that you cannot be overcome, while I am uncertain which temptations I can resist and which I cannot. Nevertheless, I have hope, because "you are faithful and do not allow us to be tempted beyond our endurance, but along with the temptation you give us the means to withstand it."

I will confess, therefore, what I know of myself, and also what I do not know. The knowledge that I have of myself, I possess because you have enlightened me; while the knowledge of myself that I do not yet possess will not be mine until my darkness shall be made as the noonday sun before your face.

Confessions 10, 1, 1–2, 2; 5, 7: CSEL 33, 226–227, 230–231

A reading from a commentary on the psalms by Ambrose,
Bishop of Milan [397]

We must always meditate on God's wisdom, keeping it in our hearts and on our lips. Your tongue must speak justice, the law of God must be in your heart. Hence Scripture tells you: "You shall speak of these commandments when you sit in your house, and when you walk along the way, and when you lie down, and when you get up." Let us then speak of the Lord Jesus, for he is wisdom, he is the word, the Word indeed of God.

It is also written: "Open your lips, and let God's word be heard." God's word is uttered by those who repeat Christ's teaching and meditate on his sayings. Let us always speak this word. When we speak about wisdom, we are speaking of Christ. When we speak about virtue, we are speaking of Christ. When we speak about justice, we are speaking of Christ. When we speak about peace, we are speaking of Christ. When we speak about truth and life and redemption, we are speaking of Christ.

"Open your lips," says Scripture, "and let God's word be heard." It is for you to open, it is for him to be heard. So David said: "I shall hear what the Lord says in me." The very Son of God says: "Open your lips, and I will fill them." Not all can attain to the perfection of wisdom as Solomon or Daniel did, but the spirit of wisdom is poured out on all according to their capacity, that is, on all the faithful. If you believe, you have the spirit of wisdom.

Meditate, then, at all times on the things of God, and speak the things of God, "when you sit in your house." By house we can understand the Church, or the secret place within us, so that we are to speak within ourselves. Speak with prudence, so as to avoid falling into sin, as by excess of talking. "When you sit in your house," speak to yourself as if you were a judge. "When you walk along the way," speak, so as never to be idle. You speak "along the way" if you speak in Christ, for Christ is the way. When you walk along the way, speak to yourself, speak to Christ. Hear him say to you: "I desire that in every place people should pray, lifting holy hands without anger or quarreling." When you lie down, speak so that the sleep of death may not steal upon you. Listen and learn how you are to speak as you lie down: "I will not give sleep to my eyes or slumber to my eyelids until I find a place for the Lord, a dwelling place for the God of Jacob."

When you get up or rise again, speak of Christ, so as to fulfill what you are commanded. Listen and learn how Christ is to awaken you from sleep. Your soul says: "I hear my brother knocking at the door." Then Christ says to you: "Open the door to me, my sister, my spouse." Listen and learn how you are to awaken Christ. Your soul says: "I charge you, daughters of Jerusalem, awaken or reawaken the love of my heart." Christ is that love.

Explanation on Psalm 36, 65–66: CSEL 64, 123–125

Week of 8 Epiphany ✠ Tuesday

A reading from a commentary on First John by Augustine, Bishop of Hippo [430]

We have been promised that "we shall be like him, for we shall see him as he is." By these words, the tongue has done its best; now we must apply the meditation of the heart. Although they are the words of Saint John, what are they in comparison with the divine reality? And how can we, so greatly inferior to John in merit, add anything of our own? Yet we have received, as John has told us, an anointing by the Holy One which teaches us inwardly more than our tongue can speak. Let us turn to this source of knowledge, and because at present you cannot see, make it your business to desire the divine vision.

The entire life of a good Christian is in fact an exercise of holy desire. You do not yet see what you long for, but the very act of desiring prepares you, so that when he comes you may see and be utterly satisfied.

Suppose you are going to fill some holder or container, and you know you will be given a large amount. Then you set about stretching your sack or wineskin or whatever it is. Why? Because you know the quantity you will have to put in it and your eyes tell you there is not enough room. By stretching it, therefore, you increase the capacity of the sack, and this is how God deals with us. Simply by making us wait he increases our desire, which in turn enlarges the capacity of our soul, making it able to receive what is to be given to us.

So let us continue to desire, for we shall be filled. Take note of Saint Paul stretching as it were his ability to receive what is to come: "Not that I have already obtained this," he said, "or am made perfect. I do not consider that I have already obtained it." We might ask: "If you have not yet obtained it, what are you doing in this life?" "This one thing I do," answers Paul, "forgetting what lies behind, and stretching forward to what lies ahead, I press on toward the prize to which I am called in the life above." Not only did Paul say he stretched forward, but he also declared that he pressed on toward a chosen goal. He realized in fact that he was still short of receiving "what no eye has seen, nor ear heard, nor the heart conceived."

Such is our Christian life. By desiring heaven we exercise the powers of our soul. Now this exercise will be effective only to the extent that we free ourselves from desires leading to infatuation with this world. Let me return to the example I have already used, of filling an empty container. God means to fill each of you with what is good; so cast out what is bad! If he wishes to fill you with honey and you are full of sour wine, where is the honey to go? The vessel must be emptied of its contents and then be cleansed. Yes, it must be cleansed even if you have to work hard and scour it. It must be made fit for the new thing, whatever it may be.

We may go on speaking figuratively of honey, gold or wine—but whatever we say we cannot express the reality we are to receive. The name of that reality is God. But who will claim that in that one syllable we utter the full expanse of our heart's desire? Therefore, whatever we say is necessarily less than the full truth. We must extend ourselves toward the measure of Christ so that when he comes he may fill us with his presence. "Then we shall be like him, for we shall see him as he is."

Treatise 4 on 1 John 6: PL 35, 2008–2009

Week of 8 Epiphany ✠ Wednesday

A reading from the Confessions of Augustine, Bishop of Hippo [430]

Where did I find you, that I came to know you? You were not within my memory before I learned of you. Where, then, did I find you before I came to know you, if not within yourself, far above me? We come to you and go from you, but no place is involved in this process. In every place, O Truth, you are present to those who seek your help, and at one and the same time you answer all, though they seek your counsel on different matters.

You respond clearly, but not everyone hears clearly. All ask what they wish, but do not always hear the answer they wish. Your best servant is intent not so much on hearing a petition answered, as rather on willing whatever that servant hears from you.

Late have I loved you, O Beauty ever ancient, ever new, late have I loved you! You were within me, but I was outside, and it was there that I searched for you. In my unloveliness I plunged into the lovely things which you created. You were with me, but I was not with you. Created things kept me from you; yet if they had not been in you they would not have been at all. You called, you shouted, and you broke through my deafness. You flashed, you shone, and you dispelled my blindness. You breathed your fragrance on me; I drew in breath and now I pant for you. I have tasted you; now I hunger and thirst for more. You touched me, and I burned for your peace.

When once I shall be united to you with my whole being, I shall at last be free of sorrow and toil. Then my life will be alive, filled entirely with you. When you fill us, you relieve us of our burdens, but because I am not yet filled with you, I am a burden to myself. My joy when I should be weeping struggles with my sorrows when I should be rejoicing. I know not where victory lies. Woe is me! Lord, have mercy on me! My evil sorrows and good joys are at war with one another. I know not where victory lies. Woe is me! Lord, have mercy! Woe is me! I make no effort to conceal my wounds. You are my physician, I your patient. You are merciful; I stand in need of mercy.

"Is not life upon earth a trial?" Who would want troubles and difficulties? You command us to endure them, not to love them. None love what they endure, though they may love the act of enduring. For even if they are happy to endure their own burdens, they would still prefer that the burdens not exist. I long for prosperity in times of adversity, and I fear adversity when times are good. Yet what middle ground is there between these two extremes where life would be other than trial? Pity the prosperity of this world, pity it once and again, for it corrupts joy and brings the fear of adversity. Pity the adversity of this world, pity it again, then a third time; for it fills us with a longing for prosperity, and because adversity itself is hard for us to bear and can even break our endurance. "Is not life upon earth a trial," a continuous trial?

There can be no hope for me except in your great mercy. Give me the grace to do as you command, and command me to do what you will! You command us to control our bodily desires. And, as we are told, when I knew that none can "be their own masters, except of God's bounty, I was wise enough already to know whence the gift came." Truly it is by continence that we are made as one and regain that unity of self which we lost by falling apart in the search for a variety of pleasures. For we love you so much the less if, besides you, we also love something else which we do not love for your sake. O Love ever burning, never quenched! O Charity, my God, set me on fire with your love! You command me to be continent. Give me the grace to do as you command, and command me to do what you will!

Confessions 10, 26–29: CSEL 33, 255–256

Week of 8 Epiphany ✠ Thursday

A reading from the Moral Reflections on Job by Gregory the Great, Bishop of Rome [604]

"Whoever is mocked by a friend, as I am, shall call upon God, and God shall hear." Weak-minded people are frequently diverted toward pursuing exterior happiness when the breath of popular favor accompanies their good actions. So they give up their own personal choices, preferring to remain at the mercy of whatever they hear from others. Thus, they rejoice not so much to become but to be called blessed. Eager for praise, they give up what they had begun to be; and so they are severed from God by the very means by which they appeared to be commendable in God.

But sometimes souls firmly strive for righteousness and yet are beset by ridicule. They do what is admirable but get only mockery. They might have gone out of themselves because of praise; they return to themselves when repelled by abuse. Finding no resting-place without, they cleave more intensely to God within. All their hope is fixed on their Creator, and amid all the ridicule and abuse they invoke their interior witness alone. Those who are afflicted in this way grow closer to God the more they turn away from human popularity. They straightway pour themselves out in prayer, and, pressured from without, they are refined with a more perfect purity to penetrate what is within.

In this context, the words apply: "Whoever is mocked by a friend, as I am, shall call upon God, and God shall hear." For while the wicked reproach the just, they show them whom they should look to as the witness of their actions. Thus afflicted, the soul strengthens itself by prayer; it is united within to one who listens from on high precisely because it is cut off externally from the praise of other people. Again, we should note how appropriately the words are inserted, "as I am." There are some people who are both oppressed by human mockery and are yet deprived of God's favorable hearing. For when the mockery is done to one's own sin, it obviously does not produce the merit that is due to virtue.

"The simplicity of the just is laughed to scorn." It is the wisdom of this world to conceal the heart with stratagems, to veil one's thoughts with words, to make what is false appear true and what is true appear false. On the other hand it is the wisdom of the just never to pretend anything for show, always to use words to express one's thoughts, to love the truth as it is and to avoid what is false, to do what is right without reward and to be more willing to put up with evil than to perpetrate it, not to seek revenge for wrong, and to consider as gain any insult for truth's sake. But this guilelessness is laughed to scorn, for the virtue of innocence is held as foolishness by the wise of this world. Anything that is done out of innocence, they doubtless consider to be stupidity, and whatever truth approves of, in practice is called folly by their worldly wisdom.

Moral Reflections on Job 10, 47–48: PL 75, 946–947

Week of 8 Epiphany ✠ Friday

A reading from a sermon of Bernard, Abbot of Clairvaux [1153]

Let us work for the food which does not perish—our salvation. Let us work in the vineyard of the Lord to earn our daily wage in the wisdom which says: "Those who work in me will not sin." Christ tells us: "The field is the world." Let us work in it and dig up wisdom, its hidden treasure, a treasure we all look for and want to obtain.

"If you are looking for it, really look. Be converted and come." Converted from what? "From your own willfulness." "But," you may say, "if I do not find wisdom in my own will, where shall I find it? My soul eagerly desires it. And I will not be satisfied when I find it, if it is not 'a generous amount, a full measure, overflowing into my hands.'" You are right, for "blessed is the one who finds wisdom and is full of prudence."

Look for wisdom while it can still be found. Call for it while it is near. Do you want to know how near it is? "The word is near you, in your heart and on your lips," provided that you seek it honestly. Insofar as you find wisdom in your heart, prudence will flow from your lips, but be careful that it flows from and not away from them, or that you do not vomit it up. If you have found wisdom, you have found honey. But do not eat so much that you become too full and bring it all up. Eat so that you are always hungry. Wisdom says: "Those who eat me continue to hunger." Do not think you have too much of it, but do not eat too much or you will throw it up. If you do, what you seem to have will be taken away from you, because you gave up searching too soon. While wisdom is near and while it can be found, look for it and ask for its help. Solomon says: "One who eats too much honey gets no good; similarly, the one who seeks personal glorification will be crushed by that same renown."

"Happy is the one who has found wisdom." Even more happy is the one "who lives in wisdom," for that person perceives its abundance.

There are three ways for wisdom or prudence to abound in you: if you confess your sins, if you give thanks and praise, and if your speech is edifying. "One believes with one's heart and so one is justified. One confesses with one's lips and so one is saved. In the beginning of the speech the just is self-accused," next the just gives glory to God, and thirdly, if wisdom extends that far, the just edifies the neighbor.

Sermon on Various, 15: PL 183, 577–579

Week of 8 Epiphany ✠ Saturday

A reading from the Catechetical Instructions of John Chrysostom, Bishop of Constantinople [407]

The Israelites witnessed marvels; you also will witness marvels, greater and more splendid than those which accompanied them on their departure from Egypt. You did not see Pharaoh drowned with his armies, but you have seen the devil with Satan's weapons overcome by the waters of baptism. The Israelites passed through the sea; you have passed from death to life. They were delivered from the Egyptians; you have been delivered from the powers of darkness. The Israelites were freed from slavery to a pagan people; you have been freed from the much greater slavery to sin.

Do you need another argument to show that the gifts you have received are greater than theirs? The Israelites could not look on the face of Moses in glory, though he was their fellow servant and kinsman. But you have seen the face of Christ in his glory. Paul cried out: "We see the glory of the Lord with faces unveiled."

In those days Christ was present to the Israelites as he followed them, but he is present to us in a much deeper sense. The Lord was with them because of the favor he showed to Moses; now he is with us not simply because of Moses but also because of your obedience. After Egypt they dwelt in desert places; after your departure you will dwell in heaven. Their great leader and commander was Moses; we have a new Moses, God himself, as our leader and commander.

What distinguished the first Moses? "Moses," Scripture tells us, "was more gentle than all who dwelt upon the earth." We can rightly say the same of the new Moses, for there was with him the very Spirit of gentleness, united to him in his inmost being. In those days Moses raised his hands to heaven and brought down manna, the bread of angels; the new Moses raises his hands to heaven and gives us the food of eternal life. Moses struck the rock and brought forth streams of water; Christ touches his table, strikes the spiritual rock of the new covenant and draws forth the living water of the Spirit. This rock is like a fountain in the midst of Christ's table, so that on all sides the flocks may draw near to this living spring and refresh themselves in the waters of salvation.

Since this fountain, this source of life, this table surrounds us with untold blessings and fills us with the gifts of the Spirit, let us approach it with sincerity of heart and purity of conscience to receive grace and mercy in our time of need. Grace and mercy be yours from the only-begotten Son, our Lord and Savior Jesus Christ; through him and with him be glory, honor and power to the Father and the life-giving Spirit, now and always and for ever.

Catechesis 3, 24–27: SC 50, 165–167

Week of Last Epiphany ✠ Sunday

A reading from a homily of Origen, Priest and Theologian [c. 254]

Christ is the "light of the world" and he enlightens the Church with his light. And as the moon receives its light from the sun so as in turn to enlighten the night, so does the Church, receiving her light from Christ, enlighten all who dwell in the night of ignorance. It is Christ, therefore, who is "the true light which gives light to every one coming into the world"; and the Church, receiving his light, becomes herself the "light of the world," "enlightening those in darkness," in accord with Christ's word to his disciples: "You are the light of the world." This goes to show that Christ is the light of the apostles, and the apostles in their turn are the light of the world.

The sun and the moon shed light on our bodies; in the same way Christ and the Church shed light on our minds. At least they enlighten them if we are not spiritually blind people. Just as the sun and the moon do not fail to shed their light on the blind who are unable to benefit by the light, so does Christ send his light into our minds; but we shall not receive any enlightenment if we meet it with blindness. If that is so, let the blind first follow Christ crying out: "Son of David, have pity on us." Then once they have recovered their sight, thanks to his favor, they will be able to benefit by the radiation of the splendor of the light.

Again, all who see are not equally illumined by Christ, but all are enlightened according to their capacity to receive the light. The eyes of our body are not equally enlightened by the sun. Also, the higher we climb in high places, and the higher the spot from which we contemplate the sunrise, the better we also perceive the sun's splendor and its warmth. The same is true of our mind.

The more we go up and rise Christward and expose ourselves to the splendor of his light, the more wonderfully and brilliantly we too shall be flooded with his brightness, as he said himself through the Prophet: "Come near to me and I shall come near to you, says the Lord." And elsewhere: "Am I a God near at hand only, says the Lord, and not a God far off?"

It is not by the same road, however, that all of us go to him, but "according to each one's abilities." We might go to him with the crowds and he would feed us with parables lest we faint in the way because we are fasting; or we might remain constantly at his feet intently listening to his words, without being anxious about diverse services, "having chosen the better portion" and we "shall not be deprived of it."

By coming closer to him we also receive more light from him. And if, like the apostles, we do not separate ourselves in the least from him and faithfully remain with him in all his tribulations, he then explains to us secretly what he had said to the crowds, and greater is the brightness with which he enlightens us.

Finally, if we can ascend with him to the top of the mountain, like Peter, James, and John, not only do we receive the enlightenment from Christ, but we hear the very voice of the Father.

Homily 1 on Genesis 5–7: SC 7, 70–73

Week of Last Epiphany ✠ Monday

A reading from the Catechetical Instructions of Cyril, Bishop of Jerusalem [386]

It is not alone among us, who are stamped with the name of Christ, that the dignity of faith is great. All the business of the world, even of those who are outside the Church, is accomplished by faith.

By faith, marriage joins together persons who are strangers to one another; the spouses, though they were formerly strangers, bestow their bodies and material possessions on one another because of their faith in the marriage contracts. By faith, agriculture is sustained; for a person endures the labor involved only because one believes that one will reap a harvest. By faith, seafarers entrust themselves to a tiny wooden vessel and exchange the solid land surface for the erratic movement of the waves; they surrender themselves to uncertain hopes and take with them a faith that is surer than any anchor.

Thus, most of human affairs depend on faith; and this holds good not only among us, but also, as I have already mentioned, among those who are outside the fold. Although they do not accept the Scriptures but advance certain doctrines of their own, they nonetheless receive these doctrines on faith!

Faith is the eye that enlightens every conscience and gives understanding; for the Prophet says: "Unless your faith is firm, you shall not understand." Faith closes the mouths of lions, according to Daniel; for Scripture says of him: "Daniel was removed from the den, unhurt because he trusted in his God."

Is anything more terrible than the devil? Yet, even against the devil, all we have is the armor of faith, a spiritual shield against an invisible enemy. For Satan lets fly manifold arrows, and shoots in the dark at those who are not vigilant. However, although the enemy remains invisible, we have our faith as a strong protection, according to the saying of the Apostle: "In all circumstances hold faith up before you as your shield; it will help you extinguish the fiery darts of the evil one."

Catechesis 5, 3–4: PG 33, 507–510

Week of Last Epiphany ✠ Tuesday

A reading from the First Letter to the Corinthians by Clement, Bishop of Rome [c. 100]

Let the one truly possessed by the love of Christ keep his commandments. Who can express the binding power of divine love? Who can find words for the splendor of its beauty? Beyond all description are the heights to which it lifts us. Love unites us to God; "it cancels innumerable sins," has no limits to its endurance, bears everything patiently. Love is neither servile nor arrogant. It does not provoke schisms or form cliques, but always acts in harmony with others. By it all God's chosen ones have been sanctified; without it, it is impossible to please him. Out of love the Lord took us to himself; because he loved us and it was God's will, our Lord Jesus Christ gave his life's blood for us—he gave his body for our body, his soul for our soul.

See then, beloved, what a great and wonderful thing love is, and how inexpressible its perfection. Who are worthy to possess it unless God makes them so? To him therefore we must turn, begging of his mercy that there may be found in us a love free from human partiality and beyond reproach. Every generation from Adam's time to ours has passed away; but those who by God's grace were made perfect in love have a dwelling now among the saints, and when at last the kingdom of Christ appears, they will be revealed. "Take shelter in your rooms for a little while," says Scripture, "until my wrath subsides. Then I will remember the good days, and will raise you from your graves."

Happy are we, beloved, if love enables us to live in harmony and in the observance of God's commandments, for then it will also gain for us the remission of our sins. Scripture pronounces "happy those whose transgressions are pardoned, whose sins are forgiven. Happy the one," it says, "to whom the Lord imputes no fault, on whose lips there is no guile." This is the blessing given those whom God has chosen through Jesus Christ our Lord. To him be glory for ever and ever.

First Letter to the Corinthians 49–50: Funk 1, 123–125

Week of Last Epiphany ✠ Ash Wednesday

A reading from a sermon of Peter Chrysologus, Bishop of Ravenna [450]

There are three things by which faith stands firm, devotion remains constant, and virtue endures. They are prayer, fasting and mercy. Prayer knocks at the door, fasting obtains, mercy receives. Prayer, mercy and fasting: these three are one, and they give life to each other.

Fasting is the soul of prayer, mercy is the lifeblood of fasting. Let no one try to separate them; they cannot be separated. If you have only one of them or not all together, you have nothing. So if you pray, fast; if you fast, show mercy; if you want your petition to be heard, hear the petition of others. If you do not close your ear to others you open God's ear to yourself.

When you fast, see the fasting of others. If you want God to know that you are hungry, know that another is hungry. If you hope for mercy, show mercy. If you look for kindness, show kindness. If you want to receive, give. If you ask for yourself what you deny to others, your asking is a mockery.

Let this be the pattern for all when they practice mercy: show mercy to others in the same way, with the same generosity, with the same promptness, as you want others to show mercy to you.

Therefore, let prayer, mercy and fasting be one single plea to God on our behalf, one speech in our defense, a threefold united prayer in our favor.

Let us use fasting to make up for what we have lost by despising others. Let us offer our souls in sacrifice by means of fasting. There is nothing more pleasing that we can offer to God, as the psalmist said in prophecy: "A sacrifice to God is a broken spirit; God does not despise a bruised and humbled heart."

Offer your soul to God, make him an oblation of your fasting, so that your soul may be a pure offering, a holy sacrifice, a living victim, remaining your own and at the same time made over to God. Whoever fails to give this to God will not be excused, for if you are to give him yourself you are never without the means of giving.

To make these acceptable, mercy must be added. Fasting bears no fruit unless it is watered by mercy. Fasting dries up when mercy dries up. Mercy is to fasting as rain is to the earth. However much you may cultivate your heart, clear the soil of your nature, root out vices, sow virtues. If you do not release the springs of mercy, your fasting will bear no fruit.

When you fast, if your mercy is thin your harvest will be thin; when you fast, what you pour out in mercy overflows into your barn. Therefore, do not lose by saving, but gather in by scattering. Give to the poor, and you give to yourself. You will not be allowed to keep what you have refused to give to others.

Sermon 43: PL 52, 320, 322

Week of Last Epiphany ✠ Thursday

A reading from the First Letter to the Corinthians by Clement, Bishop of Rome [c. 100]

Let us fix our attention on the blood of Christ and recognize how precious it is to God his Father, since it was shed for our salvation and brought the grace of repentance to all the world.

If we review the various ages of history, we will see that in every generation the Lord has "offered the opportunity of repentance" to any who were willing to turn to him. When Noah preached God's message of repentance, all who listened to him were saved. Jonah told the Ninevites they were going to be destroyed, but when they repented, their prayers gained God's forgiveness for their sins, and they were saved, even though they were not of God's people.

Under the inspiration of the Holy Spirit, the ministers of God's grace have spoken of repentance; indeed, the Master of the whole universe himself spoke of repentance with an oath: "As I live," says the Lord, "I do not wish the death of the sinner but the sinner's repentance." He added this evidence of his goodness: "House of Israel, repent of your wickedness. Tell my people: If their sins should reach from earth to heaven, if they are brighter than scarlet and blacker than sackcloth, you need only turn to me with your whole heart and say, 'Father,' and I will listen to you as to a holy people."

In other words, God wanted all his beloved ones to have the opportunity to repent and he confirmed this desire by his own almighty will. That is why we should obey his sovereign and glorious will and prayerfully entreat his mercy and kindness. We should be suppliant before him and turn to his compassion, rejecting empty works and quarreling and jealousy which only lead to death.

We should be humble in mind, putting aside all arrogance, pride and foolish anger. Rather, we should act in accordance with the Scriptures, as the Holy Spirit says: "The wise must not glory in wisdom nor the strong in strength nor the rich in riches. Rather, let the one who glories glory in the Lord, by seeking him and doing what is right and just." Recall especially what the Lord Jesus said when he taught gentleness and forbearance. "Be merciful," he said, "so that you may have mercy shown to you. Forgive, so that you may be forgiven. As you treat others, so you will be treated. As you give, so you will receive. As you judge, so you will be judged. As you are kind to others, so you will be treated kindly. The measure of your giving will be the measure of your receiving."

Let these commandments and precepts strengthen us to live in humble obedience to his sacred words. As Scripture asks: "Whom shall I look upon with favor except the humble, peaceful one who trembles at my words?"

Sharing then in the heritage of so many vast and glorious achievements, let us hasten toward the goal of peace, set before us from the beginning. Let us keep our eyes firmly fixed on the Father and Creator of the whole universe, and hold fast to his splendid and transcendent gifts of peace and all his blessings.

First Letter to The Corinthians 7, 4–8, 3; 8, 5–9, 1; 13, 1–4; 19, 2: Funk 1, 71–73, 77–78, 87

Week of Last Epiphany ✠ Friday

A reading from the Moral Reflections on Job by Gregory the Great, Bishop of Rome [604]

Since the daybreak or the dawn is changed gradually from darkness into light, the Church, which comprises the elect, is fittingly styled daybreak or dawn. While she is being led from the night of infidelity to the light of faith, she is opened gradually to the splendor of heavenly brightness, just as dawn yields to the day after darkness. The Song of Songs says aptly: "Who is this who moves forward like the advancing dawn?" Holy Church, inasmuch as she keeps searching for the rewards of eternal life, has been called the dawn. While she turns her back on the darkness of sins, she begins to shine with the light of righteousness.

This reference to the dawn conjures up a still more subtle consideration. The dawn intimates that the night is over; it does not yet proclaim the full light of day. While it dispels the darkness and welcomes the light, it holds both of them, the one mixed with the other, as it were. Are not all of us who follow the truth in this life daybreak and dawn? While we do some things which already belong to the light, we are not free from the remnants of darkness. In Scripture the prophet says to God: "No living being will be justified in your sight." Scripture also says: "In many ways all of us give offense."

When he writes: "the night is passed," Paul does not add, "the day is come," but rather, "the day is at hand." Since he argues that after the night has passed, the day as yet is not come but is rather at hand, he shows that the period before full daylight and after darkness is without doubt the dawn, and that he himself is living in that period.

It will be fully day for the Church of the elect when she is no longer darkened by the shadow of sin. It will be fully day for her when she shines with the perfect brilliance of interior light. This dawn is aptly shown to be an ongoing process when Scripture says: "And you showed the dawn its place." A thing which is shown its place is certainly called from one place to another. What is the place of the dawn but the perfect clearness of eternal vision? When the dawn has been brought there, it will retain nothing belonging to the darkness of night. When the Psalmist writes: "My soul thirsts for the living God; when shall I go and see the face of God?," does the psalm not refer to the effort made by the dawn to reach its place? Paul was hastening to the place which he knew the dawn would reach when he said he wished to die and to be with Christ. He expressed the same idea when he said: "For me to live is Christ, and to die is gain."

Moral Reflections on Job 29, 2–4: PL 76, 478–480

Week of Last Epiphany ✠ Saturday

A reading from a sermon of Augustine, Bishop of Hippo [430]

Stretching out his hand over his disciples, the Lord Christ declared: "Here are my mother and my brothers; anyone who does the will of my Father who sent me is my brother and sister and my mother." I would urge you to ponder these words. Did the Virgin Mary, who believed by faith and conceived by faith, who was the chosen one from whom our Savior was born among us, who was created by Christ before Christ was created in her—did she not do the will of the Father? Indeed the blessed Mary certainly did the Father's will, and so it was for her a greater thing to have been Christ's disciple than to have been his mother, and she was more blessed in her discipleship than in her motherhood. Hers was the happiness of first bearing in her womb him whom she would obey as her master.

Now listen and see if the words of Scripture do not agree with what I have said. The Lord was passing by and crowds were following him. His miracles gave proof of divine power and a woman cried out: "Happy is the womb that bore you, blessed is that womb!" But the Lord, not wishing people to seek happiness in a purely physical relationship, replied: "More blessed are those who hear the word of God and keep it." Mary heard God's word and kept it, and so she is blessed. She kept God's truth in her mind, a nobler thing than carrying his body in her womb. The truth and the body were both Christ: he was kept in Mary's mind insofar as he is truth, he was carried in her womb insofar as he is human; but what is kept in the mind is of a higher order than what is carried in the womb.

The Virgin Mary is both holy and blessed, and yet the Church is greater than she. Mary is a part of the Church, a member of the Church, a holy, an eminent—the most eminent—member, but still only a member of the entire body. The body undoubtedly is greater than she, one of its members. This body has the Lord for its head, and head and body together make up the whole Christ. In other words, our head is divine—our head is God.

Now, beloved, give me your whole attention, for you also are members of Christ; you also are the body of Christ. Consider how you yourselves can be among those of whom the Lord said: "Here are my mother and my brothers." Do you wonder how you can be the mother of Christ? He himself said: "Whoever hears and fulfills the will of my Father in heaven is my brother and my sister and my mother." As for our being the brothers and sisters of Christ, we can understand this because although there is only one inheritance and Christ is the only Son, his mercy would not allow him to remain alone. It was his wish that we too should be heirs of the Father, and co-heirs with himself.

Now having said that all of you are brothers and sisters of Christ, shall I not dare to call you his mother? Much less would I dare to deny his own words. Tell me how Mary became the mother of Christ, if it was not by giving birth to the members of Christ? You, to whom I am speaking, are the members of Christ. Of whom were you born? "Of Mother Church," I hear the reply of your hearts. You became children of this mother at your baptism, you came to birth then as members of Christ. Now you in your turn must draw to the font of baptism as many as you possibly can. You became children when you were born there yourselves, and now by bringing others to birth in the same way, you have it in your power to become the mothers of Christ.

Sermon 25, 7–8: PL 46, 937–938

1 Lent
To Trinity Sunday

Week of 1 Lent ✠ Sunday

A reading from a commentary on the psalms by Augustine,
Bishop of Hippo [430]

The body of Christ, the one Church of Christ, the unity which is ourselves, cries out from the end of the earth: "Hear, O God, my cry; listen to my prayer! From the earth's end I call to you." From the earth's end, that is, from everywhere. But why have I called? Because "my heart grows faint."

One who prays thus is present to the nations of the whole world, which is a great glory, but in the midst of great trials. Our life in this earthly pilgrimage cannot be without trials, our progress can only be by way of our trials, and we do not know ourselves if we have not suffered temptation. There is no reward for the one who has not persevered, no victory for the one who has not fought, no fighting except in face of the enemy or in temptation.

This person crying out from the end of the earth, then, is faint, but not left alone. For it is ourselves, that is to say our body, which the Savior willed to prefigure in his own body in which he died, rose again, and ascended into heaven, so that the members could be sure of reaching where the head had gone before. So he had represented us in his own person when he willed to be tempted by Satan.

We read in the gospel that our Lord Jesus Christ was tempted in the wilderness by the devil. In Christ you were tempted, because Christ had taken his flesh from you to give you his salvation, his death from you to give you his life, his insults from you to give you his honor, and the temptations from you to give you his victory.

If we have been tempted in him, in him also we triumph over the devil. You are perfectly aware that Christ was tempted, but do you not see that he has carried off the victory? Recognize yourself in him in his temptation, recognize yourself in him in his victory. He could have prevented the devil from coming to him; but had he not been tempted how could he have taught us how to overcome temptation?

Moreover, there is nothing surprising in the fact that, harassed by temptations, he cried out from the end of the earth. But how is it that he is not overcome? "You will set me high upon a rock." From this we see who it is that is crying out from the earth's end. Remember the gospel: "On this rock I will build my Church." She it is, then, who cries out from the earth's end, the Church whom he had wished to build on the rock.

But who became rock so that the Church could be built on the rock? Listen to St. Paul who says: "The rock was Christ." So on him we are built up. That is why this rock on which we are constructed was the first to be buffetted by winds, flood and rains when Christ was tempted by the devil. This is the immovable foundation on which he willed to set us. So our voice does not cry out in vain, but it is heard. We are in a place of hope: "You will set me on a rock."

Commentary on Psalm 60, 2–3: CCL 39, 766–767

Week of 1 Lent ✠ Monday

A reading from the Travels of Egeria, Abbess, and Pilgrim to Jerusalem [late fourth century]

When the season of Lent is at hand, it is observed in the following manner. Now whereas with us the forty days preceding Easter are observed, here they observe the eight weeks before Easter. This is the reason why they observe eight weeks: On Sundays and Saturdays they do not fast, except on the one Saturday which is the vigil of Easter, when it is necessary to fast. Except on that day, there is absolutely no fasting here on Saturdays at any time during the year. And so, when eight Sundays and seven Saturdays have been deducted from the eight weeks—for it is necessary, as I have just said, to fast on one Saturday—there remain forty-one days which are spent in fasting, which are called here "eortae," that is to say, Lent.

This is a summary of the fasting practices here during Lent. There are some who, having eaten on Sunday after the dismissal, that is, at the fifth or the sixth hour, do not eat again for the whole week until Saturday, following the dismissal from the Anastasis. These are the ones who observe the full week's fast. Having eaten once in the morning on Saturday, they do not eat again in the evening, but only on the following day, on Sunday, that is, do they eat after the dismissal from the church at the fifth hour or later. Afterwards, they do not eat again until the following Saturday, as I have already said. Such is their fate during the Lenten season that they take no leavened bread (for this cannot be eaten at all), no olive oil, nothing which comes from trees, but only water and a little flour soup. And this is what is done throughout Lent.

Pilgrimage 27–28: SC 296, 256–258, 264–266

Week of 1 Lent ✠ Tuesday

A reading from a sermon of Leo the Great, Bishop of Rome [461]

Our understanding, which is enlightened by the Spirit of truth, should receive with purity and freedom of heart the glory of the cross as it shines in heaven and on earth. It should see with inner vision the meaning of the Lord's words when he spoke of the imminence of his passion: "The hour has come for the Son of Man to be glorified." Afterward he said: "Now my soul is troubled, and what am I to say? Father, save me from this hour. But it was for this that I came to this hour. Father, glorify your Son." When the voice of the Father came from heaven, saying: "I have glorified him, and will glorify him again," Jesus said in reply to those around him: "It was not for me that this voice spoke, but for you. Now is the judgment of the world, now will the prince of this world be cast out. And I, if I am lifted up from the earth, will draw all things to myself."

How marvelous the power of the cross; how great beyond all telling the glory of the passion: here is the judgment-seat of the Lord, the condemnation of the world, the supremacy of Christ crucified.

Lord, you drew all things to yourself so that the devotion of all peoples everywhere might celebrate, in a sacrament made perfect and visible, what was carried out in the one temple of Judaea under obscure fore-shadowings.

Now there is a more distinguished order of levites, a greater dignity for the rank of elders, a more sacred anointing for the priesthood, because your cross is the source of all blessings, the cause of all graces. Through the cross the faithful receive strength from weakness, glory from dishonor, life from death.

The different sacrifices of animals are no more: the one offering of your body and blood is the fulfillment of all the different sacrificial offerings, for you are the true "Lamb of God: you take away the sins of the world." In yourself you bring to perfection all mysteries, so that, as there is one sacrifice in place of all other sacrificial offerings, there is also one kingdom gathered from all peoples.

Dearly beloved, let us then acknowledge what Saint Paul, the teacher of the nations, acknowledged so exultantly: "This is a saying worthy of trust, worthy of complete acceptance: Christ Jesus came into this world to save sinners."

God's compassion for us is all the more wonderful because Christ died, not for the righteous or the holy but for the wicked and the sinful, and, though the divine nature could not be touched by the sting of death, he took to himself, through his birth as one of us, something he could offer on our behalf.

The power of his death once confronted our death. In the words of Hosea the prophet: "Death, I shall be your death; grave, I shall swallow you up." By dying he submitted to the laws of the underworld; by rising again he destroyed them. He did away with the everlasting character of death so as to make death a thing of time, not of eternity. "As all die in Adam, so all will be brought to life in Christ."

Sermon 8 for the Lord's Passion 6–8: PL 54, 340–342

Week of 1 Lent ✠ Wednesday

A reading from the treatise On the Lord's Prayer by Cyprian, Bishop and Martyr of Carthage [258]

The Master of peace and unity would not have each of us pray singly and severally, since when we pray we are not to pray only for ourselves. For we neither say: "My Father, who art in heaven" nor "Give me this day my bread"; nor does each one of us individually pray for our own debt to be forgiven, nor do we ask that we ourselves alone should not be led into temptation, nor that we only should be delivered from evil.

Our prayer is general and for all; and when we pray, we pray not for one person but for us all, because we are all one. God, the Master of peace and concord, so willed that one should pray for all, even as he himself bore us all.

The three youths in the fiery furnace kept this rule of prayer, being in unison in prayer and agreeing in spirit. The authority of the Scriptures tells us this, and in teaching how they prayed it gives an example which we ought to imitate in our prayers, so that we might become like them. "Then these three," it says: "with one voice sang, glorifying and blessing God." They sang with one voice although Christ had not yet taught them to pray. Hence their words in prayer were effectual, because the Lord was gained by simple, peaceful, and spiritual praying.

We find that the apostles too prayed in this way after the Lord's ascension: "Together," we are told: "they devoted themselves: [with one accord] to constant prayer."

"This is how you are to pray," Christ said: " Our Father in heaven. " This new person, born again, restored to God by grace, says first of all "Father" because this one has now become an heir. "To his own he came, yet his own did not accept him. Any who did accept him he empowered to become children of God." So any who have believed in his name and have become children of God ought now to begin to offer thanks and to declare themselves God's children, when they speak of God as their Father in heaven.

How indulgent it is of the Lord, what exuberance of condescension and goodness toward us, to permit us when praying in God's presence to address ourselves to God as Father, and name ourselves children of God, even as Christ is Son of God—a name which none of us would have dared to reach in prayer, had he himself not allowed us so to pray.

We should therefore recollect and feel that, when we call God a Father, we ought to act like children of God, and if it comforts us to regard him as our Father, let us so act that he may be comforted in us. Let us conduct ourselves as temples of God, and God will remain in us.

On the Lord's Prayer 8-9, 11: CSEL 3, 271-272, 274

Week of 1 Lent ✠ Thursday

A reading from the Five Hundred Chapters by Maximus the Confessor, Abbot [662]

Charity is a right attitude of mind which prefers nothing to the knowledge of God. If we possess any strong attachment to the things of this earth, we cannot possess true charity. For anyone who really loves God prefers to know and experience God rather than his creatures. The whole set and longing of such a person's mind is ever directed toward God.

For God is far superior to all his creation, since everything which exists has been made by God and for God. And so, in deserting God, who is beyond compare, for the inferior works of creation, we show that we value God, the author of creation, less than creation itself.

The Lord himself reminds us: "Whoever loves me will keep my commandments. And this is my commandment: that you love one another." So the one who does not love a neighbor does not obey God's command. But one who does not obey his command cannot love God. One is blessed if one can love all people equally. Moreover, if one truly loves

God, one must love one's neighbor absolutely. Such a one cannot hoard wealth. Rather, like God himself, one generously gives from one's own resources to all according to their needs.

Since one imitates God's generosity, the only distinction one draws is the person's need. Such a person does not distinguish between a good person and a bad one, a just person and one who is unjust. Yet personal goodness of will makes the one who strives after virtue preferred to the one who is depraved.

A charitable mind is not displayed simply in giving money; it is manifested still more by personal service as well as by the communication of God's word to others. In fact, if service toward one's brothers and sisters is genuine and if one really renounces worldly concerns, one is freed from selfish desires. For one now shares in God's own knowledge and love. Since one does possess God's love, one does not experience weariness as one follows the Lord God. Rather, after the prophet Jeremiah, one withstands every type of reproach and hardship without even harboring an evil thought toward any person.

For Jeremiah warns us: "Do not say: 'We are the Lord's temple.'" Neither should you say: "Faith alone in our Lord Jesus Christ can save me." By itself faith accomplishes nothing. For even the devils believe and shudder. No, faith must be joined to an active love of God which is expressed in good works. The charitable person is distinguished by sincere and long-suffering service to others: it also means using things aright.

Five Hundred Chapters 1, 4–5, 16–17, 23–24, 26–28, 30–40: PG 90, 962–967

Week of 1 Lent ✠ Friday

A reading from a commentary on the Song of Songs by Gregory, Bishop of Nyssa [c. 394]

No one who has given thought to the way we talk about God can adequately grasp the terms pertaining to God. "Mother," for example, is mentioned [in the Song of Songs 3:11] instead of "father." Both terms mean the same, because there is neither male nor female in God. How, after all, could anything transitory like this be attributed to the Deity, when this is not permanent even for us human beings, since when we all become one in Christ we are divested of the signs of this difference along with the whole of our old humanity? Therefore every name we invent is of the same adequacy for indicating God's ineffable nature, since neither "male" nor "female" can defile the meaning of God's pure nature. Hence, in the Gospel [Matthew 22:2] a father is said to give a marriage feast for his son , while the prophet addresses God [Psalm 21:3] saying "You have set a crown of precious stones upon his head" and the Song asserts that the crown was put on the bridegroom's head by his mother. Since, then, there is one wedding feast and the bride is one and the crown is placed on the head of the bridegroom by a single agent, it does not make much difference whether God calls his Only-begotten "Son of God" or "Son of his love" as Paul puts it [Colossians 1:13].

Homily 7 on the Song of Songs: Jaeger 6, 212–213; PG 44, 916.

Week of 1 Lent ✠ Saturday

A reading from the Travels of Egeria, Abbess, and Pilgrim to Jerusalem [late fourth century]

I must also describe how those who are baptized at Easter are instructed. Those who give their names do so the day before Lent, and the priest notes down all their names; and this is before those eight weeks during which, as I have said, Lent is observed here. When the priest has noted down everyone's name, then on the following day, the first day of Lent, on which the eight weeks begin, a throne is set up for the bishop in the center of the major church, the Martyrium. The priests sit on stools on both sides, and all the clergy stand around. One by one the candidates are led forward, in such a way that the men come with their godfathers and the women with their godmothers.

Then the bishop questions individually the neighbors of the one who has come up, inquiring: "Does this person lead a good life? Obey parents? Is this person a drunkard or a liar?" And the bishop seeks out in the candidate other vices which are more serious. If the person proves to be guiltless in all these matters concerning which the bishop has questioned the witnesses who are present, the bishop notes down the candidate's name. If, however, the candidate is accused of anything, the bishop orders the person to go out and says: "Let such a one amend their life, and when this is done, then approach the baptismal font." He makes the same inquiry of both men and women. If, however, some are strangers, such people cannot easily receive baptism, unless they have witnesses who know them.

Ladies, my sisters, I must describe this, lest you think that it is done without explanation. It is the custom here, throughout the forty days on which there is fasting, for those who are preparing for baptism to be exorcised by the clergy early in the morning, as soon as the dismissal from the morning service has been given at the Anastasis. Immediately a throne is placed for the bishop in the major church, the Martyrium. All those who are to be baptized, both men and women, sit closely around the bishop, while the godmothers and godfathers stand there; and indeed all of the people who wish to listen may enter and sit down, provided they are of the faithful. A catechumen, however, may not enter at the time when the bishop is teaching them the law. The bishop does so in this way: beginning with Genesis and going through the whole of Scripture during these forty days, expounding first its literal meaning and then explaining the spiritual meaning. In the course of these days everything is taught not only about the Resurrection but concerning the body of faith. This is called catechetics.

When five weeks of instruction have been completed, they then receive the Creed. The bishop explains the meaning of each of the phrases of the Creed in the same way as Holy Scripture was explained, expounding first the literal and then the spiritual sense. In this fashion the Creed is taught.

And thus it is that in these places all the faithful are able to follow the Scriptures when they are read in the churches, because all are taught through those forty days, that is, from the first to the third hours, for during the three hours instruction is given. God knows, ladies, my sisters, that the voices of the faithful who have come to catechetics to hear instruction on those things being said or explained by the bishop are louder than when the bishop sits down in church to preach about each of those matters which are explained in this fashion. The dismissal from catechetics is given at the third hour, and immediately, singing hymns, they lead the bishop to the Anastasis, and the office of the third hour takes place. And thus they are taught for three hours a day for seven weeks. During the eighth week, the one which is called the Great Week, there remains no more time for them to be taught, because what has been mentioned above must be carried out.

Now when seven weeks have gone by and there remains only Holy Week, which is here called the Great Week, then the bishop comes in the morning to the major church, the Martyrium. To the rear, at the apse behind the altar, a throne is placed for the bishop, and one by one they come forth, the men with their godfathers, the women with their godmothers. And each one recites the Creed back to the bishop. After the Creed has been recited back to the bishop, the bishop delivers a homily to them all, and says: "During these seven weeks you have been instructed in the whole law of the Scriptures, and you have heard about the faith. You have also heard of the resurrection of the flesh. But as for the whole explanation of the Creed, you have heard only that which you are able to know while you are still catechumens. Because you are still catechumens, you are not able to know those things which belong to a still higher mystery, that of baptism. But that you may not think that anything would be done without explanation, once you have been baptized in the name of God, you will hear of them during the eight days of Easter in the Anastasis following the dismissal from church. Because you are still catechumens, the most secret of the divine mysteries cannot be told to you.''

Pilgrimage 45–46; SC 296, 304–312

Week of 2 Lent ✠ Sunday

A reading from the Compendium of Theology by Thomas Aquinas, Priest and Friar [1274]

According to God's providential design, everything which exists is given the means to attain the end befitting its nature. Human beings too, in order to obtain what they hope for from God, have received a means adapted to the human condition. This condition obliges us to use a humble form of request or prayer to obtain what we hope for from others, especially if the person addressed is our superior.

For this cause people are exhorted to pray in order to obtain from God those things which they hope to receive from him. But the requisite prayer is different according to whether it is a question of obtaining something from another person or from God.

When a request is addressed to a person, it must first of all express the desire and need of the petitioner. We also need to move the heart of the person implored into granting the request. Now these two elements have no place in prayer made to God. When we pray, we do not have to worry about making our desires and needs plain to God who knows them all. In the words of the psalmist: "Lord, all my desire is before you." And we read in the gospel: "Your Father knows what you need."

There is no question either of moving the divine will, by the power of human words, into willing something other than the original divine purpose, for it is written in the Book of Numbers: "God is not a human that he should speak falsely, nor mortal, that he should change," and in the Book of Samuel: "He is not a human that he should repent."

Yet prayer is necessary to us in order to obtain grace from God; and this on account of the petitioner's own self, so that we can reflect on our own deficiencies and move our hearts to desire fervently and devotedly what we hope to obtain by prayer. This is how we make ourselves fit to receive.

There is another difference distinguishing prayer made to God from that addressed to people. Prayer addressed to a human being demands at the outset a certain degree of familiarity thanks to which the petitioner is sure of access to the one implored. However, prayer to God by itself makes us intimates of God, as our souls rise toward him, converse affectionately with him, and adore him in spirit and in truth.

This intimacy acquired through prayer encourages us to apply ourselves to prayer with confidence. For this cause it is written in the Psalm: "I call upon you" (that is, I pray confidently), "for you will answer me, O God." At the first prayer, the psalmist was received into the intimacy of God, and returns to pray thereafter with increased confidence. And so, in prayer to God, perseverance in or insistence on the request is not wearisome but indeed acceptable to God; as it is written in the gospel: "You ought always to pray and not lose heart"; and elsewhere the Lord bids us: "Ask, and you will receive. Knock, and it will be opened to you."

Compendium of Theology 2, 1: Vives 5, 27; Lynch, 314–315

Week of 2 Lent ✠ Monday

A reading from the Catechetical Instructions of Cyril, Bishop of Jerusalem [386]

The Catholic Church glories in every deed of Christ. Her supreme glory, however, is the cross. Well aware of this, Paul says: "God forbid that I glory in anything but the cross of our Lord Jesus Christ!"

At Siloam, there was a sense of wonder, and rightly so. A man born blind recovered his sight. But of what importance is this, when there are so many blind people in the world? Lazarus rose from the dead, but even this only affected Lazarus. What of those countless numbers who have died because of their sins? Those five miraculous loaves fed five thousand people. Yet this is a small number compared to those all over the world who were starved by ignorance. After eighteen years a woman was freed from the bondage of Satan. But are we not all shackled by the chains of our own sins?

For us all, however, the cross is the crown of victory! It has brought light to those blinded by ignorance. It has released those enslaved by sin. Indeed, it has redeemed the whole of humankind!

Do not, then, be ashamed of the cross of Christ; rather, glory in it. Although it is a stumbling block to the Jews and folly to the Gentiles, the message of the cross is our salvation. Of course it is folly to those who are perishing, but to us who are being saved it is the power of God. For it was not a mere human being who died for us, but the Son of God, God-made-human.

In the Mosaic law a sacrificial lamb banished the destroyer. But now "it is the Lamb of God who takes away the sin of the world." Will he not free us from our sins even more? The blood of an animal, a sheep, brought salvation. Will not the blood of the only-begotten Son bring us greater salvation?

He was not killed by violence, he was not forced to give up his life. His was a willing sacrifice. Listen to his own words: "I have the power to lay down my life and to take it up again." Yes, he willingly submitted to his own passion. He took joy in his achievement; in his crown of victory he was glad and in the salvation of humanity he rejoiced. He did not blush at the cross for by it he was to save the world. No, it was not a lowly human being who suffered, but God incarnate. He entered the contest for the reward he would win by his patient endurance.

Certainly in times of tranquillity the cross should give you joy. But maintain the same faith in times of persecution. Otherwise you will be a friend of Jesus in times of peace and his enemy during war. Now you receive the forgiveness of your sins and the generous gift of grace from your king. When war comes, fight courageously for him.

Jesus never sinned; yet he was crucified for you. Will you refuse to be crucified for him, who for your sake was nailed to the cross? You are not the one who gives the favor; you have received one first. For your sake he was crucified on Golgotha. Now you are returning his favor; you are fulfilling your debt to him.

Catechesis 13, 1, 3, 6, 23: PG 33, 771–774, 779, 802

Week of 2 Lent ✠ Tuesday

A reading from The City of God by Augustine, Bishop of Hippo [430]

We Christians call rulers happy if they rule with justice; if amid the voices of exalted praise and the reverent salutations of excessive humility, they are not inflated with pride, but remember that they are but mortal; if they put their power at the service of God's majesty, to extend his worship far and wide; if they fear God, love him and worship him; if, more than their earthly kingdom, they love that realm where they do not fear to share the kingship; if they are slow to punish, but ready to pardon; if they take vengeance on wrong because of the necessity to direct and protect the state, and not to satisfy their personal animosity; if they grant pardon not to allow impunity to wrong-doing but in the hope of amendment of the wrong-doer; if, when they are obliged to take severe decisions, as must often happen, they compensate this with the gentleness of their mercy and the generosity of their benefits; if they restrain their self-indulgent appetites all the more because they are more free to gratify them, and prefer to have command over their lower desires than over any number of subject peoples; and if they do all this not for a burning desire for empty glory, but for the love of eternal blessedness; and if they do not fail to offer to their true God, as a sacrifice for their sins, the oblation of humility, compassion, and prayer.

It is Christian rulers of this kind whom we call happy.

City of God 5, 24: CCL 47, 160

Week of 2 Lent ✠ Wednesday

A reading from the treatise On the Six Days of Creation by Ambrose, Bishop of Milan [397]

If evil is not something that has no principle from which it springs, as is the case of the uncreated Being; and if it is not something that God has made, where does it come from? For no wise person will deny the existence of evil in this world. We are all familiar with the evil of death. But from what we have said it is evident that evil is not a living substance. It is a pervasion of mind and spirit, swerving from the way of true virtue, which frequently overtakes the unwary.

We see also that the greater danger does not come from outside us. It comes from our very selves. The enemy is within us. Within us is the progenitor of our error; within us, I say, dwells our adversary. Hence, we must examine our aims, explore the habits of our minds, be watchful over our thoughts and over the desires of our heart.

You yourself are the cause of your wickedness. You yourself are the commander of your shameful acts, and the instigator of your crimes. Why blame another agent as an excuse for your own faults? Oh! that you would not incite yourself, that you would not rush heedlessly on, that you would not entangle yourself in immoderate endeavors, or in indignation and passionate desires, for these hold you captive as in nets.

Most certainly it belongs to us, and we are able to moderate our endeavors, to restrain our anger, to curb our desires. But we can also yield to wantonness, foster evil passions, inflame our anger or give ear to those who incite to anger, become puffed up with pride, or give in to fits of anger instead of humbly lowering ourselves and lovingly practicing gentleness.

Hence, why should we accuse "nature"? There are impediments in nature; there is old age and infirmity. But both have also advantages: old age brings more friendly manners, gives more useful counsels, inspires more readiness to accept death, and helps curb evil passions more easily. The weakness of the body too has as counterpart the sobriety of mind. Hence, the Apostle says: "When I am powerless, it is then I am strong." Accordingly, he gloried in his infirmities, and not in his powers. And there came to him the luminous and salutary answer that "in weakness power is made perfect."

Let us therefore not seek for causes outside ourselves nor blame others for them. Let us acknowledge our guilt. For we must willingly attribute to ourselves, not to others, whatever evil we can avoid doing when we so choose.

The Six Days of Creation 1, 31–32: CSEL 32, 1, 29–33

Week of 2 Lent ✠ Thursday

A reading from the book addressed to Autolycus by
Theophilus, Bishop of Antioch [late second century]

If you say: "Show me your God," I will say to you: "Show me what kind of person you are, and I will show you my God." Show me then whether the eyes of your mind can see, and the ears of your heart hear.

It is like this. Those who can see with the eyes of their bodies are aware of what is happening in this life on earth. They get to know things that are different from each other. They distinguish light and darkness, ugliness and beauty, elegance and inelegance, proportion and lack of proportion, excess and defect. The same is true of the sounds we hear: high or low or pleasant. So it is with the ears of our heart and the eyes of our mind in their capacity to hear or see God.

God is seen by those who have the capacity to see him, provided that they keep the eyes of their mind open. All have eyes, but some have eyes that are shrouded in darkness, unable to see the light of the sun. Because the blind cannot see it, it does not follow that the sun does not shine. The blind must trace the cause back to themselves and their eyes. In the same way, you have eyes in your mind that are shrouded in darkness because of your sins and evil deeds.

A person's soul should be clean, like a mirror reflecting light. If there is rust on the mirror one's face cannot be seen in it. In the same way, no one who has sin within can see God.

But if you will you can be healed. Hand yourself over to the doctor, who will open the eyes of your mind and heart. Who is to be the doctor? It is God, who heals and gives life through his Word and wisdom. Through his Word and wisdom he created the universe, for "by his Word the heavens were established, and by his Spirit all their array." His wisdom is supreme. God "by wisdom founded the earth, by understanding he arranged the heavens, by his knowledge the depths broke forth and the clouds poured out the dew."

If you understand this, and live in purity and holiness and justice, you may see God. But, before all, faith and the fear of God must take the first place in your heart, and then you will understand all this. When you have laid aside mortality and been clothed in immortality, then you will see God according to your merits. God raises up your flesh to immortality along with your soul, and then, once made immortal, you will see the immortal One, if you believe in him now.

To Autolycus 1, 2, 7: PG 6, 1026–1027, 1035

Week of 2 Lent ✠ Friday

A reading from the treatise Against Heresies by Irenaeus, Bishop of Lyons [c. 202]

In the book of Deuteronomy Moses says to the people: "The Lord your God made a covenant on Horeb; he made this covenant, not with your ancestors but with you." Why did God not make this covenant with their ancestors? Because "the law is not aimed at the righteous." Their ancestors were righteous: they had the power of the Decalogue implanted in their hearts and in their souls. That is, they loved the God who made them and did nothing unjust against their neighbor. For this reason they did not need to be admonished by written rebukes: they had the righteousness of the law in their hearts.

When this righteousness and love for God had passed into oblivion and been extinguished in Egypt, God had necessarily to reveal himself through his own voice, out of his great love for us. He led the people out of Egypt in power, so that they might once again become God's disciples and followers. He made them afraid as they listened, to warn them not to hold their Creator in contempt.

He fed them with manna, that they might receive spiritual food. In the book of Deuteronomy Moses says: "He fed you with manna, which your parents did not know, that you might understand that humanity will not live by bread alone but will live by every word of God coming from the mouth of God."

He commanded them to love himself and trained them to practice righteousness toward their neighbor, so that they might not be unrighteous or unworthy of God. Through the Decalogue he prepared them for friendship with himself and for harmony with their neighbors. This was to their advantage, though God needed nothing from them.

This raised humans to glory, for it gave them what they did not have, friendship with God. But it brought no advantage to God, for God did not need their love. Humankind did not possess the glory of God, nor could they attain it by any other means than through obedience to God. This is why Moses said to the people: "Choose life, that you may live and your descendants too; love the Lord your God, hear his voice and hold fast to him, for this is life for you and length of days."

This was the life that the Lord was preparing humanity to receive when he spoke in person and gave the words of the Decalogue for all alike to hear. These words remain with us as well; they were extended and amplified through his coming in the flesh, but not annulled.

God gave to the people separately through Moses the commandments that enslave: these were precepts suited to their instruction or their condemnation. As Moses said: "The Lord commanded me at that time to teach you precepts of righteousness and of judgment." The precepts that were given them to enslave and to serve as a warning have been cancelled by the new covenant of freedom. The precepts that belong to human nature and to freedom and to all alike have been enlarged and broadened. Through the adoption of heirs God had enabled humanity so generously and bountifully to know him as Father, to love him with the whole heart, and to follow his Word unfailingly.

Against Heresies 4, 16, 2–5: SC 100, 564–572

Week of 2 Lent ✠ Saturday

A reading from the Exhortation to Martyrdom by Origen,
Priest and Theologian [c. 254]

If passing from unbelief to faith means that we have "passed from death to life," we should not be surprised to find that "the world hates us." Anyone who has not "passed from death to life" is incapable of loving those who have departed from death's dark dwelling place to enter a dwelling "made of living stones" and filled with the light of life. Jesus "laid down his life for us;" so we too should lay down our lives, I will not say for him, but for ourselves and also, surely, for those who will be helped by the example of our martyrdom.

Now is the time for Christians to rejoice, since Scripture says that "we should rejoice in our sufferings, knowing that suffering trains us to endure with patience, patient endurance makes us pleasing to God, and being pleasing to God gives us ground for a hope that will not be disappointed." Only let "the love of God be poured forth in our hearts through the Holy Spirit."

"The more we share in the sufferings of Christ, the more we share, through him, in his consolation." We should be extremely eager to share in Christ's sufferings and to let them be multiplied in us if we desire the superabundant consolation that will be given to those who mourn. This consolation will not perhaps be the same for all, for if it were, Scripture would not say: "The more we share in the sufferings of Christ, the more we share in his consolation." Sharing in his consolation will be proportionate to our sharing in his suffering. We learn this from one who could say with all confidence: "We know that as you share in the sufferings, so you will share in the consolation as well."

God says through the prophet: "At an acceptable time I heard you; on the day of salvation I helped you." What time could be more acceptable than when, for our fidelity to God in Christ, we are made a public spectacle and led away under guard, not defeated but triumphant?

In Christ and with Christ the martyrs disarm the principalities and powers and share in his triumph over them, for their share in Christ's sufferings makes them sharers also in the mighty deeds those sufferings accomplished. What could more appropriately be called the day of salvation than the day of such a glorious departure from this world? But I entreat you "not to give offense to anyone, so that our ministry may not be blamed. Be very patient and show in every way that you are servants of God." Say: "And now, what do I wait for? Is it not the Lord?"

Exhortation to Martyrdom 41–42: PG 11, 618–619

Week of 3 Lent ✠ Sunday

A reading from a commentary on John by Augustine, Bishop of Hippo [430]

Let us applaud and give thanks that we have become not only Christians but Christ himself. Do you understand, beloved, the grace that God our head has given us? Be filled with wonder and joy—we have become veritable Christs. If he is the head and we are the members, we form one complete human being with him. This is what the apostle Paul says: "Let us, then, be children no longer, tossed here and there, carried about by every wind of doctrine."

He had said previously: "Till we become one in faith and in the knowledge of God's Son, and form that perfect human who is Christ come to full stature." "Christ come to full stature" is made up of head and members. What is meant by the head and members? Christ and his Church. It would be arrogance on our part to arrogate this prerogative to ourselves if he himself had not promised it to us by telling us through his Apostle: "You are the body of Christ. Every one of you is a member of it."

Thus, when the Father shows his works to Christ's members, it is to Christ that he shows them. This constitutes an astounding but true prodigy; the Father shows to Christ something that Christ knows, and he shows it to Christ through Christ. It is a remarkable and surprising prodigy, but one confirmed by sacred Scripture. Are we going to contradict its teachings? Should we not rather try to understand them and render thanks to the author of this precious gift?

What does it mean to say that the Father shows his works to Christ through Christ? He shows them to the members through the head. Here is an example taken from yourself. Suppose you wish to take hold of some object with your eyes closed. Your hand does not know where to go, yet your hand is a member of yours, for it has not been separated from your body. Open your eyes, and your hand will now see where it must go; the member follows the way indicated to it by the head.

Therefore, if an example can be found in you of the truth that your body can show something to your body, do not be surprised that I have said that the Father shows his works to Christ through Christ. For the head shows so that the members might see, and the head teaches so that the members might learn; yet head and members constitute only one person.

Far from separating himself from us he willed to unite himself to us by the closest of unions. He was far from us, and an immense distance existed between us. What greater distance is there than the one existing between God and us, between justice and iniquity, between eternity and mortality? This is how far removed was the Word who was God and in God from the beginning, and through whom all things were made. How then did he get close enough to us to become what we are and to unite himself so intimately to us? "The Word became flesh and made his dwelling among us."

Treatise 21 on John 8–9: CCL 36, 216–217

Week of 3 Lent ✠ Monday

A reading from a sermon of Baldwin, Archbishop of Canterbury [1190]

The Lord knows the thoughts and intentions of our hearts. Without a doubt, every one of them is known to him, while we know only those which he lets us read by the grace of discernment. Our spirit does not know all that is in us, nor all of the thoughts which we have, willingly or unwillingly. We do not always perceive our thoughts as they really are. Having clouded vision, we do not discern them clearly with our mind's eye.

Often under the guise of devotion a suggestion occurs to our mind—coming from our own thoughts or from another person or from the tempter—and in God's eyes we do not deserve any reward for our virtue. For there are certain imitations of true virtues as also of vices which play tricks with the heart and bedazzle the mind's vision. As a result, the appearance of goodness often seems to be in something which is evil, and equally the appearance of evil seems to be in something good. This is part of our wretchedness and ignorance, causing us anguish and anxiety.

It has been written: "There are paths which seem to be right, but which in the end lead to hell." To avoid this peril, Saint John gives us these words of advice: "Test the spirits to see if they are from God." Now no one can test the spirits to see if they are from God unless God has given us discernment of spirits to enable us to investigate spiritual thoughts, inclinations and intentions with honest and true judgment. Discernment is the mother of all the virtues; everyone needs it either to guide the lives of others or to direct and reform our own lives.

In the sphere of action, a right thought is one ruled by the will of God, and intentions are holy when directed single-mindedly toward him. In a word, we could see clearly through any action of ours, or into our entire lives, if we had a simple eye. A simple eye is an eye, and it is simple. This means that we see by right thinking what is to be done, and by our good intention we carry it out with simple honesty, because deceitful action is wrong. Right thinking does not permit mistakes; a good intention rules out pretense. This then is true discernment, a combination of right thinking and good intention.

Therefore, we must do all our actions in the light of discernment as if in God and in his presence.

Treatise 6: PL 204, 466–467

A reading from a sermon of Gregory of Nazianzus, Bishop of Constantinople [389]

Recognize to whom you owe the fact that you exist, that you breathe, that you understand, that you are wise, and, above all, that you know God and hope for the kingdom of heaven and the vision of glory, now darkly and as in a mirror but then with greater fullness and purity. You have been made a child of God, co-heir with Christ. Where did you get all this, and from whom?

Let me turn to what is of less importance: the visible world around us. What benefactor has enabled you to look out upon the beauty of the sky, the sun in its course, the circle of the moon, the countless number of stars, with the harmony and order that are theirs, like the music of a harp? Who has blessed you with rain, with the art of husbandry, with different kinds of food, with the arts, with houses, with laws, with states, with a life of humanity and culture, with friendship and the easy familiarity of kinship?

Who has given you dominion over animals, those that are tame and those that provide you with food? Who has made you master of everything on earth? In short, who has endowed you with all that makes humankind superior to all other living creatures?

Is it not God who asks you now in your turn to show yourself generous above all other creatures and for the sake of all other creatures? Because we have received from him so many wonderful gifts, will we not be ashamed to refuse him this one thing only, our generosity? Though he is God and Lord he is not afraid to be known as our Father. Shall we for our part repudiate those who are our kith and kin?

Friends, let us never allow ourselves to misuse what has been given us by God's gift. If we do, we shall hear Saint Peter say: "Be ashamed of yourselves for holding on to what belongs to someone else. Resolve to imitate God's justice, and no one will be poor." Let us not labor to heap up and hoard riches while others remain in need. If we do, the prophet Amos will speak out against us with sharp and threatening words: "Come now, you that say: When will the new moon be over, so that we may start selling? When will sabbath be over, so that we may start opening our treasures?"

Let us put into practice the supreme and primary law of God. He sends down rain on just and sinful alike, and causes the sun to rise on all without distinction. To all earth's creatures he has given the broad earth, the springs, the rivers and the forests. He has given the air to the birds, and the waters to those who live in water. He has given abundantly to all the basic needs of life, not as a private possession, not restricted by law, not divided by boundaries, but as common to all, amply and in rich measure. His gifts are not deficient in any way, because he wanted to give equality of blessing to equality of worth, and to show the abundance of his generosity.

Oration 14, On the Love of the Poor, 23-25: PG 35, 887-890

Week of 3 Lent ✠ Wednesday

A reading from the reconstructed Primitive Rule of 1210 by Francis of Assisi, Friar [1226]

The Rule and Life of the brothers is this: to live in obedience, in chastity and without property, and to follow the teaching and the footsteps of Christ, who says: "If you will be perfect, go and sell what you have, and give to the poor, and you will have treasure in heaven; and come, and follow me"; and: "If any want to become my followers, let them deny themselves and take up the cross daily, and follow me"; and again: "If anyone come to me, and hate not father, and mother, and wife, and children, and brothers, and sisters, yea, and life also, that one cannot be my disciple"; and: "Everyone that has forsaken father, or mother, or brothers, or sisters, or wife, or children, or houses, or lands for my name's sake, shall receive an hundredfold, and shall inherit eternal life."

If anyone, by divine inspiration and willing to accept this life, shall come to the brothers, let him be kindly received by them; and he must sell all his goods and be careful to give everything to the poor. And let all the brothers be dressed in simple clothes and let them patch them with sackcloth or other rags with the blessing of God; for our Lord says: "They which are gorgeously apparelled, and live delicately, are in royal courts." And they may eat anything that is set before them according to the Gospel: "Eat such things as are set before you."

None of the brothers shall have any power or domination, especially among themselves. As our Lord says in the Gospel: "The princes of the Gentiles exercise dominion over them, and they that are great exercise authority over them, but it shall not be so among" the friars; but "whosoever would be the greatest" among them "let that one be their minister" and servant; and, " whoever is greatest among them let that one be as the younger." And no one is to be called prior; but all alike shall be called brothers. And let them wash one another's feet.

Moorman, Sources, 38-54: Mandic 1924, 122-123

A reading from the treatise On Prayer by Tertullian,
Theologian [c. 225]

Prayer is the offering in spirit that has done away with the sacrifices of old. "What good do I receive from the multiplicity of your sacrifices?" asks God. "I have had enough of burnt offerings of rams, and I do not want the fat of lambs and the blood of bulls and goats. Who has asked for these from your hands?"

What God has asked for we learn from the Gospel. "The hour will come," he says: "when true worshipers will worship the Father in spirit and in truth. God is a spirit," and so he looks for worshipers who are like himself.

We are true worshipers and true priests. We pray in spirit, and so offer in spirit the sacrifice of prayer. Prayer is an offering that belongs to God and is acceptable to him: it is the offering he has asked for, the offering he planned as his own.

We must dedicate this offering with our whole heart, we must fatten it on faith, tend it by truth, keep it unblemished through innocence and clean through chastity, and crown it with love. We must escort it to the altar of God in a procession of good works to the sound of psalms and hymns. Then it will gain for us all that we ask of God.

Since God asks for prayer offered in spirit and in truth, how can he deny anything to this kind of prayer? How great is the evidence of its power, as we read and hear and believe.

Of old, prayer was able to rescue from fire and beasts and hunger, even before it received its perfection from Christ. How much greater then is the power of Christian prayer. No longer does prayer bring an angel of comfort to the heart of a fiery furnace, or close up the mouths of lions, or transport to the hungry food from the fields. No longer does it remove all sense of pain by the grace it wins for others. But it gives the armor of patience to those who suffer, who feel pain, who are distressed. It strengthens the power of grace, so that faith may know what it is gaining from the Lord, and understand what it is suffering for the name of God.

In the past prayer was able to bring down punishment, rout armies, withhold the blessing of rain. Now, however, the prayer of the just turns aside the whole anger of God, keeps vigil for its enemies, pleads for persecutors. Is it any wonder that it can call down water from heaven when it could obtain fire from heaven as well? Prayer is the one thing that can conquer God. But Christ has willed that it should work no evil, and has given it all power over good.

Its only art is to call back the souls of the dead from the very journey into death, to give strength to the weak, to heal the sick, to exorcise the possessed, to open prison cells, to free the innocent from their chains. Prayer cleanses from sin, drives away temptations, stamps out persecutions, comforts the faint-hearted, gives new strength to the courageous, brings travelers safely home, calms the waves, confounds robbers, feeds the poor, overrules the rich, lifts up the fallen, supports those who are falling, sustains those who stand firm.

All the angels pray. Every creature prays. Cattle and wild beasts pray and bend the knee. As they come from their barns and caves they look up to heaven and call out, lifting up their spirit in their own fashion. The birds too rise and lift themselves up to heaven: they open out their wings, instead of hands, in the form of a cross, and give voice to what seems to be a prayer.

What more need be said on the duty of prayer? Even the Lord himself prayed. To him be honor and power for ever and ever.

On Prayer 28–29: CCL 1, 273–274

Week of 3 Lent ✠ Friday

A reading from a homily of Basil the Great, Bishop of Caesarea [379]

"The wise must not boast of wisdom, nor the strong of strength, nor the rich of riches." What then is the right kind of boasting? What is the source of human greatness? Scripture says: "The one who boasts must boast of this, of knowing and understanding that I am the Lord." Here is our greatness, here is our glory and majesty: to know in truth what is great, to hold fast to it, and to seek glory from the Lord of glory. The Apostle tells us: "The one who boasts must boast of the Lord." He has just said: "Christ was appointed by God to be our wisdom, our righteousness, our sanctification, our redemption, so that, as it is written, one who boasts must boast of the Lord."

Boasting of God is perfect and complete when we take no pride in our own righteousness but acknowledge that we are utterly lacking in true righteousness and have been made righteous only by faith in Christ.

Paul boasts of the fact that he holds his own righteousness in contempt and seeks the righteousness in faith that comes through Christ and is from God. He wants only to know Christ and the power of his resurrection and to have fellowship with his sufferings by taking on the likeness of his death, in the hope that somehow he may arrive at the resurrection of the dead.

Here we see all overweening pride laid low. Humanity, there is nothing left for you to boast of, for your boasting and hope lie in putting to death all that is your own and seeking the future life that is in Christ. Since we have its firstfruits we are already in its midst, living entirely in the grace and gift of God.

"It is God who is active within us, giving us both the will and the achievement, in accordance with his good purpose." Through his Spirit, God also reveals his wisdom in the plan he has preordained for our glory.

God gives power and strength in our labors. "I have toiled harder than all others," Paul says: "but it is not I but the grace of God, which is with me."

God rescues us from dangers beyond all human expectation. "We felt within ourselves that we had received the sentence of death, so that we might not trust in ourselves but in God, who raises the dead; from so great a danger did he deliver us, and does deliver us; we hope in him, for he will deliver us again."

Homily 20, on Humility, 3: PG 31, 530–531

Week of 3 Lent ✠ Saturday

A reading from a sermon of Gregory of Nazianzus, Bishop of Constantinople [389]

"Blessed are the merciful, because they shall obtain mercy," says the Scripture. Mercy is not the least of the beatitudes. Again: "Blessed is the one who is considerate to the needy and the poor." Once more: "Generous is the one who is merciful and lends." In another place: "All day the just is merciful and lends." Let us lay hold of this blessing, let us earn the name of being considerate, let us be generous.

Not even night should interrupt you in your duty of mercy. Do not say: "Come back and I will give you something tomorrow." There should be no delay between your intention and your good deed. Generosity is the one thing that cannot admit of delay.

"Share your bread with the hungry, and bring the needy and the homeless into your house," with a joyful and eager heart. "Whoever who does acts of mercy should do so with cheerfulness." The grace of a good deed is doubled when it is done with promptness and speed. What is given with bad grace or against one's will is distasteful and far from praiseworthy.

When we perform an act of kindness we should rejoice and not be sad about it. "If you undo the shackles and the thongs," says Isaiah, that is, if you do away with miserliness and counting the cost, with hesitation and grumbling, what will be the result? Something great and wonderful! What a marvelous reward there will be: "Your light will break forth like the dawn, and your healing will rise up quickly." Who would not aspire to light and healing?

If you think that I have something to say, servants of Christ, his co-heirs, let us visit Christ whenever we may; let us care for him, feed him, clothe him, welcome him, honor him, not only at a meal, as some have done, or by anointing him, as Mary did, or only by lending him a tomb, like Joseph of Arimathaea, or by arranging for his burial, like Nicodemus, who loved Christ half-heartedly, or by giving him gold, frankincense and myrrh, like the Magi before all these others. The Lord of all asks for mercy, not sacrifice, and mercy is greater than myriads of fattened lambs. Let us then show him mercy in the persons of the poor and those who today are lying on the ground, so that when we come to leave this world they may receive us into everlasting dwelling places, in Christ our Lord himself, to whom be glory for ever and ever.

Oration 14, On the Love of the Poor, 38, 40: PG 35, 907, 910

Week of 4 Lent ✠ Sunday

A reading from a sermon of Augustine, Bishop of Hippo [430]

Christ gave sight to one blind from birth; why do we marvel? Christ is the Savior; by an act of mercy he imparted a benefit which he had failed to give in the womb. Now when he failed to give that man eyes, it was surely not a mistake on his part; he simply deferred doing so until another time when he would give them to him through a miracle. You might be saying to yourselves: "How do you know this?" I know it from the Lord himself; he just said so, and we all heard it together.

When his disciples asked him: "Rabbi, was it his sin or that of his parents that caused him to be born blind," you yourselves heard, as I did, what answer he made. "It was no sin, either of this man or of his parents. Rather, it was to let God's works show forth in him." This was the reason why he had put off granting him the use of his eyes. He did not give then what he could give—and which he knew he would give—later, when the right moment would arrive.

Do not suppose that this man's parents had no sin, or that he himself had not at birth contracted original sin, for the remission of which sin infants are baptized. But this blindness was not the result of his parents' sin or of his own; "it was only to let God's works show forth in him."

Listen to the testimony of one who was blind and has recovered sight. Consider what misfortune it is for those who have stumbled against the cross because they did not want to confess their blindness to the Physician! The law had continued with them. But what good was the law without grace? Unhappy ones, what can the law do without grace? What can the earth accomplish without the spittle of Christ? What does the earth do without grace except make them more guilty? Why? Because those who hear the law and do not keep it are by that very fact sinners and prevaricators!

What can the law do without grace? What does the Apostle say to us—the ones who now see and have been enlightened from blindness? "If the law that was given was such that it could impart life, then justice would be a consequence of the law." If it could not impart life, why was it given? The Apostle goes on to add: "In fact, however, Scripture has locked all things in under the constraint of sin. Why? So that the promise might be fulfilled in those who believe, in consequence of faith in Jesus Christ."

You have received the law, and you wished to keep it, but you were not able; you have fallen through pride and realized your weakness. Run to the Physician and wash your face. Long for Christ, confess Christ, believe in Christ; the Spirit will be added to the letter, and you will be saved. If you take away the Spirit from the letter, the letter kills, and then what hope will remain? But the Spirit gives life.

Sermon 136, 1, 5: PL 38, 750-751, 753

Week of 4 Lent ✠ Monday

A reading from a homily of Origen, Priest and Theologian [c. 254]

Once a year the high priest, leaving the people outside, entered that place where no one except the high priest might enter. In it was the mercy-seat, and above the mercy-seat the cherubim, as well as the ark of the covenant and the altar of incense.

Let me turn to my true high priest, the Lord Jesus Christ. In our human nature he spent the whole year in the company of the people, the year that he spoke of when he said: "He sent me to bring good news to the poor, to announce the acceptable year of the Lord, and the day of forgiveness." Notice how once in that year, on the day of atonement, he enters into the holy of holies. Having fulfilled God's plan, he passes through the heavens and enters into the presence of the Father to make him turn in mercy to the human race and to pray for all who believe in him.

John the apostle, knowing of the atonement that Christ makes to the Father for all humanity, says this: "Little children, I say these things so that you may not sin. But if we have sinned we have an advocate with the Father, Jesus Christ, the righteous, and he is the atonement for our sins." In the same way Paul refers to this atonement when he says of Christ: "God appointed him to be the atonement for our sins in his blood, through faith." We have then a day of atonement that remains until the world comes to an end.

God's word tells us: "The high priest shall put incense on the fire in the sight of the Lord. The smoke of the incense shall cover the mercy-seat above the tokens of the covenant, so that he may not die. He shall take some of the blood of the bull-calf and sprinkle it with his finger over the mercy-seat toward the east."

God taught the people of the old covenant how to celebrate the ritual offered to him in atonement for sins. But you have come to Christ, the true high priest. Through his blood he has made God turn to you in mercy and has reconciled you with the Father. You must not think simply of ordinary blood but you must learn to recognize instead the blood of the Word. Listen to him as he tells you: "This is my blood, which will be shed for you for the forgiveness of sins."

There is a deeper meaning in the fact that the high priest sprinkles the blood toward the east. Atonement comes to you from the east. From the east comes the one whose name is Dayspring, he who is mediator between God and humankind. You are invited then to look always to the east: it is there that the sun of righteousness rises for you, it is there that the light is always being born for you. You are never to walk in darkness; the great and final day is not to enfold you in darkness. Do not let the night and mist of ignorance steal upon you. So that you may always enjoy the light of knowledge, keep always in the daylight of faith, hold fast always to the light of love and peace.

Homily 9 on Leviticus 5, 10: PG 12, 515, 523

Week of 4 Lent ✠ Tuesday

A reading from a sermon of Leo the Great, Bishop of Rome [461]

In the gospel of John the Lord says: "In this will all know that you are my disciples, if you have love for each other." In a letter of the same apostle we read: "Beloved, let us love one another, for love is from God, and everyone who loves is born of God and knows God; whoever does not love does not know God, for God is love."

The faithful should therefore enter into themselves and make a true judgment on their attitudes of mind and heart. If they find some store of love's fruit in their hearts, they must not doubt God's presence within them. If they would increase their capacity to receive so great a guest, they should practice greater generosity in doing good, with persevering charity.

If God is love, charity should know no limit, for God cannot be confined.

Any time is the right time for works of charity, but these days of Lent provide a special encouragement. Those who want to be present at the Lord's Passover in holiness of mind and body should seek above all to win this grace, for charity contains all other virtues and covers a multitude of sins.

As we prepare to celebrate that greatest of all mysteries, by which the blood of Jesus Christ did away with our sins, let us first of all make ready the sacrificial offerings of works of mercy. In this way we shall give to those who have sinned against us what God in his goodness has already given to us.

Let us now extend to the poor and those afflicted in different ways a more open-handed generosity, so that God may be thanked through many voices and the relief of the needy supported by our fasting. No act of devotion on the part of the faithful gives God more pleasure than that which is lavished on his poor. Where he finds charity with its loving concern, there he recognizes the reflection of his own fatherly care.

In these acts of giving do not fear a lack of means. A generous spirit is itself great wealth. There can be no shortage of material for generosity where it is Christ who feeds and Christ who is fed. In all this activity there is present the hand of him who multiplies the bread by breaking it, and increases it by giving it away.

The givers of alms should be free from anxiety and full of joy. Their gain will be greatest when they keep back least for themselves. The holy apostle Paul tells us: "He who provides seed for the sower will also provide bread for eating; he will provide you with more seed, and will increase the harvest of your goodness," in Christ Jesus our Lord, who lives and reigns with the Father and the Holy Spirit for ever and ever.

Sermon 10 for Lent 3–5: PL 54, 299–301

Week of 4 Lent ✠ Wednesday

A reading from a letter by Maximus the Confessor, Abbot [662]

God's will is to save us, and nothing pleases him more than our coming back to him with true repentance. The heralds of truth and the ministers of divine grace have told us this from the beginning, repeating it in every age. Indeed, God's desire for our salvation is the primary and preeminent sign of his infinite goodness. It was precisely in order to show that there is nothing closer to God's heart that the divine Word of God the Father, with untold condescension, lived among us in the flesh, and did, suffered, and said all that was necessary to reconcile us to God the Father, when we were at enmity with him, and to restore us to the life of blessedness from which we had been exiled. He healed our physical infirmities by miracles; he freed us from our sins, many and grievous as they were, by suffering and dying, taking them upon himself as if he were answerable for them, sinless though he was. He also taught us in many different ways that we should wish to imitate him by our own kindness and genuine love for one another.

So it was that Christ proclaimed that he had come to call sinners to repentance, not the righteous, and that it was not the healthy who required a doctor, but the sick. He declared that he had come to look for the sheep that was lost, and that it was to the lost sheep of the house of Israel that he had been sent. Speaking more obscurely in the parable of the silver coin, he tells us that the purpose of his coming was to reclaim the royal image, which had become coated with the filth of sin. "You can be sure that there is joy in heaven," he said, "over one sinner who repents."

To give the same lesson he revived the man who, having fallen into the hands of brigands, had been left stripped and half-dead from his wounds; he poured wine and oil on the wounds, bandaged them, placed the man on his own mule and brought him to an inn, where he left sufficient money to have him cared for, and promised to repay any further expense on his return.

Again, he told of how that Father, who is goodness itself, was moved with pity for his profligate son who returned and made amends by repentance; how he embraced him, dressed him once more in the fine garments that befitted his own dignity, and did not reproach him for any of his sins.

So too, when he found wandering in the mountains and hills the one sheep that had strayed from God's flock of a hundred, he brought it back to the fold, but he did not exhaust it by driving it ahead of him. Instead, he placed it on his own shoulders and so, compassionately, he restored it safely to the flock.

So also he cried out: "Come to me, all you that toil and are heavy of heart. Accept my yoke," he said, by which he meant his commands, or rather, the whole way of life that he taught us in the Gospel. He then speaks of a burden, but that is only because repentance seems difficult. In fact, however: "my yoke is easy," he assures us, "and my burden is light."

Then again he instructs us in divine justice and goodness, telling us to be like our heavenly Father, holy, perfect and merciful. "Forgive," he says: "and you will be forgiven. Behave toward other people as you would wish them to behave toward you."

Letter 11: PG 91, 454–455

Week of 4 Lent ✠ Thursday

A reading from a sermon of Leo the Great, Bishop of Rome [461]

Dear friends, at every moment "the earth is full of the mercy of God," and nature itself is a lesson for all the faithful in the worship of God. The heavens, the sea and all that is in them bear witness to the goodness and omnipotence of their Creator, and the marvelous beauty of the elements as they obey him demands from the intelligent creation a fitting expression of its gratitude.

But with the return of that season marked out in a special way by the mystery of our redemption, and of the days that lead up to the paschal feast, we are summoned more urgently to prepare ourselves by a purification of spirit.

The special note of the paschal feast is this: the whole Church rejoices in the forgiveness of sins. It rejoices in the forgiveness not only of those who are then reborn in holy baptism but also of those who are already numbered among God's adopted children.

Initially, we are made new by the rebirth of baptism. Yet there is still required a daily renewal to repair the shortcomings of our mortal nature, and whatever degree of progress has been made there is no one who should not be more advanced. All must therefore strive to ensure that on the day of redemption no one may be found in the sins of the former life.

Dear friends, what the Christian should be doing at all times should be done now with greater care and devotion, so that the Lenten fast enjoined by the apostles may be fulfilled, not simply by abstinence from food but above all by the renunciation of sin.

There is no more profitable practice as a companion to holy and spiritual fasting than that of almsgiving. This embraces under the single name of mercy many excellent works of devotion, so that the good intentions of all the faithful may be of equal value, even where their means are not. The love that we owe both God and each other is always free from any obstacle that would prevent us from having a good intention. The angels sang: "Glory to God in the highest, and peace to his people on earth." The person who shows love and compassion to those in any kind of affliction is blessed, not only with the virtue of good will but also with the gift of peace.

The works of mercy are innumerable. Their very variety brings this advantage to those who are true Christians, that in the matter of almsgiving not only the rich and affluent but also those of average means and the poor are able to play their part. Those who are unequal in their capacity to give can be equal in the love within their hearts.

Sermon 6 for Lent 1–2: PL 54, 285–287

Week of 4 Lent ✠ Friday

A reading from a homily of John Chrysostom, Bishop of Constantinople [407]

Prayer and converse with God is a supreme good: it is a partnership and union with God. As the eyes of the body are enlightened when they see light, so our spirit, when it is intent on God, is illumined by his infinite light. I do not mean the prayer of outward observance but prayer from the heart, not confined to fixed times or periods but continuous throughout the day and night.

Our spirit should be quick to reach out toward God, not only when it is engaged in meditation; at other times also, when it is carrying out its duties, caring for the needy, performing works of charity, giving generously in the service of others, our spirit should long for God and call him to mind, so that these works may be seasoned with the salt of God's love, and so make a palatable offering to the Lord of the universe. Throughout the whole of our lives we may enjoy the benefit that comes from prayer if we devote a great deal of time to it.

Prayer is the light of the spirit, true knowledge of God, mediating between God and humanity. The spirit, raised up to heaven by prayer, clings to God with the utmost tenderness; like a child crying tearfully for its mother, it craves the milk that God provides. It seeks the satisfaction of its own desires, and receives gifts outweighing the whole world of nature.

Prayer stands before God as an honored ambassador. It gives joy to the spirit, peace to the heart. I speak of prayer, not words. It is the longing for God, love too deep for words, a gift given to us only by God's grace. The apostle Paul says: "We do not know how we are to pray but the Spirit himself pleads for us with inexpressible longings."

When the Lord gives this kind of prayer to us, he gives us riches that cannot be taken away, heavenly food that satisfies the spirit. One who tastes this food is set on fire with an eternal longing for the Lord: such a person's spirit burns as in a fire of the utmost intensity.

Supp. Homily 6, on Prayer: PG 64, 462–465

Week of 4 Lent ✠ Saturday

A reading from the treatise Against Heresies by Irenaeus, Bishop of Lyons [c. 202]

Our Lord, the Word of God, first drew human beings to God as servants, but later he freed those made subject to him. He himself testified to this: "I do not call you servants any longer, for a servant does not know what the master is doing. Instead I call you friends, since I have made known to you everything that I have learned from my Father." Friendship with God brings the gift of immortality to those who accept it.

In the beginning God created Adam, not because he needed humans, but because he wanted to have someone on whom to bestow his blessings. Not only before Adam but also before all creation, the Word was glorifying the Father in whom he dwelt, and was himself being glorified by the Father. The Word himself said: "Father, glorify me with that glory that I had with you before the world was."

Nor did the Lord need our service. He commanded us to follow him, but his was the gift of salvation. To follow the Savior is to share in salvation; to follow the light is to enjoy the light. Those who are in the light do not illuminate the light but are themselves illuminated and enlightened by the light. They add nothing to the light; rather, they are beneficiaries, for they are enlightened by the light.

The same is true of service to God: it adds nothing to God, nor does God need our service. Rather, he gives life and immortality and eternal glory to those who follow and serve him. He confers a benefit on his servants in return for their service and on his followers in return for their loyalty, but he receives no benefit from them. He is rich, perfect and in need of nothing.

The reason why God requires service from us is this: because he is good and merciful he desires to confer benefits on those who persevere in his service. In proportion to God's need of nothing is our need for communion with God.

This is the glory of humanity: to persevere and remain in the service of God. For this reason the Lord told his disciples: "You did not choose me but I chose you." He meant that his disciples did not glorify him by following him, but in following the Son of God they were glorified by him. As he said: "I wish that where I am they also may be, that they may see my glory."

Against Heresies 4, 13, 4–14, 1: SC 100, 534–540

Week of 5 Lent ✠ Sunday

A reading from the treatise On Works and Almsgiving by
Cyprian, Bishop and Martyr of Carthage [258]

You who are rich and wealthy, buy for yourself from Christ gold that has been tried by fire. Then, after your impurities have been burnt out as if by fire, you may be pure gold if you are cleansed by almsgiving and just works.

Buy for yourself white garments, that you who were naked according to Adam and were previously frightful and unsightly may be clothed with the white garment of Christ. And you who are wealthy and rich in Christ's Church, do not anoint your eyes with the eyewash of the devil. Anoint them, rather, with the eye-salve of Christ, that you may merit the vision of God, by obtaining his favor through your almsgiving and good conduct.

However, I am not surprised that a person such as you cannot avail yourself of the opportunity to perform works of charity. Your eyes are so painted and shadowed that a kind of dark night hangs over them and prevents them from seeing the poor and needy. You are wealthy and rich, and yet you think that you worthily celebrate the Lord's Supper although you do not even look at the poor-box, come to church without a sacrifice, and take only part of the sacrifice which the poor have offered!

Consider the woman in the gospel who was mindful of the heavenly precepts amid the most dire poverty and cast into the treasury two copper coins—all that she had. Seeing her, our Lord paid less attention to her good action than to the intention behind it; he considered not so much the amount she gave but the amount from which she took what she gave.

Thus, he declares: "I assure you, this poor widow has put in more than all the rest. They make contributions out of their surplus, but she from her want has given what she could not afford—every penny she had to live on." What a highly blessed and glorious woman, who even before the day of judgment merited to be praised by the voice of the Judge!

Let the rich be ashamed of their barrenness and lack of faith; here is a widow—and a poverty-stricken one at that—who is generous in works. Everything that we give is conferred on widows and orphans, yet here is one who gives instead of receiving; we can therefore realize what punishment lies in store for the rich when by this teaching even the poor are not exempt from almsgiving.

Furthermore, to demonstrate that it is to God himself that these charities are made—and that whoever makes them draws down grace and merits a reward—Christ calls them "gifts of God." He points out that this widow has placed two copper coins among the gifts of God, showing ever more clearly that the one who has pity on the poor lends to God.

Treatise on Works and Almsgiving 14–15: PL 4, 634–637

Week of 5 Lent ✠ Monday

A reading from an Easter Letter by Athanasius, Bishop of Alexandria [373]

The Word who became all things for us is close to us, our Lord Jesus Christ who promises to remain with us always. He cries out, saying: "See, I am with you all the days of this age." He is himself the shepherd, the high priest, the way and the door, and has become all things at once for us. In the same way, he has come among us as our feast and holy day as well. The blessed Apostle says of him who was awaited: "Christ has been sacrificed as our Passover." It was Christ who shed his light on the psalmist as he prayed: "You are my joy, deliver me from those surrounding me." True joy, genuine festival, means the casting out of wickedness. To achieve this one must live a life of perfect goodness and, in the serenity of the fear of God, practice contemplation in one's heart.

This was the way of the saints, who in their lifetime and at every stage of life rejoiced as at a feast. Blessed David, for example, not once but seven times rose at night to win God's favor through prayer. The great Moses was full of joy as he sang God's praises in hymns of victory for the defeat of Pharaoh and the oppressors of the Hebrew people. Others had hearts filled always with gladness as they performed their sacred duty of worship, like the great Samuel and the blessed Elijah. Because of their holy lives they gained freedom, and now keep festival in heaven. They rejoice after their pilgrimage in shadows, and now distinguish the reality from the promise.

When we celebrate the feast in our own day, what path are we to take? As we draw near to this feast, who is to be our guide? Beloved, it must be none other than the one whom you will address with me as our Lord Jesus Christ. He says: "I am the way." As blessed John tells us: it is Christ "who takes away the sin of the world." It is he who purifies our souls, as the prophet Jeremiah says: "Stand upon the ways; look and see which is the good path, and you will find in it the way of amendment for your souls."

In former times the blood of goats and the ashes of a calf were sprinkled on those who were unclean, but they were able to purify only the body. Now through the grace of God's Word everyone is made abundantly clean. If we follow Christ closely we shall be allowed, even on this earth, to stand as it were on the threshold of the heavenly Jerusalem, and enjoy the contemplation of that everlasting feast, like the blessed apostles, who in following the Savior as their leader, showed, and still show, the way to obtain the same gift from God. They said: "See, we have left all things and followed you." We too follow the Lord, and we keep his feast by deeds rather than by words.

Easter Letter 14, 1–2: PG 26, 1419–1420

Week of 5 Lent ✠ Tuesday

A reading from the Letter of the Churches of Lyons and Vienne [177]

The whole fury of crowd, governor, and soldiers fell with crushing force on Sanctus, the deacon from Vienne; on Maturus, very recently baptized but heroic in facing his ordeal; on Attakus, who had always been a pillar and support of the church in his native Pergamon; and on Blandina, through whom Christ proved that things which people regard as mean, unlovely, and contemptible are by God deemed worthy of great glory, because of her love for Him shown in power and not vaunted in appearance.

When we were all afraid, and her earthly mistress, who was herself facing the ordeal of martyrdom, was in agony lest she should be unable even to make a bold confession of Christ because of bodily weakness, Blandina was filled with such power that those who took it in turns to subject her to every kind of torture from morning to night were exhausted by their efforts and confessed themselves beaten—they could think of nothing else to do to her. They were amazed that she was still breathing, for her whole body was mangled and her wounds gaped; they declared that torment of any one kind was enough to part soul and body, let alone a succession of torments of such extreme severity. But the blessed woman, wrestling magnificently, grew in strength as she proclaimed her faith, and found refreshment, rest, and insensibility to her sufferings in uttering the words: "I am a Christian: we do nothing to be ashamed of."

Blandina was hung on a post and exposed as food for the wild beasts let loose in the arena. She looked as if she was hanging in the form of a cross, and through her ardent prayers she stimulated great enthusiasm in those undergoing their ordeal, who in their agony saw with their outward eyes in the person of their sister the One who was crucified for them, that He might convince those who believe in Him that any one who has suffered for the glory of Christ has fellowship for ever with the living God.

To crown all this, on the last day of the sports Blandina was again brought in, and with her Ponticus, a lad of about fifteen. Day after day they had been taken in to watch the rest being punished, and attempts were made to make them swear by the heathen idols. When they stood firm and treated these efforts with contempt, the mob was infuriated with them, so that the boy's tender age called forth no pity and the woman no respect. They subjected them to every horror and inflicted every punishment in turn, attempting again and again to make them swear, but to no purpose. Ponticus was encouraged by his sister in Christ, so that the heathen saw that she was urging him on and stiffening his resistance, and he bravely endured every punishment till he gave back his spirit to God.

Last of all, like a noble mother who had encouraged her children and sent them before her in triumph to the King, blessed Blandina herself passed through all the ordeals of her children and hastened to rejoin them, rejoicing and exulting at her departure as if invited to a wedding supper, not thrown to the beasts. After the whips, after the beasts, after the griddle, she was finally dropped into a basket and thrown to a bull. Time after time the animal tossed her, but she was indifferent now to all that happened to her, because of her hope and sure hold on all that her faith meant, and of her communing with Christ. Then she, too, was sacrificed, while the heathen themselves admitted that never yet had they known a woman suffer so much or so long.

Eusebius, Ecclesiastical History 5, 1: PG 20, 416, 425, 432

Week of 5 Lent ✠ Wednesday

*A reading from a commentary on John by Thomas Aquinas,
Priest and Friar [1274]*

"I am the Good Shepherd." Surely it is fitting that Christ should be a shepherd, for just as a flock is guided and fed by a shepherd so the faithful are fed by Christ with spiritual food and with his own body and blood. The Apostle said: "You were once like sheep without a shepherd, but now you have returned to the shepherd and guardian of your souls." The prophet has said: "As a shepherd he pastures his flock."

Christ said that the shepherd enters through the gate and that he is himself the gate as well as the shepherd. Then it is necessary that he enter through himself. By so doing, he reveals himself, and through himself he knows the Father. But we enter through him because through him we find happiness.

Take heed: no one else is the gate but Christ. Others reflect his light, but no one else is the true light. John the Baptist "was not the light, but he bore witness to the light." It is said of Christ, however: "He was the true light that enlightens everyone." For this reason no one says that they are the gate; this title is Christ's own. However, he has made others shepherds and given that office to his members; for Peter was a shepherd, and so were the other apostles and all good bishops after them. Scripture says: "I shall give you shepherds according to my own heart." Although the bishops of the Church, who are her children, are all shepherds, nevertheless Christ refers only to one person in saying: "I am the Good Shepherd," because he wants to emphasize the virtue of charity. Thus, no one can be a good shepherd unless he is one with Christ in charity. Through this we become members of the true shepherd.

The duty of a good shepherd is charity; therefore Christ said: "The good shepherd gives his life for the sheep." Know the difference between a good and a bad shepherd: the good shepherd cares for the welfare of the flock, but the bad shepherd cares only for personal welfare.

The Good Shepherd does not demand that shepherds lay down their lives for a real flock of sheep. But every spiritual shepherd must endure the loss of bodily life for the salvation of the flock, since the spiritual good of the flock is more important than the bodily life of the shepherd, when danger threatens the salvation of the flock. This is why the Lord says: "The good shepherd lays down his life," that is, physical life, "for the sheep"; this the shepherd does because of the shepherd's authority and love. Both, in fact, are required: that they should be ruled by the shepherd, and that the shepherd should love them. The first without the second is not enough.

Christ stands out for us as the example of this teaching: "If Christ laid down his life for us, so we also ought to lay down our lives for one another."

Chapter 10, lectio 3, 1–2: Marietti 1952, ed. Cai, 261

Week of 5 Lent ✠ Thursday

A reading from a homily of John Chrysostom, Bishop of Constantinople [407]

The cross used to denote punishment but it has now become a focus of glory. It was formerly a symbol of condemnation but it is now seen as a principle of salvation. For it has now become the source of innumerable blessings: it has delivered us from error, enlightened our darkness, and reconciled us to God; we had become God's enemies and were foreigners afar off, and it has given us his friendship and brought us close to him. For us it has become the destruction of enmity, the token of peace, the treasury of a thousand blessings.

Thanks to the cross we are no longer wandering in the wilderness, because we know the right road; we are no longer outside the royal palace, because we have found the way in; we are not afraid of the devil's fiery darts, because we have discovered the fountain. Thanks to the cross we are no longer in a state of widowhood, for we are reunited to the Bridegroom; we are not afraid of the wolf, because we have the good shepherd: "I am the good shepherd," he said. Thanks to the cross we dread no usurper, since we are sitting beside the King.

That is why we keep festival as we celebrate the memory of the cross. St. Paul himself invites us to this festival in honor of the cross: "Let us celebrate the feast not with the old leaven, that of corruption and wickedness, but with the unleavened bread of sincerity and truth." And he tells us why, saying: "Christ, our Passover, has been sacrificed."

Now do you see why he appoints a festival in honor of the cross? It is because Christ was immolated on the cross. And where he was sacrificed, there is found abolition of sins and reconciliation with the Lord; and there, too, festivity and happiness are found: "Christ, our Passover, has been sacrificed."

Where was he sacrificed? On a gibbet. The altar of this sacrifice is a new one because the sacrifice himself is new and extraordinary. For he is at one and the same time both victim and priest; victim according to the flesh and priest according to the spirit.

This sacrifice was offered outside the camp to teach us that it is a universal sacrifice, for the offering was made for the whole world; and to teach us that it effected a general purification and not just that of the Jews. God commanded the Jews to leave the rest of the world and to offer their prayers and sacrifices in one particular place; because all the rest of the world was soiled by the smoke and smell of all the impurities of pagan sacrifices. But for us, since Christ has now come and purified the whole world, every place has become an oratory.

Homily 1 on the Cross and the Thief 1: PG 49, 399–401

Week of 5 Lent ✠ Friday

A reading from a sermon of Gregory of Nazianzus, Bishop of Constantinople [389]

We are soon going to share in the Passover, and although we still do so only in a symbolic way, the symbolism already has more clarity than it possessed in former times because, under the law, the Passover was, if I may dare to say so, only a symbol of a symbol. Before long, however, when the Word drinks the new wine with us in the kingdom of his Father, we shall be keeping the Passover in a yet more perfect way, and with deeper understanding. He will then reveal to us and make clear what he has so far only partially disclosed. For this wine, so familiar to us now, is eternally new.

It is for us to learn what this drinking is, and for him to teach us. He has to communicate this knowledge to his disciples, because teaching is food, even for the teacher.

So let us take our part in the Passover prescribed by the law, not in a literal way, but according to the teaching of the Gospel; not in an imperfect way, but perfectly; not only for a time, but eternally. Let us regard as our home the heavenly Jerusalem, not the earthly one; the city glorified by angels, not the one laid waste by armies. We are not required to sacrifice young bulls or rams, beasts with horns and hoofs that are more dead than alive and devoid of feeling; but instead, let us join the choirs of angels in offering God upon his heavenly altar a sacrifice of praise. We must now pass through the first veil and approach the second, turning our eyes toward the Holy of Holies. I will say more: we must sacrifice ourselves to God, each day and in everything we do, accepting all that happens to us for the sake of the Word, imitating his passion by our sufferings, and honoring his blood by shedding our own. We must be ready to be crucified.

If you are a Simon of Cyrene, take up your cross and follow Christ. If you are crucified beside him like one of the thieves, now, like the good thief, acknowledge your God. For your sake, and because of your sin, Christ himself was regarded as a sinner; for his sake, therefore, you must cease to sin. Worship him who was hung on the cross because of you, even if you are hanging there yourself. Derive some benefit from the very shame; purchase salvation with your death. Enter paradise with Jesus, and discover how far you have fallen. Contemplate the glories there, and leave the other scoffing thief to die outside in blasphemy.

If you are a Joseph of Arimathea, go to the one who ordered his crucifixion, and ask for Christ's body. Make your own the expiation for the sins of the whole world. If you are a Nicodemus, like the one who worshiped God by night, bring spices and prepare Christ's body for burial. If you are one of the Marys, or Salome, or Joanna, weep in the early morning. Be the first to see the stone rolled back, and even the angels perhaps, and Jesus himself.

Oration 45, 23–24: PG 36, 654–655

Week of 5 Lent ✠ Saturday

A reading from the Travels of Egeria, Abbess, and Pilgrim to Jerusalem [late fourth century]

The following day, Sunday, marks the beginning of Holy Week, which they call here the Great Week. On this Sunday morning, at the completion of those rites which are customarily celebrated at the Anastasis or the Cross from the first cockcrow until dawn, everyone assembles for the liturgy according to custom in the major church, called the Martyrium. It is called the Martyrium because it is on Golgotha, behind the Cross, where the Lord suffered His Passion, and is therefore a shrine of martyrdom. As soon as everything has been celebrated in the major church as usual, but before the dismissal is given, the archdeacon raises his voice and first says: "Throughout this whole week, beginning tomorrow at the ninth hour, let us all gather in the Martyrium, in the major church." Then he raises his voice a second time, saying: "Today let us all be ready to assemble at the seventh hour at the Eleona." When the dismissal has been given in the Martyrium or major church, the bishop is led to the accompaniment of hymns to the Anastasis, and there all ceremonies are accomplished which customarily take place every Sunday at the Anastasis following the dismissal from the Martyrium. Then everyone retires home to eat hastily, so that at the beginning of the seventh hour everyone will be ready to assemble in the church on the Eleona, by which I mean the Mount of Olives, where the grotto in which the Lord taught is located.

At the seventh hour all the people go up to the church on the Mount of Olives, that is, to the Eleona. The bishop sits down, hymns and antiphons appropriate to the day and place are sung, and there are likewise readings from the Scriptures. As the ninth hour approaches, they move up, chanting hymns, to the Imbomon, that is, to the place from which the Lord ascended into heaven; and everyone sits down there. When the bishop is present, the people are always commanded to be seated, so that only the deacons remain standing. And there hymns and antiphons proper to the day and place are sung, interspersed with appropriate readings from the Scriptures and prayers.

As the eleventh hour draws near, that particular passage from Scripture is read in which the children bearing palms and branches came forth to meet the Lord, saying: "Blessed is He who comes in the name of the Lord." The bishop and all the people rise immediately, and then everyone walks down from the top of the Mount of Olives, with the people preceding the bishop and responding continually with "Blessed is He who comes in the name of the Lord" to the hymns and antiphons. All the children who are present here, including those who are not yet able to walk because they are too young and therefore are carried on their parents' shoulders, all of them bear branches, some carrying palms, others olive branches. And the bishop is led in the same manner as the Lord once was led. From the top of the mountain as far as the city, and from there through the entire city as far as the Anastasis, everyone accompanies the bishop the whole way on foot, and this includes distinguished ladies and men of consequence, reciting the responses all the while; and they move very slowly so that the people will not tire. By the time they arrive at the Anastasis, it is already evening. Once they have arrived there, even though it is evening, vespers is celebrated; then a prayer is said at the Cross and the people are dismissed.

Pilgrimage 30–31: SC 296, 270–274

Holy Week ✠ Palm Sunday

A reading from a sermon of Andrew of Crete, Bishop and Hymnographer [740]

Let us go together to meet Christ on the Mount of Olives. Today he returns from Bethany and proceeds of his own free will toward his holy and blessed passion, to consummate the mystery of our salvation. He who came down from heaven to raise us from the depths of sin, to raise us with himself, we are told in Scripture: "above every sovereignty, authority and power, and every other name that can be named," now comes of his own free will to make his journey to Jerusalem. He comes without pomp or ostentation. As the psalmist says: "He will not dispute or raise his voice to make it heard in the streets." He will be meek and humble, and he will make his entry in simplicity.

Let us run to accompany him as he hastens toward his passion, and imitate those who met him then, not by covering his path with garments, olive branches or palms, but by doing all we can to prostrate ourselves before him by being humble and by trying to live as he would wish. Then we shall be able to receive the Word at his coming, and God, whom no limits can contain, will be within us.

In his humility Christ entered the dark regions of our fallen world and he is glad that he became so humble for our sake, glad that he came and lived among us and shared in our nature in order to raise us up again to himself. And even though we are told that he has now ascended above the highest heavens—the proof, surely, of his power and godhead—his love for us will never rest until he has raised our earthbound nature from glory to glory, and made it one with his own in heaven.

So let us spread before his feet, not garments or soulless olive branches, which delight the eye for a few hours and then wither, but ourselves, clothed in his grace, or rather, clothed completely in him. We who have been baptized into Christ must ourselves be the garments that we spread before him. Now that the crimson stains of our sins have been washed away in the saving waters of baptism and we have become white as pure wool, let us present the conqueror of death, not with mere branches of palms but with the real rewards of his victory. Let our souls take the place of the welcoming branches as we join today in the children's holy song: "Blessed is he who comes in the name of the Lord. Blessed is the king of Israel."

Sermon 9 for Palm Sunday: PG 97, 990–994

Holy Week ✠ Monday

A reading from a commentary on the psalms by Jerome,
Priest, and Monk of Bethlehem [420]

The cross of Christ is the support of humankind. Our dwelling is built on this column. When I speak of the cross, I am not speaking of the wood but of the Passion. This cross is found as much in Britain as in India, and in the whole universe. For what does Christ say in the gospel? "If you do not take up your cross each day and follow in my footsteps, if your soul is not ready to take up the cross as mine was taken up for you, you cannot be my disciple."

Blessed are those who bear the cross and the resurrection in their hearts, as well as the place of the birth and that of the ascension of Christ. Blessed are they who possess Bethlehem in their hearts and in whose hearts Christ is born daily. For what is the meaning of Bethlehem if not "house of bread"? Let us too be a house of bread, of that bread which came down from heaven.

Every day Christ is crucified, for we are crucified to the world, and Christ is crucified in us. Blessed is the one in whose heart Christ rises every day because every day such a one does penance even for the smallest sins. Blessed is the one who every day ascends from the Mount of Olives to the kingdom of heaven, where the olives are large and the light of Christ is born.

It is not a question of having been in Jerusalem but what matters is to have lived well in Jerusalem and it is for this that we must be happy. The city we must seek is not the city that has killed the prophets and shed the blood of Christ, but the city that can rejoice in a powerful river, the city that, built on a mountain, cannot be hid, the city that the Apostle proclaims to be the mother of saints and that he wishes to dwell in with the righteous.

In saying this, I am not accusing myself of inconstancy. I do not repudiate what I am doing as if I considered it useless to have left my own and my country after the example of Abraham, for I would not dare to restrict the almighty power of God and confine it to a small country or confine to a small corner of the earth the one whom heaven cannot contain. Every believer is estimated according to the merit of faith and not on account of where a person lives. And the true adorers do not need Jerusalem or Mount Garizim to adore the Father. For God is spirit and his adorers must adore in spirit and in truth. Now, the Spirit blows where it wills and "The Lord's are the earth and its fullness."

Treatise on Psalm 95: CCL 78, 154–155; Letter 58, 2–4: PL 22, 580–582

Holy Week ✠ Tuesday

A reading from the treatise On the Holy Spirit by Basil the Great, Bishop of Caesarea [379]

When humankind was estranged by disobedience, God our Savior made a plan for raising us from our fall and restoring us to friendship with himself. According to this plan Christ came in the flesh, he showed us the gospel way of life, he suffered, died on the cross, was buried and rose from the dead. He did this so that we could be saved by imitation of him, and recover our original status as children of God by adoption.

To attain holiness, then, we must not only pattern our lives on Christ's by being gentle, humble and patient, we must also imitate him in his death. Taking Christ for his model, Paul said that he wanted to become like him in his death in the hope that he too would be raised from death to life.

We imitate Christ's death by being buried with him in baptism. If we ask what this kind of burial means and what benefit we may hope to derive from it, it means first of all making a complete break with our former way of life, and our Lord himself said that this cannot be done unless we are born again. In other words, we have to begin a new life, and we cannot do so until our previous life has been brought to an end. When runners reach the turning point on a racecourse, they have to pause briefly before they can go back in the opposite direction. So also when we wish to reverse the direction of our lives there must be a pause, or a death, to mark the end of one life and the beginning of another.

Our descent into hell takes place when we imitate the burial of Christ by our baptism. The bodies of the baptized are in a sense buried in the water as a symbol of their renunciation of the sins of their unregenerate nature. As the Apostle says: "The circumcision you have undergone is not an operation performed by human hands, but the complete stripping away of your unregenerate nature. This is the circumcision that Christ gave us, and it is accomplished by our burial with him in baptism." Baptism cleanses the soul from the pollution of worldly thoughts and inclinations: "You will wash me," says the psalmist, "and I shall be whiter than snow." We receive this saving baptism only once because there was only one death and one resurrection for the salvation of the world, and baptism is its symbol.

On the Holy Spirit 15, 35: PG 32, 127–130

Holy Week ✠ Wednesday

A reading from the Easter Homily of Melito, Bishop of Sardis [c. 190]

There was much proclaimed by the prophets about the mystery of the Passover. That mystery is Christ, and to him be glory for ever and ever.

For the sake of suffering humanity he came down from heaven to earth, clothed himself in that humanity in the Virgin's womb, and was born as one of us. Having then a body capable of suffering, he took the pain of fallen humanity upon himself; he triumphed over the diseases of soul and body that were its cause, and by his Spirit, which was incapable of dying, he dealt our destroyer, death, a fatal blow.

He was led forth like a lamb; he was slaughtered like a sheep. He ransomed us from our servitude to the world, as he had ransomed Israel from the hand of Egypt; he freed us from our slavery to the devil, as he had freed Israel from the hand of Pharaoh. He sealed our souls with his own Spirit, and the members of our body with his own blood.

He is the One who covered death with shame and cast the devil into mourning, as Moses cast Pharaoh into mourning. He is the One who smote sin and robbed iniquity of offspring, as Moses robbed the Egyptians of their offspring. He is the One who brought us out of slavery into freedom, out of darkness into light, out of death into life, out of tyranny into an eternal kingdom; who made us a new priesthood, a people chosen to be his own for ever. He is the Passover that is our salvation.

It is he who endured every kind of suffering in all those who foreshadowed him. In Abel he was slain, in Isaac bound, in Jacob exiled, in Joseph sold, in Moses exposed to die. He was sacrificed in the Passover lamb, persecuted in David, dishonored in the prophets.

It is he who was made flesh of the Virgin, he who was hung on the tree; it is he who was buried in the earth, raised from the dead, and taken up to the heights of heaven. He is the mute lamb, the slain lamb, the lamb born of Mary, the fair ewe. He was seized from the flock, dragged off to be slaughtered, sacrificed in the evening, and buried at night. On the tree no bone of his was broken; in the earth his body knew no decay. He is the One who rose from the dead, and who raised us from the depths of the tomb.

Easter Homily 65–71: SC 123, 95–101

Holy Week ✠ Maundy Thursday

A reading from a sermon of Thomas Aquinas, Priest and Friar [1274]

The happy commemoration of today's feast with its immense concourse of people invites us to prolong fervently our praises of the Most Holy Body of Christ. What could be sweeter, what more pleasing to the heart of the faithful than to exalt the abyss of his divine charity, and to glorify the overflowing torrent of his love! At the table of the new grace the hand of the priest distributes ceaselessly his Flesh as food and his precious Blood as drink, to those who are his children and heirs of the kingdom promised by God to those who love him.

O endless Emanation of the goodness of God and of his immense love for us, admirable and worthy of all praise! In this sacrament, where all former sacrifices are done away with, he remains with us to the end of the world; he feeds the children of adoption with the bread of angels and inebriates them with filial love.

This is the food and drink for the elect, living bread and spiritual nourishment, remedy for daily weaknesses! It is the table which Christ has prepared for his friends and guests, like the one the father prepared for his son on the day of his return, to replace the symbolic lamb. This is the Passover in which the victim immolated is Christ; O Christ our Passover, you want us too to pass over from vice to virtue; as once you delivered the Jews, so now you set us free in spirit. You are the food that satisfies all but the most hardened; food that is eaten by faith, tasted by fervor, assimilated by charity. O viaticum of our pilgrimage, you lead travellers to the height of virtue. Confirm my heart in good, assure it in the paths of life, give joy to my soul, purify my thoughts.

The Eucharist is bread, real bread; we eat it without consuming or dividing it; it converts but itself is not changed; it gives strength without ever losing it; it gives perfection and suffices for salvation; it gives life, it confers grace, it remits sins. It is the food of souls, a food which enlightens the intelligence of the faithful, inflames their hearts, purifies them from their shortcomings, elevates their desires.

O chalice that holy souls love to drink of, chalice of fervor, chalice changed into the Blood of Christ, to seal the new Alliance, withdraw from us the old leaven, fill our souls with yourself, that we may become a new paste and that we may go to the feast with the unleavened bread of sincerity and truth. For the Lamb without spot, who knows no touch or stain of any sin, ought to be eaten with unleavened bread. We should not approach without being cleansed by confession, without having a solid foundation of faith, without being in charity.

Come to the Lord's supper, if you wish to come to the nuptials of the Lamb; there, we shall be inebriated with the riches of the house of God, we shall see the King of glory and the God of hosts in all his beauty, we shall eat this bread in the kingdom of the Father.

Lectionary and Martyrology, ed. Encalcat 1956, 288–289

Holy Week ✠ Good Friday

A reading from the Travels of Egeria, Abbess, and Pilgrim to Jerusalem [late fourth century]

[On Good Friday] following the dismissal from the Cross, which occurs before sunrise, everyone now stirred up goes immediately to Sion to pray at the pillar where the Lord was whipped. Returning from there then, all rest for a short time in their own houses, and soon all are ready. A throne is set up for the bishop on Golgotha behind the Cross, which now stands there. The bishop sits on the throne, a table covered with a linen cloth is set before the bishop, and the deacons stand around the table. The gilded silver casket containing the sacred wood of the cross is brought in and opened. Both the wood of the cross and the inscription are taken out and placed on the table. As soon as they have been placed on the table, the bishop, remaining seated, grips the ends of the sacred wood, while the deacons, who are standing about, keep watch over it. There is a reason why it is guarded in this manner. It is the practice here for all the people to come forth one by one, the faithful as well as the catechumens, to bow down before the table, kiss the holy wood, and then move on. It is said that someone (I do not know when) took a bite and stole a piece of the holy cross. Therefore, it is now guarded by the deacons standing around, lest there be anyone who would dare come and do that again.

All the people pass through one by one; all of them bow down, touching the cross and the inscription, first with their foreheads, then with their eyes; and, after kissing the cross, they move on. No one, however, puts out a hand to touch the cross. As soon as they have kissed the cross and passed on through, a deacon, who is standing, holds out the ring of Solomon and the phial with which the kings were anointed. They kiss the phial and venerate the ring from more or less the second hour; and thus until the sixth hour all the people pass through, entering through one door, exiting through another. All this occurs in the place where the day before, on Thursday, the sacrifice was offered.

When the sixth hour is at hand, everyone goes before the Cross, regardless of whether it is raining or whether it is hot. This place has no roof, for it is a sort of very large and beautiful courtyard lying between the Cross and the Anastasis. The people are so clustered together there that it is impossible for anything to be opened. A chair is placed for the bishop before the Cross, and from the sixth to the ninth hours nothing else is done except the reading of passages from Scripture.

First, whichever Psalms speak of the Passion are read. Next, there are readings from the apostles, either from the Epistles of the apostles or the Acts, wherever they speak of the Passion of the Lord. Next, the texts of the Passion from the Gospels are read. Then there are readings from the prophets, where they said that the Lord would suffer; and then they read from the Gospels, where He foretells the Passion. And so, from the sixth to the ninth hour, passages from Scripture are continuously read and hymns are sung, to show the people that whatever the prophets had said would come to pass concerning the Passion of the Lord can be shown, both through the Gospels and the writings of the apostles, to have taken place. And so, during those three hours, all the people are taught that nothing happened which was not first prophesied, and that nothing was prophesied which was not completely fulfilled. Prayers are continually interspersed, and the prayers themselves are proper to the day. At each reading and at every prayer, it is astonishing how much emotion and groaning there is from all the people. There is no one, young or old, who on this day does not sob more than can be imagined for the whole three hours, because the Lord suffered all this for us. After this, when the ninth hour is at hand, the passage is read from the Gospel according to Saint John where Christ gave up His spirit. After this reading, a prayer is said and the dismissal is given.

As soon as the dismissal has been given from before the Cross, everyone gathers together in the major church, the Martyrium, and there everything which they have been doing regularly throughout this week from the ninth hour when they came together at the Martyrium, until evening, is then done. After the dismissal from the Martyrium, everyone comes to the Anastasis, and, after they have arrived there, the passage from the Gospel is read where Joseph seeks from Pilate the body of the Lord and places it in a new tomb. After this reading a prayer is said, the catechumens are blessed, and the faithful as well; then the dismissal is given.

On this day no one raises a voice to say the vigil will be continued at the Anastasis, because it is known that the people are tired. However, it is the custom that the vigil be held there. And so, those among the people who wish, or rather those who are able, to keep the vigil, do so until dawn; whereas those who are not able to do so, do not keep watch there. But those of the clergy who are either strong enough or young enough, keep watch there, and hymns and antiphons are sung there all through the night until morning. The greater part of the people keep watch, some from evening on, others from midnight, all doing what they can.

Pilgrimage 37: SC 296, 284–290

Holy Week ✠ Holy Saturday

A reading from The Easter Homily of John Chrysostom, Bishop of Constantinople [407]

Everyone who is devout and a lover of God, let them enjoy this beautiful and radiant Feast of Feasts!

If anyone is a wise servant, rejoice and enter into the joy of the Lord.

If anyone has been wearied in fasting, now receive your recompense.

If anyone has labored from the first hour, today receive your just reward. If anyone has come at the third hour, with thanksgiving keep the feast. If anyone has arrived at the sixth hour, have no misgivings; for you shall suffer no loss. If anyone has delayed until the ninth hour, draw near without hesitation. If anyone has arrived even at the eleventh hour, do not fear on account of your delay. For the Lord is gracious, and receives the last even as the first; He gives rest to the one that comes at the eleventh hour, just as to the one who has labored from the first. He has mercy upon the last, and cares for the first; to the one He gives, and to the other He is gracious. He both honors the work, and praises the intention.

Enter all of you, therefore, into the joy of our Lord, and whether first or last receive your reward. O rich and poor, one with another, dance for joy! O you ascetics and you negligent, celebrate the Day! You that have fasted and you that have disregarded the fast, rejoice today! The table is rich-laden; feast royally, all of you! The calf is fattened; let no one go forth hungry!

Let all partake of the Feast of Faith. Let all receive the riches of goodness.

Let none lament their poverty, for the Universal Kingdom has been revealed.

Let none mourn their transgressions, for Pardon has dawned from the Tomb!

Let no one fear Death, for the Savior's death has set us free!

He that was taken by Death has annihilated it!

He descended into Hell, and took Hell captive!

He embittered it when it tasted of His Flesh! And anticipating this Isaiah exclaimed, "Hell was embittered when it encountered thee in the lower regions." It was embittered, for it was abolished! It was embittered, for it was mocked! It was embittered, for it was purged! It was embittered, for it was despoiled! It was embittered, for it was bound in chains!

It took a body, and face to face met God! It took earth, and encountered Heaven! It took what it saw, but crumbled before what it had not seen!

"O Death, where is your sting? O Hell, where is your victory?"

Christ is risen, and you are overthrown!

Christ is risen, and the demons are fallen!

Christ is risen, and the Angels rejoice!

Christ is risen, and Life reigns!

Christ is risen, and not one dead remains in the tombs!

For Christ being raised from the dead, has become the first-fruits of them that slept. To Him be glory and dominion through all the ages of ages!

Trans. Wright and Kelley: PG 52, 765–772

Easter Week ✠ Easter Day

A reading from the Easter Homily of Melito, Bishop of Sardis [c. 190]

We should understand, beloved, that the paschal mystery is at once old and new, transitory and eternal, corruptible and incorruptible, mortal and immortal. In terms of the Law it is old, in terms of the Word it is new. In its figure it is passing, in its grace it is eternal. It is corruptible in the sacrifice of the lamb, incorruptible in the eternal life of the Lord. It is mortal in his burial in the earth, immortal in his resurrection from the dead.

The Law indeed is old, but the Word is new. The type is transitory, but grace is eternal. The lamb was corruptible, but the Lord is incorruptible.

He was slain as a lamb; he rose again as God. "He was led like a sheep to the slaughter," yet he was not a sheep. He was silent as a lamb, yet he was not a lamb. The type has passed away; the reality has come. The lamb gives place to God, the sheep gives place to a person, and the person is Christ, who fills the whole of creation. The sacrifice of the lamb, the celebration of the Passover, and the prescriptions of the Law have been fulfilled in Jesus Christ. Under the old Law, and still more under the new dispensation, everything pointed toward him.

Both the Law and the Word came forth from Zion and Jerusalem, but now the Law has given place to the Word, the old to the new. The commandment has become grace, the type a reality. The lamb has become a Son, the sheep a human, and the human, God.

The Lord, though he was God, became human. He suffered for the sake of those who suffer, he was bound for those in bonds, condemned for the guilty, buried for those who lie in the grave; but he rose from the dead, and cried aloud: "Who will contend with me? Confront me." I have freed the condemned, brought the dead back to life, raised the dead from their graves. Who has anything to say against me? I, he said, am the Christ; I have destroyed death, triumphed over the enemy, trampled hell underfoot, bound the strong one, and taken humanity up to the heights of heaven: I am the Christ.

Come, then, all you nations, receive forgiveness for the sins that defile you. I am your forgiveness. I am the Passover that brings salvation. I am the lamb who was immolated for you. I am your ransom, your life, your resurrection, your light, I am your salvation and your king. I will bring you to the heights of heaven. With my own right hand I will raise you up, and I will show you the eternal Father.

Easter Homily 2–7, 100–103; SC 123, 60–64, 120–122

Easter Week ✠ Monday

A reading from the treatise Against Heresies by Irenaeus,
Bishop of Lyons [c. 202]

There is one God, who by his word and wisdom created all things and set them in order. His Word is our Lord Jesus Christ, who in this last age became human among us to unite the end and the beginning, that is, humanity and God.

The prophets, receiving the gift of prophecy from this same Word, foretold his coming in the flesh, which brought about the union and communion between God and humankind ordained by the Father. From the beginning the word of God prophesied that God would be seen by people and would live among them on earth; he would speak with his own creation and be present to it, bringing it salvation and being visible to it. He would "free us from the hands of all who hate us," that is, from the universal spirit of sin, and enable us "to serve him in holiness and righteousness all our days." Humankind was to receive the Spirit of God and so attain to the glory of the Father.

The prophets, then, foretold that God would be seen by human beings. As the Lord himself says: "Blessed are the pure in heart, for they shall see God." In his greatness and inexpressible glory "no one can see God and live," for the Father is beyond our comprehension. But in his love and generosity and omnipotence God allows even this to those who love him, that is, even to see God, as the prophets foretold. "For what is impossible for humans is possible to God."

By our own powers we cannot see God, yet God will be seen by us because he wills it. He will be seen by those he chooses, at the time he chooses, and in the way he chooses, for God can do all things. He was seen of old through the Spirit in prophecy; he is seen through the Son by our adoption as his children, and he will be seen in the kingdom of heaven in his own being as the Father. The Spirit prepares us to receive the Son of God, the Son leads us to the Father, and the Father, freeing us from change and decay, bestows the eternal life that comes to everyone from seeing God.

As those who see light are in the light sharing its brilliance, so those who see God are in God sharing his glory, and that glory gives them life. To see God is to share in life.

Against Heresies 4, 20, 4–5: SC 100, 634–640

Easter Week ✠ Tuesday

A reading from the treatise On the Trinity by Hilary, Bishop of Poitiers [367]

We believe that the Word became flesh and that we receive his flesh in the Lord's Supper. How then can we fail to believe that he really dwells within us? When he became human, he actually clothed himself in our flesh, uniting it to himself for ever. In the sacrament of his body he actually gives us his own flesh, which he has united to his divinity. This is why we are all one, because the Father is in Christ, and Christ is in us. He is in us through his flesh and we are in him. With him we form a unity which is in God.

The manner of our indwelling in him through the sacrament of his body and blood is evident from the Lord's own words: "This world will see me no longer but you shall see me. Because I live you shall live also, for I am in my Father, you are in me, and I am in you." If it had been a question of a mere unity of will, why should he have given us this explanation of the steps by which it is achieved? He is in the Father by reason of his divine nature, we are in him by reason of his human birth, and he is in us through the mystery of the sacraments. This, surely, is what he wished us to believe; this is how he wanted us to understand the perfect unity that is achieved through our Mediator, who lives in the Father while we live in him, and who, while living in the Father, lives also in us. This is how we attain to unity with the Father. Christ is in very truth in the Father by his eternal generation; we are in very truth in Christ, and he likewise is in us.

Christ himself bore witness to the reality of this unity when he said: "You who eat my flesh and drink my blood live in me and I in you." No one will be in Christ unless Christ himself has been in that one: Christ will take to himself only the flesh of those who have received his flesh.

He had already explained the mystery of this perfect unity when he said: "As the living Father sent me and I draw life from the Father, so he who eats my flesh will draw life from me." We draw life from his flesh just as he draws life from the Father. Such comparisons aid our understanding, since we can grasp a point more easily when we have an analogy. And the point is that Christ is the wellspring of our life. Since we who are in the flesh have Christ dwelling in us through his flesh, we shall draw life from him in the same way as he draws life from the Father.

On the Trinity 8, 13–16: PL 10, 246–249

Easter Week ✠ Wednesday

A reading from the Mystagogical Catecheses of Cyril, Bishop of Jerusalem [386]

Having been "baptized into Christ," and "put on Christ," you have been made conformable to the Son of God; for God having "predestinated us to the adoption of heirs" made us "share the fashion of Christ's glorious body." Being therefore made "partakers of Christ," you are properly called Christs, and of you God said, "Touch not my Christ," or anointed. Now you were made Christs, by receiving the emblem of the Holy Spirit, and all things were in a figure wrought in you, because you are figures of Christ. He also bathed himself in the river Jordan, and having imparted of the fragrance of his Godhead to the waters, he came up from them; and the Holy Spirit lighted on him, like resting upon like. In the same manner to you also, after you had come up from the pool of the sacred streams, was given the unction, the emblem of that wherewith Christ was anointed; and this is the Holy Spirit; of whom also the blessed Isaiah in his prophecy says in the person of the Lord: "The Spirit of the Lord is upon me, because he has anointed me to preach glad tidings to the poor."

For Christ was not anointed by human hands with oil or material ointment, but the Father, having appointed him to be the Savior of the whole world, anointed him with the Holy Spirit, as Peter says: "Jesus of Nazareth, whom God anointed with the Holy Spirit." And David the Prophet cried, saying: "Your throne, O God, is for ever and ever; a scepter of righteousness is the scepter of your kingdom; you have loved righteousness and hated iniquity; therefore God even your God has anointed you with the oil of gladness above your fellows." And as Christ was in truth crucified, and buried, and raised, and you in likeness are in baptism accounted worthy of being crucified, buried, and raised together with him, so is it with the unction also. As he was anointed with the spiritual oil of gladness, the Holy Spirit, who is so called, because he is the author of spiritual gladness, so you were anointed with ointment, having been made partakers and "fellows" of Christ.

But beware of supposing this to be plain ointment. For as the Bread of the Eucharist, after the invocation of the Holy Spirit, is mere bread no longer, but the Body of Christ, so also this body ointment is no more simple ointment, nor (so to say) common, after the invocation, but the gift of Christ; and by the presence of his Godhead, it causes in us the Holy Spirit. It is symbolically applied to your forehead and your other senses; and while your body is anointed with visible ointment, your soul is sanctified by the Holy and lifegiving Spirit.

Mystagogical Catechesis 3, 1–3: SC 126, 120–125

Easter Week ✠ Thursday

A reading from the Mystagogical Catecheses of Cyril, Bishop of Jerusalem [386]

You were led to the holy pool of divine baptism, as Christ was carried from the cross to the sepulchre which is before our eyes. And each of you was asked, whether you believed in the name of the Father, and of the Son, and of the Holy Spirit, and you made that saving confession, and descended three times into the water, and ascended again; here also covertly pointing by a figure at the three-days burial of Christ. For as our Savior passed three days and three nights in the heart of the earth, so you also in your first ascent out of the water represented the first day of Christ in the earth, and by your descent, the night; for as he who is in the night sees no more, but he who is in the day remains in the light, so in descending you saw nothing as in the night, but in ascending again you were as in the day. And at the self-same moment, you died and were born; and that water of salvation was at once your grave and your mother. And what Solomon spoke of others will suit you also: for he said: "There is a time to be born and a time to die"; but to you, on the contrary, the time to die is also the time to be born; and one and the same season brings about both of these, and your birth went hand in hand with your death.

O strange and inconceivable thing! We did not really die, we were not really buried, we were not really crucified and raised again, but our imitation was merely in a figure, while our salvation is in reality. Christ was actually crucified, and actually buried, and truly rose again; and all these things have been vouchsafed to us, that we, by imitation communicating in his sufferings, might gain salvation in reality. O surpassing loving-kindness! Christ received the nails in his undefiled hands and feet, and endured anguish; while to me without suffering or toil, by the fellowship of his pain he vouchsafes salvation.

Let no one then suppose that baptism is merely the grace of remission of sins, or further, that of adoption, as John's baptism bestowed only the remission of sins. Indeed we know full well, that as it purges our sins, and conveys to us the gift of the Holy Spirit, so also it is the counterpart of Christ's sufferings. For, for this cause Paul cried aloud and says: "Know you not that as many of us as were baptized into Christ Jesus were baptized into his death? Therefore we are buried with him by baptism into death."

Mystagogical Catechesis 2, 4–6; SC 126, 110–115

Easter Week ✠ Friday

A reading from the treatise On Flight from the World by Ambrose, Bishop of Milan [397]

Where your heart is, there is your treasure also. God is not accustomed to refusing a good gift to those who ask for one. Since he is good, and especially to those who are faithful to him, let us hold fast to him with all our soul, our heart, our strength, and so enjoy his light and see his glory and possess the grace of supernatural joy. Let us reach out with our hearts to possess that good, let us exist in it and live in it, let us hold fast to it, that good which is beyond all we can know or see and is marked by perpetual peace and tranquility, a peace which is beyond all we can know or understand.

This is the good that permeates creation. In it we all live, on it we all depend. It has nothing above it; it is divine. No one is good but God alone. What is good is therefore divine, what is divine is therefore good. Scripture says: "When you open your hand all things will be filled with goodness." It is through God's goodness that all that is truly good is given us, and in it there is no admixture of evil.

These good things are promised by Scripture to those who are faithful: "The good things of the land will be your food."

We have died with Christ. We carry about in our bodies the sign of his death, so that the living Christ may also be revealed in us. The life we live is not now our ordinary life but the life of Christ: a life of sinlessness, of chastity, of simplicity and every other virtue. We have risen with Christ. Let us live in Christ, let us ascend in Christ, so that the serpent may not have the power here below to wound us in the heel.

Let us take refuge from this world. You can do this in spirit, even if you are kept here in the body. You can at the same time be here and present to the Lord. Your soul must hold fast to him, you must follow after him in your thoughts, you must tread his ways by faith, not in outward show. You must take refuge in him. He is your refuge and your strength. David addresses him in these words: "I fled to you for refuge, and I was not disappointed."

Since God is our refuge, God who is in heaven and above the heavens, we must take refuge from this world in that place where there is peace, where there is rest from toil, where we can celebrate the great sabbath, as Moses said: "The sabbaths of the land will provide you with food." To rest in the Lord and to see his joy is like a banquet, and full of gladness and tranquility.

Let us take refuge like deer beside the fountain of waters. Let our soul thirst, as David thirsted, for the fountain. What is that fountain? Listen to David: "With you is the fountain of life." Let my soul say to this fountain: "When shall I come and see you face to face?" For the fountain is God himself.

Treatise on Flight from the World 6, 36; 7, 44; 8, 45; 9, 52: CSEL 32, 192, 198–199, 204

Easter Week ✠ Saturday

A reading from the Mystagogical Catecheses of Cyril, Bishop of Jerusalem [386]

"Our Lord Jesus Christ the same night in which he was betrayed, took bread, and when he had given thanks he broke it, and said, 'Take, eat, this is my body'; and having taken the cup and given thanks, he said, 'Take, drink, this is my blood.' " Since he himself has declared and said of the bread: "This is my body," who shall dare to doubt any longer? And since he has affirmed and said: "This is my blood," who shall ever hesitate, saying that it is not his blood?

Therefore with fullest assurance let us partake as of the Body and Blood of Christ: for in the figure of bread is given to you his Body, and in the figure of wine his Blood; that you, by partaking of the Body and Blood of Christ, might be made of the same body and the same blood with him. For thus we come to bear Christ in us, because his Body and Blood are diffused through our members; thus it is that, according to the blessed Peter: "we become partakers of the divine nature."

Christ on a certain occasion discoursing with the Jews said: "Except you eat my flesh and drink my blood, you have no life in you." Not receiving his saying spiritually, they were offended, and went backward, supposing that he was inviting them to eat flesh.

Even under the Old Testament there was shewbread; but this, as it belonged to the Old Testament, came to an end; but in the New Testament there is the Bread of heaven, and the Cup of salvation, sanctifying soul and body; for as the Bread has respect to our body, so is the Word appropriate to our soul.

Contemplate therefore the bread and wine not as bare elements, for they are, according to the Lord's declaration, the Body and Blood of Christ; though sense suggests this to you, let faith steady you. Judge not the matter from taste, but from faith be fully assured without misgiving, that you have been vouchsafed the Body and Blood of Christ.

Having learned these things, and being fully persuaded that what seems bread is not bread, though bread by taste, but the Body of Christ; and that what seems wine is not wine, though the taste will have it so, but the Blood of Christ; and that of this David sang of old, saying: "And bread which strengthens our heart, and oil to make our face to shine," so I bid you "strengthen your heart," partaking thereof as spiritual, and "make the face of your soul to shine." And thus having it unveiled by a pure conscience, may you "behold as in a glass the glory

of the Lord," and proceed from "glory to glory," in Christ Jesus our
Lord:—To whom be honor, and might, and glory, for ever and ever.

Mystagogical Catechesis 4: SC 126, 134–145

Week of 2 Easter ✠ Sunday

A reading from a sermon of Augustine, Bishop of Hippo [430]

I speak to you who have just been reborn in baptism, my little children
in Christ, you who are the new offspring of the Church, gift of the Father,
proof of Mother Church's fruitfulness. All of you who stand fast in the
Lord are a holy seed, a new colony of bees, the very flower of our ministry
and fruit of our toil, my joy and my crown. The words of the Apostle I
address to you: "Put on the Lord Jesus Christ, and make no provision
for the flesh and its desires," so that you may be clothed with the life of
him whom you have put on in this sacrament. "You have all been clothed
with Christ by your baptism in him. There is neither Jew nor Greek; there
is neither slave nor free; there is neither male nor female; you are all one
in Christ Jesus."

Such is the power of this sacrament: it is a sacrament of new life which
begins here and now with the forgiveness of all past sins, and will be
brought to completion in the resurrection of the dead. "You have been
buried with Christ by baptism into death in order that, as Christ has risen
from the dead, you also may walk in newness of life."

You are walking now by faith, still on pilgrimage in a mortal body away
from the Lord; but he to whom your steps are directed is himself the sure
and certain way for you: Jesus Christ, who for our sake became human.
For all who fear him he has stored up abundant happiness, which he will
reveal to those who hope in him, bringing it to completion when we have
attained the reality which even now we possess in hope.

This is the octave day of your new birth. Today is fulfilled in you the
sign of faith that was prefigured in the Old Testament by the circumcision
of the flesh on the eighth day after birth. When the Lord rose from the
dead, he put off the mortality of the flesh; his risen body was still the
same body, but it was no longer subject to death. By his resurrection he
consecrated Sunday, or the Lord's day. Though the third after his passion, this day is the eighth after the Sabbath, and thus also the first day
of the week.

And so your own hope of resurrection, though not yet realized, is sure
and certain, because you have received the sacrament or sign of this
reality, and have been given the pledge of the Spirit. "If, then, you have

risen with Christ, seek the things that are above, where Christ is seated at the right hand of God. Set your hearts on heavenly things, not the things that are on earth. For you have died and your life is hidden with Christ in God. When Christ, your life, appears, then you too will appear with him in glory."

Sermon 8 for the Octave of Easter 1, 4: PL 46, 838, 841

Week of 2 Easter ✠ Monday

A reading from a commentary on John by Augustine, Bishop of Hippo [430]

The Lord has marked out for us the fullness of love that we ought to have for each other. He tells us: "No one has greater love than those who lay down their lives for their friends." In these words, the Lord tells us what the perfect love we should have for one another involves. John, the evangelist who recorded them, draws the conclusion in one of his letters: As Christ laid down his life for us, so we too ought to lay down our lives for our sisters and brothers. We should indeed love one another as he loved us, he who laid down his life for us.

This is surely what we read in the Proverbs of Solomon: "If you sit down to eat at the table of a ruler, observe carefully what is set before you; then stretch out your hand, knowing that you must provide the same kind of meal yourself." What is this ruler's table if not the one at which we receive the body and blood of him who laid down his life for us? What does it mean to sit at this table if not to approach it with humility? What does it mean to observe carefully what is set before you if not to meditate devoutly on so great a gift? What does it mean to stretch out one's hand, knowing that one must provide the same kind of meal oneself, if not what I have just said: as Christ laid down his life for us, so we in our turn ought to lay down our lives for our sisters and brothers? This is what the apostle said: "Christ suffered for us, leaving us an example, that we might follow in his footsteps."

This is what is meant by providing "the same kind of meal." This is what the blessed martyrs did with such burning love. If we are to give true meaning to our celebration of their memorials, to our approaching the Lord's table in the very banquet at which they were fed, we must, like them, provide "the same kind of meal."

At this table of the Lord we do not commemorate the martyrs in the same way as we commemorate others who rest in peace. We do not pray for the martyrs as we pray for those others, rather, they pray for us, that we may follow in their footsteps. They practiced the perfect love of which the Lord said there could be none greater. They provided "the same kind of meal" as they had themselves received at the Lord's table.

This must not be understood as saying that we can be the Lord's equals by bearing witness to him to the extent of shedding our blood. He had the power of laying down his life; we by contrast cannot choose the length of our lives, and we die even if it is against our will. He, by dying, destroyed death in himself; we are freed from death only in his death. His body did not see corruption; our body will see corruption and only then be clothed through him in incorruption at the end of the world. He needed no help from us in saving us; without him we can do nothing. He gave himself to us as the vine to the branches; apart from him we cannot have life.

Finally, even if kindred die for kindred, yet no martyr by shedding blood brings forgiveness for the sins of others, as Christ brought forgiveness to us. In this he gave us, not an example to imitate but a reason for rejoicing. Inasmuch, then, as they shed their blood for their sisters and brothers, the martyrs provided "the same kind of meal" as they had received at the Lord's table. Let us then love one another as Christ also loved us and gave himself up for us.

Treatise 84 on John 1–2: CCL 36, 536–538

Week of 2 Easter ✠ Tuesday

A reading from the treatise On the Trinity by Didymus the Blind, Theologian of Alexandria [398]

The Holy Spirit renews us in baptism through his godhead, which he shares with the Father and the Son. Finding us in a state of deformity, the Spirit restores our original beauty and fills us with his grace, leaving no room for anything unworthy of our love. The Spirit frees us from sin and death, and changes us from the earthly people we were, people of dust and ashes, into spiritual people, sharers in the divine glory, and heirs of God the Father who bear a likeness to the Son and are his co-heirs and kindred, destined to reign with him and to share his glory. In place of earth the Spirit re-opens heaven to us and gladly admits us into paradise, giving us even now greater honor than the angels.

We are conceived twice: to the human body we owe our first conception; to the divine Spirit, our second. John says: "To all who received him, who believed in his name, he gave power to become children of God. These were born not by human generation, not by the desire of the flesh, not by the will of humankind, but of God." All who believed in Christ, he says, received power to become children of God, that is, of the Holy Spirit, and to gain kinship with God. To show that their parent was God the Holy Spirit, he adds these words of Christ: "I give you this solemn warning, that without being born of water and the Spirit, no one can enter the kingdom of God."

Visibly, through the ministry of priests, the font gives symbolic birth to our visible bodies. Invisibly, through the ministry of angels, the Spirit of God, whom even the mind's eye cannot see, baptizes into himself both our souls and bodies, giving them a new birth.

Speaking quite literally, and also in harmony with the words "of water and the Spirit," John the Baptist says of Christ: "He will baptize you with the Holy Spirit and with fire." Since we are only vessels of clay, we must first be cleansed in water and then hardened by spiritual fire—for "God is a consuming fire." We need the Holy Spirit to perfect and renew us, for spiritual fire can cleanse us, and spiritual water can recast us as in a furnace and make us into new people.

Treatise on the Trinity 2, 12: PG 39, 667–674

Week of 2 Easter ✠ Wednesday

A reading from a commentary on John by Cyril, Bishop of Alexandria [444]

All who receive the sacred flesh of Christ are united with him as members of his body. This is the teaching of Saint Paul when he speaks of the mystery of our religion "that was hidden from former generations, but has now been revealed to the holy apostles and prophets by the Spirit; namely, that the Gentiles are joint-heirs with the Jews, that they are members of the same body, and that they have a share in the promise made by God in Christ Jesus."

If, in Christ, all of us, both ourselves and he who is within us by his own flesh, are members of the same body, is it not clear that we are one, both with one another and with Christ? He is the bond that unites us, because he is at once both God and human.

With regard to our unity in the Spirit, we may say, following the same line of thought, that all of us who have received one and the same Spirit, the Holy Spirit, are united intimately, both with one another and with God. Taken separately, we are many, and Christ sends the Spirit, who is both the Father's Spirit and his own, to dwell in each of us. Yet that Spirit, being one and indivisible, gathers together those who are distinct from each other as individuals, and causes them all to be seen as a unity in himself. Just as Christ's sacred flesh has power to make those in whom it is present into one body, so the one, indivisible Spirit of God, dwelling in all, causes all to become one in spirit.

Therefore, Saint Paul appeals to us to "bear with one another charitably, and to spare no effort in securing, by the bonds of peace, the unity that comes from the Spirit. There is but one body and one Spirit, just as there is but one hope held out to us by God's call. There is one Lord, one faith, one baptism, one God and Father of all, who is above all, and works through all, and is in all." If the one Spirit dwells in us, the one God and Father of all will be in us, and he, through his Son, will gather together into unity with one another and with himself all who share in the Spirit.

There is also another way of showing that we are made one by sharing in the Holy Spirit. If we have given up our worldly way of life and submitted once for all to the laws of the Spirit, it must surely be obvious to everyone that by repudiating, in a sense, our own life, and taking on the supernatural likeness of the Holy Spirit, who is united to us, our nature is transformed so that we are no longer merely human, but also children of God, spiritual folk, by reason of the share we have received in the divine nature. We are all one, therefore, in the Father and the Son and the Holy Spirit. We are one in mind and holiness, we are one through our communion in the sacred flesh of Christ, and through our sharing in the one Holy Spirit.

Commentary on John 11, 11: PG 74, 559–562

Week of 2 Easter ✠ Thursday

A reading from a commentary on Daniel by Hippolytus, Priest or Bishop of Rome [c. 236]

It is precisely because Daniel had made himself small and had given himself out as the most insignificant of all people that the king honored him and established him as prince over the whole land of Babylon. This reminds us of what the Pharaoh had done for Joseph establishing him as ruler over the whole land of Egypt. As a matter of fact, only Joseph had been found in the whole land of Egypt who was able to interpret the meaning of Pharaoh's dreams. In Babylon similarly, no wise person had been able to explain the visions of the king except Daniel. This goes to show that God, in the course of generations, raises up for himself holy personages who glorify him in the whole world.

Are we not justified then in recognizing in those events, predicted by Daniel in Babylon, the things that are being accomplished in today's world? The statue that was then described for the benefit of Nebuchadnezzar represented the empire of the world. In that period of history the Babylonians held sway: they were the golden head of the statue. After them the Persians were the masters for 245 years. This goes to show that they represent the silver [in the statue].

After that the supreme rule was transferred to the Greeks for 300 years; this began with Alexander of Macedonia and is symbolized by the brass. They were followed by the Romans represented by the iron legs, for the Romans have iron strength. Then come the toes that point to the future democracies, which will be separated from one another as are the fingers of the statue, and they are partly iron and partly tile.

What does Daniel say after that? "A stone which was hewn from a mountain without a hand being put to it, struck its iron and tile feet." When iron becomes mingled with clay, when this mixture will have reached the fingers, when people no longer will agree among themselves, will any other king remain than Christ? He came from heaven like the stone detached from the mountain, to overthrow the earthly kingships, to initiate the heavenly kingdom of the saints "which will never be destroyed"; he himself will become the "mountain" and the city of the saints, and will cover the whole earth.

That is why blessed Daniel has said: "In the lifetime of those kings the God of heaven will set up a kingdom that shall never be destroyed or delivered up to another people." And that no one might have a doubt about those words and that no one might ask if truly this will come to pass, yes or no, the prophet put the seal to his prediction saying: "This is exactly what you dreamed, and its meaning is sure."

Commentary on Daniel 2, 9, 12-13: SC 14, 141-142, 144-147

Week of 2 Easter ✠ Friday

A reading from a homily of John Chrysostom, Bishop of Constantinople [407]

"God did not send the Son into the world to condemn the world, but that the world might be saved through him."

Many rather careless persons who are inclined to abuse God's loving kindness to increase the magnitude of their sins and indulge in excessive negligence mouth such words as these: "There is no hell; there is no future judgment; God forgives all our sins." To reduce them to silence a wise man states: "Say not: 'Great is his mercy; my many sins he will forgive.' For mercy and anger alike are with him; upon the wicked alights his wrath." And again: "Great as his mercy is his punishment."

"Where then," you ask, "are the proofs of his lovingkindness, if we receive the punishment deserved by our sins?" In testimony that we shall receive the punishment "deserved by our sins," pay heed to the words of both the Prophet and Paul. The former declares: "You render to all according to their deeds," and the latter states: "He will repay all for what they have done."

Yet it is also clear from this fact that God's lovingkindness is nonetheless great. In dividing our existence into two periods—the present life and that which is to come—and making the first a succession of trials and the second a place of crowning, God has shown great lovingkindness. How, and in what way? Because, although we have committed many and grievous sins, and have not ceased from youth to extreme old age to defile our souls with ten thousand evil deeds, he has not demanded from us a reckoning for any one of these sins but has granted us pardon for them by the bath of regeneration and has freely bestowed on us justice and holiness.

"What then," you ask, "if one who from earliest years has been deemed worthy of the mysteries should commit ten thousand sins afterward?" Such a one certainly deserves greater punishment. For we do not pay the same penalties for the same sins; the penalties are much more severe when we offend after partaking of the mysteries. This is what Paul means when he says: "Anyone who rejects the law of Moses is put to death without mercy on the testimony of two or three witnesses. Do you not suppose that a much worse punishment is due the one who disdains the Son of God, thinks the covenant-blood by which the soul was sanctified to be ordinary, and insults the Spirit of grace?" Such a one therefore is deserving of severer punishment.

Yet even for this person God has opened the doors of repentance and has granted even this sinner many means to wash away offences, if the sinner desires. Consider then what great proofs of lovingkindness these constitute: to remit sin by grace, and to refrain from punishing the one who after grace has sinned and deserves punishment but rather to give the sinner the opportunity and the time to make amends!

Homily 28 on John 1: PG 59, 162–163

Week of 2 Easter ✠ Saturday

A reading from the Demonstration of the Apostolic Preaching by Irenaeus, Bishop of Lyons [c. 202]

This is the rule of our faith, the foundation of our building, and the consolidation of our way of life.

God, the Father, uncreated, unlimited, invisible, one God, the creator of the universe—this is the first article of our faith. The second article is the Word of God, the Son of God, Jesus Christ our Lord, who was revealed by the prophets in accord with the genre of their prophecies and in accord with the plan of the Father; through him all things have been made. At the end of times, in order to recapitulate all things, he has become a human among humans, visible and palpable, so as to destroy death, bring life to light, and effect the reconciliation of God and humanity.

And the third article is the Holy Spirit; through the Spirit the prophets prophesied, our ancestors were taught the things of God, and the just were led along the path of justice. At the end of times, the Spirit has been poured forth in a new manner upon all flesh, in order to renew them for God over the whole earth.

Therefore, the baptism of our new birth is placed under the sign of these three articles. God the Father grants it to us in view of our new birth in his Son through the Holy Spirit. For those who are bearers of the Holy Spirit are led to the Word who is the Son, and the Son leads them to the Father, and the Father confers incorruptibility on us. Without the Spirit it is impossible to see the Word of God, and without the Son one cannot approach the Father. For the Son is the knowledge of the Father, and the knowledge of the Son is had through the Holy Spirit; and the Son gives the Spirit according to the Father's good pleasure.

Through the Spirit, the Father is called Most High, Almighty, and Lord of Hosts. Thus, we come to the knowledge of God: we know that God exists, that he is the creator of heaven and earth and all things, the maker of angels and humans, the Lord, through whom all things come into existence, and from whom all things proceed, rich in mercy, grace, compassion, goodness, and justice.

He is the God of all, both of Jews and of Gentiles and of the faithful. To the faithful he is a Father, for in the end of times he has opened the testament of their adoptive inheritance. To the Jews, he is Lord and Lawgiver, for in the intermediate times, when humankind had forgotten and fallen away and rebelled against God, God subjected them to the law so that he might teach them that they have a Lord who is their creator and author, who has given them the breath of life, and to whom we are bound to render worship day and night. To the Gentiles, he is the creator, author, and supreme master. But for all alike he is sustainer and nourisher and king and judge—for none shall escape his judgment, neither Jew nor Gentiles nor sinner among the faithful, nor angelic spirit.

This is he who in the law is called the God of Abraham, the God of Isaac, and the God of Jacob: the God of the living. The sublimity and greatness of this God surpass all description.

Demonstration of the Apostolic Preaching 6–8: SC 62, 39–44

Week of 3 Easter ✠ Sunday

A reading from the First Apology of Justin, Martyr at Rome [c. 167]

Through Christ we received new life and we consecrated ourselves to God. I will explain the way in which we did this. Those who believe what we teach is true and who give assurance of their ability to live according to that teaching are taught to ask God's forgiveness for their sins by prayer and fasting and we pray and fast with them. We then lead them to a place where there is water and they are reborn in the same way as we were reborn; that is to say, they are washed in the water in the name of God, the Father and Lord of the whole universe, of our Savior Jesus Christ and of the Holy Spirit. This is done because Christ said: "Unless you are born again you will not enter the kingdom of heaven," and it is obviously impossible for anyone, having once been born, to re-enter their mother's womb.

An explanation of how repentant sinners are to be freed from their sins is given through the prophet Isaiah in the words: "Wash yourselves and be clean. Remove the evil from your souls; learn to do what is right. Be just to the orphan, vindicate the widow. Come, let us reason together, says the Lord. If your sins are like scarlet, I will make them white as wool; if they are like crimson, I will make them white as snow. But if you do not heed me, you shall be devoured by the sword. The mouth of the Lord has spoken."

The apostles taught us the reason for this ceremony of ours. Our first birth took place without our knowledge or consent because our parents came together, and we grew up in the midst of wickedness. So if we were not to remain children of necessity and ignorance, we needed a new birth of which we ourselves would be conscious, and which would be the result of our own free choice. We needed, too, to have our sins forgiven. This is why the name of God, the Father and Lord of the whole universe, is pronounced in the water over anyone who chooses to be born again and who has repented of sin. The person who leads the candidate for baptism to the font calls upon God by this name alone, for God so far surpasses our powers of description that no one can really give a name to him. Any who dare to say that they can must be hopelessly insane.

This baptism is called "illumination" because of the mental enlightenment that is experienced by those who learn these things. The person receiving this enlightenment is also baptized in the name of Jesus Christ, who was crucified under Pontius Pilate, and in the name of the Holy Spirit, who through the prophets foretold everything concerning Jesus.

First Apology 61: PG 6, 419–422

Week of 3 Easter ✠ Monday

A reading from the First Apology of Justin, Martyr at Rome [c. 167]

No one may share the eucharist with us unless they believe that what we teach is true, unless they are washed in the regenerating waters of baptism for the remission of sins, and unless they live in accordance with the principles given us by Christ.

We do not consume the eucharistic bread and wine as if it were ordinary food and drink, for we have been taught that as Jesus Christ our Savior became a human being of flesh and blood by the power of the Word of God, so also the food that our flesh and blood assimilate for their nourishment becomes the flesh and blood of the incarnate Jesus by the power of his own words contained in the prayer of thanksgiving.

The apostles, in their recollections, which are called gospels, handed down to us what Jesus commanded them to do. They tell us that he took bread, gave thanks and said: "Do this in memory of me. This is my body." In the same way he took the cup, he gave thanks and said: "This is my blood." The Lord gave this command to them alone. Ever since then we have constantly reminded one another of these things. The rich among us help the poor and we are always united. For all that we receive we praise the Creator of the universe through his Son Jesus Christ and through the Holy Spirit.

On Sunday we have a common assembly of all our members, whether they live in the city or in the outlying districts. The recollections of the apostles or the writings of the prophets are read, as long as there is time. When the reader has finished, the president of the assembly speaks to us urging everyone to imitate the examples of virtue we have heard in the readings. Then we all stand up together and pray.

On the conclusion of our prayer, bread and wine and water are brought forward. The president offers prayers and gives thanks as well as possible, and the people give their assent by saying: "Amen." The eucharist is distributed, everyone present communicates, and the deacons take it to those who are absent.

The wealthy, if they wish, may make a contribution, and they themselves decide the amount. The collection is placed in the custody of the president, who uses it to help the orphans and widows and all who for any reason are in distress, whether because they are sick, in prison, or away from home. In a word, the president takes care of all who are in need.

We hold our common assembly on Sunday because it is the first day of the week, the day on which God put darkness and chaos to flight and created the world, and because on that same day our savior Jesus Christ rose from the dead. For he was crucified on Friday and on Sunday he appeared to his apostles and disciples and taught them the things that we have passed on for your consideration.

First Apology 66–67: PG 6, 427–431

Week of 3 Easter ✠ Tuesday

A reading from the commentary on First Peter by Bede, the Venerable, Priest, and Monk of Jarrow [735]

"You are a chosen race, a royal priesthood." This praise was given long go by Moses to the ancient people of God, and now the apostle Peter rightly gives it to the Gentiles, since they have come to believe in Christ who, as the cornerstone, has brought the nations together in the salvation that belonged to Israel.

Peter calls them "a chosen race" because of their faith, to distinguish them from those who by refusing to accept the living stone have themselves been rejected. They are "a royal priesthood" because they are united to the body of Christ, the supreme king and true priest. As sovereign he grants them his kingdom, and as high priest he washes away their sins by the offering of his blood. Peter says they are "a royal priesthood;" they must always remember to hope for an everlasting kingdom and to offer to God the sacrifice of a blameless life.

They are also called "a consecrated nation, a people claimed by God as his own," in accordance with the apostle Paul's explanation of the prophet's teaching: "My righteous ones live by faith; but if they draw back, I will take no pleasure in them. But we," he says: "are not the sort of people who draw back and are lost; we are those who remain faithful until we are saved." In the Acts of the Apostles we read: "The Holy Spirit has made you overseers, to care for the Church of God which he bought with his own blood." Thus, through the blood of our Redeemer, we have become "a people claimed by God as his own," as in ancient times the people of Israel were ransomed from Egypt by the blood of a lamb.

In the next verse, Peter also makes a veiled allusion to the ancient story, and explains that this story is to be spiritually fulfilled by the new people of God, "so that," he says, "they may declare his wonderful deeds." Those who were freed by Moses from slavery in Egypt sang a song of triumph to the Lord after they had crossed the Red Sea, and Pharaoh's army had been overwhelmed; in the same way, now that our sins have been washed away in baptism, we too should express fitting gratitude for the gifts of heaven. The Egyptians who oppressed the people of God, and who can also stand for darkness or trials, are an apt symbol of the sins that once oppressed us but have now been destroyed in baptism.

The deliverance of the children of Israel and their journey to the long-promised land correspond with the mystery of our redemption. We are making our way toward the light of our heavenly home with the grace of Christ leading us and showing us the way. The light of his grace was also symbolized by the cloud and the pillar of fire, which protected the Israelites from darkness throughout their journey, and brought them by a wonderful path to their promised homeland.

Commentary on 1 Peter 2: PL 93, 50–51

Week of 3 Easter ✠ Wednesday

A reading from the Catechetical Instructions of Theodore,
Bishop of Mopsuestia [428]

When the bishop and the congregation have exchanged blessings, the bishop begins to give the Kiss of Peace, and the church herald, that is to say, the deacon, in a loud voice orders all the people to exchange the Kiss of Peace, following the bishop's example. This kiss which all present exchange constitutes a kind of profession of the unity and charity that exists among them. Each of us gives the Kiss of Peace to the person next to us, and so in effect gives it to the whole assembly, because this act is an acknowledgement that we have all become the single body of Christ our Lord, and so must preserve with one another that harmony that exists among the limbs of a body, loving one another equally, supporting and helping one another, regarding the individual's needs as concerns of the community, sympathizing with one another's sorrows and sharing in one another's joys.

The new birth that we underwent at baptism is unique for this reason, that it joins us into a natural unity; and so we all share the same food when we partake of the same body and the same blood, for we have been linked in the unity of baptism. St. Paul says: "Because there is one loaf, we who are many are one body, for we all partake of the same loaf." This is why before we approach the sacrament of the liturgy we are required to observe the custom of giving the Kiss of Peace, as a profession of unity and mutual charity. It would certainly not be right for those who form a single body, the body of the Church, to entertain hatred towards a brother or sister in the faith, who has shared the same birth so as to become a member of the same body, and whom we believe to be a member of Christ our Lord just as we are, and to share the same food at the spiritual table. Our Lord said: "Every one who is angry with a brother [or sister] without cause shall be liable to judgment." This ceremony, then, is not only a profession of charity, but a reminder to us to lay aside all unholy enmity, if we feel that our cause of complaint against one of our brothers or sisters in the faith is not just. After our Lord had forbidden any unjust anger, he offered the following remedy to sinners of every kind: "If you are offering your gift at the altar, and there remember that your brother [or sister] has something against you, leave your gift there before the altar and go; first be reconciled to your brother [or sister], and then come and offer your gift." He tells the sinner to seek immediately every means of reconciliation with the one offended, and not to presume to make an offering until amends are made to the one wronged and the sinner has done all that is possible to placate the offended person; for we all make the offering by the agency of the bishop.

Baptismal Homily 4, 39–40: Yarnold 233–234

Week of 3 Easter ✠ Thursday

A reading from the Catechetical Instructions of John Chrysostom, Bishop of Constantinople [407]

If we wish to understand the power of Christ's blood, we should go back to the ancient account of its prefiguration in Egypt. "Sacrifice a lamb without blemish," commanded Moses, "and sprinkle its blood on your doors." If we were to ask him what he meant, and how the blood of an irrational beast could possibly save humans endowed with reason, his answer would be that the saving power lies not in the blood itself, but in the fact that it is a sign of the Lord's blood.

If you desire further proof of the power of this blood, remember where it came from, how it ran down from the cross, flowing from the Master's side. The gospel records that when Christ was dead, but still hung on the cross, a soldier came and pierced his side with a lance and immediately there poured out water and blood. Now the water was a symbol of baptism, and the blood of the holy eucharist. The soldier pierced the Lord's side, he breached the wall of the sacred temple, and I have found the treasure and made it my own. So also with the lamb: the Jews sacrificed the victim and I have been saved by it.

"There flowed from his side water and blood." Beloved, do not pass over this mystery without thought; it has yet another hidden meaning, which I will explain to you. I said that water and blood symbolized baptism and the holy eucharist. From these two sacraments the Church is born: from baptism, "the cleansing water that gives rebirth and renewal through the Holy Spirit," and from the holy eucharist. Since the symbols of baptism and the eucharist flowed from his side, it was from his side that Christ fashioned the Church, as he had fashioned Eve from the side of Adam. Moses gives a hint of this when he tells the story of the first man and makes him exclaim: "Bone from my bones and flesh from my flesh!" As God then took a rib from Adam's side to fashion a woman, so Christ has given us blood and water from his side to fashion the Church. God took the rib when Adam was in a deep sleep, and in the same way Christ gave us the blood and the water after his own death.

Do you understand, then, how Christ has united his bride to himself and what food he gives us all to eat? By one and the same food we are both brought into being and nourished. As a woman nourishes her child with her own blood and milk, so does Christ unceasingly nourish with his own blood those to whom he himself has given life.

Catechesis 3, 13–19: SC 50, 174–177

A reading from a sermon of Ephrem of Edessa, Deacon [373]

Death trampled our Lord underfoot, but he in his turn treated death as a highroad for his own feet. He submitted to it, enduring it willingly, because by this means he would be able to destroy death in spite of itself. Death had its own way when our Lord went out from Jerusalem carrying his cross; but when by a loud cry from that cross he summoned the dead from the underworld, death was powerless to prevent it.

Death slew him by means of the body which he had assumed, but that same body proved to be the weapon with which he conquered death. In slaying our Lord, death itself was slain. It was able to kill natural human life, but was itself killed by the life that is above the nature of mortals.

Death could not devour our Lord unless he possessed a body, neither could hell swallow him up unless he bore our flesh; and so he came in search of a chariot in which to ride to the underworld. This chariot was the body which he received from the Virgin; in it he invaded death's fortress, broke open its strongroom and scattered all its treasure.

At length he came upon Eve, the mother of all the living. She was that vineyard whose enclosure her own hands had enabled death to violate, so that she could taste its fruit; thus the mother of all the living became the source of death for every living creature. But in her stead Mary grew up, a new vine in place of the old. Christ, the new life, dwelt within her. When death, with its customary impudence, came foraging for her mortal fruit, it encountered its own destruction in the hidden life that fruit contained. All unsuspecting, it swallowed him up, and in so doing released life itself and set free a multitude.

He who was also the carpenter's glorious son set up his cross above death's all-consuming jaws, and led the human race into the dwelling place of life. Since a tree had brought about the downfall of humankind, it was upon a tree that humankind crossed over to the realm of life. Bitter was the branch that had once been grafted upon that ancient tree, but sweet the young shoot that has now been grafted in, the shoot in which we are meant to recognize the Lord whom no creature can resist.

We give glory to you, Lord, who raised up your cross to span the jaws of death like a bridge by which souls might pass from the region of the dead to the land of the living. We give glory to you who put on the body of a single mortal and made it the source of life for every other mortal. You are incontestably alive. Your murderers sowed your living body in the earth as farmers sow grain, but it sprang up and yielded an abundant harvest of people raised from the dead.

Come then, my brothers and sisters, let us offer our Lord the great and all-embracing sacrifice of our love, pouring out our treasury of hymns and prayers before him who offered his cross in sacrifice to God for the enrichment of us all.

Sermon on our Lord 3–4, 9: ed. Lamy 1, 152–158, 166–168

Week of 3 Easter ✠ Saturday

A reading from a commentary on Daniel by Hippolytus,
Priest or Bishop of Rome [c. 236]

Look well; behold three youths who have set an example for all of us. They were unafraid of the numerous satraps and of the words of the king; they did not tremble when they heard about the fiery flames of the furnace, but they spurned all human force and the whole world for they thought only of the fear of God.

You see how the Spirit of the Father teaches eloquence to the martyrs, consoling them and exhorting them to despise death in this world, to hasten their attainment of heavenly goods. But one who is without the Holy Spirit is frightened of the struggle. Such a one hides, takes precautions against a death that is only temporal, is afraid of the sword, falls into a panic at the thought of the torture. The coward no longer sees any other thing than the world here below, worries only about the present life, prefers a spouse to everything else, is bothered only about care for offspring, and seeks nothing but wealth.

Such a person, because not endowed with heavenly strength, is quickly lost. That is why anyone who desires to come near the Word listens to the behest of the King and Lord of heaven: "Whoever does not bear the cross and follow me is not worthy of me and whoever does not renounce all possessions cannot be my disciple."

Scripture tells us that after this "those three youths, Shadrach, Meshach and Abednego fell into the white-hot furnace and walked about in the flames, singing to God and blessing the Lord." The fire had no difficulty in devouring the fetters with which they had been bound by order of the king, but it did not touch "their coats, hats, shoes and other garments." This miracle brought out the wonderful power of God.

But someone might say: "Why did God of old rescue martyrs when he does not rescue martyrs of our own day? For we see that blessed Daniel was cast twice into the den, and that he was not devoured by the beasts, just as the three youths were cast into the furnace and suffered not the least damage from the fire."

Think it over, skeptic! At that time, God saved those he wanted, in order that the wonders of his works might be revealed to the whole world. But those whom he desired to undergo martyrdom, he crowned and let them come to him. If he drew the three youths out of their predicament, it was to show the emptiness and folly of Nebuchadnezzar's boastfulness and prove at the same time that "what is impossible to humans is possible to God." Nebuchadnezzar had proudly declared: "Who is the God that can deliver you out of my hands?" God proved to him that he can free his servants when he wishes to do so.

That is why it is improper for us to oppose the decisions of God. "For if we live, we live for the Lord. And if we die, we die for the Lord. Whether we live or whether we die, we belong to the Lord." He drew Jonah from the belly of a monster because he willed it. He rescued Peter from the hand of Herod and let him escape from prison because he wanted Peter to live somewhat longer. He received Peter and made him come near him at the appointed time, after he had been crucified for the Lord's name. This happened only when he wanted it.

Commentary on Daniel 2, 18, 21, 28, 35–36: SC 14, 150–151, 156–157, 170, 189

Week of 4 Easter ✠ Sunday

A reading from a sermon of Leo the Great, Bishop of Rome [461]

The blessedness of seeing God is justly promised to the pure of heart. For the eye that is unclean would not be able to see the brightness of the true light, and what would be happiness to clear minds would be a torment to those that are defiled. Therefore, let the mists of worldly vanities be dispelled, and the inner eye be cleansed of all the filth of wickedness, so that the soul's gaze may feast serenely upon the great vision of God.

It is to the attainment of this goal that the next words refer: "Blessed are the peacemakers, for they shall be called children of God." This blessedness, dearly beloved, does not derive from any casual agreement or from any and every kind of harmony, but it pertains to what the Apostle says: "Be at peace before the Lord," and to the words of the prophet: "Those who love your law shall enjoy abundant peace; for them it is no stumbling block."

Even the most intimate bonds of friendship and the closest affinity of minds cannot truly lay claim to this peace if they are not in agreement with the will of God. Alliances based on evil desires, covenants of crime and pacts of vice—all lie outside the scope of this peace. Love of the world cannot be reconciled with love of God, and those who do not separate themselves from the children of this generation cannot join the company of the children of God. But those who keep God ever in their hearts, and are "anxious to preserve the unity of the spirit in the bond of peace," never dissent from the eternal law as they speak the prayer of faith. "Your will be done on earth as it is in heaven."

These then are the peacemakers; they are bound together in holy harmony and are rightly given the heavenly title of "children of God, co-heirs with Christ." And this is the reward they will receive for their love of God and neighbor: when their struggle with all temptation is finally over, there will be no further adversaries to suffer or scandal to fear; but they will rest in the peace of God undisturbed, through our Lord who lives and reigns with the Father and the Holy Spirit for ever and ever.

Sermon 95, 8–9: PL 54, 465–466

Week of 4 Easter ✠ Monday

A reading from a sermon of Leo the Great, Bishop of Rome [461]

Beloved, the days which passed between the Lord's resurrection and his ascension were by no means uneventful; during them great sacramental mysteries were confirmed, great truths revealed. In those days the fear of death with all its horrors was taken away, and the immortality of both body and soul affirmed. It was then that the Lord breathed on all his apostles and filled them with the Holy Spirit; and after giving the keys of the kingdom to blessed Peter, whom he had chosen and set above all the others, he entrusted him with the care of his flock.

During these days the Lord joined two of his disciples as their companion on the road, and by chiding them for their timidity and hesitant fears he swept away all the clouds of our uncertainty. Their lukewarm hearts were fired by the light of faith and began to burn within them as the Lord opened up the Scriptures. And as they shared their meal with him, their eyes were opened in the breaking of bread, opened far more happily to the sight of their own glorified humanity than were the eyes of our first parents to the shame of their sin.

Throughout the whole period between the resurrection and ascension, God's providence was at work to instill this one lesson into the hearts of the disciples, to set this one truth before their eyes, that our Lord Jesus Christ, who was truly born, truly suffered and truly died, should be recognized as truly risen from the dead. The blessed apostles together with all the others had been intimidated by the catastrophe of the cross, and their faith in the resurrection had been uncertain; but now they were so strengthened by the evident truth that when their Lord ascended into heaven, far from feeling any sadness, they were filled with great joy.

Indeed that blessed company had a great and inexpressible cause for joy when it saw human nature rising above the dignity of the whole heavenly creation, above the ranks of angels, above the exalted status of archangels. Nor would there be any limit to its upward course until humanity was admitted to a seat at the right hand of the eternal Father, to be enthroned at last in the glory of him to whose nature it was wedded in the person of the Son.

Sermon 1 for the Ascension 2–4: PL 54, 395–396

Week of 4 Easter ✠ Tuesday

A reading from the Letter to the Philippians by Polycarp, Bishop and Martyr of Smyrna [156]

From Polycarp and his fellow presbyters to the church of God sojourning in Philippi: May you have mercy and peace in abundance from Almighty God and Jesus Christ our Savior.

I rejoice with you greatly in the Lord Jesus Christ because you have assumed the pattern of true love and have rightly helped on their way those who were in chains. Such chains are becoming to the faithful; they are the rich crown of the chosen ones of our Lord and God. I am glad, too, that your deep-rooted faith, proclaimed of old, still abides and continues to bear fruit in the life-giving power of our Lord Jesus Christ. He, for our sins, did not refuse to go down to death, and God "raised him up after destroying the pains of hell. With a glorious joy that no words can express you believe in Christ without seeing him." This is the joy in which many wish to share "knowing that it is by grace that you are saved and not by works," for so God has willed through Jesus Christ.

So prepare yourselves for the struggle, serve the Lord in fear and truth. Put aside empty talk and popular errors; your faith must be in him who raised our Lord Jesus Christ from the dead and gave him a share in his own glory and a seat at his right hand. To him everything was made subject in heaven and on earth; all things obey him, who will come as judge of the living and the dead. All who refuse to believe in him must answer to God for the blood of his Son.

He who raised him from the dead will raise us too if we do his will and keep his commandments, loving what he loved, refraining from all wrongdoing, fraud, avarice, malice and slander. We must abstain from false witness, "not returning evil for evil, nor curse for curse," nor blow for blow, nor denunciation for denunciation. Always remember the words of the Lord, who taught: "Do not judge and you will not be judged; forgive and you will be forgiven; be merciful and you will find mercy; the amount you measure out to others will be the amount measured out to you. Blessed are the poor and those who suffer persecution, for theirs is the kingdom of God."

To the Philippians 1, 1–2, 3: Funk 1, 267–269

Week of 4 Easter ✠ Wednesday

A reading from a commentary on John by Augustine, Bishop of Hippo [430]

"A new commandment I give you, that you love one another." This commandment that he is giving them is a new one, the Lord Jesus tells his disciples. Yet was it not contained in the Old Law, where it is written: "You shall love your neighbor as yourself"? Why does the Lord call it new when it is clearly so old? Or is the commandment new because it divests us of our former selves and clothes us with the new person? Love does indeed renew the one who hears, or rather obeys, its command; but only that love which Jesus distinguished from a natural love by the qualification: "As I have loved you."

This is the kind of love that renews us. When we love as he loved us we become new people, heirs of the new covenant and singers of the new song. My beloved, this was the love that even in bygone days renewed the holy ones, the patriarchs and prophets of old. In later times it renewed the blessed apostles, and now it is the turn of the Gentiles. From the entire human race throughout the world this love gathers together into one body a new people, to be the bride of God's only Son. She is the bride of whom it is asked in the Song of Songs: "Who is this who comes clothed in white?" White indeed are her garments, for she has been made new; and the source of her renewal is none other than this new commandment.

And so all her members make each other's welfare their common care. When one member suffers, all the members suffer too, and if one member is glorified all the rest rejoice. They hear and obey the Lord's words: "A new commandment I give you, that you love one another," not as people love one another for their own selfish ends, nor merely on account of their common humanity, but because they are all gods and children of the Most High. They love one another as God loves them so that they may be brothers and sisters of his only Son. He will lead them to the goal that alone will satisfy them, where all their desires will be fulfilled. For when God is all in all, there will be nothing left to desire.

This love is the gift of the Lord who said: "As I have loved you, you also must love one another." His object in loving us, then, was to enable us to love each other. By loving us himself, our mighty head has linked us all together as members of his own body, bound to one another by the tender bond of love.

Treatise 65 on John 1–3: CCL 36, 490–492

Week of 4 Easter ✠ Thursday

A reading from a treatise by Clement of Alexandria, Priest [c. 210]

"Awake, O sleeper, arise from the dead, and Christ will give you light." He is the sun of the resurrection, begotten before the dawn, he who gives life through his own rays. So let no one spurn the Word, for fear of spurning the self without knowing it. For Scripture says: "Oh, that today you would hear the voice: 'Harden not your hearts.' " And this "today" extends to each new day as long as "today" will be said.

This "today" remains until the end of times, as long as there is a possibility of being understood. At that moment the real today, God's day without ending, will merge with eternity. So let us always obey the voice of the divine Word, for "today" is always a figure of eternity and the day is a symbol of light; now the Word is for us the light in which we see God.

Because he loves humankind, the Lord invites them "to come to know the truth," and he sends them the Spirit, the Paraclete. What is this knowledge? It is the discipline of religion. According to St. Paul, the discipline of religion is incalculably more valuable than physical training, with its promise of life here and hereafter. This discipline assimilates and likens us to God as far as is possible, and it gives us God as Master; God alone has the right and power to make us like himself. The Apostle, who had experienced this divine formation, will say to Timothy: "From your infancy you have known the sacred Scriptures, the source of the wisdom which through faith in Jesus Christ leads to salvation." For these Scriptures which sanctify and deify are truly sacred. Their sacred letters and syllables constitute the works concerning which the same Apostle says a bit later: "All Scripture is inspired of God and is useful for teaching—for reproof, correction, and training in holiness so that the child of God may be fully competent and equipped for every good work." No one could be moved by the exhortations of other saints as much as by the Lord himself who loves us and works for one single end: to save us.

"Taste and see how good the Lord is." Faith will introduce you. Experience will teach you. Scripture, like a schoolteacher, will guide you. "Come, children, hear me," it says; "I will teach you the fear of the Lord." Then, as though addressing those who already believe, Scripture adds: "Which of you desires life, and takes delight in prosperous days?" We do, you will say, the worshipers of the Good and the sharers of goodness.

Then listen, both you who are far off and you who are near. The Word does not hide from anyone. He is our shared light, he shines for all. Let us hasten, then, toward salvation, toward the new birth. Let us who are many make haste to unite ourselves in the unity of love. Thus this multitude of so many different voices, after obtaining divine unison and harmony, will produce a unique symphony; and the choir, obeying one single master, the Word, will find its rest in Truth itself and be able to say: "Abba, Father." And God will garner this sound, full of truth, as the first fruit of his children.

Protrepticus 9: PG 8, 195–201

Week of 4 Easter ✠ Friday

A reading from a sermon of Leo the Great, Bishop of Rome [461]

Among all the days honored in various ways by Christian devotion none has greater importance than the feast of Easter, because it consecrates all the other festivals of God's Church. Even the Lord's birth from his mother has this mystery as its fulfillment. And there was no other reason for the birth of the Son of God save that of being able to die on the cross.

He assumed mortal flesh in the Virgin's womb. The progress of the passion was accomplished in this mortal flesh, which through the ineffable purpose of God's mercy became for us redemptive sacrifice, abolition of sin, and the ground of resurrection to eternal life.

When we think of what the whole world has received through the cross of the Lord, we recognize that it is right to prepare for the celebration of Easter by a fast of forty days, in order to take part worthily in the celebration of the divine mysteries.

Not only the bishops, priests, and ministers of the sacraments, but the whole body of the Church, the whole company of the faithful, must be cleansed from all dirt, so that the temple of God, whose foundation is its Founder himself, may be beautiful in every stone and shining in every part.

Doubtless the purification of this temple can be neither undertaken nor finished without the builder; yet he who built it has also given it power to seek its growth by its own labor. For a living and intelligent material is used in the construction of this temple, and the Spirit of grace has inspired its voluntary gathering into one building.

This material has been loved and sought after, so that we who did not love nor seek after might begin to love and seek in our turn, according to the saying of blessed John the apostle: "We, for our part, love because he first loved us."

Therefore, so that the whole company of the faithful and each one in particular may form one and the same temple of God, this temple must be perfect in each member, just as it is to be perfect in the whole. For although there may not be the same beauty in all the members, nor equal merit in so great a diversity of parts, yet the bond of charity ensures a communion of beauty.

Those who are united by holy love, even though they may not have received the same gifts of grace, rejoice mutually in their blessings; and that which they love is not foreign to them, because they gain treasure by finding their joy in the progress of others.

Sermon 48, 1: PL 54, 298A–299A

Week of 4 Easter ✠ Saturday

A reading from the commentary on the Apostles' Creed by Rufinus of Aquileia, Monk [410]

On the third day he rose again from the dead. The glory of his resurrection brought out in Christ the splendor of everything that previously seemed feeble and weak. If a few moments ago you thought it impossible for One who was immortal to reach death, you can now perceive the impossibility of his being mortal who is declared to have vanquished death and to have risen again. Herein you should discern the Creator's goodness, in his readiness to follow you down to the depths to which your sins have plunged you.

You should not, either, suggest that anything is impossible for God, the Creator of all things, imagining that his work could have been brought to an end by falling into an abyss to which he could not penetrate in order to accomplish salvation. "Underworld" and "upper world" are terms which we employ, limited as we are by the fixed circumference of our bodies and confined within the limits of the space assigned to us. But what is underworld or upper world to God, who is present everywhere and is nowhere absent?

Notwithstanding, when he assumed a body, those dimensions found their place. The flesh which had been laid in the tomb was resuscitated in fulfillment of the Prophet's words: "Because you will not give your Holy One to see corruption." So he returned victoriously from the dead, bringing with him spoils from hell. For he conducted forth those whom death held prisoners, as he himself had prophesied in the words: "When I am lifted up from the earth, I will draw all people unto myself." The gospel bears witness to this when it states: "The graves were opened, and many bodies of the saints that slept arose, and they appeared to many, and entered into the holy city." By this is meant, I am sure, the city intended by the Apostle when he wrote: "But that Jerusalem which is above is free: which is mother of us all." He made the same point again to the Hebrews: "For it became him for whom are all things, and by whom are all things, who had brought many children to glory, to perfect the author of their salvation by his passion."

By his passion, therefore, he made perfect that human flesh which had been brought down to death by the first man's sin, and restored it by the power of his resurrection: sitting on God's right hand, he placed it in the highest heavens. In view of this the Apostle says: "Who has raised us up together, and has made us sit together in the heavenly places." It was he, you see, who was the potter mentioned by the prophet Jeremiah: "The vessel which had fallen from his hand and was broken, he again raised up with his hands and formed anew, as it seemed good in his eyes." So it seemed good to him to raise the mortal and corruptible body he had assumed from the rocky tomb, and rendering it immortal and incorruptible to place it, no longer in an earthly environment, but in heaven at his Father's right hand.

Commentary on the Apostles' Creed 29: PL. 21, 364-365

A reading from the Letter to Diognetus [c. 124]

Christians are indistinguishable from others either by nationality, language or customs. They do not inhabit separate cities of their own, or speak a strange dialect, or follow some outlandish way of life. Their teaching is not based upon reveries inspired by the curiosity of human beings. Unlike some other people, they champion no purely human doctrine. With regard to dress, food and manner of life in general, they follow the customs of whatever city they happen to be living in, whether it is Greek or foreign.

And yet there is something extraordinary about their lives. They live in their own countries as though they were only passing through. They play their full role as citizens, but labor under all the disabilities of aliens. Any country can be their homeland, but for them their homeland, wherever it may be, is a foreign country. Like others, they marry and have children, but they do not expose them. They share their meals, but not their wives. They live in the flesh, but they are not governed by the desires of the flesh. They pass their days upon earth, but they are citizens of heaven. Obedient to the laws, they yet live on a level that transcends the law.

Christians love all people, but all people persecute them. Condemned because they are not understood, they are put to death, but raised to life again. They live in poverty, but enrich many; they are totally destitute, but possess an abundance of everything. They suffer dishonor, but that is their glory. They are defamed, but vindicated. A blessing is their answer to abuse, deference their response to insult. For the good they do they receive the punishment of malefactors, but even then they rejoice, as though receiving the gift of life. They are attacked by the Jews as aliens, they are persecuted by the Greeks, yet no one can explain the reason for this hatred.

To speak in general terms, we may say that the Christian is to the world what the soul is to the body. As the soul is present in every part of the body, while remaining distinct from it, so Christians are found in all the cities of the world, but cannot be identified with the world. As the visible body contains the invisible soul, so Christians are seen living in the world, but their religious life remains unseen. The body hates the soul and wars against it, not because of any injury the soul has done it, but because of the restriction the soul places on its pleasures. Similarly, the world hates the Christians, not because they have done it any wrong, but because they are opposed to its enjoyments.

Christians love those who hate them just as the soul loves the body and all its members despite the body's hatred. It is by the soul, enclosed within the body, that the body is held together, and similarly, it is by the Christians, detained in the world as in a prison, that the world is held together. The soul, though immortal, has a mortal dwelling place; and Christians also live for a time amidst perishable things, while awaiting the freedom from change and decay that will be theirs in heaven. As the soul benefits from the deprivation of food and drink, so Christians flourish under persecution. Such is the lofty and divinely appointed function of Christians, from which they are not permitted to excuse themselves.

Chapters 5–6: Funk 1, 397–401

Week of 5 Easter ✠ Monday

A reading from the treatise On the Holy Spirit by Basil the Great, Bishop of Caesarea [379]

Our Lord made a covenant with us through baptism in order to give us eternal life. There is in baptism an image both of death and of life, the water being the symbol of death, the Spirit giving the pledge of life. The association of water and the Spirit is explained by the twofold purpose for which baptism was instituted, namely, to destroy the sin in us so that it could never again give birth to death, and to enable us to live by the Spirit and so win the reward of holiness. The water into which the body enters as into a tomb symbolizes death; the Spirit instills into us life-giving power, awakening our souls from the death of sin to the life that they had in the beginning. This then is what it means to be born again of water and the Spirit: we die in the water, and we come to life again through the Spirit.

To signify this death and to enlighten the baptized by transmitting to them knowledge of God, the great sacrament of baptism is administered by means of a triple immersion and the invocation of each of the three divine Persons. Whatever grace there is in the water comes not from its own nature but from the presence of the Spirit, since "baptism is not a cleansing of the body, but a pledge made to God from a clear conscience."

As a preparation for our life after the resurrection, our Lord tells us in the gospel how we should live here and now. He teaches us to be peaceable, long-suffering, undefiled by desire for pleasure, and detached from worldly wealth. In this way we can achieve, by our own free choice, the kind of life that will be natural in the world to come.

Through the Holy Spirit we are restored to paradise, we ascend to the kingdom of heaven, and we are reinstated as adopted children. Thanks to the Spirit we obtain the right to call God our Father, we become sharers in the grace of Christ, we are called children of light, and we share in everlasting glory. In a word, every blessing is showered upon us, both in this world and in the world to come. As we contemplate them even now, like a reflection in a mirror, it is as though we already possessed the good things our faith tells us that we shall one day enjoy. If this is the pledge, what will the perfection be? If these are the firstfruits, what will the full harvest be?

On the Holy Spirit 15, 35–36: SC 17bis, 364–370

Week of 5 Easter ✠ Tuesday

A reading from a sermon of Leo the Great, Bishop of Rome [461]

The whole of the mystery of Easter has been given us in the gospel narratives; the impious betrayal of our Lord Jesus Christ, his condemnation, his cruel crucifixion, his glorious resurrection. Now you must implant in your hearts the words of the gospel.

The cross, of which Christ made use to save humankind, is both a mystery, and an example: a mystery in which the fullness of the divine power is involved, an example which leads us to generosity.

When all the human race had fallen, God determined in his mercy to give aid, through his only-begotten Son Jesus Christ, to the creatures made in his own image; he wished that the restoration of their nature should not come from without, but that it should be raised at the same time to a dignity superior to that of their origin. Happy they would have been, if they had not fallen from this first dignity in which he had placed them, but far happier still will they be, if they remain in that to which he has elevated them. It was already much to have recovered their beauty from the hands of Christ, but it is still better to be incorporated in Christ for ever.

The divine nature in him has indeed captured us; we have become his property. In himself, in the unity of the one person, he has united human nature to the divine nature. Infirmity and mortality, which were not sin, but the punishment of sin, were taken by the Redeemer of the world that he might be able to suffer and pay our ransom. Hence, that which is in others the heritage of condemnation, is in Christ the mysterious witness to his loving kindness. For he, who owed nothing, offered himself to the pitiless demands of his creditor; he abandoned his sinless flesh to be tortured by the hands of his enemies, the devil's instruments. He wished to possess a mortal body until his resurrection, so that faith in him would make persecutions bearable, and even death incapable of depressing us; sure of sharing the same nature, we are certain of receiving the same glory.

It follows then, that if we firmly believe in our heart what we profess with our lips, then in Christ we have been crucified, have died, been buried and have also been raised the third day. The Apostle says: "Risen, then, with Christ, you must lift your thoughts above, where Christ now sits at the right hand of God. You must be heavenly-minded, not earthly-minded; you have undergone death, and your life is hidden away now with Christ in God. Christ is your life, and when he is made manifest, you too will be made manifest in glory with him."

And that the faithful may know how to raise their thoughts to such lofty heights and despise worldly lusts, our Lord pledges to us his presence, saying: "And behold I am with you all through the days that are coming, until the consummation of the world."

We must, therefore, neither lose our heads among vanities, nor tremble at adversities. Doubtless, false pleasures have their attractions and work is hard. But since "the earth is filled with the Lord's kindness," the victory of Christ which is ours is everywhere. It is the fulfillment of his words: "Take courage, I have overcome the world."

Sermon 72: PG 54, 390-392

Week of 5 Easter ✠ Wednesday

A reading from a commentary on John by Cyril, Bishop of Alexandria [444]

The Lord calls himself the vine and those united to him branches in order to teach us how much we shall benefit from our union with him, and how important it is for us to remain in his love. By receiving the Holy Spirit, who is the bond of union between us and Christ our Savior, those who are joined to him, as branches are to a vine, share in his own nature.

On the part of those who come to the vine, their union with him depends upon a deliberate act of the will; on his part, the union is effected by grace. Because we had good will, we made the act of faith that brought us to Christ, and received from him the dignity of adoption that made us his own kin, according to the words of Saint Paul: "Whoever is joined to the Lord is one spirit with him."

The prophet Isaiah calls Christ the foundation, because it is upon him that we as living and spiritual stones are built into a holy priesthood to be a dwelling place for God in the Spirit. Upon no other foundation than Christ can this temple be built. Here Christ is teaching the same truth by calling himself the vine, since the vine is the parent of its branches, and provides their nourishment.

From Christ and in Christ, we have been reborn through the Spirit in order to bear the fruit of life; not the fruit of our old, sinful life but the fruit of a new life founded upon our faith in him and our love for him. Like branches growing from a vine, we now draw our life from Christ, and we cling to his holy commandment in order to preserve this life. Eager to safeguard the blessing of our noble birth, we are careful not to grieve the Holy Spirit who dwells in us, and who makes us aware of God's presence in us.

Let the wisdom of John teach us how we live in Christ and Christ lives in us: "The proof that we are living in him and he is living in us is that he has given us a share in his Spirit." Just as the trunk of the vine gives its own natural properties to each of its branches, so, by bestowing on them the Holy Spirit, the Word of God, the only-begotten Son of the Father, gives Christians a certain kinship with himself and with God the Father because they have been united to him by faith and determination to do his will in all things. He helps them to grow in love and reverence for God, and teaches them to discern right from wrong and to act with integrity.

Commentary on John 10, 2: PG 74, 331–334

Week of 5 Easter ✠ Thursday

A reading from the Confessions of Augustine, Bishop of Hippo [430]

Our Life himself came down into this world and took away our death. He slew it with his own abounding life, and with thunder in his voice he called us from this world to return to him in heaven. From heaven he came down to us, entering first the Virgin's womb, where humanity, our mortal flesh, was wedded to him so that it might not be for ever mortal. Then "as a bridegroom coming from his bed, he exulted like some great runner who sees the track before him." He did not linger on his way but ran, calling us to return to him, calling us by his words and deeds, by his life and death, by his descent into hell and his ascension into heaven. He departed from our sight, so that we should turn to our hearts and find him there. He departed, but he is here with us. He would not stay long with us, but he did not leave us. He went back to the place which he had never left, because "he, through whom the world was made, was in the world and he came into the world to save sinners."

Confessions 4, 12: CSEL 33, 79

Week of 5 Easter ✠ Friday

A reading from a commentary on the psalms by Augustine,
Bishop of Hippo [430]

Our thoughts in this present life should turn on the praise of God, because it is in praising God that we shall rejoice for ever in the life to come; and one cannot be ready for the next life unless trained for it now. So we praise God during our earthly life, and at the same time we make our petitions to him. Our praise is expressed with joy, our petitions with yearning. We have been promised something we do not yet possess, and because the promise was made by one who keeps his word, we trust him and are glad; but insofar as possession is delayed, we can only long and yearn for it. It is good for us to persevere in longing until we receive what was promised, and yearning is over; then praise alone will remain.

Because there are these two periods of time—the one that now is, beset with the trials and troubles of this life, and the other yet to come, a life of everlasting serenity and joy—we are given two liturgical seasons, one before Easter and the other after. The season before Easter signifies the troubles in which we live here and now, while the time after Easter which we are celebrating at present signifies the happiness that will be ours in the future. What we commemorate before Easter is what we experience in this life; what we celebrate after Easter points to something we do not yet possess. This is why we keep the first season with fasting and prayer; but now the fast is over and we devote the present season to praise. Such is the meaning of the "Alleluia" we sing.

Both these periods are represented and demonstrated for us in Christ our head. The Lord's passion depicts for us our present life of trial— shows how we must suffer and be afflicted and finally die. The Lord's resurrection and glorification show us the life that will be given to us in the future.

Now therefore, we urge you to praise God. That is what we are all telling each other when we say "Alleluia." You say to your neighbor:

"Praise the Lord!" and your neighbor says the same to you. We are all urging one another to praise the Lord, and all thereby doing what each of us urges the other to do. But see that your praise comes from your whole being; in other words, see that you praise God not with your lips and voices alone, but with your minds, your lives and all your actions.

We are praising God now, assembled as we are here in church; but when we go our various ways again, it seems as if we cease to praise God. But provided we do not cease to live a good life, we shall always be praising God. You cease to praise God only when you swerve from justice and from what is pleasing to God. If you never turn aside from the good life, your tongue may be silent but your actions will cry aloud, and God will perceive your intentions; for as our ears hear each other's voices, so do God's ears hear our thoughts.

Commentary on Psalm 148, 1–2: CCL 40, 2165–2166

Week of 5 Easter ✠ Saturday

A reading from a scriptural commentary of Ephrem of Edessa, Deacon [373]

At nightfall, when he is about to deliver himself, Jesus distributes his body to his apostles, gives them his blood, and tells them to do what he has done in memory of his Passion. Then he who had urged his disciples not to fear death—"Do not fear those who deprive the body of life"—strangely shows fear of death and prays that the cup might be taken away from him.

"If it is possible, let this cup pass me by." This Jesus says because of the weakness he has put on, because he has truly clothed himself with our nature and there is no make-believe in this. For he has made himself small, and truly assumed our weakness; and we know that human beings normally tremble and are troubled. Having assumed our flesh and put on our weakness, he ate when he was hungry, was tired because of labor, was overcome by sleep. Hence, when the moment of death is at hand, he must undergo all that belongs to the flesh.

So, indeed, the anguish of death enters into him, to manifest that he is a son of Adam, for "from Adam death reigned," as the Apostle tells us. Hence, he says to his disciples: "Be on guard, and pray that you may not undergo the test. The spirit is willing but nature is weak." "If it is true to say, then, that when you are in the grip of fear it is not your spirit that is fearful but the weakness of your human nature, recall that I too have feared death to prove by that fear that I had truly assumed human nature."

Jesus did indeed experience fear, just as he experienced hunger and thirst, became tired and slept. He experienced fear so that the world might not have an occasion to say: "It is without suffering and pain that he paid our debts." It was also to make his disciples commit their life and their death to God. For, if he who possesses the very wisdom of God prayed for that which was good for him, how much more ought those who lack wisdom commit themselves to him who knows all things.

That he might give comfort to his disciples by his Passion, Jesus chose to experience their sentiments. He put their fear into his heart to show, through his resemblance with them, that we should not boast about the willingness to give up our life before death is actually undergone. He who feared nothing experienced fear and asked to be freed from death although he knew it was impossible. How much more must the others persevere in prayer before temptation assails them in order to be freed when the test has come. At the hour of temptation our spirits are plagued and our thoughts wander. That is why Jesus persevered in prayer.

Commentary on the Diatesseron 20, 3–4, 6–7: CSCO 145, 201–204

Week of 6 Easter ✠ Sunday

A reading from a sermon of Gregory, Bishop of Nyssa [c. 394]

The reign of life has begun, the tyranny of death is ended. A new birth has taken place, a new life has come, a new order of existence has appeared, our very nature has been transformed! This birth is not brought about "by human generation, by the will of humankind, or by the desire of the flesh, but by God."

If you wonder how, I will explain in clear language. Faith is the womb that conceives this new life, baptism the rebirth by which it is brought forth into the light of day. The Church is its nurse; her teachings are its milk, the bread from heaven is its food. It is brought to maturity by the practice of virtue; it is wedded to wisdom; it gives birth to hope. Its home is the kingdom; its rich inheritance the joys of paradise; its end, not death, but the blessed and everlasting life prepared for those who are worthy.

"This is the day the Lord has made"—a day far different from those made when the world was first created and which are measured by the passage of time. This is the beginning of a new creation. On this day, as the prophet says, God makes a new heaven and a new earth. What is this new heaven? you may ask. It is the firmament of our faith in Christ. What is the new earth? A good heart, a heart like the earth, which drinks up the rain that falls on it and yields a rich harvest.

In this new creation, purity of life is the sun, the virtues are the stars, transparent goodness is the air, and "the depths of the riches of wisdom and knowledge," the sea. Sound doctrine, the divine teachings are the grass and plants that feed God's flock, the people whom he shepherds; the keeping of the commandments is the fruit borne by the trees.

On this day is created the true human, the one made in the image and likeness of God. For "this day the Lord has made" is the beginning of this new world. Of this day the prophet says that it is not like other days, nor is this night like other nights. But still we have not spoken of the greatest gift it has brought us. This day destroyed the pangs of death and brought to birth the firstborn of the dead.

"I ascend to my Father and to your Father, to my God and to your God." O what wonderful good news! He who for our sake became like us in order to make us his brothers and sisters, now presents to his true Father his own humanity in order to draw all his kindred up after him.

Oration 1 on the Resurrection: PG 46, 603, 606, 626–627

Week of 6 Easter ✠ Monday

A reading from the commentary on Second Corinthians by Cyril, Bishop of Alexandria [444]

Those who have a sure hope, guaranteed by the Spirit, that they will rise again lay hold of what lies in the future as though it were already present. They say: Outward appearances will no longer be our standard in judging others. Our lives are all controlled by the Spirit now, and are not confined to this physical world that is subject to corruption. The light of the Only-begotten has shone on us, and we have been transformed into the Word, the source of all life. While sin was still our master, the bonds of death had a firm hold on us, but now that the righteousness of Christ has found a place in our hearts we have freed ourselves from our former condition of corruptibility.

This means that none of us lives in the flesh any more, at least not insofar as living in the flesh means being subject to the weaknesses of the flesh, which include corruptibility. "Once we thought of Christ as being in the flesh, but we do not do so any longer," says Saint Paul. By this he meant that the Word became flesh and dwelt among us; he suffered death in the flesh in order to give life to all. It was in this flesh that we knew him before, but we do so no longer. Even though he remains in the flesh, since he came to life again on the third day and is now with the Father in heaven, we know that he has passed beyond the life of the flesh; for "having died once, he will never die again, death has no power over him any more. His death was a death to sin, which he died once for all; his life is life with God."

Since Christ has in this way become the source of life for us, we who follow in his footsteps must not think of ourselves as living in the flesh any longer, but as having passed beyond it. Saint Paul's saying is absolutely true that "whoever is in Christ becomes a completely different person: their old life is over and a new life has begun." We have been justified by our faith in Christ and the power of the curse has been broken. Christ's coming to life again for our sake has put an end to the sovereignty of death. We have come to know the true God and to worship him in spirit and in truth, through the Son, our mediator, who sends down upon the world the Father's blessings.

And so Saint Paul shows deep insight when he says: "This is all God's doing: it is he who has reconciled us to himself through Christ." For the mystery of the incarnation and the renewal it accomplished could not have taken place without the Father's will. Through Christ we have gained access to the Father, for as Christ himself says, no one comes to the Father except through him. "This is all God's doing," then. "It is he who has reconciled us to himself through Christ, and who has given us the ministry of reconciliation."

Commentary on 2 Corinthians 5, 5–6, 2: PG 74, 942–943

Week of 6 Easter ✠ Tuesday

A reading from the treatise Against Heresies by Irenaeus, Bishop of Lyons [c. 202]

If our flesh is not saved, then the Lord has not redeemed us with his blood, the eucharistic chalice does not make us sharers in his blood, and the bread we break does not make us sharers in his body. There can be no blood without veins, flesh and the rest of the human substance, and this the Word of God actually became: it was with his own blood that he redeemed us. As the Apostle says: "In him, through his blood, we have been redeemed, our sins have been forgiven."

We are his members and we are nourished by creation, which is his gift to us, for it is he who causes the sun to rise and the rain to fall. He declared that the chalice, which comes from his creation, was his blood, and he makes it the nourishment of our blood. He affirmed that the bread, which comes from his creation, was his body, and he makes it the nourishment of our body. When the chalice we mix and the bread we bake receive the word of God, the eucharistic elements become the body and blood of Christ, by which our bodies live and grow. How then can it be said that flesh belonging to the Lord's own body and nourished by his body and blood is incapable of receiving God's gift of eternal life? Saint Paul says in his letter to the Ephesians that "we are members of his body," of his flesh and bones. He is not speaking of some spiritual and incorporeal kind of person, "for spirits do not have flesh and bones." He is speaking of a real human body composed of flesh, sinews and bones, nourished by the chalice of Christ's blood and receiving growth from the bread which is his body.

The slip of a vine planted in the ground bears fruit at the proper time. The grain of wheat falls into the ground and decays only to be raised up again and multiplied by the Spirit of God who sustains all things. The Wisdom of God places these things at the service of human beings and when they receive God's word they become the eucharist, which is the body and blood of Christ. In the same way our bodies, which have been nourished by the eucharist, will be buried in the earth and will decay, but they will rise again at the appointed time, for the Word of God will raise them up to the glory of God the Father. Then the Father will clothe our mortal nature in immortality and freely endow our corruptible nature with incorruptibility, for God's power is shown most perfectly in weakness.

Against Heresies 5, 2, 2–3: SC 153, 30–38

Week of 6 Easter ✠ Wednesday

A reading from the Life of St. Macrina by Gregory, Bishop of Nyssa [c. 394]

Macrina no longer spoke to us who were present, but to that One alone upon whom she held her eyes intently. Her bed had been turned toward the east, and she stopped conversing with us and addressed herself to God, and this was her prayer:

"Lord, you have released us from the fear of death. You have made the end of life here on earth the beginning of true life for us. For a little while you will let our bodies rest in sleep, and then you will wake them again from their sleep at the sound of the last trumpet. You give back to the earth for safekeeping our bodies of dust which you have made with your own hands, and you will restore again what you have given, transforming with incorruptibility and grace that which is mortal and formless in us. You redeemed us from the curse and from sin, having taken both upon yourself. You have crushed the heads of the serpent that had seized us with diabolical jaws in the abyss of our disobedience. When you had shattered the gates of hell and reduced to impotence the one who ruled over death, you opened for us the path to resurrection. To those who fear you you have given a visible token, the sign of the holy cross, for the destruction of the enemy and the protection of our life.

"O God eternal, you have been my refuge ever since I left my mother's womb. My soul has loved you with all its strength. I have consecrated my body and soul to you from infancy up to this very moment. Set beside me a shining angel who will lead me by the hand to the place of refreshment, where there is water of repose beside the dwelling of the holy ones. You who broke the flaming sword and restored to paradise the thief who was crucified with you and sought your mercy, remember me also in your kingdom, for I too have been crucified with you and the nails have pierced my flesh out of reverence for you and fear of your judgements. Let not the dreadful abyss separate me from your chosen ones. Let not the slanderer stand in my way nor my sins be discovered before your eyes, if out of the weakness of human nature I have fallen and sinned in word or deed or thought. You who have the power on earth to forgive sins, forgive me, that I may have breath again and may stand before you without stain or blemish in the form of my soul once I am divested of my body. May my soul be received in your hands, blameless and spotless, as an offering of incense in your sight."

As she spoke this prayer, she traced the sign of the cross on her eyes, her mouth, and her heart, and with this prayer she died.

The Life of St. Macrina 23–25: Jaeger 8/1; SC 178, 216–227.

Week of 6 Easter ✠ Eve of Ascension

A reading from a sermon of Leo the Great, Bishop of Rome [461]

At Easter, it was the Lord's resurrection which was the cause of our joy; our present rejoicing is on account of his ascension into heaven. With all due solemnity we are commemorating that day on which our poor human nature was carried up, in Christ, above all the hosts of heaven, above all the ranks of angels, beyond the highest heavenly powers to the very throne of God the Father. It is upon this ordered structure of divine acts that we have been firmly established, so that the grace of God may show itself still more marvelous when, in spite of the withdrawal from our sight of everything that is rightly felt to command our reverence, faith does not fail, hope is not shaken, charity does not grow cold.

For such is the power of great minds, such the light of truly believing souls, that they put unhesitating faith in what is not seen with the bodily eye; they fix their desires on what is beyond sight. Such fidelity could never be born in our hearts, nor could anyone be justified by faith, if our salvation lay only in what was visible.

And so our Redeemer's visible presence has passed into the sacraments. Our faith is nobler and stronger because sight has been replaced by a doctrine whose authority is accepted by believing hearts, enlightened from on high. This faith was increased by the Lord's ascension and strengthened by the gift of the Spirit; it would remain unshaken by fetters and imprisonment, exile and hunger, fire and ravening beasts, and the most refined tortures ever devised by brutal persecutors. Throughout the world women no less than men, girls as well as boys, have given their life's blood in the struggle for this faith. It is a faith that has driven out devils, healed the sick and raised the dead.

Even the blessed apostles, though they had been strengthened by so many miracles and instructed by so much teaching, took fright at the cruel suffering of the Lord's passion and could not accept his resurrection without hesitation. Yet they made such progress through his ascension that they now found joy in what had terrified them before. They were able to fix their minds on Christ's divinity as he sat at the right hand of the Father, since what was presented to their bodily eyes no longer hindered them from turning all their attention to the realization that he had not left his Father when he came down to earth, nor had he abandoned his disciples when he ascended into heaven.

The truth is that the Son of Man was revealed as Son of God in a more perfect and transcendent way once he had entered into the Father's glory; he now began to be indescribably more present in divinity to those from whom he was further removed in humanity. A more mature faith enabled their minds to stretch upward to the Son in his equality with the Father; it no longer needed contact with Christ's tangible body, in which as a human being he is inferior to the Father. For while his glorified body retained the same nature, the faith of those who believed in him was now summoned to heights where, as the Father's equal, the only-begotten Son is reached not by physical handling but by spiritual discernment.

Sermon 2 for the Ascension 1–4: Pl. 54, 397–399

Week of 6 Easter ✠ Ascension Day

A reading from a sermon of Augustine, Bishop of Hippo [430]

Today our Lord Jesus Christ ascended into heaven; let our hearts ascend with him. Listen to the words of the Apostle: "If you have risen with Christ, set your hearts on the things that are above where Christ is, seated at the right hand of God; seek the things that are above, not the things that are on earth." For just as he remained with us even after his ascension, so we too are already in heaven with him, even though what is promised us has not yet been fulfilled in our bodies.

Christ is now exalted above the heavens, but he still suffers on earth all the pain that we, the members of his body, have to bear. He showed this when he cried out from above: "Saul, Saul, why do you persecute me?" and when he said: "I was hungry and you gave me food."

Why do we on earth not strive to find rest with him in heaven even now, through the faith, hope and love that unites us to him? While in heaven he is also with us; and we while on earth are with him. He is here with us by his divinity, his power and his love. We cannot be in heaven, as he is on earth, by divinity, but in him, we can be there by love.

He did not leave heaven when he came down to us; nor did he withdraw from us when he went up again into heaven. The fact that he was in heaven even while he was on earth is borne out by his own statement: "No one has ever ascended into heaven except the one who descended from heaven, the Son of Man, who is in heaven."

These words are explained by our oneness with Christ, for he is our head and we are his body. No one ascended into heaven except Christ because we also are Christ: he is the Son of Man by his union with us, and we by our union with him are children and heirs of God. So the Apostle says: "Just as the human body, which has many members, is a unity, because all the different members make one body, so is it also with Christ." He too has many members, but one body.

Out of compassion for us he descended from heaven, and although he ascended alone, we also ascend, because we are in him by grace. Thus, no one but Christ descended and no one but Christ ascended; not because there is no distinction between the head and the body, but because the body as a unity cannot be separated from the head.

Sermon for the Lord's Ascension: PLS 2, 494–495

Week of 6 Easter ✠ Friday

A reading from the commentary on First John by Augustine,
Bishop of Hippo [430]

Ascending into heaven on the fortieth day, our Lord Jesus Christ commended to us his Body where it would continue to lie, because he saw that many would honor him for his ascent into heaven. And he saw that their honoring him is useless if they trample upon his members who are here on earth. And lest anyone should err, and while adoring the head in heaven should trample upon the feet on earth, he told us where his members would be. When he was about to ascend, he spoke his last words on earth; after that, he spoke no more on earth.

The Head about to ascend to heaven commended to us his members on earth and departed. Thenceforth, you do not find Christ speaking on earth; you find him speaking, but from heaven. And even from heaven, why? Because his members on earth were trampled upon. For to Saul the persecutor he said from on high: "Saul, Saul, why do you persecute me?" I have ascended to heaven, but I still remain on earth; here I sit at the right hand of the Father, but there I still hunger, thirst, and am a stranger.

In what manner, then, did he commend his Body to us, when he was about to ascend to heaven? When the disciples asked him: "Lord, are you going to restore the rule to Israel now?" he answered them on the very point of departure: "The exact time is not yours to know. The Father has reserved that to himself. You will receive power when the Holy Spirit comes down on you; then you are to be my witnesses." See where his Body is spread abroad, see where he does not will to be trampled upon: "You are to be my witnesses in Jerusalem, throughout Judea and Samaria, yes, even to the ends of the earth."

See then where I lie who am about to ascend. For I ascend because I am the Head; my Body still lies beneath. Where does it lie? Throughout the whole earth. Be careful that you do not strike it, that you do not hurt it, that you do not trample upon it. These are the last words of Christ about to go to heaven.

Think with Christian hearts; if to the heirs of a person, words spoken when about to go to the tomb are so sweet, so grateful, so weighty, what must we account of the last words of Christ, spoken not when about to go back to the tomb but to ascend to heaven! As for the one who lived and is dead, the soul is hurried off to other places, the body is laid in the earth, and it makes no difference whether words be carried out or not. The dead person has now something else to do or something else to suffer. Either that one rejoices in Abraham's bosom or longs for a drop of water in eternal fire, while the corpse lies there senseless in the grave. Yet the last words of the dying are kept. What have those to look for who do not keep the last words of the One who sits in heaven and sees from on high whether they are despised or not despised?

Treatise 10 on 1 John 9: PL 35, 2060–2061

Week of 6 Easter ✠ Saturday

A reading from a commentary on John by Augustine, Bishop of Hippo [430]

The Church recognizes two kinds of life as having been commended to her by God. One is a life of faith, the other a life of vision; one is a life passed on pilgrimage in time, the other in a dwelling place in eternity; one is a life of toil, the other of repose; one is spent on the road, the other in our homeland; one is active, involving labor, the other contemplative, the reward of labor.

The first kind of life is symbolized by the apostle Peter, the second by John. All of the first life is lived in this world, and it will come to an end with this world. The second life will be imperfect till the end of this world, but it will have no end in the next world. And so Christ says to Peter: "Follow me"; but of John he says: "If I wish him to remain until I come, what is that to you? Your duty is to follow me."

You are to follow me by imitating my endurance of transient evils; John is to remain until my coming, when I will bring eternal blessings. A way of saying this more clearly might be: Your active life will be perfect if you follow the example of my passion, but to attain its full perfection John's life of contemplation must wait until I come.

Perfect patience is to follow Christ faithfully, even to death, but for perfect knowledge we must await his coming. Here, in the land of the dying, the sufferings of the world must be endured; there, in the land of the living, shall be seen the good things of the Lord.

Christ's words, "I wish him to remain until I come," should not be taken to imply that John was to remain on earth until Christ's coming, but rather that he was to wait because it is not now but only when Christ comes that the life he symbolizes will find fulfillment. On the other hand, Christ says to Peter: "Your duty is to follow me," because the life Peter symbolizes can attain its goal only by action here and now.

Yet we should make no mental separation between these great apostles. Both lived the life symbolized by Peter; both were to attain the life symbolized by John. Symbolically, one followed, the other remained, but living by faith they both endured the sufferings of this present life of sorrow and they both longed for the joys of the future life of happiness.

Nor were they alone in this. They were one with the whole Church, the bride of Christ, which will in time be delivered from the trials of this life and live for ever in the joy of the next. These two kinds of life were represented respectively by Peter and John, yet both apostles lived by faith in this present, passing life, and in eternal life both have the joy of vision.

And so for the sake of all the saints inseparably united to the body of Christ, to guide them through the storms of this life, Peter, the chief of the apostles, received the keys of the kingdom of heaven with the power to bind and loose sins; and for the sake of those same saints, to plumb the depths of that other, hidden life, John the evangelist reclined on the breast of Christ.

For it is not only Peter but the whole Church that binds and looses from sin; and as for the sublime teaching of John about the Word, who in the beginning was God with God, and everything else he told us about Christ's divinity, and about the trinity and unity of the Godhead, which now, until the Lord comes, is all like a faint reflection in a mirror, but which will be seen face to face in the kingdom of heaven—it was not only John who drank in this teaching that came forth from the Lord's breast as from a fountain. All who belong to the Lord are to drink it in, according to their several capacities, and this is why the Lord himself has spread John's gospel throughout the world.

Treatise 124 on John 5, 7: CCL 36, 685–687

Week of 7 Easter ✠ Sunday

A reading from a homily of Gregory, Bishop of Nyssa [c. 394]

When love has entirely cast out fear, and fear has been transformed into love, then the unity brought us by our Savior will be fully realized, for all will be united with one another through their union with the one supreme Good. They will possess the perfection ascribed to the dove, according to our interpretation of the text: "One alone is my dove, my perfect one. She is the only child of her mother, her chosen one."

Our Lord's words in the gospel bring out the meaning of this text more clearly. After conferring all power on his disciples by his blessing, he obtained many other gifts for them by his prayer to the Father. Among these was included the greatest gift of all, which was that they were no longer to be divided in their judgment of what was right and good, for they were all to be united to the one supreme Good. As the Apostle says, they were to be bound together with the bonds of peace in the unity that comes from the Holy Spirit. They were to be made one body and one spirit by the one hope to which they were all called. We shall do better, however, to quote the sacred words of the gospel itself. "I pray," the Lord says, "that they all may be one; that as you, Father, are in me and I am in you, so they also may be one in us."

Now the bond that creates this unity is glory. That the Holy Spirit is called glory no one can deny if one thinks carefully about the Lord's words: "The glory you gave to me, I have given to them." In fact, he gave this glory to his disciples when he said to them: "Receive the Holy Spirit." Although he had always possessed it, even before the world existed, he himself received this glory when he put on human nature. Then, when his human nature had been glorified by the Spirit, the glory of the Spirit was passed on to all his kin, beginning with his disciples. This is why he said: "The glory you gave to me, I have given to them, so that they may be one as we are one. With me in them and you in me, I want them to be perfectly one."

Whoever has grown from infancy to adulthood and attained to spiritual maturity possesses the mastery over passions and the purity that makes it possible to receive the glory of the Spirit. Such a one is that perfect dove upon whom the eyes of the bridegroom rest when he says: "One alone is my dove, my perfect one."

Homily on the Song of Songs 15: Jaeger VI, 466–468

Week of 7 Easter ✠ Monday

A reading from The City of God by Augustine, Bishop of Hippo [430]

We Christians do not assign to the martyrs temples, priests, ceremonies and sacrifices. They are not gods for us; their God is our God. We certainly honor the memory of our martyrs, as holy men and women of God, who have contended for the truth as far as the death of their bodies, so that the true religion might be made known and fiction and falsehood convicted. There may have been some in previous times who thought as they did, but if so, fear kept them silent.

But has any of the faithful ever heard the priest say, in prayers while standing at the altar, even if that altar has been erected for the glory and worship of God over the body of a holy martyr: "I offer sacrifice to you

Peter, or Paul, or Cyprian?" No. For at the memorials of martyrs the sacrifice is offered to God who made them human and made them martyrs, and has brought them into fellowship with his holy angels in the glory of heaven. And so in this solemn celebration we offer thanks to the true God for their victories, and by renewing their memory we encourage ourselves to emulate their crowns and palms of victory, calling upon God to help us. Thus all the acts of reverence which the devout perform at the shrines of the martyrs are acts of respect to their memory. They are not ceremonies or sacrifices offered to the dead as to gods.

There are some Christians who bring banquets to the memorials. This is not the custom of the better-instructed, and in most parts of the world the practice is unknown. But even those who do this first lay the food at the tomb, then say their prayers and then remove the viands, which they either eat themselves, or distribute to the poor. Their intention is that the food should be sanctified through the merits of the martyrs in the name of the Lord of the martyrs. That this is not a sacrifice to the martyrs is well known to anyone who knows of the one and only Christian sacrifice, which is offered there also.

City of God 8, 27: CCL 47, 248

Week of 7 Easter ✠ Tuesday

A reading from the Catechetical Instructions of Cyril, Bishop of Jerusalem [386]

"The water that I shall give you will become in you a fountain of living water, welling up into eternal life." This is a new kind of water, a living, leaping water, welling up for those who are worthy. But why did Christ call the grace of the Spirit water? Because all things are dependent on water; plants and animals have their origin in water. Water comes down from heaven as rain, and although it is always the same in itself, it produces many different effects, one in the palm tree, another in the vine, and so on throughout the whole of creation. It does not come down, now as one thing, now as another, but while remaining essentially the same, it adapts itself to the needs of every creature that receives it.

In the same way the Holy Spirit, whose nature is always the same, simple and indivisible, apportions grace to each as the Spirit wills. Like a dry tree which puts forth shoots when watered, the soul bears the fruit of holiness when repentance has made it worthy of receiving the Holy Spirit. Although the Spirit never changes, the effects of the Spirit's action, by the will of God and in the name of Christ, are both many and marvelous.

The Spirit makes one a teacher of divine truth, inspires another to prophesy, gives another the power of casting out devils, enables another to interpret holy Scripture. The Spirit strengthens one's self-control, shows another how to help the poor, teaches another to fast and lead a life of asceticism, makes another oblivious to the needs of the body, trains another for martyrdom. This action is different in different people, but the Spirit is always the same. "In each person," Scripture says, "the Spirit reveals his presence in a particular way for the common good."

The Spirit comes gently and makes himself known by his fragrance. The Spirit is not felt as a burden, for the Spirit is light, very light. Rays of light and knowledge stream before him as he approaches. The Spirit comes with the tenderness of a true friend and protector to save, to heal, to teach, to counsel, to strengthen, to console. The Spirit comes to enlighten the mind first of the one who receives him, and then, through that one, the minds of others as well.

As light strikes the eyes of those who come out of darkness into the sunshine and enables them to see clearly things they could not discern before, so light floods the souls of those counted worthy of receiving the Holy Spirit and enables them to see things beyond the range of human vision, things hitherto undreamed of.

Catechesis 16, 1, 11–12, 16: PG 33, 931–935, 939–942

Week of 7 Easter ✠ Wednesday

A reading from the Cento of Proba, Christian laywoman of the city of Rome [c. 351]

Where the lifeless body had been placed—neither bolts nor guards themselves were strong enough to keep it there—they see the rocks torn from rocks, tight fitting joints loosened.

There is a roar, the earth is shaken by the huge weight. There was terror in every heart; the very silence was horrifying. But behold from beneath the eaves the first songs of birds; leaving the tomb He strode, glorious in His victory; He went forth in triumph, and the earth shrilled, shook with the beat of His feet.

Bearing those wounds He entered through lofty doors. And here to His surprise He found that a great number of disciples had gathered, and without warning He spoke, "I whom you seek am here." Piety and living virtue have overcome the difficult road.

Hasten now, be on guard and let there be no fear. Behold my return, my longed for triumph. Behold my great faith. O thrice and four times blessed, what rewards should I deem worthy for your glorious deeds? What gifts? Take this to heart: the earth which first bore you from your parents' stock, the same will welcome you with joyful breast. Recall your courage; banish gloomy fear, and save yourselves for better things. Be happy with what you have done and pray that peace be at hand. Praise peace, highminded ones, wherever you are. The pledge of peace is alone inviolable. And with these words He showed them His face and mouth, His head, both hands and breast pierced by iron. They joined hands, rejoicing to gaze at Him.

Nor was it enough to see Him once; they took joy in delaying Him, keeping step with Him, and joining hand to hand. These rites at last completed, He parts the breeze's breath, and is born through thin air towards the open sky. He vanished from mortal view in the midst of His teaching, and the palace of starry heaven welcomed Him to His throne, and holds through the ages His name undying. From this moment His glory has been celebrated, and posterity rejoices to observe the day.

Probae Cento 652–688: CSEL 16, 607–609

Week of 7 Easter ✠ Thursday

A reading from a commentary on Romans by Cyril, Bishop of Alexandria [444]

Though many, we are one body, and members one of another, united by Christ in the bonds of love. "Christ has made Jews and Gentiles one by breaking down the barrier that divided us and abolishing the law with its precepts and decrees." This is why we should all be of one mind and if one member suffers some misfortune, all should suffer alongside; if one member is honored, all should be glad.

Paul says: "Accept one another as Christ accepted you, for the glory of God." Now accepting one another means being willing to share one another's thoughts and feelings, bearing one another's burdens, and "preserving the unity of the Spirit in the bond of peace." This is how God accepted us in Christ, for John's testimony is true and he said that "God" the Father "loved the world so much that he gave his own Son for us." God's Son was given as a ransom for the lives of us all. He has delivered us from death, redeemed us from death and from sin.

Paul throws light on the purpose of God's plan when he says that Christ became the servant of the circumcised to show God's fidelity. God had promised the Jewish patriarchs that he would bless their offspring and make it as numerous as the stars of heaven. This is why the divine

Word himself, who as God holds all creation in being and is the source of its well-being, appeared in the flesh and became human. He came into this world in human flesh not to be served, but, as he himself said, to serve and to give his life as a ransom for many.

Christ declared that his coming in visible form was to fulfill the promise made to Israel. "I was sent only to the lost sheep of the house of Israel," he said. Paul was perfectly correct, then, in saying that Christ became a servant of the circumcised in order to fulfill the promise made to the patriarchs and that God the Father had charged him with this task, as also with the task of bringing salvation to the Gentiles, so that they too might praise their Savior and Redeemer as the Creator of the universe. In this way God's mercy has been extended to all, including the Gentiles, and it can be seen that the mystery of the divine wisdom contained in Christ has not failed in its benevolent purpose. In the place of those who fell away the whole world has been saved.

Commentary on Romans 15, 7: PG 74, 854–855

Week of 7 Easter ✠ Friday

A reading from a commentary on John by Cyril, Bishop of Alexandria [444]

After Christ had completed his mission on earth, it still remained necessary for us to become sharers in the divine nature of the Word. We had to give up our own life and be so transformed that we would begin to live an entirely new kind of life that would be pleasing to God. This was something we could do only by sharing in the Holy Spirit.

It was most fitting that the sending of the Spirit and his descent upon us should take place after the departure of Christ our Savior. As long as Christ was with them in the flesh, it must have seemed to believers that they possessed every blessing in him; but when the time came for him to ascend to his heavenly Father, it was necessary for him to be united through his Spirit to those who worshiped him, and to dwell in our hearts through faith. Only by his own presence within us in this way could he give us confidence to cry out: "Abba, Father," make it easy for us to grow in holiness and, through our possession of the all-powerful Spirit, fortify us invincibly against the wiles of the devil and the assaults of human beings.

It can easily be shown from examples both in the Old Testament and the New that the Spirit changes those in whom he comes to dwell; he so transforms them that they begin to live a completely new kind of life.

Saul was told by the prophet Samuel: "The Spirit of the Lord will take possession of you, and you shall be changed into another person." Saint Paul writes: "As we behold the glory of the Lord with unveiled faces, that glory, which comes from the Lord who is the Spirit, transforms us all into his own likeness, from one degree of glory to another."

Does this not show that the Spirit changes those in whom he comes to dwell and alters the whole pattern of their lives? With the Spirit within them it is quite natural for people who had been absorbed by the things of this world to become entirely other-worldly in outlook, and for cowards to become people of great courage. There can be no doubt that this is what happened to the disciples. The strength they received from the Spirit enabled them to hold firmly to the love of Christ, facing the violence of their persecutors unafraid. Very true, then, was our Savior's saying that it was to their advantage for him to return to heaven: his return was the time appointed for the descent of the Holy Spirit.

Commentary on John 10: PG 74, 434

Week of 7 Easter ✠ Saturday

A reading from the treatise On the Holy Spirit by Basil the Great, Bishop of Caesarea [379]

The titles given to the Holy Spirit must surely stir the soul of anyone who hears them, and make one to realize that they speak of nothing less than the supreme Being. Is he not called the Spirit of God, the Spirit of truth who proceeds from the Father, the steadfast Spirit, the guiding Spirit? But his principal and most personal title is the Holy Spirit.

To the Spirit all creatures turn in their need for sanctification; all living things seek him according to their ability. His breath empowers each to achieve its own natural end.

The Spirit is the source of holiness, a spiritual light, and he offers his own light to every mind to help it in its search for truth. By nature the Spirit is beyond the reach of our mind, but we can know him by his goodness. The power of the Spirit fills the whole universe, but the Spirit gives himself only to those who are worthy, acting in each according to the measure of faith.

Simple in himself, the Spirit is manifold in his mighty works. The whole of his being is present to each individual; the whole of his being is present everywhere. Though shared in by many, he remains unchanged; his self-giving is no loss to himself. Like the sunshine, which permeates all the atmosphere, spreading over land and sea, and yet is enjoyed by each person as though it were for each alone, so the Spirit pours forth his grace in full measure, sufficient for all, and yet is present as though exclusively to everyone who can receive him. To all creatures that share in him he gives a delight limited only by their own nature, not by his ability to give.

The Spirit raises our hearts to heaven, guides the steps of the weak, and brings to perfection those who are making progress. He enlightens those who have been cleansed from every stain of sin and makes them spiritual by communion with himself.

As clear, transparent substances become very bright when sunlight falls on them and shine with a new radiance, so also souls in whom the Spirit dwells, and who are enlightened by the Spirit, become spiritual themselves and a source of grace for others.

From the Spirit comes foreknowledge of the future, understanding of the mysteries of faith, insight into the hidden meaning of Scripture, and other special gifts. Through the Spirit we become citizens of heaven, we are admitted to the company of the angels, we enter into eternal happiness, and abide in God. Through the Spirit we acquire a likeness to God; indeed, we attain what is beyond our most sublime aspirations—we become God.

On the Holy Spirit 9, 22–23: PG 32, 107–110

Week of 7 Easter ✠ Eve of Pentecost

A reading from the Travels of Egeria, Abbess, and Pilgrim to Jerusalem [late fourth century]

On the feast of Pentecost, which falls on Sunday, the day on which there is the greatest strain on the people, everything is done exactly according to custom from the first cockcrow. The vigil is held in the Anastasis, so that the bishop may read the passage from the Gospel which is always read on Sundays, that of the Resurrection of the Lord. Afterwards, the customary ritual is carried out in the Anastasis, just as it is throughout the year. As soon as it is morning, all the people assemble for the liturgy in the major church, in the Martyrium, where everything customarily done is accomplished. The priests preach and afterwards the bishop. All the prescribed rites are accomplished, that is, the sacrifice is offered in the manner in which it is customarily done on Sundays. On this one day, however, the dismissal is moved up in the Martyrium, so that it is given before the third hour.

As soon as the dismissal has been given in the Martyrium, all the people without exception, singing hymns, lead the bishop to Sion, but in such a manner that they are in Sion at precisely the third hour. When they arrive, there is read from the Acts of the Apostles that passage in which the Holy Spirit came down so that all tongues might be heard and all might understand what was being said. Afterwards the divine service is celebrated in the prescribed manner. Now the priests read there from the Acts of the Apostles that passage which is read because this is the place on Sion—the church now is something else—where at an earlier time, after the Passion of the Lord, the multitude was gathered with the apostles, and where that which we mentioned above was done. Afterwards, the divine service is celebrated in the prescribed manner, and the sacrifice is offered. Then, just before the people are dismissed, the archdeacon raises his voice to say: "Today, immediately after the sixth hour, let us all be ready at the Imbomon on the Eleona." All the people then return home, each one to rest.

Immediately after lunch, everyone, insofar as is possible, goes up to the Mount of Olives, that is to the Eleona, with the result that not a single Christian remains in the city, for they have all gone. As soon as they have climbed the Mount of Olives, the Eleona, that is, they go first of all to the Imbomon, that is, to the place from which the Lord ascended into heaven. The bishop sits down there, and the priests and all the people, too. Passages from Scripture are read, hymns are interspersed and sung, and also antiphons proper to the day itself and the place are sung. The prayers which are interspersed are said in such a manner that they fit both the day and the place. Then the passage from the Gospel is read which speaks of the Ascension of the Lord; then there is the reading from the Acts of the Apostles which speaks of the Ascension of the Lord into Heaven after the Resurrection. When this has been done, the catechumens are blessed and then the faithful. Then at the ninth hour everyone comes down from there and goes, singing hymns, to the church which is also on the Eleona, that is to say, in that grotto where the Lord sat teaching the apostles. By the time they arrive there it is already past the tenth hour. Vespers is held there, a prayer is said, the catechumens and then the faithful are blessed.

Then all the people without exception come down from there singing hymns, everyone together with the bishop singing hymns and antiphons proper to the day itself. And in this fashion they make their way slowly and easily to the Martyrium. When they reach the city gate, it is already night, and around two hundred church candles are brought out for the people. Since it is quite far from the city gate to the major church or Martyrium, it is definitely around the second hour of the night when they arrive, because they move slowly and easily all the way so that the people will not be tired out from walking. And when the great doors which are on the market street side are opened, then all the people, singing hymns, enter the Martyrium with the bishop.

After they have entered the church, hymns are sung, a prayer is said, and the catechumens and then the faithful are blessed. From there, everyone, singing hymns, then goes to the Anastasis. When they have arrived at the Anastasis, in like manner hymns and antiphons are sung, a prayer is said, and the catechumens and then the faithful are blessed. And the same thing is done at the Cross.

Then all the Christian people without exception, singing hymns, lead the bishop to Sion. When they get there, appropriate passages from Scripture are read, Psalms and antiphons as well are sung, and a prayer is said. The catechumens are blessed and then the faithful, and the dismissal is given. Once the dismissal has been given, everyone comes forth to kiss the bishop's hand. Everyone then returns to his own home around midnight.

And so a great deal of toil is borne on this day, for the vigil at the Anastasis starts with the first cockcrow, and from then on throughout the whole day there is no stopping. Everything that is celebrated is drawn out to the point that only at midnight, after the dismissal has been given at Sion, does everyone return home.

Pilgrimage 43: SC 296, 298–302

The Day of Pentecost

A reading from the treatise Against Heresies by Irenaeus, Bishop of Lyons [c. 202]

When the Lord told his disciples "to go and teach all nations" and to "baptize them in the name of the Father and of the Son and of the Holy Spirit," he conferred on them the power of giving people new life in God.

He had promised through the prophets that in these last days he would pour out his Spirit on his servants and handmaids, and that they would prophesy. So when the Son of God became the Son of Man, the Spirit also descended upon him, becoming accustomed in this way to dwelling with the human race, to living in them and to inhabiting God's creation. The Spirit accomplished the Father's will in people who had grown old in sin, and gave them new life in Christ.

Luke says that the Spirit came down on the disciples at Pentecost, after the Lord's ascension, with power to open the gates of life to all nations and to make known to them the new covenant. So it was that people of every language joined in singing one song of praise to God, and scattered tribes, restored to unity by the Spirit, were offered to the Father as the firstfruits of all the nations.

This was why the Lord had promised to send the Advocate: he was to prepare us as an offering to God. Like dry flour, which cannot become one lump of dough, one loaf of bread, without moisture, we who are many could not become one in Christ Jesus without the water that comes down from heaven. And like parched ground, which yields no harvest unless it receives moisture, we who were once like a waterless tree could never have lived and borne fruit without this abundant rainfall from above. Through the baptism that liberates us from change and decay we have become one in body; through the Spirit we have become one in soul.

"The Spirit of wisdom and understanding, the Spirit of counsel and strength, the Spirit of knowledge and the fear of God" came down upon the Lord, and the Lord in turn gave this Spirit to his Church, sending the Advocate from heaven into all the world into which, according to his own words, the devil too had been cast down like lightning.

If we are not to be scorched and made unfruitful, we need the dew of God. Since we have our accuser, we need an Advocate as well. And so the Lord in his pity for us, who had fallen into the hands of brigands, having himself bound up our wounds and left for our care two coins bearing the royal image, entrusted us to the Holy Spirit. Now, through the Spirit, the image and inscription of the Father and the Son have been given to us, and it is our duty to use the coin committed to our charge and make it yield a rich profit for the Lord.

Against Heresies 3, 17, 1–3: SC 34, 302–306

Eve of Trinity Sunday

A reading from the treatise On the Trinity by Hilary, Bishop of Poitiers [367]

Our Lord commanded us to baptize in the name of the Father and of the Son and of the Holy Spirit. In baptism, then, we profess faith in the Creator, in the only-begotten Son and in the gift which is the Spirit. There is one Creator of all things, for in God there is one Father from whom all things have their being. And there is one only-begotten Son, our Lord Jesus Christ, through whom all things exist. And there is one Spirit, the gift who is in all. So all follow their due order, according to the proper operation of each: one power, which brings all things into being, one Son, through whom all things come to be, and one gift of perfect hope. Nothing is wanting to this flawless union: in Father, Son and Holy Spirit, there is infinity of endless being, perfect reflection of the divine image, and mutual enjoyment of the gift.

Our Lord has described the purpose of the Spirit's presence in us. Let us listen to his words: "I have yet many things to say to you, but you cannot bear them now. It is to your advantage that I go away; if I go, I will send you the Advocate." And also: "I will ask the Father and he will give you another Counselor to be with you for ever, the Spirit of truth. He will guide you into all the truth; for he will not speak on his own authority, but whatever he hears he will speak, and he will declare to you the things that are to come. He will glorify me, for he will take what is mine."

From among many of our Lord's sayings, these have been chosen to guide our understanding, for they reveal to us the intention of the giver, the nature of the gift and the condition for its reception. Since our weak minds cannot comprehend the Father or the Son, we have been given the Holy Spirit as our intermediary and advocate, to shed light on that hard doctrine of our faith, the incarnation of God.

We receive the Spirit of truth so that we can know the things of God. In order to grasp this, consider how useless the faculties of the human body would become if they were denied their exercise. Our eyes cannot fulfill their task without light, either natural or artificial; our ears cannot react without sound vibrations, and in the absence of any odor our nostrils are ignorant of their function. Not that these senses would lose their own nature if they were not used; rather, they demand objects of experience in order to function. It is the same with the human soul. Unless it absorbs the gift of the Spirit through faith, the mind has the ability to know God but lacks the light necessary for that knowledge.

This unique gift which is in Christ is offered in its fullness to everyone. It is everywhere available, but it is given to each in proportion to our readiness to receive it. Its presence is the fuller, the greater our desire to be worthy of it. This gift will remain with us until the end of the world, and will be our comfort in the time of waiting. By the favors it bestows, it is the pledge of our hope for the future, the light of our minds, and the splendor that irradiates our understanding.

On the Trinity 2, 1, 33, 35: PL 10, 50–51, 73–75

Trinity Sunday

A reading from a letter by Athanasius, Bishop of Alexandria [373]

It will not be out of place to consider the ancient tradition, teaching and faith of the Catholic Church, which was revealed by the Lord, proclaimed by the apostles and guarded by the fathers. For upon this faith the Church is built, and if anyone were to lapse from it, they would no longer be Christian either in fact or in name.

We acknowledge the Trinity, holy and perfect, to consist of the Father, the Son and the Holy Spirit. In this Trinity there is no intrusion of any alien element or of anything from outside, nor is the Trinity a blend of creative and created being. It is a wholly creative and energizing reality, self-consistent and undivided in its active power, for the Father makes all things through the Word and in the Holy Spirit, and in this way the unity of the holy Trinity is preserved. Accordingly, in the Church, one God is preached, one God who is "above all things and through all things and in all things." God is "above all things" as Father, for he is principle and source; he is "through all things" through the Word; and he is "in all things" in the Holy Spirit.

Writing to the Corinthians about spiritual matters, Paul traces all reality back to one God, the Father, saying: "Now there are varieties of gifts, but the same Spirit; and varieties of service, but the same Lord; and there are varieties of working, but it is the same God who inspires them all in everyone."

Even the gifts that the Spirit dispenses to individuals are given by the Father through the Word. For all that belongs to the Father belongs also to the Son, and so the graces given by the Son in the Spirit are true gifts of the Father. Similarly, when the Spirit dwells in us, the Word who bestows the Spirit is in us too, and the Father is present in the Word. This is the meaning of the text: "My Father and I will come to him and make our home with him." For where the light is, there also is the radiance; and where the radiance is, there too are its power and its resplendent grace.

This is also Paul's teaching in his second letter to the Corinthians: "The grace of our Lord Jesus Christ and the love of God and the fellowship of the Holy Spirit be with you all." For grace and the gift of the Trinity are given by the Father through the Son in the Holy Spirit. Just as grace is given from the Father through the Son, so there could be no communication of the gift to us except in the Holy Spirit. But when we share in the Spirit, we possess the love of the Father, the grace of the Son and the fellowship of the Spirit himself.

First Letter to Serapion 28–30: PG 26, 594–595, 599

Propers 1–29

Proper 1 ✠ Monday

A reading from an Easter Letter by Athanasius, Bishop of Alexandria [373]

How fine a thing it is to move from festival to festival, from prayer to prayer, from holy day to holy day. The time is now at hand when we enter on a new beginning: the proclamation of the blessed Passover, in which the Lord was sacrificed. We feed as on the food of life, we constantly refresh our souls with his precious blood, as from a fountain. Yet we are always thirsting, burning to be satisfied. But he himself is present for those who thirst and in his goodness invites them to the feast day. Our Savior repeats his words: "If anyone thirsts, let him come to me and drink."

He quenched the thirst not only of those who came to him then. Whenever any seek him they are freely admitted to the presence of the Savior. The grace of the feast is not restricted to one occasion. Its rays of glory never set. It is always at hand to enlighten the minds of those who desire it. Its power is always there for those whose minds have been enlightened and who meditate day and night on the holy Scriptures, like the one who is called blessed in the holy psalm: "Blessed is the one who has not followed the counsel of the wicked, or stood where sinners stand, or sat in the seat of the scornful, but whose delight is in the law of the Lord, and who meditates on his law day and night."

Moreover, my friends, the God who first established this feast for us allows us to celebrate it each year. He who gave up his Son to death for our salvation, from the same motive gives us this feast, which is commemorated every year. This feast guides us through the trials that meet us in this world. God now gives us the joy of salvation that shines out from this feast, as he brings us together to form one assembly, uniting us all in spirit in every place, allowing us to pray together and to offer common thanksgiving, as is our duty on the feast. Such is the wonder of his love: he gathers to this feast those who are far apart, and brings together in unity of faith those who may be physically separated from each other.

Easter Letter 5, 1–2: PG 26, 1379–1380

Proper 1 ✠ Tuesday

A reading from a Prayer to St. Paul by Anselm, Archbishop of Canterbury [1109]

And you, Jesus, are you not also a mother? Are you not the mother who, like a hen, gathers her chickens under her wings? Truly, Lord, you are a mother; for both they who are in labor and they who are brought forth are accepted by you. You have died more than they, that they may labor to bear. It is by your death that they have been born, for if you had not been in labour, you could not have borne death; and if you had not died, you would not have brought forth. For, longing to bear children into life, you tasted of death, and by dying you begot them. You did this in your own self, your servants by your commands and help. You as the author, they as the ministers. So you, Lord God, are the great mother.

Then both of you [Jesus and Paul] are mothers. Even if you are fathers, you are also mothers. For you have brought it about that those born to death should be reborn to life—you by your own act, you by his power. Therefore you are fathers by your effect and mothers by your affection. Fathers by your authority, mothers by your kindness. Fathers by your teaching, mothers by your mercy. Then you, Lord, are a mother, and you, Paul, are a mother too. If in quantity of affection you are unequal, yet in quality you are not unalike. Though in the greatness of your kindness you are not co-equal, yet in will you are of one heart. Although you have not equal fullness of mercy, yet in intention you are not unequal.

And you, my soul, dead in yourself, run under the wings of Jesus your mother and lament your griefs under his feathers. Ask that your wounds may be healed and that, comforted, you may live again.

Christ, my mother, you gather your chickens under your wings; this dead chicken of yours comes to shelter under those wings. For by your gentleness the badly frightened are comforted, by your sweet smell the despairing are revived, your warmth gives life to the dead, your touch justifies sinners. Mother, know again your dead child, both by the sign of your cross and the voice of my confession. Warm your chicken, give life to your dead, justify your sinner. Let your terrified one be consoled by you; despairing, be comforted by you; and in your whole and unceasing grace be refashioned by you. For from you flows consolation for sinners; to you be blessing for ages and ages.

Prayer to St. Paul, Oratio 10: Opera Omnia, ed. Schmitt, 3, 40–41

Proper 1 ✠ Wednesday

A reading from the treatise On the Value of Patience by Cyprian, Bishop and Martyr of Carthage [258]

Patience begins at the source of its dignity and glory. The origin and grandeur of patience are found in God, its author. We should love what is dear to God and what the majesty of God recommends. If God is our Lord and Father, we must imitate the patience of the Master as well as of the Father; for it is the task of servants to be docile and children not to be unworthy.

But in truth what great patience God has! He makes the day dawn and the light of the sun rise both over the good and over the wicked; he waters the earth with his rain, and no one is excluded from its benefits, since water is given to the just and unjust alike. We see him act with equal patience toward the guilty and the innocent, the faithful and the wicked, the thankful and the ungrateful. For all of them, the seasons obey God's commands, the elements place themselves at their service, the winds blow, the waters flow, crops grow in abundance, grapes ripen, trees swell with fruit, forests take on greenery, and meadows blossom with flowers.

Although God is exacerbated by frequent and ever continual offenses, he tempers his indignation and waits patiently for the day fixed for retribution. And although he has the power of vengeance, he prefers to have patience for a long time. He waits and graciously differs so that if it were possible the malice might become less with time and we who are mired in the infection of our errors and crimes might finally turn to God, in accord with what he himself tells us in these terms: "I take no pleasure in the death of the wicked, but rather in the wicked's conversion, so that life may triumph." And again: "Return to me," says the Lord: "return to the Lord, your God. For gracious and merciful is he, slow to anger, rich in kindness, and relenting in punishment."

Jesus said: "You must be made perfect as your heavenly Father is perfect." By these words he shows us that we who are children of God and regenerated by a heavenly birth will attain the summit of perfection when the patience of God the Father dwells in us and the divine likeness that was lost through Adam's sin is manifested and shines in our actions.

What glory it is to be like God and what happiness it is to have that virtue which is worthy of the divine praises!

On the Value of Patience 3–5: CSEL 3, 1, 398–401

Proper 1 ✠ Thursday

A reading from a commentary on the psalms by Hilary, Bishop of Poitiers [367]

"The river of God is brimming with water. You have provided their food, for this is your way of preparing them." There can be no doubt about the river referred to, for the prophet says: "There is a river whose streams make glad the city of God"; and in the gospel the Lord himself says: "Streams of living water welling up to eternal life will flow from the heart of anyone who drinks the water I shall give him." He was speaking of the Holy Spirit, whom those who believed in him were to receive. The river of God is brimming with water; that is to say, we are inundated by the gifts of the Holy Spirit, and from that fountain of life the river of God pours into us in full flood.

We also have food prepared for us. And who is this food? It is he in whom we are prepared for life with God, for by receiving his holy body we receive a place in the communion of his holy body. This is what is meant by the words of the psalm: "You have provided their food, for this is your way of preparing them." For as well as refreshing us now, that food also prepares us for the life to come.

We who have been reborn through the sacrament of baptism experience intense joy when we feel within us the first stirrings of the Holy Spirit. We begin to have an insight into the mysteries of faith, we are able to prophesy and to speak with wisdom. We become steadfast in hope and receive the gift of healing. Demons are made subject to our authority. These gifts enter us like a gentle rain, and once having done so, little by little, they bring forth fruit in abundance.

Discourse on Psalm 64, 14–15: CSEL 22, 245–246

Proper 1 ✠ Friday

A reading from an instruction by Columbanus, Celtic Abbot [615]

Who, I ask, will search out the Most High in his own being, for he is beyond words or understanding? Who will penetrate the secrets of God? Who will boast that he knows the infinite God, who fills all things, yet encompasses all things, who pervades all things, yet reaches beyond all things, who holds all things in his hand, yet escapes the grasp of all things? "No one has ever seen him as he is." No one must then presume to search for the unsearchable things of God: his nature, the manner of his existence, his selfhood. These are beyond telling, beyond scrutiny, beyond investigation. With simplicity, but also with fortitude, only believe that this is how God is and this is how he will be, for God is incapable of change.

Who then is God? He is Father, Son and Holy Spirit, one God. Do not look for any further answers concerning God. Those who want to understand the unfathomable depths of God must first consider the world of nature. Knowledge of the Trinity is rightly compared with the depth of the sea. Wisdom asks: "Who will find out what is so very deep?" As the depths of the sea are invisible to human sight, so the godhead of the Trinity is found to be beyond the grasp of human understanding. If any one, I say, wants to know what you should believe, you must not imagine that you understand better through speech than through belief; the knowledge of God that you seek will be all the further off than it was before.

Seek then the highest wisdom, not by arguments in words but by the perfection of your life, not by speech but by the faith that comes from simplicity of heart, not from the learned speculations of the unrighteous. If you search by means of discussions for the God who cannot be defined in words, he will depart further from you than he was before. If you search for him by faith, wisdom will stand where wisdom lives, "at the gates." Where wisdom is, wisdom will be seen, at least in part. But wisdom is also to some extent truly attained when the invisible God is the object of faith, in a way beyond our understanding, for we must believe in God, invisible as he is, though he is partially seen by a heart that is pure.

Instruction 1 on the Faith 3–5: Opera, Dublin 1957, 62–66

Proper 1 ✠ Saturday

A reading from a commentary on the psalms by Hilary,
Bishop of Poitiers [367]

On the sabbath everyone without exception was commanded to do no work and to rest, inactive. Why then did the Lord break the sabbath by saying: "Have you not read in the law how the priests on temple duty can break the sabbath rest without incurring guilt?"

Great, indeed, are the works of God: he holds the sky in his hands, and he gives light to the sun and other planets, gives growth to the plants of the earth, maintains us in life. Yes, everything in heaven and on earth has its being and lives through the will of God the Father; everything comes from God, and everything exists through the Son. He is, in fact, the head and the principle of all things. In him everything was made. And it is out of the fullness contained in himself, according to the initiative of his eternal power, that he has created everything.

If Christ is active in all things, it follows that it is the Father's action which acts in Christ. That is why he said: "My Father is at work until now, and I am at work as well." Because all that Christ does, as the Son of God indwelt by God the Father, is the work of the Father. Thus everything in each day is created by the Son. Thus, Christ's action goes on every day; and, it seems to me, the principles of life, the formation of bodies, and the development and growth of living things manifest this action.

Does God then work on the sabbath? He certainly does; otherwise the sky would disappear, the light of the sun would go out, the earth would fall apart, all its fruits would dry up, and the life of humankind would perish if, because of the sabbath, the moving power of the universe were to stop working. But in fact there is no cessation: during the sabbath, just as during the other six days, the elements of the universe continue to fulfil their function. For through them the Father is working now and always.

But he acts in the Son who is begotten of him and through whom everything is his work. For through the Son the Father's action goes on during the sabbath. And consequently there is no rest for God since there is no day that sees the cessation of God's works.

So it is with God's action. But what of his rest? God's work is Christ's work. And God's rest is Christ as God, because all that pertains to God is truly in Christ to such a degree that the Father can find rest in him.

Commentary on Psalm 91, 3–8: PL 9, 495–498

Proper 2 ✠ Monday

A reading from a sermon of Bernard, Abbot of Clairvaux [1153]

"I will be with you in distress," says God. What else then should I long for but distress? "For me, to be near God is my good"; and even more, "to make the Lord God my refuge," for he says, "I will deliver you and glorify you."

"I will be with you in distress." And he adds: "I found delight in humankind." Emmanuel, God with us. He came down to be near those whose heart is distressed, to be with us in distress. But a day will come when we "will be caught up in the clouds to meet the Lord. Thenceforth we shall be with the Lord unceasingly." If we take care to have him always as a companion along the way, he will give us the kingdom in return; better still, he will be the Kingdom for us, provided that he is now our Way.

Lord, it is good for me to be in distress, provided that you are there with me; that is much better for me than to reign without you, rejoice without you, or be glorified without you. It is far better for me to cleave to you in distress, to have you with me in the crucible than to be without you in heaven. For what have I in heaven, and from you what have I wished upon earth? "Gold is tried in fire and the just in the trials of distress." It is there, among those who are gathered in your name that you are present, as once you were with the three young men.

Why should we be afraid and make every effort to flee from the crucible? The fire burns, but the Lord is with us in distress. "If God is for us, who can be against us?" If it is also he who saves, who can charm us out of his hand? Who could snatch us from his hand? Finally, if it is God who glorifies, who can deprive us of glory and humiliate us?

"With length of days will I gratify you," answers the Lord. This says clearly: I know what you desire, what you thirst for, and what you crave. You do not crave gold or silver, sensual pleasures, curiosities, or dignities of any kind. All of these are no help to you; there is no cure except for you to humble yourself in the depths of your heart and refuse to give your attention to what cannot satisfy you. You are not unaware in whose image you have been created and of what greatness you are capable; you do not want a meager profit to be for you the occasion of an immense frustration. Hence, "with length of days will I gratify you," for only the true Light can restore you, only the eternal Light can satisfy you—that Light whose length knows no end, whose brightness knows no dimming, and whose fullness knows no completion.

Commentary on Psalm 91, sermon 17, 4–6: PL 183, 252–253

Proper 2 ✠ Tuesday

A reading from the Detailed Rules for Monks by Basil the
Great, Bishop of Caesarea [379]

What words can adequately describe God's gifts? They are so numerous that they defy enumeration. They are so great that any one of them demands our total gratitude in response.

Yet even though we cannot speak of it worthily, there is one gift which no thoughtful person can pass over in silence. God fashioned us in his own image and likeness; he gave us knowledge of himself; he endowed us with the ability to think which raised us above all living creatures; he permitted us to delight in the unimaginable beauties of paradise, and gave us dominion over everything upon earth.

Then, when we fell into sin, which led to death and to all the sufferings associated with death, God still did not forsake us. God first gave us the law to help us; he set angels over us to guard us; he sent the prophets to denounce vice and to teach virtue; he restrained humanity's evil impulses by warnings and roused our desire for virtue by promises. Frequently, by way of warning, God showed us the respective ends of virtue and of vice in the lives of others. Moreover, when we continued in disobedience even after he had done all this, God did not desert us.

No, we were not abandoned by the goodness of the Lord. Even the insult we offered to our Benefactor by despising his gifts did not destroy his love for us. On the contrary, although we were dead, our Lord Jesus Christ restored us to life again, and in a way even more amazing than the fact itself, "for his state was divine, yet he did not cling to his equality with God, but emptied himself to assume the condition of a slave."

"He bore our infirmities and endured our sorrows. He was wounded for our sake so that by his wounds we might be healed. He redeemed us from the curse by becoming a curse for our sake," and he submitted to the most ignominious death in order to exalt us to the life of glory. Nor was he content merely to summon us back from death to life; he also bestowed on us the dignity of his own divine nature and prepared for us a place of eternal rest where there will be joy so intense as to surpass all human imagination.

How, then, shall we repay the Lord for all his goodness to us? He is so good that he asks no recompense except our love: that is the only payment he desires. To confess my personal feelings, when I reflect on all these blessings I am overcome by a kind of dread and numbness at the very possibility of ceasing to love God and of bringing shame upon

Christ because of my lack of recollection and my preoccupation with trivialities.

Detailed Rules for Monks, Resp. 2, 2–4: PG 31, 914–915

Proper 2 ✠ Wednesday

A reading from the Proslogion of Anselm, Archbishop of Canterbury [1109]

My soul, have you found what you were seeking? You were seeking God, and you have found that he is a being superior to all beings, a being than which nothing greater can be conceived. You have found that this being is life itself, light, wisdom, goodness, eternal blessedness, and blessed eternity; and that it is eternal and omnipresent.

If you have not found your God, how is he this being which you have found, and which you have conceived him to be, with such certain truth and such true certainty? But if you have found him, why do you not feel that you have found him? Why, O Lord, our God, does not my soul feel you, if she has found you? Has she not found him whom she found to be light and truth? For how did my soul understand this, except by seeing light and truth? Could she understand anything at all about you, except through your light and your truth?

Hence, if my soul has seen light and truth, she has seen you; if she has not seen you, she has not seen light and truth. Is the light and truth that she has seen, without however seeing you, the result of her seeing you only in part but not as you are? Lord, my God, my creator and renewer, tell my longing soul what you are other than what she has seen, so that she may clearly see what she desires.

My soul strains to see you more; but she sees nothing except darkness beyond what she has already seen. Rather, she does not see darkness for there is none in you; but she sees that she cannot see farther because of her own darkness.

Why is this, O Lord, why is this? Is the eye of the soul darkened by its infirmity, or dazzled by your glory? Surely it is both darkened in itself and dazzled by you. Doubtless it is both obscured by its own insignificance and overwhelmed by your infinity. Truly, it is both contracted by its own narrowness and overcome by your greatness.

Indeed, how great is that light from which shines every truth which gives light to the rational mind! How great is that truth in which is everything that is true and outside of which is only nothingness and the false! How boundless is the truth which sees at a glance whatever has been made and by whom, and how it has been made out of nothing! What purity, what certainty, what splendor where it is! Assuredly, more than a creature can conceive.

Proslogion 14: Opera Omnia, ed. Schmitt, 1, 111–112

Proper 2 ✠ Thursday

A reading from the treatise Against Heresies by Irenaeus, Bishop of Lyons [c. 202]

The Word of God became human, the Son of God became the Son of Man, in order to unite us with himself and make us, by adoption, children and heirs of God. Only by being united to one who is himself immune could we be preserved from corruption and death, and how else could this union have been achieved if he had not first become what we are? How else could what is corruptible and mortal in us have been swallowed up in his incorruptibility and immortality, to enable us to receive adoptive sonship? Therefore, the Son of God, our Lord, the Word of the Father, is also the Son of Man; he became the Son of Man by a human birth from Mary, a member of the human race.

The Lord himself has given us a sign here below and in the heights of heaven, a sign that we did not ask for because we never dreamt that such a thing would be possible. A virgin was with a child and she bore a son who is called Emmanuel, which means "God with us." He came down to the earth here below in search of the sheep that was lost, the sheep that was in fact his own creature, and then ascended into the heights of heaven to offer to the Father and entrust to his care the human race that he had found again. The Lord himself became the firstfruits of the resurrection of humankind, and when its time of punishment for disobedience is over the rest of the body, to which the whole human race belongs, will rise from the grave as the head has done. By God's aid it will grow and be strengthened in all its joints and ligaments, each member having its own proper place in the body. There are many rooms in the Father's house because the body has many members.

God bore with us patiently when we fell because he foresaw the victory that would be won through the Word. Weakness allowed strength its full play, and so revealed God's kindness and great power.

Against Heresies 3, 19, 1, 3–20, 1: SC 34, 332, 336–338

A reading from the treatise Against Faustus by Augustine,
Bishop of Hippo [430]

We, the Christian community, assemble to celebrate the memory of the martyrs with ritual solemnity because we want to be inspired to follow their example, share in their merits, and be helped by their prayers. Yet we erect no altars to any of the martyrs, even in the martyrs' burial chapels themselves.

No bishop, when celebrating at an altar where these holy bodies rest, has ever said: "Peter, we make this offering to you," or "Paul, to you," or "Cyprian, to you." No, what is offered is offered always to God, who crowned the martyrs. We offer in the chapels where the bodies of those he crowned rest, so the memories that cling to those places will stir our emotions and encourage us to greater love both for the martyrs whom we can imitate and for God whose grace enables us to do so.

So we venerate the martyrs with the same veneration of love and fellowship that we give to the holy ones of God still with us. We sense that the hearts of these latter are just as ready to suffer death for the sake of the Gospel, and yet we feel more devotion toward those who have already emerged victorious from the struggle. We honor those who are fighting on the battlefield of this life here below, but we honor more confidently those who have already achieved the victor's crown and live in heaven.

But the veneration strictly called "worship," or "latria," that is, the special homage belonging only to the divinity, is something we give and teach others to give to God alone. The offering of a sacrifice belongs to worship in this sense (that is why those who sacrifice to idols are called idol-worshipers), and we neither make nor tell others to make any such offering to any martyr, any holy soul, or any angel. If any among us fall into this error, they are corrected with words of sound doctrine and must then either mend their ways or else be shunned.

The saints themselves forbid anyone to offer them the worship they know is reserved for God, as is clear from the case of Paul and Barnabas. When the Lycaonians were so amazed by their miracles that they wanted to sacrifice to them as gods, the apostles tore their garments, declared that they were not gods, urged the people to believe them, and forbade them to worship them.

Yet the truths we teach are one thing, the abuses thrust upon us are another. There are commandments that we are bound to give; there are breaches of them that we are commanded to correct, but until we correct them we must of necessity put up with them.

Against Faustus 20, 21: CSEL 25, 562-563

Proper 2 ✠ Saturday

A reading from the Detailed Rules for Monks by Basil the Great, Bishop of Caesarea [379]

Love of God is not something that can be taught. We did not learn from someone else how to rejoice in light or want to live, or to love our parents or guardians. It is the same—perhaps even more so—with our love for God: it does not come by another's teaching. As soon as the living creature (that is, humanity) comes to be, a power of reason is implanted in us like a seed, containing within it the ability and the need to love. When the school of God's law admits this power of reason, it cultivates it diligently, skillfully nurtures it, and with God's help brings it to perfection.

For this reason, as by God's gift, I find you with the zeal necessary to attain this end, and you on your part help me with your prayers. I will try to fan into flame the spark of divine love that is hidden within you, as far as I am able through the power of the Holy Spirit.

First, let me say that we have already received from God the ability to fulfill all his commands. We have then no reason to resent them, as if something beyond our capacity were being asked of us. We have no reason either to be angry, as if we had to pay back more than we had received. When we use this ability in a right and fitting way, we lead a life of virtue and holiness. But if we misuse it, we fall into sin.

This is the definition of sin: the misuse of powers given us by God for doing good, a use contrary to God's commandments. On the other hand, the virtue that God asks of us is the use of the same powers based on a good conscience in accordance with God's command.

Since this is so, we can say the same about love. Since we received a command to love God, we possess from the first moment of our existence an innate power and ability to love. The proof of this is not to be sought outside ourselves, but we can learn this from ourselves and in ourselves. It is natural for us to want things that are good and pleasing to the eye, even though at first different things seem beautiful and good to different people. In the same way, we love what is related to us or near to us, though we have not been taught to do so, and we spontaneously feel well disposed to our benefactors.

What, I ask, is more wonderful than the beauty of God? What thought is more pleasing and satisfying than God's majesty? What desire is as urgent and overpowering as the desire implanted by God in a soul that is completely purified of sin and cries out in its love: "I am wounded by love"? The radiance of the divine beauty is altogether beyond the power of words to describe.

Detailed Rules for Monks, Resp. 2, 1: PG 31, 908–910

Proper 3 ✠ Sunday

A reading from the Letter to the Magnesians by Ignatius, Bishop of Antioch, and Martyr [c. 115]

I saw and loved in faith your whole community; and so I urge you to strive to do all things in the harmony of God. The bishop is to preside as God's representative, the presbyters are to perform the rule of the apostolic council, and the deacons, who are so dear to me, are to be entrusted with the service of Jesus Christ, who was with the Father before time began and has now at last manifested himself to us. Follow the ways of God, and have respect for one another; let none judge their neighbor as the world does, but love one another always in Jesus Christ. Let there be nothing among you that could divide you, but live in accord with the bishop and those who are over you as a sign and a pattern of eternal life.

The Lord did nothing either of himself or through his apostles without his Father, with whom he is united; so too, you should undertake nothing without the bishop and the presbyters. Do not attempt to persuade yourselves that what you do on your own account is right and proper, but when you meet together there must be one petition, one prayer, one mind, one hope in love and in holy joy, for Jesus Christ is one and perfect before all else. You must all be quick to come together, as to one temple of God, one altar, to the one Jesus Christ, who came forth from the one Father while still remaining one with him, and returned to him.

Do not be led astray by false doctrines or by old and idle tales. For if we still live by the law, we admit that we have not received grace. But the holy prophets lived according to Jesus Christ, and that is why they were persecuted. They were inspired by his grace to convince an unbelieving world that there is one God, manifested now through Jesus Christ his Son, his Word, who came forth from the Father and was in all things pleasing to the one who sent him.

Those who lived by the ancient customs attained a fresh hope; they no longer observed Saturday, but Sunday, the Lord's day, for on that day life arose for us through Christ and through his death. Some deny this mystery, but through it we have received our faith and because of it we persevere, that we may prove to be disciples of our only teacher, Jesus Christ. Even the prophets awaited him as their teacher, since they were his disciples in spirit. That is why Christ, whom they rightly awaited, raised them from the dead when he appeared. How then can we live without him?

Letter to the Magnesians 6, 1–9, 2: Funk 1, 195–199

Proper 3 ✠ Monday

A reading from the Letter to the Magnesians by Ignatius,
Bishop of Antioch, and Martyr [c. 115]

Let us not be insensible of Christ's loving kindness. For if he had acted as we do, we would have been lost indeed. Therefore let us become his disciples and learn to live in the Christian way; those who are called by any other name are not of God. Cast out the evil leaven that has become old and sour, and replace it with the new leaven, which is Jesus Christ. He must be the salt of your lives, so that none of you may become corrupt, since it is by your wholesomeness that you will be judged.

I do not write this to you, my dear friends, because I have heard that any one of you is thus disaffected, but because, though I am less than yourselves, I would have you all guard against falling into the snares of false doctrine. Have a firm faith in the reality of the Lord's birth and passion and resurrection which took place when Pontius Pilate was procurator. All these deeds were truly and certainly accomplished by Jesus Christ, who is our hope; may none of you ever be turned away from him!

May you be my joy in all things, if I am worthy of it. For although I am in chains, I do not deserve to be compared with any of you who live in freedom. I know that you are not inflated with pride, for you have Jesus Christ within you. And I know that you blush when I praise you, as the Scripture says: "The just is self-accused." Take care, then, to be firmly grounded in the teachings of the Lord and his apostles so that "you may prosper in all your doings" both in body and in soul, in faith and in love, in the Son and in the Father and in the Spirit, in the beginning and in the end, along with your most worthy bishop and his spiritual crown, your presbyters, and with the deacons, who are servants of God. Be obedient to the bishop and to one another, as Jesus Christ was in the flesh to the Father, and the apostles to Christ and to the Father and to the Spirit, so that there may be unity in flesh and in spirit.

I have exhorted you only briefly, for I am aware that you are filled with God. Remember me in your prayers, that I may attain to God. And remember the church in Syria, from which I am unworthy to be called. How I need your united prayer and love in God! Remember, then, the church in Syria, that it may be strengthened through your prayers.

The Ephesians at Smyrna, where I write these lines, send their greetings. They have come together here like yourselves for the glory of God; they have consoled me in every way and so has Polycarp, their bishop. The other churches, too, greet you for the glory of Jesus Christ. Farewell; may you abide in God's harmony, possessing that undivided spirit which is Jesus Christ.

Letter to the Magnesians 10, 1–15: Funk 1, 199–203

Proper 3 ✠ Tuesday

A reading from the treatise On Cain and Abel by Ambrose, Bishop of Milan [397]

"Offer God a sacrifice of praise and fulfill your vows to the Most High." If you praise God you offer your vow and fulfill the promise you have made. So the Samaritan leper, healed by the Lord's word of command, gained greater credit than the other nine; he alone returned to Christ, praising God and giving thanks. Jesus said of him: "There was no one to come back and thank God except this foreigner. He tells the thankful one: Stand up and go on your way, for your faith has made you whole."

The Lord Jesus, in his divine wisdom, taught you about the goodness of the Father, who knows how to give good things, so that you might ask for the things that are good from Goodness itself. He urges you to pray earnestly and frequently, not offering long and wearisome prayers, but praying often, and with perseverance. Lengthy prayers are usually filled with empty words, while neglect of prayer results in indifference to prayer.

Again, Christ urges you, when you ask forgiveness for yourself, to be especially generous to others, so that your actions may commend your prayer. The Apostle, too, teaches you how to pray: you must avoid anger and contentiousness, so that your prayer may be serene and wholesome. He tells you also that every place is a place of prayer, though our Savior says: "Go into your room."

But by "room" you must understand, not a room enclosed by walls that imprison your body, but the room that is within you, the room where you hide your thoughts, where you keep your affections. This room of prayer is always with you, wherever you are, and it is always a secret room, where only God can see you.

You are told to pray especially for the people, that is, for the whole body, for all its members, the family of your mother the Church; the badge of membership in this body is love for each other. If you pray only for yourself, you pray for yourself alone. If each of you prays for yourself, you receive less from God's goodness than the one who prays on behalf of others. But as it is, because each prays for all, all are in fact praying for each one.

To conclude, if you pray only for yourself, you will be praying, as we said, for yourself alone. But if you pray for all, all will pray for you, for you are included in all. In this way there is a great recompense; through the prayers of each individual, the intercession of the whole people is gained for each individual. There is here no pride, but an increase of humility and a richer harvest from prayer.

Treatise on Cain and Abel 1, 9, 34, 38–39: CSEL 32, 369, 371–372

Proper 3 ✠ Wednesday

A reading from the treatise On Pastoral Care by Gregory the Great, Bishop of Rome [604]

A spiritual guide should be silent when discretion requires and speak when words are of service. Otherwise you may say what you should not or be silent when you should speak. Indiscreet speech may lead people into error and an imprudent silence may leave in error those who could have been taught. Pastors who lack foresight hesitate to say openly what is right because they fear losing the favor of their people. As the voice of truth tells us, such leaders are not zealous pastors who protect their flocks, rather they are like mercenaries who flee by taking refuge in silence when the wolf appears.

The Lord reproaches them through the prophet: "They are dumb dogs that cannot bark." On another occasion he complains: "You did not advance against the foe or set up a wall in front of the house of Israel, so that you might stand fast in battle on the day of the Lord." To advance against the foe involves a bold resistance to the powers of this world in defense of the flock. To stand fast in battle on the day of the Lord means to oppose the wicked enemy out of love for what is right.

When a pastor has been afraid to assert what is right, has that shepherd not turned back and fled by remaining silent? Whereas if you intervene on behalf of the flock, you set up a wall against the enemy in front of the house of Israel. Therefore, the Lord again says to his unfaithful people: "Your prophets saw false and foolish visions and did not point out your wickedness, that you might repent of your sins." The name of the prophet is sometimes given in the sacred writings to teachers who both declare the present to be fleeting and reveal what is to come. The word of God accuses them of seeing false visions because they are afraid to reproach people for their faults and thereby lull the evildoer with an empty promise of safety. Because they fear reproach, they keep silent and fail to point out the sinner's wrongdoing.

The word of reproach is a key that unlocks a door, because reproach reveals a fault of which the evildoer is often unaware. That is why Paul says: "A bishop must be able to encourage people in sound doctrine and refute those who oppose it." For the same reason God tells us through Malachi: "The lips of the priest are to preserve knowledge, and people shall look to the priest for the law, for the priest is the messenger of the Lord of hosts." Finally, that is also the reason why the Lord warns us through Isaiah: "Cry out and be not still; raise your voice in a trumpet call."

All who are ordained priest undertake the task of preaching, so that with a loud cry they may go on ahead of the terrible judge who follows. If, then, a priest does not know how to preach, what kind of cry can such a dumb herald utter? It was to bring this home that the Holy Spirit descended in the form of tongues on the first pastors, for the Spirit causes those who are thus filled, to speak out spontaneously.

Treatise on Pastoral Care 2, 4: PL 77, 30–31

Proper 3 ✠ Thursday

A reading from The Imitation of Christ by Thomas a Kempis, Priest [1471]

Turn to the Lord with your whole heart and leave behind this wretched world. Then your soul shall find rest. For the kingdom of God is the peace and joy of the Holy Spirit. If you prepare within your heart a fitting dwelling place, Christ will come to you and console you.

His glory and beauty are within you, and he delights in dwelling there. The Lord frequently visits our hearts. There he shares with us pleasant conversations, welcome consolation, abundant peace and a wonderful intimacy.

So come, faithful soul. Prepare your heart for your spouse to dwell within you. For the spouse says: "If you love me, you will keep my word and we shall come to you and make our dwelling within you."

Make room for Christ. When you possess Christ you are rich, for he is sufficient for you. He himself shall provide for you and faithfully administer all your cares. You will not have to place your hope in people. Put all your trust in God; let him be both your fear and your love. He will respond on your behalf and will do whatever is in your best interest.

You have here no lasting city. For wherever you find yourself, you will always be a pilgrim from another city. Until you are united intimately with Christ, you will never find your true rest.

Let your thoughts be with the Most High and direct your prayers continually to Christ. If you do not know how to contemplate the glory of heaven, take comfort in the passion of Christ, and dwell willingly in his sacred wounds. Endure with Christ, suffer for him, if you wish to reign with him.

Once you have entered completely into the depths of Jesus, and have a taste of his powerful love, then you will not care about your own convenience or inconvenience. Rather you will rejoice all the more in insults and injuries, for the love of Jesus us scorn our own needs.

The Imitation of Christ 2, 1–6

Proper 3 ✠ Friday

*A reading from a commentary on the psalms by Ambrose,
Bishop of Milan [397]*

"Why do you turn away your face?" We think that God is turning his face away from us when we find ourselves in such distress that our senses are clouded in darkness and we cannot see the glory of him who is truth. We are convinced that if God would pay attention to our condition and be pleased to visit our souls, nothing could plunge us in gloom. If a person's face is more enlightening than other parts of the body—so that when we look at someone we either see a stranger or recognize the person as someone we know, whom our glance will not allow to pass unrecognized—how much more does the face of God enlighten those on whom he directs his gaze.

In his usual way Saint Paul has something striking to say on this subject. He employs his gift for making Christ better understood to bring him closer to us through the use of appropriate ideas and expressions. He tells us: "God, who commanded light to shine out of darkness, has caused light to shine in our hearts, so that we might receive the revelation of God's glory in the face of Jesus Christ." We know, then, the place where Christ is shining within us. He is the eternal splendor enlightening our minds and hearts. He was sent by the Father to shine on us in the glory of his face, and so enable us to see what is eternal and heavenly, where before we were imprisoned in the darkness of this world.

There should be no need for me to speak of Christ when even Peter the apostle said to the man born lame: "Look at us." He looked at Peter and was enlightened by the grace of faith. He would not have received healing had he not believed with faith.

Such was the glory possessed by the apostles. Yet Zachaeus, hearing that the Lord Jesus was passing by, climbed a tree, for he was small in stature and could not see him because of the crowd. He saw Christ and discovered the light. He saw Christ and gave up what was his own, though he was one who took what belonged to others.

"Why do you turn away your face?" We may say it in another way. Even if, Lord, you turn your face away from us, yet "we are sealed with the glory of your face." Your glory is in our hearts and shines in the deep places of our spirit. Indeed, no one can live if you should turn away your face.

Explanation on Psalm 43, 89–90: CSEL 64, 324–326

Proper 3 ✠ Saturday

A reading from a sermon of Gregory the Great, Bishop of Rome [604]

Let us listen to what the Lord says as he sends the preachers forth: "The harvest is great but the laborers are few. Pray therefore the Lord of the harvest to send laborers into his harvest." We can speak only with a heavy heart of so few laborers for such a great harvest, for although there are many to hear the good news there are only a few to preach it. Look about you and see how full the world is of priests, yet in God's harvest a laborer is rarely to be found; for although we have accepted the priestly office, we do not fulfill its demands.

Beloved, consider what has been said: "Pray the Lord of the harvest to send laborers into his harvest." Pray for us so that we may have the strength to work on your behalf, that our tongue may not grow weary of exhortation, and that after we have accepted the office of preaching, our silence may not condemn us before the just judge. For frequently the preacher's tongue is bound fast on account of personal wickedness; while on the other hand it sometimes happens that because of the people's sins, the word of preaching is withdrawn from those who preside over the assembly. With reference to the former situation, the psalmist says: "But God asks the sinner: Why do you recite my commandments?" And with reference to the latter, the Lord tells Ezekiel: "I will make your tongue cleave to the roof of your mouth, so that you shall be dumb and unable to reprove them, for they are a rebellious house." He clearly means this: the word of preaching will be taken away from you because as long as this people irritates me by their deeds, they are unworthy to hear the exhortation of truth. It is not easy to know for whose sinfulness the preacher's word is withheld, but it is indisputable that the shepherd's silence, while often injurious to the shepherd, will always harm the flock.

There is something else about the life of the shepherds, beloved, which discourages me greatly. But lest what I claim should seem unjust to anyone, I accuse myself of the very same thing, although I fall into it unwillingly—compelled by the urgency of these barbarous times. I speak of our absorption in external affairs; we accept the duties of office, but by our actions we show that we are attentive to other things. We abandon the ministry of preaching and, in my opinion, are called bishops to our detriment, for we retain the honorable office but fail to practice the virtues proper to it. Those who have been entrusted to us abandon God, and we are silent. They fall into sin, and we do not extend a hand of rebuke.

But how can we who neglect ourselves be able to correct someone else? We are wrapped up in worldly concerns, and the more we devote ourselves to external things, the more insensitive we become in spirit.

For this reason the Church rightfully says about her own feeble members: "They made me keeper of the vineyards, but my own vineyard I have not kept." We are set to guard the vineyards but do not guard our own, for we get involved in irrelevant pursuits and neglect the performance of our ministry.

Homily on the Gospels 17, 3, 14: PL 76, 1139–1140, 1146

Proper 4 ✠ Sunday

A reading from the treatise On the Unity of the Catholic Church by Cyprian, Bishop and Martyr of Carthage [258]

It is particularly incumbent upon those of us who preside over the Church as bishops to uphold this unity firmly and to be its champions, so that we may prove the episcopate also to be itself one and undivided.

Let no one deceive the faithful with lies or corrupt the true faith with faithless treachery.

The episcopate is a single whole, in which each bishop's share gives a right to, and a responsibility for, the whole. So is the Church a single whole, though she spreads far and wide into a multitude of churches as her fertility increases. We may compare the sun, many rays but one light, or a tree, many branches but one firmly rooted trunk. When many streams flow from one spring, although the bountiful supply of water welling out has the appearance of plurality, unity is preserved in the source. Pluck a ray from the body of the sun, and its unity allows no division of the light. Break a branch from the tree, and when it is broken off it will not bud. Cut a stream off from its spring, and when it is cut off it dries up. In the same way the Church, bathed in the light of the Lord, spreads her rays throughout the world, yet the light everywhere diffused is one light and the unity of the body is not broken. In the abundance of the Church's plenty she stretches her branches over the whole earth, far and wide she pours her generously flowing streams. Yet there is one head, one source, one mother boundlessly fruitful. Of her womb are we born, by her milk we are nourished, by her breath we are quickened.

On the Unity of the Catholic Church 5: PL 4, 516–518

Proper 4 ✠ Monday

A reading from the Life of Moses by Gregory, Bishop of Nyssa [c. 394]

Let no one think that there is a complete, point-by-point correspondence between the narrative text [of Scripture] and the mind's contemplative understanding of it; for then you might reject the whole understanding of a passage if one detail of the text's language did not fit in with it. Rather it is necessary to remember the precise aim which we have before our eyes as we go through this exposition—the aim, stated to begin with in the preface, of setting out the lives of famous people as examples of virtue to their posterity. It is, however, impossible for those who desire to be like such people to undergo experience of the very same physical events as they. For where will we find again that nation which grew and multiplied after its departure from Egypt?—or a slave-driving tyrant who is hostile to male babies and wants the weaker sex to increase?—or any of the other particular circumstances which this story contains?

Since, then, it is demonstrably impossible to imitate the splendid deeds of the saints in a literal or material way, what one must do is to take those events which are patient of such treatment, and in their case transpose from the level of their material sequence to the level of moral teaching. By this means, people who are eager for virtue will find assistance towards their goal. And if some event in the narrative falls by its very nature outside the scheme of interpretation adopted, because it is irrelevant in that framework, we do not, just for that reason, break off the inquiry about virtue where it remains possible.

Life of Moses 2, 48–50: PG 44, 340

Proper 4 ✠ Tuesday

A reading from a homily of Gregory, Bishop of Nyssa [c. 394]

If the soul will fix its eyes heavenward on its head, who is Christ, as Paul urges, it will have to be regarded as blest through its keenness of vision, because it has its eyes where there is no obscurity of evil. The great apostle Paul, and others if there are any equal to him, had his eyes on the head; so also do all those who live and move and are in Christ.

Just as it cannot happen that the person who is in the light sees darkness, so it cannot happen that the one who has eyes on Christ will fix them on something lacking value. Hence, the person who has eyes fixed on the head—and by head we mean the principle of all things—has eyes on every virtue (indeed, Christ is the perfect virtue, and absolute in every way), on truth, justice, incorruptibility, and every good. "The wise person has eyes on the head, but the fool walks in darkness." Indeed, the person who does not place a lamp on the lampstand but places it under a bushel basket makes darkness take the place of light.

How much more numerous, on the contrary, are those who delight in striving for the things on high, and through contemplation dwell on those things that really exist, whereas they are regarded as blind and useless, just as Paul gloried in being such, terming himself foolish for Christ. For his prudence and wisdom was not directed toward any of the things with which we are concerned. Hence, he says: "We are fools on Christ's account" as if he were saying: "We are blind toward the things that concern what is here below, but have our life and our eyes on the head because we keep our gaze heavenward." For this reason, he was without home or food, poor, wandering, and naked, wracked by hunger and thirst.

Indeed, who would not have regarded Paul as wretched on seeing him in chains and afflicted with the blows of invective, immersed in the midst of the huge waves of the sea after the ship split in two, and led every-where in chains. Yet, although he was in such a state among people, he did not turn his eyes elsewhere but kept them ever on the head, declar-ing: "Who will separate us from the love of Christ which is in Christ Jesus? Trial, or distress, or persecution, or hunger, or nakedness, or danger, or the sword?" And this is equivalent to saying: "Who will wrest my eyes from the head to transfer them on something that will be tram-pled under foot?"

He urges us to do the same when he tells us "to seek the things that are above"; which is equivalent to telling us to keep our eyes on Christ.

Sermon 5 on Ecclesiastes: PG 44, 683–686

Proper 4 ✠ Wednesday

A reading from a homily of Gregory, Bishop of Nyssa [c. 394]

Ecclesiastes says: "There is a time to be born and a time to die." Right from the beginning he fittingly compressed this necessary etymological relation, bringing together death and procreation. For death necessarily follows upon birth and every birth ends in destruction.

"There is a time," he says, "to be born and a time to die." May we also receive the grace to be born at the right time and die at the opportune moment. For no one could assert that Ecclesiastes is here presenting this procreation as involuntary and death as spontaneous, as if such were the ordinary process of virtue. Neither the act of giving birth takes place by the will of the woman, nor is death subject to the free choice of those who must die. What does not depend on us cannot be reckoned as virtue or vice by anyone. Hence, it is necessary to inquire about what is the birth that happens at a right time and what is the death that comes at an opportune moment.

I believe that a birth is right and not out of its time when—as Isaiah says—someone has conceived out of the fear of God and through the travails of the soul in birth generates salvation. For we are in a certain sense our own parents, when through the good disposition of our soul and complete freedom of our will we form and generate and bring ourselves to the light.

We do this by the fact that we bring God into ourselves, having become children of God, children of virtue, and children of the Most High. On the other hand, we bring ourselves into the world out of due time and form ourselves in an imperfect and immature manner when there has not been formed in us "the image of Christ," to use the words of the Apostle.

For it is necessary that the child of God be without reproach and perfect.

If the manner in which we are born at the right time is evident, equally clear to all is the way we die at the opportune moment and the way every moment was in the eyes of St. Paul opportune for a good death. For he cries out in his writing, pronouncing in a certain way an oath when he says: "For your sake we are being slain all the day long." And we bear within our very selves the sentence of death.

Furthermore, the manner in which Paul dies each day is not obscure; he never lives in sin; he always mortifies the members of the flesh and ever bears within him the mortification of the body of Christ, for he is always crucified with Christ and never lives for himself but ever has Christ living in him. This in my opinion was the favorable death which was leading to true life.

Sermon 6 on Ecclesiastes: PG 44, 701–703

Proper 4 ✠ Thursday

A reading from a sermon of Caesarius, Bishop of Arles [543]

"Blessed are the merciful, for they shall receive mercy." My brothers and sisters, sweet is the thought of mercy, but even more so is mercy itself. It is what all hope for, but unfortunately, not what all deserve. For while all wish to receive it, only a few are willing to give it.

How can we ask for ourselves what we refuse to give to another? If we expect to receive any mercy in heaven, we should give mercy on earth. Do we all desire to receive mercy? Let us make mercy our patroness now, and she will free us in the world to come. Yes, there is mercy in heaven, but the road to it is paved by our merciful acts on earth. As Scripture says: "Lord, your mercy is in heaven."

There is, therefore, an earthly as well as heavenly mercy, that is to say, a human and a divine mercy. Human mercy has compassion on the miseries of the poor. Divine mercy grants forgiveness of sins. Whatever human mercy bestows here on earth, divine mercy will return to us in our homeland. In this life God feels cold and hunger in all who are stricken with poverty; for, remember, he once said: "What you have done to the least of my brothers and sisters you have done to me." Yes, God who sees fit to give his mercy in heaven wishes it to be a reality here on earth.

What kind of people are we? When God gives, we wish to receive, but when he begs, we refuse to give. Remember, it was Christ who said: "I was hungry and you gave me nothing to eat." When the poor are starving, Christ too hungers. Do not neglect to improve the unhappy conditions of the poor, if you wish to ensure that your own sins be forgiven you. Christ hungers now, beloved; it is he who deigns to hunger and thirst in the persons of the poor. And what he will return in heaven tomorrow is what he receives here on earth today.

What do you wish for, what do you pray for, my dear brothers and sisters, when you come to church? Is it mercy? How can it be anything else? Show mercy, then, while you are on earth, and mercy will be shown to you in heaven. A poor person asks you for something; you ask God for something. The poor person begs for a morsel of food; you beg for eternal life. Give to the beggar so that you may merit to receive from Christ. For he it is who says: "Give and it will be given to you." It baffles me that you have the impudence to ask for what you do not want to give. Give when you come to church. Give to the poor. Give them whatever your resources will allow.

Sermon 25, 1: CCL 103, 111–112

Proper 4 ✠ Friday

A reading from the Revelations of Divine Love by Dame Julian of Norwich [c. 1417]

So when he made us God almighty was our kindly Father, and God all-wise our kindly Mother, and the Holy Spirit their love and goodness; all one God, one Lord. In this uniting together he is our real, true husband, and we his loved wife and sweetheart. He is never displeased with his wife: "I love you and you love me," he says, "and our love will never be broken."

I saw the blessed Trinity working. I saw that there were these three attributes: fatherhood, motherhood, and lordship—all in one God. In the almighty Father we have been sustained and blessed with regard to our created natural being from before all time. By the skill and wisdom of the Second Person we are sustained, restored, and saved with regard to our sensual nature, for he is our Mother, Brother, and Savior. In our good Lord the Holy Spirit we have, after our life and hardship is over, that reward and rest which surpasses for ever any and everything we can possibly desire—such is his abounding grace and magnificent courtesy.

Our life too is threefold. In the first stage we have our being, in the second our growth, and in the third our perfection. The first is nature, the second mercy, and the third grace. For the first I realized that the great power of the Trinity is our Father, the deep wisdom our Mother, and the great love our Lord. All this we have by nature and in our created and essential being. Moreover I saw that the Second Person who is our Mother with regard to our essential nature, that same dear Person has become our Mother in the matter of our sensual nature. We are God's creation twice: essential being and sensual nature. Our being is that higher part which we have in our Father, God almighty, and the Second Person of the Trinity is Mother of this basic nature, providing the substance in which we are rooted and grounded. But he is our Mother also in mercy, since he has taken our sensual nature upon himself. Thus "our Mother" describes the different ways in which he works, ways which are separate to us, but held together in him. In our Mother, Christ, we grow and develop; in his mercy he reforms and restores us; through his passion, death, and resurrection he has united us to our being. So does our Mother work in mercy for all his children who respond to him and obey him.

Grace works with mercy too, and especially in two ways. The work is that of the Third Person, the Holy Spirit, who works by "rewarding" and "giving." Rewarding is the generous gift of truth that the Lord makes to him who has suffered. Giving is a magnanimous gesture which he makes freely by his grace: perfect, and far beyond the deserts of any of his creatures.

Thus in our Father, God almighty, we have our being. In our merciful Mother we have reformation and renewal, and our separate parts are integrated into perfect humanity. In yielding to the gracious impulse of the Holy Spirit we are made perfect. Our essence is in our Father, God almighty, and in our Mother, God all-wise, and in our Lord the Holy Spirit, God all-good. Our essential nature is entire in each Person of the Trinity, who is one God. Our sensual nature is in the Second Person alone, Jesus Christ. In him is the Father too, and the Holy Spirit. In and by him have we been taken out of hell with a strong arm; and out of earth's wretchedness have been wonderfully raised to heaven, and united, most blessedly, to him who is our true being. And we have developed in spiritual wealth and character through all Christ's virtues, and by the gracious work of the Holy Spirit.

Revelation 14, chapter 58: Colledge and Walsh 2, 582–588

Proper 4 ✠ Saturday

A reading from a sermon of Basil the Great, Bishop of Caesarea [379]

Human beings should be like the earth and bear fruit; they should not let inanimate matter appear to surpass them. The earth bears crops for your benefit, not for its own, but when you give to the poor, you are bearing fruit which you will gather in for yourself, since the reward for good deeds goes to those who perform them. Give to a hungry person, and what you give becomes yours, and indeed it returns to you with interest. As the sower profits from wheat that falls onto the ground, so will you profit greatly in the world to come from the bread that you place before a hungry person.

You are going to leave your money behind you here whether you wish to or not. On the other hand, you will take with you to the Lord the honor that you have won through good works. In the presence of the universal judge, all the people will surround you, acclaim you as a public benefactor, and tell of your generosity and kindness.

Do you not see how people throw away their wealth on theatrical performances, boxing contests, mimes and fights between humans and wild beasts, which are sickening to see, and all for the sake of fleeting honor and popular applause? If you are miserly with your money, how can you expect any similar honor? Your reward for the right use of the things of this world will be everlasting glory, a crown of righteousness, and the kingdom of heaven; God will welcome you, the angels will praise you, all who have existed since the world began will call you blessed. Do you care nothing for these things, and spurn the hopes that lie in the future for the sake of your present enjoyment? Come, distribute your wealth freely, give generously to those who are in need. Earn for yourself the psalmist's praise: "You gave freely to the poor; your righteousness will endure for ever."

How grateful you should be to your own benefactor; how you should beam with joy at the honor of having other people come to your door, instead of being obliged to go to theirs! But you are now ill-humored and unapproachable; you avoid meeting people, in case you might be forced to loosen your purse-strings even a little. You can say only one thing: "I have nothing to give you. I am poor." Poor you certainly are, and destitute of all real riches; you are poor in love, generosity, faith in God and hope of eternal happiness.

Sermon on Charity 3, 6: PG 31, 266–267, 275

Proper 5 ✠ Sunday

A reading from the Catechetical Instructions of Cyril, Bishop of Jerusalem [386]

The Church is called Catholic or universal because it has spread throughout the entire world, from one end of the earth to the other. Again, it is called Catholic because it teaches fully and unfailingly all the doctrines which ought to be brought to people's knowledge, whether concerned with visible or invisible things, with the realities of heaven or the things of earth. Another reason for the name Catholic is that the Church brings under religious obedience all classes of people, rulers and subjects, learned and unlettered. Finally, it deserves the title Catholic because it heals and cures unrestrictedly every type of sin that can be committed in soul or in body, and because it possesses within itself every kind of virtue that can be named, whether exercised in actions or in words or in some kind of spiritual charism.

It is most aptly called a church, which means an "assembly of those called out," because it "calls out" all people and gathers them together, just as the Lord says in Leviticus: "Assemble all the congregation at the door of the tent of meeting." It is worth noting also that the word "assemble" is used for the first time in the Scriptures at this moment when the Lord appoints Aaron high priest. So in Deuteronomy God says to Moses: "Assemble the people before me and let them hear my words, so that they may learn to fear me." There is a further mention of the assembly in the passage about the tablets of the Law: "And on them were written all the words which the Lord had spoken to you on the mountain out of the midst of the fire, on the day of the assembly"; it is as though he had said, even more clearly, "on the day when you were called out by God and gathered together." So too the psalmist says: "I will give thanks to you in the great assembly, O Lord; in the mighty throng I will praise you."

Long ago the psalmist sang: "Bless God in the assembly; bless the Lord, you who are Israel's heirs." But now the Savior has built a second holy assembly, our Christian Church, from the Gentiles. It was of this that he spoke to Peter: "On this rock I will build my Church, and the powers of death shall not prevail against it."

The churches of Christ are already multiplying throughout the world, and of them it is said in the psalms: "Sing a new song to the Lord, let his praise be sung in the assembly of the saints." Taking up the same theme the prophet says: "From the rising of the sun to its setting my name is glorified among the nations." Of this holy Catholic Church Paul writes to Timothy: "That you may know how one ought to behave in the household of God, which is the Church of the living God, the pillar and bulwark of the truth."

Catechesis 18, 23–25: PG 33, 1043–1047

Proper 5 ✠ Monday

A reading from the Catechetical Instructions of Cyril, Bishop of Jerusalem [386]

The Catholic Church is the distinctive name of this holy Church which is the mother of us all. She is the bride of our Lord Jesus Christ, the only-begotten Son of God (for Scripture says: "Christ loved the Church and gave himself up for her"). She is the type and she bears the image of "the Jerusalem above that is free and is the mother of us all," that Jerusalem which once was barren but now has many children.

In the Catholic Church, "God has appointed first, apostles, second, prophets, third, teachers, then workers of miracles, then healers, helpers, administrators and speakers in various kinds of tongues," as Paul says; and together with these is found every sort of virtue—wisdom and understanding, self-control and justice, mercy and kindness, and invincible patience in persecution. "With the weapons of righteousness in the right hand and in the left, in glory and dishonor," this Church in earlier days, when persecution and afflictions abounded, crowned her holy martyrs with the varied and many-flowered wreaths of endurance. But now when God has favored us with times of peace, she receives her due honor from kings and those of high station, and from every condition and race of humankind. And while the rulers of the different nations have limits to their sovereignty, the holy Catholic Church alone has a power without boundaries throughout the entire world. For, as Scripture says: God "has made peace her border."

Instructed in this holy Catholic Church and bearing ourselves honorably, we shall gain the kingdom of heaven and inherit eternal life. For the sake of enjoying this at the Lord's hands, we endure all things. The goal set before us is no trifling one; we are striving for eternal life. In the Creed, therefore, after professing our faith "in the resurrection of the body," that is, of the dead, which I have already discussed, we are taught to believe "in life everlasting," and for this as Christians we are struggling.

Now real and true life is none other than the Father, who is the fountain of life and who pours forth his heavenly gifts on all creatures through the Son in the Holy Spirit, and the good things of eternal life are faithfully promised to us also, because of his love for us.

Catechesis 18, 26–29: PG 33, 1047–1050

Proper 5 ✠ Tuesday

A reading from the Revelations of Divine Love by Dame Julian of Norwich [c. 1417]

It is the way of God to set good against evil. So Jesus Christ who sets good against evil is our real Mother. We owe our being to him—and this is the essence of motherhood!—and all the delightful, loving protection which ever follows. God is as really our Mother as he is our Father. He showed this throughout, and particularly when he said that sweet word, "It is I." In other words, It is I who am the strength and goodness of Fatherhood; I who am the wisdom of Motherhood; I who am light and grace and blessed love; I who am Trinity; I who am Unity; I who am the sovereign goodness of every single thing; I who enable you to love; I who enable you to long. It is I, the eternal satisfaction of every genuine desire.

For the soul is at its best, its most noble and honorable, when it is most lowly, and humble, and gentle. Springing from this fundamental source and as part of our natural endowment, are all the virtues of our sensual nature, aided and abetted as they are by mercy and grace. Without such assistance we should be in a poor way!

Our great Father, God almighty, who is Being, knew and loved us from eternity. Through his knowledge, and in the marvellous depths of his charity, together with the foresight and wisdom of the whole blessed Trinity, he willed that the Second Person should become our Mother, Brother, and Saviour. Hence it follows that God is as truly our Mother as he is our Father. Our Father decides, our Mother works, our good Lord, the Holy Spirit, strengthens. So we ought to love our God in whom we have our own being, reverently thanking him, and praising him for creating us, earnestly beseeching our Mother for mercy and pity, and our Lord, the Spirit, for help and grace. For in these three is contained our life: nature, mercy, grace. From these we get our humility, gentleness, patience and pity. From them too we get our hatred of sin and wickedness—it is the function of virtue to hate these.

So we see that Jesus is the true Mother of our nature, for he made us. He is our Mother, too, by grace, because he took our created nature upon himself. All the lovely deeds and tender services that beloved motherhood implies are appropriate to the Second Person. In him the godly will is always safe and sound, both in nature and grace, because of his own fundamental goodness. I came to realize that there were three ways of looking at God's motherhood: the first is based on the fact that our nature is "made"; the second is found in the assumption of that nature—there begins the motherhood of grace; the third is the motherhood of work which flows out over all by that same grace—the length and breadth and height and depth of it is everlasting. And so is his love.

Revelation 14, chapter 59: Colledge and Walsh 2, 589–593

Proper 5 ✠ Wednesday

A reading from the treatise Against Heresies by Irenaeus, Bishop of Lyons [c. 202]

From the beginning God created humanity out of his own generosity. He chose the patriarchs to give them salvation. He took his people in hand, teaching them, unteachable as they were, to follow him. He gave them prophets, accustoming them to bear his Spirit and to have communion with God on earth. He who stands in need of no one gave communion with himself to those who need him. Like an architect he outlined the plan of salvation to those who sought to please him. By his own hand he gave food in Egypt to those who did not see him. To those who were restless in the desert he gave a law perfectly suited to them. To those who entered the land of prosperity he gave a worthy inheritance. He killed the fatted calf for those who turned to him as Father, and clothed them with the finest garment. In so many ways he was training the human race to take part in the harmonious song of salvation.

For this reason John in the book of Revelation says: "His voice was as the voice of many waters." The Spirit of God is indeed a multitude of waters, for the Father is rich and great. As the Word passed among all these people he provided help in generous measure for those who were obedient to him, by drawing up a law that was suitable and fitting for every circumstance.

He established a law for the people governing the construction of the tabernacle and the building of the temple, the choice of Levites, the sacrifices, the offerings, the rites of purification and the rest of what belonged to worship.

He himself needs none of these things. He is always filled with all that is good. Even before Moses existed he had within himself every fragrance of all that is pleasing. Yet he sought to teach his people, always ready though they were to return to their idols. Through many acts of indulgence he tried to prepare them for perseverance in his service. He kept calling them to what was primary by means of what was secondary, that is, through foreshadowings to the reality, through things of time to the things of eternity, through things of the flesh to the things of the spirit, through earthly things to the heavenly things. As he said to Moses: "You will fashion all things according to the pattern that you saw on the mountain."

For forty days Moses was engaged in remembering the words of God, the heavenly patterns, the spiritual images, the foreshadowings of what was to come. Saint Paul says: "They drank from the rock that followed them, and the rock was Christ." After speaking of the things that are in the law he continues: "All these things happened to them as symbols: they were written to instruct us, on whom the end of the ages has come."

Through foreshadowings of the future they were learning reverence for God and perseverance in his service. The law was therefore a school of instruction for them, and a prophecy of what was to come.

Against Heresies 4, 14, 2–3; 15, 1: SC 100, 542, 548

Proper 5 ✠ Thursday

A reading from the Letter to Polycarp by Ignatius, Bishop of Antioch, and Martyr [c. 115]

Ignatius, also called Theophorus, to Polycarp, who is bishop of the Church in Smyrna, or rather who has for his bishop God the Father and the Lord Jesus Christ, greetings and all good wishes.

Recognizing your devotion to God, firmly built as if upon a solid rock, I am full of thanksgiving to him for allowing me to see your blessed countenance—may I for ever enjoy the sight of it in God! I beseech you by the grace with which you are endowed to press forward on your course and to exhort all people to salvation. Justify your episcopal dignity by your unceasing concern for the spiritual and temporal welfare of your flock; let unity, the greatest of all goods, be your preoccupation. Carry the burdens of all as the Lord carries yours; have patience with all in charity, as indeed you do. Give yourself to prayer continually, ask for wisdom greater than you now have, keep alert with an unflagging spirit. Speak to each person individually, following God's example; bear the infirmities of all, like a perfect athlete of God. The greater the toil, the richer the reward.

If you love only your good disciples, you gain no merit; rather you must win over the more troublesome of them by kindness. The same medication does not heal all wounds; convulsions should be allayed with poultices. "Be prudent as the serpent" in all things, and "innocent as the dove" always. You are both body and soul; treat gently the manifestations of human fault, even as you pray for the knowledge of things invisible, and then you will lack nothing but abound in every blessing. Do as the circumstances require, like the pilot looking to the wind and the storm-tossed sailor to the harbor, that you may win your way to God with your people. Exercise self-discipline, for you are God's athlete; the prize is immortality and eternal life, as you know full well. In everything I am your devoted friend—I and my chains, which you have kissed.

Do not be overwhelmed by those who seem trustworthy and yet teach heresy. Remain firm, like the anvil under the hammer. The good athlete must take punishment in order to win. And above all we must bear with everything for God, so that he in turn may bear with us. Increase your zeal. Read the signs of the times. Look for him who is outside time, the eternal one, the unseen, who became visible for us; he cannot be touched and cannot suffer, yet he became subject to suffering and endured so much for our sake.

Do not neglect widows; after the Lord, it is you who must be their guardian. Nothing must be done without your approval, and you must do nothing without God's approval, as indeed is the case; stand firm. Services should be held often; seek out everyone by name. Do not look down upon slaves, whether men or women; yet they too should not be arrogant, but should give better service for the glory of God so as to gain from him a better freedom. They should not be anxious for their freedom to be bought at the community's expense, for they might then prove to be the slaves of their own desires.

Letter to Polycarp 1, 1–4, 3: Funk 1, 247–249

Proper 5 ✠ Friday

A reading from the Letter to Polycarp by Ignatius, Bishop of Antioch, and Martyr [c. 115]

Avoid evil practices; indeed, preach against them. Tell my sisters to love the Lord and be content with their husbands in the flesh and in the spirit, and in the same way bid my brothers in Christ's name to love their wives as the Lord loves his Church. If any can remain chaste in honor of the Savior's flesh, then let them do so without boasting. For if they boast of it, they are lost; and if they think themselves for this reason better than the bishop, they are lost. Those who marry should be united with the bishop's approval, so that the marriage may follow God's will and not merely the prompting of the flesh. Let everything be done for God's honor.

Hear your bishop, that God may hear you. My life is a sacrifice for those who are obedient to the bishop, the presbyters and the deacons; and may it be my lot to share with them in God. Work together in harmony, struggle together, run together, suffer together, rest together, rise together, as stewards, advisors and servants of God. Seek to please him whose soldiers you are and from whom you draw your pay; let none of you prove a deserter. Let your baptism be your armor, your faith your helmet, your charity your spear, your patience your panoply. Let your good works be your deposits, so that you may draw out well-earned savings. So be patient and gentle with one another, as God is with you. May I have joy in you for ever!

Since I have heard that the church of Antioch in Syria is in peace through your prayers, I too am more tranquil in my reliance upon God. If only I may find my way to God through my passion and at the resurrection prove to be your disciple! My most blessed Polycarp, you should convene a godly council and appoint someone whom you consider dear and especially diligent to be called God's courier and to have the honor of going into Syria and advancing God's glory by speaking of your untiring charity. Christians are not their own masters; their time is God's. This is God's work, and it will be yours as well when you have performed it. I have trust in the grace of God that you are ready to act generously when it comes to God's work. Since I knew so well your zeal for truth, I have limited my appeal to these few words.

I could not write to all the churches because I am sailing at once from Troas to Neapolis as is required of me. I want you, therefore, as one who knows God's purpose, to write to the churches of the East and bid them to do the same. Those who can should send representatives, while the rest should send letters through your delegates. Thus your community will be honored for a good work which will be remembered for ever, as their bishop deserves.

I wish all of you well for ever in Jesus Christ; through him may you all remain in God's unity and in his care. Farewell in the Lord!

Letter to Polycarp 5, 1–8, 1, 3: Funk 1, 249–253

Proper 5 ✠ Saturday

A reading from the Second Discourse against the Arians by Athanasius, Bishop of Alexandria [373]

The likeness of Wisdom has been stamped upon creatures in order that the world may recognize in it the Word who was its maker and through the Word come to know the Father. This is Paul's teaching: "What can be known about God is clear to them, for God has shown it to them. Ever since the creation of the world his invisible nature has been there for the mind to perceive in things that have been made." Accordingly the Word is not a creature, for the passage that begins: "The Lord created me" is to be understood as referring to that wisdom which is truly in us and is said to be so.

But if this fails to persuade our opponents, let them tell us whether there is any wisdom in created things. If there is none, why does the apostle Paul allege as the cause of human sins: "By God's wisdom, the world failed to come to a knowledge of God through wisdom"? And if there is no created wisdom, how is it that the expression "a multitude of the wise" is found in Scripture? And again, Scripture testifies that "the wise one is wary and turns away from evil," and "by wisdom is a house built." Further, Ecclesiastes says: "Wise people's wisdom will light up their faces." He also rebukes presumptuous persons with the warning: "Do not say: How is it that former days were better than these? For it is not in wisdom that you ask this."

So there is a wisdom in created things, as the son of Sirach too bears witness: "The Lord has poured it out upon all his works, to be with humankind as his gift, and with wisdom he has abundantly equipped those who love him." This quality of being "poured out" belongs not to the essence of that self-existent Wisdom who is the Only-begotten, but to that wisdom which reflects the only-begotten one in the world. Why then is it beyond belief if the creative and archetypal Wisdom, whose likeness is the wisdom and understanding poured out in the world, should say, as though speaking directly of himself: "The Lord created me in his works"? For the wisdom in the world is not creative, but is itself created in God's works, and in the light of this wisdom "the heavens declare the glory of God," and "the firmament proclaims the work of his hands."

Second Discourse against the Arians 78, 79: PG 26, 311, 314

Proper 6 ✠ Sunday

A reading from the treatise On the Holy Spirit by Basil the Great, Bishop of Caesarea [379]

Of the beliefs and practices whether generally accepted or publicly enjoined which are preserved in the Church, some we possess derived from written teaching; others we have received delivered to us "in a mystery" by the tradition of the apostles; and both of these in relation to true religion have the same force. And were we to attempt to reject such customs as have no written authority, on the ground that the importance they possess is small, we should unintentionally injure the Gospel.

For instance, what writing has taught us to turn to the East at prayer? What was the meaning of the mighty Moses in not making all parts of the tabernacle open to every one? Moses was wise enough to know that contempt attaches to the trite and to the obvious, while a keen interest is naturally associated with the unusual and the unfamiliar. In the same manner the Apostles and Fathers who laid down laws for the Church from the beginning thus guarded the awful dignity of the mysteries in secrecy and silence, for what is bruited abroad at random is no mystery at all. This is the reason for our tradition of unwritten precepts and practices, that the knowledge of our dogmas may not become neglected and condemned by the multitude through familiarity. "Dogma" and "Kerygma" are two distinct things; the former is observed in silence; the latter is proclaimed to all the world. One form of this silence is the obscurity employed in Scripture, which makes the meaning of "dogmas" difficult to be understood for the very advantage of the reader.

Thus we all look to the East at our prayers, but few of us know that we are seeking our own ancient country, Paradise, which God planted in Eden in the East. We pray standing on the first day of the week, but we do not all know the reason. On the day of the resurrection [Greek *ana-stasis*, 'standing again'] we remind ourselves of the grace given to us by standing at prayer, not only because we rose with Christ [Greek *sun-ana-stantes*, 'stood again with'] and are bound to "seek those things which are above"; but also because the day seems to us to be in some sense an image of the age which we expect. Of necessity, then, the Church teaches her own foster children to offer their prayers on that day standing, to the end that through continual reminder of the endless life we may not neglect to make provision for our removal thither.

Moreover, all Pentecost is a reminder of the resurrection expected in the age to come. On this day the rules of the Church have educated us to prefer the upright attitude of prayer, for by their plain reminder they, as it were, make our mind to dwell no longer in the present but in the future. Moreover, every time we fall upon our knees and rise from off them we show by the very deed that by our sin we fell down to earth, and by the loving kindness of our Creator were called back to heaven.

On the Holy Spirit 2", 66: PG 32, 188–192

Proper 6 ✠ Monday

A reading from the treatise On the Lord's Prayer by Cyprian, Bishop and Martyr of Carthage [258]

When we pray, our words should be calm, modest and disciplined. Let us reflect that we are standing before God. We should please him both by our bodily posture and the manner of our speech. It is characteristic of the vulgar to shout and make a noise, not those who are modest. On the contrary, they should employ a quiet tone in their prayer.

Moreover, in the course of his teaching, the Lord instructed us to pray in secret. Hidden and secluded places, even our own rooms, give witness to our belief that God is present everywhere; that he sees and hears all; that in the fullness of his majesty, he penetrates hidden and secret places. This is the teaching of Jeremiah: "Am I God when I am near, and not God when I am far away? Can anyone hide in a dark corner without being seen by me? Do I not fill heaven and earth?" Another passage of Scripture says: "The eyes of the Lord are everywhere, observing both the good and the wicked."

The same modesty and discipline should characterize our liturgical prayer as well. When we gather to celebrate the divine mysteries with God's priest, we should not express our prayer in unruly words; the petition that should be made to God with moderation is not to be shouted out noisily and verbosely. For God hears our heart not our voice. He sees our thoughts; he is not to be shouted at. The Lord showed us this when he asked: "Why do you think evil in your hearts?" The Book of Revelation testifies to this also: "And all the churches shall know that I am the one who searches the heart and the desires."

Hannah maintained this rule; in her observance of it she is an image of the Church. We are told that she prayed quietly and modestly to God in the recesses of her heart. Her prayer was secret but her faith was evident. She did not pray with her voice, but with her heart, for she knew that in this way the Lord would hear her. She prayed with faith and obtained what she sought. Scripture makes this clear in the words:

"She was speaking in her heart; her lips were moving but her voice could not be heard; and the Lord heard her prayer." The psalmist also reminds us: "Commune within your own hearts, and in the privacy of your own room keep silence." This is the teaching of the Holy Spirit. Through Jeremiah he suggests this: "Say in your hearts: Lord, it is you that we have to worship."

My friends, anyone who worships should remember the way in which the tax-collector prayed in the temple alongside the Pharisee. He did not raise his eyes immodestly to heaven or lift up his hands arrogantly. Instead he struck his breast and confessing the sins hidden within his heart he implored the assistance of God's mercy. While the Pharisee was pleased with himself, the tax-collector deserved to be cleansed much more because of the manner in which he prayed. For he did not place his hope of salvation in the certainty of his own innocence; indeed, no one is innocent. Rather he prayed humbly, confessing his sins. And the Lord who forgives the lowly heard his prayer.

On The Lord's Prayer 4–6: CSEL 3, 268–270

Proper 6 ✠ Tuesday

A reading from the Revelations of Divine Love by Dame Julian of Norwich [c. 1417]

Our Mother by nature and grace—for he would become our Mother in everything—laid the foundation of his work in the Virgin's womb with great and gentle condescension. This was shown in the first revelation when I received a mental picture of the Virgin's genuine simplicity at the time she conceived. In other words, it was in this lowly place that God most high, the supreme wisdom of all, adorned and arrayed himself with our poor flesh, ready to function and serve as Mother in all things.

A mother's is the most intimate, willing, and dependable of all services, because it is the truest of all. None has been able to fulfil it properly but Christ, and he alone can. We know that our own mother's bearing of us was a bearing to pain and death, but what does Jesus, our true Mother, do? Why, he, All-love, bears us to joy and eternal life! Blessings on him! Thus he carries us within himself in love. And he is in labor until the time has fully come for him to suffer the sharpest pangs and most appalling pain possible—and in the end he dies. And not even when this is over, and we ourselves have been born to eternal bliss, is his marvellous love completely satisfied. This he shows in that overwhelming word of love, "If I could possibly have suffered more, indeed I would have done so."

He might die no more, but that does not stop him working, for he needs to feed us. It is an obligation of his dear, motherly, love. The human mother will suckle her child with her own milk, but our beloved Mother, Jesus, feeds us with himself, and, with the most tender courtesy, does it by means of the Blessed Sacrament, the precious food of all true life. And he keeps us going through his mercy and grace by all the sacraments. This is what he meant when he said, "It is I whom Holy Church preaches and teaches." In other words, "All the health and life of sacraments, all the virtue and grace of my word, all the goodness laid up for you in Holy Church—it is I." The human mother may put her child tenderly to her breast, but our tender Mother Jesus simply leads us into his blessed breast through his open side, and there gives us a glimpse of the Godhead and heavenly joy—the inner certainty of eternal bliss. The tenth revelation showed this, and said as much with that word, "See how I love you," as looking into his side he rejoiced.

This fine and lovely word "Mother" is so sweet and so much its own that it cannot properly be used of any but him, and of her who is his own true Mother—and ours. In essence "motherhood" means love and kindness, wisdom, knowledge, goodness. Though in comparison with our spiritual birth our physical birth is a small, unimportant, straightforward sort of thing, it still remains that it is only through his working that it can be done at all by his creatures. A kind, loving mother who understands and knows the needs of her child will look after it tenderly just because it is the nature of a mother to do so. As the child grows older she changes her methods—but not her love. Older still, she allows the child to be punished so that its faults are corrected and its virtues and graces developed. This way of doing things, with much else that is right and good, is our Lord at work in those who are doing them. Thus he is our Mother in nature, working by his grace in our lower part, for the sake of the higher. It is his will that we should know this, for he wants all our love to be fastened on himself. Like this I could see that our indebtedness, under God, to fatherhood and motherhood—whether it be human or divine—is fully met in truly loving God. And this blessed love Christ himself produces in us. This was shown in all the revelations, and especially in those splendid words that he uttered, "It is I whom you love."

Revelation 14, chapter 60: Colledge and Walsh 2, 594–600

Proper 6 ✠ Wednesday

A reading from the Letter to the Trallians by Ignatius, Bishop of Antioch, and Martyr [c. 115]

Ignatius, also called Theophorus, to the holy church at Tralles in the province of Asia, dear to God the Father of Jesus Christ, elect and worthy of God, enjoying peace in body and in the Spirit through the passion of Jesus Christ, who is our hope through our resurrection when we rise to him. In the manner of the apostles, I too send greetings to you with the fullness of grace and extend my every best wish.

Reports of your splendid character have reached me: how you are beyond reproach and ever unshaken in your patient endurance—qualities that you have not acquired but are yours by nature. My informant was your own bishop Polybius, who by the will of God and Jesus Christ visited me here in Smyrna. He so fully entered into my joy at being in chains for Christ that I came to see your whole community embodied in him. Moreover, when I learned from him of your God-given kindliness toward me, I broke out in words of praise for God. It is on him, I discovered, that you pattern your lives.

Your submission to your bishop, who is in the place of Jesus Christ, shows me that you are not living as people usually do but in the manner of Jesus himself, who died for us that you might escape death by belief in his death. Thus one thing is necessary, and you already observe it, that you do nothing without your bishop; indeed, be subject to the presbytery as well, seeing in them the apostles of Jesus Christ our hope, for if we live in him we shall be found in him.

Deacons, too, who are ministers of the mysteries of Jesus should in all things be pleasing to all. For they are not mere servants with food and drink, but emissaries of God's Church; hence they should guard themselves against anything deserving reproach as they would against fire.

Similarly, all should respect the deacons as Jesus Christ, just as all should regard the bishop as the image of the Father, and the presbyters as God's senate and the college of the apostles. Without these three orders you cannot begin to speak of a church. I am confident that you share my feelings in this matter, for I have had an example of your love in the person of your bishop who is with me now. His whole bearing is a great lesson, and his very gentleness wields a mighty influence.

By God's grace there are many things I understand, but I keep well within my limitations for fear that boasting should be my undoing. At the moment, then, I must be more apprehensive than ever and pay no attention at all to those who flatter me; their praise is as a scourge. For though I have a fierce desire to suffer martyrdom, I know not whether I am worthy of it. Most people are unaware of my passionate longing, but it assails me with increasing intensity. My present need, then, is for that humility by which the prince of this world is overthrown.

And so I strongly urge you, not I so much as the love of Jesus Christ, to be nourished exclusively on Christian fare, abstaining from the alien food that is heresy. And this you will do if you are neither arrogant nor cut off from God, from Jesus Christ, and from the bishop and the teachings of the apostles. Whoever is within the sanctuary is pure; but whoever is not is unclean. That is to say, whoever acts apart from the bishop and the presbytery and the deacons is not pure in conscience. In writing this, it is not that I am aware of anything of the sort among you; I only wish to forewarn you, for you are my dearest children.

Letter to the Trallians 1, 1–8, 1: Funk 1, 203–209

Proper 6 ✠ Thursday

A reading from the Letter to the Trallians by Ignatius, Bishop of Antioch, and Martyr [c. 115]

Make yourselves gentle, and be born again in the faith which is the body of the Lord and in the love which is the blood of Jesus Christ. No one must bear a grudge against a neighbor. Never give the pagans the slightest pretext, so that the great majority who serve God will not be mocked because of the folly of a few. "Woe to the one on account of whose folly my name is blasphemed."

So turn a deaf ear to the talk of anyone whose language has nothing to do with Jesus Christ. Descended from David, he was truly born of Mary, he really ate and drank. He was really persecuted under Pontius Pilate, and truly died by crucifixion, while heavenly and earthly beings and those under the earth looked on. He truly rose from the dead, being raised by his Father. Those who believe in him will be raised like him by the Father. We shall rise again in Christ without whom we do not have true life.

Avoid, then, those poisonous growths that bear deadly fruit; the mere taste of them is sudden death. Such growths are not of the Father's planting; if they were they would be recognized as branches of the cross, their fruit would be imperishable. The cross of Christ's passion is his invitation to you who are the members of his body. The head cannot come to life without the members, since God, the very ground of unity, has foretold such a union.

I send you greetings from Smyrna and from all God's churches which are here with me. They have been a comfort to me in every way, both physically and spiritually. The chains which I wear for the sake of Jesus Christ, praying all the time that I may come to God, are my plea. Continue to live together in that harmony of yours and persevere in prayer together. It is fitting that everyone, and especially the presbyters, should comfort the bishop and thereby honor the Father and Jesus Christ, and his apostles.

I beg you, if you love me, listen to me, so that this letter of mine may not witness against you. And pray for me, too, lest I be found unfit, for in God's mercy I need your love to make me worthy of the destiny that is mine.

The communities of Smyrna and Ephesus send greetings. In all your prayers remember the church in Syria. I am unworthy to claim membership in it, being the least of them all. And now, farewell in Jesus Christ. Be submissive to your bishop, as you would to God's command, and also to the presbytery. As individuals, love one another with undivided affection. My life is being sacrificed for you, not only at this moment, but also when I shall come before God. Though I am still in danger, God the Father, through Jesus Christ, is my pledge that my prayer and yours will be heard. My desire is that, through him, you may be found without fault.

Letter to the Trallians 8, 1–13, 3: Funk 1, 209–211

Proper 6 ✠ Friday

A reading from a sermon of Augustine, Bishop of Hippo [430]

Solicitude about my office as bishop has engrossed me since the time this burden was placed upon my shoulders, for I shall have to give a rigorous account. But what ought we to fear after receiving this grace of the episcopacy? We must fear the danger of being led astray by the honor it brings to us, instead of using that office for a fruitful ministry. Help me, therefore, by your prayers that he who has deigned to give me this charge may also deign to help me to bear my burden.

When you pray in this way for me, it is really for yourselves that you are praying. For what is the burden of which I am speaking but you? Pray that I may be strong, as I myself pray that you may not be burdensome. For, indeed, our Lord Jesus Christ would never have said that his burden was light if he did not bear it with the one who is charged with it. And you too, support me. In that way, according to the commandment of the Apostle, we shall bear one another's burdens, thus accomplishing the law of Christ. If he does not bear the burden with us, we succumb. If he does not carry us, we fall.

If what I am "for" you frightens me, what I am "with" you reassures me. For you, I am the bishop; with you, I am a Christian. "Bishop," this is the title of an office one has accepted to discharge; "Christian," that is the name of the grace one receives. Dangerous title! Salutary name! We are tossed around in the whirlpool of that activity as in an immense sea. But, reminding ourselves of the blood with which we were ransomed, and calmed by this thought, we enter, as it were, into a safe harbor.

Laboring in a personal task, we find rest in the blessing that is common to all. If I am more pleased to have been redeemed with you, than to be your head, I shall more fully be your servant, and this is what the Lord commands. May I thus not be accountable for the price in virtue of which I have received the favor of being your companion in serving.

For I must love my Redeemer and I know what he said to Peter: "Simon, son of John, do you love me? Feed my sheep." He said that once, twice, three times. He questioned him about love; he commanded the labor, for the greater the love, the lighter the burden. "How shall I make a return to the Lord for all the good he has done for me?"

Should I dare to say that I reimburse him because I lead his flock to pasture? I am doing that, of course, but not I, "The grace of God with me." Where then can I discover what is due to me if he goes before me everywhere? For one cannot ask any salary from him whom he loves gratuitously unless the salary is the very one who is loved!

Sermon on the Anniversary of his Episcopal Consecration: CCL 104, 919–920

Proper 6 ✠ Saturday

A reading from a sermon of Augustine, Bishop of Hippo [430]

The day I became a bishop, a burden was laid on my shoulders for which it will be no easy task to render an account. The honors I receive are for me an ever present cause of uneasiness. Indeed, it terrifies me to think that I could take more pleasure in the honor attached to my office, which is where its danger lies, than in your salvation, which ought to be its fruit. This is why being set above you fills me with alarm, whereas being with you gives me comfort. Danger lies in the first; salvation in the second.

To be honest with you, my obligations involve me in so much turmoil that I feel as though I were tossed by storms on a great ocean. When I remember by whose blood I have been redeemed, this thought brings me peace, as though I were entering the safety of a harbor; and I am consoled, as I carry out the arduous duties of my own particular office, by the blessings which we all have in common. By finding my chief joy therefore in the redemption which I share with you, and not in my office, which has placed me over you, I shall the more truly be your servant; and so not only fulfill the Lord's command, but also show myself not ungrateful to him for making me your fellow servant. For my Redeemer has a claim upon my love, and I do not forget how he questioned Peter, and asked: "Do you love me, Peter? Then feed my sheep." He asked this once, then again and then a third time. He inquired about his love, and then he gave him work to do; for the greater one's love is, the easier is the work.

"How shall I repay the Lord for all the blessings he has given me?" I could say perhaps that I repay him by feeding his sheep, but even though I do this, "it is not really I who do it, but the grace of God within me." So when all that I do is the gift of God's grace, how can I possibly repay him? As a matter of fact, I hope to be repaid myself, and this for the very reason that I love him freely and feed his sheep. But, you may ask, if I feed his sheep because I love him freely, how can I demand payment for feeding them? It is indeed unthinkable to ask for a recompense for love freely given unless that recompense is the loved one.

But even if feeding his sheep could repay him for redeeming me, what could repay him for having made me his shepherd? To be a good shepherd I depend entirely on his grace, for without his help I should be a very bad one, there is so much evil in me. Pray, then, that I may not be a bad shepherd, but a good one.

And for you, "I also pray and warn you against failing to cooperate with the grace you receive from God." Make my ministry a fruitful one. You are God's garden, and you should therefore welcome the laborer who does the visible work of planting and watering the seed, even though the growth comes from one who works invisibly within you. Help me both by your prayers and by your obedience, for then it will be a pleasure for me, not to preside over you, but to serve you.

Sermon 340, 1: PL 38, 1483–1484

Proper 7 ✠ Sunday

A reading from the Letter to the Romans by Ignatius, Bishop of Antioch, and Martyr [c. 115]

Ignatius, called Theophorus, to the church which has found mercy in the generosity of the Father on high and of Jesus Christ, his only Son; to the church which is loved and enlightened by the Father, who wills all that exists in accordance with the love of Jesus Christ our God; to the church which rules over the land of the Romans, a church worthy of God, worthy of honor and of praise, worthy to be called blessed, worthy to receive the answer to its prayer, pure, and preeminent in love among Christian communities, observing the law of Christ and bearing the Father's name. I greet this church in the name of Jesus Christ, Son of the Father. To those who were in union, body and soul, with his every command, and filled inalienably with the grace of God, and cleansed wholly from all foreign stain, I wish every blameless joy in Jesus Christ our Lord.

Through my prayers I have been granted the favor of seeing you, face to face, as indeed I have constantly asked. I now hope to embrace you as a prisoner in Christ Jesus, provided that it is God's will for me to be found worthy to the end. For a good start has been made, if only I may gain the grace to secure my prize without hindrance. For I fear that your love may harm me. It is easy for you to do as you wish, but hard for me to attain to God if you should not allow me to be martyred.

I wish you to please God and not people—as indeed you are doing. I shall never again have such an opportunity to get to God, nor will you if you keep silent ever have the credit for a greater achievement. If you keep silent about me, I become a word of God; but if you love me in the flesh, I become a meaningless cry. Grant me no more than to be made a sacrifice to God while there is still an altar at hand. Thus you may form a choir of love and sing praise to the Father in Christ Jesus for so graciously summoning the bishop of Syria from the sun's rising to come to the place of its setting. It is a fine thing for me to set with the sun, leaving the world and going to God, that I may rise in him.

Letter to the Romans 1, 1–2, 2: Funk 1, 213–215

Proper 7 ✠ Monday

A reading from the Letter to the Romans by Ignatius, Bishop of Antioch, and Martyr [c. 115]

The delights of this world and all its kingdoms will not profit me. I would prefer to die in Jesus Christ than to rule over all the earth. I seek him who died for us, I desire him who rose for us. I am in the throes of being born again. Bear with me, beloved; do not keep me from living, do not wish me to die. I desire to belong to God; do not give me over to the world, and do not seduce me with perishable things. Let me see the pure light; when I am there, I shall be truly fulfilled at last. Let me imitate the sufferings of my God. If anyone has God within, understand what I want and have sympathy for me, knowing what drives me on.

The prince of this world would snatch me away and destroy my desire to be with God. So let none of you who will be there give satan help; side rather with me, that is, with God. Do not have Jesus Christ on your lips and the world in your hearts. Give envy no place among you. And if, when I get there, I should beg for your intervention, pay no attention to me; no, believe instead what I am writing to you now. For I write to you while I yet live, but I long for death. My earthly desires have been crucified, and there no longer burns in me the love of perishable things, but a living water speaks within me, saying: "Come to the Father."

I take no delight in corruptible food or in the pleasures of this life. I want the bread of God, which is the flesh of Jesus Christ, who was of David's seed, and for drink I want his blood, the sign of his imperishable love.

I no longer wish to live, as people count life. And I shall have my way, if you wish it so. Wish it, then, so that you too may have God's favor. With these few words I beg you to believe me. Jesus Christ will make plain to you the truth of what I say; he is the true voice that speaks the Father's truth. Pray for me that I may reach my goal. I have written to you not prompted by merely human feelings and values, but by God's purpose for me. If I am to suffer, it will be because you loved me well; if I am rejected, it will be because you hated me.

Remember in your prayers the church of Syria: it now has God for its shepherd instead of me. Jesus Christ alone will be its bishop, along with your love. For myself, I am ashamed to be counted among its members, for I do not deserve it, being the least of all, born out of due time. Yet, if I attain to God, by his mercy I shall be something. I greet you from my heart, and so do the churches that have welcomed me in love not as a mere passerby but as the representative of Jesus Christ. Yes, even the churches that were not on my route humanly speaking, though spiritually on the same journey, were there to meet me in city after city.

Letter to the Romans 6, 1–9, 3: Funk 1, 219–223

Proper 7 ✠ Tuesday

A reading from the treatise On Prayer by Origen, Priest and Theologian [c. 254]

People cannot obtain their requests if they do not pray with the requisite dispositions and faith, and if they do not conduct themselves in a fitting manner before praying. It is not a case of saying a great deal or coming to prayer with a soul filled with resentments.

No one can think of devoting time to prayer without being purified, no more than one will imagine that those who pray can obtain the pardon of their sins unless they have first wholeheartedly forgiven the brothers or sisters who ask their pardon. I think that they will profit in many ways from their prayer who desire to conduct themselves in this way and do so as well as they can.

First of all, they who dispose themselves to pray in this manner will have great advantage in adopting an attitude of prayer which places them in God's presence and engages them to pray to him as to someone who is present and looking at them. For just as certain mental images and remembrances of things which are recalled encumber the mind which lets itself be inundated by them, so can we believe that it is useful to recall that God is present and knows the most secret movements of the soul. Thus, the soul is disposing herself to please him who is present to her, who sees her, and anticipates her every thought, the one who searches hearts and reins.

Even if we suppose that no other advantage comes to those who prepare their minds to pray, it is clear that such an attitude bears fruits that are far from negligible. Those who give themselves continually to prayer know by experience that through this frequent practice many sins are avoided and many good deeds carried out.

The remembrance of a good-hearted and wise person induces us to imitation and restrains our impulses toward evil. How much more, then, will the remembrance at prayer, of God, the Father of us all, benefit us, if we are convinced that he is present, hears us, and speaks to us!

And now we must prove from the sacred Scripture what we have said, as follows. Those who pray should lift up pure hands by forgiving everyone who has offended them, banishing whatever troubles their souls, and being irritated against no one. Again, in order that one's mind may not be troubled by thinking about other things, one should while praying forget everything that is foreign to it.

Who can doubt that this state of soul is the most favorable? Paul teaches this in his First Epistle to Timothy when he declares: "It is my wish, then, that in every place the faithful should offer prayers with blameless hands held aloft, and be free from anger and dissension."

Treatise on Prayer 8–9: PG 11, 442–443

Proper 7 ✠ Wednesday

A reading from the Dialogue of Divine Providence by Catherine of Siena, Dominican Sister and Mystic [1380]

You are my laborers, for I have sent you to work in the vineyard of holy Church. You are laboring in the general body of Christian people, where I set you, by grace, when I gave you the light of holy baptism which, in turn, you received in the mystical body of holy Church at the hands of my ministers, whom I have set working along with you. You are in the general body, they in the mystical body; their task being to nourish your souls with the Blood administered in the sacraments which you receive from holy Church, and to draw out the thorns of mortal sin and plant grace in your souls. They are my labourers in the vineyard of your souls. They form a unity in the vineyard of holy Church.

All rational creatures have their own vineyards, their souls, their wills being the laborers appointed to work in them with freedom of choice, and in time, that is, for as long as they live. Once this time is past they can work no more, whether well or ill, but while they live they can work at their vineyards in which I had placed them. And these laborers in the soul have been given a strength no devil or any other creature can take from them unless they choose; for their baptism made them strong and equipped them with a knife of love of virtue and hatred of sin. This love and hatred they find in the Blood, for it was out of love for you and hatred for sin that my only-begotten Son gave his Blood and died; and it was through this Blood that you received life at baptism. You have this knife, then, to be used with your free will while you have time, to cut out the thorns of mortal sin and put in the virtues; otherwise you cannot hope to receive the fruit of the Blood from those laborers I have placed in holy Church who, as I said, remove mortal sin from the soul's vineyard and dispense grace in the Blood they administer to you in the sacraments of holy Church.

The first thing to do, then, is to bestir yourself with heartfelt contrition, with sorrow for sin and love of virtue. This done, you will receive the fruit of the Blood. You could not do so otherwise, not if you neglect to prepare yourselves, on your side, as branches of the vine of my Son who said: "I am the true vine and you are the branches, and my Father is the vinedresser." For so it is. I am the Vinedresser, since all that has being comes from me. My power is measureless and with it I rule the universe; nothing is made or ruled except through me. And it was I who planted the true vine of my only-begotten Son in the earth of humanity, in order that you, as branches abiding in the vine, should bear fruit.

The Dialogue of Divine Providence 23: ed. Foster and Ronayne, London 1980, 295–296

Proper 7 ✠ Thursday

A reading from the Dialogue of Divine Providence by
Catherine of Siena, Dominican Sister and Mystic [1380]

Do you know what I do, once my servants are united in following the doctrine of the sweet loving Word? I prune them, that they may bear more fruit, and their fruit be tested and not turn into wild fruit. As the vinedresser prunes the shoots of the vine so as to get better and more wine from them, cutting off the barren shoots and burning them, so do I, the true Vinedresser, with my vine, pruning with much suffering my servants who abide in me, that they may bear more fruit and better fruit, and their virtues be tested. But the barren ones are cut off and thrown into the fire, as I have said.

The true laborers toil away at their souls, uprooting all self-love and turning over in me the earth of their affections. They nurture and foster the growth of the seed of grace they received in holy baptism. And as they work their own vineyard, they work their neighbor's too, since the two go together—as you remember, I have explained that all evil and all good are done by way of one's neighbor; that you are my laborers who have come forth from me, the supreme eternal Laborer, and that by the union I have made with you I have grafted you into the Vine.

Bear in mind that all rational creatures have their own vineyard, and that this is joined to their neighbor's without anything in between. All are so joined together that none can do any good to themselves without benefiting their neighbors, nor any evil to themselves without harming their neighbors. And all of you together form one great vineyard which is the whole body of Christians, united in the vineyard of the mystical body of holy Church, whence you draw your life. And within this vineyard is planted the vine of my only-begotten Son, into which you must be grafted—otherwise you at once become rebels against holy Church and are like limbs that are cut off from the body and immediately decay.

Even so, while you have time you can get up out of the stench of sin with true repentance, and have recourse to my ministers, the laborers who hold the keys of the wine, that is of the Blood, that has flowed from that Vine, a blood so perfect that no defect in its ministers can deprive you of its fruit.

It is the bond of charity that binds my servants, together with true humility acquired through knowledge of self and of me. So you see, I have made you all my laborers. And now I call on you again, because the world is already at its last gasp, so much have thorns multiplied and smothered the seed that it will not produce any fruit of grace. I want you then to be true laborers, zealously helping to tend souls in the mystical body of holy Church. For this I have chosen you, for it is my will to have mercy on the world, the world for which you pray to me so earnestly.

The Dialogue of Divine Providence 24: ed. Foster and Ronayne, London 1980, 297–298

Proper 7 ✠ Friday

A reading from the First Letter to the Corinthians by Clement, Bishop of Rome [c. 100]

Beloved, Jesus Christ is our salvation, he is the high priest through whom we present our offerings and the helper who supports us in our weakness. Through him our gaze penetrates the heights of heaven and we see, as in a mirror, the most holy face of God. Through Christ the eyes of our hearts are opened, and our weak and clouded understanding reaches up toward the light. Through him the Lord God willed that we should taste eternal knowledge, for Christ "is the radiance of God's glory, and as much greater than the angels as the name God has given him is superior to theirs."

So then, let us do battle with all our might under his unerring command. Think of the soldiers serving under our military commanders. How well disciplined they are! How readily and submissively they carry out orders! Not everyone can be a prefect, a tribune, a centurion, or a captain of fifty, but each rank executes the orders of the emperor and the officers in command. The great cannot exist without those of humble condition, nor can those of humble condition exist without the great. Always it is the harmonious working together of its various parts that insures the well-being of the whole. Take our own body as an example:

the head is helpless without the feet; and the feet can do nothing without the head. Even our least important members are useful and necessary to the whole body, and all work together for its well-being in harmonious subordination.

Let us, then, preserve the unity of the body that we form in Christ Jesus, and let all give their neighbors the deference to which their particular gifts entitle them. Let the strong care for the weak and the weak respect the strong. Let the wealthy assist the poor and the poor thank God for giving them someone to supply their needs. The wise should show wisdom not by eloquence but by good works; the humble should not proclaim their own humility, but leave others to do so; nor must the one who preserves chastity ever boast of it, but recognize that the ability to control desires has been given by another.

Think of how we first came into being, of what we were at the first moment of our existence. Think of the dark tomb out of which our Creator brought us into his world where he had his gifts prepared for us even before we were born. All this we owe to him and for everything we must give him thanks. To him be glory for ever and ever.

First Letter to the Corinthians 36, 1–2, 37–38: Funk 1, 145–149

Proper 7 ✠ Saturday

A reading from a sermon of Gregory the Great, Bishop of Rome [604]

Two disciples were walking together. They did not believe, yet they were talking about Jesus. Suddenly, he appeared, but under characteristics which they could not recognize. To their bodily eyes the Lord thus manifested externally what was taking place in their innermost depths, in the thoughts of their heart. The disciples were inwardly divided between love and doubt. The Lord was really present at their side, but he did not let himself be recognized. He offered his presence to these disciples who spoke of him, but because they doubted him he hid his true visage from them. He spoke to them and reproached them for their little sense. He interpreted for them every passage of Scripture which referred to him, but since he was still a stranger to the faith of their heart he acted as if he were going farther.

In acting in such a manner, the Truth who is sincere was not being deceitful: he was showing himself to the eyes of his disciples as he appeared in their minds. And the Lord wished to see whether these disciples, who did not yet love him as God, would at least be friendly to him under the guise of a stranger. But those with whom Truth walked could not have been far from charity; they invited him to share their lodging, as one does with a traveler. Can we say simply that they invited him? The Scripture says that "they pressed him." It shows us by this example that when we invite strangers under our roof, our invitation must be a pressing one.

They thus set the table, serve the food, and in the breaking of bread discover the God whom they had failed to come to know in the explanation of the Scriptures. It was not in hearing the precepts of God that they were enlightened, but in carrying them out: "It is not those who hear the law who are just in the sight of God; it is those who keep it who will be declared just." If anyone wishes to understand what you have heard, hasten to put into practice whatever you have grasped. The Lord was not recognized while he was speaking; he was pleased to make himself known while he was offered something to eat. Let us then, beloved, love to practice charity. It is of this that Paul speaks to us: "Love your fellow Christians always. Do not neglect to show hospitality, for by that means some have entertained angels without knowing it." Peter also says: "Be mutually hospitable without complaining." And Truth himself speaks to us of it: "I was a stranger and you welcomed me." "As often as you did it for one of my least brothers [or sisters]," the Lord will declare on the day of judgment, "you did it for me."

Despite this, we are so slothful in the face of the grace of hospitality! Let us appreciate the greatness of this virtue. Let us receive Christ at our table so as to be welcomed at his eternal supper. Let us show hospitality to Christ present in the stranger now so that at the judgment he will not ignore us as strangers but will welcome us as brothers and sisters into his Kingdom.

Homily 23: PL 76, 1182–1183

Proper 8 ✠ Sunday

A reading from the Letter to the Philadelphians by Ignatius,
Bishop of Antioch, and Martyr [c. 115]

Ignatius, also called Theophorus, to the church of God the Father and the Lord Jesus Christ located at Philadelphia in the province of Asia. You have found mercy and have been strengthened in the peace of God; you are now filled with gladness because of the passion of our Lord, and by his mercy you are made believers in his resurrection. I greet you in the blood of Jesus Christ. You are my abiding and unshakable joy, especially if your members remain united with the bishop and with the presbyters and deacons, all appointed in accordance with the mind of Christ who by his own will has strengthened them in the firmness which the Spirit gives.

I know that this bishop has obtained his ministry, which serves the community, neither by his own efforts, nor from people nor even out of vainglory, but from the love of God the Father and of the Lord Jesus Christ. I am deeply impressed by his gentleness, and by his silence he is more effective than the empty talkers. He is in harmony with the commandments as is a lute with its strings. I call him blessed, then, for his sentiments toward God, since I know these to be virtuous and perfect, and for his stability and calm, in which he imitates the gentleness of the living God.

As children of the light of truth, flee divisions and evil doctrines; where your shepherd is, follow him as his flock.

For all who belong to God and Jesus Christ are with the bishop; all who repent and return to the unity of the Church will also belong to God, that they may live according to Jesus Christ. Do not be deceived. If anyone follows a schismatic, "you will not obtain the inheritance of God's kingdom"; if anyone lives by an alien teaching, you do not assent to the passion of the Lord.

Be careful, therefore, to take part only in the one eucharist; for there is only one flesh of our Lord Jesus Christ and one cup to unite us with his blood, one altar and one bishop with the presbyters and deacons, who are his fellow servants. Then, whatever you do, you will do according to God.

I overflow with love for you and with a joyous heart I make you strong—although it is not so much I but Jesus Christ. Although imprisoned for his sake, I fear more because of my imperfection. But your prayers will perfect me in the eyes of God so that I might yet receive the inheritance promised me by the merciful God. I seek refuge in the person of Christ through the Gospels and I appeal to the true ministry of the Church through the apostles.

Letter to the Philadelphians 1, 1–2, 1; 3, 2–5: Funk 1, 226–229

Proper 8 ✠ Monday

A reading from a sermon of Augustine, Bishop of Hippo [430]

"Sing to the Lord a new song; his praise is in the assembly of the saints."
We are urged to sing a new song to the Lord, as new singers who have
learned a new song. A song is a thing of joy; more profoundly, it is a thing
of love. Anyone, therefore, who has learned to love the new life has
learned to sing a new song, and the new song reminds us of our new
life. The new singer, the new song, the new covenant, all belong to the
one kingdom of God, and so the new singer will sing a new song and
will belong to the new covenant.

There is not one who does not love something, but the question is,
what to love. The psalms do not tell us not to love, but to choose the
object of our love. But how can we choose unless we are first chosen?
We cannot love unless someone has loved us first. Listen to the apostle
John: "We love him, because he first loved us." The source of our love
for God can only be found in the fact that God loved us first. He has given
us himself as the object of our love, and he has also given us its source.
What this source is you may learn more clearly from the apostle Paul who
tells us: "The love of God has been poured into our hearts." This love
is not something we generate ourselves; it comes to us "through the
Holy Spirit who has been given to us."

Since we have such an assurance, then, let us love God with the love
he has given us. As John tells us more fully: "God is love, and those who
abide in love abide in God, and God in them." It is not enough to say:
"Love is from God." Which of us would dare to pronounce the words of
Scripture: "God is love"? They alone could say it who knew what it was
to have God dwelling within them. God offers us a short route to the
possession of himself. He cries out: Love me and you will have me, for
you would be unable to love me if you did not possess me already.

All you who have been born again in Christ and whose life is from
above, listen to me; or rather, listen to the Holy Spirit saying through me:
"Sing to the Lord a new song." Look, you tell me, I am singing. Yes indeed,
you are singing; you are singing clearly, I can hear you. But make sure
that your life does not contradict your words. Sing with your voices, your
hearts, your lips and your lives: "Sing to the Lord a new song."

Now it is your unquestioned desire to sing of him whom you love, but
you ask me how to sing his praises. You have heard the words: "Sing to
the Lord a new song," and you wish to know what praises to sing. The
answer is: "His praise is in the assembly of the saints"; it is in the singers

themselves. If you desire to praise him, then live what you express. Live good lives, and you yourselves will be his praise.

Sermon 34, 1–3, 5–6: CCL 41, 424–426

Proper 8 ✠ Tuesday

A reading from the Confessions of Augustine, Bishop of Hippo [430]

Victorinus was an old man of great learning, with a profound knowledge of all the liberal sciences. He had studied a great many books of philosophy and published criticisms of them. He had been master to many distinguished members of the Senate, and to mark his outstanding ability as a teacher, he had even been awarded a statue in the Roman forum—a great honor in the eyes of the world. He had always been a worshiper of idols and had taken part in the sacrilegious rites which were then in vogue amongst most of the nobility of Rome. Rome, in fact, had become the suppliant of the gods whom she had once defeated, for her leaders now talked only of "prodigies, monstrous deities of every sort, and Anubis who barked like a dog—all the gods who had once battled against Neptune, Venus, and Minerva." For many years Victorinus, now an old man, had never ceased to defend these practices with all the fire of his oratory, and yet he was not ashamed to be the child of Christ and to become an infant at your font, submitting his neck to the yoke of humility and bowing his head before the ignominy of the Cross.

O Lord, Lord, "who bade heaven stoop and came down to earth, at whose touch the mountains were wreathed in smoke," how did you find the way to his heart? He read the Holy Scriptures, so Simplicianus told me, and made the most painstaking and careful study of all Christian literature. Privately as between friends, though never in public, Victorinus used to say to Simplicianus, "I want you to know that I am now a Christian." Simplicianus used to reply, "I shall not believe it or count you as a Christian until I see you in the Church of Christ." At this Victorinus would laugh and say, "Is it then the walls of the church that make the Christian?"

He often repeated his claim to be a Christian, and each time Simplicianus gave him the same answer, only to receive the same rejoinder about the walls. He was afraid of offending his proud friends who worshiped heathen gods, and he thought that a storm of hostility would break upon him from the peak of their Babylonian dignity, as though it were from the cedars of Lebanon which the Lord had not yet brought down. But later on, as a result of his attentive reading, he became resolute. He was seized by the fear that Christ might deny him before the holy angels if he was too faint-hearted to acknowledge Christ before the people, and he felt himself guilty of a great crime in being ashamed of the sacraments instituted by your Word in his lowly state, whereas he was not ashamed of the impious rites devoted to those proud deities whom his own pride had led him to follow and accept. So he repudiated vanity and turned in shame to the truth. Simplicianus told me that quite unexpectedly and without warning he said, "Let us go to the church. I want to be made a Christian." So Simplicianus, unable to contain his joy, went with him to the church. He was instructed in the first mysteries of the faith and soon afterwards, to the wonder of Rome and the joy of the Church, he gave in his name to be reborn through baptism.

Eventually the time came for making his profession of faith. At Rome those who are about to enter into your grace usually make their profession in a set form of words which they learn by heart and recite from a raised platform in view of the faithful, but Simplicianus said that the priests offered to allow Victorinus to make his profession in private, as they often did for people who seemed likely to find the ceremony embarrassing. But Victorinus preferred to declare his salvation in full sight of the assembled faithful. For there was no salvation in the rhetoric which he taught, and yet he had professed it in public. If he was not afraid of uttering his own words before a crowd of lunatics, why should he be frightened to name your Word before your meek flock?

Confessions 8, 2: CSEL 33, 171–174

Proper 8 ✠ Wednesday

A reading from the First Letter to the Corinthians by Clement, Bishop of Rome [c. 100]

Let us fix our gaze on the Father and Creator of the whole world, and let us hold on to his peace and blessings, his splendid and surpassing gifts. Let us contemplate him in our thoughts and with our mind's eye reflect upon the peaceful and restrained unfolding of his plan; let us consider the care with which he provides for the whole of his creation.

By his direction the heavens are in motion, and they are subject to him in peace. Day and night fulfill the course he has established without interfering with each other. The sun, the moon and the choirs of stars revolve in harmony at his command in their appointed paths without deviation. By his will the earth blossoms in the proper seasons and produces abundant food for humans and animals and all the living things on it without reluctance and without any violation of what he has arranged.

Yet unexplored regions of the abysses and inexpressible realms of the deep are subject to his laws. The mass of the boundless sea, joined together by his ordinance in a single expanse, does not overflow its prescribed limits but flows as he commanded it. For he said: "Thus far shall you come, and your waves will be halted here." The ocean, impassable for humans, and the worlds beyond it are governed by the same edicts of the Lord.

The seasons, spring, summer, autumn and winter, follow one another in harmony. The quarters from which the winds blow function in due season without the least deviation. And the ever-flowing springs, created for our health as well as our enjoyment, unfailingly offer their breasts to sustain human life. The tiniest of living creatures meet together in harmony and peace. The great Creator and Lord of the universe commanded all these things to be established in peace and harmony, in his goodness to all, and in overflowing measure to us who seek refuge in his mercies through our Lord Jesus Christ; to him be glory and majesty for ever and ever.

First Letter to the Corinthians 19, 2–20, 12: Funk 1, 125–129

Proper 8 ✠ Thursday

A reading from the Confessions of Augustine, Bishop of Hippo [430]

I felt that I was still the captive of my sins, and in my misery I kept crying "How long shall I go on saying 'tomorrow, tomorrow'? Why not now? Why not make an end of my ugly sins at this moment?"

I was asking myself these questions, weeping all the while with the most bitter sorrow in my heart, when all at once I heard the singsong voice of a child in a nearby house. Whether it was the voice of a boy or a girl I cannot say, but again and again it repeated the refrain: "Take it and read, take it and read." At this I looked up, thinking hard whether there was any kind of game in which children used to chant words like these, but I could not remember ever hearing them before. I stemmed my flood of tears and stood up, telling myself that this could only be a divine command to open my book of Scripture and read the first passage on which my eyes should fall. For I had heard the story of Antony, and I remembered how he had happened to go into a church while the

Gospel was being read and had taken it as a counsel addressed to himself when he heard the words: "Go home and sell all that belongs to you. Give it to the poor, and so the treasure you have shall be in heaven; then come back and follow me." By this divine pronouncement he had at once been converted to you.

So I hurried back to the place where Alypius was sitting, for when I stood up to move away I had put down the book containing Paul's Epistles. I seized it and opened it, and in silence I read the first passage on which my eyes fell: "Not in revelling and drunkenness, not in lust and wantonness, not in quarrels and rivalries. Rather, arm yourselves with the Lord Jesus Christ; spend no more thought on nature and nature's appetites." I had no wish to read more and no need to do so. For in an instant, as I came to the end of the sentence, it was as though the light of confidence flooded into my heart and all the darkness of doubt was dispelled.

Confessions 8, 12: CSEL 33, 194–195

Proper 8 ✠ Friday

A reading from the First Letter to the Corinthians by Clement, Bishop of Rome [c. 100]

Consider, beloved, how the Lord keeps reminding us of the resurrection that is to come, of which he has made the Lord Jesus Christ the firstfruits by raising him from the dead. Let us look, beloved, at the resurrection that occurs at its appointed time. Day and night show us a resurrection; the night lies in sleep, day rises again; the day departs, night takes its place. Let us think about the harvest; how does the sowing take place, and in what manner? The sower goes out and casts each seed onto the ground. Dry and bare, they fall into the earth and decay. Then the greatness of the Lord's providence raises them up again from decay, and out of one many are produced and yield fruit.

In this hope, then, let our hearts be bound fast to him who is faithful in his promises and just in his judgments. He forbade us to tell lies; still less will he himself tell a lie. Nothing is impossible for God except to tell a lie. Then let our faith in him be awakened; let us reflect that everything is close to him.

By the word of his power he established all things, and by his word he can reduce them to ruin. "Who shall say to him: What have you done? Who shall stand up against the power of his might?" He will accomplish everything when he wills and as he wills, and nothing that he has decreed shall pass away. All things stand in his presence, and nothing lies hidden from his counsel. "If the heavens tell forth the glory of God, the firmament reveals the work of his hands, day speaks to day, and night shares knowledge with night; there are no words, no speeches, and their voices are not heard."

Since all things lie open to his eyes and ears, let us hold him in awe and rid ourselves of impure desires to do works of evil, so that we may be protected by his mercy from the judgment that is to come. Which of us can escape his mighty hand? What world will give asylum to one who deserts him? "Where will I go, where will I hide from his face? If I go up to heaven, you are there; if I go to the limits of the earth, your right hand is there; if I lie down in the deep, your spirit is there." Where, then, can one go, where can one escape to, from the presence of him whose hands embrace the universe?

Let us then approach him in holiness of soul, raising up to him hands pure and undefiled, out of love for our good and merciful Father who made us a chosen portion for himself.

First Letter to the Corinthians 24, 1–5; 27, 1–29, 1: Funk 1, 93–97

Proper 8 ✠ Saturday

A reading from the treatise On Death as a Blessing by Ambrose, Bishop of Milan [397]

The Apostle tells us: "The world is crucified to me, and I to the world." We are to understand that this death by crucifixion takes place in this life, and that this death is a blessing. So he goes on to urge us "to bear the death of Jesus with us in our bodies, for whoever bears the death of Jesus in the body will bear also in the body the life of the Lord Jesus."

Death must be active within us if life also is to be active within us. "Life" is life after death, a life that is a blessing. This blessing of life comes after victory, when the contest is over, when the law of our fallen nature no longer rebels against the law of our reason, when we no longer need to struggle against the body that leads to death, for the body already shares in victory. It seems to me that this "death" is more powerful than "life." I accept the authority of the Apostle when he says: "Death is therefore active within us, but life also is active within you." Yet the "death" of this one was building up life for countless multitudes of peoples! He therefore teaches us to seek out this kind of death even in this life, so that the death of Christ may shine forth in our lives—that blessed death by which our outward self is destroyed and our inmost self renewed, and our earthly dwelling crumbles away and a home in heaven opens before us.

Those who cut themselves off from this fallen nature of ours and free themselves from its chains are imitating death. These are the bonds spoken of by the Lord through Isaiah: "Loose the bonds of injustice, untie the thongs of the yoke, set free the oppressed and break every yoke of evil."

The Lord allowed death to enter this world so that sin might come to an end. But he gave us the resurrection of the dead so that our nature might not end once more in death; death was to bring guilt to an end, and the resurrection was to enable our nature to continue for ever.

"Death" in this context is a passover to be made by all humankind. You must keep facing it with perseverance. It is a passover from corruption, from mortality to immortality, from rough seas to a calm harbor. The word "death" must not trouble us; the blessings that come from a safe journey should bring us joy. What is death but the burial of sin and the resurrection of goodness? Scripture says: "Let my soul die among the souls of the just"; that is, let me be buried with the just, so that I may cast off my sins and put on the grace of the just, of those who bear the death of Christ with them, in their bodies and in their souls.

Treatise on Death as a Blessing 3, 9; 4, 15: CSEL 32, 710, 716–717

Proper 9 ✠ Sunday

A reading from a commentary on the psalms by Augustine, Bishop of Hippo [430]

God could give no greater gift to us than to make his Word, through whom he created all things, our head and to join us to him as his members, so that the Word might be both Son of God and Son of Man, one God with the Father, and one human being with all humankind. The result is that when we speak with God in prayer we do not separate the Son from him, and when the body of the Son prays it does not separate its head from itself: it is the one Savior of his body, our Lord Jesus Christ, the Son of God, who prays for us and in us and is himself the object of our prayers.

He prays for us as our priest, he prays in us as our head, he is the object of our prayers as our God.

Let us then recognize both our voice in his, and his voice in ours. When something is said, especially in prophecy, about the Lord Jesus Christ that seems to belong to a condition of lowliness unworthy of God, we must not hesitate to ascribe this condition to one who did not hesitate to unite himself with us. Every creature is his servant, for it was through him that every creature came to be.

We contemplate his glory and divinity when we listen to these words: "In the beginning was the Word, and the Word was with God, and the Word was God. He was in the beginning with God. All things were made through him, and without him nothing was made." Here we gaze on the divinity of the Son of God, something supremely great and surpassing all the greatness of his creatures. Yet in other parts of Scripture we hear him as one sighing, praying, giving praise and thanks.

We hesitate to attribute these words to him because our minds are slow to come down to his humble level when we have just been contemplating him in his divinity. It is as though we were doing him an injustice in acknowledging in a human being the words of one with whom we spoke when we prayed to God; we are usually at a loss and try to change the meaning. Yet our minds find nothing in Scripture that does not go back to him, nothing that will allow us to stray from him.

Our thoughts must then be awakened to keep their vigil of faith. We must realize that the one whom we were contemplating a short time before in his nature as God took to himself the nature of a servant; he was made in the likeness of humankind and found to be a human like others; he humbled himself by being obedient even to accepting death; as he hung on the cross he made the psalmist's words his own: "My God, my God, why have you forsaken me?"

We pray to him as God, he prays for us as a servant. In the first case he is the Creator, in the second a creature. Himself unchanged, he took to himself our created nature in order to change it, and made us one with himself, head and body. We pray then to him, through him, in him, and we speak along with him and he along with us.

Commentary on Psalm 85, 1: CCL 39, 1176–1177

Proper 9 ✠ Monday

A reading from the Confessions of Augustine, Bishop of Hippo [430]

But what is my God? I put my question to the earth. It answered, "I am not God," and all things on earth declared the same. I asked the sea and the chasms of the deep and the living things that creep in them, but they answered, "We are not your God. Seek what is above us." I spoke to the winds that blow, and the whole air and all that lives in it replied, "Anaximenes is wrong. I am not God." I asked the sky, the sun, the moon, and the stars, but they told me, "Neither are we the God whom you seek." I spoke to all the things that are about me, all that can be admitted by the door of the senses, and I said, "Since you are not my God, tell me about him. Tell me something of my God." Clear and loud they answered, "God is the one who made us." I asked these questions simply by gazing at these things, and their beauty was all the answer they gave.

Then I turned to myself and asked, "Who are you?" "A human being," I replied. But it is clear that I have both body and soul, the one the outer, the other the inner part of me. Which of these two ought I to have asked to help me find my God? With my bodily powers I had already tried to find him in earth and sky, as far as the sight of my eyes could reach, like an envoy sent upon a search. But my inner self is the better of the two, for it was to the inner part of me that my bodily senses brought their messages. They delivered to their arbiter and judge the replies which they carried back from the sky and the earth and all that they contain, those replies which stated "We are not God" and "God is he who made us." The inner part of me knows these things through the agency of the outer part. I, the inner part, know these things; I, the soul, know them through the senses of my body. I asked the whole mass of the universe about my God, and it replied, "I am not God. God is the one who made me."

Confessions 10, 6: CSEL 33, 232–233

Proper 9 ✠ Tuesday

A reading from a treatise by Baldwin, Archbishop of Canterbury [1190]

"The word of God is both living and powerful and much more piercing than a two-edged sword." The word of God is plainly shown in all its strength and wisdom to those who seek out Christ, who is the word, the power and the wisdom of God. This word was with the Father in the beginning, and in its own time was revealed to the apostles, then preached by them and humbly received in faith by believers. So, the word is in the Father, as well as on our lips and in our hearts.

This word of God is living; the Father gave it life in itself, just as he has life in himself. For this reason it not only is alive, but it is life, as he says of himself: "I am the way, the truth and the life." Since he is life, he is both living and life-giving. For, "as the Father raises up the dead and gives them life, so also the Son gives life to those he chooses." He is life-giving when he calls the dead from the grave and says: "Lazarus, come forth."

When this word is preached, in the very act of preaching it gives to its own voice which is heard outwardly a certain power which is perceived inwardly, so much so that the dead are brought back to life and by these praises the children of Abraham are raised from the dead. This word then is alive in the heart of the Father, on the lips of the preacher, and in the hearts of those who believe and love him. Since this word is so truly alive, undoubtedly it is full of power.

It is powerful in creation, powerful in the government of the universe, powerful in the redemption of the world. For what is more powerful, more effective? Who shall speak of its power; who shall make all its praises heard? It is powerful in what it accomplishes, powerful when preached. It does not come back empty; it bears fruit in all to whom it is sent.

It is powerful and "more piercing than any two-edged sword" when it is believed and loved. For what is impossible to the believer? What is difficult for a lover? When this word is spoken, its message pierces the heart like the sharp arrows of a strong archer, like nails driven deep; it enters so deeply that it penetrates to the innermost recess. This word is much more piercing than any two-edged sword, inasmuch as it is stronger than any courage or power, sharper than any shrewdness of human ingenuity, keener than all human wisdom, or the subtlety of learned argument.

Treatise 6: PL 204, 451–453

Proper 9 ✠ Wednesday

A reading from the Confessions of Augustine, Bishop of Hippo [430]

"You are great, Lord, and worthy of our highest praise; your power is great and there is no limit to your wisdom." Humankind, a tiny part of your creation, wishes to praise you. Though we bear about us our mortality, the evidence of sin and the evidence that "you resist the proud," yet we who are a tiny part of your creation wish to praise you. It is you who move us to delight in your praise. For you have made us for yourself, and our heart is restless until it rests in you.

Lord, help me to know and understand which is the soul's first movement, to call upon you for help or to praise you; or if it must first know you before it can call upon you. But if someone does not know you, how can they call upon you? For, not knowing you, they might call upon someone else instead of you. Or must you first be called upon in order to be known? But Scripture says: "Unless they believe in him, how shall they call upon him? And how shall they believe unless someone preaches to them?"

"Those who seek the Lord will praise him." Seeking the Lord they will find him, and finding him they will praise him. Lord, let me seek you by calling upon you, and let me call upon you believing in you, for you have been preached to us. Lord, my faith calls upon you, the faith you have given me, the faith you have inspired in me by the incarnation of your Son and through the ministry of your preacher.

How shall I call upon my God, my Lord and my God? For when I call upon him, I am really calling him into myself. Where within me can my God come? How can God who made heaven and earth come into me? Lord my God, is there anything in me that can contain you? Can heaven and earth, which you have made and in which you have made me, contain you? Or is it true that whatever exists contains you since without you nothing would exist?

Since I do indeed exist and yet would not exist unless you were in me, why do I ask you to come to me? I am not now in hell, yet you are there. For the psalmist says: "If I descend into hell you are there." Therefore, my God, I would not exist at all, unless you were in me; or rather, I would not exist unless I were in you "from whom and by whom and in whom all things exist." Yes, Lord, it is so. To what place do I call you to come, since I am in you? Or from what place are you to come to me? Where can I go beyond the bounds of heaven and earth, that my God may come to me, for he has said: "I fill heaven and earth?"

Who will help me to find rest in you? Who will send you into my heart to inebriate it, so that I will forget my evil ways and embrace you, my only good? What are you to me? Have mercy on me, that I may speak. What am I to you that you command me to love you, and grow angry and threaten me with terrible punishment if I do not? Is it then a small sorrow not to love you?

In your mercy, Lord my God, tell me what you are to me. "Say to my soul, I am your salvation." So speak that I may hear you. The ears of my heart are turned to you, Lord; open them and say to my soul: "I am your salvation." I will run after your voice and I will lay hold of you. Do not hide your face from me. Let me see your face even if I die, for if I see it not, I shall die of longing.

Confessions 1, 1–2; 2, 5; 5: CSEL 33, 1–5

Proper 9 ✠ Thursday

A reading from a sermon of Augustine, Bishop of Hippo [430]

Goliath was a Philistine, that is, one of the aliens who were making war on the children of Israel. Now, at this same time, David (the author of the psalms, or rather the instrument of the Holy Spirit who inspired them) was a child or at most a youth, who tended his father's sheep. His brothers who were older fought in the army of the king. One day, David was sent by his parents to take them their food. He thus found himself in the midst of the war.

Also present at that time, was the Goliath already mentioned—gigantic in stature, bristling with weapons, unsurpassed in strength, and consumed with arrogance; in his insolence, he challenged any one of his enemies to individual combat. He demanded that one chosen by them should meet him so that the issue of the war would rest on the result and victory would go to the army of the contestant who prevailed.

Now the king of the Jewish people and the children of Israel was at the time Saul. This proposal threw him into great distress, and he searched his entire army for a man resembling this giant, but he found none who combined the same great stature with similar boldness. While Saul was thus agitated, the youthful David—not presuming on his own strength but trusting in the name of God—dared to offer to stand up against this giant.

The king was informed of this and saw in such resolution not the temerarious presumption of a child but the assurance that comes from piety; and he did not reject the suggestion. He realized, looking at the daring youth, that he had something of God in him and that one so young could not conceive such an idea without an inspiration from on high. He thus accepted David's offer and the youth went out to confront Goliath.

They wanted to arm David so that his weapons might supply for his lack of years and the inequality of his strength. But these armaments intended for an older man, far from helping him, were too heavy for one so young. He did not want a man's armor, and rejected it as a weight that would impede his movements. He wanted to go to the combat, free and untrammelled, because he put his strength in God rather than in himself, and he was armed with faith rather than the sword.

All human strength lies in the knowledge of God and the reception of his grace, in which David placed all his confidence. Goliath, on the contrary, only counted on himself, on his own strength; this proud, this boasting, this arrogant man wished to have the sole honor of the victory of his people. Like all the proud, his pride showed itself in his face and it was in his face that the stone cast by David struck him and felled him.

Those who spout vain words and are true Philistines do not form part of the family of Christ; they do not belong to the kingdom of the One who said: "Our Father"—but are strangers. "Who can equal me? Who dares attack me?" Is not this the language of those who pride themselves on their own resources? Is not this their invariable sentiment? But David goes forth without armor, furnished only with a few small stones, and this just man will bring low all that pride. This is what the martyrs did; they vanquished the wicked at the very moment when the wicked appeared to be victorious.

Sermon 32, 3–4, 12, 25–26: PL 38, 197–198, 201, 205–206

Proper 9 ✠ Friday

A reading from the treatise On Christian Perfection by
Gregory, Bishop of Nyssa [c. 394]

No one has known Christ better than Paul, nor surpassed him in the careful example he gave of what anyone should be who bears Christ's name. So precisely did he mirror his Master that he became his very image. By a painstaking imitation, he was transformed into his model and it seemed to be no longer Paul who lived and·spoke, but Christ himself. He shows his keen awareness of this grace when he refers to the Corinthians' desire for proof that Christ was speaking in him; as he says: "It is no longer I who live: it is Christ who lives in me."

Paul teaches us the power of Christ's name when he calls him the power and wisdom of God, our peace, the unapproachable light where God dwells, our expiation and redemption, our great high priest, our paschal sacrifice, our propitiation; when he declares him to be the radiance of God's glory, the very pattern of his nature, the creator of all ages, our spiritual food and drink, the rock and the water, the bedrock of our faith, the cornerstone, the visible image of the invisible God. He goes on to speak of him as the mighty God, the head of his body, the Church, the firstborn of the new creation, the firstfruits of those who have fallen asleep, the firstborn of the dead, the eldest of many children; he tells us that Christ is the mediator between God and humankind, the only-begotten Son crowned with glory and honor, the Lord of glory, the beginning of all things, the king of justice and of peace, the king of the whole universe, ruling a realm that has no limits.

Paul calls Christ by many other titles too numerous to recall here. Their cumulative force will give some conception of the marvelous content of the name "Christ," revealing to us his inexpressible majesty, insofar as our minds and thoughts can comprehend it. Since, by the goodness of God, we who are called "Christians" have been granted the honor of sharing this name, the greatest, the highest, the most sublime of all names, it follows that each of the titles that express its meaning should be clearly reflected in us. If we are not to lie when we call ourselves "Christians," we must bear witness to it by our way of living.

Treatise on Christian Perfection: PG 46, 254–255

Proper 9 ✠ Saturday

A reading from The City of God by Augustine, Bishop of Hippo [430]

Every work that effects our union with God in a holy fellowship is a true sacrifice; every work, that is, which is referred to that final end, that ultimate good, by which we are able to be in the true sense happy. As a consequence even that mercy by which aid is given to us is not a sacrifice unless it is done for the sake of God. Sacrifice, though performed or offered by us, is something divine; that is why the ancient Latin authors gave it this name of "sacrifice," of something sacred. We ourselves, consecrated in the name of God and vowed to God, are therefore a sacrifice insofar as we die to the world in order to live for God. This too is part of mercy, the mercy that each one has. Scripture tells us: "Have mercy on your soul by pleasing God."

Works of mercy, then, done either to ourselves or to our neighbor and referred to God are true sacrifices. Works of mercy, however, are intended to free us from wretchedness and by this means to bring us to happiness. For we cannot be happy except through that good of which Scripture says: "For me, my true good is to cling to God." It clearly follows that the whole redeemed city, that is, the assembly and fellowship of the saints, is offered to God as a universal sacrifice through the great high priest, who in the nature of a slave offered even himself for us in his passion, in order that we might be the body of so great a head. He offered this nature of a slave; he was offered in that nature, because in that nature he is the mediator, in that nature he is the high priest, in that nature he is the sacrifice.

The Apostle urges us to present our bodies "as a living sacrifice, holy and pleasing to God, and as our spiritual worship," and not to follow the pattern of this world but to be transformed by the renewal of our minds and hearts, so that we may discern what is the will of God, what is good and pleasing and perfect, the total sacrifice that is ourselves. "By the grace of God that has been given me," he says, "I say to all who are among you: Do not think more highly of yourselves than you should, but judge yourselves with moderation according to the measure of faith God has given to each of you. As we have in the same body many members, yet all the members do not have the same functions, so we are many, but are one body in Christ; we are each of us members of one another, having different gifts according to the grace that has been given us."

This is the sacrifice of Christians, "the many who are one body in Christ." This is the sacrifice which the Church celebrates in the sacrament of the altar, that sacrament known to the faithful; in that sacrament it is made clear to the Church that in the sacrifice she offers, she herself is offered.

Hence it is that the true Mediator receives the sacrifice "in the form of God", in union with the Father, with whom he is one God. And yet "in the form of a servant" he preferred to be himself the sacrifice rather than to receive it, to prevent anyone from supposing that sacrifice, even in this circumstance, should be offered to any created being. Thus he is both the priest, himself making the offering, and the oblation. This is the reality, and he intended the daily sacrifice of the Church to be the sacramental symbol of this; for the Church, being the body of which he is the head, learns to offer itself through him. This is the true sacrifice; and the sacrifices of the saints in earlier times were many different symbols of it. This one sacrifice was prefigured by many rites, just as many words are used to refer to one thing, to emphasize a point without inducing boredom. This was the supreme sacrifice, and the true sacrifice, and all the false sacrifices yielded place to it.

And yet it is we ourselves—we, his city—who are his best, his most glorious sacrifice.

City of God 10, 6, 20; 19, 23: CCL 47, 278–279, 294; CCL 48, 695

Proper 10 ✠ Sunday

A reading from the Exposition of the Orthodox Faith by John of Damascus, Priest [c. 760]

It is not without reason or by chance that we worship towards the East. Since God is spiritual light, and Christ in the Scriptures is called the Sun of Righteousness and the Dayspring, the East is the direction that must be assigned to his worship. Indeed the holy David also says "Sing unto God, ye kingdoms of the earth, O sing praises unto the Lord, to him that rideth upon the Heaven of Heavens towards the East." Moreover the Scripture also says that God planted a garden eastward in Eden, and there He put the man and woman whom he had formed, and when they had transgressed his command he expelled them and made them dwell over against the delights of Paradise, which clearly is the West. So then, we worship God seeking and striving after our old homeland. Moreover, the tent of Moses had its veil and mercy seat towards the East. Also the tribe of Judah as the most precious pitched their camp on the East. Also in the celebrated temple of Solomon the Gate of the Lord was placed eastward. Moreover, Christ, when he hung on the cross, had his face turned towards the West, and so we worship, striving after him. And when he was received again into Heaven he was borne towards the East, and thus his apostles worship him, and thus he will come again in the way in which they beheld him going towards Heaven; as the Lord himself said, "As the lightning cometh out of the East and shineth even unto the West, so also shall the coming of the Son of Man be." So then, in expectation of his coming we worship towards the East. But this tradition of the apostles is unwritten. For much that has been handed down to us by tradition is unwritten.

The Fount of Knowledge 3, On the Orthodox Faith 4, 12: PG 94, 1133-1136

Proper 10 ✠ Monday

A reading from the sermon On Pastors by Augustine, Bishop of Hippo [430]

You have already been told about the wicked things shepherds desire. Let us now consider what they neglect. "You have failed to strengthen what was weak, to heal what was sick, and to bind up what was injured," that is, what was broken. "You did not call back the straying sheep, nor seek out the lost. What was strong you have destroyed." Yes, you have cut it down and killed it. The sheep is weak, that is to say, its heart is weak, and so, incautious and unprepared, it may give in to temptations.

The negligent shepherd fails to say to the believer: "My child, come to the service of God, stand fast in fear and in righteousness, and prepare your soul for temptation." A shepherd who does say this strengthens the one who is weak and makes him strong. Such a believer will then not hope for the prosperity of this world. For if one has been taught to hope for worldly gain, one will be corrupted by prosperity. When adversity comes, that believer will be wounded or perhaps destroyed.

The builder who builds in such manner is not building the believer on a rock but upon sand. "But the rock was Christ." Christians must imitate Christ's sufferings, not set their hearts on pleasures. The weak will be strengthened when told: "Yes, expect the temptations of this world, but the Lord will deliver you from them all if your heart has not abandoned him. For it was to strengthen your heart that he came to suffer and die, came to be spit upon and crowned with thorns, came to be accused of shameful things, yes, came to be fastened to the wood of the cross. All these things he did for you, and you did nothing. He did them not for himself, but for you."

But what sort of shepherds are they who for fear of giving offense not only fail to prepare the sheep for the temptations that threaten, but even promise them worldly happiness? God himself made no such promise to this world. On the contrary, God foretold hardship upon hardship in this world until the end of time. And you want the Christian to be exempt from these troubles? Precisely because one a Christian, one is destined to suffer more in this world.

For the Apostle says: "All who desire to live a holy life in Christ will suffer persecution." But you, shepherd, seek what is yours and not what is Christ's, you disregard what the Apostle says: "All who want to live a holy life in Christ will suffer persecution." You say instead: "If you live a holy life in Christ, all good things will be yours in abundance. If you do not have children, you will embrace and nourish all people, and none of them shall die." Is this the way you build up the believer? Take note of what you are doing and where you are placing them. You have built them on sand. The rains will come, the river will overflow and rush in, the winds will blow, and the elements will dash against that house of yours. It will fall, and its ruin will be great.

Lift them up from the sand and put them on the rock. Let them be in Christ, if you wish them to be Christians. Let them turn their thoughts to sufferings, however unworthy they may be in comparison to Christ's. Let them center their attention on Christ, who was without sin, and yet made restitution for what he had not done. Let them consider Scripture, which says to them: "He chastises every child whom he receives." Let them prepare to be chastised, or else not seek to be received as children.

Sermon 46, on Pastors, 10–11: CCL 41, 536–538

Proper 10 ✠ Tuesday

A reading from a letter by Augustine, Bishop of Hippo [430]

This is the one, true and only life of happiness, that, immortal and incorruptible in body and spirit, we should contemplate the Lord's graciousness for ever. It is for the sake of this one thing that everything else is sought and without impropriety requested. The person who has this will have all that one wants; in heaven, such a person will be unable to want, because unable to possess anything that is unfitting.

In heaven is the fountain of life, that we should now thirst for in prayer as long as we live in hope and do not yet see the object of our hope, under the protection of his wings in whose presence is all our desire, so that we may drink our fill from the plenty of his house and be given drink from the running stream of his delights. For with him is the fountain of life, and in his light we shall see light, when our desire will be satisfied with good things, and there will be nothing to ask for with sighs but only what we possess with joy.

Yet, since this is that peace that surpasses all understanding, even when we ask for it in prayer we do not know how to pray for what is right. Certainly we do not know something if we cannot think of it as it really is; whatever comes to mind we reject, repudiate, find fault with; we know that this is not what we are seeking, even if we do not yet know what kind of thing it really is.

There is then within us a kind of instructed ignorance, instructed, that is, by the Spirit of God who helps our weakness. When the Apostle said: "If we hope for something we do not see, we look forward to it with patience," he added: "In the same way the Spirit helps our weakness; we do not know what it is right to pray for, but the Spirit pleads with sighs too deep for words. He who searches hearts knows what the Spirit means, for the Spirit pleads for the saints according to God's will."

We must not understand by this that the Holy Spirit of God pleads for the saints as if the Spirit were someone different from what God is: in the Trinity the Spirit is the unchangeable God and one God with the Father and the Son. Scripture says that the Spirit "pleads for the saints" because the Spirit moves the saints to plead, just as it says: "The Lord your God tests you, to know if you love him," in this sense, that he does it to enable you to know. So the Spirit moves the saints to plead with sighs too deep for words by inspiring in them a desire for the great and as yet unknown reality that we look forward to with patience. How can words express what we desire when it remains unknown? If we were entirely ignorant of it we would not desire it; again, we would not desire it or seek it with sighs, if we were able to see it.

Letter 130, to Proba, 14, 27–15, 28: CSEL 44, 71–73

Proper 10 ✠ Wednesday

A reading from the Confessions of Augustine, Bishop of Hippo [430]

O Lord God, grant us peace, for all that we have is your gift. Grant us the peace of repose, the peace of the Sabbath, the peace which has no evening. For this worldly order in all its beauty will pass away. All these things that are very good will come to an end when the limit of their existence is reached. They have been allotted their morning and their evening.

But the seventh day is without evening and the sun shall not set upon it, for you have sanctified it and willed that it shall last for ever. Although your eternal repose was unbroken by the act of creation, nevertheless, after all your works were done and you had seen that they were very good, you rested on the seventh day. And in your Book we read this as a forecast that when our work in this life is done, we too shall rest in you in the Sabbath of eternal life, though our works are very good only because you have given us the grace to perform them.

In that eternal Sabbath you will rest in us, just as now you work in us. The rest that we shall enjoy will be yours, just as the work that we now do is your work done through us. But you, O Lord, are eternally at work and eternally at rest. It is not in time that you see or in time that you move or in time that you rest: yet you make what we see in time; you make time itself and the repose which comes when time ceases.

You, who are the one God, the good God, have never ceased to do good. By the gift of your grace some of the works that we do are good, but they are not everlasting. After them we hope that we shall find rest, when you admit us to the great holiness of your presence. But you are Goodness itself and need no good besides yourself. You are for ever at rest, because you are your own repose.

Confessions 13, 35–38: CSEL 33, 386–388

Proper 10 ✠ Thursday

A reading from a homily of Origen, Priest and Theologian [c. 254]

The ark of the covenant led the people of God across the Jordan. The priests and the levites halted, and the waters, as though out of reverence to the ministers of God, stopped flowing. They piled up in a single mass, thus allowing the people of God to cross in safety. As a Christian, you should not be amazed to hear of these wonders performed for people of the past. The divine Word promises much greater and more lofty things to you who have passed through Jordan's stream by the sacrament of baptism: he promises you a passage even through the sky. Listen to what Paul says concerning the just: "We shall be caught up in the clouds to meet Christ in heaven, and so we shall always be with the Lord." There is absolutely nothing for the just to fear; the whole of creation serves the just. Listen to another promise that God makes the just through the prophet: "If you pass through fire, the flame shall not burn you, for I am the Lord your God." The just is everywhere welcome, and everything renders the just due service.

So you must not think that these events belong only to the past, and that you who now hear the account of them do not experience anything of the kind. It is in you that they all find their spiritual fulfillment. You have recently abandoned the darkness of idolatry, and you now desire to come and hear the divine law. This is your departure from Egypt. When you became a catechumen and began to obey the laws of the Church, you passed through the Red Sea; now at the various stops in the desert, you give time every day to hear the law of God and to see the face of Moses unveiled by the glory of God. But once you come to the baptismal font and, in the presence of the priests and deacons, are initiated into those sacred and august mysteries which only those know who should, then, through the ministry of the priests, you will cross the Jordan and enter the promised land. There Moses will hand you over to Jesus, and he himself will be your guide on your new journey.

Mindful, then, of all the mighty works of God, remembering that he divided the sea for you and held back the waters of the river, you will turn to them and say: "Why was it, sea, that you fled? Jordan, why did you turn back? Mountains, why did you skip like rams, and you hills, like young sheep?" And the word of the Lord will reply: "The earth is shaken at the face of the Lord, at the face of the God of Jacob, who turns stones into a pool and rock into springs of water."

Homily 4 on Joshua the Son of Nun 1: SC 71, 146–151

Proper 10 ✠ Friday

A reading from a letter by Cyprian, Bishop and Martyr of Carthage [258]

As we do battle and fight in the contest of faith, God and his angels and Christ himself watch us. How exalted is the glory, how great the joy of engaging in a contest with God presiding, of receiving a crown with Christ as judge.

Beloved, let us arm ourselves with all our might, let us prepare ourselves for the struggle by innocence of heart, integrity of faith, dedication to virtue.

The blessed Apostle teaches us how to arm and prepare ourselves: "Put round you the belt of truth; put on the breastplate of righteousness; for shoes wear zeal for the Gospel of peace; take up the shield of faith to extinguish all the burning arrows of the evil one; take the helmet of salvation, and the sword of the spirit, which is the word of God."

Let us take this armor and defend ourselves with these spiritual defenses from heaven, so that we may be able to resist the threats of the devil, and fight back on the evil day.

Let us put on the breastplate of righteousness so that our hearts may be safeguarded, proof against the arrows of the enemy. Let our feet be protected by the shoes of the teaching of the Gospel so that when we begin to trample on the serpent and crush it, we may not be bitten and tripped up by it.

Let us with fortitude bear the shield of faith to protect us by extinguishing all the burning arrows that the enemy may launch against us.

Let us wear on our head the helmet of the spirit to defend our ears against the proclamations of death, our eyes against the sight of accursed idols, our forehead so that God's sign may be kept intact, our lips so that our tongue may proclaim victoriously its faith in Christ its Lord.

Let us arm our right hand with the sword of the spirit so that it may courageously refuse the daily sacrifices, and like the hand—mindful of the eucharist—that receives the body of the Lord, stretch out to embrace him, and so gain from the Lord the future prize of a heavenly crown.

Have all this firmly fixed in your hearts. If the day of persecution finds us thinking on these things and meditating upon them, the soldier of

Christ, trained by Christ's commands and instructions, does not begin to panic at the thought of battle, but is ready for the crown of victory.

Letter 58, 8–9, 11: CSEL 3, 663–666

Proper 10 ✠ Saturday

A reading from a homily of Origen, Priest and Theologian [c. 254]

Once Jericho was surrounded it had to be stormed. How then was Jericho stormed? No sword was drawn against it, no battering ram was aimed at it, no javelins were hurled. The priests merely sounded their trumpets, and the walls of Jericho collapsed.

In the Scriptures Jericho is often represented as an image of the world. There can be no doubt that the man whom the gospel describes as going down from Jerusalem to Jericho and falling into the hands of brigands is an image of Adam being driven out of paradise into the exile of this world. Likewise the blind in Jericho, to whom Jesus came to give sight, signified the people in this world who were blinded by ignorance, to whom the Son of God came.

Jericho will fall, then; this world will perish. Indeed in the sacred books the end of the world was proclaimed long ago. How will the world be brought to an end, and by what means will it be destroyed? The answer of Scripture is: "By the sound of trumpets." If you ask what trumpets, then let Paul reveal the secret. Listen to what he says: "The trumpet will sound, and the dead who are in Christ will rise incorruptible. The voice of the archangel and the trumpet of God will give the signal, and the Lord himself will come down from heaven." Then the Lord Jesus will conquer Jericho with trumpets and destroy it, saving only the harlot and her household.

Jesus our Lord "will come," says Paul, and he will come with the sound of trumpets. He will save only the woman who received his spies, that is, his apostles, in faith and obedience, and hid them on the roof of her house; and he will join this harlot to the house of Israel. But let us not bring up her past sins again or impute them to her. She was a harlot once, but now she is joined to Christ, chaste virgin to one chaste husband. Listen to what the Apostle says of her: "He has determined to present you to Christ as a chaste virgin to her one and only husband." Indeed, Paul himself had been born of her: "Misled by our folly and disbelief," he said, "we too were once slaves to our passions and to pleasures of every kind."

If you wish to learn more fully about how this harlot ceased to be a harlot then listen to Paul once again: "And such were you also, but you have been cleansed and made holy in the name of our Lord Jesus Christ and in the Spirit of our God." To assure her escape when Jericho was destroyed, the harlot was given that most effective symbol of salvation, the scarlet cord. For it is by the blood of Christ that the entire Church is saved, in the same Jesus Christ our Lord, to whom belongs glory and dominion for ever and ever.

Homily 6 on Joshua the Son of Nun 4: SC 71, 188–193

Proper 11 ✠ Sunday

A reading from a sermon of Augustine, Bishop of Hippo [430]

The words we have sung contain our declaration that we are God's flock: "For he is the Lord our God who made us." He is our God, "and we are the people of his pasture and the sheep of his hands." Human shepherds did not make the sheep they own; they did not create the sheep they pasture. Our Lord God, however, because he is God and Creator, made for himself the sheep which he has and pastures. No one else created the sheep he pastures, nor does anyone else pasture the sheep he created.

In this song we have declared that we are his flock, the people of his pasture, and the sheep of his hands. Let us listen therefore to the words he addresses to us as his sheep. Earlier he addressed the shepherds, but now he speaks to the sheep. We listened to those earlier words of his and we—the shepherds—trembled, but you listened without a qualm.

What is to happen when we hear these words today? Are we in turn to be without a qualm while you tremble? By no means! We are shepherds, and the shepherd listens and trembles not only at what is said to the shepherds but also at what is said to the sheep. If the shepherd does listen without a qualm to what is said to the sheep, the shepherd is not concerned for them. And further, on that occasion we asked you in your charity to remember two points about us: first, that we are Christians, and second, that we are placed in charge. Because we are placed in charge, we are ranked among the shepherds, if we are good; but because we are Christians, we too are members of the flock with you. Therefore, whether the Lord is addressing the shepherds or the sheep, we must listen to all his words and tremble; our hearts must always remain concerned.

And so, beloved, let us listen to the words with which the Lord upbraids the wicked sheep and to the promises he makes to his own flock.

"You are my sheep," he says. Even in the midst of this life of tears and tribulations, what happiness, what great joy it is to realize that we are God's flock! To him were spoken the words: "You are the shepherd of Israel." Of him it was said: "The guardian of Israel will not slumber, nor will he sleep." He keeps watch over us when we are awake; he keeps watch over us when we sleep. A flock belonging to a person feels secure in the care of its human shepherd; how much safer should we feel when our shepherd is God. Not only does he lead us to pasture, but he even created us.

"You are my sheep, says the Lord God. See, I judge between one sheep and another, and between rams and goats." What are goats doing here in the flock of God? In the same pastures, at the same springs, goats—though destined for the left—mingle with those on the right. They are tolerated now, but will be separated later. In this way the patience of the flock develops and becomes like God's own patience. For it is he who will do the separating, placing some on the left and others on the right.

Sermon 47, 1, 2, 3, 6: CCL 41, 572-573, 575-576

Proper 11 ✠ Monday

*A reading from the Revelations of Divine Love by Dame
Julian of Norwich [c. 1417]*

A mother may allow her child sometimes to fall, and to learn the hard way, for the child's own good. But because she loves the child she will never allow the situation to become dangerous. Admittedly earthly mothers have been known to let their children die, but our heavenly Mother, Jesus, will never let us, his children, die. He and none but he is almighty, all wisdom, all love. Blessings on him! But often when we are shown the extent of our fall and wretchedness we are so scared and dreadfully ashamed that we scarcely know where to look. But our patient Mother does not want us to run away: nothing would be more displeasing to him. His desire is that we should do what a child does: for when a child is in trouble or is scared it runs to mother for help as fast as it can. Which is what he wants us to do, saying with the humility of a child, "Kind, thoughtful, dearest Mother, do be sorry for me. I have got myself into a filthy mess, and am not a bit like you. I cannot begin to put it right without your special and willing help." Even if we do not feel immediate relief we can still be sure that he behaves like a wise mother. If he sees it is better for us to mourn and weep he lets us do so—with pity and sympathy, of course, and for the right length of time—because he loves us. And he wants us to copy the child who always and naturally trusts mother's love through thick and thin.

Moreover he wills that we should hold tight to the Faith of Holy Church, and find there in that Communion of Saints our dearest Mother, who comforts us because she really understands. Individuals may often break down—or so it seems to them—but the whole body of Holy Church is unbreakable, whether in the past, present, or future. So it is a good, sound, grace-bringing thing to resolve, humbly but firmly, to be fastened and united to Holy Church our Mother,—in other words, to Jesus Christ. For the merciful ample flood of his precious blood and water suffices to make us sweet and clean; the Saviour's blessed wounds are open, and rejoice to heal us; the dear, gracious hands of our Mother are ever about us, and eager to help.

In all this work he functions as a kindly nurse who has no other business than to care for the well-being of her charge. It is his business to save us; it is his glory to do this for us; and it is his will that we should know it. For it is also his will that we should love him dearly, and trust him humbly and wholeheartedly. All this he showed in those gracious words, "I will keep you safe and sound."

Revelation 14, chapter 61: Colledge and Walsh 2, 604–609

Proper 11 ✠ Tuesday

A reading from the treatise On The Lord's Prayer by Cyprian, Bishop and Martyr of Carthage [258]

The gospel precepts are none other than instructions of God, foundations on which hope is built, firm bases of faith, fuel to rekindle the heart, guides to point out the way, and aids to the attainment of salvation. They instruct the minds of the faithful on earth in order to lead them to the kingdom of heaven. The words which God willed to let us hear from the prophets are many, but much greater are the words uttered by the Son, those which the word of God who dwelled within the prophets attests with his own voice. He no longer asks that the way be prepared for one who comes, but he comes himself to show us the way and to open it for us. Thus, we who were once blind and lacking foresight, wandering in the shadows of death, can now be enlightened by the light of grace and walk along the paths of life under the Lord's leadership and direction.

Among other saving instructions and divine teachings intended for the salvation of his people, the Lord gave us the form of prayer and urged us to pray as he has instructed us. He who gave us life also taught us to pray, with that same benevolence by which he has given and bestowed on us everything else. Thus, when we speak to the Father in the prayer that his Son has taught us, we are more readily heard. Jesus had already announced that the hour would come when the true worshipers would adore the Father in spirit and in truth and he accomplished what he promised. Having received the Spirit and the truth by his sanctifying action, we can now worship in spirit and in truth through the transmission of his teaching. Indeed, could there be a more spiritual prayer than the one left us by Christ who has also sent us his Spirit? Is there a truer manner of praying to the Father than the one which has come from the lips of Christ who is Truth?

Let us pray, then, as God our Master has taught us. Affectionate and familiar is the prayer with which we implore God in the words of God and reach his ear through the words of his Son. Let the Father recognize his Son's words when we offer up our prayer; and let him who dwells in our heart be also on our lips. And since we have him as an advocate with the Father for our sins, let us make the words of our advocate be heard when we as sinners beg pardon for our offenses. Since he has said that the Father will give us whatever we ask in his name, how much more surely will we obtain what we ask in Christ's name if we ask with his prayer as well!

On the Lord's Prayer 1-3: PL 4, 519-521

Proper 11 ✠ Wednesday

A reading from a homily of Gregory, Bishop of Nyssa [c. 394]

The happiness God promises certainly knows no limits. When one has gained such a blessing, what is left to desire? In seeing God one possesses all things. In the language of Scripture, to see is to have. "May you see the good things of Jerusalem" is the same as "May you possess the good things of Jerusalem." When the prophet says: "May the wicked be carried off and not see the glory of the Lord," it means: "May they not share in the glory of the Lord."

One who has seen God has, in the act of seeing, gained all that is counted good: life without end, everlasting freedom from decay, undying happiness, a kingdom that has no end, lasting joy, true light, a voice to sing pleasingly in the spirit, unapproachable glory, perpetual rejoicing, in a word, the totality of blessing.

Such is the wonderful hope held out by the beatitudes. As we have seen, the condition for seeing God is purity of heart, and now once more my mind is in confusion, as from an attack of giddiness, wondering if purity of heart is something impossible, something beyond the capacity of human nature. If the vision of God is dependent on purity of heart, and if Moses and Paul did not attain this vision—they state that neither they nor anyone else can see God—then the promise of the beatitude spoken by the Word seems to be something impossible of realization.

What do we gain from knowing the means by which God may be seen if we have not the power to see him? It is like saying that one is blessed if one is in heaven because in heaven things are seen that are not seen on earth. If we were told beforehand how to get to heaven, it would be helpful to know that one is blessed if one is in heaven. But as long as the way to heaven is impossible what do we gain by knowing about the happiness of heaven? This only saddens and annoys us when we realize the good things we are deprived of, because it is impossible to get there.

Surely the Lord does not encourage us to do something impossible to human nature, because the magnitude of what he commands is beyond the reach of our human strength? The truth is different. He does not command those creatures to whom he has not given wings to become birds, nor those to whom he has assigned a life on land to live in water. If then in the case of all other creatures the command is according to the capacity of those who receive it, and does not oblige them to anything beyond their nature, we shall come to the conclusion that we are not to give up hope of gaining what is promised by the beatitude. John and Paul and Moses, then, and any others like them, did not fail to achieve that sublime happiness that comes from the vision of God: not Paul, who said: "There is stored up for me a crown of righteousness, which the judge who judges justly will give me"; nor John, who leaned on the breast of Jesus; nor Moses, who heard God saying to him: "I know you above all others."

If it is clear that those who taught that the contemplation of God was beyond their powers are themselves blessed, and if blessedness consists in the vision of God and is granted to the pure in heart, then purity of heart, leading to blessedness, is certainly not among the things that are impossible.

Hence it can be said that those who with Paul teach that the vision of God is beyond our powers are right in what they say, and that the voice of the Lord does not contradict them when he promises that the pure in heart will see God.

Oration 6 on the Beatitudes: PG 44, 1266–1267

Proper 11 ✠ Thursday

A reading from a commentary on the psalms by Augustine,
Bishop of Hippo [430]

"Praise the Lord with the lyre, make melody to him with the harp of ten strings! Sing to him a new song." Rid yourself of what is old and worn out, for you know a new song. A new singer, a new covenant—a new song. This new song does not belong to the old singer. Only the new one learns it: the person restored from a fallen condition through the grace of God, and now sharing in the new covenant, that is, the kingdom of heaven. To it all our love now aspires and sings a new song. Let us sing a new song not with our lips but with our lives.

"Sing to him a new song, sing to him with joyful melody." Every one of us tries to discover how to sing to God. You must sing to God, but you must sing well. He does not want your voice to come harshly to his ears, so sing well, beloved!

If you were asked, "Sing to please this musician," you would not like to do so without having taken some instruction in music, because you would not like to offend an expert in the art. An untrained listener does not notice the faults a musician would point out to you. Who, then, will offer to sing well for God, the great artist whose discrimination is faultless, whose attention is on the minutest detail, whose ear nothing escapes? When will you be able to offer him a perfect performance so that you will in no way displease such a supremely discerning listener?

See how God himself provides you with a way of singing. Do not search for words, as if you could find a lyric which would give God pleasure. Sing to him "with songs of joy." This is singing well to God, just singing with songs of joy.

But how is this done? You must first understand that words cannot express the things that are sung by the heart. Take the case of people singing while harvesting in the fields or in the vineyards or when any other strenuous work is in progress. Although they begin by giving expression to their happiness in sung words, yet shortly there is a change. As if so happy that words can no longer express what they feel, they discard the restricting syllables. They burst out into a simple sound of joy, of jubilation. Such a cry of joy is a sound signifying that the heart is bringing to birth what it cannot utter in words.

Now, who is more worthy of such a cry of jubilation than God himself, whom all words fail to describe? If words will not serve, and yet you must not remain silent, what else can you do but cry out for joy? Your heart must rejoice beyond words, soaring into an immensity of gladness, unrestrained by syllabic bonds. "Sing to God with songs of joy."

Commentary on Psalm 32, 1, 7–8: CCL 38, 253–254

Proper 11 ✠ Friday

A reading from a commentary on the psalms by Ambrose,
Bishop of Milan [397]

Though all Scripture is fragrant with God's grace, the Book of Psalms has a special attractiveness.

Moses wrote the history of Israel's ancestors in prose, but after leading the people through the Red Sea—a wonder that remained in their memory—he broke into a song of triumph in praise of God when he saw King Pharaoh drowned along with his forces. His genius soared to a higher level, to match an accomplishment beyond his own powers.

Miriam too raised her timbrel and sang encouragement for the rest of the women, saying: "Let us sing to the Lord, for he has triumphed gloriously; he has cast horse and rider into the sea."

In the Book of Psalms there is profit for all, with healing power for our salvation. There is instruction from history, teaching from the law, prediction from prophecy, chastisement from denunciation, persuasion from moral preaching. All who read it may find the cure for their own individual failings. All with eyes to see can discover in it a complete gymnasium for the soul, a stadium for all the virtues, equipped for every kind of exercise; it is for each to choose the kind each judges best to help gain the prize.

If you wish to read and imitate the deeds of the past, you will find the whole history of the Israelites in a single psalm: in one short reading you can amass a treasure for the memory. If you want to study the power of the law, which is summed up in the bond of charity ("Who loves their neighbor has fulfilled the law"), you may read in the psalms of the great love with which one person faced serious dangers singlehandedly in order to remove the shame of the whole people. You will find the glory of charity more than a match for the parade of power.

What am I to say of the grace of prophecy? We see that what others hinted at in riddles was promised openly and clearly to the psalmist alone: the Lord Jesus was to be born of David's seed, according to the word of the Lord: "I will place upon your throne one who is the fruit of your flesh."

In the psalms, then, not only is Jesus born for us, he also undergoes his saving passion in his body, he lies in death, he rises again, he ascends into heaven, he sits at the right hand of the Father. What no one would have dared to say was foretold by the psalmist alone, and afterward proclaimed by the Lord himself in the Gospel.

Explanation on Psalm 1, 4, 7–8: CSEL 64, 4–7

Proper 11 ✠ Saturday

A reading from a funeral oration by Ambrose, Bishop of Milan [397]

The Lord shows in the gospel how a person will rise again. He not only quickened Lazarus, he quickened the faith of all. For if people believe, as they read, their spirits, which were dead, also are quickened with that same Lazarus. For when the Lord went to the sepulcher and loudly cried out: "Lazarus, come forth," what other meaning is there in this except that he wished to give visible proof of our future resurrection?

Why did he cry out loudly? Was it because he was not used to working through the Spirit, or because he was not accustomed to command in silence? No, he intended rather to emphasize the Scriptural statement "that in a moment, in the twinkling of an eye, at the last trumpet, the dead shall rise again incorruptible." For the lifting of his voice corresponds to the peal of trumpets. He added the name of Lazarus lest the resurrection might seem to be accidental rather than something commanded.

The dead man, therefore, heard and came forth from the tomb. He was bound and his face was covered with a cloth. But he who arose and walked, had sight. For, where the power of a divine command was operating, nature no longer followed its own course, but obeyed the divine will.

If anyone is astonished at this, inquire who gave the command and your astonishment will cease. It was Jesus Christ, the Power of God, the Life, the Light, the Resurrection of the dead. The Power lifted up a man lying in the grave; the Life made him walk; the Light dispelled the darkness and restored his sight; the Resurrection renewed the gift of life.

Perhaps you are concerned by the fact that Jesus took away the stone and loosened the bands, and you are worried that there will be no one to take away the stone from your grave. As if he who could restore life could not remove a stone, or that he who made a bound man walk could not break bonds, or that he who shed light upon covered eyes could not uncover a face, or that he who could renew nature could not split a rock!

But in order that they who refused to believe in their hearts might at least believe their eyes, they removed the stone, they saw the corpse, they smelled the stench, they broke the bands. They could not deny that he was dead whom they saw rising again. They saw the marks of death and the proofs of life.

What wonder if, as they worked, they had a change of heart in the process, and, as they heard, they at least believed their ears! What wonder if, as they looked, they were forced to believe their eyes, and, as they broke the bonds, they loosened the shackles of their minds! What wonder if, as Lazarus was being unbound, the people were set free, and, as they allowed him to go off, they themselves returned to God! Therefore, many who had come to Mary, seeing what was done, believed.

Nor was this the only instance our Lord Jesus Christ afforded us, but he raised others, also, that we might believe.

Second Oration on the Death of his Brother Satyrus 77–81: CSEL 73, 291–294

Proper 12 ✠ Sunday

A reading from a commentary on the psalms by Ambrose, Bishop of Milan [397]

What is more pleasing than a psalm? David expresses it well: "Praise the Lord, for a song of praise is good: let there be praise of our God with gladness and grace." Yes, a psalm is a blessing on the lips of the people, a hymn in praise of God, the assembly's homage, a general acclamation, a word that speaks for all, the voice of the Church, a confession of faith in song. It is the voice of complete assent, the joy of freedom, a cry of happiness, the echo of gladness. It soothes the temper, distracts from care, lightens the burden of sorrow. It is a source of security at night, a lesson in wisdom by day. It is a shield when we are afraid, a celebration of holiness, a vision of serenity, a promise of peace and harmony. It is like a lyre, evoking harmony from a blend of notes. Day begins to the music of a psalm. Day closes to the echo of a psalm.

In a psalm, instruction vies with beauty. We sing for pleasure. We learn for our profit. What experience is not covered by a reading of the psalms? I come across the words: "A song for the beloved," and I am aflame with desire for God's love. I go through God's revelation in all its beauty, the intimations of resurrection, the gifts of his promise. I learn to avoid sin. I see my mistake in feeling ashamed of repentance for my sins.

What is a psalm but a musical instrument to give expression to all the virtues? The psalmist of old used it, with the aid of the Holy Spirit, to make earth re-echo the music of heaven. The psalmist used the dead gut of strings to create harmony from a variety of notes, in order to send up to heaven the song of God's praise. In doing so the psalmist taught us that we must first die to sin, and then create in our lives on earth a harmony through virtuous deeds, if the grace of our devotion is to reach up to the Lord.

David thus taught us that we must sing an interior song of praise, like Saint Paul, who tells us: "I shall pray in spirit, and also with understanding; I shall sing in spirit, and also with understanding." We must fashion our lives and shape our actions in the light of the things that are above. We must not allow pleasure to awaken bodily passions, which weigh our soul down instead of freeing it. The holy prophet told us that his songs of praise were to celebrate the freeing of his soul, when he said: "I shall sing to you, God, on the lyre, holy one of Israel; my lips will rejoice when I have sung to you, and my soul also, which you have set free."

Explanation on Psalm 1, 9–12: CSEL 64, 7, 9–10

Proper 12 ✠ Monday

A reading from The City of God by Augustine, Bishop of Hippo [430]

After recalling the great promise of God to David and the assurances by which he so strongly confirmed it, the prophet feared that people might think this promise was fulfilled in Solomon. To counter this hope and the disillusion that it would give rise to, he continues: "Yet you, O Lord, have rejected and spurned."

What he is referring to here is what happened to Solomon's kingdom in his successors, down to the devastation of the earthly Jerusalem which was the capital of his kingdom, and especially down to the destruction of the very temple that Solomon had built. But lest anyone might think that God had been unfaithful to his promises, the prophet immediately adds: "You have postponed the coming of your Anointed." If the coming of the Anointed of the Lord has been postponed, he cannot therefore be identified with Solomon or even with David himself.

It is indeed true that all the kings of the Jews, who were anointed with the mystic chrism, were called the anointed of the Lord. Not only David and his successors were thus described, but Saul also, who was the first to be anointed as king of the people of the Jews and whom David himself called the Lord's anointed.

There was, however, but one true Christ or "Anointed," of whom David and his successors were but types by virtue of their prophetic anointing. In saying that his coming was postponed, the prophet is merely speaking from the viewpoint of those who had identified him in their thoughts with David or Solomon, whereas according to the plan and preparations of God he was to come at his own proper time.

The psalm here continues with a narrative of what happened during the interval of this delay to the kingdom of the earthly Jerusalem where hope in the eventual reign of the Anointed one, promised by the Lord, was kept alive and strong: "You have renounced the covenant with your servant, and defiled his crown in the dust. You have broken down all his walls; you have laid his strongholds in ruins. All who pass by the way have plundered him; he is made the reproach of his neighbors. You have exalted the right hands of his foes, you have gladdened all his enemies. You have turned back his sharp sword and have not sustained him in battle. You have deprived him of his luster and hurled his throne to the ground. You have shortened the days of his youth; you have covered him with shame."

All these misfortunes were visited upon the enslaved Jerusalem, though some of her kings reigned as heirs of the free Jerusalem from on high; they regarded their office as a role in a divine dispensation that was temporary and preparatory; they believed with a true faith that God would eventually establish the kingdom of the heavenly Jerusalem, of which they were heirs; they placed all their hope in the one true Christ, who was to come. As to how the events referred to in the psalm actually came to pass, one need but read the history of the dynasty of David and Solomon.

City of God 17, 10: CCL 48, 574

Proper 12 ✠ Tuesday

A reading from the Revelations of Divine Love by Dame Julian of Norwich [c. 1417]

We make our humble complaint to our beloved Mother, and he sprinkles us with his precious blood, and makes our soul pliable and tender, and restores us to our full beauty in course of time. This is his glory and our eternal joy. And this sweet and lovely work he will never cease from doing until all his beloved children are born and delivered. This was showed in the explanation of his spiritual thirst, that longing that loves and lasts until the Day of Judgment.

Thus in Jesus, our true Mother, has our life been grounded, through his own uncreated foresight, and the Father's almighty power, and the exalted and sovereign goodness of the Holy Spirit. In taking our nature he restored us to life; in his blessed death upon the cross he bore us to eternal life; and now, since then, and until the Day of Judgment, he feeds and helps us on—just as one would expect the supreme and royal nature of motherhood to act, and the natural needs of childhood to require.

Beautiful and sweet is our heavenly Mother in the sight of our souls; and, in the sight of our heavenly Mother, dear and lovely are the gracious children; gentle and humble, with all the lovely natural qualities of children. The natural child does not despair of mother's love; the natural child does not give itself airs; the natural child loves mother, and the other children. These are beautiful qualities, and there are many others as well, and with them all our heavenly Mother is served and pleased. And I understood that there is no higher state in this life than that of childhood, because of our inadequate and feeble capacity and intellect, until such time as our gracious Mother shall bring us up to our Father's bliss. And then the true meaning of those lovely words will be made known to us, "It is all going to be all right. You will see for yourself that everything is going to be all right." And then shall the blessedness of our motherhood in Christ begin anew in the joys of our God: a new beginning and an eternal one. To this new beginning all his blessed children born to him by nature shall be brought to him again by grace.

Revelation 14, chapter 63: Colledge and Walsh 2, 615–618

Proper 12 ✠ Wednesday

A reading from the treatise On the Priesthood by John Chrysostom, Bishop of Constantinople [407]

The work of the priesthood is done on earth, but it is ranked among heavenly ordinances. And this is only right, for no human being, no angel, no archangel, no other created power, but the Paraclete himself ordained this succession, and persuaded us, while still remaining in the flesh to represent the ministry of angels. The priest, therefore, must be as pure as if standing in heaven itself, in the midst of those powers.

When you see the Lord sacrificed and lying before you, and the High Priest standing over the sacrifice and praying, and all who partake being tinctured with that precious blood, can you think that you are still among mortals and still standing on earth? Are you not at once transported to heaven, and, having driven out of your soul every carnal thought, do you not with soul naked and mind pure look round upon heavenly things? Oh, the wonder of it! Oh, the loving-kindness of God to us! He who sits above with the Father is at that moment held in our hands, and gives himself to those who wish to clasp and embrace him—which they do, all of them, with their eyes. Do you think this could be despised? or that it is the kind of thing anyone can be superior about?

On the Priesthood 3, 4: PG 48, 642

Proper 12 ✠ Thursday

A reading from a sermon of Augustine, Bishop of Hippo [430]

"This is our glory: the witness of our conscience." There are those who rashly judge, who slander, whisper and murmur, who are eager to suspect what they do not see, and eager to spread abroad things they have not even a suspicion of. Against people of this sort, what defense is there save the witness of our own conscience?

We do not seek, nor should we seek, our own glory even among those whose approval we desire. What we should seek is their salvation, so that if we walk as we should they will not go astray in following us. They should imitate us if we are imitators of Christ; and if we are not, they should still imitate him. He cares for his flock, and he alone is to be found with those who care for their flocks, because they are all in him.

And so we seek no advantage for ourselves when we aim to please people. We want to take our joy in them—and we rejoice when they take pleasure in what is good, not because this exalts us, but because it benefits them.

It is clear who is intended by the apostle Paul: "If I wanted to please people, I would not be a servant of Christ." You have listened to our Lord Jesus Christ as he taught his apostles: "Let your actions shine before people so that they may see your good deeds, and give glory to your Father who is in heaven," for it is the Father who made you thus. "We are the people of his pasture, the sheep of his hands." If then you are good, praise is due to him who made you so; it is no credit to you, for if you were left to yourself, you could only be wicked. Why then do you try to pervert the truth, in wishing to be praised when you do good, and blaming God when you do evil? For though he said: "Let your works shine before people," in the same Sermon on the Mount he also said: "Do not parade your good deeds before people." So if you think there are contradictions in Saint Paul, you will find the same in the Gospels; but if you refrain from troubling the waters of your heart, you will recognize here the peace of the Scriptures and with it you will have peace.

And so our concern should be not only to live as we ought, but also to do so in the sight of all; not only to have a good conscience but also, so far as we can in our weakness, so far as we can govern our frailty, to do nothing which might lead our weak sister or brother into thinking evil of us.

Sermon 47, 12–14; CCL 41, 582–584

Proper 12 ✠ Friday

A reading from the Letter to the Romans by Ignatius, Bishop of Antioch, and Martyr [c. 115]

You have never begrudged the martyrs their triumph but rather trained them for it. And so I am asking you to be consistent with the lessons you teach them. Just beg for me the courage and endurance not only to speak but also to will what is right, so that I may not only be called a Christian, but prove to be one. For if I prove myself to be a Christian by martyrdom, then people will call me one, and my loyalty to Christ will be apparent when the world sees me no more. Nothing you can see is truly good. For our Lord Jesus Christ, now that he has returned to his Father, has revealed himself more clearly. Our task is not one of producing persuasive propaganda; Christianity shows its greatness when it is hated by the world.

I am writing to all the churches to declare to them all, that I am glad to die for God, provided you do not hinder me. I beg you not to show me a misplaced kindness. Let me be the food of beasts that I may come to God. I am his wheat, and I shall be ground by the teeth of beasts, that I may become Christ's pure bread.

I would rather that you coaxed the beasts to become my tomb and to leave no scrap of me behind; then when I have died I will be a burden to no one. I shall be a true disciple of Christ when the world no longer sees my body. Pray to Christ for me that by these means I may become a sacrifice to God. I do not give you orders like Peter and Paul. They were apostles, I am a condemned criminal; they were free, I am still a slave. But if I suffer, I shall become the freedman of Jesus Christ and I shall rise again to freedom in him.

Now as a prisoner I am learning to give up my own wishes. All the way from Syria to Rome I am fighting wild beasts, by land and by sea, by day and by night, chained as I am to ten leopards, I mean the detachment of soldiers who guard me; the better you treat them, the worse they become. I am more and more trained in discipleship by their ill-usage of me, "but I am not therefore justified." How happy I will be with the beasts which are prepared for me! I hope that they will make short work of me. I shall even coax them to devour me quickly and not to be afraid of touching me, as sometimes happens; in fact, if they hold back, I shall force them to it. Bear with me, for I know what is good for me. Now I am beginning to be a disciple. May nothing visible or invisible rob me of my prize, which is Jesus Christ! The fire, the cross, packs of wild beasts, lacerations, rendings, wrenching of bones, mangling of limbs, crushing of the whole body, the horrible tortures of the devil—let all these things come upon me, if only I may gain Jesus Christ!

To the Romans 3, 1–5, 3: Funk 1, 215–219

Proper 12 ✠ Saturday

A reading from a sermon of Jerome, Priest, and Monk of Bethlehem [420]

"As the deer longs for running water, so my soul longs for you, my God." Just as the deer longs for running water, so do our newly baptized members, our young deer, so to speak, also yearn for God. By leaving Egypt and the world, they have put Pharaoh and his entire army to death in the waters of baptism. After slaying the devil, their hearts long for the springs of running water in the Church. These springs are the Father, the Son and the Holy Spirit. Jeremiah testifies that the Father is like a fountain when he says: "They have forsaken me, the fountain of living water, to dig for themselves cisterns, broken cisterns that can hold no water." In another passage we read about the Son: "They have forsaken the fountain of wisdom." And again, John says of the Holy Spirit: "Whoever drinks the water I will give, that water shall become in that person a fountain, springing up into eternal life." The evangelist explains that the Savior said this of the Holy Spirit. The testimony of these texts establishes beyond doubt that the three fountains of the Church constitute the mystery of the Trinity.

These are the waters that the heart of the believer longs for, these are the waters that the heart of the newly baptized yearns for when saying: "My heart thirsts for God, the living fountain." This is not a weak, faint desire to see God; rather the newly baptized actually burn with desire and thirst for God. Before they received baptism, they used to ask one another: "When shall I go and see the face of God?" Now their quest has been answered. They have come forward and they stand in the presence of God. They have come before the altar and have looked upon the mystery of the Savior.

Having received the body of Christ, and being reborn in the life-giving waters, they speak up boldly and say: "I shall go into God's marvelous dwelling place, his house." The house of God is the Church, his marvelous dwelling place, filled with joyful voices giving thanks and praise, filled with all the sounds of festive celebration.

This is the way you should speak, you newly baptized, for you have now put on Christ. Under our guidance, by the word of God you have been lifted out of the dangerous waters of this world like so many little fish. In us the nature of things has been changed. Fish taken out of the sea die; but the apostles have fished for us and have taken us out of the sea of this world so we could be brought from death to life. As long as we were in the world, our eyes looked down into the abyss and we lived in filth. After we were rescued from the waves, we began to look upon the sun and look up at the true light. Confused in the presence of so much joy, we say: "Hope in God, for I shall again praise him, in the presence of my Savior and my God."

Sermon on Psalm 41, to the newly baptized: CCL 78, 542–544

Proper 13 ✠ Sunday

A reading from a homily of John Chrysostom, Bishop of Constantinople [407]

Beloved, let us therefore learn to ask God for the things which it is fitting for us to seek from him. Then those other things—I mean the things of this life—will do us no harm no matter which way they may occur. For if we are rich, it is only here that we shall enjoy our luxury; and if we fall into poverty, we shall suffer nothing terrible.

Neither the splendors nor the pains of the present life have much power to fix us in a state of unhappiness or happiness; both are equally contemptible and slip away very swiftly. Hence, they are rightly termed "a way," since they are fleeting and by their nature do not long perdure; but the things which are to come endure forever: both those of punishment and those of the kingdom.

Let us then make vigorous efforts to avoid the first and obtain the last. For what is the advantage of this world's luxury? It is here today and gone tomorrow; today a bright flower, and tomorrow scattered dust; today a blazing fire, and tomorrow smoldering ashes.

Spiritual things, on the other hand, are not like this, but they ever remain shining and blooming, and become brighter every day. That wealth never perishes, never departs, never ceases, never brings with it care or envy or blame, does not utterly destroy the body, does not corrupt the soul, does not cause jealousy, does not heap up malice—yet all these things accompany the wealth of this world.

That other glory does not lift people into folly, does not puff them up, never ceases, and does not grow dim. The rest and enjoyment of heaven continue forever and are ever the same, since they are perpetually unchanged and immortal, for their limit or end is impossible to find.

Let us then desire this life. For if we do so, we shall make no account of present things but shall despise and scorn them all. Even if someone should call us to enter into the court of the king, we shall not while we have this hope choose to do so. Although nothing seems to be a happier lot than such a calling, even this seems little and worthless and of no account to those possessed by the love for heaven. Nothing which comes to an end is to be much desired; whatever comes to an end—and is here today but gone tomorrow—even if it be very great, seems actually to be very little and contemptible.

Let us, therefore, not cleave to fleeting things which slip away and depart, but to those which are enduring and immovable. May we all attain them through the grace and loving kindness of our Lord Jesus Christ, through whom and with whom, be glory to the Father and the Holy Spirit, now and always, forever and ever.

Homily 44 on John 2: PG 59, 250

Proper 13 ✠ Monday

A reading from the treatise On the Prescription of Heretics by Tertullian, Theologian [c. 225]

Now, with regard to this rule of faith—that we may from this point acknowledge what it is which we defend—it is, you must know, that by which we believe that there is one only God, and that He is none other than the Creator of the world, who produced all things out of nothing through His own Word, sent forth before all things; that this Word is called His Son, and, under the name of God, was seen in various ways by the patriarchs, heard at all times in the prophets, at last brought down by the Spirit and Power of the Father into the Virgin Mary, was made flesh in her womb, and, being born of her, went forth as Jesus Christ; thenceforth He preached the new law and the new promise of the kingdom of heaven, worked miracles, was crucified, and rose again the third day; then having ascended into the heavens, He sat at the right hand of the Father; sent in his place the Power of the Holy Spirit to lead such as believe; will come with glory to take the saints to the enjoyment of everlasting life and of the heavenly promises and to condemn the wicked to everlasting fire, after the resurrection of both good and evil, together with the restoration of their flesh. This rule, as it will be proved, was taught by Christ, and raises amongst ourselves no other questions than those which heresies introduce, and which make people heretics.

On the Prescription of Heretics 13: CCL 1, 197–198

Proper 13 ✠ Tuesday

A reading from the treatise On the Unity of the Catholic Church by Cyprian, Bishop and Martyr of Carthage [258]

Heresies have frequently arisen and continue to do so because of the fact that disgruntled minds find no peace and faithless rabble-rousers undermine unity. But the Lord allows and endures these things, while not touching our freedom, so that when our hearts and minds are examined by the norm of truth, the sound faith of those who are approved may clearly stand out. This is foretold by the Holy Spirit through the Apostle when he says: "There may even have to be factions among you for the tried and true to stand out clearly."

Thus are the faithful approved, thus are the faithless detected; thus even here, before the day of judgment, are the souls of the just and the unjust set apart, and the chaff separated from the wheat. This explains why some, of their own accord and without divine appointment, set themselves over daring strangers, making themselves into prelates regardless of the rules of ordination, and assume the title of bishop on their own authority, although no one confers the episcopate on them.

In the Psalms, the Holy Spirit designates these as sitting in the chair of pestilence; they are the plague and disease for the faith, serpent-tongued deceivers and skilled corruptors of the truth, spewing forth lethal venom from their poisonous tongues; their speech resembles a creeping cancer and their preaching injects a fatal virus in the heart and breast of everyone.

Against such persons the Lord cries out, and from these he restrains and recalls his wandering people, saying: "Listen not to the voice of your [false] prophets, who fill you with emptiness; visions of their own fancy they speak, not from the mouth of the Lord. They say to those who despise the word of the Lord: 'Peace shall be yours'; and to everyone who walks in hardness of heart, 'No one shall overtake you.' I did not speak to them, yet they prophesied. Had they stood in my counsel, and did they but proclaim to my people my words, they would have brought them back from evil ways and from their wicked deeds."

It is these same persons whom the Lord designates and censures when he says: "They have forsaken me, the source of living waters; they have dug themselves cisterns, broken cisterns, that hold no water." Although there can be only the one baptism, they think they can baptize: and although they forsake the fountain of life, they still promise the grace of life and saving water. People are not cleansed by them but simply made foul; and sins are not taken away but only accumulated.

Such a "new birth" does not bring forth children for God but for the devil. Born by a lie, they do not receive the promises of truth. Begotten by perfidy, they lose the grace of faith. They cannot attain to the reward of peace, since they have broken the peace of the Lord with the madness of discord.

On the Unity of the Catholic Church 10–11: PL 4, 523–524

Proper 13 ✠ Wednesday

A reading from the Catechetical Instructions of Cyril, Bishop of Jerusalem [386]

If there are any slaves of sin here present, they should at once prepare themselves through faith for the rebirth into freedom that makes us God's adopted children. They should lay aside the wretchedness of slavery to sin, and put on the joyful slavery of the Lord, so as to be counted worthy to inherit the kingdom of heaven. By acknowledging your sins you strip away your former self, seduced as it is by destructive desires, and put on the new self, renewed in the likeness of its Creator. Through faith you receive the pledge of the Holy Spirit, so that you may be welcomed into the everlasting dwelling places. Draw near, to be marked with the supernatural seal, so that you may be easily recognized by your master. Become a member of Christ's holy and spiritual flock, so that one day you may be set apart on his right hand, and so gain the life prepared as your inheritance.

Those whose sins still cling to them like a goatskin will stand on his left hand because they did not approach Christ's fountain of rebirth to receive God's grace. By rebirth I mean, not rebirth of the body, but the spiritual rebirth of the soul. Our bodies are brought into being by parents who can be seen, but our souls are reborn through faith: "the Spirit breathes where he wills." At the end, if you are made worthy, you may hear the words: "Well done, good and faithful servant," when, that is, you are found with no stain of hypocrisy on your conscience.

If any here present are thinking of putting God's grace to the test, they are deceiving themselves, and they do not understand the nature of things. You are but human; there is one who searches out human thoughts and hearts. You must keep your soul innocent and free from deceit.

The present is a time for the acknowledgment of sins. Acknowledge what you have done, in word or deed, by night or day. Acknowledge your sins at a time of God's favor, and on the day of salvation you will receive the treasures of heaven.

Wash yourself clean, so that you may hold a richer store of grace. Sins are forgiven equally for all, but communion in the Holy Spirit is given in the measure of each one's faith. If you have done little work, you will receive little; if you have achieved a great deal, great will be your reward. The race you are running is for your own advantage; look after your own interests.

If you have a grudge against anyone, forgive that person. You are drawing near to receive forgiveness for your own sins; you must yourself forgive those who have sinned against you.

Catechesis 1, 2–3, 5–6: PG 33, 371, 375–378

Proper 13 ✠ Thursday

A reading from the treatise In Defense of the Prophet David
by Ambrose, Bishop of Milan [397]

We have undertaken to write a defense of the prophet David, not because he, distinguished as he was by such great merits and virtues, should be considered to be in need of this service. We have done so because many, who read what is narrated concerning him but without any penetrating appreciation of the power of the Scriptures or of the mysteries hidden therein, wonder how so great a Prophet could have fallen into the sin of adultery and afterward into the sin of murder.

Therefore, we have set ourselves the task of examining with a critical eye the story of the events and circumstances that seem to have opened the way to that sin. We read in the Second Book of Samuel that David, while strolling about in his palace, saw from the roof a woman bathing; the name of the woman was Bathsheba. She was extraordinarily attractive in her figure and bearing and in the singular beauty of her facial features and expression.

Captivated by these charms, David was stricken with a great desire to have her. The woman, however, was already married to a man, whose name was Uriah. At the bidding of the king the stage was set up to have Uriah killed; for his life, while it did not inhibit the king's lust, was regarded by him as an obstacle to be rid of to protect him against the stigma of adultery.

To begin our discussion, therefore, with considerations that should be evident to all, let us be on our guard not to condemn anyone whom God has justified. "It matters little to me," says St. Paul, "whether you or any human court pass judgment on me. I do not even pass judgment on myself." He said this while he was still in the flesh and still subject to temptation. The reason why he would not pass judgment on himself was because the spiritual person can be appraised by no one except by God alone. He then adds: "The Lord is the one to judge me, so stop passing judgment before the time of his return."

As for David, he has already fulfilled the time, has been found worthy of God's favor, and has been justified by Christ, since the Lord himself was proud to be called Son of David, while those who confessed him to be the Son of David were enlightened to do so from above. How then, after he has been so rewarded by God, can you judge and condemn this man of God? The Lord himself expressed his judgment concerning him, when he said to Solomon: "If you live in my presence as your father David lived, sincerely and uprightly, doing just as I commanded him."

Is this man, therefore, who did all that God commanded him and who lived in holiness and uprightness of heart, to be considered deserving of condemnation or of commendation?

Treatise in Defense of the Prophet David 1, 1–3: CSEL 32, 299–301

Proper 13 ✠ Friday

A reading from a sermon of Augustine, Bishop of Hippo [430]

"I acknowledge my transgression," says David. If I admit my fault, then you will pardon it. Let us never assume that if we live good lives we will be without sin; our lives should be praised only when we continue to beg for pardon. But we are hopeless creatures, and the less we concentrate on our own sins, the more interested we become in the sins of others. We seek to criticize, not to correct. Unable to excuse ourselves, we are ready to accuse others. This was not the way that David showed us how to pray and make amends to God, when he said: "I acknowledge my transgression, and my sin is ever before me." He did not concentrate on others' sins; he turned his thoughts upon himself. He did not merely stroke the surface, but he plunged inside and went deep down within himself. He did not spare himself, and therefore was not impudent in asking to be spared.

Do you want God to be appeased? Learn what you are to do that God may be pleased with you. Consider the psalm again: "If you wanted sacrifice, I would indeed have given it; in burnt offerings you will take no delight." Are you then to be without sacrifice? Are you to offer nothing? Will you please God without an offering? Consider what you read in the same psalm: "If you wanted sacrifice, I would indeed have given it; in burnt offerings you will take no delight." But continue to listen, and say with David: "A sacrifice to God is a contrite spirit; God does not despise a contrite and humble heart." Cast aside your former offerings, for now you have found out what you are to offer. In the days of your parents you would have made offerings of cattle—these were the sacrifices. "If you wanted sacrifice, I would indeed have given it." These then, Lord, you do not want, and yet you do want sacrifice.

"You will take no delight in burnt offerings," David says. If you will not take delight in burnt offerings, will you remain without sacrifice? Not at all. "A sacrifice to God is a contrite spirit; God does not despise a contrite and humble heart."

You now have the offering you are to make. No need to examine the herd, no need to outfit ships and travel to the most remote provinces in search of incense. Search within your heart for what is pleasing to God. Your heart must be crushed. Are you afraid that it might perish so? You have the reply: "Create a clean heart in me, O God." For a clean heart to be created, the unclean one must be crushed.

We should be displeased with ourselves when we commit sin, for sin is displeasing to God. Sinful though we are, let us at least be like God in this, that we are displeased at what displeases him. In some measure then you will be in harmony with God's will, because you find displeasing in yourself what is abhorrent to your Creator.

Sermon 19, 2–3: CCL 41, 252–254

Proper 13 ✠ Saturday

*A reading from the treatise In Defense of the Prophet David
by Ambrose, Bishop of Milan [397]*

How many sins each of us commits from one hour to the next! And yet among ordinary men and women who would think there is any obligation to admit to these sins? But this king, great and powerful though he was, could not for even the briefest moment endure to keep hidden within himself the consciousness of his crime, confessing his guilt to the Lord without delay and with intense sorrow.

Where could you now easily find me a person wealthy and in a position of great prestige who, if accused as guilty of some fault, would not at once resent it? But David, distinguished though he was by his royal office and the beneficiary of so many divine oracles, far from reacting with rage and indignation when he was reprehended by an ordinary subject for having gravely sinned, confessed his guilt with great mourning and sorrow.

So great was the sorrow of his inmost heart that the Lord was moved to say to him through Nathan: "Because of your repentance, the Lord has forgiven your sin; you shall not die." The readiness with which God pardoned him is a clear indication of the depth of the king's repentance, which wiped away the offense of so great a crime.

Others, when reproved by a priest because of their sins, only aggravate their guilt when they seek to deny or excuse it, with the result that their hoped for correction has only made their sin greater. Saintly folk, however, who strive to fight the good fight to the end and to run the race of salvation to the finish, are nevertheless and remain human.

Should it happen that they fall into sin more by reason of the frailty of their nature than by reason of any desire to sin, they rise up to continue the race with even greater eagerness and, under the stimulus of sorrow, to gain even greater victories. Hence, their sin is not to be regarded as an obstacle to their progress but rather as an incentive to hasten it all the more.

These saintly ones, should they happen to fall into sin, do not slacken their pace in the race or relax their efforts in the fight but carry on the contest unremittingly or even, as in the case of many after one or the other fall, receive greater grace to bring them to victory. How much more, then, should we refrain from judging because of one fall into sin those who are striving earnestly to lead a holy life, since they are blessed who have been able to recover themselves after a fall; for resurrection also after death is the reward of the blessed.

We can also understand that good results are occasioned by sin in other ways and that it is according to the providence of the Lord that even saintly people fall victims to sins. For they have been set before us as models to be imitated, and God has therefore let it happen that they also should sometimes fall into sin. God therefore withdrew his grace from them for a short while, that they might teach us by their life to imitate them and that we might learn from their repentance as well as from their innocence.

Treatise in Defense of the Prophet David 1, 5–6: CSEL 32, 301–303

Proper 14 ✠ Sunday

A reading from a commentary on John by Augustine, Bishop of Hippo [430]

"I myself am the living bread come down from heaven." I am the "living" bread precisely because I came down from heaven. The manna also came down from heaven; but the manna was only a shadow, whereas this is the truth. "Whoever eats this bread shall live forever; the bread that I will give is my flesh for the life of the world."

How could flesh comprehend that the Lord was giving the name flesh to bread? He calls that flesh which flesh cannot comprehend, and for that reason all the more flesh does not comprehend it, that it is called flesh. For they were horrified at this: they said it was too much for them; they thought it impossible. "It is my flesh," he says, "for the life of the world."

Believers know the body of Christ, if they do not neglect to be the body of Christ. Let them become the body of Christ, if they wish to live by the Spirit of Christ. None lives by the Spirit of Christ but the body of Christ.

Understand what I am trying to say. You are a human being; you have both a spirit and a body. I call that a spirit which is called the soul; that which makes you human, for you consist of soul and body. And so you have an invisible spirit and a visible body.

Tell me which lives from the other; does your spirit live from the body, or your body from your spirit? Every living person can answer; and if any cannot answer it, I do not know whether they are alive. What does everyone alive answer? My body, of course, lives by my spirit.

If you would then live by the spirit of Christ, be in the body of Christ. For surely my body does not live by your spirit. My body lives by my spirit, and your body by your spirit. The body of Christ can live only by the Spirit of Christ.

That is why the Apostle Paul, expounding this bread, says: "One head—we, many though we are, are one body."

O sacrament of goodness! O sign of unity! O bond of charity! Whoever would live knows wherein the source of life resides. Draw near, believe; be embodied, that you may be made to live. Do not flee from close union with the members; do not be a rotten member that deserves to be cut off. Do not be a deformed member of which to be ashamed.

Be a fair, fit, and sound member; cleave to the body, live for God by God. Labor now on earth, that hereafter you may reign in heaven.

Treatise 26 on John 13: CCL 36, 266–267

Proper 14 ✠ Monday

A reading from a commentary on the psalms by Ambrose,
Bishop of Milan [397]

Let your door stand open to receive him, unlock your soul to him, offer him a welcome in your mind, and then you will see the riches of simplicity, the treasures of peace, the joy of grace. Throw wide the gate of your heart, stand before the sun of the everlasting light that shines on every one. This true light shines on all, but if any close their windows they will deprive themselves of eternal light. If you shut the door of your mind, you shut out Christ. Though he can enter, he does not want to force his way in rudely, or compel us to admit him against our will.

Born of a virgin, he came forth from the womb as the light of the whole world in order to shine on all. His light is received by those who long for the splendor of perpetual light that night can never destroy. The sun of our daily experience is succeeded by the darkness of night, but the sun of holiness never sets, because wisdom cannot give place to evil.

Blessed then is the person at whose door Christ stands and knocks. Our door is faith; if it is strong enough, the whole house is safe. This is the door by which Christ enters. So the Church says in the Song of Songs: "The voice of my brother is at the door." Hear his knock, listen to him asking to enter: "Open to me, my sister, my betrothed, my dove, my perfect one, for my head is covered with dew, and my hair with the moisture of the night."

When does God the Word most often knock at your door?—When his head is covered with the dew of night. He visits in love those in trouble and temptation, to save them from being overwhelmed by their trials. His head is covered with dew or moisture when those who are his body are in distress. That is the time when you must keep watch so that when the bridegroom comes he may not find himself shut out, and take his departure. If you were to sleep, if your heart were not wide awake, he would not knock but go away; but if your heart is watchful, he knocks and asks you to open the door to him.

Our soul has a door; it has gates. "Lift up your heads, O gates, and be lifted up, eternal gates, and the King of glory will enter." If you open the gates of your faith, the King of glory will enter your house in the triumphal procession in honor of his passion. Holiness too has its gates. We read in Scripture what the Lord Jesus said through his prophet: "Open for me the gates of holiness."

It is the soul that has its door, its gates. Christ comes to this door and knocks; he knocks at these gates. Open to him; he wants to enter, to find his bride waiting and watching.

Explanation on Psalm 118, 12, 13–14: CSEL 62, 258–259

Proper 14 ✠ Tuesday

A reading from The City of God by Augustine, Bishop of Hippo [430]

Miracles are the work of martyrs, or rather they are the work of God, with the co-operation of the martyrs or in response to their prayers; and the purpose of those miracles is the advancement of that faith by which we believe, not that the martyrs are our gods, but that we and they have the same God. It comes to this: the pagans have built temples for their gods, they have set up altars, established priesthoods and offered sacrifices, whereas we Christians construct, in honor of our martyrs, not temples, as if to gods, but memorial shrines, as to those who are dead, but whose spirits are living with God. We do not in those shrines raise altars on which to sacrifice to the martyrs, but to the one God, who is the martyrs' God and ours; and at this sacrifice the martyrs are named, in their own place and in the appointed order, as people of God who have overcome the world in the confession of his name. They are not invoked by the priest who offers the sacrifice. For, of course, he is offering the sacrifice to God, not to the martyrs (although he offers it at their shrine), because the priest is God's priest, not theirs. Indeed, the sacrifice itself is the Body of Christ, which is not offered to them, because they themselves are that Body.

And among all the truths they speak this is the most important: that Christ rose from the dead and first displayed the immortality of the resurrection in his own body, and promised that it would come to us at the beginning of the new age or (which is the same) at the end of this world.

City of God 22, 10: CCL 48, 828

Proper 14 ✠ Wednesday

A reading from a commentary on John by Augustine, Bishop of Hippo [430]

"A woman came." She is a symbol of the Church not yet made righteous but about to be made righteous. Righteousness follows from the conversation. She came in ignorance, she found Christ, and he enters into conversation with her. Let us see what it is about, let us see why "a Samaritan woman came to draw water." The Samaritans did not form part of the Jewish people: they were foreigners. The fact that she came from a foreign people is part of the symbolic meaning, for she is a symbol of the Church. The Church was to come from the Gentiles, of a different race from the Jews.

We must then recognize ourselves in her words and in her person, and with her give our own thanks to God. She was a symbol, not the reality; she foreshadowed the reality, and the reality came to be. She found faith in Christ, who was using her as a symbol to teach us what was to come. "She came" then "to draw water." She had simply come to draw water, in the normal way of man or woman.

"Jesus says to her: Give me water to drink. For his disciples had gone to the city to buy food. The Samaritan woman therefore says to him: How is it that you, though a Jew, ask me for water to drink, though I am a Samaritan woman? For Jews have nothing to do with Samaritans."

The Samaritans were foreigners; Jews never used their utensils. The woman was carrying a pail for drawing water. She was astonished that a Jew should ask her for a drink of water, a thing that Jews would not do. But the one who was asking for a drink of water was thirsting for her faith.

Listen now and learn who it is that asks for a drink. "Jesus answered her and said: If you knew the gift of God, and who it is that is saying to you, 'Give me a drink,' perhaps you might have asked him and he would have given you living water."

He asks for a drink, and he promises a drink. He is in need, as one hoping to receive, yet he is rich, as one about to satisfy the thirst of others. He says: "If you knew the gift of God." The gift of God is the Holy Spirit. But he is still using veiled language as he speaks to the woman and gradually enters into her heart. Or is he already teaching her? What could be more gentle and kind than the encouragement he gives? "If you knew the gift of God, and who it is that is saying to you, 'Give me a drink,' perhaps you might ask and he would give you living water."

What is this water that he will give if not the water spoken of in Scripture: "With you is the fountain of life?" How can those feel thirst who "will drink deeply from the abundance in your house?"

He was promising the Holy Spirit in satisfying abundance. She did not yet understand. In her failure to grasp his meaning, what was her reply? "The woman says to him: Master, give me this drink, so that I may feel no thirst or come here to draw water." Her need forced her to this labor, her weakness shrank from it. If only she could hear those words: "Come to me, all who labor and are burdened, and I will refresh you." Jesus was saying this to her, so that her labors might be at an end; but she was not yet able to understand.

Treatise 15 on John 10–12, 16–17: CCL 36, 154–156

Proper 14 ✠ Thursday

A reading from the treatise On the Lord's Prayer by Cyprian, Bishop and Martyr of Carthage [258]

How merciful the Lord is to us, how kind and richly compassionate! He wished us to repeat this prayer in God's sight, to call the Lord our Father and, as Christ is God's Son, be called in turn children of God! None of us would ever have dared to utter this name unless he himself had allowed us to pray in this way. And therefore, dear friends, we should bear in mind and realize that when we call God our Father we ought also to act like God's children. If we are pleased to call him Father, let him in turn be pleased to call us his children.

We should live like the temples of God we are, so that it can be seen that God lives in us. No act of ours should be unworthy of the spirit. Now that we have begun to live in heaven and in the spirit, all our thoughts and actions should be heavenly and spiritual; for, as the Lord God himself has said: "Those who honor me I will honor, and those who despise me shall be despised." And the blessed Apostle wrote in his letter: "You are not your own; you were bought with a great price. So glorify and bear God in your body."

We go on to say: "May your name be hallowed." It is not that we think to make God holy by our prayers; rather we are asking God that his name may be made holy in us. Indeed, how could God be made holy, he who is the source of holiness? Still, because he himself said: "Be holy, for I am holy," we pray and beseech him that we who have been hallowed in baptism may persevere in what we have begun. And we pray for this every day, for we have need of daily sanctification; sinning every day, we cleanse our faults again and again by constant sanctification.

The apostle Paul instructs us in these words concerning the sanctification which God's loving kindness confers on us: "None of these: fornicators, idolaters, adulterers, male prostitutes, sodomites, thieves, the greedy, drunkards, revilers, robbers—none will inherit the kingdom of God. And this is what some of you were. But you have been washed, you have been sanctified, you have been justified in the name of the Lord Jesus Christ and in the Spirit of our God." We were sanctified, he says, "in the name of the Lord Jesus Christ and in the Spirit of our God." Hence we make our prayer that this sanctification may remain in us. But further, our Lord who is also our judge warns those who have been cured and brought back to life by him to sin no more lest something worse happen to them. Thus we offer constant prayers and beg night and day that this sanctification and new life which is ours by God's favor may be preserved by his protection.

On the Lord's Prayer 11–12: CSEL 3, 274–275

Proper 14 ✠ Friday

A reading from the treatise On the Lord's Prayer by Cyprian,
Bishop and Martyr of Carthage [258]

The prayer continues: "Your kingdom come." We pray that God's kingdom will become present for us in the same way that we ask for his name to be hallowed among us. For when does God not reign, when could there be in him a beginning of what always was and what will never cease to be? What we pray for is that the kingdom promised to us by God will come, the kingdom won by Christ's blood and passion. Then we who formerly were slaves in this world will reign from now on under the dominion of Christ, in accordance with his promise: "Come, O blessed of my Father, receive the kingdom which was prepared for you from the foundation of the world."

However, my dear friends, it could also be that the kingdom of God whose coming we daily wish for is Christ himself, since it is his coming that we long for. He is our resurrection, since we rise again in him; so too he can be thought of as the kingdom of God because we are to reign in him. And it is good that we pray for God's kingdom; for though it is a heavenly kingdom, it is also an earthly one. But those who have already renounced the world are made greater by holding positions of authority in that kingdom.

After this we add: "Your will be done on earth as it is in heaven"; we pray not that God should do his will, but that we may carry out his will. How could anyone prevent the Lord from doing what he wills? But in our prayer we ask that God's will be done in us, because the devil throws up obstacles to prevent our mind and our conduct from obeying God in all things. So if his will is to be done in us we have need of his will, that is, his help and protection. No one can be strong by his own strength or secure save by God's mercy and forgiveness. Even the Lord, to show the weakness of the human nature which he bore, said: "Father, if it be possible, let this cup pass from me," and then, by way of giving example to his disciples that they should do God's will and not their own, he added: "Nevertheless, not as I will, but as you will."

All Christ did, all he taught, was the will of God. Humility in our daily lives, an unwavering faith, a moral sense of modesty in conversation, justice in acts, mercy in deed, discipline, refusal to harm others, a readiness to suffer harm, peaceableness with one another, a wholehearted love of the Lord, loving in him what is of the Father, fearing him because he is God, preferring nothing to him who preferred nothing to us, clinging tenaciously to his love, standing by his cross with loyalty and courage whenever there is any conflict involving his honor and his name, manifesting in our speech the constancy of our profession and under torture confidence for the fight, and in dying the endurance for which we will be crowned—this is what it means to wish to be a fellow heir with Christ, to keep God's command; this is what it means to do the will of the Father.

On the Lord's Prayer 13–15: CSEL 3, 275–278

Proper 14 ✠ Saturday

A reading from the treatise On the Lord's Prayer by Cyprian, Bishop and Martyr of Carthage [258]

As the Lord's Prayer continues, we ask: "Give us this day our daily bread." We can understand this petition in a spiritual and in a literal sense. For in the divine plan both senses may help toward our salvation. For Christ is the bread of life; this bread does not belong to everyone, but is ours alone. When we say, our Father, we understand that he is the father of those who know him and believe in him. In the same way we speak of our daily bread, because Christ is the bread of those who touch his body.

Now, we who live in Christ and receive his eucharist, the food of salvation, ask for this bread to be given us every day. Otherwise we may be forced to abstain from this communion because of some serious sin. In this way we shall be separated from the body of Christ, as he taught us in the words: "I am the bread of life which has come down from heaven. Anyone who eats my bread will live for ever and the bread that I will give is my flesh for the life of the world." Christ is saying, then, that anyone who eats this bread will live for ever. Clearly they possess life who approach his body and share in the eucharistic communion. For this reason we should be apprehensive and pray that no one has to abstain from this communion, lest they be separated from the body of Christ and be far from salvation. Christ has warned of this: "If you do not eat the flesh of the Son of Man and drink his blood you will have no life in you." We pray for our daily bread, Christ, to be given to us. With his help, we who live and abide in him will never be separated from his body and his grace.

After this we ask pardon for our sins, in the words: "and forgive us our trespasses." The gift of bread is followed by a prayer for forgiveness. To be reminded that we are sinners and forced to ask forgiveness for our faults is prudent and sound. Even while we are asking God's forgiveness, our hearts are aware of our state! This command to pray daily for our sins reminds us that we commit sin every day. None should complacently think themselves innocent, lest their pride lead to further sin. Such is the warning that John gives us in his letter: "If we say we have no sin, we deceive ourselves, and the truth is not in us. If we confess our sins, the Lord is faithful and just, and will forgive our sins." His letter includes both points, that we should beg for forgiveness for our sins, and that we receive pardon when we do. He calls the Lord faithful, because he remains loyal to his promise, by forgiving us our sins. He both taught us to pray for our sins and our faults, and also promised to show us a father's mercy and forgiveness.

On the Lord's Prayer 18–22: CSEL 3, 280–281, 283–284

Proper 15 ✠ Sunday

A reading from the treatise On the Unity of the Catholic Church by Cyprian, Bishop and Martyr of Carthage [258]

Unanimity once prevailed among the apostles; this was the spirit in which the new community of believers obeyed our Lord's commands and maintained its charity. Sacred Scripture shows this, when it says: "The community of believers were of one heart and one mind." And again: "Together they devoted themselves to constant prayer." That was the reason why their prayers were efficacious, and why they could be confident of obtaining whatever they asked from the Lord's mercy.

But among us this unanimity has diminished in proportion as the generosity of our charity has degenerated. In those days, they used to put their houses and estates up for sale, and lay up for themselves treasures in heaven by giving the proceeds to the apostles for distribution to the poor. But now we do not even give a tenth of our patrimony; and whereas our Lord bids us to sell, we buy instead and increase our store. Thus has the vigor of faith diminished away among us; thus has the strength of believers weakened. That is why our Lord declares in his gospel with respect to our time: "When the Son of Man comes, will he find any faith on the earth?"

We see that what he foretold has come to pass. There is no faith in the fear of God, in the law of justice, in love, in works. No one thinks of fear of the future: the day of the Lord and the wrath of God, the punishment that awaits unbelievers and the eternal torments decreed for the faithless. Whatever a believing conscience should fear our conscience fears not at all—because it no longer believes. But if it believed, it would also take heed; and if it took heed, it would escape.

Let us do our best, beloved, to rouse ourselves; breaking the sleep of our past inertia, let us awake to the observance and fulfillment of our Lord's precepts. Let us be what he himself has bidden us to be by his words: "Let your belts be fastened around your waists and your lamps be burning ready. Be like servants awaiting their master's return from a wedding so that when he arrives and knocks, you will open for him without delay. It will go well with those servants whom the master finds wide-awake on his return."

We ought to have our belts tightened, so that when the day of departure comes we may not be found burdened and entangled. Let our light shine forth brightly in good works, so that it may lead us from the darkness of this world into the daylight of eternal brightness. Let us be ever wide-awake, solicitous and watchful, for the Lord's sudden coming, so that when he shall knock, our faith may be on the watch, ready to receive from the Lord the reward of its vigilance.

If these mandates are kept, if these warnings and precepts are observed, we cannot be overtaken in slumber by the devil's deceit. To the contrary, we will reign as vigilant servants with Christ as our Lord.

On the Unity of the Catholic Church 26–27: PL 4, 535–536

Proper 15 ✠ Monday

A reading from a commentary on the psalms by Augustine,
Bishop of Hippo [430]

"And in your name I will lift up my hands": Lift up, therefore, hands in prayer. Our Lord has lifted up for us his hands on the cross, and stretched out were his hands for us, and therefore were his hands stretched out on the cross, in order that our hands might be stretched out with good works; because his cross has brought us mercy. Behold, he has lifted up hands, and has offered for us himself a sacrifice to God, and through that sacrifice have all our sins been effaced. Let us also lift up our hands to God in prayer: and our hands being lifted up to God shall not be confounded, if they be exercised in good works. For what does one do in lifting up hands? Whence has it been commanded that with hands lifted up we should pray to God? For the Apostle says, "Lifting up pure hands without anger and dissension." It is in order that when you lift up your hands to God, your own works may come to mind. For whereas those hands are lifted up so that you may obtain what you wish, you should think to exercise those same hands in good works that they may not blush to be lifted up to God.

Commentary on Psalm 62 (5), 13: CCL 39, 801–802

Proper 15 ✠ Tuesday

A reading from a commentary on John by Origen, Priest and
Theologian [c. 254]

I think that both the temple and the body of Jesus can be seen in a single perspective as a type of the Church. For the Church is being built out of living stones; it is in process of becoming a "spiritual dwelling for a holy priesthood, raised on the foundations of apostles and prophets, with Christ as its chief cornerstone." Hence it bears the name "temple." On the other hand, it is written: "You are the body of Christ, and individually members of it." Thus even if the harmonious alignment of the stones should seem to be destroyed and fragmented and, as described in the twenty-first psalm, all the bones which go to make up Christ's body should seem to be scattered by insidious attacks in persecutions or times of trouble, or by those who in days of persecution undermine the unity of the temple, nevertheless the temple will be rebuilt and the body will rise again on the third day, after the day of evil which threatens it and the day of consummation which follows. For the third day will dawn upon a new heaven and a new earth when these bones that form the whole house of Israel are raised up on that great day of the Lord, when death has been defeated. So the resurrection of Christ, accomplished after his suffering on the cross, embraces the mystery of the resurrection of his whole body.

For just as that physical body of Christ was crucified and buried, and afterward raised up, so in the same way the whole body of Christ's holy ones has been crucified and lives no longer with its own life. For each of them, like Paul, makes his boast of nothing else but the cross of our Lord Jesus Christ, by which he has been crucifed to the world, and the world to him. But each Christian has not only been crucified to the world; he has been buried with Christ too, as Paul tells us: "We have been buried with Christ". But as though already in possession of some pledge of the resurrection, Paul goes on to say: "And we have risen with him".

Commentary on John 10, 20: PG 14, 370-371

Proper 15 ✠ Wednesday

A reading from a homily of John Chrysostom, Bishop of Constantinople [407]

"At that, Jesus realized that they would come and carry him off to make him king, so he fled back to the mountain alone."

How great is the tyranny of gluttony and how great the fickleness of human minds! No longer were they concerned to vindicate the law, no longer did they care for the violation of the sabbath, no longer were they zealous for God; all such considerations were cast aside once their bellies had been filled. He was a prophet in their eyes, and they were going to choose him as their king; but Christ fled. Why did he? To teach us to despise worldly dignities, and to show us that he needed nothing on earth. He who had chosen all lowly things—mother, home, city, rearing, and clothing—was not going to make himself illustrious now by worldly means.

The things which he had from heaven were glorious and great: angels, a star, the Father rendering testimony, the Spirit bearing witness, and the prophets heralding him from afar; those on earth were all lowly, that thus his power might be more apparent. He came also to teach us to despise the things of the world, and not to be amazed or astonished by the splendors of this life, but to scorn all of them and to desire those things which are to come.

He who makes much of the things which are here will not esteem those of heaven. That is why he said to Pilate: "My kingdom does not belong to this world," so that he might not afterwards appear to have employed mere human terror or dominion for the purpose of persuasion. How is it, then, that the Prophet declares: "See, your king shall come to you, meek and riding on an ass"? It was because he spoke of that other kingdom, the one in heaven—not this one on earth. And that is also why Christ says: "I do not receive praise from humans."

Let us, then, beloved, learn to despise the honor that comes from people, and not to desire it. We have been singled out for the greatest of honors, in comparison with which that honor is actually insult and ridicule, and caricature. Hence, just as the riches of this world are as poverty compared to that, and this life apart from that is death, so this honor is shame and ridicule when compared with that. Let us then not pursue it. If those who confer it are of less account than a shadow or a dream, how much more so is the honor itself! "The glory of humans is like the flower of the field"; and what is more perishable than the flower of the field?

Even if this glory were everlasting, how could it profit the soul? In no way! On the contrary, it does us great harm by making us slaves, slaves in worse condition than those bought with money, slaves who obey not one single master but two or three or ten thousand masters, all giving different commands.

Homily 42 on John 3–4: PG 59, 245

Proper 15 ☩ Thursday

A reading from a commentary on John by Cyril, Bishop of Alexandria [444]

"They wanted to take him into the boat, but suddenly it came aground on the shore they had been approaching."

The Lord not only releases the voyagers from dangers, by unexpectedly appearing to them, but also frees them from all strain and sweat when he propels the ship forward to the opposite shore through his God-befitting power. For they were expecting that by continuously rowing they would reach the shore only with difficulty; but he releases them from their toils, revealing himself to them in a very little time as the worker of many miracles to their full assurance.

Hence, when Christ appears and shines upon us, we shall without any labor succeed even against our hope; and we who are in danger through not having him shall have no more need of toil to be able to accomplish what is profitable for us, when he is present. Thus, Christ is our deliverance from all danger, and the accomplishment of achievements beyond hope to those who receive him.

We said that Jesus ascended to heaven as to a mountain, that is, after his resurrection from the dead. But when this has taken place, then his disciples alone and by themselves, a type of ecclesiastical teachers in succession throughout all time, swim through the billows of this present life in a kind of sea, meeting with varied and great temptations, and enduring no contemptible dangers of teaching at the hands of those who oppose the faith and war against the preaching of the gospel. But they shall be freed from all fear and every danger, and shall rest from their toils and misery, when Christ shall appear to them hereafter also in God-befitting power with the whole world under his feet. This is in my estimation the meaning of his walking on the sea, since the sea is often taken as a type in the Psalms: "The sea also, great and wide, in which are schools without number of living things both small and great."

Hence, when Christ comes "with the Father's glory," as it is written, then shall the ship of the holy apostles, that is, the Church, and those who are therein, that is, those who through faith and love in God are above the things of the world, without delay and without any toil gain the land "they had been approaching." For it is their aim to reach the kingdom of heaven, as some fair haven. And our Savior confirms this understanding of all that has been said when at a particular time he declares to his disciples: "Within a short time you will lose sight of me, but soon after that you will see me again," and at another time: "You will suffer in the world. But take courage! I have overcome the world."

Commentary on John 3, 4: PG 73, 470–471

Proper 15 ✠ Friday

A reading from a homily of John Chrysostom, Bishop of Constantinople [407]

"Those who seize what belongs to another bring ruin upon themselves." Have some unjustly appropriated the property of others? They have then brought ruin upon themselves. It may turn out that those who have been the victims of the injustice may even be benefited as a result. But the perpetrators of the injustice can only succeed in doing harm to their own souls.

Have some inflicted an injury on the person of others? What they have done is like a sword, by which they themselves have been pierced. For those who are injured most by wrongdoing are not the victims but rather the perpetrators of the act. Paul, therefore, advised the Corinthians to be ready to suffer injustice from their fellow-Christians rather than to inflict it on them. Christ himself bids us, not to strike back when someone strikes us on the cheek, but to turn and offer the other.

To conduct ourselves in this way is virtue of the highest kind; it helps us to become more perfect in patience and fortitude, while it strengthens us to keep our passions under control. Those who injure or strike or insult others show that they themselves have been overcome by passion and have become enslaved by it. Whereas it is their neighbors only who seem to be injured, they themselves suffer far more serious harm and are reduced to the abject status of slaves.

"Their mischief shall recoil upon their own head; upon the crowns of their heads their violence shall rebound." It is thought that these words refer to Ahithophel and Absalom. In the case of both it was what happened to their head that brought about their death. Ahithophel died by hanging himself. Absalom, when the mule on which he was mounted passed beneath a tree, was caught fast in the branches of the tree by the hair of his head and there, the mule running off, he hung for a long time.

Thus also did Judas hang himself and end his life, knowingly doing violence to his head to accomplish his purpose. Ahithophel strangled himself, because he clearly foresaw that David would ultimately triumph over him. It was not Absalom's intention to hang himself, nor did he die at once. But he hung there, fastened to the wood of the tree, as one awaiting judgment.

It was by God's will and decree that he should hang there for so long a time, his conscience all the while tortured by remorse. He had been plotting to raise his hand against his father to strangle him. Yet even in these circumstances his father pleaded with his soldiers to spare his life. What is more, his father's affection for him was so forgetful of self that he even mourned for him after his death.

What happened to Absalom was not the work of people but from beginning to end a divine judgment. This becomes clear when we stop to consider that instead of a soldier it was a mule that betrayed him, that instead of a rope it was the hair of his head that bound him, and that instead of a stake it was a tree to which he was bound.

Homily on Psalm 7, 14: PG 55, 103

Proper 15 ✠ Saturday

A reading from the Moral Reflections on Job by Gregory the Great, Bishop of Rome [604]

Holy Job is a type of the Church. At one time he speaks for the body, at another for the head. As he speaks of its members he is suddenly caught up to speak in the name of their head. So it is here, where he says: "I have suffered this without sin on my hands, for my prayer to God was pure."

Christ suffered without sin on his hands, for he committed no sin and deceit was not found on his lips. Yet he suffered the pain of the cross for our redemption. His prayer to God was pure, his alone out of all humanity, for in the midst of his suffering he prayed for his persecutors: "Father, forgive them, for they do not know what they are doing."

Is it possible to offer, or even to imagine, a purer kind of prayer than that which shows mercy to one's torturers by making intercession for them? It was thanks to this kind of prayer that the frenzied persecutors who shed the blood of our Redeemer drank it afterward in faith and proclaimed him to be the Son of God.

The text goes on fittingly to speak of Christ's blood: "Earth, do not cover over my blood, do not let my cry find a hiding place in you." When humankind sinned, God had said: "Earth you are, and to earth you will return." Earth does not cover over the blood of our Redeemer, for all sinners, as they drink the blood that is the price of their redemption, offer praise and thanksgiving, and to the best of their power make that blood known to all around them.

Earth has not hidden away his blood, for holy Church has preached in every corner of the world the mystery of its redemption.

Notice what follows: "Do not let my cry find a hiding place in you." The blood that is drunk, the blood of redemption, is itself the cry of our Redeemer. Paul speaks of "the sprinkled blood that calls out more eloquently than Abel's." Of Abel's blood Scripture had written: "The voice of your brother's blood cries out to me from the earth." The blood of Jesus calls out more eloquently than Abel's, for the blood of Abel asked for the death of Cain the fratricide, while the blood of the Lord has asked for, and obtained, life for his persecutors.

If the sacrament of the Lord's passion is to work its effect in us, we must imitate what we receive and proclaim to humanity what we revere. The cry of the Lord finds a hiding place in us if our lips fail to speak of this, though our hearts believe in it. So that his cry may not lie concealed in us it remains for us all, each in our own measure, to make known to those around us the mystery of our new life in Christ.

Moral Reflections on Job 13, 21–23: PL 75, 1028–1029

Proper 16 ✠ Sunday

A reading from a funeral oration by Ambrose, Bishop of Milan [397]

A great good is the virtue of humility, which rescues those who are in danger and raises up those who have fallen. It was because he understood this that David cried out: "It is I who have sinned; it is I, the shepherd, who have done wrong. But these are sheep; what have they done? Punish me." Well does he speak thus, who as king recognized his subjection to God, repented and, having confessed his sin, prayed for forgiveness. Thus it was by humility that he was saved. Christ humbled himself, in order to raise up all humanity. Only they can enter into the rest of Christ, who have followed Christ in his humility.

The emperor Theodosius proved himself a humble man by praying for forgiveness after he had sinned. It is for this reason that his soul has returned to its place of tranquil repose, as Sacred Scripture expresses it: "Return, O my soul, to your tranquility, for the Lord has been good to you." How beautifully chosen is the word "return," which is here addressed to the soul as to an athlete exhausted after a long race and now invited to relax from his exertion and to rest. The horse returns to its stall, after it has run its course; and the ship returns to its port as to a secure haven, after it has been tossed about by heavy seas.

As for the words "your tranquility," how otherwise are they to be understood except as a reference to that of which the Lord Jesus speaks, saying: "Come. You have my Father's blessing! Inherit the kingdom prepared for you from the creation of the world." What has been promised is a possession, qualified as an inheritance. God is faithful and does not take back what he once prepared for those who serve him. If we remain true to him in faith, he remains true to us in his promise.

Behold the grace of Christ, which encompasses you! Even now, though still tossed about by the tempests of life here on earth, you have a secure possession in heaven. Where your treasure is, let your heart therefore also be. Promised to the just, this rest is denied to the unworthy, as the Lord has said: "Therefore, I swore in my anger: they shall not enter into my rest."

As the Lord has said, those who "know not my ways" shall not enter into the rest of the Lord. It is only to the one, who has "fought the good fight" and has "finished the race," that the invitation "return to your tranquility" is addressed. How satisfying the rest, to leave behind the things of the world and to find repose beyond and above this world in sharing with the blessed in the enjoyment of the as yet unrevealed realities of heaven.

This is the rest toward which the Prophet hastens, saying: "Had I but wings like a dove, I would fly away and be at rest." This is the rest which the holy Psalmist knew to be his very own and to which he invites his soul to return. His soul, therefore, was already in possession of the rest, to which he says it must return. This is the rest of the great sabbath, the spiritual and hidden goal, to the attainment of which the saints devote themselves entirely, rising above the material things of the world and united to God. This is the rest of that sabbath, on which God rested from all his works in the creation of this world.

Oration on the Death of the Emperor Theodosius 27–29: CSEL 73, 384–386

Proper 16 ✠ Monday

A reading from a letter by Jerome, Priest, and Monk of Bethlehem [420]

There is a "mysterious and hidden Wisdom of God. God planned it before all ages for our glory." And this wisdom of God is Christ; he is the power of God and the wisdom of God.

In fact, in the Son are found all the treasures of wisdom and knowledge; he himself, hidden in this mystery, was destined from of old, before the ages, predestined and prefigured in the Law and the Prophets. That is why the prophets bore the name of "seers": they saw him whom others could not see.

Abraham also saw his day, and he was glad. For Ezekiel the heavens were opened whereas for the sinful people they were closed. "Open my eyes," said David, "that I may consider the wonders of your law." For, in fact, the law is spiritual, and in order to understand it the veil must be taken away and the glory of God must be contemplated with unveiled face.

In the Book of Revelation we are shown a scroll sealed with seven seals. If you were to give it to a learned person to read, the scholar would say: I cannot, because it is sealed. How many people today, who claim to be learned, hold a sealed Book in their hands! And they cannot open it until the seals are broken by him "who wields David's key, who opens and no one can close, who closes and no one can open." Understand from this that you cannot begin to follow the Scriptures without a guide to show you the way.

So tell me: to live in the atmosphere of these holy books, to think about them constantly, neither to know nor to look for anything beside them, is this not to live in the kingdom of heaven already, here on earth? And do not be put off, in the Scriptures, by the simplicity and bluntness of language which may be the translators' fault or even intentional. They are always set forth in such a way that whoever comes along can find instruction and so that, in one and the same sentence, both the learned and the ignorant can find the plain meaning.

I am not by any means making so wild and foolish a claim as to flatter myself that I understand everything in the Scriptures: this would be like trying to gather fruit from trees whose roots were fixed in heaven; but I confess that I long to understand and I am pressing on with my endeavor. So here on earth let us study those things, the understanding of which is laid up for us in heaven.

Letter 53, to Paulinus of Nola: trans. Verbraken, 6–8

Proper 16 ✠ Tuesday

A reading from the First Letter to the Corinthians by Clement, Bishop of Rome [c. 100]

Beloved, see what a marvelous thing love is; its perfection is beyond our expression. Who can truly love save those to whom God grants it? We ought to beg and beseech him in his mercy that our love may be genuine, unmarred by any too human inclination. From Adam down to the present time all generations have passed away; but those who were perfected in love by God's grace have a place among the saints who will be revealed when the kingdom of Christ comes to us. As it is written: "Enter your chambers for a little while, until my wrath and anger pass away; and I shall remember a good day and raise you from your graves." We are blessed, beloved, if we fulfill the commands of the Lord in harmonious, loving union, so that through love our sins may be forgiven. For it is written: "Blessed are those whose transgressions are forgiven, whose sins are covered. Blessed is the one to whom the Lord imputes not iniquity, and in whose mouth there is no deceit." This is the blessing that has been given to those who have been chosen by God through our Lord Jesus Christ, to whom be glory for ever.

We should pray then that we may be granted forgiveness for our sins and for whatever we may have done when led astray by our adversary's servants. And as for those who were the leaders of the schism and the sedition, they too should look to the common hope. For those who live in pious fear and in love are willing to endure torment rather than have their neighbor suffer; and they more willingly suffer their own condemnation than the loss of that harmony that has been so nobly and righteously handed down to us. For it is better to confess one's sins than to harden one's heart.

Who then among you is generous, who is compassionate, who is filled with love? You should speak out as follows: If I have been the cause of sedition, conflict and schisms, then I shall depart; I shall go away wherever you wish, and I shall do what the community wants, if only the flock of Christ live in peace with the presbyters who are set over them. Whoever acts thus would win great glory in Christ, and would be received everywhere, "for the earth is the Lord's and the fullness thereof." Thus have they acted in the past and will continue to act in the future who live without regret as citizens in the city of God.

First Letter to the Corinthians 50, 1–51, 3; 55, 1–4: Funk 1, 125–127, 129

Proper 16 ✠ Wednesday

A reading from a letter by Cyprian, Bishop and Martyr of Carthage [258]

If Christ alone is to be heard, we ought not to attend to what anyone else before us thought ought to be done, but what Christ, who is before all, did first. Neither ought we to follow human customs, but the truth of God.

But if it is not allowed to break the least of the commandments of the Lord, how much more important is it not to infringe upon matters which are so great, so tremendous, so closely connected to the very Sacrament of the Passion of the Lord and of our Redemption, or in any way to change for human tradition what has been divinely instituted? For, if Christ Jesus, our Lord and God, is Himself the High Priest of God the Father and first offered Himself as a Sacrifice to His Father and commanded this to be done in commemoration of Himself, certainly that priest acts truly in the place of Christ who imitates that which Christ did and then offers the true and full Sacrifice in the Church to God the Father, if the priest thus begins to offer after the manner that Christ Himself offered.

Letter 63, 14: CSEL 3; FC 51, 212–213; ACW 46, 106

Proper 16 ✠ Thursday

A reading from a commentary on the psalms by Augustine,
Bishop of Hippo [430]

"And he shall live and unto him shall be given the gold of Arabia." The Prophet would not have said "he shall live," were he speaking of Christ's life here on earth; for these words could then be said of any human, however brief life here below might be.

He is speaking of that life, in which Christ does not die and in which death has no more power over him. "He shall live" was, therefore, said of him who died an object of contempt, because, as another Prophet says: "his life" shall be "cut off from the land of the living."

But what is the meaning of the words: "they shall give him gold of Arabia"? Solomon also received gold from Arabia. But what was true of Solomon is here figuratively applied to Christ, who is the true Solomon, the true man of peace. For it was not Solomon, but Christ alone, who has established his rule "from the river to the ends of the earth."

These words, therefore, foretold that even the wise of this world would believe in Christ. For Arabia is to be understood as referring to the Gentiles, and gold as referring to wisdom. Hence, just as gold is the most precious of all metals, so wisdom is the noblest of all the sciences, since it is written: "Receive prudence as silver and wisdom as proven gold."

"And he shall be a firm support on earth, on the summits of mountains." For "whatever promises God has made have been fulfilled in him," that is, were confirmed in Christ, because in him has been realized whatever was foretold concerning our salvation. As for the summits of the mountains, these are fittingly identified with the authors of the divine Scriptures, the ministers namely by whom the Scriptures were given to us.

Christ is their firm support, because it is to him that everything they wrote under divine inspiration refers. It was on earth, however, that he willed to be their firm support, because it was for the salvation of those who inhabit the earth that the Scriptures were written.

It was for this same reason that he himself came upon earth, in order namely to substantiate all that was written or, in other words, to show that all things written were realized in himself. He himself has said: "Everything written about me in the law of Moses and the prophets and psalms" (that is, on the summits of mountains) "had to be fulfilled." Thus has the mountain of the Lord become visible in these last days, the mountain established on the peak of mountains or, in the equivalent words of our Prophet, "on the summits of mountains."

Commentary on Psalm 71 (72), 17–18: CCL 39, 982

Proper 16 ✠ Friday

A reading from "The Teaching of the Twelve Apostles"
[probably second century]

Celebrate the eucharist as follows: Say over the cup: "We give you thanks, Father, for the holy vine of David, your servant, which you made known to us through Jesus your servant. To you be glory for ever."

Over the broken bread say: "We give you thanks, Father, for the life and the knowledge which you have revealed to us through Jesus your servant. To you be glory for ever. As this broken bread scattered on the mountains was gathered and became one, so too, may your Church be gathered together from the ends of the earth into your kingdom. For glory and power are yours through Jesus Christ for ever."

Do not let anyone eat or drink of your eucharist except those who have been baptized in the name of the Lord. For the statement of the Lord applies here also: "Do not give to dogs what is holy."

When you finish the meal, offer thanks in this manner: "We thank you, Holy Father, for your name which you enshrined in our hearts. We thank you for the knowledge and faith and immortality which you revealed to us through your servant Jesus. To you be glory for ever. Almighty ruler, you created all things for the sake of your name; you gave us food and drink to enjoy so that we might give you thanks. Now you have favored us through Jesus your servant with spiritual food and drink as well as with eternal life. Above all we thank you because you are mighty. To you be glory for ever.

"Remember, Lord, your Church and deliver her from all evil. Perfect her in your love; and, once she has been sanctified, gather her together from the four winds into the kingdom which you have prepared for her. For power and glory are yours for ever.

"May grace come and this world pass away! Hosanna to the God of David. If any are holy, let them come. If any are not, let them repent. Maranatha. Amen."

On the Lord's day, when you have been gathered together, break bread and celebrate the eucharist. But first confess your sins so that your offering may be pure. If anyone has a quarrel with a neighbor, that person should not join you until the quarrel has been reconciled. Your sacrifice must not be defiled. In this regard, the Lord has said: "In every place and time offer me a pure sacrifice. I am a great king, says the Lord, and my name is great among the nations."

Didache 9, 1–10, 6; 14, 1–3: Funk 2, 19–22, 26

Proper 16 ✠ Saturday

A reading from a commentary on the psalms by Hilary, Bishop of Poitiers [367]

God chose Zion for his abode and his dwelling place. But Zion was ultimately destroyed. Where, then, is the everlasting throne of the Lord, where his eternal resting place, where the temple on which he can reside? It is that temple about which is written: "You are the temple of God, and the Spirit of God dwells in you."

This is the house and this is the temple of God, filled with the knowledge and power of God; made fit for God's indwelling by holiness of heart—to which the Prophet bore witness: "Holy is your temple, wonderful in justice." The holiness, justice, and purity of the human race constitute a temple for the Lord.

Hence, this temple must be built by God. Erected by human labor, it will never last; founded on worldly wisdom, it will never hold together; kept by our foolish labors and care, it will never be preserved. It is not to be erected on shifting sand but firmly founded on the prophets and the apostles; with living stones must it take shape, solidified by the cornerstone. With its materials securely linked together it must grow to perfect maturity, to the stature of the body of Christ, and is to be adorned with the beauty and splendor of spiritual gifts.

For a long time already, the Lord has been keeping watch over this city. He guards Abraham on his pilgrimage, rescues Isaac from immolation, rewards Jacob for his years of service, and makes a powerful figure of Joseph sold into Egypt. He strengthens Moses in his conflict with Pharaoh, delegates Joshua to wage wars, delivers David from all dangers, and bestows the gift of wisdom on Solomon.

The Lord is there among his prophets; he snatches up Elijah, chooses Elisha, gives food to Daniel, and refreshes the youths in the fiery furnace. He informs Joseph by an angel of his virgin birth, reassures Mary, and sends John before him.

He chooses apostles, and prays to his Father with the words: "Holy Father, protect them; as long as I was with them, I guarded them in your name." Finally, after his passion, he promises that he himself will have an eternal care for us: "Behold, I am with you always, until the end of the world."

Such is the never-ending protection of this blessed and holy city, which—formed as it is of many come together into one and found in each of us—is indeed the city of God.

Commentary on Psalm 126 (127), 7–9: PL 9, 695–697

Proper 17 ✠ Sunday

A reading from the Moral Reflections on Job by Gregory the Great, Bishop of Rome [604]

How must we interpret this law of God? How, if not by love? The love that stamps the precepts of right-living on the mind and bids us put them into practice. Listen to Truth speaking of this law: "This is my commandment, that you love one another." Listen to Paul: "The whole law," he declares, "is summed up in love"; and again: "Help one another in your troubles, and you will fulfill the law of Christ." The law of Christ—does anything other than love more fittingly describe it? Truly we are keeping this law when, out of love, we go to the help of a brother or sister in trouble.

But we are told that this law is manifold. Why? Because love's lively concern for others is reflected in all the virtues. It begins with two commands, but it soon embraces many more. Paul gives a good summary of its various aspects. "Love is patient," he says, "and kind; it is never jealous or conceited; its conduct is blameless; it is not ambitious, not selfish, not quick to take offense; it harbors no evil thoughts, does not gloat over other people's sins, but is gladdened by an upright life."

The one ruled by this love shows patience by bearing wrongs with equanimity, kindness by generously repaying good for evil. Jealousy is foreign to such a person. It is impossible to envy worldly success when people have no worldly desires. Such people are not conceited. The prizes they covet lie within; outward blessings do not elate them. Their conduct is blameless, for they cannot do wrong in devoting themselves entirely to love of God and their neighbor. They are not ambitious. The welfare of their own souls is what they care about. Apart from that they seek nothing. They are not selfish. Unable to keep anything they have in this world, they are as indifferent to it as if it were another's. Indeed, in their eyes nothing is their own but what will be so always. They are not quick to take offense. Even under provocation, thought of revenge never crosses their minds. The reward they seek hereafter will be greater in proportion to their endurance. They harbor no evil thoughts. Hatred is utterly rooted out of a heart whose only love is goodness. Thoughts that defile a person can find no entry. They do not gloat over other people's sins. No; an enemy's fall affords them no delight, for loving all, they long for their salvation.

On the other hand, "they are gladdened by an upright life." Since they love others as themselves, they take as much pleasure in whatever good they see in them as if the progress were their own. That is why this law of God is manifold.

Moral Reflections on Job 10, 7–8, 10: PL 75, 925–926

Proper 17 ✠ Monday

A reading from a commentary on the psalms by Augustine, Bishop of Hippo [430]

The temple that Solomon built to the Lord was a type and figure of the future Church as well as of the body of the Lord. For this reason Christ says in the gospel: "Destroy this temple and in three days I will raise it up again." For just as Solomon built the ancient temple, so the true Solomon, the true peacemaker, our Lord Jesus Christ, built a temple for himself. Now Solomon means peacemaker; Jesus, however, is the true peacemaker, of whom Saint Paul says: "He is our peace, uniting the two into one." The true peacemaker brought together in himself two walls coming from different angles and himself became the cornerstone. One wall was formed of the circumcised believers and the other of the uncircumcised gentiles who had faith. And of these two peoples he made one Church, with himself as the cornerstone and, therefore, the true peacemaker.

And so when Solomon the king of Israel, the son of David and Bathsheba, built his temple, he acted as a figure of Christ, the true Solomon and peacemaker. But I do not think it was Solomon of old, the type of Christ, who really built God's dwelling. As the beginning of the psalm tells us: "Unless the Lord build the house, in vain have the builders labored on it." Thus it is the Lord who builds the house; it is the Lord Jesus who builds his own dwelling. Many may toil on its building, but unless he builds it, "in vain have the builders labored on it."

And who are those who labor on it? All those who preach God's word in the Church, who are ministers of his sacraments. All of us now rush, work and build, and before us others rushed, worked and built; still, "unless the Lord build the house, in vain have the builders labored on it."

The apostles, and Paul specifically, saw some of them fail, and said: "You observe the days, the years, the months and the seasons; I fear that I may have toiled for you to no purpose." For realizing that he was the result of the Lord's building from within, he was sorrowful because he had toiled for them to no avail. Hence, we are the ones who speak from without, but he builds from within. We notice the fact that you are listening, but he alone knows what you are thinking, for he sees our thoughts. He is the one who builds, admonishes, instills fear, opens the mind, and bends the perceptions to the act of belief. Yet we too, his ministers, labor, and are as it were his workers.

Commentary on Psalm 126, 2: CCL 40, 1857–1858

Proper 17 ✠ Tuesday

A reading from the treatise On Works and Almsgiving *by Cyprian, Bishop and Martyr of Carthage [258]*

The Lord is the Teacher of our life and Master of eternal salvation, who not only quickens the assembly of believers but also provides for them forever when quickened.

Among his divine mandates and heavenly precepts in the gospel, he commands and prescribes nothing more frequently than that we should devote ourselves to almsgiving and not depend on earthly possessions but rather store up heavenly treasures.

"Sell," he says, "what you have and give alms." And again: "Do not lay up for yourselves treasure on earth where moths and rust corrupt and thieves break in and steal. Make it your practice instead to store up heavenly treasure, which neither moths nor rust corrupt, nor thieves break in and steal. Remember, where your treasure is, there will your heart be also."

In addition, when he wished to set forth a person who had been made perfect and complete by the observance of the law, he said: "If you will be perfect, go, sell your possessions, and give to the poor. You will then have treasure in heaven. Afterward, come back and follow me." Moreover, in another place he declares that merchants of the heavenly grace and purchasers of eternal salvation ought to part with all possessions and purchase from their wealth eternal life, namely, that precious pearl for which the blood of Christ has paid such a great price. He says: "The kingdom of heaven is like the merchants' search for fine pearls. When they found one really valuable pearl, they went back and put up for sale all that they had and bought it."

Lastly, he applies the name children of Abraham to those whom he sees actively helping and nourishing the poor. For when Zacchaeus exclaimed: "I give half my belongings, Lord, to the poor. If I have defrauded anyone in the least, I pay back fourfold," Jesus replied: "Today salvation has come to this house, for this is what it means to be a child of Abraham."

If Abraham believed in God and it was accounted to him for righteousness, certainly the one who gives alms according to God's precept believes in God, and the one who has the truth of faith maintains the fear of God; moreover, the one who maintains the fear of God considers God in showing mercy to the poor. You labor thus because you believe—since you know that what is foretold in God's word is true and that the sacred Scriptures cannot lie—that unfruitful trees, that is, sterile folk, are lopped off and thrown into the fire but the merciful are called into the kingdom.

Thus, in another place our Lord applies the word faithful to those who are industrious and fruitful but he denies faith to unfruitful and barren ones, saying: "If you cannot be trusted with elusive wealth, who will trust you with that which endures? And if you have not been faithful with someone else's money, who will give you what is your own?"

Treatise on Works and Almsgiving 7–8: PL 4, 630–631

Proper 17 ✠ Wednesday

A reading from a sermon of Gregory, Bishop of Nyssa [c. 394]

Despite the fact that through every word of divine Scripture we are invited to imitate the Lord who created us in his beneficence, we divert everything to our own utility and measure everything by our pleasure. We assign some goods to our own life and we place the rest in reserve for our heirs. As for the people who are in misery, we accord them no thought at all! And as for the poor, we do not have the slightest concern. O hearts without mercy!

You see your neighbors lacking bread and the means of obtaining indispensable food for themselves; instead of hastening to offer them help to deliver them out of this misery, you observe them as one would observe a verdant plant in the process of piteously drying up for want of water. And yet you overflow with riches and would be capable of helping many with your goods. Just as the flow of one single spring can water numerous fields over a vast area, so the opulence of one single house is capable of saving a large number of poor people from misery, unless parsimony and avarice arise to put an obstacle in the way, in the same manner that a boulder which has fallen into a brook diverts its course.

Let us not live solely according to the flesh, let us live according to God. Mercy and beneficence are God's friends. And if they come to establish themselves in the heart, they will divinize our humanity and mold it after the likeness of the sovereign Good, that we may be the image of that Essence which is primary and without mixture and surpasses all knowledge.

You, therefore, rational creatures endowed with intelligence which interprets and teaches divine things, do not let yourselves be seduced by temporal things. Try rather to gain the one which possesses what is eternal. Limit yourselves in using the goods of life. Everything does not belong to you; may a part be left for the poor who are loved by God. For everything belongs to God, our common Father, and we are sisters and brothers.

In the case of siblings, the most just ideal would be that each one enjoy an equal share of the inheritance. But if this does not come about and some claim more of this inheritance for themselves, let all the others obtain at least a part of it. And if someone wants to possess it all to the exclusion of numerous kin, such a one is a pitiless tyrant, a heartless barbarian, an insatiable beast.

Therefore, use the goods of the earth, but do not abuse them.

Sermon 1, on The Love of the Poor: PG 46, 463–466

Proper 17 ✠ Thursday

A reading from the treatise On Works and Almsgiving by Cyprian, Bishop and Martyr of Carthage [258]

Do you believe that Christ does not feed those who feed him or that earthly things will be wanting for those to whom heavenly and divine things are given? Is this not an unbelieving thought, an impious and sacrilegious consideration? What is an unbeliever doing in the home of faith? Why is one who does not really believe in Christ called and spoken of as a Christian? The name Pharisee fits you much better!

In the gospel when our Lord was speaking about almsgiving, and faithfully and wholesomely warning us to make friends for ourselves of our earthly lucre by providing good works, so that they might afterward receive us into eternal dwellings, the Scripture added to this: "The Pharisees, who were avaricious, heard all this and began to deride him."

We presently see in the Church some persons like these, whose closed ears and darkened hearts admit no light from spiritual and saving warnings. We should not marvel that they condemn the servants in their discourses when we see the Lord himself despised by them.

You are the captive and slave of your money. You are bound with the chains and bonds of avarice, and you have fallen back into the captivity from which Christ had freed you.

You save your money which, when saved, does not save you. You heap up an inheritance which burdens you with its weight; and you do not remember what God replied to the rich farmer who boasted with foolish elation over the abundance of his luxuriant harvest: "You fool! This very night shall your life be required of you. To whom will this piled-up wealth of yours go?"

Why do you keep a lonely vigil over your riches? Why do you increase your burdens by increasing your wealth? Why do you want to become so rich when you will only have to become that much poorer before God? Divide your returns with the Lord your God. Share your gains with Christ. Make Christ a partner in your earthly possessions, so that he may also make you co-heir of his heavenly kingdom.

You are mistaken and deceived, if you think of yourself as rich in this world. Listen to the voice of your Lord in the book of Revelation as he rebukes people of your ilk with just reproaches: "You keep saying: 'I am so rich and secure that I want for nothing.' Little do you realize how wretched you are, how pitiable and poor, how blind and naked. Take my advice. Buy from me gold refined by fire if you would be truly rich. Buy white garments in which to be clothed, if the shame of your nakedness is to be clothed. Buy ointment to smear on your eyes, if you would see once more."

Treatise on Works and Almsgiving 12–14: PL 4, 633–634

Proper 17 ✠ Friday

A reading from the treatise On the Lord's Prayer by Cyprian, Bishop and Martyr of Carthage [258]

Christ clearly laid down an additional rule to bind us by a certain contractual condition: we ask that our debts be forgiven insofar as we forgive our own debtors. Thus we are made aware that we cannot obtain what we ask regarding our own trespasses unless we do the same for those who trespass against us. This is why he says elsewhere: "The measure you give will be the measure you get." And the servant who, after the master forgives all debt, refuses to forgive a fellow servant is thrown into prison. Because that one refused to be kind to a fellow servant, that servant lost the favor the master had given.

Along with his other precepts Christ lays this down even more forcefully with a most vigorous condemnation. He says: "When you stand up to pray, if you have anything against anyone, let it go, so that your heavenly Father may also forgive you; but if you do not forgive others their trespasses, neither will your Father forgive you your trespasses." You will have no excuse on the day of judgment, for then you will be judged just as you have judged, and you will suffer whatever you have done to others.

God bids us to be peace-loving, harmonious "and of one mind in his house"; he wants us to live with the new life he gave us at our second birth. As children of God, we are to abide in peace; as we have one Spirit, we should be one in mind and heart. Thus God does not receive the sacrifice of one who lives in conflict; and he orders us to turn back from the altar and be first reconciled with our neighbor, that God too may be appeased by the prayers of one who is at peace. The greatest offering we can make to God is our peace, harmony among fellow Christians, a people united with the unity of the Father, the Son and the Holy Spirit.

When Cain and Abel first offered their sacrifices, God considered not so much the gifts as the spirit of the giver: God was pleased with Abel's offering because he was pleased with his spirit. Thus Abel the just one, the peacemaker, in his blameless sacrifice taught us that when we offer our gift at the altar we should approach as he did, in the fear of God, simplicity of heart, ruled by justice and peaceful harmony. Since this was the character of Abel's offering, it was only right that he himself should afterward become a sacrifice. As martyrdom's first witness and possessing the Lord's qualities of justice and peace, he foreshadowed the Lord's passion in the glory of his own death. Such, then, are those who are crowned by the Lord and will be justified with him on the day of judgment.

But Saint Paul and the sacred Scriptures tell us that the quarrelsome and the troublemaker, who is never at peace with anyone, cannot escape the charge of internal dissension even though that person may die for Christ's name. For it is written: "If you hate your brother [or sister] you are a murderer," nor can you attain the kingdom of heaven. God cannot abide a murderer. A person cannot be united with Christ, who has preferred to imitate Judas rather than Christ.

On the Lord's Prayer 23–24: CSEL 3, 284–285

Proper 17 ✠ Saturday

A reading from a sermon of Zeno, Bishop of Verona [c. 375]

Is Job a type of Christ? If I am right, he is, and the comparison will reveal the truth of my claim. But while Job was called just by God, God himself is the fountain of justice from whom all the saints drink. See what Scripture says: "The sun of righteousness will rise for you." Job was called truthful, but the Lord is, as he says in the Gospel, "the way, the truth and the life." And while Job was rich, the Lord is far richer, "for the earth is the Lord's and everything in it; the world and all who dwell in it." All the rich are his servants, and the whole world and all of nature as well.

But we may compare Job and Christ in many ways. As Job was tempted by the devil three times, so too Christ was tempted three times. The Lord set aside his riches out of love for us and chose poverty so that we might become rich, while Job lost all that he possessed. A violent wind killed Job's sons, while the sons of God, the prophets, were killed by the fury of the Pharisees. Job became ulcerated and disfigured, while the Lord, by becoming human, took on the defilement of the sins committed by all humanity. The wife of Job tempted him to sin, much as the synagogue tried to force the Lord to yield to corrupt leadership. Thus he was insulted by the priests, the servants of his altar, as Job was insulted by his friends. And as Job sat on a dunghill of worms, so all the evil of the world is really a dunghill which became the Lord's dwelling place, while people that abound in every sort of crime and base desire are really worms.

The restoration of health and riches to Job prefigures the resurrection, which gives health and eternal life to those who believe in Christ. Regaining lordship over all the world, Christ says: "All things have been given to me by my Father." And just as Job fathered other children so too did Christ, for the apostles, the children of the Lord, succeeded the prophets.

Job died happily and in peace, but there is no death for the Lord. He is praised for ever, just as he was before time began, and as he always will be as time continues and moves into eternity.

Sermon 15, 2: PL 11, 441–443

Proper 18 ✠ Sunday

A reading from the Letter to the Philippians by Polycarp,
Bishop and Martyr of Smyrna [156]

It is not out of presumption that I write to you, my friends, on what righteousness means, but rather because you asked me to do so. For neither I nor anyone like me can equal the wisdom of the blessed and glorious Paul. When he was in your city, he fully and courageously taught the people of that time the word of truth; when he was absent, he wrote you letters. By carefully studying these letters, you can strengthen yourselves in the faith that has been given to you. This faith is "the mother of us all," followed by hope, preceded by love—love of God, of Christ, of our neighbor. Whoever lives within this framework has fulfilled the commandment of righteousness. For anyone who has love is far from sin.

"Now the source of all evil is the desire to possess." Mindful that we "brought nothing into this world and can take nothing out of it," let us put on the armor of righteousness. We must begin by teaching ourselves how to walk in the commandment of the Lord. Then you should teach your wives to walk in the faith that has been handed down to them, in love and in chastity. They must love their husbands with complete fidelity, but they must cherish all others equally, and with self-control; they must raise their children in the discipline that comes from fear of God. We must teach widows to be discreet in all that concerns the faith of the Lord; they must pray without ceasing for all, shunning all calumny, gossip, false witness, greed, in a word, every sort of evil. They must bear in mind that they are God's sacrificial altar. He sees everything clearly, nothing escapes his vigilance, be it calculation, thought or some secret desire of the heart.

"God," as we know, "is not mocked." Let us walk in a way that is worthy of his commands and his purposes. Deacons, in the same way, must be blameless in the sight of his goodness, for they are servants of God and of Christ, not of people. They must avoid calumny, hypocritical talk and greed. Merciful and diligent, they must control all their desires, walking according to the truth of the Lord who became the servant of all. If we please him in this life, we shall receive the life to come; for he has promised us that he will raise us from the dead, and that, if we lead lives worthy of him, we shall reign along with him. This is what our faith tells us.

Letter to the Philippians 3, 1–5, 2: Funk 1, 269–273

Proper 18 ✠ Monday

A reading from the treatise On the Lord's Prayer by Cyprian,
Bishop and Martyr of Carthage [258]

Dear friends, why does the fact that God has taught us such a prayer as this astonish us? Did he not express all of our prayers in his own words of life? Indeed this was already foretold by Isaiah. Filled with the Holy Spirit, he spoke of the majesty and fidelity of God: "The Lord will speak a final brief word of justice, a word throughout the world." Our Lord Jesus Christ came for all humankind. He gathered together male and female, the learned and the unlearned, the old and the young and taught them his saving doctrine. He did not want his disciples to be burdened by memorizing his teaching; he made a complete summary of his commands such as was necessary for a trusting faith, and could be quickly learned.

Thus he summarized his teaching on the mystery of eternal life and its meaning with an admirable, divine brevity: "And eternal life is this: to know you, the only true God, and Jesus Christ whom you have sent." Again, in quoting the first and the greatest precept of the law and the prophets, he spoke in the same way: "Listen, Israel, the Lord your God is one Lord," and: "you shall love the Lord your God with all your heart, with all your soul, and with all your strength. This is the first commandment. The second is like it: You must love your neighbor as yourself. On these two commandments depends all that is contained in the law and the prophets." On another occasion the Lord said: "Always treat others as you would like them to treat you: that is the meaning of the law and the prophets."

God taught us to pray not only by his words, but also by his actions. He taught us by his own example for he often prayed on our behalf. The Scripture says: "He withdrew to the wilderness and prayed." And again: "He went into the hills to pray and he spent the whole night in prayer to God."

Was the sinless Lord praying for himself? No, he was praying and interceding on our behalf. He explained this to Peter: "Behold Satan demanded that he might sift you like wheat, but I have prayed for you that your faith may not fail." Later on he prayed to the Father for everyone: "I am not praying for these only, but also for those who will believe in me through their preaching, that they may be one; just as you, Father, are in me, and I in you, that they also may be one in us." God loves us; for the sake of our salvation he is generous toward us. He is not satisfied with redeeming us by his blood. He also prays to the Father on our behalf. Consider the love exemplified in that prayer. The Father and Son are one; we too are to abide in that oneness.

On the Lord's Prayer 28–30: CSEL 3, 287–289

Proper 18 ✠ Tuesday

A reading from the treatise On the Mysteries by Ambrose, Bishop of Milan [397]

We gave a daily instruction on right conduct when the readings were taken from the history of the patriarchs or the maxims of Proverbs. These readings were intended to instruct and train you, so that you might grow accustomed to the ways of our ancestors, entering into their paths and walking in their footsteps, in obedience to God's commands.

We must now speak of the mysteries, setting forth the meaning of the sacraments. If we had thought fit to teach these things to those not yet initiated through baptism, we should be considered traitors rather than teachers. Then, too, the light of the mysteries is of itself more effective where people do not know what to expect than where some instruction has been given beforehand.

Open then your ears. Enjoy the fragrance of eternal life, breathed on you by means of the sacraments. We explained this to you as we celebrated the mystery of "the opening" when we said: "Effetha, that is, be opened." All who were to come for the grace of baptism had to understand what they were to be asked, and to remember what they were to answer. This mystery was celebrated by Christ when he healed the one who was deaf and dumb, in the Gospel which we proclaimed to you.

After this, the holy of holies was opened up for you; you entered into the sacred place of regeneration. Recall what you were asked; remember what you answered. You renounced the devil and all Satan's works, the world and its dissipation and sensuality. Your words are recorded, not on a monument to the dead but in the book of the living.

There you saw the levite, you saw the priest, you saw the high priest. Do not consider their outward form but the grace given by their ministries. You spoke in the presence of angels, as it is written: "The lips of a priest guard knowledge, and people seek the law from the mouth of the priest, for the priest is the angel of the Lord almighty." There is no room for deception, no room for denial. One is an angel whose message is the kingdom of Christ and eternal life. You must judge the priest, not by the appearance but by the priestly office. Remember what the priests handed on to you, weigh up their value, and so acknowledge their standing.

You entered to confront your enemy, for you intended to renounce Satan to his face. You then turned toward the east, for one who renounces the devil turns toward Christ and fixes the gaze directly on him.

On the Mysteries 1–7: SC 25 bis, 156–158

Proper 18 ✠ Wednesday

A reading from the treatise On the Mysteries by Ambrose, Bishop of Milan [397]

What did you see in the baptistry? Water certainly, but not water alone. You saw the levites ministering there, the high priest asking questions and consecrating. First of all, the Apostle taught you that we must fix our eyes, "not on the things that are seen but on the things that are unseen, for the things that are seen are for a time, but the things that are unseen are eternal." In another place you may read that "the invisible things" of God "from the creation of the world, can be understood through the things that have been created, and his everlasting power and godhead" can be known through his works. The Lord himself says: "If you do not believe me, believe at least my works." Then believe that the presence of the godhead is there. You believe in its activity, and refuse to believe in its presence? How could there be activity if there were no presence beforehand?

Consider how ancient the mystery is, prefigured as it was in the creation of the world itself. In the very beginning, when God made heaven and earth, "the Spirit," God tells us, "moved over the waters." Was the Spirit not active in moving over the waters? When the prophet tells you that "by the word of the Lord the heavens were established, and by the spirit of his mouth all their array," realize that the Spirit was active in this making of the world. The fact that the Spirit moved over the waters, and the fact the Spirit was active, both rest on prophetic testimony. Moses tells us that the Spirit moved over the waters; David testifies that the Spirit was active.

Listen to another testimony. All flesh had become corrupt because of its sins. God said: "My Spirit will not remain in human beings, for they are flesh." God thus shows that spiritual grace is repelled by uncleanness of the flesh and by the stain of more serious sin. So God resolved to restore the gift he had given. He sent the flood and ordered Noah, the righteous one, into the ark. When the flood began to subside Noah sent first a raven, then a dove, which, as we read, came back with an olive branch. You see water, you see wood, you look on a dove, and you hesitate to believe the mystery?

The water is that in which the flesh is dipped, to wash away all its sin. In it all wickedness is buried. The wood is that to which the Lord Jesus was fastened when he suffered for us. The dove is the one in whose likeness the Holy Spirit descended, as you have learned from the New Testament: the Spirit who breathes into you peace of soul, tranquility of mind.

On the Mysteries 8–11; SC 25 bis, 158–160

Proper 18 ✠ Thursday

A reading from the treatise On the Mysteries by Ambrose,
Bishop of Milan [397]

The Apostle teaches you "that our ancestors were all covered by the cloud, all passed through the sea, all were baptized into Moses in the cloud and in the sea." Further, Moses in his canticle says: "You sent your Spirit, and the sea overwhelmed them." Observe that in this crossing by the Hebrews there was already a symbol of holy baptism. The Egyptian perished; the Hebrew escaped. What else is the daily lesson of this sacrament than that guilt is drowned, and error destroyed, while goodness and innocence pass over unharmed?

You are taught that our ancestors were covered by the cloud, a cloud of blessing that cooled the fire of bodily passions. A cloud of blessing: it is with a cloud of blessing that the Holy Spirit came at last upon the Virgin Mary, and the power of the Most High overshadowed her, when she conceived for all Him who is our redemption. This great miracle was prefigured through Moses. If then the Spirit was prefigured, is the Spirit not now present in truth? Scripture tells you that "the law was given through Moses, but grace and truth came through Jesus Christ."

Marah was a spring of bitter water. When Moses threw wood into it, its water became sweet. Water, you see, is of no avail for future salvation without the proclamation of the Lord's cross. But when it has been consecrated through the saving mystery of the cross, it is then ready for use in the laver of the Spirit and in the cup of salvation. Therefore, as Moses in his role of prophet threw wood into the spring of Marah, so also the priest sends out into the fountain of baptism the proclamation of the Lord's cross, and the water becomes sweet, ready for the giving of grace.

Do not then believe only what the eyes of your body tell you. What is not seen is here more truly seen, for what is seen belongs to time but what is not seen belongs to eternity. What is not comprehended by the eyes but is seen by the mind and the soul is seen in a truer and deeper sense.

Finally, learn from the readings we have gone through from the Books of the Kings. Naaman was a Syrian; he was a leper, and could not be healed by anyone. Then a girl from among the captives said that there was a prophet in Israel who could cleanse him from the disease of leprosy. Taking gold and silver, we are told, he went to see the king of Israel. The king, on learning the reason for his coming, rent his garments, saying that it was really to find an excuse against him, for what he was being asked was beyond the power of a king.

Elisha, however, told the king to send the Syrian to him, and he would learn that there was a God in Israel. When he came, Elisha ordered him to bathe seven times in the river Jordan. Then Naaman began to reflect that the rivers of his own country had better waters, and that he had often bathed in them, and had never been cleansed of his leprosy. This gave him pause, and he refused to obey the prophet's instructions. But on the advice and persuasion of his servants he yielded and bathed, and was instantly made clean. He realized then that it is not waters that make clean but grace.

Here was one who doubted before being made whole. You are already made whole, and so ought not to have any doubt.

On the Mysteries 12–16: SC 25 bis, 162–164

Proper 18 ✠ Friday

A reading from the Moral Reflections on Job by Gregory the Great, Bishop of Rome [604]

"Listen, Job, to what I say and ponder all my words." The teaching of the arrogant has this characteristic: they do not know how to introduce their teaching humbly and they cannot convey correctly to others the things they understand correctly themselves. With their words they betray what . they teach; they give the impression that they live on lofty heights from which they look down disdainfully on those whom they are teaching; they regard the latter as inferiors, to whom they do not deign to listen as they talk; indeed they scarcely deign to talk to them at all—they simply lay down the law.

To teachers of this kind the Lord through the prophet says rightly:

"But you will rule them with severity and with power." There is no doubt that such as are prone not to correct their subjects with quiet reasoning, but to compel them to change by rough and domineering methods, rule with severity and power.

On the contrary true doctrine all the more effectively shuns the voice of arrogance through reflection, in which it pursues the arrogant teacher with the arrows of its words. It ensures that the pride which it attacks in the hearts of those listening to the sacred words will not in fact be preached by arrogant conduct. For true doctrine tries both to teach by words and to demonstrate by living example—humility, which is the mother and mistress of virtues. Its goal is to express humility among the disciples of truth more by deeds than by words.

Accordingly, when addressing the Thessalonians, Paul is oblivious of his own eminent dignity as an apostle; he actually says: "We became as little children in your midst." Similarly, the apostle Peter enjoins: "Be always prepared to satisfy everybody who asks a reason for the hope which is in you"; and by adding the words: "with a good conscience, speak gently and respectfully," Peter draws attention to the manner in which sacred doctrine should be taught.

When he tells his disciples: "These things command and teach with all power," Paul really recommends the credibility that goes hand in hand with good behavior rather than the domineering exercise of power. When one practices first and preaches afterwards, one is really teaching with power. Doctrine loses credibility, if conscience tethers the tongue. Paul, therefore, in the saying quoted above, does not refer to the power of lofty rhetoric but to the confidence elicited by good deeds. Of the Lord, too, it is said: "He taught with authority unlike the Scribes and the Pharisees." He alone in a unique and sovereign way spoke from the power of his goodness because no evil weakness led him into sin. For he had from the power of his own divine nature what he gave to us through the sinlessness of his human nature.

Moral Reflections on Job 23, 23–24: PL 76, 265–266

Proper 18 ✠ Saturday

A reading from the treatise On Works and Almsgiving by Cyprian, Bishop and Martyr of Carthage [258]

What more could Christ have said to us? How more could he have inspired us to works of mercy than by saying that whatever is given to the poor and needy is given to himself, and by saying that he is offended unless the poor and needy are supplied? Thus, any who belong to the Church and are not moved by consideration for brothers and sisters might be moved by contemplation of Christ; and any who fail to think of their fellow-servants in suffering and poverty might yet think of their Lord abiding in the very person whom they are despising.

We have a holy fear directed toward God and our minds—having already despised and trampled underfoot the world—are raised to heavenly and divine things. Let us, therefore, give our obedience to the Lord with full faith, devoted mind, and ceaseless labor in order to acquire new riches.

Let us give to Christ earthly clothing so that he may one day clothe us with immortality. Let us feed him in this world, so that in the next we may be seated at the heavenly banquet together with Abraham, Isaac, and Jacob. Let us sow in abundance, so that we may also reap in abundance.

Let us, while there is time, strive to assure our salvation, in accord with the advice of the Apostle: "While we have the opportunity, let us do good to all people—but especially to those of the household of the faith. Let us not grow weary of doing good, for in due time we shall reap our harvest."

What will be the glory of the charitable; how great and lofty the joy when the Lord begins to number his people, and to reward our merits and good works in accord with his promises! He will grant heavenly things for earthly, eternal things for temporal, great things for small. He will present us to the Father to whom he restored us by his sanctification, bestow on us the eternal immortality which he purchased at the price of his blood, and bring us back to paradise and open up the kingdom of heaven. Let these open up the kingdom of heaven.

Let these things be imprinted firmly on our soul, totally grasped by our faith, loved by our whole heart, and purchased by a continuous stream of charitable deeds.

Charity is something excellent and divine; it is the consolation of believers, the pledge of our salvation, the basis of our hope, the safeguard of our faith, and the remedy for our sins. It is something within the power of the doer, great in itself yet easy to do. It is a crown worn in continual peacetime, exempt from dangers and persecutions. It is one of God's greatest gifts, needful for the weak, and glorious for the strong, enabling all Christians to obtain graces from heaven, to merit Christ's favor on judgment day, and to make a debtor of God himself.

Let us joyously and readily strive for this palm of saving works. Let us all run in the race for righteousness with God and Christ as spectator, and since we are already above the world may none of its false goods be able to retard our course. Then if the day of death or persecution finds us thus engaged, prompt and occupied in doing good, the Lord will never fail to bestow on us the reward we deserve.

Treatise on Works and Almsgiving 23–24, 26: PL 4, 643–646

Proper 19 ✠ Sunday

A reading from the Second Discourse against the Arians by Athanasius, Bishop of Alexandria [373]

Wisdom in person, God's only-begotten Son, is the creator and framer of all things. The Psalm says: "In wisdom you have wrought them all—the earth is full of your creatures." But to insure that whatever came into being might also be good, it pleased God that his own Wisdom should come down among creatures. Then the universe as a whole and every being in particular would bear its impress and semblance, manifesting itself as a wise work and one worthy of God.

For as the Son of God, considered as the Word, has his image in our human word, so, as Wisdom, he is reflected in our created wisdom; and when this gives us knowledge and thought, we become recipients of the creative Wisdom who in turn gives us knowledge of the Father, in accord with the promise of the gospel: "You who acknowledge the Son can claim the Father as well," and: "You who welcome me welcome him who sent me." Hence, this impress of Wisdom in creatures is the means by which the world knows the creative Word, and through it the Father.

Thus, those who examine the world honestly, in accord with the wisdom given them, may say: "In virtue of your ordinance all things have their being." However, those who make light of this duty will hear the words: "They claimed to be wise, but turned into fools instead." Indeed, as St. Paul says: "Whatever can be known about God is clear to them; he himself made it so. Since the creation of the world, invisible realities, God's eternal power and divinity, have become visible, recognized through the things he has made. Therefore these persons are inexcusable. They certainly had knowledge of God, yet they did not glorify him as God."

They will hear further for their confusion: "Since in God's wisdom the world did not come to know him through 'wisdom' " (which bears on what we have just said), "it pleased God to save those who believe through the absurdity of the preaching of the gospel." For God no longer wills to be known, as formerly, through an image and shadow of his wisdom present in creatures; he has made the true Wisdom himself to take flesh, and to become human, and to undergo the death of the cross, that henceforth all should be saved by faith in him.

It was the divine Wisdom who up to that time had shown himself to souls and manifested the Father by his image impressed on things. It is the same divine Wisdom who "became flesh," as St. John puts it, and who after abolishing death and saving our race, still more revealed himself and through him his own Father, saying: "Grant them to know you, the only true God, and Jesus Christ whom you have sent."

Hence, the whole earth is filled with the knowledge of him; for the knowledge of Father through Son and Son from Father is one and the same, and the Father delights in him, and in the same joy the Son rejoices in the Father, saying: "I was beside him as his craftsman, and I was his delight day by day."

Second Discourse against the Arians 78, 81–82: PG 26, 311–320

Proper 19 ✠ Monday

A reading from the treatise On the Mysteries by Ambrose, Bishop of Milan [397]

You were told before not to believe only what you saw. This was to prevent you from saying: Is this the great mystery "that eye has not seen nor ear heard nor the human's heart conceived"? I see the water I used to see every day; does this water in which I have often bathed without being sanctified really have the power to sanctify me? Learn from this that water does not sanctify without the Holy Spirit.

What is water without the cross of Christ? Only an ordinary element without sacramental effect. Again, without water there is no sacrament of rebirth: "Unless you are born again of water and the Spirit you cannot enter into the kingdom of God." The catechumens believe in the cross of the Lord with which they too are signed, but unless they are baptized in the name of the Father, and of the Son and of the Holy Spirit they cannot receive the forgiveness of sins or the gift of spiritual grace.

The Syrian Naaman bathed seven times under the old law, but you were baptized in the name of the Trinity. You proclaimed your faith in the Father—recall what you did—and the Son and the Spirit. Mark the sequence of events. In proclaiming this faith you died to the world, you rose again to God, and, as though buried to sin, you were reborn to eternal life. Believe, then, that the water is not without effect.

The paralytic at the pool was waiting for someone. Who was this if not the Lord Jesus, born of a virgin? At his coming it is not a question of a shadow healing an individual, but Truth himself healing the universe. He is the one whose coming was expected, the one of whom God the Father spoke when he said to John the Baptist: "He on whom you see the Spirit coming down from heaven and resting, this is the one who baptizes in the Holy Spirit." He is the one witnessed to by John: "I saw the Spirit coming down from heaven as a dove and resting on him." Why did the Spirit come down as a dove if not to let you see and understand that the dove sent out by holy Noah from the ark was a figure of this dove? In this way you were to recognize a type of this sacrament.

Is there any room left for doubt? The Father speaks clearly in the Gospel: "This is my beloved Son, in whom I am well pleased"; the Son too, above whom the Holy Spirit showed himself in the form of a dove; and also the Holy Spirit, who came down as a dove. David too speaks clearly: "The voice of the Lord is above the waters; the God of glory has thundered; the Lord is above the many waters." Again, Scripture bears witness for you that fire came down from heaven in answer to Gideon's prayers, and that when Elijah prayed, God sent fire which consumed the sacrifice.

You went down into the water. Remember what you said: I believe in the Father and the Son and the Holy Spirit. Not: I believe in a greater, a lesser and a least. You are committed by this spoken understanding of yours to believe the same of the Son as of the Father, and the same of the Holy Spirit as of the Son, with this one exception: you proclaim that you must believe in the cross of the Lord Jesus alone.

On the Mysteries 19–21, 24, 26–38: SC 25 bis, 164–170

Proper 19 ✠ Tuesday

A reading from the sermons of Peter Chrysologus, Bishop of Ravenna [450]

"I will break away and return to my father." The prodigal who spoke these words was lying prostrate on the ground. He has pondered his fall, taken stock of his ruin, found himself mired in sin, and so he exclaims: "I will break away and return to my father." What is the basis for such hope, such assurance, and such confidence on his part? The very fact that it is his father to whom he will return. "I have forfeited my sonship," he tells himself, "but he has not forfeited his fatherhood. There is no need for a stranger to intercede with a father: it is the father's own affection which intervenes and supplicates in the depths of his heart. His paternal instinct yearns to beget his child anew through forgiveness. Therefore, guilty though I am, I will return to my father."

And the father, on sighting his son, immediately covers over his sin. He prefers his role as father to his role as judge. At once, he transforms the sentence into pardon, for he desires his son's return, not his ruin. He "threw his arms around his neck, and kissed him." This is how the father judges and corrects: he gives a kiss in place of a beating. The power of love takes no account of sin; that is why the Father pardons his child's guilt with a kiss and covers it over with an embrace. The father does not reveal his child's sin, neither does he stigmatize his son; he nurses his wounds in such a way that they leave no scar or dishonor whatever. "Happy is the one whose fault is taken away."

If the past behavior of this youngster has filled us with disgust and if the prodigal's escapade has shocked us, we must ourselves be careful not to become estranged from such a Father. The sight alone of the Father suffices to put sin to flight, to keep transgression away, and to repel every kind of evil and temptation. But if we have drifted away from the Father, if we have squandered all his goods by a dissolute life, if we have happened to commit some sin or misdeed, if we have fallen into the bottomless pit of impiety and into absolute ruin, we must finally arise and return to such a Father, encouraged by such an example.

"His father caught sight of him and was deeply moved. He ran out to meet him, threw his arms around his neck, and kissed him." Now I ask what place there is here for despair, what occasion for an excuse or for any kind of fear. Unless perhaps we dread meeting the Father and his kiss makes us afraid; unless perhaps we believe that it is only to get hold of him and take revenge rather than to welcome and forgive him that the Father comes and takes his son by the hand, that he presses him to his heart and embraces him.

But this life-destroying thought, this enemy of our salvation, is completely disarmed by the words that follow: "The father said to his servants: 'Quick! bring out the finest robe and put it on him; put a ring on his finger and shoes on his feet. Take the fatted calf and kill it. Let us eat and celebrate because this son of mine was dead and has come back to life. He was lost and is found.'" After hearing this, can we still put off our own return to the Father?

Sermons 2–3: Pl. 52, 188–189, 192

Proper 19 ✠ Wednesday

A reading from a letter by Augustine, Bishop of Hippo [430]

Why in our fear of not praying as we should, do we turn to so many things, to find what we should pray for? Why do we not say instead, in the words of the psalm: "I have asked one thing from the Lord, this is what I will seek: to dwell in the Lord's house all the days of my life, to see the graciousness of the Lord, and to visit his temple." There, the days do not come and go in succession, and the beginning of one day does not mean the end of another; all days are one, simultaneously and without end, and the life lived out in these days has itself no end.

So that we might obtain this life of happiness, he who is true life itself taught us to pray, not in many words as though speaking longer could gain us a hearing. After all, we pray to one who, as the Lord himself tells us, knows what we need before we ask for it.

Why he should ask us to pray, when he knows what we need before we ask him, may perplex us if we do not realize that our Lord and God does not want to know what we want (for he cannot fail to know it) but wants us rather to exercise our desire through our prayers, so that we may be able to receive what he is preparing to give us. His gift is very great indeed, but our capacity is too small and limited to receive it. That is why we are told: "Enlarge your desires, do not bear the yoke with unbelievers."

The deeper our faith, the stronger our hope, the greater our desire, the larger will be our capacity to receive that gift, which is very great indeed. "No eye has seen it"; it has no color. "No ear has heard it"; it has no sound. "It has not entered the human heart"; the human heart must enter into it.

In this faith, hope and love we pray always with unwearied desire. However, at set times and seasons we also pray to God in words, so that by these signs we may instruct ourselves and mark the progress we have made in our desire, and spur ourselves on to deepen it. The more fervent the desire, the more worthy will be its fruit. When the Apostle tells us: "Pray without ceasing," he means this: Desire unceasingly that life of happiness which is nothing if not eternal, and ask it of him who alone is able to give it.

Letter 130, to Proba 8, 15, 17–9, 18: CSEL 44, 56–57, 59–60

Proper 19 ✠ Thursday

A reading from a sermon of Leo the Great, Bishop of Rome [461]

After preaching the blessings of poverty, the Lord went on to say: "Blessed are they who mourn, for they shall be comforted." But the mourning for which he promises eternal consolation, dearly beloved, has nothing to do with ordinary worldly distress; for the tears which have their origin in the sorrow common to all humanity do not make anyone blessed. There is another cause for the sighs of the saints, another reason for their blessed tears. Religious grief mourns for sin, one's own or another's; it does not lament because of what happens as a result of God's justice, but because of what is done by human malice. Indeed, those who do wrong are more to be lamented than those who suffer it, for their wickedness plunges the sinner into punishment, whereas endurance can raise the just to glory.

Next the Lord says: "Blessed are the meek, for they shall inherit the earth." To the meek and gentle, the lowly and the humble, and to all who are ready to endure any injury, he promises that they will possess the earth. Nor is this inheritance to be considered small or insignificant, as though it were distinct from our heavenly dwelling; for we know that it is the kingdom of heaven which is also the inheritance promised to the meek. The earth that is promised to the meek and which will be given to the gentle for their own possession is none other than the bodies of the saints. Through the merit of their humility their bodies will be transformed by a joyous resurrection and clothed in the glory of immortality. No longer opposed in any way to their spirits, their bodies will remain in perfect harmony and unity with the will of the soul. Then, indeed, the outer self will be the peaceful and unblemished possession of the inner self.

Then, truly will the meek inherit the earth in perpetual peace, and nothing will be taken from their rights; for "this perishable nature shall put on the imperishable and this mortal nature shall put on immortality." Their risk will turn into reward; what was a burden will have become an honor.

Sermon 95, 4–6: PL 54, 462–464

Proper 19 ✠ Friday

A reading from the treatise On the Mysteries *by Ambrose,*
Bishop of Milan [397]

We see that grace can accomplish more than nature, yet so far we have been considering instances of what grace can do through a prophet's blessing. If the blessing of a human being had power even to change nature, what do we say of God's action in the consecration itself, in which the very words of the Lord and Savior are effective? If the words of Elijah had power even to bring down fire from heaven, will not the words of Christ have power to change the natures of the elements? You have read that in the creation of the whole world "he spoke and they came to be; he commanded and they were created." If Christ could by speaking create out of nothing what did not yet exist, can we say that his words are unable to change existing things into something they previously were not? It is no lesser feat to create new natures for things than to change their existing natures.

What need is there for argumentation? Let us take what happened in the case of Christ himself and construct the truth of this mystery from the mystery of the incarnation. Did the birth of the Lord Jesus from Mary come about in the course of nature? If we look at nature we regularly find that conception results from the union of man and woman. It is clear then that the conception by the Virgin was above and beyond the course of nature. And this body that we make present is the body born of the Virgin. Why do you expect to find in this case that nature takes its ordinary course in regard to the body of Christ when the Lord Jesus himself was born of the Virgin in a manner above and beyond the order of nature? This is indeed the true flesh of Christ, which was crucified and buried. This is then in truth the sacrament of his flesh.

The Lord Jesus himself declares: "This is my body." Before the blessing contained in these words a different thing is named; after the consecration a body is indicated. He himself speaks of his blood. Before the consecration something else is spoken of; after the consecration blood is designated. And you say: "Amen," that is: "It is true." What the mouth utters, let the mind within acknowledge; what the word says, let the heart ratify.

So the Church, in response to grace so great, exhorts her children, exhorts her neighbors, to hasten to these mysteries: "Neighbors," she says, "come and eat; friends, drink and be filled." In another passage the Holy Spirit has made clear for you what you are to eat, what you are to drink. "Taste," the prophet says, "and see that the Lord is good; blessed is the one who trusts in him." Christ is in that sacrament, for it is the body of Christ. It is therefore not bodily food but spiritual. Thus the Apostle too says, speaking of its symbol: "Our ancestors ate spiritual food and drank spiritual drink." For the body of God is spiritual; the body of Christ is that of a divine spirit, for Christ is a spirit. We read: "The spirit before our face is Christ the Lord." And in the letter of Saint Peter we have this: "Christ died for you." Finally, it is this food that gives strength to our hearts, this drink which "gives joy to the heart," as the prophet has written.

On the Mysteries 52–54, 58: SC 25 bis, 186–188, 190

Proper 19 ✠ Saturday

A reading from a Prayer to St. Mary by Anselm, Archbishop of Canterbury [1109]

Mary, great Mary, most blessed of all Marys, greatest among all women, great Lady, great beyond measure, I long to love you with all my heart, I want to praise you with my lips, I desire to venerate you in my understanding, I love to pray to you from my deepest being, I commit myself wholly to your protection.

All nature is created by God and God is born of Mary. God created all things, and Mary gave birth to God. God who made all things made himself of Mary, and thus he refashioned everything he had made. He who was able to make all things out of nothing refused to remake it by force, but first became the Son of Mary. So God is the Father of all created things, and Mary is the mother of all re-created things. God is the Father of all that is established, and Mary is the mother of all that is re-established. For God gave birth to him by whom all things were made and Mary brought forth him by whom all are saved. God brought forth him without whom nothing is, Mary bore him without whom nothing is good. O truly, "the Lord is with you," to whom the Lord gave himself, that all nature in you might be in him.

Prayer to St. Mary 3, Oratio 7: Opera Omnia, ed. Schmitt, 3, 18, 22

Proper 20 ✠ Sunday

A reading from a treatise by Clement of Alexandria, Priest [c. 210]

We are commanded to reverence and honor the one who we are persuaded is Word, Savior, and Leader, and to honor the Father through him—not on special days, as some others do, but continually in all our life, and in every way.

Hence, it is not in a specified place, or in a special shrine, or at certain festivals and on appointed days, but during their whole lives and in every place that the truly spiritual—whether they be alone or in a community which shares their faith—honor God, that is, return their gratitude for the knowledge of the way to live.

The presence of good people, through the respect and reverence which they inspire, always improves those with whom they associate. With how much more reason, then, they who always find uninterrupted converse with God by knowledge, life, and thanksgiving grow at every step superior to themselves in all respects—in conduct, in words, and in disposition!

Holding festival, then, in all our life, in the certainty that God is completely present on every side of us, we cultivate our fields, praising; we sail the sea to the sound of hymns, and we conduct ourselves as citizens of heaven.

The truly spiritual are closely allied to God, being at once grave and cheerful in all things—grave on account of their attention to God, joyful on account of their consideration of the blessings of humanity which God has bestowed on us. They always trace up to God the grave enjoyment of all things: food, drink, and pleasant fragrance; they offer their first fruits to the one who has given all things, rendering thanks to him through the one who is the Gift, Unction, and Word.

Indeed, the truly spiritual pray throughout their whole life, since prayer for them is an attempt at union with God and they reject all that is of no service, because they have attained that state in which they have already received in some way the perfection which consists in acting through love. Their whole life is one long sacred liturgy.

Stromata 7, 7, 35–36: PG 9, 450–451, 455, 470C

Proper 20 ✠ Monday

A reading from the Passion of Perpetua and her Companions, Martyrs at Carthage [202]

Certain young catechumens were arrested, Revocatus and his fellow-slave Felicitas, Saturninus, and Secundulus. Among these also Vibia Perpetua, well-born, liberally educated, honorably married, having father and mother, and two brothers, one like herself a catechumen, and an infant son at the breast. She was about twenty-two years of age. The whole story of her martyrdom is from this point onwards told by herself, as she left it written, hand and conception being alike her own.

"When I was still," she says, "with my companions, and my father in his affection for me was endeavoring to upset me by arguments and overthrow my resolution, 'Father,' I said, 'Do you see this vessel for instance lying here, waterpot or whatever it may be?' 'I see it,' he said. And I said to him, 'Can it be called by any other name than what it is?' And he answered, 'No.' 'So also I cannot call myself anything else than what I am, a Christian.'

"A few days after, we were lodged in prison; and I was in great fear, because I had never known such darkness. What a day of horror! Terrible heat, thanks to the crowds! Rough handling by the soldiers! To crown all, I was tormented there by anxiety for my baby. Then Tertius and Pomponius, those blessed deacons who were ministering to us, paid for us to be removed for a few hours to a better part of the prison and refresh ourselves. Then all went out of the prison and were left to themselves. I nursed my baby, for he was already faint for want of food. I spoke anxiously to my mother on his behalf, and strengthened my brother, and commended my son to their charge. I was pining because I saw them pine on my account. Such anxieties I suffered for many days.

"After a few days a rumor ran that we were to be examined. Moreover, my father arrived from the city, worn with trouble, and came up the hill to see me, that he might overthrow my resolution, saying: 'Daughter, pity my white hairs! Pity your father, if I am worthy to be called father by you; if with these hands I have brought you up to this your prime of life, if I have preferred you to all your brothers! Give me not over to the reproach of the people! Look upon your brothers, look upon your mother and your mother's sister, look upon your son who cannot live after you are gone! Lay aside your pride, do not ruin all of us, for none of us will ever speak freely again, if anything happen to you!' So spoke my father in his love for me, kissing my hands, and casting himself at my feet; and with tears called me by the name not of daughter but of lady. And I grieved for my father's sake, because he alone of all my kindred would not have joy in my suffering. And I comforted him, saying: 'It shall happen on that platform as God shall choose; for know well that we lie not in our own power but in the power of God.' And full of sorrow he left me.

"On another day when we were having our midday meal, we were suddenly hurried off to be examined; and we came to the marketplace. Forthwith a rumor ran through the neighboring parts of the marketplace, and a vast crowd gathered. We went up on to the platform. The others on being questioned confessed their faith. So it came to my turn. And there was my father with my child, and he drew me down from the step, beseeching me: 'Have pity on your baby.' And the procurator Hilarian, who had then received the power of life and death in the place of the late proconsul Minucius Timinianus, said to me: 'Spare your father's white hairs; spare the tender years of your child. Offer a sacrifice for the safety of the Emperors.' And I answered: 'No.' 'Are you a Christian?' said Hilarian. And I answered: 'I am.' And when my father persisted in trying to overthrow my resolution, he was ordered by Hilarian to be thrown down, and the judge struck him with his rod. And I was grieved for my father's plight, as if I had been struck myself, so did I grieve for the sorrow that had come on his old age. Then he passed sentence on the whole of us, and condemned us to the beasts; and in great joy we went down into the prison."

Passion 2–6: Musurillo, 108–114

Proper 20 ✠ Tuesday

A reading from a letter by Augustine, Bishop of Hippo [430]

We need to use words so that we may remind ourselves to consider carefully what we are asking, not so that we may think we can instruct the Lord or prevail on him.

Thus, when we say: "Hallowed be your name," we are reminding ourselves to desire that his name, which in fact is always holy, should also be considered holy among us. I mean that it should not be held in contempt. But this is a help for people, not for God.

And as for our saying: "Your kingdom come," it will surely come whether we will it or not. But we are stirring up our desires for the kingdom so that it can come to us and we can deserve to reign there.

When we say: "Your will be done on earth as it is in heaven," we are asking God to make us obedient so that his will may be done in us as it is done in heaven by his angels.

When we say: "Give us this day our daily bread," in saying "this day" we mean "in this world." Here we ask for a sufficiency by specifying the most important part of it; that is, we use the word "bread" to stand for everything. Or else we are asking for the sacrament of the faithful, which is necessary in this world, not to gain temporal happiness but to gain the happiness that is everlasting.

When we say: "Forgive us our trespasses as we forgive those who trespass against us," we are reminding ourselves of what we must ask and what we must do in order to be worthy in turn to receive.

When we say: "Lead us not into temptation," we are reminding ourselves to ask that God's help may not depart from us; otherwise we could be seduced and consent to some temptation, or despair and yield to it.

When we say: "Deliver us from evil," we are reminding ourselves to reflect on the fact that we do not yet enjoy the state of blessedness in which we shall suffer no evil. This is the final petition contained in the Lord's Prayer, and it has a wide application. In this petition Christians can utter their cries of sorrow, in it they can shed their tears, and through it they can begin, continue and conclude their prayer, whatever the distress in which they find themselves. Yes, it was very appropriate that all these truths should be entrusted to us to remember in these very words.

Whatever be the other words we may prefer to say (words which the ones praying choose so that their disposition may become clearer to themselves or which they simply adopt so that their disposition may be intensified), we say nothing that is not contained in the Lord's Prayer, provided of course we are praying in a correct and proper way. But if any say something which is incompatible with this prayer of the Gospel, they are praying in the flesh, even if they are not praying sinfully. And yet I do not know how this could be termed anything but sinful, since those who are born again through the Spirit ought to pray only in the Spirit.

Letter 130, to Proba 11, 21–12, 22: CSEL 44, 63–64

Proper 20 ✠ Wednesday

A reading from a letter by Augustine, Bishop of Hippo [430]

You may still want to ask why the Apostle said: "We do not know what it is right to pray for," because, surely, we cannot believe that either he or those to whom he wrote did not know the Lord's Prayer.

He showed that he himself shared this uncertainty. Did he know what it was right to pray for when he was given a thorn in the flesh, an angel of Satan to bruise him, so that he might not be puffed up by the greatness of what was revealed to him? Three times he asked the Lord to take it away from him, which showed that he did not know what he should ask for in prayer. At last, he heard the Lord's answer, explaining why the prayer of so great a person was not granted, and why it was not expedient for it to be granted: "My grace is sufficient for you, for my power is made perfect in weakness."

In the kind of affliction, then, which can bring either good or ill, we do not know what it is right to pray for; yet, because it is difficult, troublesome and against the grain for us, weak as we are, we do what every human would do, we pray that it may be taken away from us. We owe, however, at least this much in our duty to God: if he does not take it away, we must not imagine that we are being forgotten by him but, because of our loving endurance of evil, must await greater blessings in its place. In this way, "power is made perfect in weakness." These words are written to prevent us from having too great an opinion of ourselves if our prayer is granted, when we are impatient in asking for something that it would be better not to receive; and to prevent us from being dejected, and distrustful of God's mercy toward us, if our prayer is not granted, when we ask for something that would bring us greater affliction, or completely ruin us through the corrupting influence of prosperity. In these cases we do not know what it is right to ask for in prayer.

Therefore, if something happens that we did not pray for, we must have no doubt at all that what God wants is more expedient than what we wanted ourselves. Our great Mediator gave us an example of this. After he had said: "Father, if it is possible, let this cup be taken away from me," he immediately added, "Yet not what I will, but what you will, Father, be done" so transforming the human will that was his through taking on a human nature. As a consequence, and rightly so, through his obedience the many are made righteous.

Letter 130, to Proba 14, 25–26: CSEL 44, 68–71

Proper 20 ✠ Thursday

A reading from a sermon of Leo the Great, Bishop of Rome [461]

The Lord says: "Unless your righteousness exceeds that of the scribes and Pharisees, you will not enter into the kingdom of heaven." How indeed can righteousness exceed, unless "compassion rises above judgment"? What is as right or as worthy as a creature, fashioned in the image and likeness of God, imitating the Creator who, by the remission of sins, brought about the reparation and sanctification of believers? With strict vengeance removed and the cessation of all punishment, the guilty was restored to innocence, and the end of wickedness became the beginning of virtue. Can anything be more just than this?

This is how Christian righteousness can exceed that of the scribes and Pharisees, not by canceling out the law but by rejecting earthly wisdom. This is why, in giving his disciples a rule for fasting, the Lord said: "Whenever you fast do not become sad like the hypocrites. For they disfigure their faces in order to seem to be fasting. Amen I say to you, they have received their reward." What reward but that of human praise? Such a desire often puts on a mask of righteousness, for where there is no concern for conscience, untruthful reputation gives pleasure. The result is that lack of righteousness, when concealed, enjoys a false reputation.

For those who love God it is sufficient to please the one they love; and there is no greater recompense to be sought than the loving itself; for love is from God by the very fact that God himself is love. The good and chaste soul is so happy to be filled with God that it desires to take delight in nothing else. For what the Lord says is very true: "Where your treasure is, there also will your heart be." What is one's treasure but the heaping up of profits and the fruit of one's toil? "For whatever you sow this too will you reap," and people's gain matches their toil; and where delight and enjoyment are found, there the heart's desire is attached. Now there are many kinds of wealth and a variety of grounds for rejoicing; each person's treasure is that which the individual desires. If it is based on earthly ambitions, its acquisition makes one not blessed but wretched.

But those who enjoy the things that are above and eternal rather than earthly and perishable, possess an incorruptible, hidden store of which the prophet speaks: "Our treasure and salvation have come, wisdom and instruction and piety from the Lord: these are the treasures of righteousness." Through these, with the help of God's grace, even earthly possessions are transformed into heavenly blessings; it is a fact that many people use the wealth which is either rightfully left to them or otherwise acquired, as a tool of devotion. By distributing what might be superfluous to support the poor, they are amassing imperishable riches, so that what they have discreetly given cannot be subject to loss. They have properly placed those riches where their heart is; it is a most blessed thing to work to increase such riches rather than to fear that they may pass away.

Sermon 92, 1–3: PL 54, 454–455

Proper 20 ✠ Friday

*A reading from a commentary on the psalms by Ambrose,
Bishop of Milan [397]*

In reconciling the world to God, Christ stood in no need of reconciliation
for himself. What sin of his was there to atone for, sinless as he was?

Christ shows that he does not need to atone for sin on his own behalf:
he is no slave of sin but, as Son of God, is free from all sin. The Son sets
free, a slave remains in sin. Christ is therefore free of all sin, and does
not pay the price of his own redemption. His blood could pay the ransom
for all the sins of the whole world. The one who has no debt to pay is
the right person to set others free.

It is not only that Christ has no ransom to pay or atonement to make
for his own sins; if we apply his words to every individual they can be
taken to mean that individuals do not need to make atonement for
themselves, for Christ is the atonement for all, the redemption for all.

Is anyone's blood fit to redeem oneself, seeing that it was Christ who
shed his blood for the redemption of all? Is anyone's blood comparable
to Christ's? Is anyone great enough to make individual atonement over
and above the atonement which Christ has offered in himself, Christ who
alone has reconciled the world to God by his blood? What greater victim,
what more excellent sacrifice, what better advocate can there be than he
who became the propitiation for the sins of all, and gave his life for us
as our redemption?

We do not need, then, to look for an atonement or redemption made
by each individual, because the price paid for all is the blood of Christ,
that blood by which the Lord Jesus has redeemed us, he who alone has
reconciled us to the Father. He has labored even to the end, shouldering
our burdens himself. "Come to me," he says, "all you that labor, and I
will refresh you."

Explanation on Psalm 48, 14–15: CSEL 64, 368–370

Proper 20 ✠ Saturday

*A reading from a treatise by Baldwin, Archbishop of
Canterbury [1190]*

Death is strong, for it can rob us of the gift of life. Love too is strong, for
it can restore us to a better life.

Death is strong, for it can strip us of this robe of flesh. Love too is strong, for it can take death's spoils away and give them back to us.

Death is strong, for no one can withstand it. Love too is strong, for it can conquer death itself, soothe its sting, calm its violence, and bring its victory to naught. The time will come when death is reviled and taunted: "O death, where is your sting? O death, where is your victory?"

Love is as strong as death because Christ's love is the very death of death. Hence it is said: "I will be your death, O death! I will be your sting, O hell!" Our love for Christ is also as strong as death, because it is itself a kind of death: destroying the old life, rooting out vice, and laying aside dead works.

Our love for Christ is a return, though very unequal, for his love of us, and it is a likeness modeled on his. For "he first loved us" and, through the example of love he gave us, he became a seal upon us by which we are made like him. We lay aside the likeness of the earthly person and put on the likeness of the heavenly person; we love him as he has loved us. For in this matter "he has left us an example so that we might follow in his steps."

That is why he says: "Set me as a seal upon your heart." It is as if he were saying: "Love me as I love you. Keep me in your mind and memory, in your desires and yearnings, in your groans and sobs. Remember the kind of being I made you; how far I set you above other creatures; the dignity I conferred upon you; the glory and honor with which I crowned you; how I made you only a little less than the angels and set all things under your feet. Remember not only how much I have done for you but all the hardship and shame I have suffered for you. Yet look and see: Do you not wrong me? Do you not fail to love me? Who loves you as I do? Who created and redeemed you but I?"

Lord, take away my heart of stone, a heart so bitter and uncircumcised, and give me a new heart, a heart of flesh, a pure heart. You cleanse the heart and love the clean heart. Take possession of my heart and dwell in it, contain it and fill it, you who are higher than the heights of my spirit and closer to me than my innermost self! You are the pattern of all beauty and the seal of all holiness. Set the seal of your likeness upon my heart! In your mercy set your seal upon my heart, "God of my heart and the God who is my portion for ever!"

Treatise 10: PL 204, 513–514, 516

Proper 21 ✠ Sunday

A reading from a homily of John Chrysostom, Bishop of Constantinople [407]

Do you want to honor Christ's body? Then do not scorn him in his nakedness, nor honor him here in the church with silken garments while neglecting him outside where he is cold and naked. For he who said: "This is my body," and made it so by his words, also said: "You saw me hungry and did not feed me," and "inasmuch as you did not do it for one of these, the least of my brothers [and sisters], you did not do it for me." What we do here in the church requires a pure heart, not special garments; what we do outside requires great dedication.

Let us learn, therefore, to be people of wisdom and to honor Christ as he desires. For people being honored find greatest pleasure in the honor they desire, not in the honor we think best. Peter thought he was honoring Christ when he refused to let him wash his feet; but what Peter wanted was not truly an honor, quite the opposite! Give him the honor prescribed in his law by giving your riches to the poor. For God does not want golden vessels but golden hearts.

Now, in saying this I am not forbidding you to make such gifts; I am only demanding that along with such gifts and before them you give alms. He accepts the former, but he is much more pleased with the latter. In the former, only the giver profits; in the latter, the recipient does too. A gift to the church may be taken as a form of ostentation, but an alms is pure kindness.

Of what use is it to weigh down Christ's table with golden cups, when he himself is dying of hunger? First, fill him when he is hungry; then use the means you have left to adorn his table. Will you have a golden cup made but not give a cup of water? What is the use of providing the table with cloths woven of gold thread, and not providing Christ himself with the clothes he needs? What profit is there in that? Tell me: If you were to see Christ lacking the necessary food but were to leave him in that state and merely surround his table with gold, would he be grateful to you or rather would he not be angry? What if you were to see people clad in worn-out rags and stiff from the cold, and were to forget about clothing them and instead were to set up golden columns for them, saying that you were doing it in their honor? Would they not think they were being mocked and greatly insulted?

Apply this also to Christ when he comes along the roads as a pilgrim, looking for shelter. You do not take him in as your guest, but you decorate floor and walls and the capitals of the pillars. You provide silver chains for the lamps, but you cannot bear even to look at him as he lies chained in prison. Once again, I am not forbidding you to supply these adornments; I am urging you to provide these other things as well, and indeed to provide them first. No one has ever been accused for not providing ornaments, but for those who neglect their neighbor a hell awaits with an inextinguishable fire and torment in the company of the demons. Do not, therefore, adorn the church and ignore your afflicted sisters and brothers, for they are the most precious temple of all.

Homily 50 on Matthew 3–4; PG 58, 508–509

Proper 21 ✠ Monday

A reading from the treatise Against Heresies by Irenaeus,
Bishop of Lyons [c. 202]

That they might be saved God demanded of these people of old not sacrifices and holocausts, but faith, obedience and righteousness. God expressed his will when he taught them in the words of Hosea: "I desire mercy more than sacrifices, the knowledge of God more than holocausts." Our Lord's warning to them was the same: "If you had known what was meant by the words 'I desire mercy and not sacrifice,' you would never have condemned the guiltless." He bore witness that the prophets had spoken the truth; he also brought home to his listeners the folly of their own sin.

Moreover, he instructed his disciples to offer to God the firstfruits of creation, not because God had any need, but so that they themselves should not be unproductive and ungrateful. This is why he took bread, a part of his creation, gave thanks and said: "This is my body." In the same way he declared that the cup, an element of the same creation as ourselves, was his blood; he taught them that this was the new sacrifice of the new covenant. The Church has received this sacrifice from the apostles; throughout the world she offers to God, who feeds us, the firstfruits of his own gifts, under the new covenant. It was foretold by Malachi, one of the twelve prophets, in the words: "I take no pleasure in you, says the Lord Almighty, and no sacrifice will I accept from your hands. For, from the rising of the sun to its setting, the Gentiles glorify my name, and in every place incense and a spotless sacrifice are offered to my name; my name is great among the Gentiles, says the Lord Almighty."

But what name is glorified among the Gentiles if not that of our Lord, through whom glory is given both to the Father and to humanity. And since this name belongs to his own Son, who became human by the Father's will, the Father calls this name his own. If a king were to paint a picture of his heir, he could claim it as his own on two counts: because it is his heir's picture, and because he himself made it. In the same way, the Father declares that the name of Jesus Christ, which is glorified in the Church throughout the world, is his own, because it is his Son's name and because he wrote it to save humankind.

And so, since the Son's name belongs to the Father and since the Church makes its offerings through Jesus Christ to almighty God, for these two reasons the prophet is right when he says: "In every place incense and a pure sacrifice are offered to my name." In the book of Revelation, John speaks of incense as "the prayer of the saints."

Against Heresies 4, 17, 4–6: SC 100, 590–594

Proper 21 ✠ Tuesday

A reading from a homily of John Chrysostom, Bishop of Constantinople [407]

Would you like me to list also the paths of repentance? They are numerous and quite varied, and all lead to heaven.

A first path of repentance is the condemnation of your own sins: "Be the first to admit your sins and you will be justified." For this reason, too, the prophet wrote: "I said: I will accuse myself of my sins to the Lord, and you forgave the wickedness of my heart." Therefore, you too should condemn your own sins; that will be enough reason for the Lord to forgive you, for if you condemn your own sins you are slower to commit them again. Rouse your conscience to accuse you within your own house, lest it become your accuser before the judgment seat of the Lord.

That, then, is one very good path of repentance. Another and no less valuable one is to put out of our minds the harm done us by our enemies, in order to master our anger, and to forgive our fellow servants' sins against us. Then our own sins against the Lord will be forgiven us. Thus you have another way to atone for sin: "For if you forgive your debtors, your heavenly Father will forgive you."

Do you want to know of a third path? It consists of prayer that is fervent, careful and comes from the heart.

If you want to hear of a fourth, I will mention almsgiving, whose power is great and far-reaching.

If, moreover, one lives a modest, humble life, that no less than the other things I have mentioned takes sin away. Proof of this is the tax-collector who had no good deeds to mention, but offered humility instead and was relieved of a heavy burden of sins.

Thus I have shown you five paths of repentance: condemnation of your own sins, forgiveness of our neighbor's sins against us, prayer, almsgiving and humility.

Do not be idle, then, but walk daily in all these paths; they are easy, and you cannot plead your poverty. For, though you live out your life amid great need, you can always set aside your wrath, be humble, pray diligently and condemn your own sins; poverty is no hindrance. Poverty is not an obstacle to our carrying out the Lord's bidding, even when it comes to that path of repentance which involves giving money (almsgiving, I mean). The widow proved that when she put her two mites into the box!

Now that we have learned how to heal those wounds of ours, let us apply the cures. Then, when we have regained genuine health, we can approach the holy table with confidence, go gloriously to meet Christ, the king of glory, and attain the eternal blessings through the grace, mercy and kindness of Jesus Christ, our Lord.

Homily on the Devil the Tempter 2, 6: PG 49, 263–264

Proper 21 ✠ Wednesday

A reading from an instruction by Columbanus, Celtic Abbot [615]

Listen to my words. You are going to hear something that must be said. You quench your soul's thirst with drafts of the divine fountain. I now wish to speak of this. Revive yourself, but do not extinguish your thirst. Drink, I say, but do not entirely quench your thirst, for the fountain of life, the fountain of love calls us to him and says: "Whoever thirsts, let him come to me and drink."

Understand well what you drink. Jeremiah would tell us; the fountain of life would himself tell us: "For they abandoned me, the fountain of living water, says the Lord." The Lord himself, our God Jesus Christ, is the fountain of life, and accordingly he invites us to himself as to a fountain, that we may drink. Whoever loves him, drinks him. You drink who are filled with the Word of God. You drink who love him fully and really desire him. You drink who are on fire with the love of wisdom.

Consider the source of the fountain; bread comes down to us from the same place, since the same one is the bread and the fountain, the only-begotten son, our God, Christ the Lord, for whom we should always hunger. We may even eat him out of love for him, and devour him out of desire, longing for him eagerly. Let us drink from him, as from a fountain, with an abundance of love. May we drink him with the fullness of desire, and may we take pleasure in his sweetness and savor.

For the Lord is sweet and agreeable; rightly then let us eat and drink of him yet remain ever hungry and thirsty, since he is our food and drink, but can never be wholly eaten and consumed. Though he may be eaten, he is never consumed; one can drink of him and he is not diminished because our bread is eternal and our fountain is sweet and everlasting. Hence the prophet says: "You who thirst, go to the fountain." He is the fountain for those who are thirsty but are never fully satisfied. Therefore he calls to himself the hungry whom he raised to a blessed condition elsewhere. They were never satisfied in drinking; the more they drank, the greater their thirst.

It is right that we must always long for, seek and love the Word of God on high, the fountain of wisdom. According to the Apostle's words "all the hidden treasures of wisdom and knowledge are in him," and he calls the thirsty to drink.

If you thirst, drink of the fountain of life; if you are hungry, eat the bread of life. Blessed are they who hunger for this bread and thirst for this fountain, for in so doing they will desire ever more to eat and drink. For what they eat and drink is exceedingly sweet and their thirst and appetite for more is never satisfied. Though it is ever tasted it is ever more desired. Hence the prophet-king says: "Taste and see how sweet, how agreeable is the Lord."

Instruction 13, on Christ the Fount of Life, 1–2: Opera, Dublin 1957, 116–118

Proper 21 ✠ Thursday

A reading from an instruction by Columbanus, Celtic Abbot
[615]

Let us follow that vocation by which we are called from life to the fountain of life. He is the fountain, not only of living water, but of eternal life. He is the fountain of light and spiritual illumination; for from him come all these things: wisdom, life and eternal light. The author of life is the fountain of life; the creator of light is the fountain of spiritual illumination. Therefore, let us seek the fountain of light and life and the living water by despising what we see, by leaving the world and by dwelling in the highest heavens. Let us seek these things, and like rational and shrewd fish may we drink the living water which "wells up to eternal life."

Merciful God, good Lord, I wish that you would unite me to that fountain, that there I may drink of the living spring of the water of life with those others who thirst after you. There in that heavenly region may I ever dwell, delighted with abundant sweetness, and say: "How sweet is the fountain of living water which never fails, the water welling up to eternal life."

O God, you are yourself that fountain ever and again to be desired, ever and again to be consumed. Lord Christ, always give us this water to be for us the "source of the living water which wells up to eternal life." I ask you for your great benefits. Who does not know it? You, King of glory, know how to give great gifts, and you have promised them; there is nothing greater than you, and you bestowed yourself upon us; you gave yourself for us.

Therefore, we ask that we may know what we love, since we ask nothing other than that you give us yourself. For you are our all: our life, our light, our salvation, our food and our drink, our God. Inspire our hearts, I ask you, Jesus, with that breath of your Spirit; wound our souls with your love, so that the soul of each and every one of us may say in truth: "Show me my soul's desire," for I am wounded by your love.

These are the wounds I wish for, Lord. Blessed is the soul so wounded by love. Such a soul seeks the fountain of eternal life and drinks from it, although it continues to thirst and its thirst grows ever greater even as it drinks. Therefore, the more the soul loves, the more it desires to love, and the greater its suffering, the greater its healing. In this same way may our God and Lord Jesus Christ, the good and saving physician, wound the depths of our souls with a healing wound—the same Jesus Christ who reigns in unity with the Father and the Holy Spirit, for ever and ever.

Instruction 13, on Christ the Fount of Life, 2–3: Opera, Dublin 1957, 118–120

Proper 21 ✠ Friday

A reading from a letter by Augustine, Bishop of Hippo [430]

What merit, then, do we have before grace which could make it possible for us to receive grace, when nothing but grace produces good merit in us? When God crowns our merits, it is his own gifts that he crowns. For, just as in the beginning we obtained the mercy of faith, not because we were faithful but that we might become so, in like manner God will crown us at the end with eternal life, as the Psalm says, "with mercy and compassion." Not in vain, therefore, do we sing to God: "His mercy shall go before me," and "His mercy shall follow me." Consequently, eternal life itself, which will certainly be possessed at the end without end, is in a sense awarded to antecedent merits, yet, because the same merits for which it is awarded are not effected by us through our sufficiency, but are effected in us by grace, even this very grace is so called for no other reason than that it is given freely; not, indeed, that it is not given for merit, but because the merits themselves are given for which it is given. And when we find eternal life itself called grace, we have in the same Apostle Paul a magnificent defender of grace: "The wages of sin," he says, "is death. But [God's free gift of grace] is life everlasting in Christ Jesus our Lord."

Letter 194, 5, 19: FC 30, 313; CSEL 44.

Proper 21 ✠ Saturday

A reading from a sermon of Bernard, Abbot of Clairvaux [1153]

"He has given his angels charge over you to guard you in all your ways. Let them thank the Lord for his mercy; his wonderful works are for humankind." Let them give thanks and say among the nations, the Lord has done great things for them. O Lord, what are we that you have made yourself known to us, or why do you incline your heart to us? And you do incline your heart to us; you show us your care and your concern. Finally, you send your only Son and the grace of your Spirit, and promise us a vision of your countenance. And so, that nothing in heaven should be wanting in your concern for us, you send those blessed spirits to serve us, assigning them as our guardians and our teachers.

"He has given his angels charge over you to guard you in all your ways." These words should fill you with respect, inspire devotion and instill confidence; respect for the presence of angels, devotion because of their loving service, and confidence because of their protection. And so the angels are here; they are at your side, they are with you, present on your behalf. They are here to protect you and to serve you. But even if it is God who has given them this charge, we must nonetheless be grateful to them for the great love with which they obey and come to help us in our great need.

So let us be devoted and grateful to such great protectors; let us return their love and honor them as much as we can and should. Yet all our love and honor must go to him, for it is from him that they receive all that makes them worthy of our love and respect.

We should then show our affection for the angels, for one day they will be our co-heirs just as here below they are our guardians and trustees appointed and set over us by the Father. We are God's children although it does not seem so, because we are still but small children under guardians and trustees, and for the present little better than slaves.

Even though we are children and have a long, a very long and dangerous way to go, with such protectors what have we to fear? They who keep us in all our ways cannot be overpowered or led astray, much less lead us astray. They are loyal, prudent, powerful. Why then are we afraid? We have only to follow them, stay close to them, and we shall dwell under the protection of God's heaven.

Sermon 12, 3, 6–8: Opera Omnia 4, 458–462

Proper 22 ✠ Sunday

A reading from a sermon of Augustine, Bishop of Hippo [430]

Happy are we if we do the deeds of which we have heard and sung. Our hearing them means having them planted in us, while our doing them shows that the seed has borne fruit. By saying this, I wish to caution you, dearly beloved, not to enter the church fruitlessly, satisfied with mere hearing of such mighty blessings and failing to do good works. For "we have been saved by his grace," says the Apostle, "and not by our works, lest anyone may boast; for it is by his grace that we have been saved." It is not as if a good life of some sort came first, and that thereupon God showed his love and esteem for it from on high, saying: "Let us come to the aid of these people and assist them quickly because they are living a good life." No, our life was displeasing to him; whatever we did by ourselves was displeasing to him; but what he did in us was not displeasing to him. He will, therefore, condemn what we have done, but he will save what he himself has done in us.

We were not good, but God had pity on us and sent his Son to die, not for good people but for bad ones, not for the just but for the wicked. Yes, "Christ died for the ungodly." Notice what is written next: "One will hardly die for a righteous person, though perhaps for a good person one will dare even to die." Perhaps someone can be found who will dare to die for a good person; but for the unjust, for the wicked one, the sinner, who would be willing to die except Christ alone who is so just that he justifies even the unjust?

And so, we had no good works, for all our works were evil. Yet although our actions were such, God in his mercy did not abandon us. He sent his Son to redeem us, not with gold or silver but at the price of his blood poured out for us. Christ, the spotless lamb, became the sacrificial victim, led to the slaughter for the sheep that were blemished—if indeed one can say that they were blemished and not entirely corrupt. Such is the grace we have received! Let us live so as to be worthy of that great grace, and not do injury to it. So mighty is the physician who has come to us that he has healed all our sins! If we choose to be sick once again, we will not only harm ourselves, but show ingratitude to the physician as well.

Let us then follow Christ's paths which he has revealed to us, above all the path of humility, which he himself became for us. He showed us that path by his precepts, and he himself followed it by his suffering on our behalf. In order to die for us—because as God he could not die—"the Word became flesh and dwelt among us." The immortal One took on mortality that he might die for us, and by dying put to death our death.

This is what the Lord did, this the gift he granted to us. The mighty one was brought low, the lowly one was slain, and after he was slain, he rose again and was exalted. For he did not intend to leave us dead in hell, but to exalt in himself at the resurrection of the dead those whom he had already exalted and made just by the faith and praise they gave him. Yes, he gave us the path of humility. If we keep to it we shall confess our belief in the Lord and have good reason to sing: "We shall praise you, God, we shall praise you and call upon your name."

Sermon 23A, 1–4: CCL 41, 321–323

Proper 22 ✠ Monday

A reading from The Imitation of Christ by Thomas a Kempis, Priest [1471]

The Lord says, listen to my words, the most delightful of all words, surpassing all the knowledge of the philosophers and wise ones of this world. "My words are spirit and life" and cannot be comprehended by human senses alone.

They are not to be interpreted according to the vain pleasure of the listener, but they must be listened to in silence and received with all humility and great affection.

And I said: "Blessed are they whom you teach, Lord, and whom you instruct in your law; for them you soften the blow of the evil day," and you do not desert them on the earth.

The Lord says, I have instructed my prophets from the beginning and even to the present time I have not stopped speaking to all people, but many are deaf and obstinate in response.

Many hear the world more easily than they hear God; they follow the desires of the flesh more readily than the pleasure of God.

The world promises rewards that are temporal and insignificant, and these are pursued with great longing; I promise rewards that are eternal and unsurpassable, yet the hearts of mortals respond sluggishly.

Who serves and obeys me in all matters with as much care as the world and its princes are served?

Blush, then, you lazy, complaining servant, for people are better prepared for the works of death than you are for the works of life. They take more joy in vanity than you in truth.

Yet they are often deceived in their hope, while my promise deceives no one, and leaves empty-handed no one who confides in me. What I have promised I shall give; what I have said I will fulfill for anyone who remains faithful in my love unto the very end. I am the rewarder of all good people, the one who rigorously tests the devoted.

Write my words in your heart and study them diligently, for they will be absolutely necessary in the time of temptation. Whatever you fail to understand in reading my words will become clear to you on the day of your visitation.

I am accustomed to visit my elect in a double fashion, that is, with temptation and with consolation. And I read to them two lessons each day: one to rebuke them for their faults; the other to exhort them to increase their virtue.

"Those who possess my words yet spurn them earn their own judgment on the last day."

The Imitation of Christ 3, 3

Proper 22 ✠ Tuesday

A reading from The Imitation of Christ by Thomas a Kempis, Priest [1471]

You thunder your judgments upon me, O Lord; you shake all my bones with fear and dread, and my soul becomes severely frightened. I am bewildered when I realize that "even the heavens are not pure in your sight."

If you discovered "iniquity in the angels" and did not spare them, what will become of me? The stars fell from heaven, and I, mere dust, what should I expect? Those whose works seemed praiseworthy fell to the depths, and I have seen those who once were fed with the bread of angels delighting in the husks of swine.

There is no holiness where you have withdrawn your hand, O Lord; no profitable wisdom if you cease to rule over it; no helpful strength if you cease to preserve it. For if you forsake us, we sink and perish; but if you visit us, we rise up and live again. We are unstable, but you make us firm; we grow cool, but you inflame us.

All superficial glory has been swallowed up in the depths of your judgment upon me.

What is all flesh in your sight? "Can the clay be glorified in opposition to its Maker?"

How can any be aroused by empty talk if their hearts are subject in the truth to God?

The whole world cannot swell with pride those who are subject to truth; nor will they be swayed by the flattery of all their admirers, if they have established all their trust in God.

For those who do all the talking amount to nothing; they fail with their din of words, but "the truth of the Lord endures for ever."

The Imitation of Christ 3, 14

Proper 22 ✠ Wednesday

A reading from a letter by Clare, Abbess at Assisi [1253]

Happy indeed is she who is granted a place at the divine banquet, for she may cling with her inmost heart to him whose beauty eternally awes the blessed hosts of heaven; to him whose love inspires love, whose contemplation refreshes, whose generosity satisfies, whose gentleness delights, whose memory shines sweetly as the dawn; to him whose fragrance revives the dead, and whose glorious vision will bless all the citizens of that heavenly Jerusalem. For he is the splendor of eternal glory, "the brightness of eternal light, and the mirror without cloud."

Queen and bride of Jesus Christ, look into that mirror daily and study well your reflection, that you may adorn yourself, mind and body, with an enveloping garment of every virtue, and thus find yourself attired in flowers and gowns befitting the daughter and most chaste bride of the king on high. In this mirror blessed poverty, holy humility and ineffable love are also reflected. With the grace of God the whole mirror will be your source of contemplation.

Behold, I say, the birth of this mirror. Behold his poverty even as he was laid in the manger and wrapped in swaddling clothes. What wondrous humility, what marvelous poverty! The King of angels, the Lord of heaven and earth resting in a manger! Look more deeply into the mirror and meditate on his humility, or simply on his poverty. Behold the many labors and sufferings he endured to redeem the human race. Then, in the depths of this very mirror, ponder his unspeakable love which caused him to suffer on the wood of the cross and to endure the most shameful kind of death. The mirror himself, from his position on the cross, warned passersby to weigh carefully this act, as he said: "All of you who pass by this way, behold and see if there is any sorrow like mine." Let us answer his cries and lamentations with one voice and one spirit: "I will be mindful and remember, and my soul will be consumed within me." In this way, queen of the king of heaven, your love will burn with an ever brighter flame.

Consider also his indescribable delights, his unending riches and honors, and sigh for what is beyond your love and heart's content as you cry out: "Draw me on! We will run after you in the perfume of your ointment," heavenly spouse. Let me run and not faint until you lead me into your wine cellar; your left hand rests under my head, your right arm joyfully embraces me, and you kiss me with the sweet kiss of your lips. As you rest in this state of contemplation, remember your poor mother and know that I have indelibly written your happy memory into my heart, for you are dearer to me than all the others.

Fourth Letter to Blessed Agnes of Prague 9–33: ed. Armstrong, 48–50

Proper 22 ✠ Thursday

A reading from a sermon of Leo the Great, Bishop of Rome [461]

Dearly beloved, when our Lord Jesus Christ was preaching the Gospel of the kingdom and healing various illnesses throughout the whole of Galilee, the fame of his mighty works spread into all of Syria, and great crowds from all parts of Judea flocked to the heavenly physician. Because human ignorance is slow to believe what it does not see, and equally slow to hope for what it does not know, those who were to be instructed in the divine teaching had first to be aroused by bodily benefits and visible miracles so that, once they had experienced his gracious power, they would no longer doubt the wholesome effect of his doctrine.

In order, therefore, to transform outward healings into inward remedies, and to cure people's souls now that he had healed their bodies, our

Lord separated himself from the surrounding crowds, climbed to the solitude of a neighboring mountain, and called the apostles to himself. From the height of this mystical site he then instructed them in the most lofty doctrines, suggesting both by the very nature of the place and by what he was doing that it was he who long ago had honored Moses by speaking to him. Then his words evidenced a terrifying justice, but now they reveal a sacred compassion, in order to fulfill what was promised in the words of the prophet Jeremiah: "Behold the days are coming, says the Lord, when I shall establish a new covenant with the house of Israel and with the house of Judah. After those days, says the Lord, I shall put my laws within them and write them on their hearts."

And so it was that he who had spoken to Moses spoke also to the apostles. Writing in the hearts of his disciples, the swift hand of the Word composed the ordinances of the new covenant. And this was not done as formerly, in the midst of dense clouds, amid terrifying sounds and lightning, so that the people were frightened away from approaching the mountain. Instead, there was a tranquil discourse which clearly reached the ears of all who stood nearby so that the harshness of the law might be softened by the gentleness of grace, and the spirit of adoption might dispel the terror of slavery.

Concerning the content of Christ's teaching, his own sacred words bear witness; thus whoever longs to attain eternal blessedness can now recognize the steps that lead to that high happiness. "Blessed," he says, "are the poor in spirit, for theirs is the kingdom of heaven." It might have been unclear to which poor he was referring, if after the words "Blessed are the poor," he had not added anything about the kind of poor he had in mind. For then the poverty that many suffer because of grave and harsh necessity might seem sufficient to merit the kingdom of heaven. But when he says: "Blessed are the poor in spirit," he shows that the kingdom of heaven is to be given to those who are distinguished by their humility of soul rather than by their lack of worldly goods.

Sermon 95, 1–2: PL 54, 461–462

Proper 22 ✠ Friday

A reading from a commentary on the psalms by Augustine, Bishop of Hippo [430]

"As we have heard, so also have we seen." Truly blessed Church! You have both heard and seen. You have heard the promises, and you see their fulfillment; you have heard in prophecy, and you see in the Gospel. Yes, all that has now been brought to completion was prophesied in times past. Raise up your eyes, then, and cast your gaze around the world. See God's people, your heritage, spread to the ends of the earth. See the Scripture now fulfilled: "All the kings of the earth will adore him, all the nations will serve him." See fulfilled what has been said: "Be exalted above the heavens, O God, and your glory above all the earth." See him whose hands and feet were pierced by nails, whose bones were numbered as they hung upon the wood, and for whose garments they cast lots. See him reigning, whom they saw hanging upon the cross; see him enthroned in heaven, whom they despised when he walked on the earth. See the word fulfilled: "All the ends of the earth shall turn to the Lord, and all nations shall worship in his sight." See all this and shout with joy: "As we have heard, so also have we seen."

Deservedly then the Church is itself called from among the Gentiles: "Hear, O daughter, and see, and forget your people and your father's house." Hear and see. First you hear what you do not see; later you will see what you have heard. For he says: "A people I did not know served me, as soon as they heard me they obeyed." If they "obeyed as soon as they heard," it follows that they did not see. What then of the passage: "Those who were not told of him will see, and they who have not heard will understand"? Those to whom the prophets were not sent were the first to hear and understand the prophets, whereas those who at first did not hear them were astonished when they heard them later. Those to whom the prophets were sent remained behind, possessing the books of Scripture but not understanding the truth, possessing the tables of the law but not keeping their inheritance. "As we have heard, so also have we seen" also applies to us.

"In the city of the Lord of hosts, in the city of our God," that is where we have heard; there too we have seen. "God has made this city firm for ever." No one should say boastfully: "See, here is Christ; see, he is there." Such a claim only leads to factions. But God has promised unity. The kings were gathered together in unity, not scattered through schisms. Yet perhaps that city which had gained possession of the world will at some time be overthrown? No, "God has made it firm for ever." If God has made its foundation firm for ever, how can you fear that this foundation may collapse?

Commentary on Psalm 47, 7: CCL 38, 543–545

Proper 22 ✠ Saturday

A reading from the treatise On Christian Perfection by Gregory, Bishop of Nyssa [c. 394]

"He is our peace, for he has made both one." Since we think of Christ as our peace, we may call ourselves true Christians only if our lives express Christ by our own peace. As the Apostle says: "He has put enmity to death." We must never allow it to be rekindled in us in any way but must declare that it is absolutely dead. Gloriously has God slain enmity, in order to save us; may we never risk the life of our souls by being resentful or by bearing grudges. We must not awaken that enmity or call it back to life by our wickedness, for it is better left dead.

No, since we possess Christ who is peace, we must put an end to this enmity and live as we believe he lived. He broke down the separating wall, uniting what was divided, bringing about peace by reconciling in his single person those who disagreed. In the same way, we must be reconciled not only with those who attack us from outside, but also with those who stir up dissension within; flesh then will no longer be opposed to the spirit, nor the spirit to the flesh. Once we subject the wisdom of the flesh to God's law, we shall be re-created as one single person at peace. Then, having become one instead of two, we shall have peace within ourselves.

Now peace is defined as harmony among those who are divided. When, therefore, we end that civil war within our nature and cultivate peace within ourselves, we become peace. By this peace we demonstrate that the name of Christ, which we bear, is authentic and appropriate.

When we consider that Christ is the true light, having nothing in common with deceit, we learn that our own life also must shine with the rays of that true light. Now these rays of the Sun of Justice are the virtues which pour out to enlighten us so that "we may put away the works of darkness and walk honorably as in broad daylight." When we reject the deeds of darkness and do everything in the light of day, we become light and, as light should, we give light to others by our actions.

If we truly think of Christ as our source of holiness, we shall refrain from anything wicked or impure in thought or act and thus show ourselves to be worthy bearers of his name. For the quality of holiness is shown not by what we say but by what we do in life.

Treatise on Christian Perfection: PG 46, 259–262

Proper 23 ✠ Sunday

A reading from a sermon of Leo the Great, Bishop of Rome [461]

The Lord then goes on to say: "Blessed are those who hunger and thirst for righteousness, for they shall be filled." This hunger is not for any bodily food, this thirst is not for any earthly drink: it is a longing to be blessed with righteousness, and, by penetrating the secret of all mysteries, to be filled with the Lord himself.

Happy is the soul that longs for the food of righteousness and thirsts for this kind of drink; it would not seek such things if it had not already savored their delight. When the soul hears the voice of the Spirit saying to it through the prophet: "Taste and see that the Lord is good," it has already received a portion of God's goodness, and is on fire with love, the love that gives joy of the utmost purity. It counts as nothing all that belongs to time; it is entirely consumed with desire to eat and drink the food of righteousness. The soul lays hold of the true meaning of the first and great commandment: "You shall love the Lord God with your whole heart, and your whole mind and your whole strength," for to love God is nothing else than to love righteousness.

Finally, just as concern for one's neighbor is added to love of God, so the virtue of mercy is added to the desire for righteousness, as it is said: "Blessed are the merciful, for God will be merciful to them."

Remember, Christian, the surpassing worth of the wisdom that is yours. Bear in mind the kind of school in which you are to learn your skills, the rewards to which you are called. Mercy itself wishes you to be merciful, righteousness itself wishes you to be righteous, so that the Creator may shine forth in his creature, and the image of God be reflected in the mirror of the human heart as it imitates his qualities. The faith of those who live their faith is a serene faith. What you long for will be given you; what you love will be yours for ever.

Since it is by giving alms that everything is pure for you, you will also receive that blessing which is promised next by the Lord: "Blessed are the pure of heart, for they shall see God." Dear friends, great is the happiness of those for whom such a reward is prepared. Who are the clean of heart if not those who strive for those virtues we have mentioned above? What mind can conceive, what words can express the great happiness of seeing God? Yet human nature will achieve this when it has been transformed so that it sees the Godhead "no longer in a mirror or obscurely but face to face"—the Godhead that no one has been able to see. In the inexpressible joy of this eternal vision, human nature will possess "what eye has not seen or ear heard, what the human heart has never conceived."

Sermon 95, 6–8: PL 54, 464–465

Proper 23 ✠ Monday

A reading from a commentary on Philippians by Ambrose, Bishop of Milan [397]

God's love is calling us to the joys of eternal happiness for the salvation of our souls. You have just listened to the reading from the Apostle in which he says: "Rejoice in the Lord always." The joys of this world lead to eternal misery, but the joys that are according to the will of the Lord bring those who persevere in them to joys that are enduring and everlasting. The Apostle therefore says: "Again I say: rejoice."

He urges us to find ever increasing joy in God and in keeping his commandments. The more we try in this world to give ourselves completely to God our Lord by obeying his commands, the greater will be our happiness in the life to come, and the greater the glory that will be ours in the presence of God.

"Let your moderation be known to all." That is to say, your holiness of life must be evident, not only in the sight of God, but also in the sight of other people. It must give an example of moderation and self-control to all your contemporaries on earth and serve also as a memorial of goodness before God and other people.

"The Lord is near; have no anxiety." The Lord is always near to all who call upon his help with sincerity, true faith, sure hope, and perfect love. He knows what you need, even before you ask him. He is always ready to come to the aid of all his faithful servants in every need. There is no reason for us to be in a state of great anxiety when evils threaten; we must remember that God is very near us as our protector. "The Lord is at hand for those who are troubled in heart, and he will save those who are downcast in spirit. The tribulations of the just are many, and the Lord will rescue them from them all." If we do our best to obey and keep his commandments, he does not delay in giving us what he has promised.

"But in every prayer and entreaty let your petitions be made known to God, with thanksgiving." In time of trouble we must not grumble or be downhearted; God forbid! We must rather be patient and cheerful, "giving thanks to God always in everything."

Commentary on Philippians: PLS 1, 617–618

Proper 23 ✠ Tuesday

A reading from a letter by Augustine, Bishop of Hippo [430]

Let us always desire the happy life from the Lord God and always pray for it. But for this very reason we turn our mind to the task of prayer at appointed hours, since that desire grows lukewarm, so to speak, from our involvement in other concerns and occupations. We remind ourselves through the words of prayer to focus our attention on the object of our desire; otherwise, the desire that began to grow lukewarm may grow chill altogether and may be totally extinguished unless it is repeatedly stirred into flame.

Therefore, when the Apostle says: "Let your petitions become known before God," this should not be taken in the sense that they are in fact becoming known to God who certainly knew them even before they were made, but that they are becoming known to us before God through submission and not before human beings through boasting.

Since this is the case, it is not wrong or useless to pray even for a long time when there is the opportunity. I mean when it does not keep us from performing the other good and necessary actions we are obliged to do. But even in these actions, as I have said, we must always pray with that desire. To pray for a longer time is not the same as to pray by multiplying words, as some people suppose. Lengthy talk is one thing, a prayerful disposition which lasts a long time is another. For it is even written in reference to the Lord himself that he spent the night in prayer and that he prayed at great length. Was he not giving us an example by this? In time, he prays when it is appropriate; and in eternity, he hears our prayers with the Father.

The monks in Egypt are said to offer frequent prayers, but these are very short and hurled like swift javelins. Otherwise their watchful attention, a very necessary quality for anyone at prayer, could be dulled and could disappear through protracted delays. They also clearly demonstrate through this practice that a person must not quickly divert such attention if it lasts, just as one must not allow it to be blunted if it cannot last.

Excessive talking should be kept out of prayer but that does not mean that one should not spend much time in prayer so long as a fervent attitude continues to accompany the prayer. To talk at length in prayer is to perform a necessary action with an excess of words. To spend much time in prayer is to knock with a persistent and holy fervor at the door of the one whom we beseech. This task is generally accomplished more through sighs than words, more through weeping than speech. He "places our tears in his sight, and our sighs are not hidden from him", for he has established all things through his Word and does not seek human words.

Letter 130, to Proba 9, 18–10, 20: CSEL 44, 60–63.

Proper 23 ✠ Wednesday

A reading from a sermon of Gregory, Bishop of Nyssa [c. 394]

In our human life bodily health is a good thing, but this blessing consists not merely in knowing the causes of good health but in actually enjoying it. If we eulogize good health and then eat food that has unhealthy effects, what good is our praise of health when we find ourselves on a sickbed? Similarly, from the Lord's saying: "Blessed are the pure of heart, for they shall see God," we are to learn that blessedness does not lie in knowing something about God, but rather in possessing God within oneself.

I do not think these words mean that God will be seen face to face by the one who purifies the eye of the soul. Their sublime import is brought out more clearly perhaps in that other saying of the Lord's: "The kingdom of God is within you." This teaches us that those who cleanse their hearts of every created thing and every evil desire will see the image of the divine nature in the beauty of their own souls. I believe the lesson summed up by the Word in that short sentence was this: You have within you a desire to behold the supreme good. Now when you are told that the majesty of God is exalted above the heavens, that his glory is inexpressible, his beauty indescribable, and his nature transcendent, do not despair because you cannot behold the object of your desire. If by a diligent life of virtue you wash away the film of dirt that covers your heart, then the divine beauty will shine forth in you.

Take a piece of iron as an illustration. Although it might have been black before, once the rust has been scraped off with a whetstone, it will begin to shine brilliantly and to reflect the rays of the sun. So it is with the interior self, which is what the Lord means by the heart. Once you remove from your soul the coating of filth that has formed on it through your sinful neglect, you will regain your likeness to your Archetype, and be good. For what resembles the supreme Good is itself good. If you then look into yourself, you will see the vision you have longed for. This is the blessedness of the pure of heart: in seeing their own purity they see the divine Archetype mirrored in themselves.

Those who look at the sun in a mirror, even if they do not look directly at the sky, see its radiance in the reflection just as truly as do those who look directly at the sun's orb. It is the same, says the Lord, with you. Even though you are unable to contemplate and see the inaccessible light, you will find what you seek within yourself, provided you return to the beauty and grace of that image which was originally placed in you. For God is purity; he is free from sin and a stranger to all evil. If this can be said of you, then God will surely be within you. If your mind is untainted by any evil, free from sin, and purified from all stain, then indeed are you blessed, because your sight is keen and clear. Once purified, you see things that others cannot see. When the mists of sin no longer cloud the eye of your soul, you see that blessed vision clearly in the peace and purity of your own heart. That vision is nothing else than the holiness, the purity, the simplicity and all the other glorious reflections of God's nature, through which God himself is seen.

Oration 6: PG 44, 1270–1271

Proper 23 ✠ Thursday

*A reading from a commentary on the psalms by Augustine,
Bishop of Hippo [430]*

Let us praise the Lord in voice, understanding, and good works; and as the Psalm urges us to do, let us sing to him a new song. It begins: "Sing to the Lord a new song of praise in the assembly of the faithful." The old singer has a new song; the new singer, a new song. The person who loves earthly things sings an old song; let one who desires to sing a new song love the things of eternity. Love itself is new and eternal; hence, it is ever new, because it never grows old.

If you really think about it, love is something old. How then can it be new at the same time? Beloved, has eternal life just been born? This eternal life is Christ himself, and according to his divinity he has not just been born, for "in the beginning was the Word; the Word was in God's presence, and the Word was God. He was present to God in the beginning. Through him all things came into being, and apart from him nothing came to be." If the things which he has made are old, what is he through whom they have been made? What is he, if not eternal and co-eternal with his Father?

It is our voice which laments in another Psalm: "I have aged because of all my foes." Humankind has aged as a consequence of sin; we are renewed through grace. Hence, all those who have been renewed in

Christ sing the new song and begin to be worthy of eternal life.

It is also a song of peace and a song of love. Those who sever them-selves from the communion of the saints do not sing a new song. For they have followed the divisive inclination of the old self, not the inspiration of the new love. What is there in this new love? Peace, the bond of a holy society, a close and spiritual union, and a building of living stones! Where is this building? It is not in any one place but throughout the world. This is expressed in another Psalm: "Sing to the Lord a new song; sing to the Lord, all you lands."

The one who does sing a new song with the whole earth—sing what you will, let your tongue sound forth "Alleluia," utter it all day and all night. My ears are not so much bent to hear the voice of the singer, but I seek the deeds of the doer. For I question the singer and ask: "What is it that you are singing?" The singer answers: "Alleluia." What is "Alleluia"? "Praise the Lord." Come, let us praise the Lord together. If you praise the Lord, and I praise the Lord, why are we at variance? Love praises the Lord; discord blasphemes the Lord.

Commentary on Psalm 149, 1–2: CCL 40, 2178–2179

Proper 23 ✠ Friday

A reading from a commentary on Joel by Jerome, Priest, and Monk of Bethlehem [420]

"Return to me with all your heart" and show a spirit of repentance "with fasting, weeping and mourning"; so that while you fast now, later you may be satisfied, while you weep now, later you may laugh, while you mourn now, you may some day enjoy consolation. It is customary for those in sorrow or adversity to tear their garments. The gospel rec-ords that the high priest did this to exaggerate the charge against our Lord and Savior; and we read that Paul and Barnabas did so when they heard words of blasphemy. I bid you not to tear your garments but rather to "rend your hearts" which are laden with sin. Like wine skins, unless they have been cut open, they will burst of their own accord. After you have done this, return to the Lord your God, from whom you had been alienated by your sins. Do not despair of his mercy, no matter how great your sins, for great mercy will take away great sins.

For the Lord is "gracious and merciful" and prefers the conversion of a sinner rather than the sinner's death. Patient and generous in his mercy, he does not give in to human impatience but is willing to wait a long time for our repentance. So extraordinary is the Lord's mercy in the face of evil, that if we do penance for our sins, he regrets his own threat and does not carry out against us the sanctions he had threatened. So by the changing of our attitude, he himself is changed. But in this passage we should interpret "evil" to mean, not the opposite of virtue, but affliction, as we read in another place: "Sufficient for the day are its own evils." And, again: "If there is evil in the city, God did not create it."

In like manner, given all that we have said above—that God is kind and merciful, patient, generous with his forgiveness, and extraordinary in his mercy toward evil—lest the magnitude of his clemency make us lax and negligent, he adds this word through his prophet: "Who knows whether he will not turn and repent and leave behind him a blessing?" In other words, he says: I exhort you to repentance, because it is my duty, and I know that God is inexhaustibly merciful. As David says: "Have mercy on me, God, according to your great mercy, and in the depths of your compassion, blot out all my iniquities." But since we cannot know the depth of the riches and of the wisdom and knowledge of God, I will temper my statement, expressing a wish rather than taking anything for granted, and I will say: "Who knows whether he will not turn and repent?" Since he says, "Who," it must be understood that it is impossible or difficult to know for sure.

Commentary on Joel: PL 25, 967–968

Proper 23 ✠ Saturday

A reading from a sermon of Leo the Great, Bishop of Rome [461]

It cannot be doubted that the poor can more easily attain the blessing of humility than those who are rich. In the case of the poor, the lack of worldly goods is often accompanied by a quiet gentleness, whereas the rich are more prone to arrogance. Nevertheless, many wealthy people are disposed to use their abundance not to swell their own pride but to perform works of benevolence. They consider their greatest gain what they spend to alleviate the distress of others.

This virtue is open to all, no matter what their class or condition, because all can be equal in their willingness to give, however unequal they may be in earthly fortune. Indeed, their inequality in regard to worldly means is unimportant, provided they are found equal in spiritual possessions. Blessed, therefore, is that poverty which is not trapped by the love of temporal things and does not seek to be enriched by worldly wealth, but desires rather to grow rich in heavenly goods.

The apostles were the first after the Lord himself to provide us with an example of this generous poverty, when they all equally left their belongings at the call of the heavenly master. By an immediate conversion they were turned from the catching of fish to become fishers of souls, and by their own example they won many others to the imitation of their own faith. In these first children of the Church there was but one heart and one soul among all who believed. Abandoning all their worldly property and possessions in their dedicated poverty, they were enriched with eternal goods, and in accordance with the apostolic preaching, they rejoiced to have nothing of this world and to possess all things with Christ.

Therefore, when the apostle Peter was on his way up to the temple and was asked for alms by the lame beggar, he replied. "Silver and gold I have not; but what I have I give you. In the name of Jesus Christ of Nazareth, arise and walk." What is more sublime than this humility? And what could be richer than this poverty? Though Peter cannot assist with money, he can confer gifts of nature. With a word Peter brought healing to the one who had been lame from birth; he who did not give a coin with the emperor's image refashioned the image of Jesus in this person.

And by the riches of this treasure, not only did he help the one who recovered the power to walk, but also five thousand others who believed the preaching of the apostle because of this miraculous cure. Thus Peter, who in his poverty had no money to give to the beggar, bestowed such a bounty of divine grace that in restoring to health the feet of one person, he healed the hearts of many thousands of believers. He had found all of them lame; but he made them leap for joy in Christ.

Sermon 95, on the Beatitudes, 2–3: PL 54, 462

Proper 24 ✠ Sunday

A reading from the sermon On Pastors *by Augustine, Bishop of Hippo [430]*

There are shepherds who want to have the title of shepherd without wanting to fulfill a pastor's duties. Let us then recall what God says to his shepherds through the prophet. You must listen attentively; I must listen with fear and trembling.

"The word of the Lord came to me and said: Prophesy against the shepherds of Israel and speak to the shepherds of Israel." I have decided to speak to you on this passage. The Lord will help me to speak the truth if I do not speak on my own authority. For if I speak on my own authority, I will be a shepherd nourishing myself and not the sheep. However, if my words are the Lord's, then he is nourishing you no matter who speaks. "Thus says the Lord God: Shepherds of Israel, who have been nourishing only themselves! Should not the shepherds nourish the sheep?" In other words, true shepherds take care of their sheep, not themselves. This is the principal reason why God condemns those shepherds: they took care of themselves rather than their sheep. Who are they who nourish themselves? They are the shepherds the Apostle described when he said: "They all seek what is theirs and not what is Christ's."

I must distinguish carefully between two aspects of the role the Lord has given me, a role that demands a rigorous accountability, a role based on the Lord's greatness rather than on my own merit. The first aspect is that I am a Christian; the second, that I am a leader. I am a Christian for my own sake, whereas I am a leader for your sake; the fact that I am a Christian is to my own advantage, but I am a leader for your advantage.

Many persons come to God as Christians but not as leaders. Perhaps they travel by an easier road and are less hindered since they bear a lighter burden. In addition to the fact that I am a Christian and must give God an account of my life, I as a leader must give him an account of my stewardship as well.

Sermon 46, on Pastors, 1–2: CCL 41, 529–530

Proper 24 ✠ Monday

A reading from The City of God by Augustine, Bishop of Hippo [430]

Here, my dear Marcellinus, is the fulfillment of my promise, a book in which I have taken upon myself the task of defending the glorious City of God against those who prefer their own gods to the Founder of that City. I treat of it both as it exists in this world of time, a stranger among the ungodly, living by faith, and as it stands in the security of its everlasting seat. This security it now awaits in steadfast patience, until "justice returns to judgement"; but it is to attain it hereafter in virtue of its ascendancy over its enemies, when the final victory is won and peace established. The task is long and arduous; but God is our helper.

The City of God must bear in mind that among her very enemies are hidden her future citizens; and when confronted with them she must not think it a fruitless task to bear with their hostility until she finds them confessing the faith. In the same way, while the City of God is on pilgrimage in this world, she has in her midst some who are united with her in participation in the sacraments, but who will not join with her in the eternal destiny of the saints. Some of these are hidden; some are well known, for they do not hesitate to murmur against God, whose sacramental sign they bear, even in the company of his acknowledged enemies. At one time they join his enemies in filling the theaters, at another they join with us in filling the churches.

But, such as they are, we have less right to despair of the reformation of some of them, when some predestined friends, as yet unknown even to themselves, are concealed among our most open enemies. In truth, those two cities are interwoven and intermixed in this era, and await separation at the last judgment. My task, as far as I shall receive divine assistance, will be to say what I think necessary in explanation of the origin, development, and appointed end of those two cities. And this I shall do to enhance the glory of the City of God, which will shine the more brightly when set in contrast with cities of other allegiance.

It is therefore God, the author and giver of felicity, who, being the one true God, gives earthly dominion both to good people and to evil. And he does this not at random or, as one may say, fortuitously, because he is God, not Fortune. Rather he gives in accordance with the order of events in history, an order completely hidden from us, but perfectly known to God himself. Yet God is not bound in subjection to this order of events. He is himself in control, as the master of events, and arranges the order of things as a governor. As for felicity, he grants that only to the good. People may have this happiness—or not have it—when they are slaves, or when they are rulers. But it can only be enjoyed in its fullness in that life where no one is any longer a slave. The reason why God gives worldly dominions both to the good and the evil is this: to prevent any of his worshipers who are still infants in respect of moral progress from yearning for such gifts from him as if they were of any importance.

This is the sacrament, the hidden meaning, of the Old Testament, where the New Testament lay concealed. In the Old Testament the promises and gifts are of earthly things; but even then people of spiritual perception realized, although they did not yet proclaim the fact for all to hear, that by those temporal goods eternity was signified; they understood also what were the gifts of God which constituted true felicity.

City of God 1, Preface, 35; 4, 33: CCL 47, 1, 33–34, 126–127

Proper 24 ✠ Tuesday

A reading from The City of God by Augustine, Bishop of Hippo [430]

The heroes of Rome belonged to an earthly city, and the aim set before them, in all their acts of duty for her, was the safety of their country, and a kingdom not in heaven, but on earth; not in life eternal, but in the process where the dying pass away and are succeeded by those who will die in their turn. What else was there for them to love save glory? For, through glory, they desired to have a kind of life after death on the lips of those who praised them.

To such as these God was not going to give eternal life with his angels in his own Heavenly City, the City to which true religion leads, which renders the supreme worship [in the Greek, *latreia*] only to the one true God. If God had not granted to them the earthly glory of an empire which surpassed all others, they would have received no reward for the good qualities, the virtues, that is, by means of which they labored to attain that great glory. When such people do anything good, their sole motive is the hope of receiving glory from their fellows; and the Lord refers to them when he says, "I tell you in truth, they have received their reward in full." They took no account of their own material interests compared with the common good, that is the commonwealth and the public purse; they resisted the temptations of avarice; they acted for their country's well-being with disinterested concern; they were guilty of no offense against the law; they succumbed to no sensual indulgence. By such immaculate conduct they labored towards honors, power and glory, by what they took to be the true way. And they were honored in almost all nations; they imposed their laws on many peoples; and today they enjoy renown in the history and literature of nearly all races. They have no reason to complain of the justice of God, the supreme and true. They have received their reward in full.

Very different is the reward of the saints. Here below they endure obloquy for the City of God, which is hateful to the lovers of this world. That City is eternal; no one is born there, because there no one dies. There is the true felicity, which is no goddess, but the gift of God. From there we have received the pledge of our faith, in that we sigh for her beauty while on our pilgrimage. In that City the sun does not rise on the good and on the evil; the sun of righteousness spreads its light only on the good; there the public treasury needs no great efforts for its enrichment at the cost of private poverty; for there the common stock is the treasury of truth.

But more than this; the Roman Empire was not extended and did not attain to glory in the world's eyes simply for this, that people of this stamp should be accorded this kind of reward. It had this further purpose, that the citizens of that Eternal City, in the days of their pilgrimage, should fix their eyes steadily and soberly on those examples and observe what love they should have towards the City on high, in view of life eternal, if the earthly city had received such devotion from her citizens, in their hope of glory in the sight of others.

Let us consider all the hardships these [Roman] conquerors made light of, all the sufferings they endured, and the desires they suppressed to gain the glory of others. They deserved to receive that glory as a reward for such virtues. Let this thought avail to suppress pride in us. That City, in which it has been promised that we shall reign, differs from this earthly city as widely as the sky from the earth, life eternal from temporal joy, substantial glory from empty praises, the society of angels from the society of humans, the light of the Maker of the sun and moon from the light of the sun and moon. Therefore the citizens of so great a country should not suppose that they have achieved anything of note if, to attain that country, they have done something good, or endured some ills, seeing that those Romans did so much and suffered so much for the earthly country they already possessed.

This being so, is it such a great thing that one should despise, for the sake of that Eternal and Heavenly Country, all the attractions of this present life, however beguiling, if for the sake of this temporal and earthly country Brutus had the strength to kill his sons, a thing which that other country compels no one to do? It is surely a harder thing to put one's children to death, than to do what has to be done for that Celestial Country: to give to the poor the possessions which one had supposed should be collected and preserved for one's children, or to let them go, if a temptation should appear which made that course necessary for the sake of faith and righteousness. Happiness, whether for us or for our children, is not the result of earthly riches, which must either be lost by us in our lifetime or else must pass after our death into the possession of those we do not know or, it may be, of those whom we do not wish to have them. It is God who gives happiness; for he is the true wealth of our souls.

City of God 5, 14–18: CCL 47, 148–151

Proper 24 ✠ Wednesday

A reading from The City of God by Augustine, Bishop of Hippo [430]

The City of God is vouched for by those Scriptures whose supremacy over every product of human genius does not depend on the chance impulses of the minds of mortals, but is manifestly due to the guiding power of God's supreme providence, and exercises sovereign authority over the literature of all humanity. Now, in this Scripture we find these words, "Glorious things have been spoken of you, City of God", and in another psalm, "The Lord is great, and to be highly praised in the City of our God, in his holy mountain, spreading joy over the whole earth." And soon afterwards in the same psalm, "As we have heard, so have we seen, in the City of the Lord of Hosts, in the City of our God: God has founded that City for eternity." Again, in yet another psalm, "The swift stream of the river brings gladness to the City of God: the Most High has sanctified his tabernacle; God in her midst will not be shaken."

From such testimonies as these—and it would take too long to quote them all—we have learnt that there is a City of God: and we have longed to become citizens of that City, with a love inspired by its Founder. But the citizens of the earthly city prefer their own gods to the Founder of this Holy City, not knowing that he is the God of gods. My task is to discuss, to the best of my power, the rise, the development and the destined ends of the two cities, the earthly and the heavenly, the cities which we find, as I have said, interwoven, as it were, in this present transitory world, and mingled with one another.

Although there are many great peoples throughout the world, living under different customs in religion and morality and distinguished by a complex variety of languages, arms, and dress, it is still true that there have come into being only two main divisions, as we may call them, in human society: and we are justified in following the lead of our Scriptures and calling them two cities. There is, in fact, one city of people who choose to live by the standard of the flesh, another of those who choose to live by the standard of the spirit. The citizens of each of these desire their own kind of peace, and when they achieve their aim, that is the kind of peace in which they live.

City of God 11, 1; 14, 1; CCL 48, 321, 414

Proper 24 ✠ Thursday

A reading from The City of God by Augustine, Bishop of Hippo [430]

The two cities were created by two kinds of love: the earthly city was created by self-love reaching the point of contempt for God, the Heavenly City by the love of God carried as far as contempt of self. In fact, the earthly city glories in itself, the Heavenly City glories in the Lord. The former looks for glory from other people, the latter finds its highest glory in God, the witness of a good conscience. The earthly lifts up its head in its own glory, the Heavenly City says to its God: "My glory; you lift up my head." In the former, the lust for domination lords it over its princes as over the nations it subjugates; in the other both those put in authority and those subject to them serve one another in love, the rulers by their counsel, the subjects by obedience. The one city loves its own strength shown in its powerful leaders; the other says to its God, "I will love you, my Lord, my strength."

Consequently, in the earthly city its wise people who live by human standards have pursued the goods of the body or of their own mind, or of both. Or those of them who were able to know God "did not honor him as God, nor did they give thanks to him, but they dwindled into futility in their thoughts, and their senseless heart was darkened: in asserting their wisdom"—that is, exalting themselves in their wisdom, under the domination of pride—"they became foolish, and changed the glory of the imperishable God into an image representing a perishable human, or birds or beasts or reptiles"—for in the adoration of idols of this kind they were either leaders or followers of the general public— "and they worshiped and served created things instead of the Creator, who is blessed for ever." In the Heavenly City, on the other hand, our only wisdom is the devotion which rightly worships the true God, and looks for its reward in the fellowship of the saints, not only holy people but also holy angels, "so that God may be all in all".

One of these cities, the earthly, has created for herself such false gods as she wanted, from any source she chose—even creating them out of mortals—in order to worship them with sacrifices. The other city, the Heavenly City on pilgrimage in this world, does not create false gods. She herself is the creation of the true God, and she herself is to be his own true sacrifice. Nevertheless, both cities alike enjoy the good things, or are afflicted with the adversities of this temporal state, but with a different faith, a different expectation, a different love, until they are separated by the final judgment, and each receives her own end, of which there is no end.

City of God 14, 28; 18, 54: CCL 48, 451–452, 656

Proper 24 ✠ Friday

A reading from The City of God by Augustine, Bishop of Hippo [430]

It is clear to me that my next task is to discuss the appointed ends of these two cities, the earthly and the heavenly. My purpose is to make clear the great difference between their hollow realities and our hope, the hope given us by God. For our Final Good is that for which other things are to be desired, while it is itself to be desired for its own sake. The Final Evil is that for which other things are to be shunned, while it is itself to be shunned on its own account. Thus when we now speak of the Final Good we do not mean the end of good whereby good is finished so that it does not exist, but the end whereby it is brought to final perfection and fulfilment. And by the Final Evil we do not mean the finish of evil whereby it ceases to be, but the final end to which its harmful effects eventually lead. These two ends, then, are the Supreme Good and the Supreme Evil.

If, therefore, we are asked what reply the City of God gives when asked about each of these points, and first what view it holds about the Ultimate Good and the Ultimate Evil, the reply will be that eternal life is the Supreme Good, and eternal death the Supreme Evil, and that to achieve the one and escape the other, we must live rightly. That is why the Scripture says: "The just one lives on the basis of faith." For we do not yet see our good, and hence we have to seek it by believing; and it is not in our power to live rightly, unless while we believe and pray we receive help from him who has given us the faith to believe that we must be helped by him.

City of God 19, 1, 4: CCL 48, 657, 664

Proper 24 ✠ Saturday

A reading from The City of God by Augustine, Bishop of Hippo [430]

The peace of the Heavenly City is a perfectly ordered and perfectly harmonious fellowship in the enjoyment of God, and a mutual fellowship in God; the peace of the whole universe is the tranquillity of order—

and order is the arrangement of things equal and unequal in a pattern which assigns to each its proper position.

We see, then, that all human use of temporal things is related to the enjoyment of earthly peace in the earthly city, whereas in the Heavenly City it is related to the enjoyment of eternal peace. And so long as we are in this mortal body, we are pilgrims in a foreign land, away from God; therefore we walk by faith, not by sight. But in the household of the just who "lives on the basis of faith" and who is still on pilgrimage, far from that Heavenly City, even those who give orders are the servants of those whom they appear to command. For they do not give orders because of a lust for domination but from a dutiful concern for the interests of others, not with pride in taking precedence over others, but with compassion in taking care of others.

City of God 19, 13–14: CCL 48, 679–682

Proper 25 ✠ Sunday

A reading from a commentary on Haggai by Cyril, Bishop of Alexandria [444]

When our Savior came, he appeared as a divine temple, glorious beyond any comparison, far more splendid and excellent than the older temple. He exceeded the old as much as worship in Christ and the gospels exceeds the cult of the laws, as much as truth exceeds its shadows.

Originally there was just one temple at Jerusalem, in which one people, the Israelites, offered their sacrifices. Since the only-begotten Son became like us, and as Scripture says, though he was "Lord and God, he has shone upon us," the rest of the world has been filled with places of worship. Now there are countless worshipers who honor the universal God with spiritual offerings and fragrant sacrifices. This, surely, is what Malachi foretold, speaking, as if in the person of God: "I am a great king, says the Lord; my name is honored among the nations, and everywhere there is offered to my name the fragrance of a pure sacrifice."

With justice, therefore, do we say that the Church will be more glorious. To those who are so solicitous for the Church and labor for its construction, Haggai declares that a gift will be made, a gift from heaven given by the Savior. That gift is Christ himself, the peace of all: "through whom we have access in the one Spirit to the Father." The prophet goes on to say: "I will give peace to this place and peace of soul to save all who lay the foundation to rebuild the temple." Christ too says somewhere: "My peace I give you." Paul will teach how profitable this is for those who love: "The peace of Christ," he says, "which surpasses all understanding will keep your minds and hearts." Isaiah, the seer, made the same prayer: "O Lord our God, give us peace, for you have given us everything." Once you have been found worthy of Christ's peace, you can easily save your soul and guide your mind to carry out exactingly the demands of virtue.

Haggai, therefore, declares that peace will be given to all who build. One builds the Church either as a teacher of the sacred mysteries, as one set over the house of God, or as one who works for one's own good by setting oneself forth as a living and spiritual stone "in the holy temple, God's dwelling place in the Spirit." The results of these efforts will profit such people so that all will be able to gain their own salvation without difficulty.

Commentary on Haggai 14: PG 71, 1047–1050

Proper 25 ✠ Monday

A reading from The City of God by Augustine, Bishop of Hippo [430]

A household of human beings whose life is not based on faith is in pursuit of an earthly peace based on the things belonging to this temporal life and on its advantages, whereas a household of human beings whose life is based on faith looks forward to the blessings which are promised as eternal in the future, making use of earthly and temporal things like pilgrims in a foreign land who do not let themselves be taken in by them or be distracted from their course towards God, but rather treat them as supports which help them more easily to bear the burdens of "the corruptible body which weighs heavy on the soul." They must on no account be allowed to increase the load. Thus both kinds of people and both kinds of households alike make use of the things essential for this mortal life; but each has its own very different end in making use of them. So also the earthly city, whose life is not based on faith, aims at an earthly peace, and it limits the harmonious agreement of citizens concerning the giving and obeying of orders to the establishment of a kind of compromise between human wills about the things relevant to mortal life. In contrast, the Heavenly City—or rather that part of it which is on pilgrimage in this condition of mortality, and which lives on the basis of faith—must needs make use of this peace also, until this mortal state, for which this kind of peace is essential, passes away. And therefore, it leads what we may call a life of captivity in this earthly city as in a foreign land, although it has already received the promise of redemption, and the gift of the Spirit as a kind of pledge of it; and yet it does not hesitate to obey the laws of the earthly city by which those things which are designed for the support of this mortal life are regulated; and the purpose of this obedience is that, since this mortal condition is shared by both cities, a harmony may be preserved between them in things that are relevant to this condition.

While this Heavenly City, therefore, is on pilgrimage in this world, she calls out citizens from all nations and so collects a society of aliens, speaking all languages. She takes no account of any difference in customs, laws, and institutions, by which earthly peace is achieved and preserved—not that she annuls or abolishes any of those; rather, she maintains them and follows them (for whatever divergences there are among the diverse nations, those institutions have one single aim— earthly peace), provided that no hindrance is presented thereby to the religion which teaches that the one supreme and true God is to be worshiped. Thus even the Heavenly City in her pilgrimage here on earth makes use of the earthly peace and defends and seeks the compromise between human wills in respect of the provisions relevant to the mortal nature of humankind, so far as may be permitted without detriment to true religion and piety. In fact, that City relates the earthly peace to the heavenly peace, which is so truly peaceful that it should be regarded as the only peace deserving the name, at least in respect of the rational creation. For this peace is the perfectly ordered and completely harmonious fellowship in the enjoyment of God, and of each other in God. When we arrive at that state of peace, there will be no longer a life that ends in death, but a life that is life in sure and sober truth. This peace the Heavenly City possesses in faith while on its pilgrimage, and it lives a life of righteousness based on this faith.

City of God 19, 17: CCL 48, 683–685

Proper 25 ✠ Tuesday

A reading from The City of God by Augustine, Bishop of Hippo [430]

It is completely irrelevant to the Heavenly City what dress is worn or what manner of life adopted by each person who follows the faith that is the way to God, provided that these do not conflict with the divine instructions. Hence, when even philosophers become Christians, they are not obliged to alter their mode of dress or their dietary habits, which offer no hindrance to religion. The only change required is in their false teachings. Thus peculiar behavior is to that city a matter of no importance at all, if there is nothing indecent or immoderate in that behavior. As for the three kinds of life, the life of leisure, the life of action, and the combination of the two, any, to be sure, might spend their lives in any of these ways without detriment to their faith, and might thus attain to the everlasting rewards. What does matter is the answers to these questions: What do they possess as a result of their love of truth? And what do they pay out in response to the obligations of Christian love? For no one ought to be so leisured as to take no thought in that leisure for the interest of a neighbor, nor so active as to feel no need for the contemplation of God. The attraction of a life of leisure ought not to be the prospect of lazy inactivity, but the chance for the investigation and discovery of truth, on the understanding that each person makes some progress in this, and does not grudgingly withhold new discoveries from another.

In the life of action, on the other hand, what is to be treasured is not a place of honor or power in this life, since "everything under the sun is vanity" but the task itself that is achieved by means of that place of honor and that power—if that achievement is right and helpful, that is, if it serves to promote the well-being of the common people, for, as we have already argued, this well-being is according to God's intention. That is why the Apostle says: "Anyone who aspires to the episcopate aspires to an honorable 'task.'" He wanted to explain what *episcopate* means; it is the name of a task, not an honor. It is, in fact, a Greek word, derived from the fact that one who is put in authority over others "superintends" them, that is, has responsibility for them. For the Greek *skopos* means "intention" (in the sense of "direction of the attention"); and so we may, if we wish, translate *epi-skopein* as "super-intend". Hence "bishops" who have set their heart on a position of eminence rather than an opportunity for service should realize that they are no bishops.

City of God 19, 19: CCL 48, 686–687

Proper 25 ✠ Wednesday

A reading from The City of God by Augustine, Bishop of Hippo [430]

It is God who made the world, filled with all good things, things accessible to sense, and those perceived by the understanding; and in the world his greatest work was the creation of spirits, to whom he gave intelligence, making them capable of contemplating him, able to apprehend him; and he bound them together in one fellowship, which we call the Holy and Heavenly City, in which God himself is for those spirits the means of their life and their felicity, is, as it were, their common life and food. He has bestowed on these intellectual natures the power of free choice, which enabled them, if they so chose, to desert God, that is, to abandon their felicity, with misery to follow immediately. He foreknew that some of the angels, in their pride, would wish to be self-sufficient for their own felicity, and hence would forsake their true good; and yet he did not deprive them of this power, judging it an act of greater power and greater goodness to bring good even out of evil than to exclude the existence of evil. There would not, in fact, have been any evil at all, had not that nature which was capable of change (although good and created by the supreme God who is also the changeless good, who made all things good) produced evil for itself by sinning. This sin is itself the evidence that proves that the nature was created good; for if it had not itself been a great good, although not equal to the Creator, then assuredly this apostasy from God, as from their light, could not have been their evil.

And God made humans also upright, with the same power of free choice, as animals of earth, yet worthy of heaven if they adhered to the author of their being, but, by the same token, destined, if they abandoned God, for a misery appropriate to their kind of nature. Now God foreknew that human beings would sin by breaking God's law through their apostasy from God; and yet, as in the case of the angels, God did not deprive them of the power of free choice, foreseeing, at the same time, the good that he was to bring out of human evil. For out of this mortal progeny, so rightly and justly condemned, God by his grace is gathering a people so great that from them he may fill the place of the fallen angels and restore their number. And thus that beloved Heavenly City will not be deprived of its full number of citizens; it may perhaps rejoice in a still more abundant population.

City of God 22, 1: CCL 48, 806–807

Proper 25 ✠ Thursday

A reading from The City of God by Augustine, Bishop of Hippo [430]

Now let us see, as far as the Lord deigns to help us to see, what the saints will be doing in their immortal and spiritual bodies, when the flesh will no longer be living "according to the flesh" but "according to the Spirit."

And yet, to tell the truth, I do not know what will be the nature of that activity, or rather of that rest and leisure. I have never seen it with my physical sight; and if I were to say that I had seen it with my mind—with my intellect—what is the human understanding, in capacity or in quality, to comprehend such unique perfection? For there will be that "peace of God which," as the Apostle says, "is beyond all understanding."

But we, in our measure, are made partakers of his peace; and so we know the perfection of peace in ourselves, peace among ourselves, and peace with God, according to our standard of perfection. Likewise the angels know it, in their measure. But human beings in their present state know it in a far lower degree, however highly developed may be their intellectual powers. We must remember what a great apostle it was who said, "Our knowledge is partial, and our prophesying is partial, until perfection comes," and, "We now see a dim reflection in a mirror; but then we shall see face to face." This is how the holy angels see already, those who are called "our" angels, because we have been rescued from the power of darkness, we have received the pledge of the Spirit, and have been transferred to the kingdom of Christ, and so we already begin to belong to those angels with whom we shall share the possession of that holy and most delightful City of God. Thus those angels of God are also "our" angels, in the same way as the Christ of God is "our" Christ. They are God's angels because they have not abandoned God; they are our angels because they have begun to have us as their fellow-citizens. And the Lord Jesus said: "Take care not to despise any of these little ones; for I tell you that their angels in heaven always see the face of my Father who is in heaven." Therefore we also shall see as they see already; but we do not as yet see like this. That is why the Apostle says, as I have already quoted, "Now we see a puzzling reflection in a mirror; but then we shall see face to face." And so this vision is reserved for us as the reward of faith; and the apostle John speaks of the vision in these words: "When he is fully revealed, we shall be like him, because we shall see him as he is."

City of God 22, 29: CCL 48, 856–857

Proper 25 ✠ Friday

A reading from The City of God by Augustine, Bishop of Hippo [430]

How great will be that felicity [of the City of God in its perpetual Sabbath], where there will be no evil, where no good will be withheld, where there will be leisure for the praises of God, who will be all in all!

What other occupation could there be, in a state where there will be no inactivity of idleness, and yet no toil constrained by want? I can think of none. And this is the picture suggested to my mind by the sacred canticle, when I read or hear the words: "Blessed are those who dwell in your house; they will be always praising you!"

All the limbs and organs of the body, no longer subject to decay, the parts which we now see assigned to various essential functions, will then be freed from all such constraint, since full, secure, certain and eternal felicity will have displaced necessity; and all those parts will contribute to the praise of God. For even those elements in the bodily harmony of which I have already spoken, the harmonies which, in our present state, are hidden, will then be hidden no longer. Dispersed internally and externally throughout the whole body, and combined with other great and marvelous things that will then be revealed, they will kindle our rational minds to the praise of the great Artist by the delight afforded by a beauty that satisfies the reason.

I am not rash enough to attempt to describe what the movements of such bodies will be in that life, for it is quite beyond my power of imagination. However, everything there will be lovely in its form, and lovely in motion and in rest, for anything that is not lovely will be excluded. And we may be sure that where the spirit wills there the body will straightway be; and the spirit will never will anything but what is to bring new beauty to the spirit and the body.

There will be true glory, where no one will be praised in error or in flattery; there will be true honor, where it is denied to none who is worthy, and bestowed on none who is unworthy. And honor will not be courted by any unworthy claimant, for none but the worthy can gain admission there. There will be true peace, where none will suffer attack from within nor from any foe outside.

The reward of virtue will be God himself, who gave the virtue, together with the promise of himself, the best and greatest of all possible promises. For what did he mean when he said, in the words of the prophet, "I shall be their God, and they will be my people"? Did he not mean: "I shall be the source of their satisfaction; I shall be everything that they can honorably desire: life, health, food, wealth, glory, honor, peace and every blessing"? For that is also the correct interpretation of the Apostle's words: "so that God may be all in all." He will be the goal of all our longings; and we shall see him for ever; we shall love him without surfeit; we shall praise him without wearying. This will be the duty, the delight, the activity of all, shared by all who share the life of eternity.

City of God 22, 30: CCL 48, 862–863

Proper 25 ✠ Saturday

A reading from The City of God by Augustine, Bishop of Hippo [430]

How will they, as the psalm says: "sing the mercies of the Lord for all eternity"? Nothing will give more joy to that [Heavenly] City than this song to the glory of the grace of Christ by whose blood we have been set free. There that precept will find fulfilment: "Be still, and know that I am God." That will truly be the greatest of Sabbaths; a Sabbath that has no evening, the Sabbath that the Lord approved at the beginning of creation, where it says: "God rested on the seventh day from all his works, which he had been doing; and God blessed the seventh day and made it holy, because on that day he rested from all his works, which God had begun to do."

We ourselves shall become that seventh day, when we have been replenished and restored by his blessing and sanctification. There we shall have leisure to be still, and we shall see that he is God, whereas we wished to be that ourselves when we fell away from him, after listening to the Seducer saying: "You will be like gods." Then we abandoned the true God, by whose creative help we should have become gods, but by participating in him, not by deserting him. For what have we done without him? We have "fallen away in his anger." But now restored by him and perfected by his greater grace we shall be still and at leisure for eternity, seeing that he is God, and being filled by him when he will be all in all. For all our good works, when they are understood as being his works, not ours, are then reckoned to us for the attainment of that Sabbath rest.

After this present age God will rest, as it were, on the seventh day, and he will cause us, who are the seventh day, to find our rest in him. The important thing is that the seventh will be our Sabbath, whose end will not be an evening, but the Lord's Day, an eighth day, as it were, which is to last for ever, a day consecrated by the resurrection of Christ, foreshadowing the eternal rest not only of the spirit but of the body also. There we shall be still and see; we shall see and we shall love; we shall love and we shall praise. Behold what will be, in the end, without end! For what is our end but to reach that kingdom which has no end?

City of God 22, 30: CCL 48, 864–866

Proper 26 ✠ Sunday

A reading from the book On Christian Formation by Gregory, Bishop of Nyssa [c. 394]

"Whoever is in Christ is a new creation; the old has passed away." Now by the "new creation" Paul means the indwelling of the Holy Spirit in a heart that is pure and blameless, free of all malice, wickedness or shamefulness. For when a soul has come to hate sin and has delivered itself as far as it can to the power of virtue, it undergoes a transformation by receiving the grace of the Spirit. Then it is healed, restored and made wholly new. Indeed the two texts: "Purge out the old leaven that you may be a new one," and: "Let us celebrate the festival, not with the old leaven but with the unleavened bread of sincerity and truth," support those passages which speak about the new creation.

Yet the tempter spreads many a snare to trap the soul, and of itself human nature is too weak to defeat him. This is why the Apostle bids us to arm ourselves with heavenly weapons, when he says: "Put on the breastplate of righteousness and have your feet shod with the gospel of peace and have truth around your waist as a belt." Can you not see how many forms of salvation the Apostle indicates, all leading to the same path and the same goal? Following them to the heights of God's commandments, we easily complete the race of life. For elsewhere the Apostle says: "Let us run with fidelity the race that has been set before us, with our eyes on Jesus, the origin and the goal of our faith."

So one who openly despises the accolades of this world and rejects all earthly glory must also practice self-denial. Such self-denial means that you never seek your own will but God's, using God's will as a sure guide; it also means possessing nothing apart from what is held in common. In this way it will be easier for you to carry out your superior's commands promptly, in joy and in hope; this is required of Christ's servants who are redeemed for service to the community. For this is what the Lord wants when he says: "Whoever wishes to be first and great among you must be the last of all and a servant to all."

Our service of humanity must be given freely. One who is in such a position must be subject to everyone and serve others as if paying off a debt. Moreover, those who are in charge should work harder than the others and conduct themselves with greater submission than their own subjects. Their lives should serve as a visible example of what service means, and they should remember that those who are committed to their trust are held in trust from God.

Those, then, who are in a position of authority must look after others as conscientious teachers look after the young children who have been handed over to them by their parents. If both disciples and masters have this loving relationship, then subjects will be happy to obey whatever is commanded, while superiors will be delighted to lead their subjects to perfection. If you try to outdo one another in showing respect, your life on earth will be like that of the angels.

Book on Christian Formation: PG 46, 295–298

Proper 26 ✠ Monday

A reading from a letter by Anselm, Archbishop of Canterbury [1109]

Those who will have the grace to reign in the kingdom of heaven will see the realization of everything that they desire in heaven and on earth, and nothing that they do not want will be realized in heaven or on earth. The love which will unite God with those who will live there, and the latter among themselves, will be such that all will love one another as themselves, and all will love God more than themselves.

Hence, no one will have any other desire there than what God wills; and the desire of one will be the desire of all; and the desire of all and of each one will also be the desire of God. All together, and as one single person, will be one sole ruler with God, for all will desire one single thing and their desire will be realized. This is the good that, from the heights of heaven, God declares he will put on sale.

If someone asks at what price, here is the response: The one who offers a kingdom in heaven has no need of earthly money. No one can give God what already belongs to him, since everything that exists is his. Yet God does not give such a great thing unless one attaches value to it; he does not give it to one who does not appreciate it. For no one gives a prized posession to someone who attaches no value to it. Hence, although God has no need of your goods, he will not give you such a great thing as long as you disdain to love it: he requires only love, but without it nothing obliges him to give. Love, then, and you will receive the Kingdom. Love, and you will possess it.

And since to reign in heaven is nothing other than to adhere to God and all the saints, through love, in a single will, to the point that all together exercise only one power, love God more than yourself and you will already begin to have what you wish to possess perfectly in heaven. Put yourself at peace with God and with others—if the latter do not separate themselves from God—and you will already begin to reign with God and all the saints. For to the extent that you now conform to the will of God and to that of the others, God and all the saints will concur with your will. Hence, if you want to rule in heaven, love God and others as you should, and you will merit to be what you desire.

However, you will not be able to possess it to perfection unless you empty your heart of every other love. This is why those who fill their hearts with love for God and their neighbor have no other will than that of God—or that of another, provided it is not contrary to God. That is why they are faithful in praying as well as in carrying on a dialogue in their minds with heaven; for it is pleasing to them to desire God and to speak of someone whom they love, to hear that one spoken about, and to think of the beloved. It is also why they rejoice with those who are joyful, weep with those who are in pain, have compassion on the suffering, and give to the poor; for they love others as themselves.

Letter 112, to Hugh the Recluse: Opera Omnia, ed. Schmitt, 3, 245–246

Proper 26 ✠ Tuesday

A reading from a homily of John Chrysostom, Bishop of Constantinople [407]

Do we not offer sacrifice daily? We do indeed, but as a memorial of his death and this oblation is single and not manifold. But how can it be one and not many? Because it has been offered once for all, as was the ancient sacrifice in the holy of holies. This is the figure of that ancient sacrifice, as indeed it was of this one; for it is the same Jesus Christ we offer always, not now one victim and later another. The victim is always the same, so that the sacrifice is one. Are we going to say that because Christ is offered in many places, there are many Christs? Of course not. It is one and the same Christ everywhere; He is here in His entirety, and there in His entirety, one unique body. Just as He is one body, not many bodies, although offered in many places, so the sacrifice is one and the same. Our high-priest is the very same Christ Who has offered the sacrifice which cleanses us. The victim Who was offered then, Who cannot be consumed, is the self-same victim we offer now. "What we do is done as a memorial of what was done then." We do not offer a different sacrifice, but always the same one "or rather we accomplish the memorial of it."

Homily 17 on Hebrews 3: PG 63, 131

Proper 26 ✠ Wednesday

A reading from a sermon of Augustine, Bishop of Hippo [430]

Let me tell you plainly that you are suffering from an illusion if you have hastened to hear the Word without the intention of putting into practice what you hear. Try to realize that if it is a good thing to hear the Word, it is much better to put it into practice. If you do not listen to it, you neglect hearing it and you will not build anything. If you listen to it and fail to act accordingly, you will be constructing a ruin.

In this regard, the Lord makes a suggestion by means of a very exact comparison. He tells us: "Anyone who hears my words and puts them into practice is like the wise person who built a house on a rock. When the rainy season set in, the torrents came and the winds blew and buffeted the house. It did not collapse." Why did it not collapse? Because "it had been solidly set on rock." Hence, to listen and to put into practice is to build on rock. And by the mere fact of listening we are already in the process of building.

"Anyone," our Lord continues, "who hears my words but does not put them into practice is like the foolish person who built" also. But what did the foolish build? That one also built a house. But because the foolish one did not put into practice what was heard, this did not do any good, for the house was "built on sandy ground." One then builds on sandy ground who listens but fails to act. And one builds on rock who listens and puts into practice. But whoever refuses to listen builds neither on sandy ground nor on rock. And note what follows: "The rains fell, the torrents came, the winds blew and lashed against that house. It collapsed under all this and was completely ruined."

Someone might say to me: "What is the use of listening if there is no intention of acting upon what one hears? For if I listen without putting into practice I shall construct a ruin. Is it not safer to refrain from listening to anything?"

The Lord did not want to consider this attitude in his comparison, but he has given us what is necessary to determine its value. In this world, there are constant rains, winds, torrents. If you build neither on rock nor on sand, since you refuse to listen, it means you will be without any protection. Rain comes, torrents come: will you then be secure when you are carried away for want of a shelter? Reflect carefully, therefore, on the decision you will make. You will not be secure—as you might imagine you are—because you have failed to listen. Being without protection and having no shelter of any sort, you will, of necessity, be cast down, carried away, submerged. If it is a bad thing to build on sand, it is just as bad not to build anything. So we can conclude that there is nothing better than to build on rock. It is bad to refuse to listen, and it is just as bad to listen but to refuse to act. "Put the Word into practice. Be not satisfied with merely listening; that would be to become a victim of an illusion."

Sermon 179, 8–9: PL 38, 970–971

Proper 26 ✠ Thursday

A reading from a homily of John Chrysostom, Bishop of Constantinople [407]

Prayer, loving conversation with God, is the supreme good. It is both a relationship with God and union with him. As the eyes of the body are made sharper by the sight of light, so the soul yearning for God is illumined by his ineffable light. Prayer is not the result of an external attitude; it comes from the heart. It is not limited to set hours or minutes, but, night and day, it is a continuous activity.

It is not enough to direct one's thoughts to God when concentrating exclusively on prayer; even when absorbed in other occupations—such as, caring for the poor, or some other concern in the way of a good or useful work—it is important to combine the work with desire for and remembrance of God. For thus you will be able to offer the Lord a very pleasing food from the universe, seasoned with the salt of love for God.

Prayer is the light of the soul, true knowledge of God, a mediating activity between God and humanity. Through it, the soul rises heavenward and embraces the Savior with ineffable love. As a suckling to its mother, it cries to God, weeping, thirsting for the divine milk. It expresses its deepest desires and receives gifts greater than anything on earth. Prayer, by which we respectfully present ourselves to God, is the joy of the heart and the soul's rest.

Prayer brings the soul to the heavenly fountain, satisfies the soul with this draught, and raises up in it "a fountain leaping up to provide eternal life." Prayer gives a real assurance of the good things to come, in faith, and makes present blessings more recognizable. Do not imagine that prayer consists only in words. It is a leap to God, an inexpressible love that is not of our making, as the Apostle says: "We do not know how to pray as we ought; but the Spirit himself makes intercession for us with groanings that cannot be expressed in speech."

Such prayer, when the Lord grants it to anyone, is a treasure that cannot be taken away, a heavenly food that satisfies the soul. One who tastes it is filled with an eternal desire for God, such a devouring flame that it kindles the heart. Let this fire flare up in you in all its fullness, to adorn the dwelling place of the heart with kindness and humility, to make it shine with the light of righteousness, and to polish its floor with good deeds.

Hence, adorn your house and instead of mosaics decorate it with faith and magnanimity. And as a finishing touch put prayer at the top of your building. Then you will have prepared a house worthy to receive the Lord, as a royal place, and you yourself, through grace, will already be possessing him, in a certain manner, in the temple of your soul.

Homily 6, on Prayer: PG 64, 462D–463B, 466

Proper 26 ✠ Friday

A reading from a homily of John Chrysostom, Bishop of Constantinople [407]

Nothing is more frigid than a Christian who is not concerned with saving others. You cannot in this respect plead poverty; the woman who contributed her last two copper coins to the collection box will rise up to accuse you. So will Peter who said: "I have neither silver nor gold," and Paul who was so poor that he often went hungry for lack of necessary food. Neither can you point to your humble birth: for they were also little people of the lower class. Ignorance will serve as no better excuse for you: they also were unlettered. Even if you are a slave or a fugitive, you can still do your part; such was Onesimus, and look to what he was called. And do not bring up infirmity: Timothy was subject to frequent illness. No matter who you are, you can be useful to your neighbor if you are willing to do what you can.

Do you see how sturdy, fair, well-shaped, graceful, and magnificent are the trees that do not bear fruit? Yet if we have occasion to possess a garden, we prefer pomegranate and olive trees filled with fruit. Sterile trees are there for appearance rather than utility; and if they can be useful, it is only in a very limited way. Such are those persons who consider only their own interest. And such persons do not even attain this end, for they are good only to be rejected, whereas the trees can be used to build houses. The foolish virgins had purity, grace, and modesty, but they were not useful to anyone because they saw themselves rejected.

Such are also those persons who do not assuage Christ's hunger. Note well that none of them is reproached for private sins—fornication, perjury, and the like—but only for not having been useful to others. I ask you, is someone who acts in this fashion a Christian? If the leaven mixed with the flour does not cause it to rise, is it truly leaven? If perfume does not have a pleasing fragrance for those who come near, do we call it perfume?

Do not say that it is impossible to lead others into the fold, for if you are a Christian it is impossible not to do so. Indeed, if it is true that there is no contradiction in nature, what we have said is just as true, for it stems from the very nature of a Christian. If you claim that a Christian cannot be useful, you dishonor God and you behave like a liar. It is easier for light to be darkness than for a Christian not to send forth light. Do not declare something impossible when it is the contrary that is impossible. Do not dishonor God.

Homily 20 on Acts 3–4: PG 60, 162–164

Proper 26 ✠ Saturday

A reading from a commentary on the psalms by Hilary,
Bishop of Poitiers [367]

God had chosen Zion for his abode and the place of his rest. But Zion has been destroyed. Where will the Lord's eternal seat now be? Where his eternal rest? What temple will he inhabit? The temple about which it is stated: "You are the temple of God, and the Spirit of God dwells in you." Here we have the house and temple of God, filled with his teaching and his power, and capable of lodging God in the sanctuary of the heart. It is this temple to which the Prophet had borne witness: "Your temple is holy, O Lord; it is admirable in justice." The holiness, justice, and temperance of human beings constitute the temple of God.

Hence, God must build his house. Its foundations must rest on the prophets and apostles. It must be lifted up on living stones, be balanced on the cornerstone, be built up by the mutual union of its elements to the height of human perfection and the measure of the body of Christ, and finally be adorned with the grace and beauty of spiritual gifts. Israel, now in captivity, will continue the construction of the house when the fullness of the nations has come. This house will be multiplied into numerous houses, thanks to the labors of the faithful, and unto each of us for the adornment and the extension of the blessed city.

The Lord has been the watchful guardian of this city for a long time. He protected Abraham on his journeys, spared Isaac when he was about to be sacrificed, and called Joseph to power after he had been sold. He strengthened Moses against the Pharaoh and chose Joshua as military leader. He delivered David from all dangers and granted Solomon the gift of wisdom. He assisted the prophets, caught up Elijah to heaven and called Elisha. He fed Daniel and refreshed the young men in the furnace. Through an angel he informed Joseph of his virginal conception and reassured Mary. He sent John as the precursor and chose the apostles. He entreated his Father saying: "Holy Father, keep them"; and finally after the passion he himself promised to watch over us saying: "Know that I am with you always, until the end of the world." Such is the eternal guardianship of this blessed and holy City which is made up of a great number who have come together in unity and forms in each one of us a City for God.

Commentary on Psalm 126, 7–9: PL 9, 696–697

Proper 27 ✠ Sunday

A reading from the treatise Against Heresies by Irenaeus, Bishop of Lyons [c. 202]

Those who see God will partake of life, for the splendor of God is life-giving. It is for this reason that he who is indiscernible, incomprehensible, and invisible offers himself to be seen, comprehended, and discerned by human beings: that he may give life to those who discern him and see him. For, if his greatness is inscrutable, his kindness also is inexpressible, and it is out of his kindness that he reveals himself and gives life to those who see him. It is impossible to live without life, and there is no life except by taking part in God, a partaking which consists of seeing God and enjoying his kindness.

In this way, then, people will see God in order to live, becoming immortal through this vision and attaining to God. This is what the prophets proclaimed, in figurative speech, that God would be seen by those who hear his spirit within them and ceaselessly look to his coming, as Moses said in Deuteronomy: "We have found out today that we can still live after God has spoken with us."

He who brings about all things in everyone is invisible and inexpressible, insofar as his power and grandeur are concerned, for all those he has made; however, he is not entirely unknown to them, for all come to know through his Word that there is only one God the Father, who contains all things and gives existence to all things, in accord with our Lord's words: "No one has ever seen God. It is God the only Son, ever at the Father's side, who has revealed him."

Thus from the beginning the Son is the Revealer of the Father, since from the beginning he was with the Father: the prophetic visions, the diversity of spiritual gifts, his ministries, the glorifying of the Father, all that, like a well-composed and harmonious melody he unfolded before the eyes of all at the appointed time for their benefit. Where, in fact, there is composition, there is melody; where there is melody, there is the appointed time; where there is an appointed time, there is advantage.

That is why the Word made himself the dispenser of the Father's grace, for the benefit of humanity, for whom he accomplished such great mysteries: revealing God to us and presenting us to God, safeguarding the invisibility of the Father, so that we should not come to despise God and might have a goal toward which to move. At the same time he made God visible to us through numerous mysteries lest, totally deprived of God, we should lose everything, even our very existence. For the glory of God is a living person, and the life of the person is the vision of God. If the revelation of God through creation gives life to all who live on earth, how much more does the manifestation of the Father through the Word give life to those who see God!

Against Heresies 4, 20, 5–7: SC 100, 641–649

Proper 27 ✠ Monday

A reading from the treatise Against Heresies by Irenaeus, Bishop of Lyons [c. 202]

Because he followed the Word of God spontaneously and freely in the generosity of his faith, Abraham became "God's friend." The Word of God conferred this friendship on Abraham not out of the Word's need for a human being (since he is perfect from the beginning—"Before Abraham came to be," he says, "I am"), but to enable him, who is good, to give Abraham eternal life. For God's friendship obtains incorruptibility for all who attain it.

Likewise in the beginning God formed Adam not out of a need for human beings but so that God might have someone in whom to place his benefits. For not only before Adam but before all creation the Word glorified the Father while remaining in him, and the Word was glorified by the Father as he himself says: "Do you now, Father, glorify me with glory at your side, a glory I had with you before the world began."

Nor did he command us to follow him out of need for our services but out of the desire to bestow salvation on us. To follow the Lord is to partake of salvation just as to follow the light is to partake of light.

When people are in the light, they do not illumine the light and make it shine, but they are illumined and made resplendent by the light. Far from contributing anything to it, they benefit from the light and are illumined by it.

The same is true of service rendered to God. It gives nothing to God for God does not need our service; but God bestows life, incorruptibility, and eternal glory on those who serve and follow him. He grants his benefits to those who serve him because they serve him; and on those who follow him because they follow him; but he does not receive any benefit from them, for he is perfect and in need of nothing. If God solicits our service, it is so that he, who is good and merciful, might be able to grant his benefits to those who persevere in his service.

Just as God is in need of nothing, so we are in need of communion with God. For our human glory consists in persevering in service to God. This is why our Lord said to his disciples: "It was not you who chose me, it was I who chose you," thus indicating that they did not glorify him by following him, but that by following the Son of God they were glorified by him.

Against Heresies 4, 13, 4–14, 1: SC 100, 537–541

Proper 27 ✠ Tuesday

A reading from a sermon of Leo the Great, Bishop of Rome [461]

The Lord has said: "I have come to call, not the self-righteous, but sinners." This means that no one can be saved except in the forgiveness of sins, and we do not know to what extent the grace of the Spirit can enrich those whom the wisdom of the world despises.

Let the people of God be holy and let them be good: holy, in order to turn away from what is prohibited; good, in order to act according to the commandments. It is a great thing, no doubt, to have the right faith and possess sound doctrine; and sobriety, meekness, and purity are virtues that deserve high praise; but all these virtues remain vain if they are not coupled with charity. And we ought not to say that an excellent conduct is fruitful if it does not issue from love.

Let believers then examine their own state of mind and carefully scrutinize the intimate sentiments of their heart. If they find some fruit of charity in their conscious self, let them have no doubt that God is in them. And that they may become more and more able to welcome so great a guest, let them persevere and grow in mercy which expresses itself in acts. If God is love, charity ought not to know any limits, for nothing that is limited can contain the divinity.

It is true, that all times are good for translating the good of charity into acts, and yet the time in which we live particularly demands practical charity. Those who desire to welcome the Lord with holiness of mind and body must principally endeavor to acquire that grace which contains the sum of the virtues and "covers a multitude of sins."

As we are now making ready to celebrate the greatest of all the mysteries, namely, that of the blood of Jesus Christ which washes away our iniquities, let us prepare ourselves principally by the sacrifice of mercy. We thus render to those who have offended us that which God has given us. May insults be cast into oblivion, may errors henceforth know nothing of torture, and may all offenses be set free from the fear of vengeance! May the penitentiaries have no one in them, and may the sad groans of those found guilty be no longer heard in the gloomy dungeon cells!

If any detain such prisoners for some misdemeanor or other, let them know well that they themselves are sinners. And, that they may obtain pardon, let them be glad to have found one to whom they can give pardon. And so, when we say, following the Lord's teaching: "forgive us the wrong we have done as we forgive those who wrong us," let us not doubt that, when we express our prayer, we will obtain the pardon of God.

We must also show more generous goodness toward the poor and to those who suffer from diverse forms of weakness, that more numerous voices may render thanks to God and our fasts may contribute to the relief of those who are in need. No devotedness of believers is more pleasing to the Lord than that of the one who does good to the poor. Where God finds merciful care for others, there he recognizes the image of his goodness.

Sermon 48, 2–5; PL 54, 299–300

Proper 27 ✠ Wednesday

A reading from the treatise On Christian Perfection *by Gregory, Bishop of Nyssa [c. 394]*

The life of the Christian has three distinguishing aspects: deeds, words and thought. Thought comes first, then words, since our words express openly the interior conclusions of the mind. Finally, after thoughts and words, comes action, for our deeds carry out what the mind has conceived. So when one of these results in our acting or speaking or thinking, we must make sure that all our thoughts, words and deeds are controlled by the divine ideal, the revelation of Christ. For then our thoughts, words and deeds will not fall short of the nobility of their implications.

What then must we do, we who have been found worthy of the name of Christ? Each of us must examine our thoughts, words and deeds, to see whether they are directed toward Christ or are turned away from him. This examination is carried out in various ways. Our deeds or our thoughts or our words are not in harmony with Christ if they issue from passion. They then bear the mark of the enemy who smears the pearl of the heart with the slime of passion, dimming and even destroying the luster of the precious stone.

On the other hand, if they are free from and untainted by every passionate inclination, they are directed toward Christ, the author and source of peace. He is like a pure, untainted stream. If you draw from him the thoughts in your mind and the inclinations of your heart, you will show a likeness to Christ, your source and origin, as the gleaming water in a jar resembles the flowing water from which it was obtained.

For the purity of Christ and the purity that is manifest in our hearts are identical. Christ's purity, however, is the fountainhead; ours has its source in him and flows out of him. Our life is stamped with the beauty of his thought. The inner and the outer self are harmonized in a kind of music. The mind of Christ is the controlling influence that inspires us to moderation and goodness in our behavior. As I see it, Christian perfection consists in this: sharing the titles which express the meaning of Christ's name, we bring out this meaning in our minds, our prayers and our way of life.

Treatise on Christian Perfection: PG 46, 283–286

Proper 27 ✠ Thursday

A reading from the Catechetical Instructions of Theodore, Bishop of Mopsuestia [428]

The most important point to grasp is that the food we take is a kind of sacrifice we perform. It is true that we commemorate our Lord's death in food and drink, believing that these are the memorials of his passion, since he said himself: "This is my body which is broken for you." But it is evident also that what we perform in the liturgy is a kind of sacrifice. "The duty of the High Priest of the New Covenant is to offer this sacrifice which revealed the nature of the New Covenant." It is clearly a sacrifice, although it is not something that is new or accomplished by the efforts of the bishop: it is a recalling of this true offering. Since the bishop performs, in symbol, signs of the heavenly realities, the sacrifice must manifest them, so that the bishop presents, as it were, an image of the heavenly liturgy. For we who perform our priestly office outside the Old Law could not be priests unless we bore the image of the heavenly realities. St Paul says this of Christ our Lord: "If he were on earth, he would not be a priest at all, since there are priests who offer gifts and sacrifices according to the Law. They serve a copy and shadow of the heavenly sanctuary."

In St. Paul's words, Christ our Lord, who is the High Priest of us all, does not "serve a copy and shadow of the heavenly sanctuary," like the liturgy according to the Law; he is "a minister in the sanctuary and the true tent which is set up not by human beings but by the Lord," to teach us the heavenly mysteries. When he speaks of "the true tent which is set up not by human beings but by the Lord," he refers to heaven, because the tent prescribed by the Law was made by mortals, whereas heaven is not made by mortals but by God. This is the tent, he means, of which Christ is the minister, since he has ascended into heaven, where he performs the liturgy on our behalf, using every means to draw us there as he promised.

Since we are called by him to a New Covenant, in St. Paul's words, we have received this salvation and this life in hope. Since we do not see them, but wait to "be away from the body and at home with the Lord," "we walk by faith, not by sight;" for we have not yet attained to the realities, we have not yet reached the heavenly blessings. We continue in faith until we ascend into heaven and go to our Lord, when we shall no longer see him in a mirror dimly, but face to face. We look forward to attaining to this state in reality at the resurrection, at the time God has ordained; in the meantime we approach the first-fruits of these blessings, Christ our Lord, the High Priest of our inheritance. Accordingly we are taught to perform in this world the symbols and signs of the blessings to come, and so, as people who enter into the enjoyment of the good things of heaven by means of the liturgy, we may possess in assured hope what we look for. So just as the true new birth is the birth to which we look forward at the resurrection, while what we undergo at baptism is a new symbolic birth, so too the true food of immortality is the food we hope to receive and will truly receive later by the gift of the Holy Spirit, while for the present we receive the food of immortality only in symbols or by means of symbols, through the grace of the Holy Spirit.

Baptismal Homily 4, 15–16, 18: Yarnold, 219–223

Proper 27 ✠ Friday

A reading from a commentary on Luke by Ambrose, Bishop of Milan [397]

Virtue has more than one countenance. The example of Martha and Mary shows us active devotedness in the works of Martha, and in Mary religious attention of the heart to the word of God. If such attention is united with profound faith, it is preferable to works, for it is written: "Mary has chosen the better portion and she shall not be deprived of it." Hence, we too should strive to possess what no one can take away from us, by listening attentively and without distraction. For even the seed of the heavenly word will be taken away, if it is sown on the footpath.

Be then animated with a desire for wisdom like Mary, for that is the greater and more perfect work. Let not the cares of the ministry prevent you from learning to know the heavenly word. Do not criticize, nor consider to be idlers those whom you find engaged in the study of wisdom. Did not Solomon, the peaceful, invite her to come and dwell with him? It is not a question of reproaching Martha for her good services; nevertheless, Mary is preferred for choosing the better portion. Jesus has manifold riches and he distributes them generously. The wiser of the two women has chosen what she has recognized as being the principal thing.

We see also that the apostles did not consider it preferable to neglect the word of God and serve tables. But both functions are a work of wisdom, for Stephen too was full of wisdom and was chosen as one who had to serve. Let, then, you who are serving leave to the teacher the task of teaching and let the one who teaches exhort and inspire the one who serves. For the body of the Church is one, and if its members are diverse they on that account need one another.

"The eye cannot say to the hand: 'I do not need you,' any more than the head can say to the feet: 'I do not need you.'" And the ear cannot deny that it belongs to the body. If certain members are more important, it does not mean that others are not necessary. Wisdom resides in the head; activity in the hands. "The wise," says Ecclesiastes, "have eyes in their heads," for those who are truly wise are those whose mind is in Christ, and on that account the inner eye is raised toward the heights.

Commentary on Luke 7, 85–86: CCL 14, 241–242

Proper 27 ✠ Saturday

A reading from an instruction by Columbanus, Celtic Abbot [615]

How blessed, how fortunate, are "those servants whom the Lord will find watchful when he comes." Blessed is the time of waiting when we stay awake for the Lord, the Creator of the universe, who fills all things and transcends all things.

How I wish he would awaken me, his humble servant, from the sleep of slothfulness, even though I am of little worth. How I wish he would enkindle me with that fire of divine love. The flames of his love burn beyond the stars; the longing for his overwhelming delights and the divine fire ever burn within me!

How I wish I might deserve to have my lantern always burning at night in the temple of my Lord, to give light to all who enter the house of my God. Give me, I pray you, Lord, in the name of Jesus Christ, your Son and my God, that love that does not fail so that my lantern, burning within me and giving light to others, may be always lighted and never extinguished.

Jesus, our most loving Savior, be pleased to light our lanterns, so that they may burn for ever in your temple, receiving eternal light from you, the eternal light, to lighten our darkness and to ward off from us the darkness of the world.

Give your light to my lantern, I beg you, my Jesus, so that by its light I may see that holy of holies which receives you as the eternal priest entering among the columns of your great temple. May I ever see you only, look on you, long for you; may I gaze with love on you alone, and have my lantern shining and burning always in your presence.

Loving Savior, be pleased to show yourself to us who knock, so that in knowing you we may love only you, love you alone, desire you alone, contemplate only you day and night, and always think of you. Inspire in us the depth of love that is fitting for you to receive as God. So may your love pervade our whole being, possess us completely, and fill all our senses, that we may know no other love but love for you who are everlasting. May our love be so great that the many waters of sky, land and sea cannot extinguish it in us: "many waters could not extinguish love."

May this saying be fulfilled in us also, at least in part, by your gift, Jesus Christ, our Lord, to whom be glory for ever and ever.

Instruction 12, 2–3: Opera, Dublin 1957, 112–114

Proper 28 ✠ Sunday

A reading from a commentary on John by Augustine, Bishop of Hippo [430]

Behold, even lamps bear witness to the day because of our weakness, for we cannot bear and look at the brightness of the day. Indeed, in comparison with unbelievers, we Christians are even now light; as the Apostle says: "There was a time when you were darkness, but now you are light in the Lord. Well, then, live as children of light." And elsewhere he says: "The night is far spent; the day is at hand. Let us cast off deeds of darkness and put on the armor of light. Let us live honorably as in daylight."

Yet, in comparison with the light of that day which is to come, even the day in which we now find ourselves is still night. "We possess," says the Apostle, "the prophetic message as something altogether reliable. Keep your attention closely fixed on it, as you would on a lamp shining in a dark place until the first streaks of dawn appear and the morning star rises in your hearts."

Therefore, when our Lord Jesus Christ comes, he will as the apostle Paul also says, bring to light what is hidden in darkness and manifest the intention of hearts, that everyone may receive praise from God. Then, in the presence of such a day, lamps will not be needed. No prophet shall then be read to us; no book of an apostle shall be opened. We shall not require the witness of John; we shall have no need of the gospel itself. Accordingly, when all these are taken away, all the Scriptures—which in the night of the world were as lamps kindled for us that we might not remain in darkness—shall also be taken out of the way, that they may not shine as if we needed them. Then the messengers of God by whom these were ministered to us shall themselves, together with us, behold that true and clear light.

You shall see that very light, from which a ray was sent aslant and through many windings into your dark heart, in its purity, for the seeing and bearing of which you are being purified. John himself says: "Dearly beloved, we are God's children now; what we shall later be has not yet come to light. We know that when it comes to light we shall be like him, for we shall see him as he is."

Treatise 35 on John 8–9; CCL 36, 321–322

Proper 28 ✠ Monday

A reading from the Catechetical Instructions of Cyril, Bishop of Jerusalem [386]

The one word faith can have two meanings. One kind of faith concerns doctrines. It involves the soul's ascent to and acceptance of some particular matter. It also concerns the soul's good, according to the words of the Lord: "Whoever hears my voice and believes in him who sent me has eternal life, and will not come to be judged." And again: "Whoever believes in the Son is not condemned, but has passed from death to life."

How great is God's love for humanity! Some good people have been found pleasing to God because of years of work. What they achieved by working for many hours at a task pleasing to God is freely given to you by Jesus in one short hour. For if you believe that Jesus Christ is Lord and that God raised him from the dead, you will be saved and taken up to paradise by him, just as he brought the thief there. Do not doubt that this is possible. After all, he saved the thief on the holy hill of Golgotha because of one hour's faith; will he not save you too since you have believed?

The other kind of faith is given by Christ by means of a special grace. "To one person wise sayings are given through the Spirit, to another perceptive comments by the same Spirit, to another faith by the same Spirit, to another gifts of healing." Now this kind of faith, given by the Spirit as a special favor, is not confined to doctrinal matters, for it produces effects beyond any human capability. If one who has this faith says to this mountain: "move from here to there," it will move. For when any say this in faith, believing it will happen and having no doubt in their hearts, they then receive that grace.

It is of this kind of faith, moreover, that it is said: "If you have faith like a grain of mustard seed." The mustard seed is small in size but it holds an explosive force; although it is sown in a small hole, it produces great branches, and when it is grown birds can nest there. In the same way faith produces great effects in the soul instantaneously. Enlightened by faith, the soul pictures God and sees him as clearly as any soul can. It circles the earth; even before the end of this world it sees the judgment and the conferring of promised rewards. So may you have the faith which depends on you and is directed to God, that you may receive from him that faith too which transcends human capacity.

Catechesis 5, 10–11; PG 33, 518–519

Proper 28 ✠ Tuesday

A reading from the First Instruction by Vincent of Lerins, Priest [c. 450]

Is there to be no development of religion in the Church of Christ? Certainly, there is to be development and on the largest scale.

Who can be so grudging to humanity, so full of hate for God, as to try to prevent it? But it must truly be development of the faith, not alteration of the faith. Development means that each thing expands to be itself, while alteration means that a thing is changed from one thing into another.

The understanding, knowledge and wisdom of one and all, of individuals as well as of the whole Church, ought then to make great and vigorous progress with the passing of the ages and the centuries, but only along its own line of development, that is, with the same doctrine, the same meaning and the same import.

The religion of souls should follow the law of development of bodies. Though bodies develop and unfold their component parts with the passing of the years, they always remain what they were. There is a great difference between the flower of childhood and the maturity of age, but those who become old are the very same people who were once young. Though the condition and appearance of one and the same individual may change, it is one and the same nature, one and the same person.

The tiny members of unweaned children and the grown members of young people are still the same members. Adults have the same number of limbs as children. Whatever develops at a later age was already present in seminal form; there is nothing new in old age that was not already latent in childhood.

There is no doubt, then, that the legitimate and correct rule of development, the established and wonderful order of growth, is this: in older people the fullness of years always brings to completion those members and forms that the wisdom of the Creator fashioned beforehand in their earlier years.

If, however, the human form were to turn into some shape that did not belong to its own nature, or even if something were added to the sum of its members or subtracted from it, the whole body would necessarily perish or become grotesque or at least be enfeebled. In the same way, the doctrine of the Christian religion should properly follow these laws of development, that is, by becoming firmer over the years, more ample in the course of time, more exalted as it advances in age.

In ancient times our ancestors sowed the good seed in the harvest field of the Church. It would be very wrong and unfitting if we, their descendants, were to reap, not the genuine wheat of truth but the intrusive growth of error.

On the contrary, what is right and fitting is this: there should be no inconsistency between first and last, but we should reap true doctrine from the growth of true teaching, so that when, in the course of time, those first sowings yield an increase it may flourish and be tended in our day also.

Commonitorium 23, 28–30: ed. Moxon, 88–92

Proper 28 ✠ Wednesday

A reading from the First Instruction by Vincent of Lerins, Priest [c. 450]

I have continually given the greatest pains and diligence to inquiring, from the greatest possible number of people who are outstanding in holiness and in doctrine, how I can secure a kind of fixed and, as it were, general and guiding principle for distinguishing the true Catholic Faith from the degraded falsehoods of heresy. And the answer that I receive is always to this effect; that if I wish, or indeed if anyone wishes, to detect the deceits of heretics that arise and to avoid their snares and to keep healthy and sound in a healthy faith, we ought, with the Lord's help, to fortify our faith in a twofold manner, firstly, that is, by the authority of God's Law, then by the tradition of the Catholic Church.

Here, it may be, someone will ask: Since the canon of Scripture is complete, and is in itself abundantly sufficient, what need is there to join to it the interpretation of the Church? The answer is that because of the very depth of Scripture all persons do not place one identical interpretation upon it. The statements of the same writer are explained by different people in different ways, so much so that it seems almost possible to extract from it as many opinions as there are people. Therefore, because of the intricacies of error, which is so multiform, there is great need for the laying down of a rule for the exposition of Prophets and Apostles in accordance with the standard of the interpretation of the Church Catholic:

Now in the Catholic Church itself we take the greatest care to hold "that which has been believed everywhere, always and by all."

That is truly and properly "Catholic," as is shown by the very force and meaning of the word, which comprehends everything almost universally.

We shall hold to this rule if we follow universality, antiquity, and consent. We shall follow universality if we acknowledge that one Faith to be true which the whole Church throughout the world confesses; antiquity, if we in no wise depart from those interpretations which it is clear that our ancestors and fathers proclaimed; consent, if in antiquity itself we keep following the definitions and opinions of all, or certainly nearly all, bishops and doctors alike.

Commonitorium 2–3: ed. Moxon, 7–11

Proper 28 ✠ Thursday

A reading from a commentary on John by Augustine, Bishop of Hippo [430]

"None come unto me unless the Father draws them." Do not think that you are drawn against your will; the will is drawn also by love. We must not be afraid of those who weigh words but are far from understanding what belongs above all to divine truth. They may find fault with this passage of Scripture and say to us: "How can I believe of my own free will if I am drawn to believe?" I answer: "It is not enough that you are moved by the will, for you are drawn also by desire."

What does this mean, to be drawn by desire? "Take delight in the Lord, and he will give you the desires of your heart." The heart has its own desires; it takes delight, for example, in the bread from heaven. The poet could say: "All are drawn by their own desire," not by necessity but by desire, not by compulsion but by pleasure. We can say then with greater force that one who finds pleasure in truth, in happiness, in justice, in everlasting life, is drawn to Christ, for Christ is all these things.

Are our bodily senses to have their desires, but not the will? If the will does not have its desires, how can Scripture say: "The peoples will find their hope under the shadow of your wings, they will drink their fill from the plenty of your house, and you will give them drink from the running stream of your delights, for with you is the fountain of life, and in your light we shall see light."

Show me one who loves; the lover knows what I mean. Show me one who is full of longing, one who is hungry, one who is a pilgrim and suffering from thirst in the desert of this world, eager for the fountain in the homeland of eternity; show me people like that, and they know what I mean. But if I speak to someone without feeling, such a person does not understand what I am saying.

You have only to show a leafy branch to a sheep, and it is drawn to it. If you show nuts to a child, it is drawn to them. The child runs to them because it is drawn, drawn by love, drawn without any physical compulsion, drawn by a chain attached to the heart. "All are drawn by their own desire." This is a true saying, and earthly delights and pleasures, set before those who love them, succeed in drawing them. If this is so, are we to say that Christ, revealed and set before us by the Father, does not draw us? What does the soul desire more than truth? Why then does the soul have hungry jaws, a spiritual palate as it were, sensitive enough to judge the truth, if not in order to eat and drink wisdom, justice, truth, eternal life?

"Blessed are those who hunger and thirst for justice," that is, here on earth. "They shall be satisfied," that is, in heaven. Christ says: I give each what each loves, I give all the object of their hope; they will see what they believed in, though without seeing it. What they now hunger for, they will eat; what they now thirst for, they will drink to the full. When? At the resurrection of the dead, for "I will raise them up on the last day."

Treatise 26 on John 4–6: CCL 36, 261–263

Proper 28 ✠ Friday

A reading from the Catechetical Instructions of Cyril, Bishop of Jerusalem [386]

In learning and professing the faith, you must accept and retain only the Church's present tradition, confirmed as it is by the Scriptures. Although not everyone is able to read the Scriptures, some because they have never learned to read, others because their daily activities keep them from such study, still so that their souls will not be lost through ignorance, we have gathered together the whole of the faith in a few concise articles.

Now I order you to retain this creed for your nourishment throughout life and never to accept any alternative, not even if I myself were to change and say something contrary to what I am now teaching, not even if some angel of contradiction, changed into an angel of light, tried to lead you astray. For "even if we, or an angel from heaven, should preach to you a gospel contrary to that which you have now received, let such a one be accursed in your sight."

So for the present be content to listen to the simple words of the creed and to memorize them; at some suitable time you can find the proof of each article in the Scriptures. This summary of the faith was not composed at any human whim; the most important sections were chosen from the whole Scripture to constitute and complete a comprehensive statement of the faith. Just as the mustard seed contains in a small grain many branches, so this brief statement of the faith keeps in its heart, as it were, all the religious truth to be found in Old and New Testament alike. That is why, beloved, you must consider and preserve the traditions you are now receiving. Inscribe them across your heart.

Observe them scrupulously, so that no enemy may rob any of you in an idle and heedless moment; let no heretic deprive you of what has been given to you. Faith is rather like depositing in a bank the money entrusted to you, and God will surely demand an account of what you have deposited. In the words of the Apostle: "I charge you before the God who gives life to all things, and before Christ who bore witness under Pontius Pilate in a splendid declaration," to keep unblemished this faith you have received, until the coming of our Lord Jesus Christ.

You have now been given life's great treasure; when he comes the Lord will ask for what he has entrusted to you. "At the appointed time he will reveal himself, for he is the blessed and sole Ruler, King of kings, Lord of lords. He alone is immortal, dwelling in unapproachable light. No person has seen or ever can see him." To him be glory, honor and power for ever and ever.

Catechesis 5, 12–13: PG 33, 519–523

Proper 28 ✠ Saturday

A reading from the Book of Maxims by Isidore, Bishop of Seville [636]

Prayer purifies us, reading instructs us. Both are good when both are possible. Otherwise, prayer is better than reading.

If we want to be always in God's company, we must pray regularly and read regularly. When we pray, we talk to God; when we read, God talks to us.

All spiritual growth comes from reading and reflection. By reading we learn what we did not know; by reflection we retain what we have learned.

Reading the Holy Scriptures confers two benefits. It trains the mind to understand them; it turns our attention from the follies of the world and leads us to the love of God.

Two kinds of study are called for here. We must first learn how the Scriptures are to be understood, and then see how to expound them with profit and in a manner worthy of them. We must first be eager to understand what we are reading before we are fit to proclaim what we have learned.

Conscientious readers will be more concerned to carry out what they have read than merely to acquire knowledge of it. For it is a less serious fault to be ignorant of an objective than it is to fail to carry out what we do know. In reading we aim at knowing, but we must put into practice what we have learned in our course of study.

No one can understand Holy Scripture without constant reading, according to the words: "Love her and she will exalt you. Embrace her and she will glorify you."

The more you devote yourself to a study of the sacred utterances, the richer will be your understanding of them, just as the more the soil is tilled, the richer the harvest.

Some people have great mental powers but cannot be bothered with reading; what reading could have taught them is devalued by their neglect. Others have a desire to know but are hampered by their slow mental processes; yet application to reading will teach them things which the clever fail to learn through laziness.

Those who are slow to grasp things but who really try hard are rewarded; equally those who do not cultivate their God-given intellectual ability are condemned for despising their gifts and sinning by sloth.

Learning unsupported by grace may get into our ears; it never reaches the heart. It makes a great noise outside but serves no inner purpose. But when God's grace touches our innermost minds to bring understanding, his word which has been received by the ear sinks deep into the heart.

Book of Maxims 3, 8–10: PL 83, 679–682

Proper 29 ✠ Sunday

A reading from the Travels of Egeria, Abbess, and Pilgrim to Jerusalem [late fourth century]

Since it is Sunday, at dawn they assemble for the liturgy in the major church built by Constantine and located on Golgotha behind the Cross; and whatever is done all over customarily on Sundays is done here. Indeed it is the practice here that as many of the priests who are present and are so inclined may preach; and last of all, the bishop preaches. These sermons are given every Sunday so that the people may be instructed in the Scriptures and the love of God. Because of the sermons that are preached, there is a great delay in giving the dismissal from the church; therefore, the dismissal is not given before the fourth or fifth hour.

However, once the dismissal from the church has been given in the manner which is followed everywhere, then the monks, singing hymns, lead the bishop to the Anastasis [church of the Resurrection]. When the bishop, to the accompaniment of hymns, approaches, all the doors of the basilica of the Anastasis are opened, and all the people enter, the faithful, that is, but not the catechumens. Once the people have entered, then the bishop enters and proceeds immediately to within the railings of the grotto shrine. First, they give thanks to God, and so the sacrifice is offered; and then a prayer is said for everyone. Afterwards, the deacon cries out that all should bow their heads, wherever they are standing, and then the bishop, standing within the inner railings, blesses them; afterwards, he goes out. As the bishop is leaving, all come forth to kiss his hand. And so it is that the dismissal is delayed until as late as the fifth or sixth hour. Later at vespers everything is done exactly according to the daily ritual.

Pilgrimage 25: SC 296, 244–248

Proper 29 ✠ Monday

A reading from a sermon of Andrew of Crete, Bishop and Hymnographer [740]

Let us say to Christ: "Blessed is the one who comes in the name of the Lord, the king of Israel." Let us hold before him like palm branches those final words inscribed above the cross. Let us show him honor, not with olive branches but with the splendor of merciful deeds to one another. Let us spread the thoughts and desires of our hearts under his feet like garments, so that entering us with the whole of his being, he may draw the whole of our being into himself and place the whole of his in us. Let us say to Zion in the words of the prophet: "Have courage, daughter of Zion, do not be afraid. Behold, your king comes to you, humble and mounted on a colt, the foal of a beast of burden."

He is coming who is everywhere present and pervades all things; he is coming to achieve in you his work of universal salvation. He is coming who came to call to repentance not the righteous but sinners, coming to recall those who have strayed into sin. Do not be afraid, then: "God is in the midst of you, and you shall not be shaken."

Receive him with open, outstretched hands, for it was on his own hands that he sketched you. Receive him who laid your foundations on the palms of his hands. Receive him, for he took upon himself all that belongs to us except sin, to consume what is ours in what is his. Be glad, city of Zion, our mother, and fear not. "Celebrate your feasts." Glorify him for his mercy, who has come to us in you. Rejoice exceedingly, daughter of Jerusalem, sing and leap for joy. "Be enlightened, be enlightened," we cry to you, as holy Isaiah trumpeted: "for the light has come to you and the glory of the Lord has risen over you."

What kind of "light" is this? It is that which "enlightens every one coming into the world." It is the everlasting light, the timeless light revealed in time, the light manifested in the flesh although hidden by nature, the light that shone round the shepherds and guided the Magi. It is the light that was in the world from the beginning, through which the world was made, yet the world did not know it. It is that light which came to its own, and its own people did not receive it.

And what is this "glory of the Lord"? Clearly it is the cross on which Christ was glorified, he, the radiance of the Father's glory, even as he said when he faced his passion: "Now is the Son of Man glorified, and God is glorified in him, and will glorify him at once." The glory of which he speaks here is his lifting up on the cross, for Christ's glory is his cross and his exultation upon it, as he plainly says: "When I have been lifted up, I will draw all people to myself."

Oration 9 for Palm Sunday: PG 97, 1002

Proper 29 ✠ Tuesday

A reading from a homily of John Chrysostom, Bishop of Constantinople [407]

"I assure you, as often as you did it for one of the least of my brothers [and sisters], you did it for me." But how does Jesus in calling them his kindred say at the same time that they are "least"? It is precisely to indicate that they are his brothers and sisters only because they are "least," that is, lowly, poor, and despicable. For Jesus wants to have only the lowly as his kinfolk.

It seems to me that this is not to be understood only in reference to religious and solitaries who dwell in deserts and on mountains, but in reference to every one of the faithful living in the Church. When you see a Christian who, engaged in the world, lives therein in poverty, completely stripped of all things, Jesus wants you to regard that one as his brother or sister and care for that person as you would for your Savior. Such persons, no matter how wretched and abject they may appear, became his brothers or sisters through baptism and through participation in his mysteries.

But I beg you to notice that when Jesus wishes to heap praises on the good he begins by representing for them the eternal love which God has ever had for them. "Come," he says, "you have my Father's blessing! Inherit the kingdom prepared for you from the creation of the world." What happiness can compare with that of having a "blessing" and of having the blessing of the Father himself? Whence can such a great happiness come to anyone, and how can he merit such glory?

"For I was hungry," he declares, "and you gave me food, I was thirsty and you gave me drink." These words are filled with joy, consolation, and honor for those who will deserve to hear them! He does not say: "Receive the kingdom," but "Inherit the kingdom," take it as your inheritance—like a kingdom that belongs to you, that you have received from your Father, and that was due you from all ages. I prepared it for you even before you were born because I knew that you would be what you are.

What, then, are the acts which Jesus Christ rewards in his holy ones in so divine a manner? My friends, it is because they have harbored a stranger, clothed a poor person, given food to one who was hungry and water to one who was thirsty; finally, it is because they have visited a sick or imprisoned person. God is primarily concerned with the help we provide to those who are in need of it.

There are even cases in which he does not consider whether we have drawn them out of their wretched state. And, indeed, as I have already said, a sick person and a prisoner do not desire solely to be visited. The one wants to be cured of his evil while the other wants to get out of prison. But God, since he is so good, is content with the little that we give when we cannot give more. He does not even demand all that we could give. He leaves it to our liberty to do more if we wish, so that we can have the glory of voluntarily going beyond what we were obliged to do.

Homily 79 on Matthew: PG 58, 718–719

Proper 29 ✠ Wednesday

A reading from a commentary on the Song of Songs by
Gregory, Bishop of Nyssa [c. 394]

Where do you pasture your sheep, O Good Shepherd, you who carry on your shoulders the whole flock? For it is but one sheep, this entire human race whom you lift onto your shoulders. Show me the place where there are green pastures, let me know restful waters, lead me out to nourishing grass and call me by name so that I can hear your voice, for I am your own sheep. And through that voice calling me, give me eternal life.

"Tell me, you whom my soul loves." This is how I address you, because your true name is above all other names; it is unutterable and incomprehensible to all rational creatures. And so the name I use for you is simply the statement of my soul's love for you, and this is an apt name for making your goodness known. Very dark though I am, how could I not love you who so loved me, that you laid down your life for the sheep you tend? No greater love can be conceived than this, that you should purchase my salvation at the cost of your life.

Show me, then, says the bride, where you tend your sheep, so that I may find the saving pasture and be filled with heavenly nourishment. For whoever does not eat this food cannot enter eternal life. Let me run to you, the spring, and drink the divine draught that you cause to pour forth for the thirsty, offering water from your side opened by the spear. Whoever drinks of this becomes "a fountain of water springing up to eternal life."

If you feed me thus, then you will surely make me lie down at noonday, and I shall at once sleep in peace, resting in a light that knows no shadow. Indeed, there is no shadow at noon, for the sun shines directly over that summit where you make those you tend lie down, and take your children with you to your bed. No one is judged worthy of this noonday rest who is not a child of light and of the day. But if any make themselves equally distant from the shadows of daybreak and those of nightfall, that is, from the origin of evil and its conclusion, the sun of righteousness makes them lie down at noontide.

Show me, then, says the bride, how I should lie down; show me the path to this noonday repose, lest my ignorance of your truth cause me to stray from your good guidance and consort with flocks which are strangers to yours.

Thus speaks the bride, anxious about the beauty God has given her, and seeking to learn how her comeliness may continue for ever.

Commentary on the Song of Songs 2: PG 44, 802

Proper 29 ✠ Thursday

A reading from the Catechetical Instructions of Theodore,
Bishop of Mopsuestia [428]

It follows that, since there needs to be a representation of the High Priest, certain individuals are appointed to preside over the liturgy of these signs. For we believe that what Christ our Lord performed in reality, and will continue to perform, is performed through the sacraments by those whom divine grace has called to be priests of the New Covenant when the Holy Spirit comes down on them to strengthen them and ordain them. This is why they do not offer new sacrifices, like the repeated immolations prescribed by the Law. But with priests of the New Covenant it is just the reverse: they continue to offer the same sacrifice in every place and at every time. For there is only one sacrifice which was offered for us all, the sacrifice of Christ our Lord, who underwent death for our sake and by this sacrifice brought our perfection, as it is said: "By a single offering he has perfected for all time those who are sanctified."

In every place and at every time we continue to perform the commemoration of this same sacrifice; for as often as we eat this bread and drink this chalice, we proclaim our Lord's death until he comes. Every time, then, there is performed the liturgy of this awesome sacrifice, which is the clear image of the heavenly realities, we should imagine that we are in heaven. Faith enables us to picture in our minds the heavenly realities, as we remind ourselves that the same Christ who is in heaven, who died for us, rose again and ascended to heaven, is now being immolated under these symbols. So when faith enables our eyes to contemplate the commemoration that takes place now, we are brought again to see his death, resurrection and ascension, which have already taken place for our sake.

Christ our Lord established these awesome mysteries for us. We look forward to their perfect fulfillment in the world to come, but we have already laid hold of them by faith, so that even in this world we can struggle not to abandon any part of our faith in them. Accordingly we need this sacramental liturgy to strengthen our faith in the revelation we have received; the liturgy leads us on to what is to come, for we know that it contains, as it were, an image of the mysterious dispensation of Christ our Lord, and affords us a shadowy vision of what took place. Accordingly at the sight of the bishop we form in our hearts a kind of image of Christ our Lord sacrificing himself to save us and give us life.

At the sight of the deacons who serve at the ceremony we think of the invisible ministering powers who officiate at this mysterious liturgy; for the deacons bring this sacrifice—or rather the symbols of the sacrifice—and lay it out on the awesome altar.

Baptismal Homily 4, 19–20, 24: Yarnold, 223–224, 226–227

Proper 29 ✠ Friday

A reading from The City of God by Augustine, Bishop of Hippo [430]

We must not listen to those who say that God does not work visible miracles, since, according to their own admission, it is God who made the world, and they cannot deny that the world is a visible work. And whatever miracle happens in this world, it is certainly a lesser marvel than the whole world, that is to say, the heavens and the earth and all that is in them, which God undoubtedly made. But the manner of its making is as hidden from us and as incomprehensible to us as is he who made it. And so although the miracles of the visible world of nature have lost their value for us because we see them continually, still, if we observe them wisely they will be found to be greater miracles than the most extraordinary and unusual events. For humankind is a greater miracle than any miracle effected by human agency.

And therefore God who made the visible marvels of heaven and earth does not disdain to work visible miracles in heaven and earth, by which he arouses the soul, hitherto preoccupied with visible things, to the worship of himself, the invisible God. But where and when he does this is a secret of his unchanging counsel, in whose plan all future events are already present. For he moves events in time, while himself remaining unmoved by time. He knows what is to happen as already having happened. To him there is no difference between seeing us about to pray and listening to our prayers, for even when his angels listen, it is he himself who listens in them, being in them as in his true temple, not made with hands, as he is in his saints on earth; and his commands, which are eternal when viewed in reference to his everlasting Law, are fulfilled in time.

City of God 10, 12: CCL 47, 286–287

Proper 29 ✠ Saturday

A reading from a treatise on the Creed by Thomas Aquinas, Priest and Friar [1274]

It is fitting that the end of all our desires, namely eternal life, coincides with the words at the end of the creed: "Life everlasting. Amen."

The first point about eternal life is that humanity is united with God. For God himself is the reward and end of all our labors: "I am your protector and your supreme reward." This union consists in seeing God perfectly: "At present we are looking at a confused reflection in a mirror, but then we shall see face to face."

Next it consists in perfect praise, according to the words of the prophet: "Joy and happiness will be found in it, thanksgiving and words of praise."

It also consists in the complete satisfaction of desire, for there the blessed will be given more than they wanted or hoped for. The reason is that in this life no one can fulfill their longings, nor can any creature satisfy human desire. Only God satisfies, he infinitely exceeds all other pleasures. That is why we can rest in nothing but God. As Augustine says: "You have made us for yourself, Lord, and our hearts are restless until they rest in you."

Since in their heavenly home the saints will possess God completely, obviously their longing will be satisfied, and their glory will be even greater. That is why the Lord says: "Enter into the joy of your Lord." Augustine adds: "The fullness of joy will not enter into those who rejoice, but those who rejoice will enter into joy. I shall be satisfied when your glory is seen."

Whatever is delightful is there in superabundance. If delights are sought, there is supreme and most perfect delight. It is said of God, the supreme good: "Boundless delights are in your right hand."

Again, eternal life consists of the joyous community of all the blessed, a community of supreme delight, since everyone will share all that is good with all the blessed. Everyone will love everyone else as they love themselves, and therefore will rejoice in another's good as in their own. So it follows that the happiness and joy of each grows in proportion to the joy of all.

Collation on the Creed: Opuscula Theologica 2, 216–217

Holy Days
And Special Occasions

St. Andrew ✠ **November 30**

*A reading from a sermon of Bernard, Abbot of Clairvaux
[1153]*

Today we celebrate the feast of St. Andrew. If we attentively meditate upon it, we shall find in it much food for our spirit.

You must have noted that St. Andrew, when he came to the place where the cross was prepared, was strengthened in the Lord and started uttering fiery words, being inspired by the Spirit whom he had received together with the other apostles, in the form of tongues of fire. His mouth spoke from the abundance of the heart, and the charity that burned in him gave ardor to his voice.

And what did St. Andrew say when he saw the cross that had been put up for him? "O cross," he said, "long desired and now offered to my soul's desires! I come to you full of joy and assurance. Receive me then with gladness, for I am the disciple of him who hung from your arms."

Whence then came to that man such astonishing joy and exultation? Where did he, so frail a creature, get so much constancy? Where did he get so spiritual a soul, so fervent a charity, and so strong a will? Let us not imagine he got that great courage from himself. It was the perfect gift issued from the Father of lights, from him who alone produces marvels. It was the Holy Spirit who came to help his weakness and filled his soul with the charity strong as death, and even stronger than death.

May it please God to make us share in that Spirit! For if now the effort of conversion is painful to us, and if we are vexed by watchings, the only reason is our spiritual indigence. If the Spirit were present to us, he surely would come to help our weakness. What he has done for St. Andrew when he faced the cross and death, he would do also for us: removing from the labor of our conversion its painful character, he would render it desirable and even delicious. "My Spirit," says the Lord, "is sweeter than honey," so much so that the most bitter death could not lessen its sweetness.

We must take up our cross with St. Andrew, or rather with him whom he himself has followed, the Lord, our Savior. The cause of his joy and his exultation was that he died not only with him, but like him, and that he was so intimately united to his death and to his sufferings that he would also reign with him.

Let us too listen, with the ears of our heart, to the voice of the Lord who invites us to share his cross: "If any wish to be my followers, they must deny themselves and take up their cross, and follow in my steps." For our salvation is found on the cross, provided we courageously are attached to it. "The message of the cross," the Apostle tells us, "is complete absurdity to those who are headed for ruin, but to us, who are experiencing salvation, it is the power of God."

Second Sermon for the Feast of St. Andrew 1, 3–5, 7: PL 183, 509–512

St. Thomas ✠ December 21

A reading from a sermon of Gregory the Great, Bishop of Rome [604]

"Thomas, one of the twelve, called the Twin, was not with them when Jesus came." He was the only disciple absent; on his return he heard what had happened but refused to believe it. The Lord came a second time; he offered his side for the disbelieving disciple to touch, held out his hands, and showing the scars of his wounds, healed the wound of his disbelief.

Dearly beloved, what do you see in these events? Do you really believe that it was by chance that this chosen disciple was absent, then came and heard, heard and doubted, doubted and touched, touched and believed? It was not by chance but in God's providence. In a marvelous way God's mercy arranged that the disbelieving disciple, in touching the wounds of his master's body, should heal our wounds of disbelief. The disbelief of Thomas has done more for our faith than the faith of the other disciples. As he touches Christ and is won over to belief, every doubt is cast aside and our faith is strengthened. So the disciple who doubted, then felt Christ's wounds, becomes a witness to the reality of the resurrection.

Touching Christ, he cried out: "My Lord and my God." Jesus said to him: "Because you have seen me, Thomas, you have believed." Paul said: "Faith is the guarantee of things hoped for, the evidence of things unseen." It is clear, then, that faith is the proof of what cannot be seen.

What is seen gives knowledge, not faith. When Thomas saw and touched, why was he told: "You have believed because you have seen me"? Because what he saw and what he believed were different things. God cannot be seen by mortals. Thomas saw a human being, whom he acknowledged to be God, and said: "My Lord and my God." Seeing, he believed; looking at one who was truly human, he cried out that this was God, the God he could not see.

What follows is reason for great joy: "Blessed are those who have not seen and have believed." There is here a particular reference to ourselves; we hold in our hearts one we have not seen in the flesh. We are included in these words, but only if we follow up our faith with good works. The true believer practices what he believes. But of those who pay only lip service to faith, Paul has this to say: "They profess to know God, but they deny him in their works." Therefore James says: "Faith without works is dead."

Homily on the Gospels 26, 7–9: PL 76, 1201–1202

St. Stephen ✠ December 26

A reading from a sermon of Fulgentius, Bishop of Ruspe [533]

Yesterday we celebrated the birth in time of our eternal King. Today we celebrate the triumphant suffering of his soldier. Yesterday our king, clothed in his robe of flesh, left his place in the virgin's womb and graciously visited the world. Today his soldier leaves the tabernacle of his body and goes triumphantly to heaven.

Our king, despite his exalted majesty, came in humility for our sake; yet he did not come empty-handed. He brought his soldiers a great gift that not only enriched them but also made them unconquerable in battle, for it was the gift of love, which was to bring us to share in his divinity. He gave of his bounty, yet without any loss to himself. In a marvelous way he changed into wealth the poverty of his faithful followers while remaining in full possession of his own inexhaustible riches.

And so the love that brought Christ from heaven to earth raised Stephen from earth to heaven; shown first in the king, it later shone forth in his soldier. Love was Stephen's weapon by which he gained every battle, and so won the crown signified by his name. His love of God kept him from yielding to the ferocious mob; his love for his neighbor made him pray for those who were stoning him. Love inspired him to reprove those who erred, to make them amend; love led him to pray for those who stoned him, to save them from punishment. Strengthened by the power of his love, he overcame the raging cruelty of Saul and won his persecutor on earth as his companion in heaven. In his holy and tireless love he longed to gain by prayer those whom he could not convert by admonition.

Now at last, Paul rejoices with Stephen, with Stephen he delights in the glory of Christ, with Stephen he exalts, with Stephen he reigns. Stephen went first, slain by the stones thrown by Paul, but Paul followed after, helped by the prayer of Stephen. This, surely, is the true life, beloved, a life in which Paul feels no shame because of Stephen's death, and Stephen delights in Paul's companionship, for love fills them both with joy. It was Stephen's love that prevailed over the cruelty of the mob, and it was Paul's love that covered the multitude of his sins; it was love that won for both of them the kingdom of heaven.

Love, indeed, is the source of all good things; it is an impregnable defense, and the way that leads to heaven. Whoever walks in love can neither go astray nor be afraid: love guides, protects, and brings the one who loves to the journey's end.

Christ made love the stairway that would enable all Christians to climb to heaven. Hold fast to it, therefore, in all sincerity, give one another practical proof of it, and by your progress in it, make your ascent together.

Sermon 3, 1–3, 5–6: CCL 91A, 905–909

St. John ✠ December 27

A reading from the commentary on First John by Augustine, Bishop of Hippo [430]

"Our message is the Word of life. We announce what existed from the beginning, what we have heard, what we have seen with our own eyes, what we have touched with our own hands." Who could touch the Word with his hands unless "the Word was made flesh and lived among us"?

Now this Word, whose flesh was so real that he could be touched by human hands, began to be flesh in the Virgin Mary's womb; but he did not begin to exist at that moment. We know this from what John says: "What existed from the beginning." Notice how John's letter bears witness to his Gospel: "In the beginning was the Word, and the Word was with God."

Someone might interpret the phrase "the Word of life" to mean a word about Christ, rather than Christ's body itself which was touched by human hands. But consider what comes next: "and life itself was revealed." Christ therefore is himself the Word of life.

And how was this life revealed? It existed from the beginning, but was not revealed to mortals, only to angels, who looked upon it and feasted upon it as their own spiritual bread. But what does Scripture say? "Humans ate the bread of angels."

Life itself was therefore revealed in the flesh. In this way what was visible to the heart alone could become visible also to the eye, and so heal human hearts. For the Word is visible to the heart alone, while flesh is visible to bodily eyes as well. We already possessed the means to see the flesh, but we had no means of seeing the Word. The Word was made flesh so that we could see it, to heal the part of us by which we could see the Word.

John continues: "And we are witnesses and we proclaim to you that eternal life which was with the Father and has been revealed among us"—one might say more simply "revealed to us."

"We proclaim to you what we have heard and seen." Make sure that you grasp the meaning of these words. The disciples saw our Lord in the flesh, face to face; they heard the words he spoke, and in turn they proclaimed the message to us. So we also have heard, although we have not seen.

Are we then less favored than those who both saw and heard? If that were so, why should John add: "so that you too may have fellowship with us"? They saw, and we have not seen; yet we have fellowship with them, because we and they share the same faith.

"And our fellowship is with God the Father and Jesus Christ his Son. And we write this to you to make your joy complete"—complete in that fellowship, in that love and in that unity.

Treatise 1 on 1 John 1, 3: PL 35, 1978, 1980

Holy Innocents ✠ December 28

A reading from a sermon of Quodvultdeus, Bishop of Carthage [c. 453]

A tiny child is born, who is a great king. Wise men are led to him from afar. They come to adore one who lies in a manger and yet reigns in heaven and on earth. When they tell of one who is born a king, Herod is disturbed. To save his kingdom he resolves to kill him, though if he would have faith in the child, he himself would reign in peace in this life and for ever in the life to come.

Why are you afraid, Herod, when you hear of the birth of a king? He does not come to drive you out, but to conquer the devil. But because you do not understand this you are disturbed and in a rage, and to destroy one child whom you seek, you show your cruelty in the death of so many children.

You are not restrained by the love of weeping mothers or fathers mourning the deaths of their little ones, nor by the cries and sobs of the children. You destroy those who are tiny in body because fear is destroying your heart. You imagine that if you accomplish your desire you can prolong your own life, though you are seeking to kill Life himself.

Yet your throne is threatened by the source of grace—so small, yet so great—who is lying in the manger. He is using you, all unaware of it, to work out his own purposes in freeing souls from captivity to the devil. He has taken up the children of the enemy into the ranks of God's adopted children.

The children die for Christ, though they do not know it. The parents mourn for the death of martyrs. The children make of those as yet unable to speak fit witnesses to themselves. See the kind of kingdom that is his, coming as he did in order to be this kind of king. See how the deliverer is already working deliverance, the savior already working salvation.

But you, Herod, do not know this and are disturbed and furious. While you vent your fury against the children, you are already paying them homage, and do not know it.

How great a gift of grace is here! To what merits of their own do the children owe this kind of victory? They cannot speak, yet they bear witness to Christ. They cannot use their limbs to engage in battle, yet already they bear off the palm of victory.

Sermon 2 on the Creed: PL 40, 655

Confession of St. Peter ✠ January 18

A reading from a sermon of Leo the Great, Bishop of Rome [461]

There is no doubt that the Son of God took our human nature into so close a union with himself that one and the same Christ is present, not only in the firstborn of all creation, but in all his saints as well. The head cannot be separated from the members, nor the members from the head. Not in this life, it is true, but only in eternity will God be all in all, yet even now he dwells, whole and undivided, in his temple the Church. Such was his promise to us when he said: "See, I am with you always, even to the end of the world."

And so all that the Son of God did and taught for the world's reconciliation is not for us simply a matter of past history. Here and now we experience his power at work among us. Born of a virgin mother by the action of the Holy Spirit, Christ keeps his Church spotless and makes her fruitful by the inspiration of the same Spirit. In baptismal regeneration she brings forth children for God beyond all numbering. These are the children of whom it is written: "They are born not of blood, nor of the desire of the flesh, nor of human will, but of God."

In Christ Abraham's posterity is blessed, because in him the whole world receives the adoption of heirs, and in him the patriarch becomes the father of all nations through the birth, not from human stock but by faith, of the descendants that were promised to him. From every nation on earth, without exception, Christ forms a single flock of those he has sanctified, daily fulfilling the promise he once made: "I have other sheep, not of this fold, whom it is also ordained that I shall lead; and there shall be one flock and one shepherd."

Although it was primarily to Peter that he said: "Feed my sheep," yet the one Lord guides all pastors in the discharge of their office and leads to rich and fertile pastures all those who come to the rock. There is no counting the sheep who are nourished with his abundant love, and who are prepared to lay down their lives for the sake of the good shepherd who died for them.

But it is not only the martyrs who share in his passion by their glorious courage; the same is true, by faith, of all who are born again in baptism. That is why we are to celebrate the Lord's paschal sacrifice with the unleavened bread of sincerity and truth. The leaven of our former malice is thrown out, and a new creature is filled and inebriated with the Lord himself. For the effect of our sharing in the body and blood of Christ is to change us into what we receive. As we have died with him, and have been buried and raised to life with him, so we bear him within us, both in body and in spirit, in everything we do.

Sermon 12 for the Lord's Passion 3, 6–7: PL 54, 355–357

Conversion of St. Paul ✠ January 25

A reading from a homily of John Chrysostom, Bishop of Constantinople [407]

Paul, more than anyone else, has shown us what humanity really is, and in what our nobility consists, and of what virtue this particular animal is capable. Each day he aimed ever higher; each day he rose up with greater ardor and faced with new eagerness the dangers that threatened him. He summed up his attitude in the words: "I forget what is behind me and push on to what lies ahead." When he saw death imminent, he bade others share his joy: "Rejoice and be glad with me!" And when danger, injustice and abuse threatened, he said: "I am content with weakness, mistreatment and persecution." These he called the weapons of righteousness, thus telling us that he derived immense profit from them.

Thus, amid the traps set for him by his enemies, with exultant heart he turned their every attack into a victory for himself; constantly beaten, abused and cursed, he boasted of it as though he were celebrating a triumphal procession and taking trophies home, and offered thanks to God for it all: "Thanks be to God who is always victorious in us!" This is why he was far more eager for the shameful abuse that his zeal in preaching brought upon him than we are for the most pleasing honors, more eager for death than we are for life, for poverty than we are for wealth; he yearned for toil far more than others yearn for rest after toil. The one thing he feared, indeed dreaded, was to offend God; nothing else could sway him. Therefore, the only thing he really wanted was always to please God.

The most important thing of all to him, however, was that he knew himself to be loved by Christ. Enjoying this love, he considered himself happier than anyone else; were he without it, it would be no satisfaction to be the friend of principalities and powers. He preferred to be thus loved and be the least of all, or even to be among the damned, than to be without that love and be among the great and honored.

To be separated from that love was, in his eyes, the greatest and most extraordinary of torments; the pain of that loss would alone have been hell, and endless, unbearable torture.

So too, in being loved by Christ he thought of himself as possessing life, the world, the angels, present and future, the kingdom, the promise and countless blessings. Apart from that love nothing saddened or delighted him; for nothing earthly did he regard as bitter or sweet.

Paul set no store by the things that fill our visible world, any more than one sets value on the withered grass of the field. As for tyrannical rulers or the people enraged against him, he paid them no more heed than gnats.

Death itself and pain and whatever torments might come were but child's play to him, provided that thereby he might bear some burden for the sake of Christ.

Homily 2 on the Praises of St. Paul: PG 50, 477–480

Eve of the Presentation ✠ February 1

A reading from the Travels of Egeria, Abbess, and Pilgrim to Jerusalem [late fourth century]

The Fortieth Day after Epiphany is observed here with special magnificence. On this day they assemble in the Anastasis. Everyone gathers, and things are done with the same solemnity as at the feast of Easter. All the presbyters preach first, then the bishop, and they interpret the passage from the Gospel about Joseph and Mary taking the Lord to the Temple, and about Simeon and the prophetess Anna, daughter of Phanuel, seeing the Lord, and what they said to him, and about the sacrifice offered by his parents. When all the rest has been done in the proper way, they celebrate the sacrament and have their dismissal.

Pilgrimage 26: SC 296, 254–256

The Presentation ✠ February 2

A reading from a sermon of Sophronius, Bishop of Jerusalem [638]

In honor of the divine mystery that we celebrate today, let us all hasten to meet Christ. Everyone should be eager to join the procession and to carry a light.

Our lighted candles are a sign of the divine splendor of the one who comes to expel the dark shadows of evil and to make the whole universe radiant with the brilliance of his eternal light. Our candles also show how bright our souls should be when we go to meet Christ.

The Mother of God, the most pure Virgin, carried the true light in her arms and brought him to those who lay in darkness. We too should carry a light for all to see and reflect the radiance of the true light as we hasten to meet him.

The light has come and has shone upon a world enveloped in shadows; the Dayspring from on high has visited us and given light to those who lived in darkness. This, then, is our feast, and we join in procession with lighted candles to reveal the light that has shone upon us and the glory that is yet to come to us through him. So let us hasten all together to meet our God.

The true light has come, "the light that enlightens every person who is born into this world." Let all of us, beloved, be enlightened and made radiant by this light. Let all of us share in its splendor, and be so filled with it that no one remains in the darkness. Let us be shining ourselves as we go together to meet and to receive with the aged Simeon the light whose brilliance is eternal. Rejoicing with Simeon, let us sing a hymn of thanksgiving to God, the Father of the light, who sent the true light to dispel the darkness and to give us all a share in his splendor.

Through Simeon's eyes we too have seen the salvation of God which he prepared for all the nations and revealed as the glory of the new Israel, which is ourselves. As Simeon was released from the bonds of this life when he had seen Christ, so we too were at once freed from our old state of sinfulness.

By faith we too embraced Christ, the salvation of God the Father, as he came to us from Bethlehem. Gentiles before, we have now become the people of God. Our eyes have seen God incarnate, and because we have seen him present among us and have mentally received him into our arms, we are called the new Israel. Never shall we forget this presence; every year we keep a feast in his honor.

Sermon 3 on the Presentation 6, 7: PG 87, 3, 3291–3293

St. Matthias ✠ February 24

A reading from a homily of John Chrysostom, Bishop of Constantinople [407]

"In those days, Peter stood up in the midst of the disciples." As the fiery spirit to whom the flock was entrusted by Christ and as the leader in the band of the apostles, Peter always took the initiative in speaking: "Friends, we must choose from among our number." He left the decision to the whole body, at once augmenting the honor of those elected and avoiding any suspicion of partiality. For such great occasions can easily lead to trouble.

Did not Peter then have the right to make the choice himself? Certainly he had the right, but he did not want to give the appearance of showing special favor to anyone. Besides he was not yet endowed with the Spirit. "And they nominated two," we read, "Joseph, who was called Barsabbas and surnamed Justus, and Matthias." He himself did not nominate them; all present did. But it was he who brought the issue forward, pointing out that it was not his own idea but had been suggested to him by a scriptural prophecy. So he was speaking not as a teacher but as an interpreter.

"So," he goes on, "we must choose from those who lived in our company." Notice how insistent he is that they should be eye-witnesses. Even though the Spirit would come to ratify the choice, Peter regards this prior qualification as most important.

"Those who lived in our company," to continue the passage, "all through the time when the Lord Jesus came and went among us." He refers to those who had dwelt with Jesus, not just those who had been his disciples. For of course from the very beginning many had followed him. Notice how it is written that Peter himself was "one of the two who had listened to John, and followed Jesus."

"All through the time when the Lord Jesus came and went among us," to continue further, "beginning with the baptism of John"—rightly so, because no one knew what had happened before that time, although they were to know of it later through the Spirit.

"Up to the day," Peter added, "on which he was taken up from us— one of these must be made a witness along with us of his resurrection." He did not say "a witness of the rest of his actions" but only "a witness of the resurrection"! That witness would be more believable who could declare that he who ate and drank and was crucified also rose from the dead. He needed to be a witness not of the times before or after that event, and not of the signs and wonders, but only of the resurrection itself. For the rest happened by general admission, openly; but the resurrection took place secretly, and was known to these disciples only.

And they all prayed together, saying: "You, Lord, know our hearts; make your choice known to us." They said "You," not "we." Appropriately they said that he knew their hearts, because the choice was to be made by him, not by others.

They spoke with such confidence because someone had to be appointed. They did not say "choose" but "make known to us" the chosen one; "the one you choose," they said, fully aware that everything was pre-ordained by God. "They then drew lots." For they did not think themselves worthy to make the choice of their own accord, and therefore they wanted some sign for their instruction.

Homily 3 on Acts 1, 2, 3: PG 60, 33-36, 38

St. Joseph ✠ March 19

*A reading from a sermon of Bernardine of Siena, Franciscan
Friar and Preacher [1444]*

The general rule for all singular graces accorded a rational creature is that
when the divine mercy chooses someone for a particular grace or lofty
state it gives all the charisma needed by that chosen person and that
office.

This was verified in a particular way in the great St. Joseph, foster
father of the Lord Jesus Christ and true husband of the queen of the
world and mistress of the angels. He was chosen by the eternal Father
as faithful provider and guardian of his principal treasures—his Son and
his spouse—and Joseph carried out this task with the greatest fidelity.
Hence, the Lord says to him: "Enter, good and faithful servant, into the
joy of your Lord."

If the Lord places Joseph before the whole Church, is Joseph not the
chosen and singular man through whom and under whom Christ was
introduced to the world in an ordered and honorable fashion? If, therefore, the entire holy Church is indebted to the Virgin Mother because
through her the Church was made worthy of receiving Christ, it follows
that immediately after Mary the Church also owes to Joseph a particular
gratitude and reverence.

Indeed, Joseph is the terminus of the Old Testament in whom the
dignity of the patriarchs and the prophets attains the promised fruit. For
he is the only one who possessed what the divine condescension promised to them.

Hence, it cannot be doubted that in heaven Christ certainly did not
deny but actually increased and brought to perfect fulfillment that familiarity, reverence, and loftiest dignity which he had toward Joseph on
earth—as a son for his father.

Therefore, it is not without reason that the Lord adds: "Enter into the
joy of your Lord." Although it is the joy of eternal happiness which is to
enter into the human heart, the Lord prefers to say to him: "Enter into
the joy" to indicate mystically that this joy is not only within him but all
about him and submerges him like an infinite abyss.

Sermon 2 on St. Joseph: Opera 7, 16, 27-30

468   *St. Joseph, March 19*

Eve of the Annunciation ✠ March 24

A reading from a commentary on Luke by Ambrose, Bishop of Milan [397]

The angel revealed the message to the Virgin Mary, giving her a sign to win her trust. The angel told her of the motherhood of an old and barren woman to show that God is able to do all that he wills.

When she hears this Mary sets out for the hill country. She does not disbelieve God's word; she feels no uncertainty over the message or doubt about the sign. She goes eager in purpose, dutiful in conscience, hastening for joy.

Filled with God, where would she hasten but to the heights? The Holy Spirit does not proceed by slow, laborious efforts. Quickly, too, the blessings of her coming and the Lord's presence are made clear: as soon as "Elizabeth heard Mary's greeting, the child leapt in her womb, and she was filled with the Holy Spirit."

Notice the contrast and the choice of words. Elizabeth is the first to hear Mary's voice, but John is the first to be aware of grace. Elizabeth hears with the ears of the body, but John leaps for joy at the meaning of the mystery. She is aware of Mary's presence, but he is aware of the Lord's: a woman aware of a woman's presence, the forerunner aware of the pledge of our salvation. The women speak of the grace they have received while the children are active in secret, unfolding the mystery of love with the help of their mothers, who prophesy by the spirit of their sons.

The child leaps in the womb; the mother is filled with the Holy Spirit, but not before her son. Once the son has been filled with the Holy Spirit, he fills his mother with the same Spirit. John leaps for joy, and the spirit of Mary rejoices in her turn. When John leaps for joy Elizabeth is filled with the Holy Spirit, but we know that though Mary's spirit rejoices she does not need to be filled with the Holy Spirit. Her son, who is beyond our understanding, is active in his mother in a way beyond our understanding. Elizabeth is filled with the Holy Spirit after conceiving John, while Mary is filled with the Holy Spirit before conceiving the Lord. Elizabeth says: "Blessed are you because you have believed."

You also are blessed because you have heard and believed. A believing soul both conceives and brings forth the Word of God and acknowledges his works.

Let Mary's soul be in each of you to proclaim the greatness of the Lord. Let her spirit be in each to rejoice in the Lord. Christ has only one mother in the flesh, but we all bring forth Christ in faith. Every soul receives the Word of God if only it keeps chaste, remaining pure and free from sin, its modesty undefiled. The soul that succeeds in this proclaims the greatness of the Lord, just as Mary's soul magnified the Lord and her spirit rejoiced in God her Savior. In another place we read: "Magnify the Lord with me." The Lord is magnified, not because the human voice can add anything to God but because he is magnified within us. Christ is the image of God, and if the soul does what is right and holy, it magnifies that image of God in whose likeness it was created and, in magnifying the image of God, the soul has a share in its greatness and is exalted.

Commentary on Luke 2, 19, 22–23, 26–27: CCL 14, 39–42

Annunciation ✠ March 25

A reading from a letter by Leo the Great, Bishop of Rome [461]

Lowliness is assumed by majesty, weakness by power, mortality by eternity. To pay the debt of our sinful state, a nature that is incapable of suffering was joined to one that could suffer. Thus, in keeping with the healing that we needed, one and the same mediator between God and humanity, Jesus Christ, was able to die in one nature, and unable to die in the other.

He who is true God was therefore born in the complete and perfect nature of a true human being, whole in his own nature, whole in ours. By our nature we mean what the Creator had fashioned in us from the beginning, and took to himself in order to restore it.

For in the Savior there was no trace of what the deceiver introduced and we, being misled, allowed to enter. It does not follow that because the Savior submitted to sharing in our human weakness he therefore shared in our sins.

He took the nature of a servant without stain of sin, enlarging our humanity without diminishing his divinity. He emptied himself; though invisible he made himself visible, though Creator and Lord of all things he chose to be one of us mortals. Yet this was the condescension of compassion, not the loss of omnipotence. So he who in the nature of God had created humankind, became, in the nature of a servant, human himself.

Thus the Son of God enters this lowly world. He comes down from the throne of heaven, yet does not separate himself from the Father's glory. He is born in a new condition, by a new birth.

He was born in a new condition, for, invisible in his own nature, he became visible in ours. Beyond our grasp, he chose to come within our grasp. Existing before time began, he began to exist at a moment in time. Lord of the universe, he hid his infinite glory and took the nature of a servant. Incapable of suffering as God, he did not refuse to be a human being, capable of suffering. Immortal, he chose to be subject to the laws of death.

He who is true God is also truly human. There is no falsehood in this unity as long as the lowliness of humanity and the preeminence of God co-exist in mutual relationship.

As God does not change by his condescension, so humanity is not swallowed up by being exalted. Each nature exercises its own activity, in communion with the other. The Word does what is proper to the Word, the flesh fulfills what is proper to the flesh.

One nature is resplendent with miracles, the other falls victim to injuries. As the Word does not lose equality with the Father's glory, so the flesh does not leave behind the nature of our race.

One and the same person—this must be said over and over again—is truly the Son of God and truly the Son of Man. He is God in virtue of the fact that "in the beginning was the Word, and the Word was with God, and the Word was God." He is human in virtue of the fact that "the Word was made flesh, and dwelt among us."

Letter 28, to Flavian, 3–4: PL 54, 763–767

St. Mark ✠ April 25

A reading from the treatise Against Heresies by Irenaeus, Bishop of Lyons [c. 202]

The Church, which has spread everywhere, even to the ends of the earth, received the faith from the apostles and their disciples. By faith, we believe in one God, the almighty Father "who made heaven and earth and the sea and all that is in them." We believe in one Lord Jesus Christ, the Son of God, who became human for our salvation. And we believe in the Holy Spirit who through the prophets foretold God's plan: the coming of our beloved Lord Jesus Christ, his birth from the Virgin, his passion, his resurrection from the dead, his ascension into heaven, and his final coming from heaven in the glory of his Father, to "recapitulate all things" and to raise all mortals from the dead, so that, by the decree of his invisible Father, he may make a just judgment in all things and so that "every knee should bow in heaven and on earth and under the earth" to Jesus Christ our Lord and our God, our Savior and our King, and "every tongue confess him."

The Church, spread throughout the whole world, received this preaching and this faith and now preserves it carefully, dwelling as it were in one house. Having one soul and one heart, the Church holds this faith, preaches and teaches it consistently as though by a single voice. For though there are different languages, there is but one tradition.

The faith and the tradition of the churches founded in Germany are no different from those founded among the Spanish and the Celts, in the East, in Egypt, in Libya and elsewhere in the Mediterranean world. Just as God's creature, the sun, is one and the same the world over, so also does the Church's preaching shine everywhere to enlighten all who want to come to a knowledge of the truth.

Now of those who speak with authority in the churches, no preacher however forceful will utter anything different—for no one is above the Master—nor will a less forceful preacher diminish what has been handed down. Since our faith is everywhere the same, no one who can say more augments it, nor can anyone who says less diminish it.

Against Heresies 1, 10, 1–13: SC 264, 154–161

SS. Philip & James ✠ May 1

A reading from the treatise On the Prescription of Heretics by Tertullian, Theologian [c. 225]

Our Lord Jesus Christ himself declared what he was, what he had been, how he was carrying out his Father's will, what obligations he demanded of us. This he did during his earthly life, either publicly to the crowds or privately to his disciples. Twelve of these he picked out to be his special companions, appointed to teach the nations.

One of them fell from his place. The remaining eleven were commanded by Christ, as he was leaving the earth to return to the Father after his resurrection, to go and teach the nations and to baptize them into the Father, the Son and the Holy Spirit.

The apostles cast lots and added Matthias to their number, in place of Judas, as the twelfth apostle. The authority for this action is to be found in a prophetic psalm of David. After receiving the power of the Holy Spirit which had been promised to them, so that they could work miracles and proclaim the truth, they first bore witness to their faith in Jesus Christ and established churches throughout Judea. They then went out into the whole world and proclaimed to the nations the same doctrinal faith.

They set up churches in every city. Other churches received from them a living transplant of faith and the seed of doctrine, and through this daily process of transplanting they became churches. They therefore qualify as apostolic churches by being the offspring of churches that are apostolic.

Every family has to be traced back to its origins. That is why we can say that all these great churches constitute that one original Church of the apostles; for it is from them that they all come. They are all primitive, all apostolic, because they are all one. They bear witness to this unity by their peaceful communion, the fellowship which is their name, the hospitality to which they are pledged. The principle on which these associations are based is common tradition by which they share the same sacramental bond.

The only way in which we can prove what the apostles taught—that is to say, what Christ revealed to them—is through those same churches. They were founded by the apostles themselves, who first preached to them by what is called the living voice and later by means of letters.

The Lord had said clearly in former times: "I have many more things to tell you, but you cannot endure them now." But he went on to say: "When the Spirit of truth comes, he will lead you into the whole truth." Thus Christ shows us that the apostles had full knowledge of the truth, for he had promised that they would receive the "whole truth" through the Spirit of truth. His promise was certainly fulfilled, since the Acts of the Apostles prove that the Holy Spirit came down on them.

On the Prescription of Heretics 20, 1–9; 21, 3; 22, 8–10: CCL 1, 201–204

Eve of the Visitation ✠ May 30

A reading from the treatise On the Hail Mary by Baldwin, Archbishop of Canterbury [1190]

Every day we devoutly greet the most Blessed Virgin Mary with the angel's greeting and we usually add: "Blessed is the fruit of your womb." After she was greeted by the Virgin, Elizabeth added this phrase as if she were echoing the salutation of the angel: "Blessed are you among women and blessed is the fruit of your womb." This is the fruit of which Isaiah spoke: "On that day the shoot of the Lord shall be splendid and radiant—the sublime fruit of earth." What is this fruit but the holy one of Israel, the seed of Abraham, the shoot of the Lord, the flower arising from the root of Jesse, the fruit of life, whom we have shared?

Blessed surely in seed and blessed in the shoot, blessed in the flower, blessed in the gift, finally blessed in thanksgiving and praise, Christ, the seed of Abraham, was brought forth from the seed of David into the flesh.

Christ alone among humankind is found perfected in every good quality, for the Spirit was given to him without measure so that he alone could fulfill all justice. For his justice is sufficient for all nations, according to the Scriptures. "As the earth brings forth its buds, and as the garden germinates its own seed, so the Lord God shall bring forth justice and praise before all the nations." For this is the shoot of justice, which the flower of glory adorns with its blessings when it has grown. But how great is this glory? How can anyone think of anything more glorious, or rather, how can anyone conceive of this at all? For the flower rises from the root of Jesse. You ask: "How far?" Surely it rises even to the highest place, because "Jesus Christ is in the glory of God the Father." His magnificence is elevated above the heavens so that he, the issue of the Lord, is splendid and glorious, the sublime fruit of earth.

But what is our benefit from this fruit? What other than the fruit of blessing from the blessed fruit? From this seed, this shoot, this flower, surely the fruit of blessing comes forth. It has come even to us; first as a seed it is planted through the grace of pardon, then germinated with the increase of perfection, and finally it flowers in the hope or the attainment of glory. For the fruit was blessed by God, and in God, so that God may be glorified through it. For us, too, the fruit was blessed, so that blessed by God we may be glorified in him through the promise spoken to Abraham. God made the fruit a blessing for all nations.

Treatise 7, on the Hail Mary: PL 204, 477–478

The Visitation ✠ May 31

A reading from a sermon of Bede, the Venerable, Priest, and Monk of Jarrow [735]

"My soul proclaims the greatness of the Lord, and my spirit rejoices in God my Savior." With these words Mary first acknowledges the special gifts she has been given. Then she recalls God's universal favors, bestowed unceasingly on the human race.

When we devote all our thoughts to the praise and service of the Lord, we proclaim God's greatness. Our observance of God's commands, moreover, shows that we have God's power and greatness always at heart. Our spirit rejoices in God our savior and delights in the mere recollection of our creator who gives us hope for eternal salvation.

These words are often for all God's creations, but especially for the Mother of God. She alone was chosen, and she burned with spiritual love for the son she so joyously conceived. Above all other saints, she alone could truly rejoice in Jesus, her savior, for she knew that he who was the source of eternal salvation would be born in time in her body, in one person both her own son and her Lord.

"For the Almighty has done great things for me, and holy is his name." Mary attributes nothing to her own merits. She refers all her greatness to the gift of the one whose essence is power and whose nature is greatness, for he fills with greatness and strength the small and the weak who believe in him.

She did well to add: "and holy is his name," to warn those who heard, and indeed all who would receive his words, that they must believe and call upon his name. For they too could share in everlasting holiness and true salvation according to the words of the prophet: "and it will come to pass, that everyone who calls on the name of the Lord will be saved." This is the name she spoke of earlier: "and my spirit rejoices in God my Savior."

Therefore it is an excellent and fruitful custom of holy Church that we should sing Mary's hymn at the time of evening prayer. By meditating upon the incarnation, our devotion is kindled, and by remembering the example of God's Mother, we are encouraged to lead a life of virtue. Such virtues are best achieved in the evening. We are weary after the day's work and worn out by our distractions. The time for rest is near, and our minds are ready for contemplation.

Homilies 1, 4: CCL 122, 25–26, 30

St. Barnabas ✠ June 11

A reading from a commentary on Matthew by Chromatius, Bishop of Aquileia [407]

"You are the light of the world. A city set on a hill cannot be hidden. Nor do you light a lamp only to put it under a bushel basket; you put it on a stand where it gives light to all in the house." The Lord called his disciples the salt of the earth because they seasoned with heavenly wisdom the hearts of the people, rendered insipid by the devil. Now he calls them the light of the world as well, because they have been enlightened by him, the true and everlasting light, and have themselves become a light in the darkness.

Since he is the Sun of Justice, he fittingly calls his disciples the light of the world. The reason for this is that through them, as through shining rays, he has poured out the light of the knowledge of himself upon the entire world. For by manifesting the light of truth, they have dispelled the darkness of error from the hearts of the people.

Moreover, we too have been enlightened by them. We have been made light out of darkness as the Apostle says: "For once you were darkness, but now you are light in the Lord; walk as children of light." He says another time: "For you are not children of the night and of darkness, but you are all children of light and of the day."

Saint John also rightly asserts in his letter: "God is light," and whoever abides in God is in the light just as God himself is in the light. Therefore, because we rejoice in having been freed from the darkness of error, we should always walk in the light as children of light. This is why the Apostle says: "Among them you shine as lights in the world, holding fast to the word of life."

If we fail to live in the light, we shall, to our condemnation and that of others, be veiling over and obscuring by our infidelity the light people so desperately need. As we know from Scripture, the one who received the talent should have made it produce a heavenly profit, but instead preferred to hide it away rather than put it to work and was accordingly punished.

Consequently, that brilliant lamp which was lit for the sake of our salvation should always shine in us. For we have the lamp of the heavenly commandment and spiritual grace, to which David referred: "Your law is a lamp to my feet and a light to my path." Solomon also says this about it: "For the command of the law is a lamp."

Therefore, we must not hide this lamp of law and faith. Rather, we must set it up in the Church, as on a lampstand, for the salvation of many, so that we may enjoy the light of truth itself and all believers may be enlightened.

Treatise on Matthew 5, 1, 3–4: CCL 9, 405–407

Eve of St. John the Baptist ✠ June 23

A reading from a sermon of Bede, the Venerable, Priest, and Monk of Jarrow [735]

As forerunner of our Lord's birth, preaching and death, the blessed John showed in his struggle a goodness worthy of the sight of heaven. In the words of Scripture: "Though in the sight of the people he suffered torments, his hope is full of immortality." We justly commemorate the day of his birth with a joyful celebration, a day which he himself made festive for us through his suffering and which he adorned with the crimson splendor of his own blood. We do rightly revere his memory with joyful hearts, for he stamped with the seal of martyrdom the testimony which he delivered on behalf of our Lord.

There is no doubt that blessed John suffered imprisonment and chains as a witness to our Redeemer, whose forerunner he was, and gave his life for him. His persecutor had demanded not that he should deny Christ, but only that he should keep silent about the truth. Nevertheless, he died for Christ. Does Christ not say: "I am the truth"? Therefore, because John shed his blood for the truth, he surely died for Christ.

Through his birth, preaching and baptizing, he bore witness to the coming birth, preaching and baptism of Christ, and by his own suffering he showed that Christ also would suffer.

Such was the quality and strength of the one who accepted the end of this present life by shedding his blood after the long imprisonment. He preached the freedom of heavenly peace, yet was thrown into irons by the ungodly; he was locked away in the darkness of prison, though he came bearing witness to the Light of life and deserved to be called a bright and shining lamp by that Light itself, which is Christ. John was baptized in his own blood, though he had been privileged to baptize the Redeemer of the world, to hear the voice of the Father above him, and to see the grace of the Holy Spirit descending upon him. But to endure temporal agonies for the sake of the truth was not a heavy burden for such as John; rather it was easily borne and even desirable, for he knew eternal joy would be his reward.

Since death was ever near at hand through the inescapable necessity of nature, such people considered it a blessing to embrace it and thus gain the reward of eternal life by acknowledging Christ's name. Hence the apostle Paul rightly says: "You have been granted the privilege not only to believe in Christ but also to suffer for his sake." He tells us why it is Christ's gift that his chosen ones should suffer for him: "The sufferings of this present time are not worthy to be compared with the glory that is to be revealed in us."

Homily 23: CCL 122, 354, 356–357

Nativity of St. John the Baptist ✠ June 24

A reading from a sermon of Augustine, Bishop of Hippo [430]

The Church observes the birth of John as a hallowed event. We have no such commemoration for any other fathers; but it is significant that we celebrate the birthdays of John and of Jesus. This day cannot be passed by. And even if my explanation does not match the dignity of the feast, you may still meditate on it with great depth and profit.

John was born of a woman too old for childbirth; Christ was born of a youthful virgin. The news of John's birth was met with incredulity, and his father was struck dumb. Christ's birth was believed, and he was conceived through faith.

Such is the topic, as I have presented it, for our inquiry and discussion. But as I said before, if I lack either the time or the ability to study the implications of so profound a mystery, the Spirit who speaks within you even when I am not here will teach you better; it is the Spirit whom you contemplate with devotion, whom you have welcomed into your hearts, whose temples you have become.

John, then, appears as the boundary between the two testaments, the old and the new. That he is a sort of boundary the Lord himself bears witness, when he speaks of "the law and the prophets up until John the Baptist." Thus he represents times past and is the herald of the new era to come. As a representative of the past, he is born of aged parents; as a herald of the new era, he is declared to be a prophet while still in his mother's womb. For when yet unborn, he leapt in his mother's womb at the arrival of blessed Mary. In that womb he had already been designated a prophet, even before he was born; it was revealed that he was to be Christ's precursor, before they ever saw one another. These are divine happenings, going beyond the limits of our human frailty. Eventually he is born, he receives his name, his father's tongue is loosened. See how these events reflect reality.

Zechariah is silent and loses his voice until John, the precursor of the Lord, is born and restores his voice. The silence of Zechariah is nothing but the age of prophecy lying hidden, obscured, as it were, and concealed before the preaching of Christ. At John's arrival Zechariah's voice is released, and it becomes clear at the coming of the one who was foretold. The release of Zechariah's voice at the birth of John is a parallel to the rending of the veil at Christ's crucifixion. If John were announcing his own coming, Zechariah's lips would not have been opened. The tongue is loosened because a voice is born. For when John was preaching the Lord's coming he was asked: "Who are you?" And he replied: "I am the voice of one crying in the wilderness." The voice is John, but the Lord "in the beginning was the Word." John was a voice that lasted only for a time; Christ, the Word in the beginning, is eternal.

Sermon 293, 1-3: PL 38, 1327-1328

SS. Peter & Paul ✠ June 29

A reading from a sermon of Augustine, Bishop of Hippo [430]

This day has been made holy by the passion of the blessed apostles Peter and Paul. We are, therefore, not talking about some obscure martyrs. "For their voice has gone forth to all the world, and to the ends of the earth their message." These martyrs realized what they taught: they pursued justice, they confessed the truth, they died for it.

Saint Peter, the first of the apostles and a fervent lover of Christ, merited to hear these words: "I say to you that you are Peter," for he had said: "You are the Christ, the Son of the living God." Then Christ said: "And I say to you that you are Peter, and on this rock I will build my Church." On this rock I will build the faith that you now confess, and on your words: "You are the Christ, the Son of the living God," I will build my Church. For you are Peter, and the name Peter comes from "petra," the word for "rock," and not vice versa. "Peter" comes, therefore, from "petra," just as "Christian" comes from Christ.

As you are aware, Jesus chose his disciples before his passion and called them apostles; and among these almost everywhere Peter alone deserved to represent the entire Church. And because of that role which he alone had, he merited to hear the words: "To you I shall give the keys of the kingdom of heaven." For it was not one man who received the keys, but the entire Church considered as one. Now insofar as he represented the unity and universality of the Church, Peter's preeminence is clear from the words: "To you I give," for what was given was given to all. For the fact that it was the Church that received the keys of the kingdom of God is clear from what the Lord says elsewhere to all the apostles: "Receive the Holy Spirit," adding immediately, "whose sins you forgive, they are forgiven, and whose sins you retain, they are retained."

Rightly then did the Lord after his resurrection entrust Peter with the feeding of his sheep. Yet he was not the only disciple to merit the feeding of the Lord's sheep; but Christ in speaking only to one suggests the unity of all; and so he speaks to Peter, because Peter is first among the apostles. Therefore do not be disheartened, Peter; reply once, reply twice, reply a third time. The triple confession of your love is to regain what was lost three times by your fear. You must loose three times what you bound three times; untie by love that which your fear bound. Once, and again, and a third time did the Lord entrust his sheep to Peter.

Both apostles share the same feast day, for these two were one; and even though they suffered on different days, they were as one. Peter went first, and Paul followed. And so we celebrate this day made holy for us by the apostles' blood. Let us embrace what they believed, their life, their labors, their sufferings, their preaching and their confession of faith.

Sermon 295, 1-2, 4, 7-8: PL 38, 1348-1352

Independence Day ✠ July 4

A reading from a sermon of Gregory of Nazianzus, Bishop of Constantinople [389]

"What are we that you are mindful of us?" What is this new mystery surrounding me? I am both small and great, both lowly and exalted, mortal and immortal, earthly and heavenly. I am to be buried with Christ and to rise again with him, to become a co-heir with him, a son of God, and indeed God himself.

This is what the great mystery means for us; this is why God became human and became poor for our sake: it was to raise up our flesh, to recover the divine image, to re-create humankind, so that all of us might become one in Christ who perfectly became in us everything that he is himself. So we are no longer to be "male and female, barbarian and Scythian, slave and free"—distinctions deriving from the flesh—but are to bear within ourselves only the seal of God, by whom and for whom we were created. We are to be so formed and molded by him that we are recognized as belonging to his one family.

If only we could be what we hope to be, by the great kindness of our generous God! He asks so little and gives so much, in this life and in the next, to those who love him sincerely. In a spirit of hope and out of love for him, let us then "bear and endure all things" and give thanks for everything that befalls us, since even reason can often recognize these things as weapons to win salvation. And meanwhile let us commend to God our own souls and the souls of those who, being more ready for it, have reached the place of rest before us although they walked the same road as we do.

Lord and Creator of all, and especially of your human creatures, you are the God and Father and ruler of your children; you are the Lord of life and death, you are the guardian and benefactor of our souls. You fashion and transform all things in their due season through your creative Word, as you know to be best in your deep wisdom and providence. Receive now those who have gone ahead of us in our journey from this life.

And receive us too at the proper time, when you have guided us in our bodily life as long as may be for our profit. Receive us prepared indeed by fear of you, but not troubled, not shrinking back on that day of death or uprooted by force like those who are lovers of the world and the flesh. Instead, may we set out eagerly for that everlasting and blessed life which is in Christ Jesus our Lord. To him be glory for ever and ever.

Oration 7, in Praise of Caesar his Brother, 23–24: PG 35, 786–787

St. Mary Magdalene ✠ July 22

A reading from a sermon of Gregory the Great, Bishop of Rome [604]

When Mary Magdalene came to the tomb and did not find the Lord's body, she thought it had been taken away and so informed the disciples. After they came and saw the tomb, they too believed what Mary had told them. The text then says: "The disciples went back home," and it adds: "but Mary wept and remained standing outside the tomb."

We should reflect on Mary's attitude and the great love she felt for Christ; for though the disciples had left the tomb, she remained. She was still seeking the one she had not found, and while she sought she wept; burning with the fire of love, she longed for him whom she thought had been taken away. And so it happened that the woman who stayed behind to seek Christ was the only one to see him. For perseverance is essential to any good deed, as the voice of truth tells us: "Whoever perseveres to the end will be saved."

At first she sought but did not find, but when she persevered it happened that she found what she was looking for. When our desires are not satisfied, they grow stronger, and becoming stronger they take hold of their object. Holy desires likewise grow with anticipation, and if they do not grow they are not really desires. Anyone who succeeds in attaining the truth has burned with such a love. As David says: "My soul has thirsted for the living God; when shall I come and appear before the face of God?" And so also in the Song of Songs the Church says: "I was wounded by love"; and again: "My soul is melted with love."

"Woman, why are you weeping? Whom do you seek?" She is asked why she is sorrowing so that her desire might be strengthened; for when she mentions whom she is seeking, her love is kindled all the more ardently.

"Jesus says to her: Mary." Jesus is not recognized when he calls her "woman"; so he calls her by name, as though he were saying: "Recognize me as I recognize you; for I do not know you as I know others; I know you as yourself." And so Mary, once addressed by name, recognizes who is speaking. She immediately calls him "rabboni," that is to say, "teacher," because the one whom she sought outwardly was the one who inwardly taught her to keep on searching.

Homily 25 on the Gospels 1-2, 4-5: PL 76, 1189–1193

St. James ✠ July 25

A reading from a homily of John Chrysostom, Bishop of Constantinople [407]

The sons of Zebedee press Christ: "Promise that one may sit at your right side and the other at your left." What does he do? He wants to show them that it is not a spiritual gift for which they are asking, and that if they knew what their request involved, they would never dare make it. So he says: "You do not know what you are asking," that is, what a great and splendid thing it is and how much beyond the reach even of the heavenly powers. Then he continues: "Can you drink the cup which I must drink and be baptized with the baptism which I must undergo?" He is saying: "You talk of sharing honors and rewards with me, but I must talk of struggle and toil. Now is not the time for rewards or the time for my glory to be revealed. Earthly life is the time for bloodshed, war and danger."

Consider how by his manner of questioning he exhorts and draws them. He does not say: "Can you face being slaughtered? Can you shed your blood?" How does he put his question? "Can you drink the cup?" Then he makes it attractive by adding: "which I must drink," so that the prospect of sharing it with him may make them more eager. He also calls his suffering a baptism, to show that it will effect a great cleansing of the entire world. The disciples answer him: "We can!" Fervor makes them answer promptly, though they really do not know what they are saying but still think they will receive what they ask for.

How does Christ reply? "You will indeed drink my cup and be baptized with my baptism." He is really prophesying a great blessing for them, since he is telling them: "You will be found worthy of martyrdom; you will suffer what I suffer and end your life with a violent death, thus sharing all with me. But seats at my right and left side are not mine to give; they belong to those for whom the Father has prepared them." Thus, after lifting their minds to higher goals and preparing them to meet and overcome all that will make them desolate, he sets them straight on their request.

"Then the other ten became angry at the two brothers." See how imperfect they all are: the two who tried to get ahead of the other ten, and the ten who were jealous of the two! But, as I said before, show them to me at a later date in their lives, and you will see that all these impulses and feelings have disappeared. Read how John, the very one who here asks for the first place, will always yield to Peter when it comes to preaching and performing miracles in the Acts of the Apostles. James, for his part, was not to live very much longer; for from the beginning he was inspired by great fervor and, setting aside all purely human goals, rose to such splendid heights that he straightway suffered martyrdom.

Homily 65 on Matthew 2–4: PG 58, 619–622·

Eve of the Transfiguration ✠ August 5

A reading from a sermon of Leo the Great, Bishop of Rome [461]

The Lord reveals his glory in the presence of chosen witnesses. His body is like that of any other human, but he makes it shine with such splendor that his face becomes like the sun in glory, and his garments as white as snow.

The great reason for this transfiguration was to remove the scandal of the cross from the hearts of his disciples, and to prevent the humiliation of his voluntary suffering from disturbing the faith of those who had witnessed the surpassing glory that lay concealed.

With no less forethought he was also providing a firm foundation for the hope of holy Church. The whole body of Christ was to understand the kind of transformation that it would receive as his gift. The members of that body were to look forward to a share in that glory which first blazed out in Christ their head.

The Lord had himself spoken of this when he foretold the splendor of his coming: "Then the just will shine like the sun in the kingdom of their Father." Saint Paul the apostle bore witness to this same truth when he said: "I consider that the sufferings of the present time are not to be compared with the future glory that is to be revealed in us." In another place he says: "You are dead, and your life is hidden with Christ in God. When Christ, your life, is revealed, then you also will be revealed with him in glory."

This marvel of the transfiguration contains another lesson for the apostles, to strengthen them and lead them into the fullness of knowledge. Moses and Elijah, the law and the prophets, appeared with the Lord in conversation with him. This was in order to fulfill exactly, through the presence of these persons, the text which says: "Before two or three witnesses every word is ratified." What word could be more firmly established, more securely based, than the word which is proclaimed by the trumpets of both old and new testaments, sounding in harmony, and by the utterances of ancient prophecy and the teaching of the Gospel, in full agreement with each other?

The writings of the two testaments support each other. The radiance of the transfiguration reveals clearly and unmistakably the one who had been promised by signs foretelling him under the veils of mystery. As Saint John says: "The law was given through Moses, grace and truth came through Jesus Christ." In him the promise made through the shadows of prophecy stands revealed, along with the full meaning of the precepts of the law. He is the one who teaches the truth of prophecy through his presence, and makes obedience to the commandments possible through grace.

In the preaching of the holy Gospel all should receive a strengthening of their faith. No one should be ashamed of the cross of Christ, through which the world has been redeemed.

No one should fear to suffer for the sake of justice; no one should lose confidence in the reward that has been promised. The way to rest is through toil, the way to life is through death. Christ has taken on himself the whole weakness of our lowly human nature. If then we are steadfast in our faith in him and in our love for him, we win the victory that he has won, we receive what he has promised.

When it comes to obeying the commandments or enduring adversity, the words uttered by the Father should always echo in our ears: "This is my Son, the beloved, in whom I am well pleased; listen to him."

Sermon 51, 3–4, 8: PL 54, 310–311, 313

The Transfiguration ✠ August 6

A reading from the Chapters of Anastasius, Abbot of St. Catherine on Mt. Sinai [c. 700]

Upon Mount Tabor, Jesus revealed to his disciples a heavenly mystery. While living among them he had spoken of the kingdom and of his second coming in glory, but to banish from their hearts any possible doubt concerning the kingdom and to confirm their faith in what lay in the future by its prefiguration in the present, he gave them on Mount Tabor a wonderful vision of his glory, a foreshadowing of the kingdom of heaven. It was as if he said to them: As time goes by you may be in danger of losing your faith. To save you from this I tell you now that "some standing here" listening to me "will not taste death until they have seen the Son of Man coming in the glory of his Father." Moreover, in order to assure us that Christ could command such power when he wished, the evangelist continues: "Six days later, Jesus took with him Peter, James and John, and led them up a high mountain where they were alone. There, before their eyes, he was transfigured. His face shone like the sun, and his clothes became as white as light. Then the disciples saw Moses and Elijah appear, and they were talking to Jesus."

These are the divine wonders we celebrate today; this is the saving revelation given us upon the mountain; this is the festival of Christ that has drawn us here. Let us listen, then, to the sacred voice of God so compellingly calling us from on high, from the summit of the mountain, so that with the Lord's chosen disciples we may penetrate the deep meaning of these holy mysteries, so far beyond our capacity to express. Jesus goes before us to show us the way, both up the mountain and into heaven, and—I speak boldly—it is for us now to follow him with all speed, yearning for the heavenly vision that will give us a share in his radiance, renew our spiritual nature and transform us into his own likeness, making us for ever sharers in his Godhead and raising us to heights as yet undreamed of.

Let us run with confidence and joy to enter into the cloud like Moses and Elijah, or like James and John. Let us be caught up like Peter to behold the divine vision and to be transfigured by that glorious transfiguration. Let us retire from the world, stand aloof from the earth, rise above the body, detach ourselves from creatures and turn to the creator, to whom Peter in ecstasy exclaimed: "Lord, it is good for us to be here."

It is indeed good to be here, as you have said, Peter. It is good to be with Jesus and to remain here for ever. What greater happiness or higher honor could we have than to be with God, to be made like him and to live in his light?

Therefore, since each of us possesses God in our heart and is being transformed into the divine image, we also should cry out with joy: "It is good for us to be here"—here where all things shine with divine radiance, where there is joy and gladness and exultation; where there is nothing in our hearts but peace, serenity and stillness; where God is seen. For here, in our hearts, Christ takes up his abode together with the Father, saying as he enters: "Today salvation has come to this house." With Christ, our hearts receive all the wealth of his eternal blessings, and there where they are stored up for us in him, we see reflected as in a mirror both the firstfruits and the whole of the world to come.

Chapters 6–10: Mélanges d'archéologie et d'histoire 67, 1955, 241-244

St. Mary the Virgin ✠ August 15

A reading from a letter by Cyril, Bishop of Alexandria [444]

That anyone could doubt the right of the holy Virgin to be called the Mother of God fills me with astonishment. Surely she must be the Mother of God if our Lord Jesus Christ is God, and she gave birth to him! Our Lord's disciples may not have used those exact words, but they delivered to us the belief those words enshrine, and this has also been taught us by the holy fathers.

In the third book of his work on the holy and consubstantial Trinity, our father Athanasius, of glorious memory, several times refers to the holy Virgin as "Mother of God." I cannot resist quoting his own words: "As I have often told you, the distinctive mark of holy Scripture is that it was written to make a twofold declaration concerning our Savior; namely, that he is and has always been God, since he is the Word, Radiance and Wisdom of the Father; and that for our sake in these latter days he took flesh from the Virgin Mary, Mother of God, and became human."

Again further on he says: "There have been many holy people, free from all sin. Jeremiah was sanctified in his mother's womb, and John while still in the womb leaped for joy at the voice of Mary, the Mother of God." Athanasius is one we can trust, one who deserves our complete confidence, for he taught nothing contrary to the sacred books.

The divinely inspired Scriptures affirm that the Word of God was made flesh, that is to say, was united to a human body endowed with a rational soul. He undertook to help the descendants of Abraham, fashioning a body for himself from a woman and sharing our flesh and blood, to enable us to see in him not only God, but also, by reason of this union, a human being like ourselves.

It is held, therefore, that there are in Emmanuel two entities, divinity and humanity. Yet our Lord Jesus Christ is nonetheless one, the one true Son, both God and human; not a deified human on the same footing as those who share the divine nature by grace, but true God who for our sake appeared in human form. We are assured of this by Saint Paul's declaration: "When the fullness of time came, God sent his Son, born of a woman, born under the law, to redeem those who were under the law and to enable us to be adopted as children."

Letter 1: PG 77, 14–18, 27–30

St. Bartholomew ✠ August 24

A reading from a homily of John Chrysostom, Bishop of Constantinople [407]

It was clear through unlearned persons that the cross was persuasive, in fact, it persuaded the whole world. Their discourse was not of unimportant matters but of God and true religion, of the Gospel way of life and future judgment, yet it turned plain, uneducated folk into philosophers. How the foolishness of God is wiser than we are, and God's weakness stronger than we are!

In what way is it stronger? It made its way throughout the world and overcame all people; countless throngs sought to eradicate the very name of the Crucified, but that name flourished and grew even mightier. Its enemies lost out and perished; the living who waged war on a dead man proved helpless. Therefore, when a Greek tells me I am dead, he shows only that he is foolish indeed, for I, whom he thinks a fool, turn out to be wiser than those reputed wise. So too, in calling me weak, he but shows that he is weaker still. For the good deeds which tax-collectors and fishermen were able to accomplish by God's grace, the philosophers, the rulers, and the countless multitudes cannot even imagine.

Paul had this in mind when he said: "The weakness of God is stronger than humankind." That the preaching of these apostles was indeed divine is brought home to us in the same way. For how otherwise could twelve uneducated men, who lived on lakes and rivers and wastelands, get the idea for such an immense enterprise? How could people who perhaps had never been in a city or a public square think of setting out to do battle with the whole world? That they were fearful and timid, the evangelist makes clear; he did not reject the fact or try to hide their weaknesses. Indeed he turned these into a proof of the truth. What did he say of them? That when Christ was arrested, the others fled, despite all the miracles they had seen, while he who was leader of the others denied him!

How then account for the fact that these men, who in Christ's lifetime did not stand up to the attacks by the Jews, set forth to do battle with the whole world once Christ was dead—if, as you claim, Christ did not rise and speak to them and rouse their courage? Did they perhaps say to themselves: "What is this? He could not save himself but he will protect us? He did not help himself when he was alive, but now that he is dead he will extend a helping hand to us? In his lifetime he brought no nation under his banner, but by uttering his name we will win over the whole world?'' Would it not be wholly irrational even to think such thoughts, much less to act upon them?

It is evident, then, that if they had not seen him risen and had proof of his power, they would not have risked so much.

Homily 4 on 1 Corinthians 3–4: PG 61, 34–36

Eve of Holy Cross ✠ September 13

A reading from a sermon of Theodore of Studios, Priest and Abbot [826]

How precious the gift of the cross, how splendid to contemplate! In the cross there is no mingling of good and evil, as in the tree of paradise: it is wholly beautiful to behold and good to taste. The fruit of this tree is not death but life, not darkness but light. This tree does not cast us out of paradise, but opens the way for our return.

This was the tree on which Christ, like a king on a chariot, destroyed the devil, the lord of death, and freed the human race from tyranny. This was the tree upon which the Lord, like a brave warrior wounded in hands, feet and side, healed the wounds of sin that the evil serpent had inflicted on our nature. A tree once caused our death, but now a tree brings life. Once deceived by a tree, we have now repelled the cunning serpent by a tree. What an astonishing transformation! That death should become life, that decay should become immortality, that shame should become glory! Well might the holy Apostle exclaim: "Far be it from me to glory except in the cross of our Lord Jesus Christ, by which the world has been crucified to me, and I to the world!" The supreme wisdom that flowered on the cross has shown the folly of worldly wisdom's pride. The knowledge of all good, which is the fruit of the cross, has cut away the shoots of wickedness.

The wonders accomplished through this tree were foreshadowed clearly even by the mere types and figures that existed in the past. Meditate on these, if you are eager to learn. Was it not the wood of a tree that enabled Noah, at God's command, to escape the destruction of the flood together with his sons, his wife, his sons' wives and every kind of animal? And surely the rod of Moses prefigured the cross when it changed water into blood, swallowed up the false serpents of Pharaoh's magicians, divided the sea at one stroke and then restored the waters to their normal course, drowning the enemy and saving God's own people? Aaron's rod, which blossomed in one day in proof of his true priesthood, was another figure of the cross, and did not Abraham foreshadow the

488   *Eve of Holy Cross, September 13*

cross when he bound his son Isaac and placed him on the pile of wood?

By the cross death was slain and Adam was restored to life. The cross is the glory of all the apostles, the crown of the martyrs, the sanctification of the saints. By the cross we put on Christ and cast aside our former self. By the cross we, the sheep of Christ, have been gathered into one flock, destined for the sheepfolds of heaven.

Oration for the Adoration of the Cross: PG 99, 691–694, 695, 698–699

Holy Cross Day ✠ September 14

A reading from a sermon of Andrew of Crete, Bishop and Hymnographer [740]

We are celebrating the feast of the cross which drove away darkness and brought in the light. As we keep this feast, we are lifted up with the crucified Christ, leaving behind us earth and sin so that we may gain the things above. So great and outstanding a possession is the cross that whoever wins it has won a treasure. Rightly could I call this treasure the fairest of all fair things and the costliest, in fact as well as in name, for on it and through it and for its sake the riches of salvation that had been lost were restored to us.

Had there been no cross, Christ could not have been crucified. Had there been no cross, life itself could not have been nailed to the tree. And if life had not been nailed to it, there would be no streams of immortality pouring from Christ's side, blood and water for the world's cleansing. The bond of our sin would not be canceled, we should not have obtained our freedom, we should not have enjoyed the fruit of the tree of life and the gates of paradise would not stand open. Had there been no cross, death would not have been trodden underfoot, nor hell despoiled.

Therefore, the cross is something wonderfully great and honorable. It is great because through the cross the many noble acts of Christ found their consummation—very many indeed, for both his miracles and his sufferings were fully rewarded with victory. The cross is honorable because it is both the sign of God's suffering and the trophy of his victory. It stands for his suffering because on it he freely suffered unto death. But it is also his trophy because it was the means by which the devil was wounded and death conquered; the barred gates of hell were smashed, and the cross became the one common salvation of the whole world.

The cross is called Christ's glory; it is saluted as his triumph. We recognize it as the cup he longed to drink and the climax of the sufferings he endured for our sake. As to the cross being Christ's glory, listen to his words: "Now is the Son of Man glorified, and in him God is glorified, and God will glorify him at once." And again: "Father, glorify me with the glory I had with you before the world came to be." And once more: "Father, glorify your name. Then a voice came from heaven: I have glorified it and will glorify it again." Here he speaks of the glory that would accrue to him through the cross. And if you would understand that the cross is Christ's triumph, hear what he himself also said: "When I am lifted up, then I will draw all people to myself." Now you can see that the cross is Christ's glory and triumph.

Oration 10 for the Exaltation of the Holy Cross: PG 97, 1018–1019, 1022–1023

St. Matthew ✠ September 21

A reading from a sermon of Bede, the Venerable, Priest, and Monk of Jarrow [735]

"Jesus saw a man called Matthew sitting at the tax office, and he said to him: Follow me." Jesus saw Matthew, not merely in the usual sense, but more significantly with his merciful understanding of humankind.

He saw the tax collector and, because he saw him through the eyes of mercy and chose him, he said to him: "Follow me." This following meant imitating the pattern of his life—not just walking after him. Saint John tells us: "Whoever says he abides in Christ ought to walk in the same way in which he walked."

"And he rose and followed him." There is no reason for surprise that the tax collector abandoned earthly wealth as soon as the Lord commanded him. Nor should one be amazed that neglecting his wealth, he joined a band whose leader had, on Matthew's assessment, no riches at all. Our Lord summoned Matthew by speaking to him in words. By an invisible, interior impulse flooding his mind with the light of grace, he instructed him to walk in his footsteps. In this way Matthew could understand that Christ, who was summoning him away from earthly possessions, had incorruptible treasures of heaven in his gift.

"As he sat at table in the house, behold many tax collectors and sinners came and sat down with Jesus and his disciples." This conversion of one tax collector gave many, those from his own profession and other sinners, an example of repentance and pardon. Notice also the happy and true anticipation of his future status as apostle and teacher of the nations. No sooner was he converted than Matthew drew after him a whole crowd of sinners along the same road to salvation. He took up his appointed duties while still taking his first steps in the faith, and from that hour he fulfilled his obligation and thus grew in merit.

To see a deeper understanding of the great celebration Matthew held at his house, we must realize that he not only gave a banquet for the Lord at his earthly residence, but far more pleasing was the banquet set in his own heart which he provided through faith and love. Our Savior attests to this: "Behold I stand at the door and knock; if any hear my voice and open the door, I will come in to them and eat with them, and they with me."

On hearing Christ's voice, we open the door to receive him, as it were, when we freely assent to his promptings and when we give ourselves over to doing what must be done. Christ, since he dwells in the hearts of his chosen ones through the grace of his love, enters so that he might eat with us and we with him. He ever refreshes us by the light of his presence insofar as we progress in our devotion to and longing for the things of heaven. He himself is delighted by such a pleasing banquet.

Homily 21: CCL 122, 149–151

St. Michael & All Angels ✠ September 29

A reading from a sermon of Gregory the Great, Bishop of Rome [604]

You should be aware that the word "angel" denotes a function rather than a nature. Those holy spirits of heaven have indeed always been spirits. They can only be called angels when they deliver some message. Moreover, those who deliver messages of lesser importance are called angels; and those who proclaim messages of supreme importance are called archangels.

And so it was that not merely an angel but the archangel Gabriel was sent to the Virgin Mary. It was only fitting that the highest angel should come to announce the greatest of all messages.

Some angels are given proper names to denote the service they are empowered to perform. In that holy city, where perfect knowledge flows from the vision of almighty God, those who have no names may easily be known. But personal names are assigned to some, not because they could not be known without them, but rather to denote their ministry when they come among us. Thus, Michael means "Who is like God?"; Gabriel is "The Strength of God"; and Raphael is "God's Remedy."

Whenever some act of wondrous power must be performed, Michael is sent, so that action and name may make it clear that no one can do what God does by his own superior power. So also our ancient foe desired in pride to be like God, saying: "I will ascend into heaven; I will

exalt my throne above the stars of heaven; I will be like the Most High."
Satan will be allowed to remain in power until the end of the world when
he will be destroyed in the final punishment. Then, he will fight with the
archangel Michael, as we are told by John: "A battle was fought with
Michael the archangel."

So too Gabriel, who is called God's strength, was sent to Mary. Gabriel
came to announce the One who appeared in humility to quell the cosmic
powers. Thus God's strength announced the coming of the Lord of the
heavenly powers, mighty in battle.

Raphael means, as I have said, God's remedy, for when this angel
touched Tobit's eyes in order to cure him, Raphael banished the darkness of his blindness. Thus, since this angel is to heal, Raphael is rightly
called God's remedy.

Homily 34 on the Gospels 8–9: PL 76, 1250–1251

St. Luke ✠ October 18

*A reading from a sermon of Gregory the Great, Bishop of
Rome [604]*

Beloved, our Lord and Savior sometimes gives us instruction by words
and sometimes by actions. His very deeds are our commands; and whenever he acts silently he is teaching us what we should do. For example,
he sends his disciples out to preach two by two, because the precept of
charity is twofold—love of God and of one's neighbor.

The Lord sends his disciples out to preach in two's in order to teach
us silently that whoever fails in charity toward his neighbor should by no
means take upon himself the office of preaching.

Rightly is it said that he sent them ahead of him into every city and
place where he himself was to go. For the Lord follows after the preachers, because preaching goes ahead to prepare the way, and then when
the words of exhortation have gone ahead and established truth in our
minds, the Lord comes to live within us. To those who preach Isaiah says:
"Prepare the way of the Lord, make straight the paths of our God." And
the psalmist tells them: "Make a way for him who rises above the sunset."
The Lord rises above the sunset because from that very place where he
slept in death, he rose again and manifested a greater glory. He rises
above the sunset because in his resurrection he trampled underfoot the
death which he endured. Therefore, we make a "way for him who rises
above the sunset" when we preach his glory to you, so that when he
himself follows after us, he may illumine you with his love.

Let us listen now to his words as he sends his preachers forth: "The harvest is great but the laborers are few. Pray therefore the Lord of the harvest to send laborers into his harvest." That the harvest is good but the laborers are few cannot be said without a heavy heart, for although there are many to hear the good news there are only a few to preach it. Indeed, see how full the world is of priests, but yet in God's harvest a true laborer is rarely to be found; although we have accepted the priestly office we do not fulfill its demands.

Think over, my beloved, think over his words: "Pray the Lord of the harvest to send laborers into his harvest." Pray for us so that we may be able to labor worthily on your behalf, that our tongue may not grow weary of exhortation, that after we have taken up the office of preaching our silence may not bring us condemnation from the just judge.

Homily 17 on the Gospels 1–3: PL 76, 1139

St. James of Jerusalem ✠ October 23

A reading from Hegesippus, Church Historian [second century]

Control of the Church passed to the apostles, together with the Lord's brother James, whom everyone from the Lord's time till our own has called the Righteous, for there were many Jameses, but this one was holy from his birth; he drank no wine or intoxicating liquor and ate no animal food; no razor came near his head; he did not smear himself with oil, and took no baths. He alone was permitted to enter the Holy Place, for his garments were not of wool but of linen. He used to enter the Sanctuary alone, and was often found on his knees beseeching forgiveness for the people, so that his knees grew hard like a camel's from his continually bending them in worship of God and beseeching forgiveness for the people.

Representatives of the seven popular sects already described by me asked him what was meant by "the door of Jesus," and he replied that Jesus was the Savior. Some of them came to believe that Jesus was the Christ: the sects mentioned above did not believe either in a resurrection or in One who is coming to give all what their deeds deserve, but those who did come to believe did so because of James. Since therefore many even of the ruling class believed, there was an uproar among the Jews and Scribes and Pharisees, who said there was a danger that the entire people would expect Jesus as the Christ.

So the Scribes and Pharisees made James stand on the Sanctuary parapet and shouted to him: "Righteous one, whose word we are all obliged to accept, the people are going astray after Jesus who was crucified; so tell us what is meant by 'the door of Jesus.' " He replied as loudly as he could: "Why do you question me about the Son of Man? I tell you, He is sitting in heaven at the right hand of the Great Power, and He will come on the clouds of heaven." Many were convinced, and gloried in James's testimony, crying: "Hosanna to the Son of David!" Then again the Scribes and Pharisees said to each other: "We made a bad mistake in affording such testimony to Jesus. We had better go up and throw him down, so that they will be frightened and not believe him."

So they went up and threw down the Righteous one. Then they said to each other: "Let us stone James the Righteous," and began to stone him, as in spite of his fall he was still alive. But he turned and knelt, uttering the words: "I beseech you, Lord God and Father, forgive them; they do not know what they are doing." While they pelted him with stones, one of the descendants of Rechab the son of Rachabim—the priestly family to which Jeremiah the Prophet bore witness, called out: "Stop! what are you doing? the Righteous one is praying for you." Then one of them, a fuller, took the club which he used to beat out the clothes, and brought it down on the head of the Righteous one. Such was his martyrdom. He was buried on the spot, by the Sanctuary, and his headstone is still there by the Sanctuary. He has proved a true witness to Jews and Gentiles alike that Jesus is the Christ.

Eusebius, Ecclesiastical History 2, 23: PG 20, 195–204

SS. Simon & Jude ☩ October 28

A reading from a commentary on John by Cyril, Bishop of Alexandria [444]

Our Lord Jesus Christ has appointed certain people to be guides and teachers of the world and stewards of his divine mysteries. Now he bids them to shine out like lamps and to cast out their light not only over the land of the Jews but over every country under the sun and over people scattered in all directions and settled in distant lands.

That one has spoken truly who said: "None take honor upon themselves, except those who are called by God," for it was our Lord Jesus Christ who called his own disciples before all others to a most glorious apostolate. These holy ones became the "pillar and mainstay of the truth," and Jesus said that he was sending them just as the Father had sent him.

By these words he is making clear the dignity of the apostolate and the incomparable glory of the power given to them, but he is also, it would seem, giving them a hint about the methods they are to adopt in their apostolic mission. For if Christ thought it necessary to send out his intimate disciples in this fashion, just as the Father had sent him, then surely it was necessary that they whose mission was to be patterned on that of Jesus should see exactly why the Father had sent the Son. And so Christ interpreted the character of his mission to us in a variety of ways. Once he said: "I have come to call not the righteous but sinners to repentance." And then at another time he said: "I have come down from heaven, not to do my own will, but the will of him who sent me. For God sent his Son into the world, not to condemn the world, but that the world might be saved through him."

Accordingly, in affirming that they are sent by him just as he was sent by the Father, Christ sums up in a few words the approach they themselves should take to their ministry. From what he said they would gather that it was their vocation to call sinners to repentance, to heal those who were sick whether in body or spirit, to seek in all their dealings never to do their own will but the will of him who sent them, and as far as possible to save the world by their teaching.

Surely it is in all these respects that we find his holy disciples striving to excel. To ascertain this is no great labor; a single reading of the Acts of the Apostles or of Saint Paul's writings is enough.

Commentary on John 12, 1: PG 74, 707–710

Eve of All Saints ✠ October 31

A reading from the First Letter to the Corinthians by Clement, Bishop of Rome [c. 100]

The command has been written: "Cling to the saints, for those who cling to them will be sanctified." There is a passage in Scripture as well which states: "With the innocent you will be innocent, and with the chosen you will be chosen also; likewise with the perverse you will deal perversely." Devote yourselves, then, to the innocent and the just; they are God's chosen ones. Why are there strife and passion, schisms and even war among you? Do we not possess the same Spirit of grace which was given to us and the same calling in Christ? Why do we tear apart and divide the body of Christ? Why do we revolt against our own body? Why do we reach such a degree of insanity that we forget that we are members one of another? Do not forget the words of Jesus our Lord: "Woe to that person;

it would be better if such a one had not been born rather than to scandalize one of my chosen ones. Indeed it would be better for that one to have a great millstone round the neck and to be drowned in the sea than to lead astray one of my chosen ones." Your division has led many astray, has made many doubt, has made many despair, and has brought grief upon us all. And still your rebellion continues.

Pick up the letter of blessed Paul the apostle. What did he write to you at the beginning of his ministry? Even then you had developed factions. So Paul, inspired by the Holy Spirit, wrote to you concerning himself and Cephas and Apollos. But that division involved you in less sin because you were supporting apostles of high reputation and a person approved by them.

We should put an end to this division immediately. Let us fall down before our master and implore his mercy with our tears. Then he will be reconciled to us and restore us to the practice of loving one another as befits us. For this is the gate of justice that leads to life, as it is written: "Open to me the gates of justice. When I have entered there, I shall praise the Lord. This is the gate of the Lord; the just shall enter through it." There are many gates which stand open, but the gate of justice is the gateway of Christ. All who enter through this gate are blessed, pursuing their way in holiness and justice, performing all their tasks without discord. A person may be faithful, may have the power to utter hidden mysteries, may be discriminating in the evaluation of what is said, and pure in actions. But the greater such a one seems to be, the more humbly they ought to act, and the more zealous for the common good rather than for self-interest.

First Letter to the Corinthians 46, 2–47, 4; 48: Funk 1, 119–123

All Saints Day ✠ November 1

A reading from a sermon of Bernard, Abbot of Clairvaux [1153]

Why should our praise and glorification, or even the celebration of this feastday mean anything to the saints? What do they care about earthly honors when their heavenly Father honors them by fulfilling the faithful promise of the Son? What does our commendation mean to them? The saints have no need of honor from us; neither does our devotion add the slightest thing to what is theirs. Clearly, if we venerate their memory, it serves us, not them. But I tell you, when I think of them, I feel myself inflamed by a tremendous yearning.

Calling the saints to mind inspires, or rather arouses in us, above all else, a longing to enjoy their company, so desirable in itself. We long to share in the citizenship of heaven, to dwell with the spirits of the blessed, to join the assembly of patriarchs, the ranks of the prophets, the council of apostles, the great host of martyrs, the noble company of confessors and the choir of virgins. In short, we long to be united in happiness with all the saints. But our dispositions change. The Church of all the first followers of Christ awaits us, but we do nothing about it. The saints want us to be with them, and we are indifferent. The souls of the just await us, and we ignore them.

Come, let us at length spur ourselves on. We must rise again with Christ, we must seek the world which is above and set our mind on the things of heaven. Let us long for those who are longing for us, hasten to those who are waiting for us, and ask those who look for our coming to intercede for us. We should not only want to be with the saints, we should also hope to possess their happiness. While we desire to be in their company, we must also earnestly seek to share in their glory. Do not imagine that there is anything harmful in such an ambition as this; there is no danger in setting our hearts on such glory.

When we commemorate the saints we are inflamed with another yearning: that Christ our life may also appear to us as he appeared to them and that we may one day share in his glory. Until then we see him, not as he is, but as he became for our sake. He is our head, crowned, not with glory, but with the thorns of our sins. As members of that head, crowned with thorns, we should be ashamed to live in luxury; his purple robes are a mockery rather than an honor. When Christ comes again, his death shall no longer be proclaimed, and we shall know that we also have died, and that our life is hidden with him. The glorious head of the Church will appear and his glorified members will shine in splendor with him, when he forms this lowly body anew into such glory as belongs to himself, its head.

Therefore, we should aim at attaining this glory with a wholehearted and prudent desire. That we may rightly hope and strive for such blessedness, we must above all seek the prayers of the saints. Thus, what is beyond our own powers to obtain will be granted through their intercession.

Sermon 2: ed. Cist. 5 (1968), 364-368

Thanksgiving Day

A reading from a sermon of Basil the Great, Bishop of Caesarea [379]

Take care that the destiny of the "wicked rich" is not yours. Their history has been written to help us avoid being like them. Therefore, imitate the earth: like it, you should bring forth fruit; do not show yourselves worse than something which has no soul. It is not for her own pleasure that the earth brings forth her fruits; it is for your service.

But you have this advantage, that the benefits of your benevolence will ultimately return to you; for benefactors always reap the reward of the good they have done. You have given to the poor; what you have given is returned to you with interest. The wheat, when it falls to the ground, produces for the sower. Similarly, the bread that you give to the poor is a source of future profits. Therefore, may the end of labors be for you the beginning of celestial sowing: "Sow for yourselves righteousness," says Scripture.

Why then torment yourself so much and make so many efforts to preserve your riches behind mortar and bricks? "A good name is more desirable than great riches." You love money because of the consideration it procures for you. Think how much greater will be your renown if one can call you a parent, protector of thousands of children, rather than if you keep thousands of gold pieces hidden away. Whether you like it or not, you will surely have to leave your money behind one day; on the contrary, the glory of all the good you have done will go with you before the sovereign Master, when an entire people will hasten to defend you before the Judge of all things, and will confer titles showing that you nourished and assisted them, and that you have been good.

One sees people throw their fortune to wrestlers, to comedians, to repugnant gladiators—and all this in theaters, for a moment's glory, for the noisy acclamations of the people. And would you count the cost when you can elevate yourself to so great a glory? God will approve of you, the angels will acclaim you, and all who have lived since the creation of the world will celebrate your happiness: an imperishable glory, a crown of justice, the kingdom of heaven—such will be the prizes that you will receive.

Sermon on Love: PG 31, 266B-267A

Eve of the Dedication

A reading from a sermon of Augustine, Bishop of Hippo [430]

We are gathered together to celebrate the dedication of a house of prayer. This is our house of prayer, but we too are a house of God. If we are a house of God, its construction goes on in time so that it may be dedicated at the end of time. The house, in its construction, involves hard work, while its dedication is an occasion for rejoicing.

What was done when this church was being built is similar to what is done when believers are built up into Christ. When they first come to believe they are like timber and stone taken from woods and mountains. In their instruction, baptism and formation they are, so to speak, shaped, leveled and smoothed by the hands of carpenters and craftspeople.

But Christians do not make a house of God until they are one in charity. The timber and stone must fit together in an orderly plan, must be joined in perfect harmony, must give each other the support as it were of love, or no one would enter the building. When you see the stones and beams of a building holding together securely, you enter the building with an easy mind; you are not afraid of its falling down in ruins.

Christ the Lord wants to come in to us and dwell in us. Like a good builder he says: "A new commandment I give you: love one another." He says: "I give you a commandment." He means: Before, you were not engaged in building a house for me, but you lay in ruins. Therefore, to be raised up from your former state of ruin you must love one another.

Remember that this house is still in the process of being built in the whole world: this is the promise of prophecy. When God's house was being built after the Exile, it was prophesied, in the words of a psalm: "Sing a new song to the Lord; sing to the Lord, all the earth." For "a new song" our Lord speaks of "a new commandment." A new song implies a new inspiration of love. To sing is a sign of love. The singer of this new song is full of the warmth of God's love.

The work we see complete in this building is physical; it should find its spiritual counterpart in your hearts. We see here the finished product of stone and wood; so too your lives should reveal the handiwork of God's grace.

Let us then offer our thanksgiving above all to the Lord our God, from whom every best and perfect gift comes. Let us praise his goodness with our whole hearts. He it was who inspired in his faithful people the will to build this house of prayer; he stirred up their desire and gave them his help. He awakened enthusiasm among those who were at first uncon-

vinced, and guided to a successful conclusion the efforts of people of
good will. So God, "who gives to those of good will both the desire and
the accomplishment" of the things that belong to him, is the one who
began this work, and the one who has brought it to completion.

Sermon 336, 1, 6: PL 38, 1471–1472, 1475

Anniversary of the Dedication of a Church

*A reading from a homily of Origen, Priest and Theologian
[c. 254]*

All of us who believe in Christ Jesus are said to be living stones, according
to the words of Scripture: "But you are living stones, built as a spiritual
house in a holy priesthood, that you may offer spiritual sacrifices acceptable to God through Jesus Christ."

When we look at an earthly building, we can see that the larger and
stronger stones are the first to be set in place as the foundation, so that
the weight of the whole structure may rest on them securely. In the same
way understand that some of the living stones become the foundation
of the spiritual building. What are these living stones placed in the
foundation? They are the apostles and prophets. That is what Paul says
when he teaches: "We have been built upon the foundation of the
apostles and prophets, with our Lord Jesus Christ himself as the cornerstone."

You, my hearers, must learn that Christ himself is also the foundation
of the building we are now describing, so that you may prepare yourselves more eagerly for the construction of this building and become
stones that lie closer to the foundation. As the apostle Paul says:
"No foundation can be laid other than the one that has been laid already:
I mean Christ Jesus." Blessed are those, therefore, who build a religious
and holy structure upon such a noble foundation.

In this building of the Church, there must also be an altar. I think that
if those of you, disposed and eager for prayer, offer petitions and prayers
of supplication to God day and night, you will become the living stones
for the altar which Jesus is building.

Consider what praise is ascribed to these stones which make up the
altar. "The lawgiver Moses said that the altar was to be made of stones,
uncovered by iron." What are those stones? Perhaps those uncut and
undefiled stones are the holy apostles, all making a single altar, because
of their unity of mind and heart. For it was known that with one accord
they all opened their lips to pray: "You, Lord, know the hearts of all."

Therefore, these who were able to pray with one mind, one voice and one spirit, are perhaps worthy to form together one altar, where Jesus may offer his sacrifice to the Father.

Let us strive to agree among ourselves and to have one mind and voice. May we never quarrel or act from vainglory. But may we remain united in belief and purpose. Then even we may hope to become stones fit for the altar.

Homily 9 on Joshua the Son of Nun 1-2: SC 71, 244-246

Eve of the Patronal Feast

*A reading from a commentary on the psalms by Hilary,
Bishop of Poitiers [367]*

"Unless the Lord builds a house, the builders labor in vain. You are the temple of God. The Spirit of God dwells in you." This is the house and temple of God, full of his doctrine and his power, a dwelling place holy enough to house the heart of God. It is of this that the same inspired author is speaking, in the words: "Your temple is holy, marvelous in its goodness." Humanity's holiness, justice and self-restraint constitute God's temple.

Such a temple must be built by God; if it were constructed by human effort, it would not last; it is not held together by resting on merely worldly teachings, nor will it be protected by our own vain efforts or anxious concern. We must build it and protect it in a different way. It must not have its foundations on earth or on sand that is unstable and treacherous. Its foundations must be rooted in the prophets and apostles.

It must be built up from living stones, held together by a cornerstone; an ever-increasing unity will make it grow into a perfect harmony, to the scale of Christ's body; its beauty and its charm are the adornment given to it by supernatural grace.

A house so built by God, that is, by God's guidance, will not collapse. Through the efforts of the individual faithful this house will grow into many houses, and thus will arise the blessed and spacious city of God.

For many years now God has been watching over this city, ever on the alert. He cared for Abraham in his wanderings; he rescued Isaac when he was about to be sacrified; Jacob he enriched in his time of servitude; it is he who set Joseph over Egypt, after he had been sold into slavery; who supported Moses against Pharaoh; chose Joshua to lead his nation in war; rescued David from every peril and endowed Solomon with wisdom. He came to the aid of the prophets, he took Elijah up to heaven, chose Elisha; fed Daniel, and stood by and refreshed the three youths in the fiery furnace. He told Joseph, through an angel, of his virginal conception, he strengthened Mary, and sent John ahead to prepare the way. He chose the apostles and prayed for them, saying to his Father: "Father most holy, protect them. While I was with them, I kept them safe by the power of your name." Finally after his passion, he promised us his eternal, watchful protection, in the words: "Behold, I am with you always until the end of the world."

Such is the never-failing protection given to this blessed and holy city, a city built for God, fashioned by the coming together of many, yet seen in each one of us. It is therefore the Lord who must build this city if it is to grow to its appointed size. A building just begun is not the perfect work; final perfection is brought about only in the very process of building.

Treatise on Psalm 126, 7–10: PL 9, 696–697

The Patronal Feast

A reading from a sermon of Augustine, Bishop of Hippo [430]

Let us sing alleluia here on earth, while we still live in anxiety, so that we may sing it one day in heaven in full security. Why do we now live in anxiety? Can you expect me not to feel anxious when I read: "Is not life on earth a time of trial?" Can you expect me not to feel anxious when the words still ring in my ears: "Watch and pray that you will not be put to the test"? Can you expect me not to feel anxious when there are so many temptations here below that prayer itself reminds us of them, when we say: "Forgive us our trespasses, as we forgive those who trespass against us"? Every day we make our petitions, every day we sin. Do you want me to feel secure when I am daily asking pardon for my sins, and requesting help in time of trial? Because of my past sins I pray: "Forgive us our trespasses, as we forgive those who trespass against us," and then, because of the perils still before me, I immediately go on to add: "Lead us not into temptation." How can all be well with people who are crying out with me: "Deliver us from evil"? And yet, while we are still in the midst of this evil, let us sing alleluia to the good God who delivers us from evil.

Even here amidst trials and temptations let us, let all, sing alleluia. "God is faithful," says Holy Scripture, "and he will not allow you to be tried beyond your strength." So let us sing alleluia, even here on earth.

Humanity is still a debtor, but God is faithful. Scripture does not say that he will not allow you to be tried, but that "he will not allow you to be tried beyond your strength." Whatever the trial, he will see you through it safely, and so enable you to endure. You have entered upon a time of trial but you will come to no harm—God's help will bring you through it safely. You are like a piece of pottery, shaped by instruction, fired by tribulation. When you are put into the oven therefore, keep your thoughts on the time when you will be taken out again; for God is faithful, and "he will guard both your going in and your coming out."

But in the next life, when this body of ours has become immortal and incorruptible, then all trials will be over. "Your body is indeed dead, and why? Because of sin." Nevertheless, "your spirit lives, because you have been justified." Are we to leave our dead bodies behind then? By no means. Listen to the words of Holy Scripture: "If the Spirit of him who raised Christ from the dead dwells within you, then he who raised Christ from the dead will also give life to your own mortal bodies." At present your body receives its life from the soul, but then it will receive it from the Spirit.

O the happiness of the heavenly alleluia, sung in security, in fear of no adversity! We shall have no enemies in heaven, we shall never lose a friend. God's praises are sung both there and here, but here they are sung in anxiety, there, in security; here they are sung by those destined to die, there, by those destined to live for ever; here they are sung in hope, there, in hope's fulfillment; here they are sung by wayfarers, there, by those living in their own country.

So, then, let us sing now, not in order to enjoy a life of leisure, but in order to lighten our labors. You should sing as wayfarers do—sing, but continue your journey. Do not be lazy, but sing to make your journey more enjoyable. Sing, but keep going. What do I mean by keep going? Keep on making progress. This progress, however, must be in virtue; for there are some, the Apostle warns, whose only progress is in vice. If you make progress, you will be continuing your journey, but be sure that your progress is in virtue, true faith and right living. Sing then, but keep going.

Sermon 256, 1, 2, 3: PL 38, 1191–1193

Eves of Apostles and Evangelists

A reading from a commentary on the psalms by Augustine,
Bishop of Hippo [430]

As there are many kinds of persecution, so there are many kinds of martyrdom. Every day you are a witness to Christ. You were tempted by the spirit of fornication, but feared the coming judgment of Christ and did not want your purity of mind and body to be defiled: you are a martyr for Christ. You are tempted by the spirit of avarice to seize the property of a child and violate the rights of a defenseless widow, but you remembered God's law and saw your duty to give help, not to act unjustly: you are a witness to Christ. Christ wants witnesses like this to stand ready, as Scripture says: "Do justice for the orphan and defend the widow." You were tempted by the spirit of pride but saw the poor and the needy and looked with loving compassion on them, and loved humility rather than arrogance: you are a witness to Christ. What is more, your witness was not in word only but also in deed.

Who can give greater witness than one "who acknowledges that the Lord Jesus has come in the flesh" and keeps the commandments of the Gospel? One who hears but does not act, denies Christ. Even if one acknowledges him by words, he can be denied by deeds. How many will say to Christ: "Lord, Lord, did we not prophesy and cast out devils and work many miracles, all in your name?" On that day he will say to them: "Depart from me, all you evildoers." The true witness is one who bears witness to the commandments of the Lord Jesus and supports that witness by deeds.

How many hidden martyrs there are, bearing witness to Christ each day and acknowledging Jesus as the Lord! The Apostle knew this kind of martyrdom, this faithful witness to Christ. "This is our boast," he said, "the witness of our conscience." How many have borne witness in public but denied it in private! "Do not believe every spirit," he said, but know "from their fruits" whom you should believe. Be faithful and courageous when you are persecuted within, so that you may win approval when you are persecuted in public. Even in those unseen persecutions there are kings and governors, judges with terrible power. You have an example in the temptation endured by the Lord.

In another place we read: "Do not let sin be king in your mortal body." You see the kings before whom you are made to stand, those who sit in judgment over sinners, where sin is in control. There are as many kings as there are sins and vices; it is before these kings that we are led and before these we stand. These kings have their thrones in many hearts. But if anyone acknowledges Christ, that person immediately makes a prisoner of this kind of king and casts the usurper down from the throne of the heart. How shall the devil maintain his throne in one who builds a throne for Christ in the heart?

Commentary on Psalm 118, 20, 47–50: CSEL 62, 467–469

Select Topical and Theological Index

Each number refers to the beginning page of a selection that contains the particular topic.

For doctrinal topics related to seasons or days of the liturgical year, such as *Nativity, Pentecost, Annunciation, Transfiguration,* the reader is directed to the particular selections that are assigned for each season or feast.

Church, doctrine of, 13, 15, 20, 39, 44, 50, 60, 66, 89, 108, 111, 123, 125, 127, 142, 183, 186, 187, 196, 202, 204, 221, 222, 251, 256, 264, 273, 284, 285, 288, 291, 303, 3⎓8, 342, 344, 346, 349, 358, 401, 419, 444, 462, 465, 471, 472, 479, 496, 501

City, the heavenly, 164, 168, 253, 321, 352, 356, 412, 414, 416, 417, 418, 420, 421, 422, 423, 424, 426, 433, 491, 501

Clergy. *See* Bishops, Presbyters, Deacons.

Communion, the Church as, 40, 63, 66, 69, 108, 157, 176, 204, 229, 240, 267, 313, 330, 408, 435, 472

Creed, 1, 133, 190, 205, 265, 291, 328, 374, 447, 456, 471

Cross, 11, 25, 56, 58, 59, 76, 129, 136, 146, 147, 160, 163, 164, 165, 168, 172, 197, 198, 204, 209, 217, 230, 238, 277, 291, 344, 369, 374, 399, 449, 450, 457, 483, 487, 488, 489

Deacons, 129, 160, 165, 172, 230, 249, 250, 269, 276, 288, 309, 365, 367, 368, 382, 449, 454

Death, 12, 28, 42, 79, 85, 86, 105, 129, 141, 147, 169, 184, 197, 213, 217, 221, 259, 295, 308, 319, 371, 387, 396, 457, 476, 480, 488, 502

Ecclesiology. *See* Church, doctrine of.

Eucharist, 19, 36, 48, 63, 108, 129, 164, 168, 171, 177, 178, 182, 184, 186, 192, 194, 216, 224, 230, 240, 247, 274, 282, 284, 288, 303, 310, 323, 335, 337, 341, 349, 355, 379, 390, 392, 429, 436, 438, 454, 462

Exorcism, 133, 147, 240

Fasting, 121, 128, 133, 155, 174, 191, 204, 212, 225, 385, 409, 436

God, doctrine and names of, 7, 21, 38, 42, 43, 52, 53, 96, 112, 125, 130, 132, 139, 190, 191, 205, 238, 240, 245, 261, 266, 274, 297, 302, 339, 373, 380, 390, 412, 435

Hymns. *See* Music.

Icons, or images, 28, 56, 57, 58, 59

Justification by faith, 12, 17, 31, 62, 73, 77, 85, 89, 109, 201, 218, 325, 331, 339, 362, 391, 396, 502

Latreia (worship), 44, 46, 56, 58, 59, 190, 247, 414, 417, 420, 424

Marriage, 26, 75, 119, 198, 261, 269, 331, 365

Martrydom and martyrs, 94, 141, 160, 165, 184, 198, 224, 225, 247, 265, 276, 281, 301, 325, 337, 382, 461, 462, 476, 479, 482, 488, 493, 504

Mary, 5, 11, 20, 23, 38, 40, 41, 58, 59, 125, 197, 246, 356, 379, 380, 465, 468, 469, 473, 486

Music and musicians, 50, 61, 67, 69, 230, 281, 288, 290, 317, 318, 320, 381, 408, 449, 465, 474, 499, 502

Oil, Holy, 48, 66, 149, 158, 178, 321

Pastoral ministry, 162, 252, 255, 305, 312, 411

Peace, Kiss of, 63, 172, 194, 355, 362

Peacemaking, 22, 34, 39, 50, 54, 57, 71, 199, 226, 277, 308, 310, 358, 362, 403, 416, 418, 419, 420

Pneumatology. See Spirit, Holy.

Poverty and Wealth, 3, 5, 14, 18, 26, 43, 79, 99, 131, 146, 149, 153, 155, 158, 192, 207, 208, 260, 263, 286, 327, 342, 359, 360, 361, 371, 385, 389, 391, 400, 410, 414, 432, 436, 451, 459, 498, 504

Prayer, 7, 55, 82, 87, 101, 130, 135, 147, 156, 192, 251, 273, 283, 296, 314, 339, 340, 341, 342, 344, 349, 366, 377, 383, 384, 406, 431, 436, 448, 455, 459, 496, 499, 500. Also see below.

Prayer eastward, 82, 217, 272, 304, 367

Prayer while standing, 82, 101, 192, 272, 273, 362

Prayer with eyes open and upwards, 21, 91, 101, 431

Prayer with hands uplifted or outstretched, 82, 87, 91, 101, 117, 147, 273, 283, 344

Prayer without ceasing, 86, 87, 91, 130, 135, 156, 213, 283, 340, 342, 377, 381, 406, 431

Preaching, 26, 59, 92, 133, 192, 230, 252, 255, 298, 358, 370, 410, 449, 463, 465, 471, 472, 476, 492

Presbyters or priests, 50, 129, 133, 147, 204, 224, 230, 249, 250, 252, 255, 269, 273, 276, 277, 288, 296, 309, 323, 337, 353, 367, 369, 438, 449, 454, 465, 492

Repentance, 93, 109, 122, 154, 171, 188, 191, 194, 217, 285, 288, 330, 333, 341, 350, 355, 362, 375, 391, 409

Rulers, or public officials, 137, 187, 265, 321, 333, 350, 414, 418

Saints and sainthood, 13, 21, 58, 59, 90, 91, 125, 159, 168, 187, 203, 217, 222, 247, 307, 313, 328, 350, 352, 364, 378, 390, 408, 412, 414, 417, 423, 428, 455, 456, 462, 474, 488, 495, 496

Scriptural interpretation, 11, 15, 23, 50, 51, 76, 85, 90, 96, 99, 106, 117, 133, 172, 183, 203, 225, 229, 230, 257, 272, 287, 341, 351, 354, 358, 400, 401, 412, 442, 445, 447, 448, 465, 466, 483, 486, 488
Spirit, Holy, 44, 48, 64, 77, 81, 97, 108, 170, 178, 185, 186, 198, 208, 215, 223, 225, 228, 229, 230, 232, 233, 261, 368, 369, 374, 438, 469, 472, 477, 502
Sunday, doctrine of, 128, 165, 183, 192, 214, 241, 249, 272, 308, 350, 424, 426, 449

Tradition, as concept and doctrine, 56, 59, 99, 235, 272, 304, 353, 367, 368, 444, 445, 447, 472, 486
Trinity, 9, 33, 44, 97, 186, 190, 191, 192, 208, 222, 232, 233, 235, 240, 261, 266, 307, 326, 328, 374, 471, 486

Unction. *See* Oil, Holy.

Wealth. *See* Poverty and Wealth.
Wisdom, as concept and doctrine, 8, 30, 60, 61, 92, 111, 115, 139, 203, 216, 240, 271, 351, 354, 373, 392, 440
Women, writings about, 11, 15, 40, 41, 54, 94, 132, 158, 160, 197, 217, 218, 238, 256, 259, 261, 265, 266, 273, 274, 313, 322, 331, 338, 380, 382, 399, 408, 440, 469, 473, 474, 481, 486. *See also* Mary.
Women, writings by, 19, 55, 78, 88, 128, 133, 165, 172, 217, 226, 230, 261, 266, 274, 284, 285, 313, 318, 322, 338, 382, 399, 449

Index of Authors

Each number refers to the page upon which a reading begins. The dates in brackets are those of each author's death.

Ambrose, Bishop of Milan [397], 65, 73, 75, 77, 94, 111, 138, 180, 251, 254, 295, 318, 319, 320, 331, 333, 336, 350, 367, 368, 369, 374, 379, 387, 405, 440, 469
Anastasius, Abbot of St. Catherine on Mt. Sinai [c. 700], 484
Andrew of Crete, Bishop and Hymnographer [740], 167, 450, 489
Anselm, Archbishop of Canterbury [1109], 7, 238, 245, 380, 428
Athanasius, Bishop of Alexandria [373], 28, 40, 60, 61, 159, 235, 237, 271, 373
* Augustine, Bishop of Hippo [430], 12, 13, 26, 29, 31, 41, 43, 72, 85, 98, 109, 112, 113, 125, 127, 137, 142, 150, 183, 184, 202, 211, 212, 220, 221, 222, 224, 247, 278, 279, 290, 291, 293, 296, 297, 299, 301, 303, 305, 307, 308, 312, 317, 321, 324, 332, 335, 337, 338, 344, 354, 358, 377, 383, 384, 394, 396, 401, 406, 408, 411, 412, 414, 416, 417, 418, 420, 421, 422, 423, 424, 426, 430, 442, 446, 455, 460, 477, 479, 499, 502, 504

Baldwin, Archbishop of Canterbury [1190], 144, 298, 387, 473
Basil the Great, Bishop of Caesarea [379], 42, 44, 148, 169, 208, 229, 244, 248, 263, 272, 498
Bede, the Venerable, Priest, and Monk of Jarrow [735], 23, 64, 193, 474, 476, 490
Bernard, Abbot of Clairvaux [1153], 10, 18, 34, 116, 242, 395, 457, 496
Bernardine of Siena, Franciscan Friar and Preacher [1444], 468

Caesarius, Bishop of Arles [543], 93, 260
Catherine of Siena, Dominican Sister and Mystic [1380], 19, 284, 285

*The large number of selections from Augustine is comparatively not excessive when matched against the total bulk of his writings in the extant corpus of patristic literature.

Chromatius, Bishop of Aquileia [407], 475
Clare, Abbess at Assisi [1253], 399
Clement, Bishop of Rome [c. 100], 21, 62, 120, 122, 286, 292, 294, 352, 495
Clement of Alexandria, Priest [c. 210], 53, 54, 82, 84, 203, 381
Columbanus, Celtic Abbot [615], 57, 240, 392, 393, 441
Cyprian, Bishop and Martyr of Carthage [258], 4, 130, 158, 239, 256, 273, 310, 314, 329, 339, 340, 341, 342, 353, 359, 361, 362, 366, 371
Cyril, Bishop of Alexandria [444], 97, 108, 186, 210, 215, 227, 228, 346, 419, 486, 494
Cyril, Bishop of Jerusalem [386], 1, 119, 136, 178, 179, 182, 225, 264, 265, 330, 443, 447

Didache. *See* "The Teaching of the Twelve Apostles."
Didymus the Blind, Theologian of Alexandria [398], 185
Diognetus, the Letter to [c. 124], 17, 207

Egeria, Abbess, and Pilgrim to Jerusalem [late fourth century], 128, 133, 165, 172, 230, 449, 465
Ephrem of Edessa, Deacon [373], 2, 102, 197, 213
Eusebius, Bishop of Caesarea [373], 9, 50, 160

Francis of Assisi, Friar [1226], 146
Fulgentius, Bishop of Ruspe [533], 459

Gregory, Bishop of Nyssa [c. 394], 51, 103, 104, 105, 132, 214, 217, 223, 257, 258, 259, 302, 315, 360, 403, 407, 427, 437, 452
Gregory of Nazianzus, Bishop of Constantinople [389], 3, 5, 34, 38, 47, 79, 145, 149, 164, 480
Gregory the Great, Bishop of Rome [604], 36, 99, 107, 115, 123, 252, 255, 287, 349, 357, 370, 458, 481, 491, 492

Hegesippus, Church Historian [second century], 493
Hilary, Bishop of Poitiers [367], 66, 177, 233, 240, 241, 356, 433, 501
Hippolytus, Priest or Bishop of Rome [c. 236], 37, 187, 198

Ignatius, Bishop of Antioch, and Martyr [c. 115], 25, 67, 69, 80, 249, 250, 268, 269, 276, 277, 281, 282, 288, 325

Irenaeus, Bishop of Lyons [c. 202], 11, 24, 52, 63, 89, 140, 157, 176, 190, 216, 232, 246, 267, 390, 434, 435, 471
Isidore, Bishop of Seville [636], 448

Jerome, Priest, and Monk of Bethlehem [420], 106, 168, 326, 351, 409
John Chrysostom, Bishop of Constantinople [407], 14, 68, 71, 92, 117, 156, 163, 174, 188, 196, 323, 327, 345, 347, 389, 391, 429, 431, 432, 451, 463, 466, 482, 487
John of Damascus, Priest [c. 760], 56, 58, 304
Dame Julian of Norwich [c. 1417], 55, 78, 261, 266, 274, 313, 322
Justin, Martyr at Rome [c. 167], 191, 192

Leo the Great, Bishop of Rome [461], 8, 20, 33, 39, 46, 83, 129, 153, 155, 199, 200, 204, 209, 218, 378, 385, 400, 404, 410, 436, 462, 470, 483

Maximus the Confessor, Abbot [662], 45, 131, 154
Melito, Bishop of Sardis [c. 190], 170, 175

Origen, Priest and Theologian [c. 254], 15, 30, 76, 86, 87, 90, 91, 96, 101, 118, 141, 151, 283, 309, 311, 344, 500

The Passion of Perpetua and her Companions, Martyrs at Carthage [202], 382
Peter Chrysologus, Bishop of Ravenna [450], 48, 121, 375
Polycarp, Bishop and Martyr of Smyrna [156], 201, 365
Proba, Christian laywoman of the city of Rome [c. 351], 226

Quodvultdeus, Bishop of Carthage [c. 453], 461

Rufinus of Aquileia, Monk [410], 205

The Seventh Ecumenical Council, of Nicaea [787], 59
Sophronius, Bishop of Jerusalem [638], 465
Syncletica, Mother of the Egyptian Desert [late fourth century], 88

"The Teaching of the Twelve Apostles" [probably second century], 355
Tertullian, Theologian [c. 225], 147, 328, 472
Theodore, Bishop of Mopsuestia [428], 81, 194, 438, 454

Appendix
The Genesis of a Book

The time-honored tradition of supplementing the scriptural lessons for the Daily Office with a reading from the early church, a custom known in the Christian West as early as the sixth or seventh century,[1] was made officially possible for Anglicans (Episcopalians) in the U.S.A. by a rubric in the new, 1979 American *Book of Common Prayer* (page 142). I was contracted by the Church Hymnal Corporation, official publisher of the Episcopal Church, to compile such a volume that would complement the church's liturgical calendar and scriptural lectionary. In this way, much of the theological and devotional heritage of early and some medieval church history would be made available to a much wider reading public in the church of today. This essay is offered for the purpose of recording and sharing the problems I encountered, as well as the solutions I adopted, in selecting, editing, and translating these materials.[2]

First, selecting the material. Some of the selection problems were solved by my publisher. Was there to be one patristic reading to match every designated scriptural reading for the entire daily office calendar— which could have necessitated as many as six lessons a day for the two-year cycle? Even if surviving patristic commentaries were that extensive to allow such a choice, my publisher ruled this out on financial grounds. There was to be one selection for each day of the liturgical year that could be used with either Morning Prayer or Evening Prayer in either Year One or Year Two. This still meant, one reading for each of the 453 liturgical days in the daily office calendar of the new American Prayer Book.

As a selection guideline my publisher also asked that I re-translate and transfer as much as I thought appropriate of the post-scriptural readings from *The Liturgy of the Hours,* translated in the early 1970's by the International Committee on English in the Liturgy (ICEL), which constitute the up-dated series of post-biblical readings used officially in the Roman Catholic Church since the revision of its Divine Office mandated by the Second Vatican Ecumenical Council.[3] By removing Roman Catholic writings of the sixteenth and later centuries, as well as such writers as "pseudo-Chrysostom" who, whether genuine or spurious, would be suspect in a church not accustomed to patristic readings, I eventually was able to transfer approximately 61% of the selections from the Roman Catholic *Office of Readings,* fitting them wherever possible either to the same day, or to the same liturgical season, or to a corresponding scriptural reading, in the office lectionary and calendar of the Episcopal Church. This has meant that a large proportion of that patristic inheritance could now be shared ecumenically not only by American Episcopalians but also, if desired, by Canadian Anglicans and by American Lutherans, who both use virtually the same lectionary for the Daily Office.[4]

Beyond the principles I have now mentioned, my remaining problem in selection was how to fill in the remaining 39% of the 453 days, and here my publisher's one request was to be more inclusive of writings by and about women from the early church than had been the case with the readings chosen to accompany the Roman Catholic office. This request will be understandable in a church such as the Anglican where women can be ordained, and especially as coming from North America where this concern is great, over against the considerable weight of tradition in the Roman Catholic Church whose daily office readings, even as revised in the 1970's, include virtually no women writers apart from those on their own calendar days (none, for example, from Egeria during Lent or Holy Week). Still other readings I took from a wide variety of sources that I have encountered in over twenty years of teaching medieval and patristic church history and theology, as well as from the popular six-volume series entitled *Christian Readings* that was edited in the early 1970's by John E. Rotelle.

All told, then, my result was a spectrum of some 64 early Christian writers selected for the 453 days. The largest number of selections, as one might predict from the total bulk of the extant corpus of patristic literature, is 82 from Augustine of Hippo. There are also some 48 writings by or about women, including Egeria (seven selections), Catherine of Siena, Clare of Assisi, Julian of Norwich, Macrina, Perpetua, Proba, Syncletica of the Egyptian desert, and, of course, many that refer to Mary. The selection of themes, seen from the theological index, includes almsgiving, angels, atonement, baptism, bishops, blackness, blindness, catechesis, church as building and as doctrine, communion, creed, cross, deacons, death, eucharist, exorcism, fasting, God, icons or images, justification by faith, latreia, marriage, martyrdom, music, holy oil, kiss of peace, peacemaking, poverty and wealth, prayer, prayer eastward, prayer while standing, prayer with eyes open and upwards, prayer with hands uplifted or outstretched, prayer without ceasing, preaching, priests, repentance, rulers, sanctity, scriptural interpretation, Holy Spirit, Sunday, tradition, Trinity, and wisdom. The total number of pages in typescript was 870, and in print 514.

Next I turn to the editing of these various texts. Here I shall state the solutions adopted, from which the corresponding problems encountered will be obvious. The names, titles or descriptions, and dates of each author correspond to those already adopted officially by the Episcopal Church in its newly revised Prayer Book calendar and calendar of Lesser Feasts and Fasts, or, if the author is not in either of these calendars, the same style is followed. The date given is always the date of the author's death (when known), following the custom of the Episcopal Church's calendars, rather than the year in which the work was written. Thus, an example: "A reading from the treatise On Pastoral Care by Gregory the Great, Bishop of Rome [604]." The treatise is always called *On Pastoral Care*, rather than at times *On Pastoral Rule*, because the former is the title by which it is named in the Episcopal Church's volume of *Lesser Feasts and Fasts*. The date given is his death, 604, not when the treatise was completed. He is not called Pope or Saint, as the Episcopal's Church's calendar does not recognize the former title, nor the latter title except for New Testament figures. Generally, as seems to have been the case, sermons of Latin authors are called "sermons," those of Greek authors "homilies." Titles were standardized, so that Egeria's "Travels" does not sometimes appear as "Journey" and other times as "Pilgrimage."

Scriptural quotations, following the practice of the Episcopal Church's official *Lectionary Texts*, are always placed in quotes not italics, but, following the practice of the Roman Catholic *Office of Readings*, scriptural references are never cited. No attempt was made to force all scriptural quotations, some of which are different from the received text and in other cases are paraphrased, into one standard English Bible translation. In all texts, scriptural or otherwise, archaic English was put into modern English, and the style and spelling of American International English was followed. In order to facilitate public reading of these selections, I followed the practice of the ICEL in not using ellipsis points to indicate omissions, since the fact and extent of such omissions can be seen from any gaps in page numbers in the scholarly references placed at the end of each selection. The occasional instances of "Amen" at the end of doxologies within some texts, as well as the frequent occurrence of the vocative "brethren" *(fratres)*, which may or may not indicate an originally intended exclusively male audience, were edited out. A source reference is given at the bottom of each reading, following the practice of the ICEL, for easy location of the text in a scholarly edition and also to indicate whether there has been any ellipsis, although the reference given is not necessarily the immediate source of the translation used or adopted.

By far the greatest problem I encountered in editing was the question of copyright permissions, a process that could not even begin until I had decided which 453 texts I proposed to use. Next was the question of whether any of them needed copyright permission, since I was either translating afresh from Greek or Latin, in some cases, or, in every other case, making re-translations that involved some alterations to printed English texts based always on the Greek or Latin. How much change had to be made before an English text was no longer the property of an earlier publisher but our own? My publisher, taking legal counsel, concluded that there was no certain way of answering this question short of risking a legal proceeding in which our right to an altered English text would be challenged by an earlier publisher who claimed it was still theirs! For this reason my publisher decided, cautiously, to seek fresh permission from every publisher of every English text that I was re-translating no matter how extensive my own alterations might be. This seemed wise, but involved much more work and my publisher soon demonstrated this could not be handled without hours and days of my own time and assistance.

We assumed that everything I was using was still under copyright by someone, even though some older volumes gave no indication of copyright at all. In many cases, the publisher who owned the copyright had changed from the one under whom the text in English had been published. In other cases it was not the publisher but the author who originally owned the copyright. In many cases the publisher's address, or name, or both, had changed. In some cases, publishers were uncertain whether or not they held such copyright. And, in some cases, publishers were prepared to charge fees, no inconsequential matter, once we asked their permission and thus tacitly acknowledged that the English text in question was theirs, no matter how many changes were being made by me. This process initially involved letters to 30 different publishers, of which some never replied in spite of numerous enquiries. Also there was the question of what permission they were granting, since the texts we wanted to publish would in no cases be exactly the same English translations they had published. Would they, for example, demand to see what changes we were proposing for inclusive language, and reserve the right to pass on such changes? In the end, some demanded to see what we proposed but none the right to pass on them. From the ICEL, from which the greatest bulk of the material was taken, initially very complicated regulations were received involving the permission of Roman Catholic hierarchies in every English-speaking country where a copy of our book might be distributed, but these requirements were withdrawn once they determined that we were not publishing primarily for the Roman Catholic Church. And finally, some publishers had an exact form that they require to be printed in acknowledgment of copyright, but such forms were not parallel in wording. Moreover, would any publisher demand that their copyright to an earlier English translation of a patristic text be printed in exact proximity to our re-translation, or would a list of copyright permissions at the front of the book suffice? We opted for the latter course, and with non-parallel verbal acknowledgments simply printed one after another, and with a note reading "permission requested" for those publishers who had not replied by the time our book went to print. Moreover, in spite of my own publisher's generous original offer that I might have the copyright to this book, at my lawyer's advice I persuaded my publisher to claim the copyright on this new volume, thus reducing my own chances of legal liability if some lawsuit should ever emerge from this labyrinth of technicalities. All told, the copyright problems and solutions were a nightmare and by far the most cumbersome part of the editing process.

Finally I turn to the problems and solutions involved in translating or re-translating all of these texts, and first I mention some problems that were relatively minor. *Justicia* in Latin authors where the ultimate reference was δικαιοσύνη in the New Testament, I translated as "righteousness" even though the ICEL translations had read "justice," since "righteousness" would be more familiar if not also preferable to Anglicans accustomed to an accurate translation of the scriptural Greek text.[5] Likewise, *penitentiam gero* I translated as "repent" rather than the more scholastic "do penance" (e.g., RDOEC p. 350). And in Ignatius of Antioch, for τῷ πρεσβυτερίῳ I preferred "the presbytery" where the ICEL had read "the clergy" (RDOEC p. 276). "The Church" and "the Holy Spirit," to my surprise, did not give many problems, and usually I rendered pronouns referring back to them by simply repeating the original noun again. As for capitalization of the Spirit when not accompanied by the adjective "Holy," I had to decide whether the context called for the third person of the Trinity (capitalized) or "spirit" in a more general sense (not capitalized).

The major translation problem I encountered, which was hardly foreseen at the time I signed the contract for this volume several years ago, was that of inclusive language, now a virtual necessity for English texts in mainline churches of North America. The reasons why this is the case are not the subject of this essay, but because it is a relatively new problem there are not (yet) any generally accepted guidelines. In general, the principle I followed, which is basically that of the (1989/1990) *New Revised Standard Version* of the Bible (NRSV), was to make human terminology as inclusive as possible but to leave the language of God alone. The language of the Devil did not escape, however, and in references to Satan or the Devil I generally translated personal pronouns by repeating the noun. Thus in Augustine's psalter commentary "the devil and his angels" *(et angelis suis),* referring back to Matthew 25:41 (τῷ διαβόλῳ καὶ τοῖς 'αγγέλοις αὐτοῦ), became "and the devil's angels" (RDOEC p. 26). "The serpent that had seized us with his jaws" in Gregory of Nyssa's *Life of Moses* became "with diabolical jaws" (RDOEC p. 218).

But we must turn from the Devil to humans and then finally, to Jesus. Human language, on its own, was fairly easy, and I think most of the solutions I adopted can already be found in the principles of translators' license over the centuries. Thus, man and men often became, depending upon the context, one or they/them or we/us or humanity/humankind/the human race. I often repeated a noun antecedent in substitution for a following pronoun that was gender-specific. I used plural inclusive pronouns to refer to any antecedent noun in the collective singular. For example, in Bernard of Clairvaux's sermon on the feast of St. Andrew, I read close to the NRSV of Matthew 16:24: "If any wish to be my followers, let them deny themselves and take up their cross and follow me" (RDOEC p. 457). And generally, in my re-translations for humans, brethren became friends or beloved, craftsman became artist, steersman pilot, seaman sailor, patrimony wealth or inheritance, freeman the free, schoolmaster schoolteacher, manhood adulthood or maturity, forefathers ancestors, madmen lunatics, and mortal men mere mortals. Thus, in "The Word of God did not abandon men" of the *Christian Readings* translation of Athanasius *On the Incarnation,* τῶν 'ανθρώπων γένος became "the human race" (RDOEC p. 28). "How can a man hope for what he sees?" in Cyprian's *On the Value of Patience* 13.15, the Latin *Quod enim videt quis, quid sperat?* ultimately depending upon the Greek ὃ γὰρ βλέπει τίς ἐλπίζει of Romans 8:24, became "How can we hope for what is seen?" (RDOEC p. 4). The famous passages in Irenaeus, *Against Heresies* (3,20, 2–3 and 4, 5–7), "God is man's glory" and "The glory of God is a living man, and the life of man is the vision of God" *(Gloria enim hominis Deus* and *Gloria enim Dei vivens homo, vita autem hominis visio Dei)* became "God is the glory of humanity" and "The glory of God is living humanity and the life of humanity is the vision of God" (RDOEC pp. 24, 434). From Augustine's sermon 185, "He who glories, let him glory not in himself but in the Lord" *(Qui gloriatur, non in se, sed in domino gloriatur)* became "Let those who glory, glory not in themselves but in the Lord" (RDOEC p. 31). For Paul, an apostle "not from man, nor by any man," as found in Augustine's commentary on Galatians 1:1 (οὐκ 'ἀπ' 'ἀνθρώπων οὐδὲ δὶ 'ἀνθρώπου), I settled with the NRSV's "sent neither by human commission nor from human authorities" (RDOEC p. 72). Harder to call, was my decision for Cyprian *On the Lord's Prayer,* where I read "to name ourselves children of God," (rather than "sons of God") "even as Christ is Son of God," thus gaining human inclusivity but surrendering the parallel between us as sons of God and Christ as Son of God (RDOEC p. 130). Hilary of Poitiers *On the Trinity* quoting John 6:54–55, "He who eats my flesh and drinks my blood," became "You who eat my flesh and drink my blood" even though the Greek text of John is third person singular; the NRSV reads it "Those who . . ." (RDOEC p. 177).

Augustine's comment on I John 3:16, "As Christ laid down his life for us, so we too ought to lay down our lives for our brothers," his Latin reading *pro fratribus* and the Greek being ὕπὲρ τῶν 'ἀδελφῶν, became "for our sisters and brothers" in my translation, although I could have accepted the NRSV "for one another" (RDOEC p. 184). More difficult was the same problem in a direct quote from the Lord in Irenaeus, *Against Heresies* 4, "When you offer your gift at the altar and remember that your brother holds something against you," the Greek of Matthew 5:24 reading 'ἀδελφός. I opted for "your brother" followed by "[or sister]" in square brackets; the NRSV simply extends it to read "brother or sister" with a footnote reading "Greek, *your brother*" in italics (RDOEC p. 63; cf. p. 194). I made another similar expansion for a homily of John Chrysostom that also quoted words of the Lord, "As often as you did it for one of the least of my brothers [and sisters]" (RDOEC p. 451; cf. p. 389). And I took a similar course for Hilary of Poitiers, commenting on psalm 132, "Behold how good and pleasant it is for brothers [and sisters] to dwell in unity," even though the NRSV here reads "when kindred live together in unity" (RDOEC p. 66). This passage was made doubly difficult because Hilary continues "It is good for brothers (and I added "[and sisters]") to dwell in unity, because when they do so their association creates their singleness of purpose." Perhaps, in retrospect, "kindred" would have been better here, but I felt that the imagery of "brothers dwelling in unity" was so deeply ingrained that it was better to extend it to include "sisters" than to substitute another word. My final example of human language comes from Ignatius to the Ephesians, speaking of "your bishop," where he says "you are as united with him as the Church is to Jesus Christ." Here I left "him" as masculine because, even though my translations are intended primarily for use in churches that now ordain women to the episcopate, still the historical fact remains that the only bishops Ignatius could have been speaking of were men (RDOEC p. 67).

The many instances of "Son of Man" formed a category all their own; in my book of 453 readings there were 21 of these. I rejected the usage of the Pueblo lectionary, "Man of Heaven"; I did for a while consider the arguments for "Son of Humanity"; but in the end I voted with the NRSV to retain "Son of Man" unchanged. When it appears coupled with a human reference to "sons of God," though, this did result in surrendering several Latin theological parallels between *filius hominis* and *filii Dei*. Thus, as an example, for Leo the Great's sermon 6 for Christmas, I read "the Savior, who became the Son of Man in order that we might have the power to be the children of God," even though the Latin sentence ended *filii Dei* (RDOEC p. 20).

Most difficult of all my translation problems was the category of those few references to Jesus as "man," historically accurate in the masculine gender, where the word "man" seemed to be making a theological point that would be lost now to present North American religious consciousness if *homo* or ἄνθρωπος, occasionally even *vir* or 'ανήρ, were not translated as inclusive and gender free. These were hard cases to call, and I give some patristic examples, a few of which are also combined with "Son of Man" phrases. From Irenaeus *Against Heresies* in the ICEL text, "The Word of God became man, the Son of God became the Son of Man, in order to unite man with himself and make him, by adoption, a son of God" (the Latin for "man" being *homo*), I read, "The Word of God became human, the Son of God became the Son of Man, in order to unite us with himself and make us, by adoption, children and heirs of God" (RDOEC p. 246). Another example is from an ICEL translation of Augustine's psalter commentary, "So that the Word might be both Son of God and Son of Man, one God with the Father and one man with all men" *(unus Deus cum Patre, unus homo cum hominibus);* I re-translated "One God with the Father and one human being with all humankind" (RDOEC p. 296). A few more examples: Athanasius to Epictetus, "Our Savior truly became man, and from this has followed the salvation of men as a whole," I rendered as "Our Savior truly became human, and from this has followed the salvation of humanity as a whole" (RDOEC p. 40). Augustine, sermon 13, "God became man so that men might become God; the Lord of the angels became man today so that men could eat the bread of angels," I read "God became human like us so that we might become God. The Lord of the angels became one of us today so that we could eat the bread of Angels" (RDOEC p. 41). Maximus the Confessor, "He is born as man," I rendered "He is born as one of us" (RDOEC p. 45). Cyril of Jerusalem, Catechesis 13, went this way: "It was not a mere man (ἄνθρωπος; I read "mere human being") who died for us, but the Son of God, God made man (ἐνανθρωπήσας; I read "God made human"). It was not a lowly man (ἄνθρωπος; I read "lowly human being") who suffered, but God incarnate" (RDOEC p. 136). In Augustine's commentary on John, "If he is the head and we are the members, we form one complete man with him" *(totus homo, ille et nos)*, I translated "one complete human being with him" (RDOEC p. 142). And from the same passage, Augustine quoting Paul, "Till we become one in faith and in the knowledge of God's Son, and form that perfect man who is Christ come to full stature," I rendered Augustine's *virum perfectum* (which is the same in the Vulgate, the New Testament Greek being ἄνδρα τέλειον) as "perfect person." The NRSV is even less direct or literal. In Cyril of Alexandria commenting on John, "He is the bond that unites us, because he is at once both God and man," for "man" I read "human" (RDOEC p. 186). From a letter of Leo the Great, "He who in the nature of God had created man became in the nature of a servant man himself," I read "He who in the nature of God had created humankind became, in the nature of a servant, human himself" (RDOEC p. 470). And finally, from the Easter Homily of Melito of Sardis, "The lamb has become a Son, the Sheep a man, and man, God" (ὁ ἀμνὸς υἱός, καὶ τὸ πρόβατον ἄνθρωπος, καὶ ὁ ἄνθρωπος θεός), I translated "The lamb has become a Son (no change), the sheep a human, and the human God" (RDOEC p. 175).

These, therefore, illustrate the most difficult category of my translation problems: those few references to Jesus as "man," historically accurate in the masculine gender, where however the word "man" seemed to be making a theological point that would be lost now to the present North American religious consciousness if it were not translated as inclusive and gender free. These examples are merely exceptions, however, to the great majority of references to Jesus as *homo* or ἄνθρωπος which I took to be historical references requiring the masculine translation as "man." And the gender of God, which has been retained as masculine even in the NRSV Bible, I did not change.

Overall, these are the problems I encountered and the solutions I adopted in selecting, editing, and translating the new *Readings for the Daily Office from the Early Church.*

Notes

1. Robert Taft, *The Liturgy of the Hours in East and West. The Origins of the Divine Office and Its Meaning for Today* (Collegeville: The Liturgical Press 1986) 182; Hilaire Marot, "La Place des Lectures bibliques et patristiques dans l'Office latin," pp. 149–165 of *La Prière des Heures,* ed. Cassien and Bernard Botte (*Lex Orandi* 35, Paris: Cerf 1963), esp. pp. 155–56.

2. An abbreviated version of this essay, originally presented as a communication to the Eleventh International Conference on Patristic Studies at Oxford in August of 1991, may eventually appear in the published proceedings of that conference.

3. *Constitution on the Sacred Liturgy,* para. 92b. For the Roman Catholic principles of revision, see Henry Ashworth, "The New Patristic Lectionary," *Ephimerides Liturgicae* 85 (1971) 306–322, and esp. pp. 308–309. Also see Marot, op. cit.

4. A similar, but not the same, project has been accomplished in the Church of England by Brother Kenneth's publication, *From the Fathers to the Churches* (London: Collins 1983), to accompany the *Alternative Service Book 1980,* although the contents of his volume limit considerably the extent of patristic readings but include post-Reformation Anglican authors.

5. Examples in *Readings for the Daily Office from the Early Church* (hereinafter RDOEC), ed. J. Robert Wright (New York: The Church Hymnal Corporation 1991) 31, 359, 385; scholarly references are given *ad loc.* In all examples that follow within the narrative of this essay, references will be made to this volume and the page number upon which the cited selection begins, at the end of which selections references will be found to the original Greek or Latin texts.

CPSIA information can be obtained
at www.ICGtesting.com
Printed in the USA
LVOW03s0905190418

574051LV00001B/7/P